T0401399

Exploring the Influence of Personal Values and Cultures in the Workplace

Zlatko Nedelko
University of Maribor, Slovenia

Maciej Brzozowski
Poznan University of Economics and Business, Poland

A volume in the Advances in Human Resources
Management and Organizational Development
(AHRMOD) Book Series

www.igi-global.com

Published in the United States of America by
    IGI Global
    Business Science Reference (an imprint of IGI Global)
    701 E. Chocolate Avenue
    Hershey PA, USA 17033
    Tel: 717-533-8845
    Fax: 717-533-8661
    E-mail: cust@igi-global.com
    Web site: http://www.igi-global.com

Library of Congress Cataloging-in-Publication Data

Names: Nedelko, Zlatko, 1983- editor. | Brzozowski, Maciej, 1975- editor.
Title: Exploring the influence of personal values and cultures in the
  workplace / Zlatko Nedelko and Maciej Brzozowski, editors.
Description: Hershey : Business Science Reference, [2017]
Identifiers: LCCN 2017003787| ISBN 9781522524809 (hardcover) | ISBN
  9781522524816 (ebook)
Subjects: LCSH: Diversity in the workplace. | Leadership. | Decision making.
  | Corporate culture.
Classification: LCC HF5549.5.M5 E976 2017 | DDC 658.3008--dc23 LC record available at https://lccn.loc.
gov/2017003787

This book is published in the IGI Global book series Advances in Human Resources Management and Organizational Development (AHRMOD) (ISSN: 2327-3372; eISSN: 2327-3380)

British Cataloguing in Publication Data
A Cataloguing in Publication record for this book is available from the British Library.

For electronic access to this publication, please contact: eresources@igi-global.com.

Advances in Human Resources Management and Organizational Development (AHRMOD) Book Series

Patricia Ordóñez de Pablos
Universidad de Oviedo, Spain

ISSN:2327-3372
EISSN:2327-3380

MISSION

A solid foundation is essential to the development and success of any organization and can be accomplished through the effective and careful management of an organization's human capital. Research in human resources management and organizational development is necessary in providing business leaders with the tools and methodologies which will assist in the development and maintenance of their organizational structure.

The **Advances in Human Resources Management and Organizational Development (AHRMOD) Book Series** aims to publish the latest research on all aspects of human resources as well as the latest methodologies, tools, and theories regarding organizational development and sustainability. The **AHRMOD Book Series** intends to provide business professionals, managers, researchers, and students with the necessary resources to effectively develop and implement organizational strategies.

COVERAGE

- Skills Management
- Workplace Culture
- Employee Benefits
- Diversity in the Workplace
- Change Management
- Disputes Resolution
- Organizational Development
- Human Relations Movement
- Outsourcing HR
- Performance Improvement

IGI Global is currently accepting manuscripts for publication within this series. To submit a proposal for a volume in this series, please contact our Acquisition Editors at Acquisitions@igi-global.com or visit: http://www.igi-global.com/publish/.

Titles in this Series

For a list of additional titles in this series, please visit: www.igi-global.com

Effective Talent Management Strategies for Organizational Success
Mambo Mupepi (Grand Valley State University, USA)
Business Science Reference • copyright 2017 • 365pp • H/C (ISBN: 9781522519614) • US $210.00 (our price)

Anywhere Working and the New Era of Telecommuting
Yvette Blount (Macquarie University, Australia) and Marianne Gloet (University of Melbourne, Australia)
Business Science Reference • copyright 2017 • 295pp • H/C (ISBN: 9781522523284) • US $195.00 (our price)

Human Resources Management Solutions for Attracting and Retaining Millennial Workers
Meng-Shan Tsai (Clouder Technology Inc., Taiwan)
Business Science Reference • copyright 2017 • 269pp • H/C (ISBN: 9781522520443) • US $185.00 (our price)

Impact of Organizational Trauma on Workplace Behavior and Performance
Stanislav Háša (University of Economics, Czech Republic) and Richard Brunet-Thornton (University of Economics, Czech Republic)
Business Science Reference • copyright 2017 • 413pp • H/C (ISBN: 9781522520214) • US $190.00 (our price)

Strategic Human Capital Development and Management in Emerging Economies
Anshuman Bhattacharya (Sunbeam College for Women, India)
Business Science Reference • copyright 2017 • 321pp • H/C (ISBN: 9781522519744) • US $175.00 (our price)

Evolution of the Post-Bureaucratic Organization
Pierfranco Malizia (Libera Universita Maria SS Assunta, Italy) Chiara Cannavale (Parthenope University of Naples, Italy) and Fabrizio Maimone (Libera Universita Maria SS Assunta, Italy)
Business Science Reference • copyright 2017 • 509pp • H/C (ISBN: 9781522519836) • US $205.00 (our price)

Training Initiatives and Strategies for the Modern Workforce
Scott Frasard (Frasard Consulting, USA) and Frederick Carl Prasuhn (Tech-Wise Educational Services, LLC., USA)
Business Science Reference • copyright 2017 • 289pp • H/C (ISBN: 9781522518082) • US $180.00 (our price)

Handbook of Research on Human Resources Strategies for the New Millennial Workforce
Patricia Ordoñez de Pablos (University of Oviedo, Spain) and Robert D. Tennyson (University of Minnesota, USA)
Business Science Reference • copyright 2017 • 523pp • H/C (ISBN: 9781522509486) • US $310.00 (our price)

www.igi-global.com

701 E. Chocolate Ave., Hershey, PA 17033
Order online at www.igi-global.com or call 717-533-8845 x100
To place a standing order for titles released in this series, contact: cust@igi-global.com
Mon-Fri 8:00 am - 5:00 pm (est) or fax 24 hours a day 717-533-8661

Table of Contents

Section 4

Detailed Table of Contents

Section 1

First a traditional neo-classical model of decision making is broadened by introducing agents who interact in an organization. The resulting computational model is analyzed using virtual experiments to consider how different organizational structures (different network topologies) affect the evolutionary path of an organization's corporate culture. These computational experiments establish testable hypotheses concerning structure, culture, and performance, and those hypotheses are tested empirically using data from an international sample of firms. In addition to learning something about organizational structure and innovation, the paper demonstrates how computational models can be used to frame empirical investigations and facilitate the interpretation of results in a traditional fashion.

A person starting a professional career becomes a member of a chosen organization and begins to function among other people in a defined organizational culture and legal space. As he or she is an adult with a defined personality, knowledge and system of values, the manager can influence the employee's behavior not by changing the person but by shaping the work environment. As flexibility is the number one principle in organizational design nowadays, managers have to create a work environment making decisions on the continuum between formalization and management by values. The chapter describes the consequences of formalization and values orientation for individual organizational behavior, as well as outcomes such as commitment, job satisfaction and turnover intention rate.

Chapter 3

Anna Piekarczyk, Poznan University of Economics and Business, Poland

The article deals with organisation culture from the viewpoint of systems theory of organisation. Organisations are presented as autopoietic systems, relations between organisation and individual are discussed as well. The author attempts to define to what extent values and rules characteristic for a given culture can and should be changed.

Section 2

Chapter 4

Anne Namatsi Lutomia, University of Illinois at Urbana-Champaign, USA
Ping Li, University of Illinois at Urbana-Champaign, USA
Raghida Abdallah Yassine, University of Illinois at Urbana-Champaign, USA
Xiaoping Tong, University of Illinois at Urbana-Champaign, USA

Social networks are taking center stage in organizations for the ways they shape and inform workplace leadership. Hofstede's cultural dimensions and social capital provide a framework for enabling better cross-cultural discussion about leadership in general and understanding how leaders in globalized workplace settings tap onto existing cultural practices and values vis-à-vis social networks. In China, Kenya, and Lebanon, these cultural practices and values include Guanxi, Ubuntu, and Wasta, respectively. Responding to calls for more studies comparing social network and on cross-cultural leadership, this chapter seeks to examine how Guanxi, Ubuntu, and Wasta shape workplace leadership and culture in the three respective countries. It discusses leadership styles, reviews the way Guanxi, Ubuntu, and Wasta informs workplace leadership respectively and their intersections, generates a conceptual framework, offers recommendations, suggests future research possibilities, and provides implications for human resource development.

Chapter 5

Thais Spiegel, Rio de Janeiro State University, Brazil

Among the aspects that conform the human cognition and therefore, the behavior observed in the choices, there is the individual experience. Researches point the experience performing either positive as negative roles in the process of decision-making. Motivated by the question, What is the role of the experience in the decision-making? this text sought to check in which way the state of art and the technique of Cognitive Sciences could contribute with the better understanding of the cognitive processing in the context of decision-making. It was adopted as a start the roles' structured exposition of the cognition elements during the decision process. It was investigated through a systematic revision of the literature, the impacts of the decision-maker's experience in the manifestation of attention, categorization, memory and emotion. As a result, 17 inferences that present which is the role of the experience in the decision-making, and deeply, which are the implications of the experience in the cognitive process of the decision-maker, are presented.

Growing complexity and diversity of strategic decisions indicate the need for applying the appropriate holistic tools in strategic decision-making. Thus, the paper deals with the process of strategic decision-making from the viewpoint of systems thinking, with emphasis on the role of values and context in strategic decision-making. The main purpose is to show how systems thinking, through selected systems methodologies, can help decision-makers involve different perceptions and values in the process of strategic decision-making, as well as take into account context in which the strategic decisions are made. Considering the key internal and external factors affecting strategic decision-making (characteristics of decision-makers, organizational characteristics and environmental characteristics), Soft Systems Methodology as interpretive systems methodology and Organizational Cybernetics as functionalist systems methodology have been selected. The way in which they can be combined, aimed at improving effectiveness of strategic decision-making, has been presented.

The purpose of this chapter is to examine the role of personal values for social responsibility (SR) of higher education. Besides the core mission of higher education to create, transfer and preserve knowledge in society, the idea of SR has gained its importance also in institutions of higher education. SR has many drivers, among which personal values are considered as one of the key building blocks for SR. For enhancing SR, higher education institutions should also develop stronger ties with the community. The chapter provides an insight into discussion about community involvement of higher education, into the role of personal values for shaping SR of higher education institutions and explain how personal values can help to enhance community and social involvement of higher education. Findings may be a starting point for re-thinking and/or establishing strategies for achieving higher level of SR in higher education institutions and enhancing the link with the community.

Within the GLOBE project, CEOs from companies in East Germany, Estonia and Romania (N=129) have been interviewed about their value preferences in case of critical management decisions. Furthermore, lower level managers and employees (N=787) filled out questionnaires concerning perceived value preferences of their companies. Drawing on an extended stakeholder approach through focus on managerial values (CSV), we particularly focus on country-based contingencies of managerial values coupled with other context factors like managerial position and ownership. The findings show that there are specific country-based combinations of corporate social values in the companies studied, with strategic orientation in East Germany, shareholder focus coupled with a relatively strong religious orientation in Romania and an orientation on shareholders as well as on employees and community in Estonia. Moreover, an interaction between the country effect and organizational factors shaping managerial decisions can be observed.

Chapter 9

The main purpose of this paper is to examine the impact of prevalent management behavior on management attitudes about creativeness and innovativeness, while also considering the impact of personal values, in three Central European economies, having different development paths, namely Slovenia, Austria, and Poland. Personal values are measured using Schwartz value survey, using openness to change, conservation, self-transcendence and self-enhancement value dimensions. Results reveal that manager's behavior significantly influences on manager's attitudes regarding innovativeness, in all three countries. The impact of personal values on shaping management behavior and manager's attitudes toward innovativeness is significant only in few instances in Austrian sample, while in Slovenia and Poland it is insignificant. Regarding the mediating effect of managers' personal values on the association between management behavior and their creativeness, our results reveal marginal role of personal values.

Culture is a scheme of knowledge shared by a relatively large number of people. Hence, it is a collection of explicit as well as implicit patterns of behaviour. It makes the members of the culture feel, think act and react in a certain, predefined way, hence makes their actions predictable. The literature on cultures, especially that of national cultures has focused on cultural differences and on understanding and measuring them for long decades, but in the 21st century the attention has shifted to leveraging benefits of multicultural environments and experiences. Hence, present paper—after providing a short insight into the basic approaches of national cultures—endeavours to analyse Russian and Hungarian culture. We aim to present the similarities and differences of the two cultures, along with tools and methods that are able to lessen these differences and harvest the benefits of them.

Chapter 11

Innovation is a driver of economic growth, wealth and prosperity. On the other hand, corruption emerges as a worldwide problem responsible for sapping resources, inequality, human suffering and poverty. This study hypothesizes that national culture, measured using Hofstede's six cultural dimensions, have an impact on corruption and innovation, and that highly corrupt nations are less innovative. Data were obtained from Hofstede's, Transparency International, and Global Innovation websites for the year 2012. The findings support the claim that most national culture aspects have an impact on corruption, although their impact on innovation is less measurable. Corruption was found to have a strong and negative effect on innovation. Our results draw attention to the usefulness of Hofstede's six-dimension framework in research and the need for further analysis on how corruption influences innovation through mechanisms other than national culture.

The chapter outlines the importance and influence of organizational culture on contemporary project management in the context of variable and complex environment. The main objective of the study is to show what shapes the culture of project management and how it influences the effectiveness of managing projects in circumstances of the contemporary environment. Individual chapters disclose the essence and importance of organizational culture; besides, attention is brought to factors that form the culture of project management with a specific emphasis on social factors, which play the key role. Based on the results of research carried out in Polish companies, the last part of the chapter presents the influence of organizational culture and forming it factors on effectiveness of project management. It also displays the most important aspects of project management culture that influence the effectiveness of project management in realities of today's environment.

This chapter examines the relationship between team learning behavior and employee work related self- efficacy beliefs and further explores the moderating role of individual difference variables, such as masculinity–femininity and uncertainty avoidance values. The study tested three hypotheses using a sample of employees from a large public organization in Pakistan. The results indicated a significant positive relationship between team learning behavior and employee perceptions of their self-efficacy. Regarding the moderating role of individual differences, the data showed that the link between team learning and self-efficacy was stronger for individuals scoring high (versus low) on masculinity orientation. However, the results revealed no empirical evidence to confirm the hypothesis that employees scoring low on uncertainty avoidance will perceive a stronger relationship between team learning and self-efficacy.

Chapter 14

This chapter explores the influence of organisational culture on managerial internal career needs in small third sector social enterprises. Every organisation develops and maintains a unique culture, which provides guidelines and boundaries for the career management of members of the organisation. The research methodology was designed to allow the collection of data from three case study organisations and 24 operational managers working in these organisations. The qualitative findings of the study add to, and help to explain the inter-play between individual manager's internal career needs and organisational culture. Most importantly the findings suggest that when individual manager's internal career needs are closely supported by organisational culture, it increases their desire to stay with the organisation. The findings make an important contribution in the field of organisational career management.

Section 4

Organisations are more and more interested in ensuring flexibility of working time and space for their employees. This approach is enforced both by labour market volatility and company strategic plans, e.g. relocation. However, employers begin to realise that employees' flexibility is limited. While the reasons behind it might be objective (lack of legal regulations, commuting expenses), in some cases it is the employees' personal views that stand in the way. In such situation the company is much more limited in its attempts to offer a greater flexibility to its workforce. The research problem that arises here is as follows: is it possible to define the characteristics and situations in which employees are willing to accept flexible conditions of working time and space? Therefore, the aim of the study is to indicate how to increase work flexibility on the side of employees. The study focuses on four areas, i.e. changing the place of residence due to work, frequent business trips, long commuting and flexible work arrangements.

The main purpose of this article is to examine the relationship between the stress and labour productivity. It is recognized that high stress levels make a negative impact on the job productivity results – the incidents or errors occur because of stressful situations in the working environment. After performing the analysis of stress models, it can be stated, that stress could be assessed as a process, i.e. researches are oriented more on the person, or as the situation, i.e. researches are oriented on the causes of stress in the working environment. The metaanalysis of stress factors allow us to identificate the main causes of stress at work, whose at least partial elimination is essential for every organization to increase the productivity of employee. Analysis of the content of factors that cause stress showed that these factors can be classified into the individual and situational. The labour productivity of employees can be seen as a result of stress management, and interface among stress and job productivity are modelling.

Research about relationship between the leadership behavior and the psychological health is still limited. The effect of job dissatisfaction on health is important not only from medical but also from the economic perspective. The association between leadership behavior, job satisfaction and psychological health in nursing was tested. 640 hospital nurses from surgery and internal medicine departments in Slovenian hospitals participated. Data analysis was carried out by using SPSS, 20.0. The transformational leadership style, leaders' characteristics, job satisfaction predicted better psychological health. More frequent exposure to stress and the lack of stress management was associated with poor psychological health. Job satisfaction is at a medium level. The results indicated that 85% of employees in nursing had good psychological health. The psychological health of employees does not affect only on individual, but also on the quality and effectiveness. It is important to monitor employees' job satisfaction and take care for health by providing a healthy work environment.

The purpose of the chapter is to review the developments in the field of leadership and the concept of empathy, and to examine possible interrelation between empathy and leadership. This chapter describes the complexity of the concept of empathy according to different authors, and refers to the psychological aspects in an attempt to connect this category with organizational behavior. Further, the chapter describes developments in the field of leadership in an attempt to focus on the contribution of the identified approaches to the relations between the leader and the employee. Finally, the chapter describes a perspective that combines chosen elements of empathy and leadership theories.

Technology has pervaded our daily lives more than ever. The use of technology has become a tool to achieve competitive advantage by firms. The pervasive use of technology also has its drawbacks. Employees who cannot recognise the limits between work and leisure may have taken this opportunity to utilise companies' Internet access while at work by surfing non-work related websites to satisfy their own needs. This behaviour is known as Cyberloafing and it is thought to contribute to failures of organisations. This study introduces cyberloafing as one of the counter-productive work behaviour at the workplace. It consists of an introduction to cyberloafing, counter-productive work behaviour, and some reviews on cyberloafing research. Overall, the study provides the reader with a better understanding of cyberloafing.

Preface

Personal values and culture has gained a lot of attention during the last three decades in management and organizational behavior literature. According to Schein (1992), understanding of organizational culture is fundamental to examine what goes on in organizations, how to run them and how to improve them. A huge interest into values and cultural issues in the literature is proven with plethora of contributions examining the role and importance of culture and personal values, using different theoretical backgrounds. Based on the overview of papers are most commonly used cultural dimensions from Hofstede (2001), Schwartz theory of basic values (Schwartz, 1992), Rokeach value theory (Rokeach, 1973) and Ronen and Shenkar (1985) approach.

Studies focusing on cultural and personal values context emphasize decisive role of culture and values for behavior, decision making, strategy formulation and many other issues concerning individuals, groups or organizations. The literature dealing with the impact of cultural settings and personal values on organizational members and their actions and behavior, emphasizes several key areas of researching, ranging from organizational members actions and behavior (Hambrick & Mason, 1984), leadership styles (Brodbeck et al., 2000; Egri & Herman, 2000; Sarros & Santora, 2001; Pastor & Mayo, 2008), decision making process (Ali et al., 1995), innovativeness (Lee, 2008; Nedelko & Potocan, 2013), perception of corporate social responsibility (Dietz et al., 2005; Schultz et al., 2005; Cordano et al., 2010), strategies and goals in organizations (Bates et al., 1995), etc..

From the above mentioned areas of the interest, the most attention is dedicated to the studies addressing the link between values and behavior, since values represent a foundation for management behavior and actions (Selznick, 1957; Hambrick & Mason, 1984; Lang et al., 2000; Pastor & Mayo, 2008). The link between personal values or culture on one hand, and leadership style and behavior on another hand, is frequently examined, whereas the emphasis is often on the samples from well-developed western economies (Egri & Herman, 2000; Sarros & Santora, 2001). For instance, many studies are based on well-known GLOBE study about leadership behavior, encompassing above 60 countries worldwide (House et al., 2004) and its various repetitions (Brodbeck et al., 2000; Cater et al., 2013).

Another important stream of research is dedicated to addressing the role of values for sustainability of organizations. The mainstream literature about sustainability provides many theoretical and empirical investigations of sustainability aspects, mainly focusing on one or two out of three key underlying aspects of sustainability, where the focus is primarily on the environmental aspect (Karp, 1996; Dietz et al., 2005), while researching solely the economic or social aspect, in the context of sustainability, is rare. Considering the two-aspect studies, those dealing with both environmental and economic aspects of sustainability prevail (Munda, 1997). Meanwhile, few studies research linkages between social and other aspects of sustainability or all aspects of sustainability (Udo & Jansson, 2009; Potocan et al.,

2013). Additionally, studies are based mainly on business organizations, while significant less focus is on non-profit oriented organizations.

Next large group of contributions is describing the importance of aligning culture and strategy for organizational success (Schein, 1992; Vestal et al., 1997). Nevertheless, there are only few studies that have examined empirically, the interrelation between specific components of culture and strategy formulation (Gupta, 2011). Researchers have also indicated the importance of organizational culture in strategy implementation among the other factors such as organization structure, communication, work and information system, implementation tactics, and essential business process (Ahmadi et al., 2012). The above thoughts re-emphasize that type and elements of organizational culture need to be aligned with particular organizational strategy (Bates et al., 1995). Apart from its role in establishing competitive advantage, strategy (both intended and realized) also has social function by adjusting and reproducing organizational shared values and social relations it enunciates (Tushman & O'Reilly, 1996; Semler, 1997). The importance of ideas and their symbolic representations for culture and strategy highlight the role of leadership in the strategic management process as well (Waterman Jr et al., 1980; Mintzberg, 1994).

Based on above outlined cognitions, the link between cultural context and values on one hand, and various aspects of employees' behavior and actions on other hand, is frequently examined in the literature, whereas the emphasis is often on the samples from well-developed western economies. Fewer studies examined this link with an explicit focus on former transition or catching up Central and East Europe countries and other transformational societies, like societies form Asia and Latin America. The study of cultural context is often based on Hofstede's cultural dimensions and values based on Schwartz value survey, where values are most frequently considered as single personal values on personal level. There is also significant lack of studies addressing the role of values and culture in various types of organizations, like non-profit organizations. Additionally, there is also lack of studies addressing some promising issues for future research, taking into consideration culture and values context.

OBJECTIVES OF THE BOOK

Despite plethora of findings about the role of culture and values from various standing points, a comprehensive overview of the impact of cultural context and personal values on individual's working and behavior in different cultural settings is still rare in the literature. This book collects on one place contributions, which comprehensively address various areas on which culture and personal values have an impact.

Based on abundant literature, which consider the role of culture and personal values from various viewpoints, we want with this book to provide new insights into this field. This edited book includes: (1) conceptual and theoretical papers dealing with understanding the role of culture and values from various standing points, enabling more comprehensive understanding of the role of culture and values in various organizations and for individual's behavior in various situations, (2) empirical papers, providing evidences about the role of culture and values for organizations and individuals, also by providing examples from less frequently examined areas – like Asia and Latin America and going beyond focusing on profit organizations, with including evidences from organizations operating in non-business area, and (3) chapters addressing further research areas by emphasizing most promising areas of future research, putting in focus context of values or culture.

The aim of this book was to collect contributions about the role of culture and personal values in different areas in organizational working and behavior, and also include cognitions from under-considered viewpoints, like transformation societies and organizations operating outside business sector. This book provides necessary additional knowledge for better understanding of the impact of cultural settings and values on organizational and individuals' working and behavior in organizations in contemporary environment.

Target audience of this book are researchers and academics from all disciplines, educators, and students who are directly or indirectly involved in working of organizations and everyone that needs to become familiar with the role and importance of cultural background and values for organizations and behavior and actions of organizational members. This book provides an insight into various aspects of cultural background and values in organizations and will be helpful to understand complex relations between culture and values on one hand, and studied phenomena and concepts on the other hand. The book will inform readers with evidences from various fields and topic of interests, ranging from decision making issues, role of social networks in shaping leadership behavior, influence of personal experiences in decision-making, CEOs, value preferences, role of values of sustainability, project management culture, to the impact of organizational culture on managers' internal career needs. Besides focus on profit oriented organizations, the book provides also several evidences about the role of personal values and culture in non-profit organizations, which expand the potential target audience of the book. The book also emphasizes promising ways and areas of future research. Cognitions about the role of culture under one title will thus serve as a reference book for researchers, educators and students.

STRUCTURE OF THE BOOK

This edited book is organized into 4 sections, containing 19 chapters. First section is addressing general cognitions about the role and importance of culture in organizations and how personal values determine individual's behavior. This section concludes with a chapter addressing organizational culture from a system theory perspective.

Chapter 1 by Manoj Kumar from India discusses the role and importance of culture in organization. The author attempts to show by example, how a computational model can lead theory into areas it previously did not tread, and once that extension is complete, how to proceed down the conventional hypotheses-testing path. The specific topic under author's investigation is the relationship between innovation and organizational structure.

Chapter 2 by Ilona Swiatek-Barylska from Poland examines the consequences of formalization and core values orientation for individual organizational behavior, as well as outcomes such as commitment, job satisfaction and turnover intention rate. The author discusses the problem of management by values and formalization to answer a fundamental question: how much are values and formalization needed in managing people in an organization, and what are the consequences of this managerial choice for individual organizational behavior?

Chapter 3 by Anna Piekarczyk from Poland investigates organization culture from the viewpoint of systems theory of organization. The author discusses organizations as autopoietic systems, as well as relations between organization and individual. The author attempts to define to what extent values and rules characteristic for a given culture can and should be changed.

Second section of the book includes chapters addressing the importance of cultural context and values for behavior, by dealing with how social networks shape leadership in transitioning societies, how personal experiences influence decision making, the role of personal values and context for strategic decision making and the role of personal values for shaping social responsibility.

Chapter 4 by Anne Namatsi Lutomia, Ping Li, Raghida Abdallah Yassine, and Xiaoping Tong from United States of America addresses the role of social networks for shaping leadership. In that context authors examine how Guanxi, Ubuntu, and Wasta shape leadership and culture in China, Kenya, and Lebanon respectively. Based on the cognitions about the associations among variables of the interest, authors provide a conceptual framework, emphasizing the role of Guanxi, Ubunta, and Wasta in shaping workplace leadership and culture. The authors conclude with findings and suggestions for future research of proposed conceptual framework.

Chapter 5 by Thais Spiegel from Brazil examines the influences of personal experience in decision-making. The author investigates what is the role of experiences of the decision-makers' agents and the impact of these on the functioning of the cognitive process of a human decision maker. The author presents 17 inferences that determine the role of the experience in the in the cognitive process of decision-making.

Chapter 6 by Dejana Zlatanović and Jelena Nikolić from Serbia is tackling with growing complexity of strategic decision making, which require holistic approach in strategic-decision making process. The paper shows how system thinking may be helpful for involving different viewpoints in the process of strategic-decision making and improving effectiveness of strategic-decision making process. Among different internal and external factors influencing strategic-decision making, identified based on system approach, the focus is on the role of values and the context. Paper outlines possible improvement of strategic decision making effectiveness, based on utilization of system approach and discusses the role of values and context.

Chapter 7 by Zlatko Nedelko, Vojko Potocan and Nikša Alfirević from Slovenia and Croatia, addresses the role of personal values in fostering social responsibility of higher education organizations. The authors argue that higher education organizations should develop stronger ties with the community, which is under considered way for enhancing social responsibility of higher education organizations. In that framework, the paper theoretically discusses the role of values of key stakeholder groups – namely managers of higher education organizations, teachers, students and community, for further development of socially responsible higher education. The chapter shows important role personal values and outlines the need for further empirical investigation of considered topics.

Third section of the book encompasses empirical studies examining various aspects of culture and values, ranging from CEOs values preferences in management decisions, influence of personal values on innovativeness, analyzing Russian and Hungary culture, impact of national culture on innovation and corruption, and what shapes culture of project management. This section is concluded by two empirical chapters from non-profit organizations, addressing uncertainty avoidance values in public organization and the link between organization culture and manager's internal career needs in social enterprises.

Chapter 8 by Rainhart Lang and Irma Rybnikova from Germany based their empirical paper on the results from GLOBE project, focusing on samples of East Germany, Estonia and Romania. Authors outline results about CEOs value preferences in case of critical management decisions, based on extended stakeholder approach and through focus on corporate social values of managers in transforming societies. Results show specific country-based combinations of corporate social values and strategic orientation in East Germany, shareholder focus and religious orientation in Romania and orientation on shareholders, employees and community in Estonia. Based on the results several managerial implications are outlined.

Chapter 9 by Zlatko Nedelko and Maciej Brzozowski from Slovenia and Poland examines the association between management behavior and mangers' attitudes towards innovativeness, and the influence of personal values on this link. The authors report the results for three Central European economies with different development paths, namely Austria, Slovenia, and Poland.

Chapter 10 by Kornélia Lazányi, Péter Holicza, and Ksenia Baimakova from Russia and Hungary, deals with cultural patterns of two countries. Authors argue that culture importantly determine individuals actions and thus make individuals actions predictable. Paper analyzes Russian and Hungarian culture and outlines similarities and differences of two compared cultures. The main contribution of the paper lies in practical implications, which outline several possible instruments to lessen differences between cultures and gain the benefit of them utilization.

Chapter 11 by Pedro Silva and António Carrizo Moreira from Portugal examines how national culture influence on innovation and corruption. Utilizing Hofstede's six-dimension framework, Global innovation data and Transparency international data, authors proves that most dimensions of culture have impact on corruption, while the impact on innovation is less significant. The paper provides a fertile ground work for further examination of the impact of national culture on the association between corruption and innovation, by moderating the impact beyond national culture – i.e. Hofstede's model.

Chapter 12 by Tomasz Kopczynski from Poland outlines the importance and influence of organizational culture on contemporary project management in the context of variable and complex environment. The main objective of the author's research is to explain what shapes the culture of project management and how it influences the effectiveness of managing projects in circumstances of the contemporary business environment.

Chapter 13 by Ghulam Mustafa and Richard Glavee-Geo from Norway focuses on uncertainty avoidance values. In that context, the chapter presents an empirical examination of the relationship between team learning behavior and self-efficacy, while using masculinity vs. femininity and uncertainty avoidance values as moderating variables. The study was done in a large public organization in Pakistan. Results show significant and positive association between team learning behavior and employees' self-efficacy. The impact of uncertainty avoidance values on the relationship between team learning behavior and self-efficacy is insignificant. Authors provide several managerial implications at the end of the chapter.

Chapter 14 by Chi Maher from United Kingdom addresses the link between organization culture and managers' internal career needs. Author argues that every organization develops unique culture which creates specific guidelines and limitations for career management. Based on the answers from small third sector social enterprises, the paper helps to clarify the inter-play between individual manager's internal career needs and organizational culture. Author emphasizes that when manager's internal career needs are strongly backed up with organizational culture, managers desire to stay in organization is increased.

Final section of the book addresses possible further research directions and areas of interest, in which the role of culture and values should be considered in order to more comprehensively understand the phenomena, by addressing workplace and working conditions, stress and labor productivity, job satisfaction and psychosocial health, and empathy and finally cyberloafing.

Chapter 15 by Beata Skowron-Mielnik and Grzegorz Wojtkowiak from Poland investigates the flexibility of the workplace and working conditions. The authors analyze if it is possible to draw conclusions about preferences of job applicants or employees regarding work flexibility, based on demographic characteristics and competence. The chapter tries to define the characteristics and situations in which employees agree to flexible conditions in terms of working time and space.

Chapter 16 by Ilona Skačkauskienė and Rasa Pališkienė from Lithuania focuses on stress and labor productivity. Based on the model of job stress, organizational culture and organizational values are emphasized as an important building block of healthy, low-stress and high productive working place. It could be argued that values and organizational culture plays an important role in association with stress perception. Paper provides a fertile ground for further examination of values and organizational culture in frame of stress in organizations. Further examination of the role of values in moderating the association between stress and labor productivity can be done and reveal how values shape perception of stress.

Chapter 17 by Mateja Lorber, Sonja Treven and Damijan Mumel examines in their chapter how leadership behavior shapes employees' job satisfaction and psychological health. Their link to the value theory is leadership behavior, which is importantly depended upon individual and organizational values. Thus, this paper lays a ground work for deeper examination of the role of personal values of managers for employees' job satisfaction and psychological health, like identifying key values of managers, which are crucial for their behavior regarding job satisfaction, stress management.

Chapter 18 by Nira Shalev from Israel examines new directions in the concept of empathy and leadership theory. The author attempts to expose the two concepts and try to relate them, establishing a conceptual bridge between leadership and empathy. The specific aim of the author's study is to review the different aspects of the concept of empathy, in an attempt to position them within the organizational context.

Chapter 19 by J-Ho Siew Ching and Ramayah Thurasamy from Malaysia discusses cyberloafing as an example of the counter-productive work behavior at the workplace. The authors examine the nature of cyberfloating, activities and variables related to cyberloafing, as well as the impact of cyberloafing on organizational culture and effectiveness.

The both editors of the book cooperate in last couple of years in research about the impact of personal values on employees in organizations from various standing points. The main focus in on cross-cultural studies, including countries from Central Europe, with the aim to better understand the impact of personal values and culture background on employees' behavior, leadership styles, innovative actions in countries having different development paths in last two decades. The both editors are involved in academic training related to the management, organizations, strategic management, and business ethics.

The editing journey of this book was a delightful yet very demanding journey, and we hope that we were able to provide to the readers comprehensive insight into the issues about the role of culture and values, from different perspectives.

Zlatko Nedelko
University of Maribor, Slovenia

Maciej Brzozowski
Poznan University of Economics and Business, Poland

REFERENCES

Ahmadi, S. A. A., Salamzadeh, Y., Daraei, M., & Akbari, J. (2012). Relationship between organizational culture and strategy implementation: Typologies and dimensions. *Global Business and Management Research: An International Journal*, 4(3/4), 286–299.

Ali, A. J., Azim, A., & Krishnan, K. D. (1995). Expatriates and host country nationals: Managerial values and decision styles. *Leadership and Organizational Development*, 16(6), 27–34. doi:10.1108/01437739510092252

Bates, K. A., Amundson, S. D., Schroeder, R. G., & Morris, W. T. (1995). The crucial interrelationship between manufacturing strategy and organizational culture. *Management Science, 41*(10), 1565–1580. doi:10.1287/mnsc.41.10.1565

Brodbeck, F. C., Frese, M., Akerblom, S., Audia, G., Bakacsi, G., Bendova, H., & Wunderer, R. et al. (2000). Cultural variation of leadership prototypes across 22 european countries. *Journal of Occupational and Organizational Psychology, 73*(1), 1–29. doi:10.1348/096317900166859

Cater, T., Lang, R., & Szabo, E. (2013). Values and leadership expectations of future managers: Theoretical basis and methodological approach of the globe student project. *Journal for East European Management Studies, 18*(4), 442–462.

Cordano, M., Welcomer, S., Scherer, R., Pradenas, L., & Parada, V. (2010). Understanding cultural differences in the antecedents of pro-environmental behavior: A comparative analysis of business students in the united states and chile. *The Journal of Environmental Education, 41*(4), 224–238. doi:10.1080/00958960903439997

Dietz, T., Fitzgerald, A., & Shwom, R. (2005). Environmental values. *Annual Review of Environment and Resources, 30*(1), 335–372. doi:10.1146/annurev.energy.30.050504.144444

Egri, C. P., & Herman, S. (2000). Leadership in the north american environmental sector: Values, leadership styles, and contexts of environmental leaders and their organizations. *Academy of Management Journal, 43*(4), 571–604. doi:10.2307/1556356

Gupta, B. (2011). A comparative study of organizational strategy and culture across industry. *Benchmarking: An International Journal, 18*(4), 510–528. doi:10.1108/14635771111147614

Hambrick, D. C., & Mason, P. A. (1984). Upper echelons - the organization as a reflection of its top managers. *Academy of Management Review, 9*(2), 193–206.

Hofstede, G. (2001). *Culture's consequences. Comparing values, behaviors, institutions, and organizations across nations*. Thousand Oaks, CA: SAGE.

House, R. J., Hanges, P. J., Javidan, M., Dorfman, P. W., & Gupta, V. (2004). *Culture, leadership, and organizations: The globe study of 62 societies*. Thousand Oaks, CA: Sage.

Karp, D. G. (1996). Values and their effect on pro-environmental behavior. *Environment and Behavior, 28*(1), 111–133. doi:10.1177/0013916596281006

Lang, R., Kovač, J., & Bernik, M. (2000). *Management v tranzicijskih procesih* [management in transition processes]. Kranj: Moderna organizacija.

Lee, J. (2008). Effects of leadership and leader-member exchange on innovativeness. *Journal of Managerial Psychology, 23*(6), 670–687. doi:10.1108/02683940810894747

Mintzberg, H. (1994). The fall and rise of strategic-planning. *Harvard Business Review, 72*(1), 107–114.

Munda, G. (1997). Environmental economics, ecological economics, and the concept of sustainable development. *Environmental Values, 6*(2), 213–233. doi:10.3197/096327197776679158

Nedelko, Z., & Potocan, V. (2013). The role of management innovativeness in modern organizations. *Journal of Enterprising Communities, 7*(1), 36–49. doi:10.1108/17506201311315590

Pastor, J. C., & Mayo, M. (2008). Transformational leadership among spanish upper echelons: The role of managerial values and goal orientation. *Leadership and Organization Development Journal, 29*(4), 340–358. doi:10.1108/01437730810876140

Potocan, V., Mulej, M., & Nedelko, Z. (2013). The influence of employees ethical behavior on enterprises social responsibility. *Systemic Practice and Action Research, 26*(6), 497–511. doi:10.1007/s11213-013-9299-3

Rokeach, M. (1973). *The nature of human values*. New York: The Free Press.

Ronen, S., & Shenkar, O. (1985). Clustering countries on attitudinal dimensions: A review and synthesis. *Academy of Management Review, 10*(3), 435–454.

Sarros, J. C., & Santora, J. C. (2001). Leaders and values: A cross-cultural study. *Leadership and Organization Development Journal, 22*(5), 243–248. doi:10.1108/01437730110397310

Schein, E. (1992). *Organizational culture and leadership: A dynamic view*. San Francisco: Jossey-Bass.

Schultz, P. W., Gouveia, V. V., Cameron, L. D., Tankha, G., Schmuck, P., & Franek, M. (2005). Values and their relationship to environmental concern and conservation behavior. *Journal of Cross-Cultural Psychology, 36*(4), 457–475. doi:10.1177/0022022105275962

Schwartz, S. H. (1992). Universals in the content and structure of values - theoretical advances and empirical tests in 20 countries. *Advances in Experimental Social Psychology, 25*, 1–65. doi:10.1016/S0065-2601(08)60281-6

Selznick, P. (1957). *Leadership in administration: A sociological interpretation*. New York: Row Peterson.

Semler, S. W. (1997). Systematic agreement: A theory of organizational alignment. *Human Resource Development Quarterly, 8*(1), 23–40. doi:10.1002/hrdq.3920080105

Tushman, M. L., & OReilly, C. A. III. (1996). The ambidextrous organizations: Managing evolutionary and revolutionary change. *California Management Review, 38*(4), 8–30. doi:10.2307/41165852

Udo, V. E., & Jansson, P. M. (2009). Bridging the gaps for global sustainable development: A quantitative analysis. *Journal of Environmental Management, 90*(12), 3700–3707. doi:10.1016/j.jenvman.2008.12.020 PMID:19500899

Vestal, K. W., Fraliex, R. D., & Spreier, S. W. (1997). Organizational culture: The critical link between strategy and results. *Hospital & Health Services Administration, 42*(13), 339–365. PMID:10169292

Waterman, R. H. Jr, Peters, T. J., & Phillips, J. R. (1980). Structure is not organization. *Business Horizons, 23*(3), 14–26. doi:10.1016/0007-6813(80)90027-0

Section 1

Chapter 1
The Role and Importance of Culture in Organization

Manoj Kumar
Mother Parwati Education Services, India

ABSTRACT

First a traditional neo-classical model of decision making is broadened by introducing agents who interact in an organization. The resulting computational model is analyzed using virtual experiments to consider how different organizational structures (different network topologies) affect the evolutionary path of an organization's corporate culture. These computational experiments establish testable hypotheses concerning structure, culture, and performance, and those hypotheses are tested empirically using data from an international sample of firms. In addition to learning something about organizational structure and innovation, the paper demonstrates how computational models can be used to frame empirical investigations and facilitate the interpretation of results in a traditional fashion.

INTRODUCTION

Agent-based computational models are enormously innovative and flexible, able to incorporate non-linear relationships, stochastic dynamics, and heterogeneous decision makers. But their flexibility exacts a price. Agent-based models have so many degrees of freedom that a particular simulation can be designed to fit almost any data array. If we can always construct a computational version of some model that fits our data, is the model truly falsifiable? This malleability is especially troublesome when AB models verify their simulations by comparing a model's results to some vague stylized facts that may have been considered during the model's design. We can do better. In this chapter, we suggest that agent-based models be subjected to the same scrutiny commonly applied to neoclassical theory; their predictions should be tested empirically. Ultimately, it will be the empirical relevance of agent-based models that will lead to the broader acceptance of computational modeling as a standard theoretical tool in economics. Fagiolo, Windrum, and Moneta (2007) review the issue of empirical validation in agent-based models and provide a critical guide to the alternative validation approaches being explored in the AB modeling community. This study enters the empirical validation fray, but in a more traditional fashion. In this chapter,

DOI: 10.4018/978-1-5225-2480-9.ch001

an agent-based model extends an established, neo-classical theory, and that extended model generates empirical hypotheses which are then tested using standard econometric procedures. This approach is in the spirit of the pioneering study by Young and Burke (2011) who use an agent-based model to examine the geographic distribution of crop-sharing contracts in Illinois. Our objective is similar; to show by example, how a computational model can lead theory into areas it previously did not tread, and once that extension is complete, how we can proceed down the conventional hypotheses-testing path. Fagiolo, Windrum, and Moneta (2007) point out conventional hypothesis testing procedures also struggle with the relationship between theory and empirical data, but neo-classical economics has a consensus about testing procedures that hasn't yet emerged in AB modeling. The specific topic under investigation is the relationship between innovation and organizational structure.

INNOVATION AND ORGANIZATIONAL STRUCTURE

Ravasi and Schultz (2006) broadly define corporate culture as shared mental assumptions that define appropriate behaviors in organizations and thereby guide interpretation and action for various situations. The general agreement is that culture is a set of cognitions shared by members of a social unit (e.g., O'Reilly *et al.*, 2014; Smircich, 2013); those with strong cultures have both widely shared norms and values as well as employees who are dedicated to, and motivated to fulfilling, shared goals (O'Reilly and Chatman, 2006; Sørensen, 2012). Moreover, research links organizational culture to organizational effectiveness and shows that firms with certain cultural traits demonstrate more growth and profitability than others (e.g., Denison & Mishra, 2015). Although there are many different conceptualizations of organizational culture (Zhou *et al.*, 2006), some organizations are known to have a culture of innovation seeming to have success with round after round of new products and ideas. A history of study on innovation (Scherer, 2012; Mansfield, 2013; Cohen & Klepper, 2006) identifies size, research and development efforts, new product marketing efforts, top management support as well as the industry to which the firm belongs, and the country in which it resides as determinants of a firm's innovativeness. This study adds the potential effect of an organization's structure. Our contention is that the organization of a firm affects the evolution of that firm's decision-making processes, which affects the firm's corporate culture. Such a view is consistent with prior research examining organizational learning (March, 2011), the effects of organizational design on individual decision making (e.g., Carley & Lin, 2007), and the effects of organizational types on corporate culture (e.g., Harrington, 2008). For example, March (2011) argues that organizations store information in their forms (i.e., organizational networks), which, in turn, is used to socialize individuals in the organization. Harrington (2008) provides evidence that organizational types affect corporate culture through, among other things, recruitment and socialization. An agent-based model of the evolution of corporate culture is constructed by extending Harrington's (2008) model of rigid and flexible agents. We impose spatial constraints on a revision of his model to represent an abstract organization's decision-making environment. In our model firms are populated by agents with different decision-making philosophies; some are innovators, comfortable with change and willing to alter their strategy with changing circumstances. Others are more conservative, tradition-bound decision makers who are guided by ideology; they apply a particular set of procedures to every issue. We place these different agents into an organization and observe their performance as they are confronted with a series of decision-making situations. Formally, consider a population of N agents who are making decisions as they face one of two possible states of the world, $s \in \{0, 1\}$. In each time period agents are required to make a decision, $d \in \{0, 1\}$. Decision "1" is correct if the state of the world equals "1", and $d = 0$ is correct if $s = 0$.

Three types of agents make these decisions. Two of these types are conservative decision makers who adopt a particular philosophy and adhere to it regardless of the current environment. They are named agents C_0, those who always decide $d = 0$, and agents C_1, those who always decide $d = 1$. The third type is innovative agents, I, who are agents willing to alter their perception of a problem as the respond to the world around them. Simply, agents I always choose the action that is appropriate given the state of the world, $d = s$. So, agent C_0 is correct whenever the state of the world is $s = 0$; C_1 is correct whenever the state of the world is $s = 1$, and innovative agents, type I, always make the correct decision.

The model is initiated by randomly populating an organization with agents of each type. Then at regular intervals pairs of agents are selected, a state of the world is randomly determined, and the agents execute their decision-making algorithm. If agent i is of type C_0, his opponent, agent j, is of type C_1, and the state of the world is $s = 1$, then agent i loses and agent j wins. Winning causes the successful decision-making algorithm to spread to the losing agent, in this example, agent i switches from being type C_0 to being of type C_1. This spread of a decision-making philosophy can be thought of as the loser seeing the light and becoming a disciple of the victorious agent. Over time, the decision-making philosophy of the most frequently successful agents spreads, the distribution of agents following each decision-making algorithm adjusts, and we can track the success of a particular approach by observing its spread or contraction. In many situations the paired agents make the same decision. For example, suppose agent i is of type I, agent j is type C_1, and $s = 1$. Both agents make the correct decision, $d = 1$. In the case of draws, the agent with the greatest experience in executing that particular decision is victorious. Thus agents acquire proficiency with experience; if agent i makes decision 1 more frequently than agent j, then agent i becomes more proficient in that type of decision. If i and j meet, then agent i, being more proficient implementing decision 1, wins and agent j switches from type C_1 to I. If both agents select the correct action and both are equally experienced, both survive to participate in the next round. Similarly, if two agents of the same type meet, both survive to the next round of play. In the end, survivorship depends on both innovativeness and proficiency. To allow for this more interesting circumstance we weigh the probability that one state of the world emerges by a parameter demoted b, where $b \in (\frac{1}{2}, 1)$. On average $s = 1$ is more likely to arise than $s = 0$. Thus, the value of parameter b alters the importance of being flexible. Similarly, we tune the impact of proficiency, p, by restricting the length of each agent's memory. An agent acquires proficiency with experience, i.e., the more often an agent chooses an action the better he becomes at executing that action. However proficiency fades because the value of practice decays over time and eventually vanishes. Proficiency is assumed to deteriorate linearly, the rate of decay being set by memory length. Specifically, labeling the maximum memory length as M then agent

i's proficiency is $p^i = \sum_{m=1}^{M} (d^i_{t-M+m}) \left(\dfrac{m}{M} \right)$ where d^i_{t-M+m} is the decision ($d \in \{0, 1\}$) made by agent i in

the preceding M periods. For example, if $M = 10$, and agent i has used action 1 for the last four periods and action 0 for rest, then his proficiency value, p, for action 1 equals $1 + 0.9 + 0.8 + 0.7 + 0 + ... + 0 = 3.4$. Note that a longer memory allows for a greater proficiency advantage for rigid agents, and if $M = 0$ all agents are equally proficient. Also note that agents retain their updated proficiency for each action when they switch types because it is their decision history that determines their proficiency.

To formalize this organizational structure, we view the organization as a network. Each node of the network is occupied by an agent and the edges that connect nodes define which agents interact. Altering the architecture of the network alters the organization's structure. The question is, do these structural changes affect the evolution of the decision-making culture in some systematic fashion? To explore this possibility we do not restrict the range of organizational structures by mapping the decision-making machinery of specific firms; instead we explore the evolution of decision making in abstract organizations with exaggerated characteristics. Among these organizations are linear, well-defined organizations, rigid hierarchical structures, organic or free-flowing organizations, and random networks. This study initially reports experimental results of six vastly different networks (these would be idyllic organizational structures) and later a series of more complex networks are created by randomly severing and reattaching edges in these base structures. By repeatedly playing the conservative/innovative decision-making contest in these hypothetical networks we can observe how network structure (organizational characteristics) can affect the evolution of corporate culture. To help visualize the organizational characteristics, a small sketch of each initial network is given in Figure 1.

Consider the line network at the top of Figure 1, each agent interacts with four other "neighbors," two on each side, thus agent i interacts only with agents g, h, j, and k. One could imagine an organization in which individuals occupy offices along a hallway and pass along information with their closest office mates. But this line network is not intended to model an actual firm, more importantly it is instead used to explore the effects of a linear type of organization, one in which information would be passed along person to person to person. While there may be no firms that possess such a rigidly extreme architecture, many firms probably house some departments or areas that incorporate this sort of linear information flow. Similarly, the grid lends a two-dimensional spatial flavor to this, "talk with your office mates" construct, reminiscent perhaps of a cubicles space. The tree network can represent a standard hierarchal organization with a clear chain of command and a complete network reflects a more egalitarian structure, anyone can interact with anyone. A random network, in which edges are random, is included to provide the contrast of decision making in a disorganized organization. Finally the scale-free network is a frequently observed network consisting of a few hubs, nodes with many links, connected to nodes with few links. Small-world networks, also important in practice and theory, are added to the experiments in the next section.

It is important to reiterate that the hypothetical networks used in the computational experiments of the next section do not represent actual organizations. While it may be possible to map out precise communication networks of firms, that data and time intensive commitment would make it prohibitively expensive to attempt such a process for the 400 firms included in this study. Consequently the simplified structures of Table 1 are used for our experiments. Their exaggerated characteristics allow us to distinguish between types of organizations, hierarchal versus integrative, for example, and to see if there is a tendency for different decision-making cultures to evolve based on those characteristics.

Combining the decision-making game and alternative network architectures creates the agent-based model used here. The shape of the organization's internal network defines the set of potential agent pairings. In other words, in each round of play, agent i is matched with a randomly selected agent from his immediate neighborhood, defined as the set of agents with whom he is linked. Depending on the state of the world, agent i wins and converts his neighbor or he loses and is converted. Manipulating the pattern of connections between nodes alters the internal structure of the organization; it changes the agents' neighbors. We explore whether these alternative topologies systematically affect the evolution of a firm's innovative culture.

As the next section demonstrates, organizational structure seems to be a fundamental component of organizational decision making, that is, the same agents making the same decisions and facing the same states of the world behave differently in one organizational structure than another. The pattern of connections in an organization, or the topology of a firm's network, affects the evolution of corporate strategy and the mores of the eventual corporate culture.

THE EMERGENCE OF A CORPORATE CULTURE

There is some precedent for using agent-based models to explore corporate culture. For example, March (2011) constructs a model in which individuals adjust to a corporate code while the code evolves in response to the actions of individuals. Carley and Lin (2007) and Chang and Harrington (2005) used agent-based models to study organizational decision making and problem solving. And Harrington (2008) simulate the effects of turnover and socialization on the convergence of culture. However, none of these papers go beyond the simulation to see if those effects appear in nature. This study uses virtual experiments to construct hypotheses concerning the impact of organizational structure on innovative culture. Those hypotheses are then tested with empirical data from an international sample of firms.

Here, a series of virtual experiments explore structure and culture. In these experiments a population of agents, like amounts of each agent type, C_0, C_1, and I, are randomly dispersed across a network. An agent, a neighbor of that agent and a state of the world are all randomly selected to engage in a decision-making round. Each agent employs his decision-making philosophy (type I setting $d = s$, type C_0 setting $d = 0$, and C_1 setting $d = 1$). With the state of the world revealed, the winner survives and gains a round of proficiency, and the loser copies the victor's strategy type. Then a second agent is selected randomly; one of his neighbors is chosen; they make decisions, and so forth. The first round concludes after N random selections and in each round, agents play no more than once. This implies that if agent i is randomly selected by his neighbor he does not play again in that same round even if he is selected and consequently in some rounds some agents do not play. By restricting agents to a single play in each round, a simple snapshot of the distribution of decisions after each round of play captures every agent's decision. Removing this constraint results in a few more individual decisions in each round but has virtually no impact on the distribution of decisions given in Tables 1 and 2 or on the implications of the model. The second round begins with another random selection of players and states of the world, and the process repeats.

Before executing the cross-network experiments we align the AB model with the original analytic model developed by Harrington (2008) to see if the models yield comparable results under similar initial conditions. Thus we consider a large population of agents ($N = 900$) and a complete network (one in which every agent is connected with every other agent). Harrington's original model assumed any agent could be matched with any other agent which implies a complete network structure, although he did not identify it as such. Under these conditions our computational results readily replicate his analytical insights. For example, as the value of b increases, which increases the likelihood that $s = 1$, the benefits of being innovative and open to alternative strategies (being of type I) decline. This is intuitive; suppose $b \rightarrow 1$ so that $s = 1$ in almost every period. In such an environment there is little advantage to being an innovator because the conservative decision maker of type 1, is correct most of the time. Also consistent with Harrington, we find that a longer memory increases the advantage of being a tradition-bound decision maker. Recall that proficiency is acquired through practice; the more often an agent employs a particular decision, the more proficient he becomes. Thus, memory places a ceiling on proficiency. For example, if $M = 10$, an agent's proficiency reflects his actions in the last ten rounds of play. Thus, a conservative agent can have ten rounds of experience, which will defeat most innovators. However, if $M = 0$ there is no buildup of proficiency and the best philosophy is to be flexible. Harrington finds that even if memory is short (but > 0), rigid decision making dominates, but with less memory it takes more rounds of play for that result to emerge. These dynamics exist in our computational analysis as well.

Acs *et al.* (2008) argue for the value of aligning computational models, showing that a new model can reproduce the results of an existing model before it offers an extension. This computational model successfully replicates the dynamics and the emergent properties of Harrington's (2008) work which anchors the computational approach to his analytic results. With that foundation, we can probe more deeply into the impact of different organizational structures by introducing different networks. As we shall see, altering an organization's structure can affect the evolutionary path of its culture.

Organizational Structure Networks

To concentrate on organizational differences we fix the parameters b and M and study a variety of different network structures, starting with the simple networks shown in Figure 1. These highly idealized networks are our starting point not because they represent actual organizations but because their simplicity lets us focus on specific network attributes. We analyze more complex and more realistic networks later in the section. We fix the parameter $b = 0.6$, and so expect state of the world $s = 1$ to occur about 60% of the time and $s = 0$ about 40% of the time. Memory is set at ten periods ($M = 10$), so that proficiency in a particular action depends on the actions taken in the last ten rounds of play. Once again agents of all three types are initially scattered about the organization and the decision-making duals begin.

At this point a critical constraint is imposed; we assume an organization's network architecture does not change during the experiments. Culture evolves but networks do not. There is a vast literature on the evolution of networks, but those studies usually focus on attributes of the emergent network. See Wilhite (2006) for overviews and Chang and Harrington (2005) for an application. This is a critical decision because it constrains the degrees of freedom in the model and the universe of potential results. In short, this restriction allows us to perform controlled experiments. By fixing the topology of the network at the beginning of each experiment, we can test specific network attributes and hold all other attributes constant. The experiment can then be repeated in a different (but also fixed) network. If networks are allowed to evolve, it would be difficult to isolate the impact of specific network characteristics, and designing empirical hypotheses would be too arbitrary (Wilhite, 2006). In addition, there is a practical side to this restriction. Even though most networks evolve over time, their evolution may occur more slowly than the pace of the economic decisions being made in the network. In such cases a fixed network may be a better representation of reality than an evolving network.

Table 1 displays results of the many virtual experiments performed within this structure. Each network configuration, or organizational structure, was analyzed with different population sizes, the largest containing 900 agents and the smallest containing only 9. Then, each network/population combination was subjected to one hundred independent experiments; that is, the data in each cell of Table 1 reflect 100 different initial scatterings of the three agent types. The cells in Table 1 report the percentage of the 100 experiments that converge on various strategies. Each experiment ended with the universal adoption of a single decision-making strategy, sometimes a flexible strategy and sometimes a rigid one. Naturally larger networks take longer to converge than smaller networks, and networks with a greater diameter (measured by the longest geodesic path in the network) tend to converge more slowly. However, most networks converge quickly, in less than 500 rounds of play.

Figure 1.

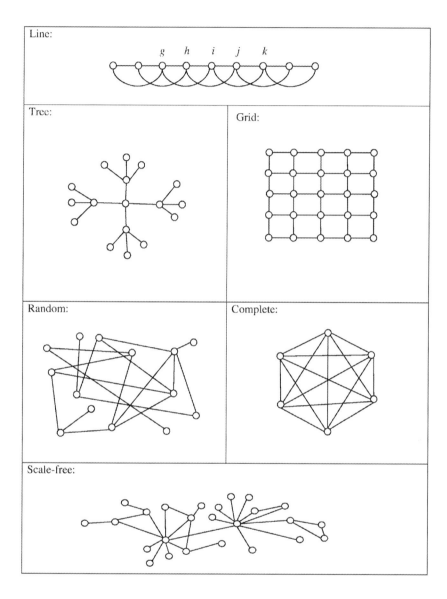

Table 1 shows that conservative decision makers of type zero, C_0, rarely survive. Extinction is the logical end for these agents, as they are making the wrong decision most of the time. In some of the very small organizations these agents occasionally survive because the less likely state-of-the-world ($s = 0$) just happens to arise frequently in the early rounds of play. In those rare cases a culture of type 0 dominates by accident.

Second, reading down the columns we see smaller organizations are more likely to evolve into flexible, innovation organizations while larger firms become more conservative. Why? As it turns out, size affects the length of the time horizon over which an organization's culture emerges, and this shorter time frame favors innovative activity. Figure 2 displays a representative firm of 900 individuals and shows the proliferation (or declination) of each type of decision maker in this organization. While the data relevant to

Table 1. Percentage of times organizations converge to a particular conservative culture (C_0 or C_1) or an innovative culture (I).

Population	Line	Tree	Grid	Random	Scale-free	Complete
900	0% C_0 100% C_1 0% I	0% C_0 100% C_1 0% I	0% C_0 100% C_1 0% I	0% C_0 100% C_1 0% I	0% C_0 100% C_1 0% I	0% C_0 100% C_1 0% I
400	0% C_0 100% C_1 0% I	0% C_0 100% C_1 0% I	0% C_0 100% C_1 0% I	0% C_0 94% C_1 6% I	0% C_0 98% C_1 2% I	0% C_0 66% C_1 34% I
100	0% C_0 100% C_1 0% I	0% C_0 98% C_1 2% I	0% C_0 96% C_1 4% I	0% C_0 73% C_1 27% I	0% C_0 77% C_1 23% I	0% C_0 56% C_1 44% I
49	0% C_0 90% C_1 10% I	0% C_0 89% C_1 11% I	0% C_0 83% C_1 17% I	0% C_0 59% C_1 41% I	0% C_0 60% C_1 40% I	0% C_0 51% C_1 49% I
25	0% C_0 64% C_1 36% I	0% C_0 77% C_1 23% I	0% C_0 66% C_1 34% I	0% C_0 58% C_1 42% I	0% C_0 46% C_1 54% I	0% C_0 55% C_1 45% I
9	2% C_0 26% C_1 72% I	3% C_0 25% C_1 72% I	2% C_0 27% C_1 71% I	2% C_0 33% C_1 65% I	0% C_0 25% C_1 75% I	1% C_0 24% C_1 75% I

Data in each cell come from 100 simulations, each with a different initial distributions of strategies.

Figure 2 emanate from a complete network, this pattern is typical of most large organizational structures. Notice how the dynamics unfold. Conservative decision makers of type 0 immediately start to decline and continue to do so until they disappear. Simultaneously, innovators grow rapidly to become the most prevalent type of decision maker in the early rounds. Over time, however, conservative decision makers of type 1 start to proliferate; innovative agents reach their peak and then decline until they too are extinct. This early proliferation of innovative agents coupled with their eventual decline reflects the shifting advantage given by innovation and proficiency. In the beginning no agent possesses proficiency in any action, and so innovators win or tie in every round. Conservative agents of type 1 win or tie most of their pairings (because $s = 1$ is more likely than $s = 0$), but they lose when $s = 0$ and they are matched with an agent C_0 or I. Over time, however, the surviving C_1 agents gain an edge in proficiency because they have a history of making the same decision in every period. From then on, C_1 agents tend to win when $s = 1$ and innovative agents win when $s = 0$. Since $s = 1$ occurs more frequently, C_1 grows and I declines.

But this proficiency advantage takes some time to develop, and in small firms the process can be truncated. In small organizations the entire population may have switched to an innovative decision philosophy before conservative agents had a chance to establish their proficiency advantage. Thus, smaller firms are less likely to get locked into a fixed ideological approach to decision making. Another observation can be gleaned from the dynamics sketched in Figure 2. Innovative decision makers tend to dominate in the early rounds of decision making. Thus, even though a firm's culture may not be fully formed, we expect younger firms to be more innovative. And, we might expect to see changes where young dynamic firms grow pedantic and conservative over time.

Third, notice how the number of firms adopting an innovative decision-making culture increases as we move horizontally to the right in Table 1. This increase in innovation stems from a more subtle

Figure 2.

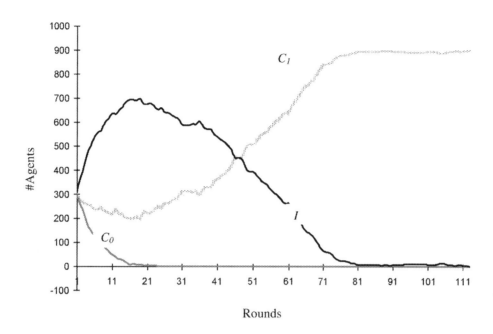

organizational characteristic; it involves the pattern of the connections in these networks. The left side of Table 1 contains relatively formal, regimented organizational structures: the line, tree, and grid. Such organizations have extreme order, lines of communication that reflect a well-defined chain of command or a formal, almost mechanistic, set of procedures and processes through which decisions are channeled. Toward the right side of Table 1 lie networks with a less systematic structure, a more informal organization. By definition random networks lack any systematic organization whatsoever. The complete network has a systematic structure because everyone is connected to everyone else, but it is not a very "organized" organization. Thus, Table 1 suggests that organizations with a formal architecture that involves well-defined chains of communication will exhibit greater rigidity in their decision-making practices while more free-flowing, open-access or organic organizations may be more conducive to a flexible decision-making culture.

To look more deeply into that possibility we investigate the impact of a more complex network structure on innovation by replicating these experiments after rewiring the networks into more irregular patterns. The rewiring process follows the small-world procedure described by Watts and Strogatz (2008): a node is randomly selected, one of its edges is severed, and then it is reattached to another randomly selected node. The amount of rewiring is controlled by a parameter, r, which is the probability that each node is rewired. If $r = 0.1$ then approximately 10 percent of the agents selected for rewiring will actually have a connection cut and another attached so higher levels of r lead to greater numbers of alterations in the networks' links. A constraint imposed on this rewiring procedure is that the network must remain connected, i.e., every node must be attainable from every other node. We do not allow rewiring to dissect a network into two or more distinct and separate networks. Because most of the agents in a tree network have a single edge (all those agents out on the end of the branches have only one neighbor), edges were only added during its rewiring. Additionally, rewiring the complete network usually just severed edges.

The rewiring process occurs before the decision-making experiments begin. Thus, rewiring simply creates new network architectures and once the rewiring is complete, these new patterns are frozen and the decision-making evolution game begins. As before, the network architecture does not change during the experiments. The emergent cultures of these more complex structures are reported in Table 2.

In the first column of Table 2 the probability that an agent is rewired equals zero and so these results replicate those of the original networks displayed in the fourth row of Table 1. Subsequent columns report the results of increased rewiring and show that rewiring affects different networks differently. For example, because the connections in a random network are random, a random rewiring has little effect. Severing a few links in the complete network also appears unimportant. However, in all three of the highly structured networks the increasing "messiness" of its rewired links leads to organizations that are much more likely to evolve innovative cultures. Something about the unruliness of these rewired networks seems compatible with innovation. In Table 1, the least innovative organizations were the line, tree, and grid. In Table 2, we see that rewiring has significant effects on all of these previously rigid organizations. While the randomness introduced by rewiring increases the survivability of innovative agents, the effect diminishes with increased rewiring. In Table 2, most of the increased flexibility brought forth by rewiring occurs by the time $r = 0.25$. Additional rewiring continues to increase the chance that the firm will develop an innovative culture, but the marginal impact of additional rewiring falls.

That excessive structure stifles creativity while a randomly rewired, less formal network is fertile ground for creativity is intuitively appealing, but there is more than intuition at work here. There is a systematic reason why a less regimented and more organic organization increases the survivability of innovative agents. Recall that in all of these organizations agents interact solely with their neighbors; however, they indirectly interact with their neighbors' neighbors and more indirectly with their neighbors' neighbors' neighbors, and so forth. For a particular decision-making strategy to spread throughout the network, it must spread neighbor by neighbor, and the pattern of connections influences this spread. As some randomly dispersed links are introduced into a regimented network, there is a greater mixing

Table 2. Rewiring* and organizational convergence to a conservative culture (C_1)** or an innovative culture (I)

	$p = 0$	$p = 0.05$	$p = 0.1$	$p = 0.25$	$p = 0.5$
RANDOM	59% C_1 41% I	59% C_1 41% I	58% C_1 42% I	55% C_1 45% I	59% C_1 41% I
COMPLETE	51% C_1 49% I	51% C_1 49% I	46% C_1 54% I	56% C_1 44% I	51% C_1 49% I
LINE	90% C_1 10% I	78% C_1 22% I	75% C_1 25% I	63% C_1 37% I	59% C_1 41% I
TREE	89% C_1 11% I	80% C_1 20% I	71% C_1 29% I	74% C_1 26% I	68% C_1 32% I
GRID	83% C_1 17% I	83% C_1 17% I	68% C_1 32% I	58% C_1 42% I	60% C_1 40% I
SCALE-FREE	60% C_1 40% I	57% C_1 43% I	64% C_1 36% I	67% C_1 33% I	76% C_1 24% I

p = probability that any particular node is rewired. Population = 49
*In the complete network edges were only severed; in the tree edges were not severed, but added.
**No simulations converged to a conservative culture of type 0, thus C_0 is omitted.

of strategies; in one structure different decision philosophies might be separated by several steps but in another structure those philosophies might be physically close.

To illustrate, consider a straight-line, $k2$ network in which half of the agents are innovative decision makers and the other half are traditionalists, and suppose a string of states of the world arise such that innovators win in every round. As shown in Figure 3, it takes a minimum of four periods for innovative agents to dominate this small organization. Compare that outcome with the same network after only one rewiring, as shown in the bottom of Figure 3. Innovative agents overtake the network in only two periods. Starting with a regimented network such as a tree, line, or grid, rewiring increases the exposure of agents to alternative decision-making philosophies. Greater exposure leads to a more rapid dispersion of strategies, and as we observed in Figure 3, speed favors innovators. Thus, these more complex networks are more likely to evolve an innovative culture.

EMPIRICAL METHODOLOGY AND MEASUREMENT

The agent-based model in the previous section suggests that smaller firms, firms with complex, small-world configurations, and younger firms are more likely to evolve an open and innovative atmosphere. These results were robust to changes in memory length and the probability weights on the state of the

Figure 3.

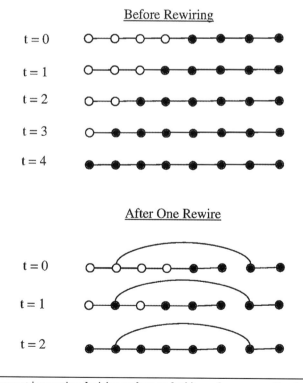

Grey nodes represent innovative decision makers and white nodes conservative decision makers

world (excluding trivial cases such as no memory). To empirically test such conjectures we use data from a new-product development study conducted by Wilhite (2006) and funded by the National Science Foundation that covers more than 400 firms located in fifteen different countries. The central objective of that study was to investigate the new product development process and so a team of researchers would enter an establishment and interview project managers of new product development efforts. The interviewers attempted to explore at least one successful and one failing new product development project in each firm. In addition to the interviews, these managers also answered a battery of survey questions that covered a range of information pertaining to the firm and to new product development. These surveys contain the information used here.

Within each of the 400 firms, one or more new-product development projects were singled out and studied in detail, providing data on more than 900 different innovation projects. Data were collected on attributes of the firm and on specific projects within each firm. One section of the survey also gathered rudimentary information on organizational structure and these parallel observations on structure and innovation allow us to test the hypothesis that structure affects innovation.

There are shortcomings to these data. For example, while certain firm characteristics are measured directly (size, industry group, etc.), much of these data represent responses to an interviewer's question. Those data capture an individual's perception of things as opposed to capturing actual things. Furthermore, the information concerning an organization's structure lacks the specificity needed to plot a company's organizational network with precision. Consequently our network measures are indirect and descriptive. Nonetheless, having firm-level and project-level data on organizational structure and innovation is uncommon, and it allows us to explore the hypothesized relationship between structure and a firm's decision-making culture.

Data were collected at two levels of aggregation; the individual firm is the initial unit of analysis and then we disaggregate to focus on specific innovation projects within firms. At each level of aggregation different measures of innovativeness are reported and different information is provided on the firms' organizational structure. This provides a variety of perspectives of the impact of structure on innovation.

In the three of the following regressions the dependent variables measuring innovation are categorical and rank-ordered. For example, one dependent variable measures the perceived commercial success of an innovation using responses in one of five categories ranked from "far below expectations" to "far above expectations." To account for the discrete nature of the dependent variables and yet still take advantage of the information provided by the ranking of responses, we use an ordered probit model to estimate the impacts of the independent variables on innovation.

Ordered probit is a generalization of the probit model. To estimate such models begin with a latent regression

$$y^* = \beta' x + e. \tag{1}$$

We do not observe y^* but instead observe responses $y = i$, if $\mu_{i-1} \leq y^* \leq \mu_i$ for a finite number of possible responses, i. The μs are unknown parameters, or cut points, that measure an intensity of feeling by the respondent. Thus, as a respondent becomes more passionate about an issue there is some point, μ_i beyond which his response shifts from "agree" to "strongly agree". Those unknown μs are estimated with β using a set of independent variables expected to influence this intensity of feeling. Assuming e is normally distributed across observations we estimate the probability of observing response i as a linear function:

$$P(response = i) = P(\mu_{i-1} \leq \beta'x + u \leq \mu_i)$$
$$= \Phi(\mu_i - \beta'x) - \Phi(\mu_{i-1} - \beta'x), \tag{2}$$

where Φ is the standard normal cumulative distribution function.

We use this ordered probit model to ask, does the organizational structure of a firm affect the level of innovation occurring in that firm?" Following others (Scherer, 2012; and Mansfield, 2013; Cohen and Klepper, 2006) the level of innovative success is expected to be related to firm size, the resources dedicated to research and development, the resources devoted to business and marketing plans for the product, the industry to which the firm belongs, and the country in which it resides. To those traditional measures we add variables that reflect some of the organizational attributes of firms so as to test whether those attributes affect innovation.

Our computational experiments suggest firms with less formal, more organic structures are more likely to be open to innovation while rigid, hierarchal organizations are more likely to become conservative decision makers and less tolerant of change. This generates our first set of empirical hypotheses and four different network measures are used to test whether the structure of the organization influences innovation. The virtual experiments suggest the size of the firm may matter as well. The question of firm size and innovativeness has received considerable scrutiny, but empirical studies have not yet reached a consensus on this issue. Scherer (2012) suggests large, profitable firms can more readily afford innovation and Cohen and Klepper (2006) argue that cost spreading gives an additional advantage to large firms, but empirical work has not provided consistent support for this relationship (see Scherer, 2012). Teece (2015) suggests that size may be a detriment to innovation, but he does not propose a formal model to support that contention. This chapter provides such a theoretical link, but faces the same empirical challenges of the past studies, that is, size may have different and opposing impacts on innovation. All else equal the computational model suggests that smaller firms are more open to flexible decision making and thus we expect them to be more innovative.

The dynamics of the virtual experiments suggests innovativeness is more pervasive early in an organization's existence. Younger organizations are more likely to tolerate and/or encourage innovation. But with the passage of time conservative decision makers gain an edge in proficiency which can allow them to eventually dominate the organization's culture. This dynamic suggests another testable hypothesis; that younger firms might be more innovative and more successful with their innovative activities than older firms.

Empirical tests require data, data require measurement, and this chapter faces considerable measurement challenges. The first is to measure innovativeness, recognizing that any measure will be indirect. Perhaps the most commonly used stand-in for innovativeness is patent awards and/or patent applications. However patent information is unreliable for international firms and patents do not reflect the incremental innovations firms introduce but do not patent. Because we are interested in all types of innovation, patent applications are not the appropriate measure for this study.

At the firm level of analysis we use two innovation metrics; the first reflects the percentage of the firm's products that are new. Interviewees were shown taxonomy of the product life cycle in which a product goes through four stages: introduction, growth, maturity, and decline. Summing the percentage of products in the introduction and growth stages yields the first measure of innovativeness. Thus more innovative firms are defined as firms with a higher proportion of new products in their product mix.

The second measure of a firm's innovativeness is based on its commercial success with innovation. Each firm was asked, "What has been your commercial success rate for new products in the last three years?" Responses were coded from one to five in which 1 = success that was "far below expectations" and 5 = success "far above expectations." The underlying assumption is that firms that are more comfortable with innovation and change are more likely to have greater commercial success with their innovation, on average, than less innovation-friendly firms.

The more disaggregated, project-level data concentrate on specific innovation projects within each firm and contain additional information on the firm's internal structure. Again, two dependent variables were used to capture different aspects of innovativeness. The first measure of innovativeness rates the "degree of innovation" of this new product. Respondents were asked to classify this product as being:

1 = *a brand new product for which a market is undefined,*
2 = *a new product for which a market is known but for which this firm is not known*
3 = *a new product in one of this firm's currently served markets,*
4 = *a product line extension to this firm's existing product line, or*
5 = *an improvement to an existing product.*

The network model suggests that firms with a structure that encourages innovative decision making are more likely to introduce radically new products and to stretch themselves into new markets. More soberly structured firms are expected to lean towards product-line extensions and improvements to existing products.

The second project-level measure of innovation mirrors the commercial success data collected at the firm level. Each respondent was asked to rate this new product's commercial success as being far below expectations to far above expectations on a five point scale. As before, we expect more irregularly structured firms to be more attuned to the challenges of innovation and thus to have greater success with their innovative endeavors.

The second quantification challenge is to find measures of the internal network structure of a firm. These data do not permit a direct mapping of a network, but at each level of aggregation there are some questions that reflect on that structure. In the more aggregated, firm-level data, managers were asked about their concerns with "shepherding ideas through the bureaucracy" rating their concerns from one (no concern) to five (a great deal of concern). In general, a higher score reflects a more rigid, stifling organization and a lower value reflects a more open, less hierarchal, or less bureaucratic structure. Managers were also asked how much they emphasize "communication between groups and functions." Those placing an emphasis on communication (an open network) recorded a five and those with no concern recorded a one. As explanatory variables, the categorical nature of these measures is problematic. This 1 – 5 scale is an ordinal ranking of opinion, not a cardinal measure of their relative importance, thus it would be inappropriate to use these data in their raw form. Consequently two dummy variables were defined, bureaucracy concerns and communication concerns. In each case the variable = 1 when respondents answered 4 (a large degree of concern) or 5 (a *very* large degree of concern). Otherwise the variables = 0.

These dummy variables are used in the analyses reported in Table 4, but to further explore the relevance of organizational structure a matching set of regressions were studied in which the organizational dummy variables concentrate on the more severe instances of concern. In this alternative specification the variables, bureaucracy concerns and communication concerns, are set = 1 if the response is 5 (a *very* large degree of concern) and is set = 0 otherwise. Because both measures yield similar results only the initial estimates are reported in full, and significant differences are noted as they arise.

The project-level survey data also yields two different organizational structure variables, the first which was adapted from Carley and Lin (2007). Respondents were asked, "How would you classify the project organization?" and were then asked to respond according to a scale that ranged from Mechanistic to Organic. A mechanistic organization was described as one characterized by "Rigid, hierarchical reporting relationships. Personnel have highly specialized jobs. There is no free flow of people and information across jobs. There are rules regarding the performance of tasks".

An organic organization was described as one characterized by Delegation and decentralization of authority. There is free flow of people and information across different jobs. There is wide latitude as to the means used to achieve objectives.

Responses were coded categorically on a one (mechanistic) to five (organic) scales. This mechanistic/organic scale and the accompanying description of each is reminiscent of the networks used in the rewiring experiments of section 2. Prior to rewiring, the line, the tree and the grid are rigid and hierarchal (mechanistic); after rewiring, they are more decentralized with a freer flow of information across distant parts of the network (organic). Because the rewiring experiments suggest that organic organizations are more conducive to an innovative culture, we hypothesize that "organic" organizations will be more innovative and more successful with their innovation.

In addition, individuals were asked to comment on the statement, "There was adequate participation in decision making by people involved in the project." Responses were ranked on a five point scale ranging from strongly agree (= 1) to strongly disagree (= 5). We expect organizations open to greater participation to evolve into innovative firms and we expect them to experience greater commercial success with those innovations. As in the firm-level data, these ordinal categories are transformed into dummy variables indicating an organic organizational structure and greater participation. Organic structure = 1 if respondents rate their organization as a 4 or 5 on the mechanistic/organic scale, and participative style = 1 if respondents agree (4) or strongly agree (5) that there is adequate participation in the decision-making hierarchy. Once again we also define a stronger version of each of these dummy variables so that organic structure = 1 only if respondents rate their organization as a 5 on the mechanistic/organic scale and participative style = 1 only if respondents strongly agree. Differences that arise because of these alternative definitions are noted in Table 4.

The computational experiments also suggest that smaller firms should be more innovative even though previous studies claim that larger firms will be more innovative because they have more resources to fund innovation. This empirical question is tested by including firm size, measured as the number of employees. While there are other potential measures of firm size (output or sales for example), the number of employees is appropriate for this study because our computational model suggests that it is the size of the organization's network of individuals that influences its culture. Thus more workers should lead to a more rigid, hierarchal system that inhibits innovation.

Table 3. Summary statistics

Dependent Variables (Innovativeness)				
proportion new products in product line	404	47.61	26.83	(0 - 100)
firm-level commercial success	438	3.087	0.955	{1, 2, ..., 5}
degree of innovation	780	2.73	1.15	{1, 2, ..., 5}
project-level commercial success	896	2.66	1.45	{1, 2, ..., 5}
Organizational Structure Measures (Hypotheses)				
bureaucracy concerns	401	0.302	0.459	{0, 1}
communication between groups	406	0.547	0.498	{0, 1}
mechanistic/organic organization	896	0.581	0.493	{0, 1}
participatory style	893	0.686	0.464	{0, 1}
firm size	819	4104	13,134	(10 - 143,000)
age of firm (years)	844	46.23	33.46	(5 - 180)
Control Variables				
% R & D expenditures	827	11.27	15.2	(0 - 90)
proportion R & D personnel	401	0.148	0.187	(0 – 0.86)
marketing strength	451	0.378	0.485	{0, 1}
top management support	842	0.749	0.433	{0, 1}

Finally, we expect younger firms to be more innovative. This hypothesis was not a parameter we planned on exploring when the computational model was initially constructed. Instead this is an emergent property of the virtual experiments. As demonstrated in Figure 2, as these virtual organizations evolve, they go through an early stage of open, innovative, decision making. Typically this fades over time so long-lived firms tend to evolve more rigid, conservative cultures that resist innovation. Firm age is calculated as the difference between 2003 and the founding year of the organization.

The remaining explanatory variables account for the influences of other market, industry, and firm attributes that earlier studies have identified as important factors in influencing the level of innovation undertaken by firms. These control variables include: a measure of funding for research and development (as a proportion of the firm's total sales). Naturally we expect greater resource investment in R & D and the percentage of the firm's workforce employed in research and development to be positively related to innovation (Acs and Audretsch, 2008). Song and Parry (2013) and Song, Souder, and Dyer (2015) demonstrate that the level of top management support for a project as well as the marketing effort put forth for the innovation have been shown to have significant effects on that innovation's success. We have measures for each. Finally we introduce a host of dummy variables for the industry and country in which the firm resides. Industry effects are long associated with different levels of innovation (see the review article by Scherer, 1982) and while cross country effects are less frequently studied, Nakata and Sivakumar (2006) document a significant cultural influence on innovative activity. Table 3 provides summary statistics of the data for these measures.

Table 4. Estimated coefficients of innovation

	Firm-level analysis		Project-level analysis	
	%New Products	Commercial Success	Degree of Innovation	Commercial Success
bureaucracy concerns	-9.973** (2.904)	-0.1795[a] (0.1330)		
Communication between groups	9.231** (2.684)	0.0880 (0.1211)		
Mechanistic/ Organic			-0.0220[a] (0.0887)	0.2638** (0.0857)
Participative style			0.0912 (0.1007)	0.7592** (0.1012)
firm size (employees)	0.000068 (0.00012)	0.00003 (0.00005)	-0.00006* (0.00003)	0.00002 (0.00003)
age of firm	-0.1237** (0.0395)	0.0011 (0.0017)	0.0026* (0.0014)	0.0011 (0.0014)
R & D expenditures	0.1878** (0.0587)	-0.0013 (0.0027)	-0.0046 (0.0033)	-0.0020 (0.0033)
R & D personnel	13.778* (8.737)	0.6831 (0.4299)		
Marketing Strength	3.021 (2.795)	0.7648** (0.1288)		
Top management support			-0.0153 (0.1090)	0.4106** (0.1075)
	n = 331 R^2 =.263	n = 365 χ^2 = 95.32	n = 630 χ^2 = 43.05	n = 734 χ^2 = 140.96

Standard errors lie below the estimated coefficients in parenthesis.

**indicates significance at the 0.05 level; * at the 0.10 level;

[a]Using the more severe measure of bureaucracy concerns and mechanistic/organic organizations these coefficients were strongly significant as well.

SOLUTIONS AND RECOMMENDATIONS

While the particular measures of network structure used here are indirect, they capture enough of the flavor of the computational model presented above to mount a test of the premise that organizational structure affects innovation. Starting with the firm-level analysis in the first two columns of Table 4, managers who express concern about the bureaucratic bottlenecks in their organizational structures tend to belong to firms that have fewer products in the early stages of the product life-cycle. These firms have not kept pace with their less rigid counterparts when it comes to introducing new products into their product mix. This result is bolstered by the similarly depressing effect of a rigid structure on the commercial success of the firm's new products. As hypothesized, a rigid decision-making culture seems to suppress the firm's ability to innovate and dampen the energy needed to make innovation successful. In addition, firms that stress communication across functional groups had significantly more new products in their product mix, but communication did not affect the firm's commercial success with innovation.

The last two columns of Table 4 report the project-level analysis. Consider the effect of an organic versus a mechanistic structure on the degree of innovativeness. Organic organizations do not seem to exhibit a greater degree of innovation, but this result changes when the more severe measure of organic/mechanistic organization is used. Firms that were rated most strongly as having an organic structure (5 on the organic/mechanistic scale) were significantly more likely to introduce new products that are a radical departure from their current product line. Alternatively, mechanistic, rigid organizations are more likely to confine their innovation to existing product line extensions and variations on products they already offer. Organic organizations also report significantly greater commercial success with their new products than mechanistic organizations. As hypothesized, because an organic organization is more conducive to an innovative culture, it achieves greater commercial success from its innovation.

The final measure of the organizational structure of a firm was its "participatory style." When firms report that a particular project was organized with a more participatory style of management, they also tended to report greater commercial success with their new products (as expected). However greater participation did not significantly affect the degree of innovation.

The impact of size is less definitive. The firm-level data did not find size to be significantly related to either the product mix or the commercial success of the firm's innovations. The project-level data suggests that smaller firms do indeed offer more radically different products than larger firms, as expected, but there was no effect on their commercial success. While the computational model in Section II suggests smaller firms are more likely to evolve a culture of innovation, *ceteris paribus*, there are other side effects that may work in the opposite fashion. Cohen and Klepper (2006) offer several reasons why larger firms may have an innovative edge: cost spreading, greater access to finance, a greater ability to internalize spillovers, and their ability to absorb the risks associated with R & D. Thus, size may alter a firm's innovative culture, but that organizational effect on innovation may be offset by other attributes of firm size. Viewed alternatively, the conventional view articulated by Scherer (2012), that size increases the level of innovation, has received mixed empirical support through the years. This study may offer an explanation as to why; size may give a firm greater access to financial capital and spread risk, but it may also foster a culture that does not promote innovation.

The computational experiments also suggested that younger firms are more likely to embrace innovative cultures and that property is present in the empirical data. Older firms have significantly fewer new products in their product line and younger firms are more likely to introduce radical innovations than are older firms. Interestingly, while younger firms are more innovative than older firms they are not more successful in commercializing those innovations. It seems that the experience of older firms allows them to be as successful with less innovation as their younger, more innovative counterparts.

The remaining explanatory variables reported in Table 4 perform as expected, consistent with the previous research on innovation. Firms that channel more money into research and development are more innovative but do not necessarily have greater commercial success with those innovations. Firms that have a higher proportion of their personnel engaged in R & D are also more innovative, but they are not more commercially successful with those products. While greater resources invested into R & D should lead to increased innovation, there is no reason to expect that R & D will translate into commercial success: engineers innovate, but don't make sales. Commercial success should follow greater investment into business and marketing activities, and Table 4 speaks to that expectation. A firms' commercial success with innovation is greater when they have a marketing department with experience with new-product development and when they have top-management support for projects. But, marketing and managerial expertise does not increase the amount of innovation. The consistency of this study's empirical results with the existing literature increases our confidence that this sample captures some of the basics of firm innovation. To those established results we suggest there may be an effect of organizational structure, specifically that irregular, small-world networks are more conducive to innovative activity.

CONCLUSION

The Achilles heel of agent-based modeling has been empirical verification. Agent-based computational models can produce captivating economic simulations, but absent testable, refutable hypotheses, such models are sometimes dismissed as little more than stories. Science is cautious, conservative. New tools and methodological innovations are scrutinized before they are embraced by the broader community. This chapter suggests that agent-based models can withstand that scrutiny.

Three critical steps help validate this model. First, we take an existing analytical model and extend it computationally to create a model of innovation and corporate structure. The first test was to see if the expanded computational model would replicate the results of the analytical model given similar initial conditions. It did. Second, we fix the architecture of the underlying network throughout each experiment. This greatly constrains the set of potential results and allows our experiments to isolate the impact of different network shapes on the evolution of culture. To agent-based modelers this may be the most egregious step because it limits one of the powerful features of computational modeling—that all things can vary. In many agent-based models such constraints may unnecessary; in this study it allows us to isolate the effects of organizational structure and to run controlled experiments. Third, the virtual experiments lead to empirically testable hypotheses that are tested using data from a sample of international firms. Empirical validation moves the model from being an interesting simulation to a plausible explanation of innovation that may have predictive power.

And the model does yield insight. Virtual experiments suggest organizations with open organic architectures topologies that possess small-world characteristics tend to evolve an open-minded culture willing to experiment with different approaches to problems. Alternatively, rigid, highly ordered, or hierarchal networks are less tolerant of new ideas and less willing to explore unique approaches to problems. The empirical results support those conjectures. Furthermore, those cultural differences seem to impact performance. Not only are mechanistic, hierarchal firms less likely to innovate, they have less commercial success with the innovations they possess.

These empirical results continue to suggest that organizational structure may have a broader effect on innovation than other, more well-known innovation factors. For example, as resources flow into R & D, firms become more innovative, but they do not necessarily benefit commercially from these innovations. Alternatively, as firms put more resources in the business side of innovation (marketing and management resources), they do not generate more innovations, but they reap greater commercial success from the innovations they have. However, organizational structure influences both: a firm with an open organic corporate structure tends to generate more innovations and tends to reap greater commercial success from those innovations.

FUTURE RESEARCH DIRECTIONS

How to study cross-cultural services is closely related to the debate over emic vs. etic research approaches. While the emic approach is based on the premise that theorizing is culture specific and favors within-culture investigation, the etic approach advocates generalization and focuses on issues that are universal and common to all cultures. We believe that both approaches contribute to our understanding of service related issues in the global context. They are simply two points of view that can converge to enrich cultural research. The critical question is which approach best addresses the issue at hand. Additionally, it is important in cross-cultural research to involve the locals. Collaborative research across countries should utilize local researchers in all steps of the process. Research teams should be drawn from the countries involved in the research to reduce chances of incorrect interpretations and to increase emic understanding. The major issue here is how culture or cultural dimensions are assessed. That is, the majority of the studies explicated culture implicitly. That is they loosely or briefly discuss what is meant by the culture construct in the context of the study, while others present a culture construct in more detail, but used it post-hoc to explain unpredicted results or pre-hoc to provide only context and background. In contrast it is important to draw cultural concepts and develop hypotheses based on strong theory and logic. How culture is operationalized and whether cultural values are measured is another issue of concern. Most often it is treated as synonymous with country or nation, perhaps for expediency; however, it is clear that cultures are not homogenous but that, in fact, layers of culture exist, and such an operationalization often shortchanges the richness of the cultural concept. Observed effects may be due to many effects other than culture, leading to erroneous conclusions. Although the nation-as-surrogate assumption has been called into question, most researchers tend not to acknowledge the potential problem. It is important for researchers to measure values and cultural orientations rather than assume differences based on where the data are collected. Very few studies reviewed here actually measured the culture construct. While few studies used cultural constructs in forming hypotheses, even fewer measured the dimensions at the individual level, with a few exceptions. In regards to measurement issues, although there are many scales to choose from, there are also a number of issues to tackle. A final issue of concern here relates to country selection in cross-cultural service research and the need for a theoretical foundation for the selection of countries. Often convenience and achieving a large variation on the dimensions of interest are the primary drivers of this issue. Our review reveals that other than convenience, the rationale for selecting countries was often not provided, and the inconsistent findings, especially in service expectation and evaluation areas, may be due to the strong variations in selection of country and within country or culture sample. Thus, countries or cultures should be selected on the basis of generalizing and building on theory. Further, some inconsistent findings may be due to variations of service contexts. Many of the studies reviewed in the service expectations area used a single industry, often in banking or retail contexts. The lack of contextual richness of these studies may reduce the generalizability of the findings. We believe there are many other service contexts that could be used in cross-cultural service research, ranging from services which involve low to high amounts of interaction opportunities and include customer service provider employee contact. These include services such as hairdressers, telecommunication services, and car repair shops. Further, since some studies found differences due to contexts, industry selection is important.

REFERENCES

Acs, Z. J., & Audretsch, D. B. (2008). Innovation in large and small firms: An empirical analysis. *The American Economic Review*, *78*(4), 678–690.

Carley, K. M., & Lin, Z. (2007). Organizational decision making and error in a dynamic task environment. *The Journal of Mathematical Sociology*, *100*(1), 720–749.

Chang, M., & Harrington, J. E. Jr. (2005). Discovery and diffusion of knowledge in an endogenous social network. *American Journal of Sociology*, *110*(1), 937–976. doi:10.1086/426555

Cohen, W. M., & Klepper, S. (2006). A reprise of size and R & D. *The Economic Journal*, *106*(1), 925–951.

Denison, D. R., & Mishra, A. K. (2015). Toward a theory of organizational culture and effectiveness. *Organization Science*, *6*(2), 204–223. doi:10.1287/orsc.6.2.204

Fagiolo, G., Paul, W., & Moneta, A. (2007). A critical guide to empirical validation of agent-based models in economics: Methodologies, procedures, and open problems. *Computational Economics*, *30*(3), 195–226. doi:10.1007/s10614-007-9104-4

Harrington, J. E. (2008). The social selection of flexible and rigid agents. *The American Economic Review*, *88*(1), 63–82.

Mansfield, E. (2013). Composition of R & D expenditures: Relationship to size of firm, concentration and innovative output. *The Review of Economics and Statistics*, *63*(1), 610–615.

March, J. G. (2011). Exploration and exploitation in organizational learning. *Organization Science*, *2*(1), 71–87. doi:10.1287/orsc.2.1.71

Nakata, C., & Sivakumar, K. (2006). National culture and new product development: An integrative review. *Journal of Marketing*, *60*(1), 61–72. doi:10.2307/1251888

O'Reilly, C. A., Chatman, J., & Caldwell, D. F. (2014). People and organizational culture: A profile comparison approach to assessing person-organization fit. *Academy of Management Journal*, *34*(1), 487–516.

O'Reilly, C. A., & Chatman, J. A. (2006). Culture as social control: Corporations, culture and commitment. *Research in Organizational Behavior*, *18*(1), 157–200.

Ravasi, D., & Schultz, M. (2006). Responding to organizational identity threats: Exploring the role of organizational culture. *Academy of Management Journal*, *49*(1), 433–458. doi:10.5465/AMJ.2006.21794663

Scherer, F. M. (2012). Inter-industry technology flows and productivity growth. *The Review of Economics and Statistics*, *64*(1), 627–634.

Scherer, F. M. (2012). Schumpeter and plausible capitalism. *Journal of Economic Literature*, *30*(3), 1416–1433.

Smircich, L. (2013). Concepts of culture and organizational analysis. *Administrative Science Quarterly*, *28*(1), 339–359.

Song, M. X., & Parry, M. E. (2013). The determinants of Japanese new product success. *JMR, Journal of Marketing Research, 34*(1), 64–76. doi:10.2307/3152065

Song, M. X., Souder, W. E., & Dyer, B. (2015). A causal model of the impact of skills, synergy, and design sensitivity on new product performance. *Journal of Product Innovation Management, 14*(2), 88–101. doi:10.1016/S0737-6782(96)00076-8

Sørensen, J. B. (2012). The strength of corporate culture and the reliability of firm performance. *Administrative Science Quarterly, 47*(1), 70–91. doi:10.2307/3094891

Teece, D. J. (2015). Firm organization, industrial structure and technological innovation. *Journal of Economic Behavior & Organization, 31*(1), 193–224.

Watts, D., & Strogatz, S. H. (2008). Collective dynamics of small world networks. *Nature, 393*(1), 440–442. PMID:9623998

Wilhite, A. (2006). Protection and social order. *Journal of Economic Behavior & Organization, 61*(1), 691–709. doi:10.1016/j.jebo.2004.07.010

Young, H. P. (2013). The evolution of conventions. *Econometrica, 61*(1), 57–84. doi:10.2307/2951778

Young, H. P., & Burke, M. A. (2011). Competition and custom in economic contracts: A case study of Illinois agriculture. *The American Economic Review, 91*(1), 559–573.

Zhou, K. Z., Tse, D. K., & Li, J. J. (2006). Organizational changes in emerging economies: Drivers and consequences. *Journal of International Business Studies, 37*(1), 248–263. doi:10.1057/palgrave.jibs.8400186

ADDITIONAL READING

Theilmann, J., & Wilhite, A. (2015). Campaign tactics and the decision to attack. *The Journal of Politics, 60*(4), 1050–1062. doi:10.2307/2647730

Wilhite, A. (2011). Bilaterial trade and small-world networks. *Computational Economics, 18*(1), 49–64. doi:10.1023/A:1013814511151

Wilhite, A., & Theilmann, J. (2013). Labor PAC contributions and labor legislation: A simultaneous logit approach. *Public Choice, 35*(3), 267–276.

KEY TERMS AND DEFINITIONS

Corporate Culture: Corporate Culture refers to the shared values, attitudes, standards, and beliefs that characterize members of an organization and define its nature. Corporate culture is rooted in an organization's goals, strategies, structure, and approaches to labor, customers, investors, and the greater community. As such, it is an essential component in any business's ultimate success or failure. Closely related concepts, discussed elsewhere in this volume, are corporate ethics (which formally state the company's values) and corporate image (which is the public perception of the corporate culture).

Corporate Governance: Corporate governance broadly refers to the mechanisms, processes and relations by which corporations are controlled and directed. Governance structures and principles identify the distribution of rights and responsibilities among different participants in the corporation (such as the board of directors, managers, shareholders, creditors, auditors, regulators, and other stakeholders) and include the rules and procedures for making decisions in corporate affairs. Corporate governance includes the processes through which corporations' objectives are set and pursued in the context of the social, regulatory and market environment.

Cross-Cultural Communication: Cross-cultural communication is a field of study that looks at how people from differing cultural backgrounds communicate, in similar and different ways among themselves, and how they endeavour to communicate across cultures. Intercultural communication is a related field of study.

Cross-Cultural Competence: Cross-cultural Competence refers to the knowledge, skills, and affect/ motivation that enable individuals to adapt effectively in cross-cultural environments. Cross-cultural competence is defined here as an individual capability that contributes to intercultural effectiveness regardless of the particular intersection of cultures. Although some aspects of cognition, behavior, or affect may be particularly relevant in a specific country or region, evidence suggests that a core set of competencies enables adaptation to any culture.

Cross-Cultural Psychology: Cross-cultural Psychology is the scientific study of human behavior and mental processes, including both their variability and invariance, under diverse cultural conditions. Through expanding research methodologies to recognize cultural variance in behavior, language, and meaning it seeks to extend and develop psychology.

Innovation: Innovation is defined simply as a new idea, device, or method. However, innovation is often also viewed as the application of better solutions that meet new requirements, unarticulated needs, or existing market needs. This is accomplished through more-effective products, processes, services, technologies, or business models that are readily available to markets, governments and society. The term innovation can be defined as something original and more effective and, as a consequence, new, that breaks into the market or society.

Organization Development: Organization development (OD) is the study of successful organizational change and performance. OD emerged from human relations studies in the 1930s, during which psychologists realized that organizational structures and processes influence worker behavior and motivation. More recently, work on OD has expanded to focus on aligning organizations with their rapidly changing and complex environments through organizational learning, knowledge management and transformation of organizational norms and values.

Organizational Behavior: Organizational Behavior (OB) or organizational behaviour is the study of human behavior in organizational settings, the interface between human behavior and the organization, and the organization itself. OB research can be categorized in at least three ways, including the study of (a) individuals in organizations (micro-level), (b) work groups (meso-level), and (c) how organizations behave (macro-level).

Organizational Culture: Organizational culture encompasses values and behaviors that contribute to the unique social and psychological environment of an organization. Organizational culture represents the collective values, beliefs and principles of organizational members and is a product of such factors as history, product, market, technology, strategy, type of employees, management style, and national culture; culture includes the organization's vision, values, norms, systems, symbols, language, assumptions, beliefs, and habits.

Organizational Structure: An organizational structure defines how activities such as task allocation, coordination and supervision are directed toward the achievement of organizational aims. It can also be considered as the viewing glass or perspective through which individuals see their organization and its environment.

Chapter 2
Core Values and Formalization as Determinants of Individual Behavior in an Organization:
A Managerial Perspective

Ilona Swiatek-Barylska
University of Lodz, Poland

ABSTRACT

A person starting a professional career becomes a member of a chosen organization and begins to function among other people in a defined organizational culture and legal space. As he or she is an adult with a defined personality, knowledge and system of values, the manager can influence the employee's behavior not by changing the person but by shaping the work environment. As flexibility is the number one principle in organizational design nowadays, managers have to create a work environment making decisions on the continuum between formalization and management by values. The chapter describes the consequences of formalization and values orientation for individual organizational behavior, as well as outcomes such as commitment, job satisfaction and turnover intention rate.

INTRODUCTION

The topic of the determinants of individual behavior has been the subject of research for many years. The traditional psychology of personality perceived behavior as a function of personal attributes (traits, emotions, attitudes, motives, and values). Matthews et al. underline that perhaps the most comprehensive contribution to the conceptual development of trait psychology is Allport's (1937) book, *Personality: A Psychological Interpretation* where he echoed the Doctrine of Traits with the following words: *In everyday life, no one, not even a psychologist, doubts that underlying the conduct of a mature person there are characteristic dispositions or traits.* Traditional social psychology, by contrast, construed behavior as a function of the environment. Classical studies of social psychology demonstrate the influence of the environment. The Stanford Prison Experiment is evidence of the Doctrine of Situationism (Zimbardo,

DOI: 10.4018/978-1-5225-2480-9.ch002

2008). The contrast between the Doctrine of Traits and the Doctrine of Situationism had an impact on the trait-situation debate over which factors were more powerful predictors of behavior. At the beginning, they were treated as two independent factors until the 1930s, when both approaches were integrated by Kurt Lewin (Kihlstrom, 2013). He expressed this idea in the equation:

$$B= f (P,E)$$

It is not a mathematical formula but a general idea about the determinants of behavior. *In this equation, the person (P) and his environment (E) have to be viewed as variables which are mutually dependent upon each other. In other words, to understand or predict behavior, the person and the environment have to be considered as one constellation of interdependent factors. We call the totality of these factors the life space* (Lewin, 1946/1951). The next step in the person-situation research was the Doctrine of Interactionism formulated by Bowers. According to this doctrine we cannot talk about the primacy of either the traits or the situation as determinants of individual behavior in an organization. *Interactionism argues that situations are as much a function of the person as the person's behavior is a function of the situation* (Bowers, 1973). Using Lewin's formula, it can be described in the following equation:

$$B= f (P \times E)$$

where personal and environmental factors are multiplicative, i.e. the person (P) and the environment (E) both affect the behavior (B), but the effect of each variable depends on the level of the other. The effect of the personality depends on the environment (the situation the person is in) and the effect of the environment (situation) depends on the person who is in it.

As the problem of individual organizational behavior is analyzed in the paper from a managerial perspective, we have to remember that managers can influence only one factor (variable) from the person-environment pair: the environment. As an employee who starts his/her job in a company is an adult human being with shaped traits, attitudes, motives and values, this element cannot be treated as an element of managerial influence. The purpose of the chapter is to examine the role of core organizational values and formalization in modelling employee behavior. On the basis of desk research, the chapter will answer three main questions: (1) what are the consequences (advantages and disadvantages) of management by values for individual behavior in organization? (2) what are advantages and disadvantages of formalization for individual behavior in an organization? and (3) what factors determine the balance between Management by Values and Formalization in an organization? The problem of Management by Values and Formalization is discussed in academic journals but it should be noted that they are analyzed as two separate phenomena while in reality one faces a more sophisticated problem: how much are values and formalization needed in managing people in an organization, and what are the consequences of this managerial choice for individual organizational behavior?

BACKGROUND

In 1961, Burns and Stalker proved that it is the environment which determines the management process in a company (Burns, Stalker, 1961). As companies face different types of changes they not only have to react to them, but also anticipate new conditions. The transformation of the organization's environment from the 1960s till now is presented in Figure 1.

Figure 1. Transformation of Organizational Environment (Swiatek-Barylska, 2013)

STABLE ENVIRONMENT	DESTABILIZATION OF ENVIRONMENT	PERMANENT CHANGE OF ENVIRONMENT	GLOBALIZATION
· Dominance of defense industry · Science and technology in the service of the army · Low number of changes (adjustment) · Management by instructions · Dominance of organizational goals · Internal recruitment · Long-term employment	· Civil industry development · Science and technology in the service of everybody · Average number of changes (adaptation, reorganization) · Management by objectives · External recruitment · Long-term employment	· New technologies (computers) · High number of changes (transformation, reengineering, restructuring) · Change as an element of normal activity · Management by objectives · Economic crisis · Massive layoffs	· Dissemination of technology (internet, mobile network) · High number of radical changes (fusions, alliances) · Management by values · Flexible employment · "Global village" · Collapse of socialist regimes
60s	70s	80s	90s — years — 21°c

Among the many different changes which can be observed in an organization's environment, globalization seems to have the widest range and impact on organizational behavior. These changes include the transition from a stable environment, in which industry was oriented towards meeting the needs of the army, into a global economy, in which companies compete to deliver value to the customer; going from a monopoly, through competition, to co-opetition (Branderburger & Nalebuff, 1996); and going from a market where the customer could have a car painted any color he wanted as long as it was black to customized products and long term relationships – it is in fact a "journey in time" to a completely new organizational world. The process of globalization left an imprint on all aspects of the management process. Outsourcing, international competition, employees who move around the world, and cultural diversity are the manifestations of globalization which influence individuals' behavior in an organization. The job in modern companies has a new character. Geography is dead. It does not matter where employees are because they can do the job using the internet. Employees' knowledge and skills become the most important strategic resource in modern organizations. The role and type of leadership is also changing. Managing well educated professionals and specialists is associated with servant leadership (McGee-Cooper & Trammel, 2002) and the *creation of an organizational climate that releases the knowledge, experience, and motivation that reside in people* (empowerment) (Blanchard, 2010). The complex and inter-connected changes can be grouped into four organizational trends which influence the changes inside companies and, at the same time, individual workplace behavior (Dolan & Garcia, 2002):

1. The need for quality and customer orientation.
2. The need for greater professionalism, autonomy, and responsibility.
3. The need for "bosses" to evolve into leaders/facilitators.
4. The need for "flatter" and more agile organizational structures.

Commensurate with the increasing need to absorb an ever-greater degree of complexity and uncertainty in business organizations, one can observe the evolution of management methods: from Management by Instructions (MBI), which was developed at the beginning of the 20th century, through Management by Objectives (MBO), described by Drucker in the 1960's and still very popular in companies now, and Management by Values (MBV), which became very popular after the publication in 1994 by Collins and Porras, the result of a six-year research project conducted in so called visionary organizations. They diagnosed the reasons for the longevity and market success of companies such as Merck, 3M, Hewlett-Packard, Walt Disney, or General Electric, and proved that what differentiates these companies from the others is the "main ideology", i.e., a collection of core values which remain unchanged despite a long history. Leaders die, products become old, the markets change, new technologies appear, management trends come and go, but the core values in the best organizations survive. They are a filter through which decisions and actions are taken (Collins & Porras, 2002). The main similarities and differences between MBI, MBO and MBV are presented in Table 1.

As the research shows, there are different types of companies operating on the market. We can find companies which use traditional management methods, which can be classified as Management by Instruction, and modern ones, which can be called "futuristic" companies, which are much more managed by values than by instructions (Swiatek-Barylska, 2016). Management by Instruction is connected with a high level of formalization. The decisions made by managers regarding which method should be used creates the organizational space for the employees. This space multiplied by the person's characteristics results in individual behavior.

Table 1. Comparison of three management methods (Dolan & Garcia, 2002)

	MBI	MBO	MBV
Preferable situation for application	Routine or emergencies	Moderate complexity	Need for creativity in the solution of complex problems
Average level of professionalism of members of the organization	Basic level of education (management of operatives)	Moderate to average professionalism (management of employees)	High level of average professionalism (management of professionalism)
Type of leadership	Traditional	Allocator of resources	Transformational
Image of customer	User-buyer	User customer	Customer with judgement and freedom of choice
Type of product market	Monopolist Standardized	Segmented	Highly diversified and dynamic
Type of organizational structure	Pyramidal with many levels	Pyramidal with few levels	Networks, functional alliances, project team structures
Need for tolerance of ambiguity	Low	Medium	High
Need for autonomy and responsibility	Low	Medium	High
Stability of environment	Stable environment	Moderately changeable environment	Very dynamic, changeable environment
Social organization	Capitalist-industrial	Capitalist post-industrial	Post-capitalist
Philosophy of control	"Top-down" control and supervision	Control and stimulus of professional performance	Encouragement of self-supervision by each individual
Purpose of the organization	Maintenance of production	Optimization of results	Continuous improvement of processes
Research of strategic vision	Short term	Medium term	Long term
Basic cultural values	Quantitative production Loyalty, conformity, and discipline	Rationalizational Motivation Efficiency Measurement of results	Developing participation, Continuous learning, Creativity, mutual trust, commitment

ISSUES, CONTROVERSIES AND PROBLEMS

Management by Formalization as a Work Environment

Formalization is defined as the degree to which rules and procedures are followed by an organization and its employees in carrying out different activities (Rai, 1983). It is often associated with Max Weber's writings on bureaucracy. To this German sociologist, bureaucracy was *a rational, efficient, ideal organization based on principles of logic.* Bureaucratic organizations are characterized by (Kinnicki & Williams, 2011):

- A well-defined hierarchy of authority.
- Formal rules and procedures.
- A clear division of labor, with parts of a complex job being handled by specialists.
- Impersonality, without reference or connection to a particular person,
- Careers based on merit.

The Weberian model contends that rules and procedures are necessary to provide guidelines to employees to conduct their everyday business. Because formalization limits an employee's discretion, workers can become more efficient, which increases motivation and satisfaction (Rai, 2013). Rules, especially written ones, are very helpful for newly-hired employees during the induction process. Clear information decreases the level of uncertainty and helps to create the individual organizational behavior which is expected by the managers. Research shows a positive correlation between the quality of the induction program and job commitment (Makowska, 2016). In subsequent years of work, the relationship between formalization and job satisfaction is not consistent and may depend upon the occupational group or organization being studied (Lambert, Paoline, & Hogan, 2006).

A high level of formalization works well in a stable environment and routine situations – in organizations in which tasks are explicit and certain. Individual organizational behavior in formalized organizations is characterized by a strong intensity of the relationship between the person and the company. People not only have the feeling that they are working in the organization, but they simply belong to it. The value and identity of employees is determined by the organization and by belonging to it. Employees see themselves through the prism of their place in the organizational hierarchy. Professional identity is built on the basis of employment in the company. It can be described in the following words: "I'm a computer specialist at firm X." A person employed in the company realizes that he or she is employed in order to achieve the company's objectives. Employees are aware that if they fulfill the conditions set by the company and are loyal to it, they will have employment with the same employer for many years. Because employees have a low level of tolerance for uncertainty and a strong need for security, they demonstrate their loyalty to the company and expect a long-term relationship in return. As it is rigid, formalization can be an effective means of ensuring that performance standards are being met. Even in a turbulent environment, organizations see the advantages of formalization and standardization and use it as a managerial tool. Total Quality Management is an example of a modern management method which is based to some extent on formalization.

Problems with a High Level of Formalization

Formalization can lead to incongruous behaviors and situations when employees do not behave rationally but as guardians of procedures. An example was described by Barry Schwartz in his lecture *"Our loss of wisdom"* presented on the TED platform (Schwartz, 2009). It is a case known as the story about lemonade. A seven-year-old boy and his father were watching a game at the ballpark. The son asked his dad for some lemonade and so the father went to the shop and bought some. The problem was that the only type of lemonade which was sold was Mike's Hard Lemonade, which is 5% alcohol. The dad, being an academic, had no idea that this lemonade contained alcohol. When the boy was drinking it, a security guard spotted it and called the police, who called an ambulance, which whisked the kid to the hospital. The emergency room ascertained that the kid had no alcohol in his blood and just when it seemed that everything would turn out well, the child welfare protection agency started to follow its own procedures. The boy was sent to a foster home for three days. After that time, when the child was due to go home, the judge allowed it but under one condition: the dad should leave the house and check into a motel. After two weeks, the family was finally reunited. Everyone involved in this event (welfare workers, ambulance people and the judge) said that they hated to do it but they had to follow the procedures. Schwartz underlined that, even if employees realize that a procedure is senseless, it spares them from thinking. An employee does not have to analyze a situation and solve the problem – the procedure tells him how to behave and what to do. Unfortunately, rules are often established as a consequence of mistakes. In Barry Schwartz's example, the rules were set down probably because a former official had been lax and let a child go back to an abusive household.

The purpose of formalization is to give order to chaos. Rules and procedures are implemented to standardize the action of the organization's members. If they do not know what their duty is and how to do their job, formalization is very helpful. As today's business world is very complicated, the number of rules and the level of formalization increase dramatically, and this creates a vicious circle of bureaucracy. It can also be a threat to individual freedoms, with the ongoing bureaucratization leading to a "polar night of icy darkness." Formalization can hamper worker creativity and interfere with professional judgment, which decreases motivation and satisfaction.

The Level of Trust

The level of formalization can be treated as a trust index in the company – the lower the level of trust, the higher the level of formalization. Trust can be perceived as an attribute of company culture – an individual makes a decision on the basis of the cultural context. Some cultures perceive putting trust in others as a standard present in their everyday life, while other cultures regard it as careless and irresponsible (Sztompka, 2007). There are many reasons to build trust in an organization. It is considered the most important premise of commitment (Civelek et al., 2015). Trust diminishes uncertainty and constitutes the basis for making decisions and actions. It encourages people to help each other, cooperate and share knowledge. What is more, it has a positive influence on building relationships between people. With trust, people willingly get to know each other and share opinions and knowledge. Moreover, trust fosters openness, spontaneous actions, and creativity. Not only does it contribute to building relationships but it also influences the need for safety. People who trust each other are convinced of the positive intentions of others (Swiatek-Barylska, 2013). A trusting relationship with a manager is also the main factor in deciding whether to stay or leave q job (Barbian, 2002). A lack of trust in the company creates a work environment which is full of behaviors oriented towards rule- and self-protection. If there is a lack of trust in the company, employees expect a document for each activity telling them what should be done, when and how. This document would absolve them of any blame should something go wrong and it does not matter if the contents of the document make any sense or are even inappropriate for the given situation. In one company, an employee who made his business trips by private car (because it was cheaper, faster, or more comfortable) could not declare it officially and had to sign a statement that he had lost the train/bus tickets. Everyone in the company knew what "losing the tickets" really meant but there was no other possibility to get the money back. How does the culture of distrust and "red tape" influence individual behavior? Employees, even if they do not accept the situation, usually sign documents just for peace of mind. The effort to fight the system is too great and the results unpredictable, thus, it is easier to pretend that nothing wrong is occurring. Some employees do not even think about it, but for some this situation creates a cognitive dissonance. Festinger defines it as the psychological discomfort a person experiences when their attitudes or beliefs are incompatible with their behavior (Festinger, 1957). Signing an organizational fiction is a situation of conflict between self-perception as an honest professional acting according to the rules and signing a formal false statement which constitutes formalization. We can observe three main methods leading to a reduction of the "dissonance":

1. A change in attitude or behavior, or both. This is the simplest solution when confronted with cognitive dissonance. Returning to our example about tickets, this would amount to either the person (a) telling himself that, although the rules are senseless, they are the rules and they should be followed or (b) simply refusing to sign the documents and taking the money back.
2. Belittle the importance of inconsistent behavior. This happens very often. In our example, the employee could belittle the consequences and importance of such behavior (everyone in the company does it).
3. Find consonant elements that outweigh dissonant ones. This approach entails rationalizing away the dissonance. The employee could explain that it would be wasting his time to fight the situation and it is much more effective and professional to spend time solving real problems and facing real challenges, as specialists do.

No matter which method is chosen, this is how companies build a culture of breaking the rules – not only small ones but also the core elements of organizational culture and law.

Formalization is not the only model of a work environment. It allows organizations to increase the predictability of human behavior, unify it and coordinate it. Formal standards determine how to proceed in a particular situation, and can be perceived as a programming-like mechanism. Weber spotted the advantages of formalization, and his concept was based on the assumption that one can predict every situation and every problem in an organization. It proved to be utopian in practice. The main disadvantage of formalization is that it limits organizational flexibility. This weakness is more acute the more turbulent the company's environment is. A highly formalized organization has a limited ability to respond to new problems. It can also cause a degradation of the role of an employee from being an active member of the organization to a passive, dependent and frustrated one (Bielski, 1992).

Management by Values as a Work Environment

The concept of Managing by Values became popular in the United States in the early nineties but it has been practiced by managers in one form or another for many years. The awareness of the significant role of developing companies' principles and core values has increased in recent years. Some even say that modern management means management of values rather than management of people (Hampden-Turner & Trompenaars, 2000). Blanchard and O'Connor describe Managing by Values as defining core values and incorporating them into everyday organizational life. Core values are a kind of a roadmap for the stakeholders (employees, customers, owners/shareholders, and significant others) (Blanchard & O'Connor, 1997). Values created and declared in the company constitute a sort of a filter used to screen routine as well as strategic decisions and actions. Individual organizational behavior in a values-driven organization has a completely different character than in a formalized work environment because it is shaped by quite different factors. The first difference lies in the type of person-organization relationship. Managers who manage by values look for candidates whose personal values are congruent with the organization's. From the individual's point of view, it looks similar. Employees apply to a place where they will feel comfortable due to the company values, goals, and prevailing relations. In such companies, employees exhibit commitment to the profession, not to the organization, and build their identity on the basis of their occupation. It can be described in the following words: "I'm a computer specialist!" It does not matter in which company. Long seniority is no longer an employee's goal. They begin to be aware that they can do their job in another company. This is facilitated by the rising level of education and qualifications of employees. Loyalty and commitment are no longer an expression of obedience and submission to the organization but are an object of exchange between employee and company. Modern companies, managed by values, offer a job which the employee may, but need not, accept. It is a completely different approach to the mutual relations. Employees receive from the company an opportunity, not a duty of employment. Flexible companies do not want to (and cannot) be obliged to the traditionally understood contract of employment. Employees also have different expectations. They offer the company not only their time and skills, but also, and perhaps above all, intellectual capital (Czarnecki, 2011). Organizations are dominated by "wise employees performing tasks wisely", which requires managers' greater sensitivity than if they were simply managing traditional, formalized factories (Handy, 1998). Companies which manage by values create a work environment which is described by values. While in formalized organizations employees have instructions which describe the expected behavior, in values-driven companies this role is played by values.

The Role of Core Values

Organizational values help employees make decisions about how to act and react. Values are treated by employees as a map which indicates the direction of behavior and shows what is really important in the company. They become the employees' internal compass. Sometimes core values are defined in the company credo, as in Johnson & Johnson, in the code of business conduct as in Coca Cola, or in the company motto as with Ritz-Carlton. For example, at Ritz Carlton, the motto "We are Ladies and Gentlemen serving Ladies and Gentlemen" exemplifies the anticipatory service provided by all staff members. These simple and attractive words influence individual organizational behavior. As it is a very general rule, employees receive some more detailed information on how to understand it, but the main difference between Management by Formalization and Management by Values lies in the number and the details of the rules. If there is no instruction for a specific situation, values inform what to do. It makes individuals responsible for their behavior and the consequences. This type of work environment is not appropriate for employees with a low tolerance to uncertainty; but for well-educated, open minded employees who tolerate uncertainty, this type of work environment is very good. It helps them to develop their competences. These values are appreciated by many professionals and young specialists. Values play a special role of life stabilizers in people's individual and social lives. They give sense to human actions, and the more one appreciates them, the more they must be protected.

Since core values have a big impact on individual organizational behavior, they should be the subject of special attention from the managers. One can even say that defining and maintaining values is one of the fundamental managerial duties (Deal & Kennedy, 1988). HR specialists who are responsible for the recruitment and selection process should select candidates not only by testing their competences, but also by verifying if their personal values are congruent with the company's values. This is a prerequisite for the effectiveness of management by values. Conflict can occur when values espoused and enacted by the organization clash with employees' personal values. Value congruence is crucial for positive outcomes such as satisfaction, commitment, performance, career success, reduced stress, and lower turnover intentions (Cable & Edwards, 2004). Having a job in a company whose core values are different from the employee's value system is a huge burden for him. It is almost certain that an employee will leave the company sooner or later. As research shows, if managers leave a company soon after receiving a job, in 80% of cases it is caused by a conflict of values (Buchhorn & Schmalholz, 2005). After a few weeks, a newly employed person realizes if they fit in at the new organization. And if they do not, the employee faces a serious problem. Should they stay in the company and try to adapt to the uncomfortable situation (but how can they do it to remain in harmony with their personal value system?) or look for another job? The costs of wrong decisions are, contrary to popular belief, borne both by the candidates and the company.

Values as Motivators

Values are also a very effective tool for motivation. The ability to work in an environment which imposes values which are important for an employee fosters an intrinsic motivation. Studies show that intrinsic reinforcements – aligned with the influence of other factors – are stronger than extrinsic reinforcements. Employees are more committed to the job when they have intrinsic motivation (Aronson & Wieczorkowska, 2001). It does not mean that salary decreases motivation and one should not pay employees who love their job. The results depend on the perception of extrinsic reinforcement by the employee. It can be perceived either as controlling or information reinforcement. Salary can be seen as an objective and a motive for acting, and in such a situation it undermines the intrinsic motivation. It can be also perceived as evidence of personal competences and it will greatly increase the intrinsic motivation. The process of motivation must be correlated with individual core values. Quantitative targets (like money) motivate people only until the moment when they are achieved. Then they lose their motivational power. Values, in contrast to quantitative targets, are never fully achieved. Values become permanent purposes which motivate people (Stachowicz-Stanusch, 2004).

The issue of motivation is combined with the job appraisal system. Standard systems are constructed to measure standard behavior. It is difficult to use them to evaluate a unique, creative job which demands flexibility and initiative. In such an organization, values become the mechanism of control. In contrast to the formal appraisal, which is done periodically, control by values runs continuously. This control method, sometimes called a social control system, is based on the need for approval. An employee who wants to be accepted by others tries to meet their expectations by behaving according to the shared values. In such circumstances, the system of social control affects employee behavior stronger than periodically held job appraisals. The reactions to this kind of modelling behavior are slightly different. While a formal appraisal is linked to the sense of compulsion and restriction of freedom, social control leaves the employee with a sense of autonomy (Steers & Porter, 1991).

Management by values is not a program with a beginning and an end. It never ends because the perfect alignment between declared values and organizational behavior is impossible. It is a process which evolves because the world is changing, and how core values are understood is changing too. Generally, if timeless core values have been properly defined they should remain unchanged, while everything else, such as practices, strategies, structures, systems, policies, and procedures, should be variable. That is the main reason why management by values seems to be an appropriate management method for globalizing and rapidly changing organizations.

SOLUTIONS AND RECOMMENDATIONS

Because the time of looking for "the best way" in management has passed and the contingency approach is commonly accepted, it will be used in analyzing the consequences of management by formalization and management by values for individual behavior in organizations. As scientists state, an individual's behavior is a function of the person and the situation.

In this chapter, the tolerance of uncertainty is taken as a criterion of a person's characteristics. On the basis of this criterion, employees are divided into two "ideal" types: (1) employees with a high tolerance of uncertainty or who are uncertainty-oriented, and (2) employees with a low tolerance of uncertainty or who are certainty-oriented. One should realize that these are artificial constructs and no organization of this pure type exists. The reduction of uncertainty is the fundamental reason (apart from the need for achievements and affiliation) directing employees' activity. People have different ways of responding to situations of uncertainty. Those who tolerate uncertainty see such situations as a challenge, and those with a low level of tolerance to uncertainty treat it as a threat. For uncertainty-oriented employees, the preferred method of dealing with it is to try to find information and engage in an activity that will directly resolve the uncertainty. They try to understand and discover aspects of the environment about which they are uncertain. Certainty-oriented ones develop a self-regulatory style that circumvents uncertainty. When given a choice, they undertake activities that maintain clarity, and when confronted with uncertainty, they rely on others or heuristic devices instead of more direct methods of resolving uncertainty (Sorretino et al., 2005).

The situation understood as the work environment is described by the dominant management method. The work environment can be described as a place located on the axis between two opposite end of a continuum, two model states of an environment: formalization and values.

Formalization and orientation towards values influence an employee's organizational behavior but, as their uncertainty orientation is different, one can observe different results in their organizational behavior (see Figure 2).

Figure 2. Work environment and individual organizational behavior. Source: own elaboration
UO – uncertainty oriented employees
CO – certainty oriented employees

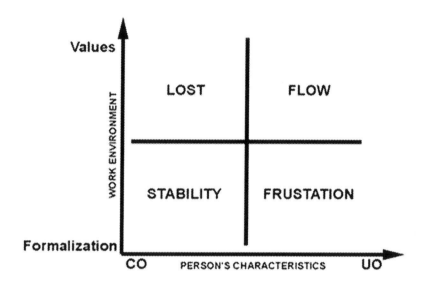

Figure 2 can be treated as a model for analyzing relationship between work environment and individual organizational behavior. The work environment is presented on the vertical axis. It is a continuum from Management by Instructions (the formalized environment) to Management by Values (not formalized). The horizontal axis presents employees' tolerance to uncertainty. It is a continuum between certainty-oriented employees and uncertainty-oriented ones. Taking into consideration these two criteria, the level of formalization of the work environment and the level of an employee's certainty, one can create four types of individual organizational behavior. The lower-left quadrant is called STABILITY. Employees who are certainty-oriented feel very comfortable in a highly formalized environment. All their duties and methods are set out so their behavior is solid, standardized, and predictable. Employees' behaviors are a reaction to the rules and procedures. The second quadrant where there is an alignment between the type of work environment and employees' certainty orientation is the upper-right one. It is called FLOW. It represents behaviors which are creative, sometime spontaneous, unique, and not standardized. Employees' behaviors are more individual and proactive. Both STABILITY and FLOW behaviors are very comfortable for employees and beneficial for the company. The following two types of behaviors are the result of incompatibility between the person and their environment. Employees do not feel comfortable in this work environment. The upper left quadrant in called LOST. Certainty-oriented employees feel lost in a non-formalized, value-oriented work environment. They do not know what to do or how to do it. They are not interested in a long-term relationship with the company and are looking for a more formalized environment. From a managerial point of view, this situation is also not effective because the management method used is not appropriate for this type of employees. There is a lack of person-organization fit. The situation in the lower-right quadrant, called FRUSTRATION, is, to some extent, similar to the LOST one. Uncertainty-oriented employees must work in a formalized work environment. They are disappointed because the rules and instructions stop their creativity and initiatives. They perceive their situation as being part of a machine and their duty as following procedures. It decreases the intrinsic motivation and commitment. Employees leave this type of company as soon as possible.

FUTURE RESEARCH DIRECTIONS

As the concept of Core Values and Formalization as Determinants of Individual Behavior in an Organization is a new one, future research and examination of the concept is recommended. The conceptual framework provides a natural guide to it (after operationalization of variables).

Moreover, although this study provides insights into relationship between employees certainty orientation, work environment and individual organizational behavior it is important to examine it in different cultures with a special attention to individualism – collectivism Hofstede's criterion.

CONCLUSION

It is worth remembering that, from a managerial perspective, the creation of an appropriate work environment is the core element for individual behavior in an organization. This chapter concentrates on the level of formalization which is the result of managerial decisions. The type of environment influences the person-organizational fit and organizational behavior. As the world is changing rapidly, companies must be flexible and they must align management methods with core values. This also has consequences for organizational behavior as it creates a space mainly for uncertainty-oriented employees. However, if the manager decides, for different reasons, to use formal rules and procedures as a dominant element of the environment, only certainty-oriented employees will be effective in such conditions. What is crucial for managers to remember is that they cannot manipulate people. They only create a work environment, and free human beings make the decision if they would like to work in this space or not. On the global market, employees can change job any time they want to find a company where the work environment will make them committed and motivated to do the job.

REFERENCES

Allport, G. W. (1937). *Personality: A psychological interpretation.* New York: Holt, Rinehart, & Winston.

Aronson, E., & Wieczorkowska, G. (2001). *Kontrola naszych myśli i uczuć.* Warsaw: Wyd. Jacek Santorski & Co.

Barbian, J. (2002). Short Shelf Life. *Training (New York, N.Y.), 25*(6).

Bielski, M. (1992). *Organziacje. Istota, struktury, procesy.* Lodz: Wydawnictwo Uniwersytetu Lodzkiego.

Blanchard, K. (2010). *Leading at a Higher Level.* Pearson Education LTD.

Blanchard, K., & O'Connor, M. (1997). *Managing By Values.* San Francisco, CA: Berrett-Kochler Publishers, Inc.

Buchhorn, E., & Schmalholz, C. G. (2005). (in press). Ciezka dola nowicjusza. *Manager Magazin.*

Burns, T., & Stalker, G. M. (1961). *The Management of Innovation.* London: Travistock Publications.

Bowers, K. S. (1973). Situationism in psychology-- Analysis and a critique. *Psychological Review, 80,* 307–336.

Branderburger, A. M., & Nalebuff, B. J. (1996). *Co-opetition*. New York: Currency Doubleday.

Cable, D. M., & Edwards, J. R. (2004). Complementary and Supplementary Fit: A Theoretical and Empirical Integration. *The Journal of Applied Psychology, 10*, 822–834.

Czarnecki, J. (2011). *Architektura korporacji. Analiza teoretyczna i metodologiczna*. Lodz: Wydawnictwo Uniwersytetu Lodzkiego.

Collins, J. C., & Porras, J. I. (2002). *Built to last. Successful Habits of Visionary Companies*. New York: HarperCollins Publishers Inc.

Civelek, M. E., Cemberci, M., & Asci, M. S. (2015). Conceptual Approach to the Organizational Trust Building in Commitment Perspective. *Doğuş Üniversitesi Dergisi, 16*(2), 217–226.

Deal, T., & Kennedy, A. (1988). *Corporate Cultures. The Rites and Rituals of Corporate life*. London: Penguin Books.

Dolan, S. L., & Garcia, S. (2002). Managing by values: Cultural redesign for strategic organizational change at the dawn of the twenty-first century. *Journal of Management Development, 21*(2), 101–117. doi:10.1108/02621710210417411

Festinger, L. (1957). *A Theory of Cognitive Dissonance*. Stanford, CA: Stanford University Press.

Handy, Ch. (2002). *The Age of Unreason*. London: Random House Group Ltd.

Hampden-Turner, Ch., & Trompenaars, A. (2000). *Siedem kultur kapitalizmu*. Krakow: Oficyna Ekonomiczna.

Kihlstrom, J. F. (2013). The person-situation interaction. In D. E. Carlston (Ed.), *The Oxford Handbook of Social Cognition*. Oxford Library of Psychology. doi:10.1093/oxfordhb/9780199730018.013.0038

Kinnicki, W., & Williams, B. K. (2011). *Management. A Practical Introduction*. New York: McGraw-Hill.

Lambert, E. G., Paoline, E. A., & Hogan, N. L. (2006). Impact of centralization and formalization on satisfaction and commitment. *Criminal Justice Studies, 19*(1), 23–44. doi:10.1080/14786010600615967

Lewin, K. (1946/1951). Behavior and development as a function of the total situation. In K. Lewin (Ed.), *Field theory in social science* (pp. 239–240). New York: Harper & Ro. doi:10.1037/10756-016

Makowska, S. (2016). *Adaptacja nowo zatrudnionych pracownikow a ich zaangazowanie w prace* (unpublished master's thesis). University of Lodz, Poland.

Matthews, G., Deary, I. J., & Whiteman, M. C. (2003). *Personality Traits*. Cambridge, UK: Cambridge University Press. doi:10.1017/CBO9780511812736

McGee-Cooper, A., & Trammell, D. (2002). From Hero-as-Leader to Servant-as-Leader. In Focus on Leadership. Servant Leadership for the 21st Century, (p. 143). New York: John Wiley & Sons, Inc.

Rai, G. S. (1983). Reducing bureaucratic inflexibility. *The Social Service Review, 57*(1), 44–58. doi:10.1086/644071

Rai, G. S. (2013). Job Satisfaction Among Long-Term Care Staff: Bureaucracy Isnt Always Bad. *Administration in Social Work, 37*(1), 90–99. doi:10.1080/03643107.2012.657750

Schwartz, B. (2009). *Our Loss of Wisdom*. Retrieved from https://www.ted.com/talks/barry_schwartz_on_our_loss_of_wisdom

Sorrentino, R. M., Hudson, G., & Huber, G. L. (2005). Umysl spoleczny a style reagowania na niepewnosc – roznice indywidualne w kontekscie interpersonalnym. In J. P. Forges, K. D. Williams, & L. Wheeler (Eds.), *Umysl spoleczny. Poznawcze i motywacyjne aspekty zachowan interpersonalnych*. Gdansk: Gdanskie Wydawnictwo Psychologiczne.

Sorrentino, R. M., Otsubo, Y., Yasunaga, S., Kouhara, S., Szeto, A., & Nezlek, J. (n.d.). *Uncertainty Orientation and Emotional Responses to Everyday Life Within and Across Cultures*. Retrieved from http://iaccp.org/ebook/xian/PDFs/5_4Sorrentino.pdf

Stachowicz-Stanusch, A. (2004). *Zarządzanie poprzez wartości. Perspektywa rozwoju wspolczesnego przedsiebiorstwa*. Gliwice: Wydawnictwo Politechniki Slaskiej.

Steers, R. M., & Porter, L. W. (1991). *Motivation and work Behavior*. New York: McGraw Hill.

Swiatek-Barylska, I. (2013). Zrodla zaufania grupowego we wspolczesnych organizacjach, *Acta Universitatis Lodziensis. Folia Oeconomica, 282,* 261–270.

Swiatek-Barylska, I. (2016 June). *Socio-demographic characteristics as determinants of person-organization relations. Results from empirical research*. Paper presented at the International Conference of Leadership and Innovations, Berlin, Germany.

Sztompka, P. (2007). *Zaufanie Fundament Spoleczenstwa*. Krakow: Wydawnictwo Znak.

Zimbardo, P. (2008). *The Lucifer Effect: How Good People Turn Evil*. New York: Random House Publishing Group.

KEY TERMS AND DEFINITIONS

Certainty/Uncertainty Orientation: The way a person responds to situations of uncertainty. Those who tolerate uncertainty see such situations as a challenge, and those with a low level of tolerance to uncertainty treat it as a threat.

Formalization: The degree to which rules and procedures determine organizational behavior.

Management by Instructions: Management methods oriented towards formalization, rules, and procedures. It is effective mainly in stable organizational environments.

Management by Values: Management method based on values. The core company values are treated as a road sign for the stakeholders. Values determines stakeholders' decisions and behavior.

Organizational Behavior: The study of individual, group, or organization behavior in a given setting. Based on the results of social science research.

Person-Organization Fit: The level of congruence between an organization's characteristics and a person in it.

Work Environment: Broadly understood conditions of the job e.g. rules, relationships, values, management methods.

Chapter 3
Organisation Culture From Systems Theory of Organisation Perspective

Anna Piekarczyk
Poznan University of Economics and Business, Poland

ABSTRACT

The article deals with organisation culture from the viewpoint of systems theory of organisation. Organisations are presented as autopoietic systems, relations between organisation and individual are discussed as well. The author attempts to define to what extent values and rules characteristic for a given culture can and should be changed.

INTRODUCTION

Different organisation culture issues have been discussed extensively for years. Nevertheless, in spite of deep interest to this phenomenon, it is still not explored completely. Organisation culture is a complex subject that extends over the whole environment of individuals who make up organisations. The core of this culture consists of values and rules that precondition all decision-making in organisation. These are hard to define, however, it is them that shape and form the entire organisation.

These values and rules are often a "tabooed" topic to discuss in organisation, as they are hard to manage – they are too "soft" and cannot be measured (Landau, 2007, p.18). Nevertheless, this social phenomenon - organisation culture - is generally considered (together with strategy and structure of organisation) to have a decisive impact on its operation, development or failure. Thus, knowledge of organisation culture nature, basics and functioning becomes very important (Balz & Arlinghaus, 2007, p.165).

The aim of this chapter is to present the essence of organisation culture from systems theory of organisation viewpoint. Steady grounds (core) are an important condition that has to be fulfilled to allow organisation to develop and succeed, as this core would help it in keeping balance under difficult circumstances. Hence, the article attempts to answer the question of the role played by culture-related factors in organisation and to what extent values and rules, accepted in a given culture, can and should be changed.

DOI: 10.4018/978-1-5225-2480-9.ch003

BACKGROUND

There is a great variety of theories of organisations. These theories are part of the huge area of social sciences that cover all aspects of private and collective life of human beings (Kieser & Ebers, 2014, p. 26). Particular topics, subjects and scientific specialisations that can be singled out within this area usually do not have clearly set boundaries – they overlap and interlace. What they all do have in common is their interest to relationship of organisation as a social entity with its members. And systems theory of organisation is focused exactly on interrelations between social system and its participants. Models of organisations produced with the help of system approach enable better understanding of logic behind any organisation's operation. On this basis it is possible to draw important conclusions and make valuable recommendations that could be applied in practice. The function of theory of organisation in relation to roles of other concepts and fields of research is often secondary. Nevertheless, taking into consideration the central role played by organisations in society, the importance of this function should not be underestimated. More and more often organisations replace family structures, tribal or ethnic links and local communities. And, whatever happens – good or bad, organisations are almost always part of this. Today they play a crucial role in the context of changes caused by increase of complexity.

Bearing that in mind, researchers, inter alia, G. Probst, P. Gomez (1997, p. 45), F. Malik (2014, pp. 21-27), J. Honegger (2008, pp. 27-28), F. Vester, (2008, pp.16-20), J. O'Connor and I. McDermott (1998, p. 34), W. Sitte and H. Wohlschlaegl (2006, p. 508), D. Meadows (2010, pp.17-18), point to the need of a broader view – the system approach to theory of organisation and the phenomenon of organisation culture.

W. Sitte and H. Wohlschlaegl at the same time note that system approach is not a priori better than other concepts, though it enables a fresh look, better understanding of processes and may lead to new conclusions (Sitte & Wohlschlaegl, 2006, p.510).

System analysis makes possible to control variability and complexity thanks to knowledge and understanding of interdependencies and links existing between different elements. Thus, it is easier to notice interrelated links and influences, which is particularly important since modern organisations are tied with their environment with an infinite number of such linkages (Schiepek et al., 1998, p. 9). Organisations are becoming more and more self-regulating, unpredictable and complex systems (Malik, 2014, p. 21). For this reason, to understand the essence and functioning of these complex systems, besides "cause and effect" thinking, a broader, all-embracing approach to research of the world is needed. According to the principles of system analysis, an organisation can be viewed as a system, a network, to be precise, within which flow and exchange of information and resources take place (von Bertalanffy, 1969, p.36). Particular parts of systems are closely related (Probst & Gomez, 1997, p.26). The main principle of the system approach is: even a minor, insignificant change within one of the smallest subsystems may have a substantial impact on the entire system in the long-term prospective, as a number of various factors exert their influence on it simultaneously (Vester, 2008, p.18). These factors are not isolated, they interact and influence each other across all boundaries set by sciences, and they are feedback links between factors of qualitative and quantitative character (Wilms, 2012, p.21). System analysis is centered on multidimensional research of essential aspects of organisation as a system and its functioning (Verster, 2008, p. 19).

ORGANISATION AS AUTOPOIETIC SYSTEM

The word (and hence, the notion) "system" originates in old Greek and means an entity composed of parts (Simon, 2013, p.16). This is why systems theory of organisation basically tries to answer two questions: what elements make up system (or could make it up) and who or what distinguishes (defines) organisation as an entity from the rest of the world (Simon, 2013, p.16).

Controversial viewpoints might appear already at this stage. Indeed, according to the most common point of view, besides buildings, machinery, devices and other means, all organisations consist of people. It might seem to be convincing, as it fits into experience of the majority of those who have dealt with organisations. Obviously, people do not interact with an abstract system - they meet particular persons, who act in a particular way, as whatever organisations do is performed by individuals in real life. K. Weick warns, however, against treating organisations as persons (Weick, 1985, p. 52). He postulates that any activity of organisation can be split into a sequence of interactions between particular individuals and it is people who define a given set of interlocking and interrelated actions. Without them, organisations would not be able to complete their tasks.

At the same time, K. Weick stresses that organisations keep to a certain model of operation, because their particular activities are properly organised and harmonized (Weick, 1979, p. 52). This allows organisations to "live" longer than their originators, and thanks to formally accepted rules operative in organisation, it is also possible to "change" personnel. This possibility of "personnel change" is a characteristic feature of organisation. Thus, formalised rules enable organisation to admit new members (i.e. individuals) without the need of changes in its functions. However, it would be interesting to know more about the way organisations adopt rules, which are kept to for a long time. In other words, what mechanisms allow for making connection and coupling actions of many individuals in organisation so that a coordinated system of action appears? And how does the process of "reproduction" of these mechanisms and rules develop with the course of time, taking into account the option of changing some members of organisation?

One might look for answers to these questions in Niklas Luhman's societal systems theory. He argues that communication is a rudimentary element of all social systems. Boundaries of communication are defined differently, not like those of actions, as an action can be attributed to a certain person, whereas it is impossible to do so with communication, because it links two or more persons. To understand it better, one could use the description of system's operation by K. Weick. In his view, the elementary unit of any organisation is the so-called "double contingency" comprising action - reaction – adaptation. Thus, an individual performs a certain action, to which another person reacts, meanwhile, initiating the interaction person also reacts to the response (reaction) of the "addressee" (Weick, 1979, p. 53). Actions of both individuals can be explained by supposition that participants of interaction attribute some meaning to both their own and the other party's actions and react to each other accordingly. Therefore, the "double contingency" gets its "cyclic" characteristics, as actions of one person can be interpreted as sending information, whereas actions of the other one as a sign of understanding. Such combination of "information", "sending/communication" and "understanding" is defined by N. Luhman as an emergent unit of communication (Luhmann, 1984, p. 193). It means that thanks to communication, a "double contingency" takes place accompanied by "interlocking" of actions. However, communication is not understood in its usual sense as an action, but as an event. It is not about communicating information in the form of signals - in the process of communication autonomous "observers" interact, their reactions to a given message can differ and cannot be predicted.

Thus, the function of human communication is not just "delivering" message, but coordination of persons and their actions. In the context of organisation it means that patterns of behavior (and action) observed there can be explained as the result of communication (though they are recognised and registered as actions). Therefore, it can be said that it is communication that turns individually acting entities (persons) into participants of a social system and only communication creates social systems. Hence, individual communications are basic elements of social systems – events that take place in the present and at the very same moment they happen, they become the past. So, to keep social systems "alive" for a long time, communication process has to be continued. The "trick" that allows organisations to live longer is: organisations with the help of their own procedures (e.g. recruitment of staff) look for possibilities to change their employees (thanks to communication) and to "reproduce" their communication patterns. This way organisation ensures the continuation of communication process, which defines it as an autonomous entity and distinguishes it from the rest of the world.

Not all social systems are "meant" to last. As they are made up of communications, there is a high probability of their decline before they become "strong". Let us imagine - a man meets another man in the street, asks him the way to the nearest library, the stranger responds, then thanks follow and the event ends – this social system has already its future "behind".

Were this social system an organisation, the event would look totally different – the communication would be continued: the message would be followed by another one, then the next one, and the communication process would continue. Thus, communication contributes to longevity of social system (in this case, organisation) and organisations make efforts to have enough "fuel" to keep it going on.

Humberto Maturana calls this type of processes "autopoietic" (Maturana, 1982, p. 280). According to his theory, autopoietic processes are the characteristic feature of living organisms. They are a specific form of self- regulation. Then, autopoietic systems are self-sufficient - they appear and reproduce themselves using only their own elements and as a result of internal processes. Thus, it is the ability of self-creation and self-regeneration which enables system to survive and develop.

INDIVIDUAL VS. ORGANISATION

F. Boos and G. Mitterer point out that modern organisation needs to distinct itself from persons (Boss & Mitterer, 2014, p. 15). It happens despite the increase of man's importance in organisation due to growing complexity. These authors also emphasise the fact that organisations want to ensure for themselves the ability to survive being able to avoid any dependencies of their structures and processes going on within them from particular individuals at the same time. They give the example of Apple Inc., a company that has been growing fast since 2000, despite untimely death of Steve Jobs, the charismatic head of the firm, in 2011. To understand well what organisation is, Boos and Mitterer suggest leaving its employees "outside", as according to the principles of system approach, organisations do not consist of their personnel (Boss & Mitterer, 2014, p. 15).

This, once radical, idea of Chester J. Barnard, an American theorist of organisation, was further developed by Niklas Luhmann, a German sociologist, in his new systems theory where he perceives people as the environment of organisation. N. Luhmann argues that it is communication patterns, not employees, which make up an organization (Luhmann, 1984, p. 42). The idea that employees are not part of organisation might make one feel uncomfortable. First, it seems to be weird and difficult to grasp, however, it is just a "side-effect" that appears only because people strongly self-identify themselves with organisations. They also often "need" organisation to feel they are part of something large.

Nontheless, the view that people are part of organisation could not be defended, if we inspect it closer. No organisation needs a "whole man" (Boss & Mitterer, 2014, p. 17; Simon, 2013, pp.17-18), it does not need all his or her wishes, health problems, interests or personal qualities. Under such a load, any organisation would slip into chaos. It can be said that more often organisations avoid being on "too human side" (Boss & Mitterer, 2014, p. 17). Some organisations prohibit any celebrations (e.g. birthdays of their employees) on their premises or block access to some web-sites. Members of staff want their private life to be separated from work as well.

F. Boos and G. Mitterer also note that if organisations consisted of their staff, then those employing the most intelligent people would be the most intelligent. Thus, universities and companies that employ people with the highest IQ, would be the most intelligent organisations. As one can see, it is not like this in reality (Boss & Mitterer, 2014, p. 18).

Yet, all the above mentioned does not mean that organisations can operate without people – just the opposite – organisations need people. But relations between an individual and an organisation differ from the generally accepted idea of it (Boss & Mitterer 2014, p. 18; Simon, 2013, pp.17-18; Luhmann, 1984, p. 289). People offer to organisations their beliefs, views, actions, their memory. Organisations are not able to think, smell, taste or watch themselves. They are tightly bonded with their employees – in a way similar to the one they are tied with their clients (Boss & Mitterer 2014, p. 18). Thus, system and its environment make a whole and thanks to it, together they can co-develop.

Positioning persons outside organisation (or any social system) is the fundamental principle of systems theory of organisation. Though it is often criticised as "diminishing" value of man, adepts of the system approach argue that it is right the opposite - as according to this school of thought, human being and organisation are equal. System exists only within its environment, and therefore, organisation needs people as part of its environment. People perform certain functions in organisation, so, there is neither a system without an environment nor an organisation without people.

F. Boos and G. Mitterer remark that focusing on decisions (or communications) instead of people means significant "relief" for organisation's staff. Thanks to this, other solutions are looked for, without focusing their attention on failures (in the first place) or successes attributed to particular employees, their qualities and style of action (Boss & Mitterer, 2014, p. 19).

Thus, organisation can be understood only when its environment is taken into consideration, as any organisation (any social system) is integrated into its environment. It exists only in relation to its environment and in separation from it at the same time. As the environment is constantly changing, the boundary between organisation and its environment has to be defined again and again continuously. This boundary is not stable, it does not stay the same long.

According to N. Luhmann, systems should be understood as identity maintained in over-complex and ever-changing environment by balancing their (systems') interior and the exterior (their environment) (Luhmann, 1973, p.175). Hence, this identity defines both internal structures with the sense of organisation's being and its relations and cooperation with the environment. Since no organisation is able to span its attention over everything that is happenning in its environment, it has to make choices. How these choices are made depends on the sense, constituted by views, values, norms, objectives etc. The sense is always specific for a particular organisation (Boss & Mitterer, 2014, p. 21); it is a necessary resource to differentiate between the communications which belong to the system and those which do not. Thus, identity of an organisation arises from relations between and cooperation of its internal structures, the sense and the environment.

But then, if organisation does not consist of its employees, what does it consist of? It is constituted by its own patterns of communication - in other words, by endless flow of decisions. Even if particular persons may come and leave, as long as organisation makes decisions, it exists. As soon as it stops making decisions, it is dead (Luhmann, 1984, p. 193). So, any living organisation must make decisions, since it re-establishes boundaries between organisation and its environment in real time, which is necessary for any system. If the boundary disappears, organisation ceases to exist and dissolves. It can be illustrated on the example of a company overtaken by another firm. Once autonomous decisions are not possible to make, the boundary disappears and this entity becomes part of another system. Thus, bankruptcy of a company (and appointment of the official receiver) can be compared to the state of coma. Therefore, organisations are intended to act and make decisions, especially in critical situations. When unexpectedly, a key person is absent, organisation must prove it is able to act, at least symbolically.

A single decision is a basic element of organisation. A decision made has to be followed by the next one. Organisations consist of a never-ending chain of decisions (even those impossible to grasp and register). J. Boss and G. Mitterer offer this example: if we imagine that any time, a decision is made in organisation, a light (immense or minor, depending on the decision's importance) is lit, an observer could enjoy a spectacular diversity of pulsing lights (Boss & Mitterer, 2014, p. 23). Yet, it would be impossible to understand, tell or predict neither what light is on at this moment and why, nor the order of their appearance.

Now, it is the right time to consider, what decisions are. Decisions are arrangements that organisation keeps to (for some time), which make a basis for further decisions. If a company makes a decision to invest in China, it makes arrangements that influence further decisions. In this example many things depend on who will work, where construction will take place and if any dotation by the state is possible. Decisions are a specific type of communication that coordinates actions. Hence, decisions define the reality rather than leave spaces for alternatives – for instance, instead in China, the company could invest in India or set up a financial reserve. This is the main difference between an act of communication in the form of decision and the rest of communications. Decisions provide certainty, whereas communication can lead to uncertainty as well (Baecker, 2003, p.35).

Organisation makes a context within which processes of management go on. This is why understanding of the essence of organisation is so important. K. Weick suggested that instead of organisation, we should speak about process of organisation. According to his views, the word "organisation" is a noun and a myth (Weick, 1985, p. 129). If you are looking for organisation you will not find it - only interrelated events and a continuous flow of decisions will be there. And as one cannot enter the same river twice, it is not possible to work twice for the same organisation.

CULTURE AS CHARACTERISTIC FEATURE OF "LIVING" SYSTEMS

Social system is made up of acts of communication (communications), whereas organisation is composed from decisions (a stream of decisions to be precise). In the context of organisation, something that is not a decision is not relevant (as background noise). Decisions are being made constantly in any organisation; they are of different meaning and importance. At the same time, it is hard to believe that in almost absolutely non-transparent stream of decisions it is possible for them to "take each other into consideration". How can it be possible that they are not in conflict with each other? There are obvious decisions, which supersede previously-made decisions and others, which are ignored. It might seem implausible, but "in spite of such diversity" it all works. It means that somehow, in one or another way, these decisions have to be "coordinated".

J. Boos and G. Mitterer postulate, that here the so-called unsolved decision premises (Boss & Mitterer, 2014, p. 51). According to N. Luhmann, these decisions make prerequisites for infinite number of other decisions (Luhmann, 2000). Therefore, they make grounds for future decisions and could be called meta-decisions, as they influence other decisions. They are essential for the whole stream and all diversity of future decisions since they are operative for a long time. Following N. Luhmann's idea, three kinds of decision premises can be distinguished and should be considered by theory of management (Luhmann, 2000, p. 222):

- Programmes,
- Structures/Processes,
- Persons.

By changing any of them, it is possible to stimulate changes in organisation. Therefore, they provide grounds for managerial actions and can serve as a "lever" of development. Organisation culture, however, plays an important role too - as the 4th element that cannot be influenced directly.

In Luhmann's terms, organisation culture is a complex, a collection of unsolved decision premises (Luhmann, 2000, pp. 241-243). In his view, this type of culture appears in self-made manner - it produces itself from itself (and anonymously). Anthropologists and sociologists discover its unknown functions – such as fulfilment of human need of feeling of belonging to a community and articulation of established values and norms.

F. B. Simon stresses the fact that rules accepted in a given culture do not appear already aimed at achievement of a set rational objective, but they develop in evolutionary way (Simon, 2013, p. 96). There is no one who could decide what rules are operative; nonetheless, those who feel members of a given culture (also organisation culture) have to meet some expectations. To belong to this culture, they have to respect and follow rules that often come into being by chance – such as some rules of communication and behaviour (i.e. descriptive and normative rules) – no one could say how and when they appeared. The fact they exist depends neither on decisions made by groups nor on those made by individuals. These rules arise in emergent, evolutionary way, however, they are in force and for this reason, they cannot be changed as a result of consciously and deliberately made decisions.

Organisation culture is interrelated with the three above mentioned types of decision premises - it can influence them but at the same time, they can have impact on this culture too. Yet, organisation culture is not predisposed to a direct influence and it is not possible to choose its form. Thus, a directive "from tomorrow our company has culture promoting innovative solutions" would make no sense. In contrast to persons, programmes and strategies, culture cannot be shaped or stimulated by making decisions (Luhmann, 2000, p. 242). Culture works differently and can be influenced only in other ways.

Every decision premise makes some options to be taken into consideration, while some others not to be. Thanks to this, decision premises serve as system of communications and decisions control. Hence, they help reduce complexity, which otherwise would be so incapacitating that organisation's activities could be stalled.

Luhmann's concept of decision premises can be presented as a "four-angled" triangle, to show interrelations between them. This "four-angled" triangle consists of programmes, processes/structures, persons and organisation culture, which is placed in the middle, because it cannot be influenced directly. Programmes are in other words strategies, visions and objectives. Processes and structures control the flow of communications in organisation. Particular values, points of view and attitude are brought into organisation by and thanks to people. Decisions made by person A would be certainly different from those made by person B. Programmes, processes/structures, persons are meta-decisions that have impact on further decisions. Particular meaning is attributed to organisation culture since, as it has been mentioned already, it is impossible to influence it directly.

E. Schein, one of the most prominent researchers of organisation culture used the image of iceberg to describe it (Schein, 2003, p.31). Huge part of what creates culture, i.e. values, norms, approach, image of human being is hidden below the waterline - it is invisible. Nevertheless, culture manifests itself in all that is visible above the waterline: such as strategies, a manner of shaping processes and structures, as well as people employed. Organisation culture requires particular attention. More and more companies discover the great importance of culture and understand how difficult it is to influence it. J. Boos and G. Mitterer remark that sometimes anything, which hides from the direct influence of management, might seem to be culture (Boss & Mitterer, 2014, p. 57). N. Luhmann calls culture an unsolved premise for decisions (Luhmann, 2000, p.242). It means it is not possible to make decision to adopt a certain culture and introduce it as the motto "from tomorrow we have a client-friendly culture". It is not possible to install it like a new piece of software. In other words, culture is not a controllable variable in organisation, as it (organisation) creates its culture and is this culture itself at the same time. From its onset, any organisation is forming its own culture. This culture lives and develops according to principles of evolution (Luhmann, 2000, p. 248).

Organisation culture comes into being as a result of multiple interactions and interdependent factors; it is visible in all dimensions of the "four-angled" triangle. This culture is often shaped by principles that proved useful in the initial stage of system's operation or helped survive a crisis. Culture is like weather – there is always some, there is no state "without" weather and neither is there environment without any culture (Boos & Mitterer, 2014, p. 58). It is impossible to imagine an organisation without any culture and for its personnel this culture is something obvious - it can be compared to a smell of a particular room – one can realise it is there only when he/she enters the room, while those who stay in the room for some time, do not notice it.

Organisation's own culture can be grasped and understood only by contrast to another culture (Luhmann, 2000, p. 246). Culture of an organisation consists of commonly shared views, beliefs and interpretations that are considered grounds for cooperation and influence social events (Simon, 2004, p. 231). It is supported by patterns of behaviour that proved useful and are forwarded to new employees as a rational and emotionally correct way of dealing with issues. This way, culture helps reduce complexity, as expected behaviour is more probable.

Organisation culture is always exceptional. Its importance and influence is the most noticeable when rules are broken. Someone, who does not know the principles of culture established in a given organisation, will find it difficult to cooperate with other members of staff. Culture always gives some sense and separates organisation from environment. Fully-fledged organisation culture facilitates its management due to higher probability of expected behaviour. However, it makes any initiatives of "external management" much more difficult to succeed. Among all four dimensions of the triangle, culture is the hardest one to change. On the other hand, to make a change lasting, it has to be deep-rooted in the culture. To be effective, management has to be successful in dealing with this paradox – the necessity to consider culture or change it without a possibility to influence it directly.

RULES AND GRAMMAR STRUCTURES

Anthropologists have been studying cultures much longer than researchers of organisations. Interesting, as it may seem, they also see cultures as communication systems. Due to this fact, some tools of analysis they use, can be useful for theory of organisation as well. According to F. B. Simon, the concept of Edward T. Hall seems to be the most compatible one in this respect (Simon, 2013, p. 97). Hall sees culture as a means of communication, similar to one's native language, and on this basis, three types of rules existing in cultures can be distinguished: technical, informal and grammar rules. Anthropologist researching an unfamiliar culture has to analyse all observed patterns of behaviour with the help of supposed rules. The ideas of rules defined by Hall as technical were adopted by theory of organisation as programmes, communication channels, formal communication, whereas informal rules are the equivalent of informal structures within organisation. The rest of the rules – grammar - can be considered as the core of organisation culture.

Whether or not a person belongs to a society, which uses a particular language, can be found out only when he/she is heard speaking (Simon, 2013, p. 98). One who did not master the rules is immediately recognised as a "stranger". Therefore, a proof of a good command of grammar rules sets boundaries between those who belong to a particular community and those who do not. Following the rules of a given organisation culture is perceived as something obvious and is taken without questions about their (rules) sense or purpose. Behaviour of this kind is expected and accepted (hence, directions and prohibitions) it is communicated within community already during the "pre-verbal" phase by communication of positive and negative emotions of respected people. Though patterns of behaviour and norms apprehended this way are learnt subconsciously, they can be re-learnt on the conscious level (as with the grammar of one's native language). Thus, thanks to this, everyone knows who belongs to this particular culture, what patterns of behavior are accepted or prohibited. Those, whose behaviour is not in accord with rules and norms, receives a negative reaction, which points to a mistake.

The same can be applied to organisation culture and its "grammar" rules (Simon, 2013, p. 99). Someone, who breaks them systematically, is either an "outsider" or does not want to be an "insider". It causes stress and emotional consequences for all members of organisation, since it becomes difficult to be sure who belongs to it and disorientation grows. To avoid this, organisation chooses a particular way of staff selection. Only persons who fit the organisation culture are employed. As organisation cannot influence primary socialisation of its employees, it needs a proper mechanism of selection. Thus, a possibility to dismiss a worker hired for a trial period helps protect the organisation culture from "unsuitable" individuals and the reasons for this may not be objective.

Grammar rules of a particular culture system cannot ensure organisation achievement of objectives. Yet, it is possible thanks to "technical" rules, i.e. organisation structures, formal communication and programmes as well as informal rules and structures. Organisations select among potential participants (i.e. candidates) persons who fit their organisation culture (obviously, not in the case, when the objective of personnel policy is to change this culture). At this moment teaching and learning of grammar rules begins similar to patterns working on the level of national cultures – i.e. breaking rules and norms causes a negative response. Thus, expressing this type of negative feelings, one communicates indirectly a threat of expulsion from the community. At the same time, positive emotions can be a signal, that one is accepted. Hence, grammar rules ensure higher level of probability of meeting expectations of the organisation as well as protection of culture system from those who do not belong to it. Therefore, these rules create and protect internal rules and the boundary with the environment (Simon, 2013, pp. 99-100).

Focus on keeping patterns and norms of behaviour and communication (directives) as well as on prevention of breaking them (prohibitions) causes them to become conservative. Norms and rules of cultures can change, but rather slowly, as there are not many objective reasons for both keeping them in their present form and changing them at the same time. Since they are accepted and "practiced" as something obvious, nobody doubts their sense. Tempo of changes in social structures and their rules depends basically on how tightly they are coupled with feelings of members of this culture. The stronger this tie is the slower and less prominent this spontaneous change. Another factor to be considered is directing organisation culture towards achievement of goals. If it takes place, it can be measured and assessed. And the more precisely it is assessed, the easier and faster this organisation's culture can be changed. Yet, self-identification of an entity/ individual changes very seldom, this is why people feel bonded with organisation - it can be a kind of protection of their identity. Thus, securing culture-based rules of organisation is a way to keep unique identity of its members. For this reason people react emotionally, when their tradition (identity) is threatened. Any actions to force organisation culture change encounter resistance, which can be expected. It is easier for members of organisations to accept changes of technical rules, i.e. programmes, structures and strategies on concrete level than changes in the realm of their own identity. Therefore, it is impossible to make decisions concerning rules of organisation culture – unsolved/ uncertain /unsettled / undefined / premises for decisions. These rules can change spontaneously as a result of self-regulating processes. F. B. Simon stresses that there is a serious risk of unexpected side-effects which can be caused by initiatives aimed at changes in organisation culture (Simon, 2013, p. 101).

ORGANISATIONAL CULTURE IN NETWORK ANALYSIS

Organisation culture can be also presented with the help of network analysis. This method was developed by P. Gomez, G. Probst and H. Ulrich professors from St. Gallen University in Switzerland (Gomez & Probst, 1995). The central idea of the method is broad, all-embracing vision and research of the world (Honneger, 2008, p.29), which essentially comes down to research of numerous factors that influence development of "a problematic situation". These factors are interrelated and interlaced like a network. To understand what organisation culture is and peculiarities of expected and accepted behaviour development process in organization, we should probably begin with defining the most important links between key-elements that have impact on this complex phenomenon.

Organisation culture can be presented as a network of interrelated factors and a dynamic network can be created, which will allow for understanding of the development of this phenomenon. The result is a clear and comprehensive picture of interrelations and interdependencies. Figure 1 shows a simplified view of development of expected and accepted patterns of behaviour in organisation.

A network, constructed in this manner can be changed and updated later and can serve as a starting point for further discussion.

Figure 1. Development of expected and accepted patterns of behavior within an organization (a simplified view/diagram)
Source: own work

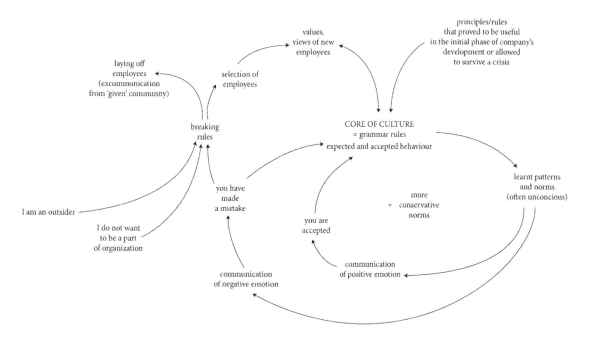

CONCLUSION

E. Schein, who was one of the first to notice and understand the importance of organisation culture, saw it as a collection of shared values, in particular, a number of consistently aligned views and aspirations (Schein, 2003, p. 34). Taken alone, they are not aimed at achievement of set objectives; nevertheless, they must be considered as essential, very important variables of the context every time actions aimed at achievement of objective are to be taken. Organisation cultures are able to "fence from" other cultures and can also reproduce and regenerate themselves by keeping to their rules. In any case, they are taken as something so obvious, that they are noticed only when broken. Often only a close encounter with rules of another culture (e.g. another organisation, branch, industry, country etc.) gives rise to awareness of the rules of one's own culture, which previously were unconscious reasons for action. Their function is separation from the exterior, joint demarcation of boundaries, in other words, "recognition" and differentiation between those who belong to the system/subsystem and those who do not. Rules and patterns of behavior that make this culture are essential for maintaining this organisation's autopoiesis, as they influence motivation and bonds with members of staff (Simon, 2013, p. 27). However, these rules and patterns are not analysed consciously, as they do not contribute to achievement of officially set goals of organisation. Their significance becomes clear no sooner than these rules are broken, as a result of shocking behaviour or unexpected decision. And then, more and more loudly asked question can be heard: WTF - are we still dealing with our "old" organisation?

FUTURE RESEARCH DIRECTIONS

The phenomenon of organisation culture has not been precisely researched in either theory or practice. It might be the consequence of lack of proper interest to it from researches.

It is still not known exactly what organisation culture characteristic functions are, what elements make it up and what kind of influence on it can be exerted and how it could be researched.

Difficulties in defining this notion could be explained, at least partly, by impossibility to program formally accepted patterns of thinking and "informal" norms of behavior.

Organisation culture grows itself from itself. This, obviously, does not mean that changes are impossible, however, "a change cannot be introduced as result of an issued directive or a decree".

This leads to an interesting question: what are (if any) possibilities to influence/change organisation culture? It may seem a paradox, but the main tool to change organisation culture could be decisions made by formal structures. Organisation culture will not change due to announcement of changes in formal structures. Nevertheless, any change in formal communication channels, setting new objectives for organisation, employment, dismissal or moving members of staff to other units will have impact on the way (also informal one) the operations are coordinated both within teams of workers and particular units and departments.

REFERENCES

Baecker, D. (2003). *Organisation und Management*. Frankfurt am Main: Suhrkamp Verlag.

Balz, U., & Arlinghaus, O. (Eds.). (2007). Praxisbuch Mergers & Akquisition. Von der strategischen Überlegung zur erfolgreichen Integration. Landsberg am Lech: mi-Fachverlag.

Boss, F., & Mitterer, G. (2014). *Einführung in das systemische Management*. Heidelberg: Carl-Auer Verlag.

Hall, E. (1959). The Silent Language. New York: Garden City.

Honneger, J. (2008). *Vernetztes Denken und Handeln in der Praxis. Mit Netmapping und Erfolgslogik schrittweise von der Vision zur Aktion. Komplexität verstehen –Ziele erreichen-Hebel wirksam nutzen.* Zürich: Versus Verlag.

Kieser, A., & Ebers, M. (2014). *Organisationstheorien*. Stuttgart: Kohlhammer Verlag.

Landau, D. (2007). *Unternehmenskultur und Organisationsberatung. Über Umgang mit Werten und Veränderungsprozessen.* Heidelberg: Carl-Auer Verlag.

Luhmann, N. (1973). *Vertrauen. Ein Mechanismus der Reduktion sozialer Komplexität.* Stuttgart: Enke Verlag.

Luhmann, N. (1984). *Soziale Systeme. Grundriss einer allgemeinen Theorie.* Frankfurt am Main: Suhrkamp Verlag.

Luhmann, N. (2000). *Organisation und Entscheidung.* Wiesbaden: Westdeutscher Verlag. doi:10.1007/978-3-322-97093-0

Malik, F. (2014). *Führen, leisten, leben. Wirksames Management für eine neue Welt.* Frankfurt, New York: Campus Verlag.

Malik, F. (2014). *Wenn Grenzen keine sind. Management und Bergsteigen.* Frankfurt am Main: Campus Verlag.

Maturana, H. (1982). *Erkennen Die Organisation und Verkörperung von Wirklichkeit.* Braunschweig: Vieweg.

Meadows, D. (2010). *Die Grenzen des Denkens. Wie wir sie mit Systemen erkennen und überwinden können.* München: Oekom Publishers.

O'Connor, J., & McDermott. (1998). *Die Lösung lauert überall. Systemisches Denken verstehen&nutzen.* Kiechzarten bei Freiburg: VAK Velag.

Probst, G., & Gomez, P. (1997). *Die Praxis des ganzheitlichen Problemlösens. Vernetz denken, unternehmerisch handeln, persönlich überzeugen.* Bern: Gabler Verlag.

Schein, E. (2003). *Organisationskultur.* Bergisch Gladbach: EHP.

Schiepek, G., Wegener, Ch., Wittig, D., & Harnischmacher, G. (1998). *Synergie und Qualität in Organisationen. Ein Fensterbilderbuch.* Tübingen: dgvt-Verlag.

Simon, F. (2004). *Gemeinsam sind wir blöd? Die Inteligenz von Unternehmen, Managern, Märkten.* Heidelberg: Carl-Auer Verlag.

Simon, F. (2013). *Einführung in die systemische Organisationstheorie.* Heidelberg: Carl-Auer Verlag.

Sitte, W., & Wohlschlägl, H. (2006). *Beiträge zur Didaktik des Geographie und Wirtschaftskunde.* Wien: Institut für Geographie und Regionalforschung der Universität Wien.

Vester, F. (2008). *Die Kunst vernetzt zu denken. Ideen und Werkzeuge für einen neuen Umgang mit Komplexität. Der neue Bericht an der Club of Rome.* München: Deutscher Taschenbuch Verlag.

von Bertalanffy, L. (1969). *General System Theory. Foundations, Development, Applications.* New York: George Braziller Inc.

Weick, K. (1979). *The Social Psychology of Organizing.* McGraw-Hill.

Weick, K. (1985). *Der Prozeß des Organiesierens.* Frankfurt am Main: Suhrkamp Verlag.

Wilms, F. (Ed.). (2012). *Wirkungsgefüge. Einsatzmöglichkeiten und Grenzen in der Unternehmungsführung.* Bern: Haupt Verlag.

KEY TERMS AND DEFINITIONS

Autopoietic System: According to Humberto Maturane theory, autopoietic processes are the characteristic feature of living organisms. They are a specific form of self- regulation. Then, autopoietic systems are self-sufficient - they appear and reproduce themselves using only their own elements and as a result of internal processes. Thus, it is the ability of self-creation and self-regeneration which enables system to survive and develop.

Network Analysis: The central idea of the method is broad, all-embracing vision and research of the world, which essentially comes down to research of numerous factors that influence development of "a problematic situation". These factors are interrelated and interlaced like a network.

System Analysis: Makes possible to control variability and complexity thanks to knowledge and understanding of interdependencies and links existing between different elements. Thus, it is easier to notice interrelated links and influences, which is particularly important since modern organisations are tied with their environment with an infinite number of such linkages.

Unsolved Decision Premises: Luhmann's concept of decision premises can be presented as a "four-angled" triangle, to show interrelations between them. This "four-angled" triangle consists of programmes, processes/structures, persons and organisation culture, which is placed in the middle, because it cannot be influenced directly. Programmes are in other words strategies, visions and objectives. Processes and structures control the flow of communications in organisation. Particular values, points of view and attitude are brought into organisation by and thanks to people.

Section 2

Chapter 4

The Role of Guanxi, Ubuntu, and Wasta in Shaping Workplace Leadership and Culture:
A Conceptual Framework

Anne Namatsi Lutomia
University of Illinois at Urbana-Champaign, USA

Raghida Abdallah Yassine
University of Illinois at Urbana-Champaign, USA

Ping Li
University of Illinois at Urbana-Champaign, USA

Xiaoping Tong
University of Illinois at Urbana-Champaign, USA

ABSTRACT

Social networks are taking center stage in organizations for the ways they shape and inform workplace leadership. Hofstede's cultural dimensions and social capital provide a framework for enabling better cross-cultural discussion about leadership in general and understanding how leaders in globalized workplace settings tap onto existing cultural practices and values vis-à-vis social networks. In China, Kenya, and Lebanon, these cultural practices and values include Guanxi, Ubuntu, and Wasta, respectively. Responding to calls for more studies comparing social network and on cross-cultural leadership, this chapter seeks to examine how Guanxi, Ubuntu, and Wasta shape workplace leadership and culture in the three respective countries. It discusses leadership styles, reviews the way Guanxi, Ubuntu, and Wasta informs workplace leadership respectively and their intersections, generates a conceptual framework, offers recommendations, suggests future research possibilities, and provides implications for human resource development.

INTRODUCTION

Whether one approaches the cultural practices of *Guanxi*, *Ubuntu*, and *Wasta* as forms of social capital and social network formation or as forces influencing leadership, this necessarily involves dichotomies of both modernity versus tradition and nationalism versus internationalism. The advent of globalization has brought about an era where understanding inter-cultural differences becomes mandatory for organi-

DOI: 10.4018/978-1-5225-2480-9.ch004

zational leadership; not having inter-cultural competence, in other words, risks losing any competitive advantage (al-Suwaidi, 2008). Understanding the effects of *Guanxi*, *Ubuntu*, and *Wasta* on international leadership styles lays a foundation for such inter-cultural competence for HRD professionals working in international contexts.

The relationship of leadership and culture both inside and outside of organizations is well documented (House, Wright, & Aditya, 1997; Kuchinke, 1999; Ardichvili & Kuchinke, 2002), but further research that includes cross-cultural experiences is required (Ardichvili & Kuchinke, 2002). This chapter is anchored on existing dialogues about cross-cultural studies, network formation, and leadership styles in different cultures. For example, inasmuch as leadership styles are informed by the culture of the leaders (GLOBE, 2016), an emphasis on procedural, status-conscious, and "face-saving" behaviors under the self-protective (or group-protective) style both reflects and shapes a leader's habit of focusing on the safety and security of the individual and the group.

The purpose of this chapter is to examine the ways that *Guanxi*, *Ubuntu*, and *Wasta* influence workplace leadership and culture in China, Kenya, and Lebanon and provide a tool for working with and within these cultures. Adapting Van De Valk's research (2008) on the relationship between leadership development and social capital, the authors pose the following questions:

1. How is *Guanxi*, *Ubuntu*, and *Wasta* practiced in various workplace settings in China, Kenya and Lebanon?
2. What intersections emerge among *Guanxi*, *Ubuntu*, and *Wasta*?
3. What are the merits and drawbacks of achieving and sustaining leadership through *Guanxi*, *Ubuntu*, and *Wasta* respectively?

To address these questions, the chapter is structured as follows. Firstly, there is an introduction that provides the definitions of the terms used and leadership views. Second, a theoretical framework anchored on the notion of cultural dimensions and social capital is provided to guide the analysis of *Guanxi*, *Ubuntu*, and *Wasta* in shaping workplace leadership and their intersection. Third, an understanding of *Guanxi*, *Ubuntu, and Wasta* that sheds light on merits and demerits of the three practices is included. Fourth, intersections of these three forms of social networks are discussed. Fifth, a conceptual framework that demonstrates the elements of *Guanxi*, *Ubuntu*, and *Wasta* and the mechanism they result in particular outcomes in leadership formation is proposed. Sixth, solutions and recommendations for resolving the problems involved in perceiving *Guanxi*, *Ubuntu*, and *Wasta* in leadership practices are provided. Seventh, implications for research, theory, and practice in human resource development (HRD) is provided. Lastly, the chapter is concluded.

BACKGROUND

On the one hand, *Guanxi*, *Ubuntu*, and *Wasta* have been defined and discussed throughout literature. Acknowledging the arguably dubious proposition of accurate translation in the first place (Zgusta, 2006), broadly speaking, *Guanxi* means "relationships" or "connections", *Ubuntu* translates as "I am because others/you are," and *Wasta* means "who you know." A commonality between these three worldviews is not simply that they implicate other people but also that they are embedded within a (culturally specific) set of social obligations vis-à-vis the other. For example, Yum (2007) observed how Confucianism offers a philosophical emphasis on collectivism, hierarchy, and social harmony that stressed the interdependency of people. This echoes the fundamental orientation of *Ubuntu* as well (Isaac, 2012). Weir (2003) and Hutchings and Weir (2006) similarly underscored the tribal affiliation that grounds *Wasta*.

More specifically, *Guanxi* in its most basic sense describes the ground of personal and social relationship in Chinese culture. It is "an indigenous Chinese construct ... defined as an informal particularistic personal connection between individuals who are bounded by implicit psychological contract to follow the norm of *Guanxi*, such as maintaining a long-term relationship, mutual commitment, loyalty and obligation" (Chen & Chen, 2004, p. 306).

Similarly, *Ubuntu* describes a humanistic orientation to community relationship that is well-suited for organizations (Le Grange, 2012) even though its introduction as a management system in Africa is comparatively recent (Fink, Holden, Karsten, & Illa, 2005; Karsten & Illa, 2001). Rametsehoa (1999) warned, however, that reducing *Ubuntu* only to a *process or technique* caricatures it,

Ubuntu embraces a set of social behaviours, which if recognised, valued and willingly incorporated into the culture of organisations could exert considerable positive outcomes on business results. Behaviours underlying Ubuntu, like sharing, seeking consensus, and interdependent helpfulness, are necessary and desirable for participative behaviours (p. 50).

Lastly, *Wasta* is how individuals achieve various goals via connections with key individuals, often in high society (Kabasakal & Bodur, 2002). These goals can be as large as securing jobs and major international contracts, or as small as cutting bureaucratic lines. On its face, it seems the least "philosophical," often likened to nepotism, cronyism, or favoritism outright. In English, it resembles "having pull." Despite these pragmatic considerations, social obligations typically undergirded by tribal affiliations enable and make *Wasta* culturally feasible (Hutchings & Weir, 2006; Weir, 2003). *Wasta* without such an underlying interconnectedness starts to look like (and can be accomplished by) simple bribery outright.

On the other hand, existent research on leadership sheds light to international leadership style. For instance, Bass (1997) argued that transformational leadership paradigm transcends organizational and national boundaries. He proposed that the most effective managers with universal potential are transformational leaders who inspire followers to perform beyond expectations while transcending self-interest for the good of the organization. Conversely, transactional leaders are individuals who exchange rewards for effort and performance, which Bass claimed to be less effective than transformational leaders.

Transformational leadership plays an important role insofar as this type of leadership tends to make leaders be seen as enigmatic and motivational (Avolio, Bass, & Jung, 1999). Such leaders usually express a strong belief in the individuals who report to them, and due to the nature of the circumstances surrounding their work environment, they tend to build trusting relationships with their subordinates in order to increase individual motivation and organizational commitment. Such engaged employees tend to add benefit to their department and increase work efficiency (Yahchouchi, 2009).

THEORETICAL UNDERPINNINGS

Throughout this chapter the authors borrow from the underpinnings of Hofstede's cultural dimensions and social capital theory as the theoretical framework. Hofstede's (1980, 2011) notion of cultural dimensions provides a framework often preferred by scholars of culture in international management and development (Ardichvili & Kuchinke, 2002). According to Hofstede, "Culture is the collective programming of the mind that distinguishes the members of one group or category of people from others" (2011. p.3). Understanding Hofstede's cultural dimensions also sheds light on leadership style. These cultural dimensions include: (1) power distance, related to the different solutions to the basic problem of human inequality, (2) individualism versus collectivism, related to the integration of individuals into primary groups, (3) masculinity versus femininity, related to the division of emotional roles between men and women, (4) uncertainty avoidance, related to the level of stress in a society in the face of an unknown future, (5) long term versus short term orientation, related to the choice of focus for people's efforts, and (6) indulgence versus restraint, related to the gratification versus control of basic human desires relevant to enjoying life (Hofstede, 1980, 2011). Hofstede (2011) cautioned that the country scores on the dimensions are relative because there is individual difference exists within nations. Hofstede (2011) encouraged the use of these dimensions when drawing meaningful comparisons. Additionally, Ardichvili and Kuchinke (2002) warned that when considering these dimensions for interventions, factors such as regional, organizational, and professional cultures as well as the political and economical climate of the country should be taken into account.

Social capital is a commodity or process by which individuals, organizations, and communities improve their economic and social positions through the exchange of knowledge, resources, and assistance (Coleman, 1988). Social capital generally relates to close interpersonal relationships between individuals, just as physical capital relates to machines, and human capital relates to education (Coleman, 1988; Lin, 1999). Adler and Kwon (2002) further described three categories of social capital: (1) the relations an actor maintains with other actors, (2) the structure of relations among actors within a collectivity, and (3) both types of linkages or the relationships characterizing the internal structure of an organization. The most overlapping part of the majority of definitions for social capital involves a focus on social relations that have productive benefits (Kreuter & Lezin, 2002). *Guanxi*, *Ubuntu*, and *Wasta* all rest on, or reflect, this sense of social capital.

In addition to this emphasis on close interpersonal relationships, however, Granovetter (1973) observed that weak ties in networks—that is, interpersonal connections with low emotional investment or infrequent contact—often play a crucial role in accessing quality information and resources for individuals, especially job opportunities. Structural hole theory similarly suggests that those who occupy structural holes between otherwise disconnected networks or organizations often have access to unique and timely information (Burt, 1992). As such, both close and distant network ties can afford access to people and resources that one can then mobilize through their own network ties (Lin, 1999). Social capital beneficially lays the groundwork for productive and approved relationships between persons and resources, including group care, better problem solving, cohesion among group members, more widespread information sharing, and satisfying psychological and safety needs.

It is noteworthy that the authors utilize the general principles behind the cultural dimensions and social capital, instead of the specific dimensions and viewpoints of the theoretic framework, in analyzing the role of *Guanxi*, *Ubuntu*, and *Wasta* in shaping workplace leadership. Hofstede's cultural dimensions in general reveals that there exist cultural differences at national level and the differences transfer into organizational practices. *Guanxi*, *Ubuntu*, and *Wasta*, representing three similar yet varying cultures are each unique in shaping workplace leadership in the respective countries. Perspectives of social capital regarding both close and distant interpersonal relationship are embedded within the practices of *Guanxi*, *Ubuntu*, and *Wasta* presumed to be influential in leadership formation and exertion.

This chapter is a conceptual manuscript on *Guanxi*, *Ubuntu*, and *Wasta* as they relate to workplace leadership and cultures. A conceptual manuscript makes "connections between multiple bodies of literature and knowledge bases to make claims toward a particular argument"(Callahan, 2010, p. 302). At one level, the chapter represents a systematic identification and analysis of otherwise disconnected literature in order to answer specific research questions about the function of social capital as a part of leadership in diverse geographic settings. This, metaphorically, resembles the comparative linguist's role as she attempts to match and distinguish the connotations and denotations of presumably similar terms across different languages—a kind of intellectual or academic version of structural hole theory itself. At another level, this involves describing the "underlying" (Platonic) human activity of social networking leadership in general. As Kropf and Newbury-Smith (2016) stated in a different but applicable context, "Comparing the two requires common sense to fossick behind academic nimbus that may be a hindrance to understanding their similarities" (p. 5).

This study has its limitations. Firstly, it does not fully take into account political and historical contexts that might have produced *Guanxi*, *Ubuntu*, and *Wasta*. Secondly, the use of a single method, namely secondary data review that relies on existing research, theories, and models, might not take into account the existing practices that might have not yet been documented (Ardichvili & Kuchinke, 2002). Lastly, this chapter does not focus on organizational behavior.

UNDERSTANDING GUANXI, UBUNTU, AND WASTA IN WORKPLACE

This section focuses on the issues, controversies, and problems that emerge when *Guanxi*, *Ubuntu*, and *Wasta* are practiced in the workplace. Special attentions are paid to ways through which various leaders practice the respective values. The intersection among *Guanxi*, *Ubuntu*, and *Wasta* is discussed at the end of this section as they share common characteristics in workplace. Notably, the authors refer to *Guanxi*, *Ubuntu*, and *Wasta* as philosophies, practices, networks, and forms of social capital interchangeably.

Guanxi

Confucian philosophy is often invoked to explain much of what can be observed in the use of *Guanxi* and its practices in China (Hong & Engeström, 2004; Hwang, Golemon, Chen, Wang, & Hung, 2009; Lin, 2011). In particular, a Confucian relationalism is rooted in *wulun*, i.e., the five traditional, hierarchical, dyadic relationships of emperor and official, father and son, husband and wife, elder and youth, and friend and friend. Bond and Hwang (2008) suggested that these dyads, particularly the familial ones, have been extended into non-familial milieus. In this way, the characteristic duties and responsibilities of one dyad—such as *xiao* (filial piety) from the father and son dyad—becomes deployed outside of that context, for example, in the manager and employee situation.

While non-Chinese outsiders often find *Guanxi* an unfathomable, almost mystical concept, *The Economist* (2000, p. 7) laconically warned, "If you don't have the patience to learn about guanxi, old boy, you might as well pack your bags and go home." In consequence, well-established and widely practiced Western leadership and motivation models do not seem to work in China (Hofstede, 1993), and a growing number of researchers realized that the *Guanxi* of the supervisor-subordinate differs substantially from Western notions about leader-member exchange or commitment to one's supervisor (Chen & Tjosvold, 2006; Hui & Graen, 1998; Law, Wong, Wang, & Wang, 2000). For example, Western leader-member exchange tends to be limited only to work-related and work-sited interactions, while supervisor-subordinate *Guanxi* typically includes non-work-related social interactions on and off-site (Cheung, Wu, Chan, & Wong, 2009). Further, whereas *Guanxi* involves "communal sharing," the core of leader-member exchange tends to be "equity-matching" (Cheung et al., 2009).

Guanxi in this work-related relational sense, which includes mutually reciprocal social (not just business or employer) obligations, can influence administrative decisions like bonus allocation and promotion, and has demonstrated positive outcomes for performance, organizational commitment, and job satisfaction (Cheung et al., 2009; Law et al., 2000). Nonetheless, it can be double-edged (Chen, Chen, & Huang, 2013). Wright, Szeto, and Cheng (2002) identified how *Guanxi* can effect a prioritization of group solidarity to the detriment of business outcomes. Nepotism and corruption (Pearce & Robinson, 2000; Xin & Pearce, 1996; Yeung & Tung, 1996), of course, readily link to *Guanxi*; a sense of moral obligation to another, even, has at times prompted an inappropriate sharing of proprietary information (Barnathan et al., 1996).

Guanxi is an indelible part of the Chinese business ethos (Chen et al., 2013) and can prompt ethical or unethical behavior depending upon the situation. The separation between Chinese private and business life is not always clear, and people are inclined to invoke *Guanxi* when they have a difficult problem not easily resolved through formal procedures (Chen & Chen, 2004). A tendency to tackle problems behind the scenes with the help of key people means maintaining good *Guanxi* with the key people, which sometimes involves appeasement even in illegal forms (Chen et al., 2013). Chinese corporate governance around business-to-government *Guanxi*, then, can at times harm a weak or unstable system and hinder its further economic growth and development (Braendle, Gasser, & Noll, 2005).

While more Western human resource norms (Warner, 1997) and the development of ethical human resource standards by Chinese professionals (Ulrich & Black, 1999) have prompted some change, Guthrie (1999) pointed to the passages of laws as better indicating a shift toward a more typically rational-legal system. In response to Guthrie's prediction that *Guanxi* would disappear from Chinese society due to obsolescence in a market economy and rational legal milieu, Yang (2002) asserted that "*Guanxi* practice may decline in some social domains, but find new areas to flourish, such as business transactions, and display new social forms and expressions" (p. 459). Yang further confirmed that *Guanxi* has not lost its importance:

[Guanxi] is in the world of business where entrepreneurs and managers still need to engage with what remains of the state economy, with official controls over state contracts, access to imports, bank loans, favorable tax incentives, access to valuable market information and influential persons, and exemptions from troublesome laws and regulations (p. 464).

Guanxi can have a gendered dimension as well. Bedford and Hwang (2013) noted that *Guanxi*-building opportunities for male-male dyads in Taiwan afforded by visiting hostess clubs was not available to women. Similarly, the level of flattery required from women in order to build business *Guanxi* tends to risk reputational damage to them (Xu & Li, 2015).

Ubuntu

According to Mbigi and Maree (2005), the traditional African view is that a person's ultimate goal in life is to become a complete person, a genuine human being, at one with *Ubuntu* as an expression of human excellence, realized by living harmoniously with others in the community. Mbigi and Maree (2005) further defined *Ubuntu* as a collective shared experience and solidarity crucial for the development of people and organizations. *Ubuntu* captures what it means to be human (Nafukho, 2006); thus, to perform humane acts in a community is *Ubuntu.* Khoza (2006) translated it as humanness, and it seems to bear a more than merely literal resemblance to supreme Confucian virtue of *rén* (humaneness). Broodryk (2006a, 2006b) employed the term to encompass the basic values of humanness, caring, sharing, respect and compassion, and a community orientation.

Scholars of *Ubuntu* in the workplace have stated that it can be a source of learning, competitive advantage, and community (Mangaliso, 2001; Mbigi & Maree, 2005; Nafukho, 2006) while also informing leadership development (Ngunjiri, 2016). Further, because *Ubuntu* calls for existence in a community, where the "we" is emphasized, it emphasizes cooperation and accomplishing things together; according to *Ubuntu*, then, a common bond exists between us all, and it is through this bond and our interactions with our fellow human beings that human qualities are discovered and that of others are affirmed (Swanson, 2009, 2010).

Ubuntu has its critics. Relatively recently, West (2014), albeit too much from an assumed "Western" point of view, rightly acknowledged the greater tendency for philosophizing about the term than doing empirical studies of it. Gathogo (2008) had earlier objected to the conceptual nebulousness of *Ubuntu*, its openness to interpretation, and its subsequent vagueness of application to virtually any aspect of life. The authors see this, however, less as a weakness of the concept and more as better affording the types of ad hoc, day-to-day, on-the-fly sorts of mediations of social behavior on an as-needed basis that leadership often requires. That is, an ad hoc declaration that such and such a behavior *is Ubuntu* or shows *Ubuntu* (both inside and outside of corporate settings, both for leadership cultures and beyond them) lends itself—when *Ubuntu* is shared as a value among community or team members—to the effective exercise of power.

Such ad hoc usage, of course, can lend itself to selfish or troubling ends. When improperly construed, or when deliberately misconstrued, *Ubuntu* can be abused for corruption; moreover, despite its emphasis on communal solidarity, it tends to privilege men and has not sufficed to date for addressing many of the concerns of African women (Gathogo, 2008). Hence, *Ubuntu* with its idealizations becomes complicit in what Ogundipe-Leslie (1993) observed:

The effect of the world-wide concern about the woman's position in [Africa] has been varied ... It is ... multi-faceted and contradictory when it is not totally false and misleading. The male-dominated society reacts in the usual fashion by denying that there is any oppression of women in Africa, glorifying an unknown pre-colonial post where our African mothers were totally happy; accusing conscious women activists of being victims of western ideas and copycats of white women; claiming that 'the family' is more important than the fate of the individual woman; brushing aside women's concern with the hypocrisy that 'national development' is a greater priority now than women's liberation; asserting that women anyhow do not need to be liberated because they have never been in bondage. So you have a compounding of historical and sociological falsification, all to the end of frightening women into quietude. The most vocal and courageous who continue to talk and act socially and politically are stigmatized (quoted in Bruner, 1993, p. 3-4).

While *Ubuntu* is at times accused of suppressing the individual (Gathogo, 2008) or reducing the individual to nothing in the community (Menkiti, 1984), Chinua Achebe reframed this recurring critique out of the character of Nigerian society generally: "For me it's not a question of [the community] imposing its will [on the individual]; it's a question of finding a balance which I think is important and which seems to be lost in the Western conception of man and his destiny" (quoted in Egejuru, 1980, p. 122).

Wasta

Kropf and Newbury-Smith (2016) noted three major strands of *Wasta:* (1) patron intercession meant to obtain privileges or resources from other parties (Cunningham & Sarayrah, 1993; Loewe, Blume, & Speer, 2008), (2) the use of tribal, family, or social affiliations broadly understood rather than merit to gain advantages (Smith et al., 2012), and (3) social networks of interpersonal relations of all sorts that bear on control, influence, or information distribution in the exercise of power (Hutchings & Weir, 2006). In Arabic settings, "succeeding or failing may depend heavily on the scale and scope [of one's *Wasta*]" (Berger, Silbiger, Herstein, & Barnes, 2015, p. 4).

More than *Guanxi* or *Ubuntu*, debate about the morality or rationality of *Wasta* seems to occupy the majority of research (Lackner, 2016; Marktanner & Wilson, 2016; Weir, Sultan, & van de Blunt, 2016). Kropf and Newbury-Smith (2016), while acknowledging the stink that *Wasta* and its non-Arabic analogs typically carry, established how the attributes of social capital and *Wasta* overlap "often to an amazing extent" (p. 4). Conversely, while *Wasta* can enhance the performance of administrative tasks, its exceptions and exceptionalism can disrupt daily business decisions and thus impact productivity (Cunningham & Sarayrah, 1993).

From the above, then, it becomes clear that the extent of research on *Guanxi*, *Ubuntu*, and *Wasta* varies both in terms of volume and approach. For *Guanxi*, there is a generally established canon of research, including a robust empirical literature about business relationships in China framed generally through the lens of Confucian ethics. For *Ubuntu*, most of the research examines it from the angle of conflict resolution, philosophy, ethics, spiritual foundations, or worldview (Gade, 2011). On the other hand, the body of literature is much limited. As Kropf and Newbury-Smith (2016) noted, "With few noteworthy exceptions (Tlaiss and Kauser 2011), *Wasta* has kept its negative image and is rather studied as a specific Middle Eastern phenomenon than as part of networking theory or social capital literature" (p. 4, italics in original).

THE INTERSECTION OF GUANXI, UBUNTU, AND WASTA

The approach of this chapter agrees with the spirit of Kropf and Newbury-Smith (2016) when they write, "The main differences between detrimental or beneficial effects of networking do not seem to lie with the particular nature of the network nor the country it takes place in, but rather with the network's overall purpose" (p. 4). The assertion here is that any claimed purpose of a network must necessarily be framed by and operate according to cultural parameters. In the desire to look at *Guanxi*, *Ubuntu*, and *Wasta* inter-culturally, this requires some degree of abstraction away from its cultural specificity in actual practice and situations, of course, but not necessarily to such a degree that the culture or country of a network becomes wholly bracketed out.

As simply one example, an underlying commonality in all three cultural practices is the assumption of personal identity through the lens of the community. To Western ears, this begins to sound like hive-mind collectivism, but at least one vehemently Western commentator rejected this. Decrying not only collectivism in the sense that the West typically imagines but also the West's rugged individualism as "pathological and inimical to life" (p. 761), Jung (1971) described *individuation* as the foundation of healthy communities, where individuation is the *personal* expression of a collective norm. As such, since "the individual is not just a single, separate being, but by his very existence presupposes a collective relationship, it follows that the process of individuation must lead to more intense and broader collective relationships and not to isolation" (p. 758). Williams (1977) underscored this, emphasizing how the bourgeois framing of the "individual" as "private" "can become complicit with a process which rejects, deforms, or actually destroys individuals in the very name of individualism" (p. 194), hence, again, "pathological and inimical to life" as Jung noted.

This bourgeois framing of the individual as private is antonymic to the individuated framing of the person implicated in *Guanxi*, *Ubuntu*, and *Wasta*, so that to analyze them through a (culturally) Western lens of individualism is at best misleading, if not actively violent when norms framed in its terms are imposed locally. At best, misunderstandings about leadership culture where *Guanxi*, *Ubuntu*, and *Wasta* are in play risk lost opportunities for business or suboptimal implementations due to cultural incompetence.

Given that Kropf and Newbury-Smith (2016) established that ultimately it is "extremely difficult to find a clear-cut differentiation between social capital and *Wasta*" (p. 5, italics in original), the authors infer something similar for *Guanxi* and *Ubuntu*. The immediate consequence of this is not so obvious: namely, that the Chinese, Kenyan, and Lebanese leadership working with Western entities assume that some sort of "Western" *Guanxi*, *Ubuntu*, or *Wasta* must be in play, even as the Western view fails or refuses to frame it as such. Therefore, "social networking" is *Wasta* "more than [what] Western proponents of professional networking who chaff at their understanding of *Wasta* might care to admit" (Kropf & Newbury-Smith, 2016, p. 4), with its own potential for use and abuse, albeit stripped in this case of an acknowledgment of its individuated ethos. It was this bourgeois failure or refusal to acknowledge the human being as ineluctably social that prompted Williams (1977) to note, "the weakness of the bourgeois concept of … 'the individual' [as 'private'] is its naivety, which in its own ways, and especially in the market, can become in practice cruel and malign" (p. 194). The authors add that, along with this potential for cruelty and malignancy, the naivety of the bourgeois concept of "the individual" in leadership is a positively dangerous and undesirable trait. Fortunately, Kropf and Newbury-Smith underscored a growing awareness around this issue; namely, that "pure meritocracy has been tempered and given way to the recognition that connections matter—and matter a lot" (p. 4). As such, the use and abuse of social capital—whether through social networking, *Guanxi*, *Ubuntu*, or *Wasta*—requires analysis and redress, in an ethical and fair sense.

PROPOSED CONCEPTUAL FRAMEWORK

The theoretical base that guides this conceptual framework includes the various philosophies embedded in *Guanxi*, *Ubuntu*, and *Wasta*. *Guanxi*, *Ubuntu*, and *Wasta* are not far from each other in as far as how communities and scholars discuss and apply them and in their relationships to discourses of social capital formation and social networks. Generally, there is an established canon of research on *Guanxi*. Part of this research includes robust theoretical and empirical literature about business relationships in China indicating that there exists business culture that privileges strong family networks, or *Guanxi* connections informed by strong Confucian ethics. In the case of *Ubuntu*, most of its research encompasses conflict resolution, philosophy, ethics, spiritual foundation, and worldview (Gade, 2011). Conversely to the case of *Guanxi*, there is a limited body of literature that has analyzed business relationships in the Arab World based on strong family networks, or *Wasta* connections, supported by Islamic ethics and values. Arguably, in the Arab World, political boundaries and government policies are surface phenomena compared to the deeper infrastructures of belief, family, kin, and obligation (Weir, 2003).

Despite the similarities that exist among these three concepts there is limited research that examines the three together or even theoretical frames, and yet more than before the Chinese, Africans, and Lebanese are involved in international business and development work. In this diagram of the conceptual framework (see Figure1), the authors suggest that the preconditions are similar to antecedents of *Guanxi*, *Ubuntu*, and *Wasta* formation-what has to be in place in order for these three forms of social network to occur. The concepts used at all levels are discussed at various points in the chapter and equally described therefore the models demonstrate the general strategy while considering the literature embedded within this chapter. Here, the authors propose a conceptual framework that can be used to explore how *Guanxi*, *Ubuntu*, and *Wasta* shapes workplace leadership and culture so as to address the lack of tools for understanding this phenomenon. The second dimension is the process that defines the mechanics of *Guanxi*, *Ubuntu*, and *Wasta*, things that people do. The last dimension outlines the outcome of the process can also be seen as the benefits that emerge from the relationships. These can be positive or negative. At the bottom are proposals of what can strengthen these process aspects of organizations and various country practices which can be infused through gender inclusion, legality, and formal relationships.

Figure 1. Conceptual Framework of the Role of Guanxi, Ubuntu, and Wasta in Shaping Workplace Leadership and Culture.

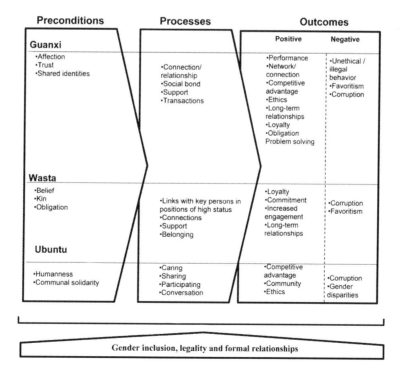

SOLUTIONS AND RECOMMENDATIONS

While the problems of "social networking" noted above include favoritism, modeling cultures of corruption in leadership, inefficiencies and de-prioritizations of policy and sound business practice, and, in general, the privileging of people along ethnic lines over others, a key problem involves analytical judgments passed on cultural practices as positive or negative.

In the case of Zhengfei Ren, who founded the now-largest telecom manufacturer worldwide in China in 1987 (Zhang & Wu, 2012), despite owning merely 1% share of the company, he retains absolute executive power, largely due to the exceptionally high loyalty that cultivating *Guanxi* with his senior management has yielded. Here, *Guanxi*—particularly the mingling of business and nonbusiness related interpersonal interactions—rather than typical property rights incentivizes commitment to Ren's charismatic leadership.

This positive use of *Guanxi* is counterbalanced by an abuse of it. While *xiahai* (i.e., former cadres become entrepreneurs) can bring about its own varieties of internal and familiar corruption (Braendle et al., 2005), Ren has also weathered criticism that he abused *Guanxi* at the time he quit his job as a colonel in the army to create his company. Indeed, *Guanxi* can often play a major role in securing the necessary governmental endorsement and providing access to business partners, in part due to the weakness of the Chinese legal system, which would otherwise constrain or moderate such activity.

In light with *Ubuntu*, a crisis in Kenya also instigated one of the more inspiring cases of social networking in Kenya. Wangari Maathai, the 2004 Nobel Peace Prize recipient, after initially starting the Green Belt Movement (GBM) in 1977 after hearing women from central Kenya complaining about drying streams and food insecurity (Kushner, 2009), gradually broadened that mission to advocate for greater democratic space and more accountability in Kenya daily life (Maathai, 2006). Eventually, GBM formalized as nongovernmental organization engaged in the intersection of environmental conservation, human rights issues, and women's empowerment, through community education. Maathai's leadership was transformational for the way that she fused adult education and environmental conservation in order to inspire community members to pursue environmentally responsible and gender-just goals. As such, Maathai's work specifically embeds human beings and cultures within an ecological worldview that acknowledges both human and non-human relationships (Ngunjiri, 2016). Maathai's work stands received international attention because she connected local women to environmental sustainability-growing trees and social justice. As discussed earlier, this act of seeing human beings as equal to nature is tied to Ubuntu's mantra of *"I am because we are"* also referring to the essence of coexistence or humanism. That is, while *Ubuntu* is expressly a humanism value, that performance makes humans the measure of all things. In contrast to Western humanism, this African humanism precludes neither spiritual considerations nor the status of the non-human world under that measure (Isaac, 2012).

In a similar manner, both the general political instability in Lebanon and the extreme blandishments of neoliberalism there, open the door for—or at times actually necessitate—*Wasta*. At one of the largest hospitals in Lebanon, for instance, a new administrative position was filled to appease an influential politician. The new hire, however, could not perform his job duties. As a result, rather than risking offending his influential patron, a second "co-director" was hired who had to do the job while mitigating the official director's shortcomings.

This broadens the scope and premises of interdependence and individuation already present in *Guanxi* and *Wasta*. Notably, simply to open up all forms of social capital—whether social networking, *Guanxi*, *Ubuntu*, or *Wasta*—beyond the "tribe" of men requires modification. Thus, as Lackner (2016) "rationalizes" *Wasta* in view of the political, economic, and cultural exigencies present in the Arabic world, the authors similarly propose to no longer "rationalize" the privileging of access to social capital for men in every context.

DIRECTIONS FOR FUTURE RESEARCH, THEORY, AND PRACTICE

Proposals for empirically studying *Ubuntu* (Marks, 2000; Murithi, 2006) and other cultural workplace practices of social networking (in the West too) are needed and welcome, along with more work to culturally situate otherwise pathologized or demonized aspects of *Wasta* (Lackner, 2016) and similar practices. In general, an acknowledgment of the fluidity of these constructs is needed, and better characterizing how emerging digital technologies are colliding traditional and more modern modes of social capital formation.

Leadership practices are not only fluid, they are culturally non-neutral as well (Bierema, 2016), so that *Guanxi*, *Ubuntu*, and *Wasta* can serve as a theory-based resource. In insisting that leadership requires innovation and accountability while solving organizational problems, Nica (2013a, 2013b) implies that a central problem is already how the problem is approached in the first place. Calls for more research on women's leadership experiences (Bierema, 2016; Stead & Elliott, 2009) not only stand to improve our understanding of *Guanxi*, *Ubuntu*, and *Wasta* as aspects of leadership but also start the needed discussion about gender differences in accessing these forms of social capital. To do so does not simply address the ethical issue of male privilege, but also stands to challenge or correct the non-beneficial instances of male cronyism, favoritism, or nepotism.

Although this chapter focuses on how *Guanxi*, *Ubuntu* and *Wasta* influence workplace leadership development and culture, it cannot be complete without examining the assumptions entailed in these practices and how they are tied to organizational behavior. Assumptions behind *Guanxi*, *Ubuntu* and *Wasta* suppose that these are good practices and should be accepted by all and that all can access them. Nonetheless, Ribot and Peluso long observed that (2003) "some people and institutions control resource access while others maintain their access through those who have control"(p.154). Secondly, understanding how *Guanxi*, *Ubuntu*, and *Wasta* works and its weaknesses has implication for the practice of socialization of newcomers in organizations set in China, Kenya and Lebanon. According to Korte (2010) newcomers enter organizations that have values and implicit and explicit norms. These leaders are assumed to have expertise and experience despite being in a new context and therefore expected to learn their responsibility and be in charge. Korte and Lin (2013) indicated that in order for the new leaders to perform well they have receive quality relationships from the team. Moreover, this process has to be facilitated by the management team, this is where the authors expect the change to be enacted - the settling of an exemplary ways of situating *good practices of Guanxi*, *Ubuntu*, and *Wasta* within workplace leadership and culture.

CONCLUSION

Admittedly, *Guanxi*, *Ubuntu*, and *Wasta* are terms that are better understood in certain milieus than others. However, there are some commonalities in *Guanxi*, *Ubuntu*, and Wasta and how they relate with leadership. Moreover, it should be remembered that aspects of these practices are also found in discourses of social capital and social networks in the Western world. The emphasis on opportunistic connections under *Guanxi* analogizes to the purpose of various Western social media as a platform for interconnectedness. As such, these cultural worldviews should not be approached with fear or prejudice but with an open mind and an acknowledgement of the good and richness that they can embody. Yet, this demands cultural competence, especially around gender; where, for example, saving face under *Guanxi* entails that the necessary level of flattery required from women in order to build business *Guanxi* actually risks losing face (Xu & Li, 2015). Similarly, boasting and "big man" politics within *Wasta* and *Ubuntu* are generally incompatible with, and are even defined in opposition to, women's modes of being, and cultural settings can preclude women, inasmuch as hostess clubs, strip clubs, and the like are unwelcoming to women at the very least (Bedford & Hwang, 2013).

In general, organizations tend to have inadequate, partial, or nonexistent cross-cultural training programs (Brewster, 1995; Selmer, 2000). This gap between research and practice emerges from difference of concerns between scholars and practitioners (Short & Shindell, 2009). To address this, ideally, would involve practitioners utilizing published research when making critical decisions in the workplace. While logistically challenging, Short and Shindell (2009) proposed HRD practical scholars as such gap closers, "[Practical scholars] ground their practice in research and theory, they are champions of research and theory in the workplace and in professional associations" (p. 478). But whatever strategy is taken up, the necessity of cultural competence for HRD and leadership internationally is necessary. To ignore the culturality of inter-cultural business loses the competitive advantage. This is true intra-culturally too, where lip service to meritocracy is corrupted by gender nepotism, thereby (once again) losing the competitive advantage meritocracy affords.

Such an opening is difficult and challenging but accomplishable and necessary. The need for HRD practitioners to produce context-based programs for leaders in cross-cultural settings is important (Hutchings & Weir, 2006; McLean, 2005; Wellins & Weaver, 2003). As this need arises both inter-culturally and intra-culturally, such examination on *Guanxi*, *Ubuntu*, and *Wasta* in relation to workplace leadership and culture sheds light on organizational consideration about factors to be addressed in designing such programs.

REFERENCES

A Survey of China: A Tangled Web. (2000). Retrieved 4 December, 2016, from http://www.economist.com/node/299613

Adler, P. S., & Kwon, S. W. (2002). Social capital: Prospects for a new concept. *Academy of Management Review, 27*(1), 17–40.

al-Suwaidi, M. (2008). *When an Arab executive says "yes": Identifying different collectivistic values that influence the Arabian decision-making process. (MSc).* University of Pennsylvania.

Ardichvili, A., & Kuchinke, K. P. (2002). Leadership styles and cultural values among managers and subordinates: A comparative study of four countries of the former Soviet Union, Germany, and the US. *Human Resource Development International, 5*(1), 99–117. doi:10.1080/13678860110046225

Avolio, B. J., Bass, B. M., & Jung, D. I. (1999). Re-examining the components of transformational and transactional leadership using the Multifactor Leadership. *Journal of Occupational and Organizational Psychology, 72*(4), 441–462. doi:10.1348/096317999166789

Barnathan, J., Crock, S., Einhorn, B., Engardio, P., Roberts, D., & Borrus, A. (1996). Rethinking China. *Business Week, 4,* 13-20.

Bass, B. M. (1997). Does the transactional–transformational leadership paradigm transcend organizational and national boundaries? *The American Psychologist, 52*(2), 130–139. doi:10.1037/0003-066X.52.2.130

Bedford, O., & Hwang, S. L. (2013). Building relationships for business in Taiwanese hostess clubs: The psychological and social processes of guanxi development. *Gender, Work and Organization, 20*(3), 297–310. doi:10.1111/j.1468-0432.2011.00576.x

Berger, R., Silbiger, A., Herstein, R., & Barnes, B. R. (2015). Analyzing business-to-business relationships in an Arab context. *Journal of World Business, 50*(3), 454–464. doi:10.1016/j.jwb.2014.08.004

Bierema, L. L. (2016). Womens Leadership Troubling Notions of the Ideal (Male) Leader. *Advances in Developing Human Resources, 18*(2), 119–136. doi:10.1177/1523422316641398

Blake, R. R., Mouton, J. S., & Bidwell, A. C. (1962). *Managerial grid.* Advanced Management-Office Executive.

Bond, M. H., & Hwang, S. (2008). *The psychology of the Chinese people.* New York: Oxford University Press.

Braendle, U. C., Gasser, T., & Noll, J. (2005). Corporate governance in China—is economic growth potential hindered by guanxi? *Business and Society Review, 110*(4), 389–405. doi:10.1111/j.0045-3609.2005.00022.x

Brewster, C. (1995). Effective expatriate training. In J. Selmer (Ed.), *Expatriate management: New ideas for international business* (pp. 57–72). Westport, CT: Quorum.

Broodryk, J. (2006a). *Ubuntu: life coping skills from Africa.* Randburg: Knowledge Resources.

Broodryk, J. (2006b). *Ubuntu: African Life Coping Skills: Theory and Practice.* Presented at the CCEAM, Lefkosia Nicosia, Cyprus.

Bruner, C. H. (1993). *The Heinemann book of African women's writing.* London: Heinemann.

Burt, R. S. (1992). *Structural holes: the social structure of competition.* Cambridge, MA: Harvard University Press.

Callahan, J. L. (2010). Constructing a manuscript: Distinguishing integrative literature reviews and conceptual and theory articles. *Human Resource Development Review, 9*(3), 300–304. doi:10.1177/1534484310371492

Chen, C., Chen, X., & Huang, S. (2013). Chinese Guanxi: An integrative review and new directions for future research. *Management and Organization Review, 9*(1), 167–207. doi:10.1111/more.12010

Chen, X.-P., & Chen, C. C. (2004). On the intricacies of the Chinese guanxi: A process model of guanxi development. *Asia Pacific Journal of Management, 21*(3), 305–324. doi:10.1023/B:APJM.0000036465.19102.d5

Chen, Y. F., & Tjosvold, D. (2006). Participative leadership by American and Chinese managers in China: The role of relationships. *Journal of Management Studies, 43*(8), 1727–1752. doi:10.1111/j.1467-6486.2006.00657.x

Cheng, B. S., Chou, L. F., Wu, T. Y., Huang, M. P., & Farh, J. L. (2004). Paternalistic leadership and subordinate responses: Establishing a leadership model in Chinese organizations. *Asian Journal of Social Psychology, 7*(1), 89–117. doi:10.1111/j.1467-839X.2004.00137.x

Cheung, M. F., Wu, W.-P., Chan, A. K., & Wong, M. M. (2009). Supervisor–subordinate guanxi and employee work outcomes: The mediating role of job satisfaction. *Journal of Business Ethics, 88*(1), 77–89. doi:10.1007/s10551-008-9830-0

Coleman, J. S. (1988). Social capital in the creation of human capital. *American Journal of Sociology, 94*, S95-S120.

Collins, J. (2005). Level 5 leadership: The triumph of humility and fierce resolve. *Harvard Business Review.* PMID:11189464

Cunningham, R., & Sarayrah, Y. K. (1993). *Wasta: The hidden force in Middle Eastern society.* Westport, CT: Praeger.

Egejuru, P. (Ed.). (1980). *Towards African literary independence: a dialogue with contemporary African writers.* Westport, CT: Greenwood Press.

Fink, G., Holden, N., Karsten, L., & Illa, H. (2005). Ubuntu as a key African management concept: Contextual background and practical insights for knowledge application. *Journal of Managerial Psychology, 20*(7), 607–620. doi:10.1108/02683940510623416

Gade, C. B. (2011). The historical development of the written discourses on ubuntu. *South African Journal of Philosophy, 30*(3), 303–329. doi:10.4314/sajpem.v30i3.69578

Gathogo, J. (2008). African philosophy as expressed in the concepts of hospitality and ubuntu. *Journal of Theology for Southern Africa, 130*(March), 39–53.

GLOBE. (2016). *Global Leadership & Organizational Behavior Effectiveness: Overview*. Retrieved 4 December, 2016, from http://globeproject.com/studies

Granovetter, M. S. (1973). The strength of weak ties. *American Journal of Sociology, 78*(6), 1360–1380. doi:10.1086/225469

Guthrie, D. (1999). Producing Guanxi: Sentiment, Self, and Subculture in a North China Village. *The China Quarterly, 158*, 509–510. doi:10.1017/S0305741000006044

Hofstede, G. (1980). *Culture's consequences: international differences in work-related values*. Beverly Hills, CA: Sage.

Hofstede, G. (1993). Cultural constraints in management theories. In J. Wren (Ed.), *The leader's companion* (pp. 253–270). New York: Free Press.

Hofstede, G. (2011). Dimensionalizing cultures: The Hofstede model in context. *Online Readings in Psychology and Culture, 2*(1).

Hong, J., & Engeström, Y. (2004). Changing principles of communication between Chinese managers and workers Confucian authority chains and guanxi as social networking. *Management Communication Quarterly, 17*(4), 552–585. doi:10.1177/0893318903262266

House, R. J., Wright, N. S., & Aditya, R. N. (1997). *Cross-cultural research on organizational leadership: A critical analysis and a proposed theory*. Academic Press.

Hui, C., & Graen, G. (1998). Guanxi and professional leadership in contemporary Sino-American joint ventures in mainland China. *The Leadership Quarterly, 8*(4), 451–465. doi:10.1016/S1048-9843(97)90024-2

Hutchings, K., & Weir, D. (2006). Guanxi and wasta: A comparison. *Thunderbird International Business Review, 48*(1), 141–156. doi:10.1002/tie.20090

Hwang, D. B., Golemon, P. L., Chen, Y., Wang, T.-S., & Hung, W.-S. (2009). Guanxi and business ethics in Confucian society today: An empirical case study in Taiwan. *Journal of Business Ethics, 89*(2), 235–250. doi:10.1007/s10551-008-9996-5

Isaac, R. J. (2012). *African Humanism: A Pragmatic Prescription For Fostering Social Justice And Political Agency*. Philadelphia, PA: Temple University.

Jung, C. G. (1971). Psychological types (4th ed.). Princeton, NJ: Princeton University Press.

Kabasakal, H., & Bodur, M. (2002). Arabic cluster: A bridge between East and West. *Journal of World Business, 37*(1), 40–54. doi:10.1016/S1090-9516(01)00073-6

Karsten, L., & Illa, H. (2001). Ubuntu as a management concept. *Quest, 15*(1-2), 111–134.

Khoza, R. J. (2006). *Let Africa lead: African transformational leadership for 21st century business*. Johannesburg: Vezubuntu.

Korte, R. (2010). First, get to know them: A relational view of organizational socialization. *Human Resource Development International, 13*(1), 27–43. doi:10.1080/13678861003588984

Korte, R., & Lin, S. (2013). Getting on board: Organizational socialization and the contribution of social capital. *Human Relations, 66*(3), 407–428. doi:10.1177/0018726712461927

Kreuter, M. W., & Lezin, N. (2002). Social capital theory: implications for community-based health promotion. In R. diClemente, R. Crosby, & M. Kegler (Eds.), *Emerging theories in health promotion practice and research: Strategies for improving public health* (pp. 228–254). San Francisco, CA: Jossey-Bass.

Kropf, A., & Newbury-Smith, T. C. (2016). Wasta as a form of social capital: an institutional perspective. In M. A. Ramady (Ed.), *The Political Economy of Wasta: Use and Abuse of Social Capital Networking* (pp. 3–22). New York: Springer International. doi:10.1007/978-3-319-22201-1_1

Kuchinke, K. P. (1999). Leadership and culture: Work-related values and leadership styles among one companys US and German telecommunication employees. *Human Resource Development Quarterly, 10*(2), 135–154. doi:10.1002/hrdq.3920100205

Kushner, J. (2009). *Wangari Maathai: Righteous leader of environmental and social change.* Presented at the Adult Education Research Conference, Chicago, IL. Retrieved from http://newprairiepress.org/cgi/viewcontent.cgi?article=3780&context=aerc

Lackner, H. (2016). Wasta: Is it such a bad thing? An anthropological perspective. In M. A. Ramady (Ed.), *The Political Economy of Wasta: Use and Abuse of Social Capital Networking* (pp. 33–46). New York: Springer International. doi:10.1007/978-3-319-22201-1_3

Law, K. S., Wong, C.-S., Wang, D., & Wang, L. (2000). Effect of supervisor–subordinate guanxi on supervisory decisions in China: An empirical investigation. *International Journal of Human Resource Management, 11*(4), 751–765. doi:10.1080/09585190050075105

Le Grange, L. (2012). Ubuntu, ukama and the healing of nature, self and society. *Educational Philosophy and Theory, 44*(sup2s2), 56–67. doi:10.1111/j.1469-5812.2011.00795.x

Lin, L.-H. (2011). Cultural and organizational antecedents of guanxi: The Chinese cases. *Journal of Business Ethics, 99*(3), 441–451. doi:10.1007/s10551-010-0662-3

Lin, N. (1999). Social networks and status attainment. *Annual Review of Sociology, 25*(1), 467–487. doi:10.1146/annurev.soc.25.1.467

Loewe, M., Blume, J., & Speer, J. (2008). How favoritism affects the business climate: Empirical evidence from Jordan. *The Middle East Journal, 62*(2), 259–276. doi:10.3751/62.2.14

Maathai, W. (2006). *Unbowed: a memoir.* New York: Alfred A. Knopf.

Mangaliso, M. P. (2001). Building competitive advantage from ubuntu: Management lessons from South Africa. *The Academy of Management Executive, 15*(3), 23–33. doi:10.5465/AME.2001.5229453

Marks, S. C. (2000). Ubuntu, Spirit of Africa: Example for the World. In S. C. Marks (Ed.), *Watching the wind: conflict resolution during South Africa's transition to democracy* (pp. 181–190). Washington, DC: United States Institute of Peace Press.

Marktanner, M., & Wilson, M. (2016). The economic cost of Wasta in the Arab world: an empirical approach. In M. A. Ramady (Ed.), *The Political Economy of Wasta: Use and Abuse of Social Capital Networking* (pp. 79–95). New York: Springer International. doi:10.1007/978-3-319-22201-1_6

Mbigi, L., & Maree, J. (2005). *Ubuntu: The spirit of African transformation management*. Randburg: Knowledge Resources.

McGregor, D. (1960). Theory X and theory Y. *Organization Theory*, 358-374.

McLean, G. N. (2005). *Organization Development: Principles, Processes, Performance*. San Francisco: Berrett-Koehler Publishers.

Menkiti, I. A. (1984). Person and community in African traditional thought. *African Philosophy: An Introduction, 3*, 171-182.

Murithi, T. (2006). Practical peacemaking wisdom from Africa: Reflections on Ubuntu. *The Journal of Pan African Studies, 1*(4), 25–34.

Nafukho, F. M. (2006). Ubuntu worldview: A traditional African view of adult learning in the workplace. *Advances in Developing Human Resources, 8*(3), 408–415. doi:10.1177/1523422306288434

Ngunjiri, F. W. (2016). I Am Because We Are Exploring Womens Leadership Under Ubuntu Worldview. *Advances in Developing Human Resources, 18*(2), 223–242. doi:10.1177/1523422316641416

Nica, E. (2013a). Ethical Challenges of Integrating Local Leadership in the Global Mindset. *Journal of Self-Governance and Management Economics, 1*(3), 32–37.

Nica, E. (2013b). The importance of leadership development within higher education. *Contemporary Readings in Law and Social Justice, 5*(2), 189–194.

Pearce, J. A. II, & Robinson, R. B. Jr. (2000). Cultivating guanxi as a foreign investor strategy. *Business Horizons, 43*(1), 31–38. doi:10.1016/S0007-6813(00)87385-1

Portes, A. (2000). Social capital: Its origins and applications in modern sociology. In E. Lesser (Ed.), *Knowledge and Social Capital* (pp. 43–67). Boston: Butterworth-Heinemann. doi:10.1016/B978-0-7506-7222-1.50006-4

Putnam, R. D. (1995). Bowling alone: Americas declining social capital. *Journal of Democracy, 6*(1), 65–78. doi:10.1353/jod.1995.0002

Rametsehoa, M. (1999). *A cultural diversity model for corporate South Africa. (Business Administration MBA)*. Johannesburg: Technikon Witwatersrand.

Selmer, J. (2000). A quantitative needs assessment technique for cross-cultural work adjustment training. *Human Resource Development Quarterly, 11*(3), 269–281. doi:10.1002/1532-1096(200023)11:3<269::AID-HRDQ5>3.0.CO;2-6

Short, D. C., & Shindell, T. J. (2009). Defining HRD scholar-practitioners. *Advances in Developing Human Resources, 11*(4), 472–485. doi:10.1177/1523422309342225

Smith, P. B., Huang, H. J., Harb, C., & Torres, C. (2011). How Distinctive Are Indigenous Ways of Achieving Influence? A Comparative Study of Guanxi, Wasta, Jeitinho, and Pulling Strings. *Journal of Cross-Cultural Psychology, 43*(1), 135–150. doi:10.1177/0022022110381430

Smith, P. B., Torres, C., Leong, C.-H., Budhwar, P., Achoui, M., & Lebedeva, N. (2012). Are indigenous approaches to achieving influence in business organizations distinctive? A comparative study of guanxi, wasta, jeitinho, svyazi and pulling strings. *International Journal of Human Resource Management, 23*(2), 333–348. doi:10.1080/09585192.2011.561232

Stead, V., & Elliott, C. (2009). *Women's leadership.* New York: Palgrave Macmillan. doi:10.1057/9780230246737

Swanson, D. M. (2009). Where have all the fishes gone?: Living uBuntu as an ethics of research and pedagogical engagement. In D. M. Caracciolo & A. M. N. Mungai (Eds.), *In the spirit of Ubuntu: stories of teaching and research* (pp. 3–21). Rotterdam: Sense.

Swanson, D. M. (2010). Value in shadows: A critical contribution to values education in our times. In T. Lovat, R. Toomey, & N. Clement (Eds.), *International research handbook on values education and student wellbeing* (pp. 137–152). Dordrecht: Springer. doi:10.1007/978-90-481-8675-4_8

Tlaiss, H., & Kauser, S. (2011). The importance of wasta in the career success of Middle Eastern managers. *Journal of European Industrial Training, 35*(5), 467–486. doi:10.1108/03090591111138026

Ulrich, D., & Black, S. (1999). Worldly Wise. *People Management,* 42-46.

Van De Valk, L. J. (2008). Leadership development and social capital: Is There a Relationship. *Journal of Leadership Education, 7*(1), 47-64.

Warner, M. (1997). Chinas HRM in Transition: Towards Relative Convergence? *Asia Pacific Business Review, 3*(4), 19–33. doi:10.1080/13602389700000041

Weir, D. (2003). Human resource development in the Middle East: A fourth paradigm. In M. Lee (Ed.), *HRD in a Complex World* (pp. 69–82). London: Routledge. doi:10.4324/9780203410158_chapter_5

Weir, D., Sultan, N., & van de Blunt, S. (2016). Wasta: a scourge or a usement management and business practice. In M. A. Ramady (Ed.), *The Political Economy of Wasta: Use and Abuse of Social Capital Networking* (pp. 23–32). New York: Springer International. doi:10.1007/978-3-319-22201-1_2

Wellins, R., & Weaver, P. (2003). From c-level to see-level leadership. *Training & Development, 57*(9), 58–65.

West, A. (2014). Ubuntu and business ethics: Problems, perspectives and prospects. *Journal of Business Ethics, 121*(1), 47–61. doi:10.1007/s10551-013-1669-3

Williams, R. (1977). *Marxism and literature* (Vol. 1). Oxford University Press.

Wright, P., Szeto, W., & Cheng, L. T. (2002). Guanxi and professional conduct in China: A management development perspective. *International Journal of Human Resource Management, 13*(1), 156–182. doi:10.1080/09585190110083839

Xin, K. K., & Pearce, J. L. (1996). Guanxi: Connections as substitutes for formal institutional support. *Academy of Management Journal, 39*(6), 1641–1658. doi:10.2307/257072

Xu, K., & Li, Y. (2015). Exploring guanxi from a gender perspective: Urban Chinese womens practices of guanxi. *Gender, Place and Culture, 22*(6), 833–850. doi:10.1080/0966369X.2014.917279

Yahchouchi, G. (2009). Employees' perceptions of Lebanese managers' leadership styles and organizational commitment. *International. The Journal of Leadership Studies, 4*(2), 127–140.

Yang, M. M. (2002). The resilience of guanxi and its new deployments: A critique of some new guanxi scholarship. *The China Quarterly, 170*, 459–476. doi:10.1017/S000944390200027X

Yeung, I. Y., & Tung, R. L. (1996). Achieving business success in Confucian societies: The importance of guanxi (connections). *Organizational Dynamics, 25*(2), 54–65. doi:10.1016/S0090-2616(96)90025-X

Yum, J. O. (2007). Confucianism and Communication: Jen, Li, and Ubuntu. *China Media Research, 3*(4), 15–22.

Zgusta, L. (2006). *Lexicography Then and Now: Selected Essays* (F. Dolezal & T. Creamer, Eds.). Tübingen: Walter De Gruyter. doi:10.1515/9783110924459

Zhang, Y., & Wu, Y. (2012). Huawei and Zhengfei Ren: leadership in a technology-innovative firm. In C. Petti (Ed.), *Technological Entrepreneurship in China: How Does it Work?* (pp. 103–122). Northampton, MA: Edward Elgar. doi:10.4337/9780857938992.00013

ADDITIONAL READING

Abalkhail, J. M., Abalkhail, J. M., Allan, B., & Allan, B. (2016). Wasta and womens careers in the Arab Gulf States. *Gender in Management: An International Journal, 31*(3), 162–180. doi:10.1108/GM-02-2015-0006

Al-Ramahi, A. (2008). Wasta in Jordan: A distinct feature of (and benefit for) Middle Eastern society. *Arab Law Quarterly, 22*(1), 35–62. doi:10.1163/026805508X286794

Brandstaetter, T., Bamber, D., & Weir, D. (2016). 'Wasta': Triadic Trust in Jordanian Business. In The Political Economy of Wasta: Use and Abuse of Social Capital Networking (pp. 65-78). Springer International Publishing.

Brubaker, T. A. (2013). Servant leadership, ubuntu, and leader effectiveness in Rwanda. *Emerging Leadership Journeys, 6*(1), 95–131.

Cunningham, R. B., Sarayrah, Y. K., & Sarayrah, Y. E. (1994). Taming" Wasta" to Achieve Development. *Arab Studies Quarterly*, 29–41.

Harbi, S. A., Thursfield, D., & Bright, D. (2016). Culture, Wasta and perceptions of performance appraisal in Saudi Arabia. *International Journal of Human Resource Management*, 1–19. doi:10.1080/0 9585192.2016.1138987

Kuah-Pearce, K. E. (2016). Migrant women entrepreneurs in the garment industry in modern China: Embedding translocality and feminised Guanxi networks. *International Journal of Business and Globalisation*, *16*(3), 335–349. doi:10.1504/IJBG.2016.075730

Li, Y., Du, J., & Van de Bunt, S. (2016). Social Capital Networking in China and the Traditional Values of Guanxi. In The Political Economy of Wasta: Use and Abuse of Social Capital Networking (pp. 173-183). Springer International Publishing. doi:10.1007/978-3-319-22201-1_12

Makhoul, J., & Harrison, L. (2004). Intercessory wasta and village development in Lebanon. *Arab Studies Quarterly*, 25–41.

Marktanner, M., & Wilson, M. (2016). The Economic Cost of Wasta in the Arab World: An Empirical Approach. In The Political Economy of Wasta: Use and Abuse of Social Capital Networking (pp. 79-94). Springer International Publishing.

Metz, T. (2016). Confucian harmony from an African perspective. *African and Asian Studies*, *15*(1), 1–22. doi:10.1163/15692108-12341354

Misumi, J., & Seki, F. (1971). Effects of Achievement Motivation on the Effectiveness of Leadership Patterns. *Administrative Science Quarterly*, *16*(1), 51–59. doi:10.2307/2391287

Niedermeier, K. E., Wang, E., & Zhang, X. (2016). The use of social media among business-to-business sales professionals in china: How social media helps create and solidify guanxi relationships between sales professionals and customers. *Journal of Research in Interactive Marketing*, *10*(1), 33–49. doi:10.1108/JRIM-08-2015-0054

Peng, H., Duysters, G., & Sadowski, B. (2016). The changing role of guanxi in influencing the development of entrepreneurial companies: A case study of the emergence of pharmaceutical companies in China. *The International Entrepreneurship and Management Journal*, *12*(1), 215–258. doi:10.1007/s11365-014-0323-6

Swanson, D. M. (2008). "Ubuntu: An African contribution to (re) search for/with a 'humble togetherness'." *Journal of contemporary*. *Issues in Education*, *2*(2).

Ta'Amnha, M., Sayce, S., & Tregaskis, O. (2016). 21. Wasta in the Jordanian context. Handbook of Human Resource Management in the Middle East, 393.

Tutu, D. (1999). *No future without forgiveness*. New York, NY: Doubleday.

Xing, Y., Liu, Y., Tarba, S. Y., & Cooper, C. L. (2016). Intercultural influences on managing African employees of Chinese firms in Africa: Chinese managers HRM practices. *International Business Review*, *25*(1), 28–41. doi:10.1016/j.ibusrev.2014.05.003

KEY TERMS AND DEFINITIONS

Guanxi: Personal connection, social network or relationship of influence which facilitates business collaboration, job promotion and other dealings.

Hofstede: Professor Geert Hofstede is a Dutch social psychologist who conducted a study of how values in the workplace are influenced by culture. He analysed a large database of employee values scores collected by IBM, between 1967, 1973, 2001, covering more than 76 countries.

Leadership: The ability to motivate other people to accomplish goals.

Leadership Style: The way a leader communicates, comports oneself, thinks in order to get things done through people.

National Culture: A formal or informal way that individuals in a nation-state are wired to view the world.

Organizational Culture: Agreed upon ways in which individuals, groups and institutions view themselves and construct their realities in order to achieve their goals.

Social Capital: The intangible product that is in the relationships and connections made by individuals or groups.

Social Network: The relationships and connections that people of the same community form in order access assets and information with an aim of producing outcomes.

Ubuntu: A spiritual, political and philosophical stance that speaks to the human interconnectedness that ties people to each other and nature on daily basis.

Wasta: "Who you know" or "one's connections." It is the use of one's individual connections or power to get things done.

Chapter 5
Influences of Personal Experience in Decision-Making

Thais Spiegel
Rio de Janeiro State University, Brazil

ABSTRACT

Among the aspects that conform the human cognition and therefore, the behavior observed in the choices, there is the individual experience. Researches point the experience performing either positive as negative roles in the process of decision-making. Motivated by the question, What is the role of the experience in the decision-making? this text sought to check in which way the state of art and the technique of Cognitive Sciences could contribute with the better understanding of the cognitive processing in the context of decision-making. It was adopted as a start the roles' structured exposition of the cognition elements during the decision process, as Spiegel's (2014) proposal. It was investigated through a systematic revision of the literature, the impacts of the decision-maker's experience in the manifestation of attention, categorization, memory and emotion. As a result, 17 inferences that present which is the role of the experience in the decision-making, and deeply, which are the implications of the experience in the cognitive process of the decision-maker, are presented.

INTRODUCTION

The decision-making study has as a target the understanding of the human ability of process multiple alternatives and choose an action course. The problem's perception and/or the responsibility attribution by the resolution the decision-maker's responsibility. The decision-maker is the individual or group on who lays the responsibility of dealing with the presented problem and, therefore, some fundamental factors linked to them change the way of how the decision occurs. The number of decision-makers, as well as the quality and the personal preference, defines the solution of the decision-making process (Spiegel, 2011).

Decisions are not equal and neither have the same difficulty degree, but they are all dependent on the mental model of their decision-makers. The agents may be evaluated by their individual knowledge about the problem, the resolution ability of each one of them, their desires and interests and the ethical and moral standards that guide them. Recognize the variety among the decision-makers is also necessary,

DOI: 10.4018/978-1-5225-2480-9.ch005

since the performance will be determined by the adjustment of the tasks' demands with the capacity, knowledge and the willingness to use effort of the decision-maker (Spiegel, 2011). Among the aspects that conform the human cognition and therefore, the observed behavior, is the personal experience. Bohanec (2003) defines the decision-making process as an "art that requires the decision-maker combines experience and education to act". Decision-makers based themselves on their personal experiences in order to make choices.

Basic researches in cognitive psychology suggest that most part of the experience's advantage of the decision-makers is placed on their greater knowledge stock, associated to the memory's processes, and mainly in the way they organize their knowledge, defined by the categorization processes, in order for it to be effectively brought to deal with the problem.

Rakow and Newell (2010) conclude their exposition presenting that this theme remains open and lacks of researches, and suggest the central point should be the question "Which is the role of the experience?" instead of "What happens in the choice based on the experience?". For them although the role of the experience has been explored in framing researches, it's still misunderstood in relation to its importance in a series of daily decisions.

Thus, this chapter proposes to investigate which is the role of experiences of the decision-makers agents and the impact of these in the functioning of the cognitive process of a human decision maker.

BACKGROUND

The Experience Definition: A First Object Approach

Rocha (2008) points out that are large and complex the variety of meanings the term experience can take and the point of views they could be studied are numerous. According to Oxford dictionary, experience refers to the "practical contact with, and the observation of facts and events. The knowledge or ability acquired by a period of practical experience in something, specially obtained by a specific profession". The Business dictionary defines it as the "familiarity with an ability or area of the knowledge acquired over months or years of practice and that, probably resulted in a superior understanding or domain".

Bondía (2002) introduces the mentioned concept that the experience is, in Spanish, "o que nos passa", in Portuguese, "o que nos acontece"; in French "*ce que nous arrive*"; in Italian, "*quello che nos succede*" or "*quello che nos acc*ade"; in English, "*that what is happening to us*"; in German, "*was passiert ist*", and not what is up, what is happening, or what touches. The author seeks to highlights with this construction, the difference between an event and the experience lived by individuals. This emphasis in the process that "occurs" with the individual is highlighted by the author by presenting the Heidegger's understanding.

[...] having an experience with something means that something happen to us, reach us; that takes hold of us, tumbles us and changes us. When we say "have" an experience, this doesn't precisely mean that we make it happen, "make' here means: suffer, feel, take what reaches us receptively, accept, as we submit to something. Make an experience means so, let us to be approached in ourselves by what challenge us, entering and being submitted to that. We can then be transformed by such experiences, from one day to the other or along the time. (Heidegger, 1987: 143 apud Bondía, 2002: 25).

The experience, as a way of knowledge, is structures by two essential poles, which are: the objective articulated to the experience object and the subjective where it stands out what the subject says about what he has lived and found in the encounter with the objects (Rocha, 2008). The object diversifies itself in an endless variety of possibilities, and in the moment of the experience, the subject commutes with the object and internalizes it in the act of knowing. Therefore, when internalized, the object starts to be part of his/her life and is marked on his/her subject singularity. Object and subject are therefore the structural poles of the notion of experience, especially the experience as a way of knowledge.

In the literature of the Organizational Theory, it's approached the "experience of specific decision" and it's defined as the experience acquired through the participation in a decision within determined configuration and built-in a personal or organizational memory (Penrose, 1959). Cho and Padmanabhan (2001) highlight the theoretical and practical importance of this kind of experience when influence the strategic decisions of the companies. The decision-making experience represents the experience acquired with the repeated application of established routines, learned with the use of similar strategies in the past. The company's past experiences are manifested in organizational routines that form the model for future actions of the company and serve as an important source of competitive advantage. The company's knowledge base will increase with repetitive experiences and it will be incorporated in the personal and organizational memory (Penrose, 1959).

According to Allen, Strathern, and Baldwin (2010), people allow their experience to guide their actions, their actions generate their results and their results confirm their experience. A feedback cycle that tends to be positive. The experience is made of an accumulation of such sequences and some of them are probably useful. However, the ones made under pressure, formed, and rapidly put into practice may be an absurd.

Cohen, Etner, and Jeleva (2010) define experience from a sequence of events occurring before the moment of decision. For the authors, the experience may embrace several events: may be events in the past, which are relevant for the decision, as accidents, when it's considered a decision aiming the safety; or other events in the past such as weather conditions when a stock market's behavior is considered.

In this text the experience is understood as a result of past events that were lived in a practical way in different situations, either making decisions or observing other people's ones, where the cognition of the human being was confirmed.

The Cognitive Sciences in Front of the Experiences: Approaches and Clippings Used

A revolution has been happening in the neurosciences since the half of the 80s. From a search on periodic basis, one may observe that the issue of the current research, related to the experience for the cognitive scientists refers to the differences in the answers that are observed whenever people face decisions from the experience and the description.

The decisions from the experience refer to the experiments that requires the participants explore an environment and learn the probabilities and results associated to each option (Rakow & Newell, 2010). The environment exploration opens space to important issues, such as: how people select the information, how much they select, the mental representation they create and the role that the memory can play. FitzGerald *et al.* (2010) follows these behavioral findings, revealing that the neural regions are differentially activated, depending if the information about options were acquired through the experience or the description.

The fact of the information that is relevant for the decision be necessarily built over the time, makes the decisions from the experience to be a good way to explore the sequential information processing (Barron & Leider, 2010). In addition, the "wealth" of the paradigm of decision from the experience with its focus on the acquisition and integration of information previous to the choice as well as the act of the choice, is available to more complete investigations in the individual differences in the cognitive processes (Rakow & Newell, 2010).

It became evident in the behavioral decision literature that these different approaches for the experimental study of decision-making, differ not only in the nature of the information provided but also in the way the acquired information is used to guide decisions (Hertwig *et al.*, 2004). In spite of this growing behavioral evidence, neurobiological studies of decision-making, haven't been able to solve the way the differences of presentation may potentially influence the neural representations underlying these variables (Jessup & O'Doherty, 2010). Results indicate the decision variables generated based on the specific provision of descriptive information are not processed neutrally the same way the decision variables acquired based on learning by trial and error. It's important notice, that the brain systems identified in the two different conditions are not likely to be exclusively involved in one or other kind of decision-making (Barron & Leider, 2010). For instance, it was identified in other researches that the prefrontal cortex ventromedial represents decision values also under conditions that involves the providing of descriptive information. While MRI studies have found there is correlation of the activity in the ventral striatum with the prediction errors, a key sign to play a role in the learning by trial and error, and particularly in the associations between stimulus-result. A similar history is valid for risk signs in the anterior insula and anterior cingulated (Chib *et al.*, 2009).

THE IMPLICATIONS OF THE DECISION-MAKER'S EXPERIENCE ON HIS COGNITIVE PROCESS

Initially, this research starts from a systematization of the human cognition's role in the decision-making process, particularly of the decision-maker's cognitive process through the elements: attention, categorization, memory and emotion; express in Spiegel (2011) and Spiegel (2014), as Figure 1.

Starting from this model, where, in a structured way, the roles that the elements of cognition assume are presented, this research was guided by stablishing one of the factors of the human being that forms the operation of the cognitive process, the experience. The option to restrict the object to the understanding of the impacts of a human being's factor on his/her cognitive process has limitations on the explanation capability. The observed behavior may be function of other not included factors. However, it's up to the researcher the cutting decisions that make feasible the research.

In this context, it was stablished as an object, the experience's impact of the agent on his/her decisions. Thus, in this text, is proceeded the literature identification and revision, guided by a structured bibliographic search procedure, as shown in Figure 2, in order to support the formulation of propositions, in the form of experience's implications in the operation of the decision-maker's cognitive process.

In the following pages there will be exposed the literature indications about the effects of the experience in the human cognition.

Figure 1. Model of the research's outgoing: the roles of cognition elements in decision-making. Source: Spiegel (2011); Spiegel (2014).

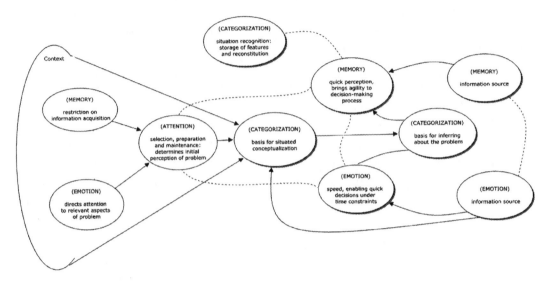

Figure 2. Method of bibliographic revision. Source: the authors

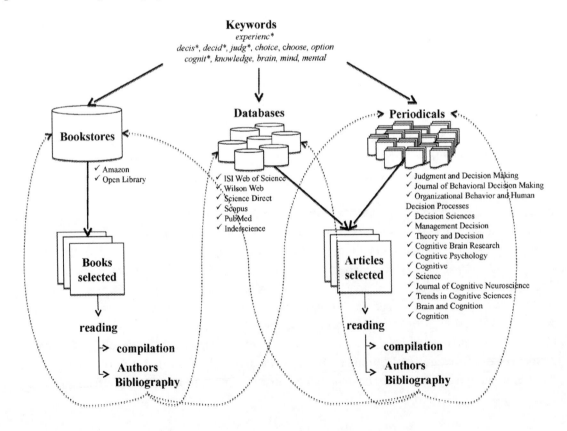

Implications of the Experience in the Decision-Maker's Attention

The Experiences Tend to Influence the Attention, Checking Perceptions That Seems to be Accurate and Fast of "Known" Objects and Ideas

The common sense suggests that the "practice leads to perfection". One of the recurrent phenomenon in the studies of shared attention (Eysenck & Keane, 2002) is the improvement that the practice many times has over the performance. A greater knowledge about what to do with different stimulus is stored with the practice, and that the automatism occurs when this information may be quickly recovered (Shepherd *et al.*, 2003). It's supposed that the automatic processes are fast, that do not reduce their available capability for other tasks and that there is no conscience of them (Dijksterhuis & Aarts, 2010).

LaBerge (1999) gives three assignments to the attention process, namely: precise and fast perceptions of objects and ideas and the support of the desired mental transformation. These are achieved three manifestations corresponding of the attention: the simple selection, the preparation and maintenance.

The experiences influence in the attention's attribution referring to accurate, fast perceptions of objects and ideas, as they stablish a "memory trace" richer for the clues (indicative signs) critics inside the future episodic processing system. This sturdier memory provides the impulse to recall this item somewhere in the future (Fiore, 2008). The practice is related to the force of the signaling assumed by specific clues, which increase the probability of being captured by attentional mechanisms.

Essentially, these specific mechanisms create a relationship of the clue with the unconscious actuation of the processing, meaning, when something (clue) in the environment is noticed, the memory is activated and increases the possibility of satisfying a need (Dijksterhuis & Aarts, 2010). Thus, due to the development of the "richer traces of memory" with the experience and their consequent activation; the shared attention is prone to a perception of the increase of performance, for instance, perception that notices precisely and fast (Fiore, 2008).

The Experiences Influence the Attention's Preparation and Maintenance

The experience also influences in the attention's manifestations, as the ones formulated by LaBerge (1999), in the way of attention's preparation and maintenance. This is because, as exposed by Eysenck & Keane (2002), the previous practice experiences facilitate the performance of the attentional mechanisms, as they: the individuals can develop new strategies (with the sense of operations' standard between the cognitive functions) to perform the tasks; the demands made by a task in attention or in other central resources may be reduced based on the practice; and beside a task initially requires the use of several resources of specific processing, the practice may allow a more economical way of operation, depending on less resources.

Coherently, Shepherd, Zacharakis & Baron (2003) indicate that the experienced decision-makers create information categories based on a deep structure that involves more ties and stronger ones among the concepts and so, they enable and facilitate the maintenance of attention. On the other hand, experienced decision-makers seem to trust in several heuristics as well as in other mental short cuts, the same way the individuals with no experience and so, this can lead them to similar mistakes.

The Recent Experiences Tend to be an Internal Focus of Attention, Being Perceived as More Relevant

An important issue refers to the reason the attention is concentrated in some components but not in others. Many factors influence this process, including the genetic, the language development, the culture and the achievement of the objective; and this is the classic problem of what limits the knowledge (Miller & Cohen, 2001).

The majority of the attention processes are moved by endogens concerns. Either the quantity as the lasting of the attention dedicated to receive information is determined by the active objectives. The attention is given more to the input information that are relevant for the achievement of the objectives than to the ones that are irrelevant (Dijksterhuis & Aarts, 2010).

In the decisions from the experience, the attention focus is on the series of lived results, with more recent results presenting more influence (Weber *et al.*, 2004). Consistent, Mcelroy and Mascari (2007) proposed the events that occur in more distant time points will be perceived as less relevant while those that occur in the near future will be perceived as more relevant. The authors use this temporal assumption to foresee when the framing effects are likely to happen from the relevance of the stimulus.

The Experiences Tend to Direct the Focus of Foreign Attention and Influence the Sub Ponderation of Rare Events

There are evidences that rare events are sub pondered in the decisions from the experience, as captured by the Perspective Theory; what confers to the experience positive and negative valence, meaning contributions and losses to complete the task (Shepherd, Zacharakis, & Baron, 2003). The sub ponderation of the rare events may be explained by the differences in the attention focus during information acquisition, because the direction of attention, either to the external as the internal factors, has been pointed as the responsible by translating the weight of decision (Kamenica, 2012). The first found information capture the attention, leading the depending references in the evaluations and subsequent comparisons (Kahneman, 2003).

As the individuals become more experienced in a particular task, they tend to increase their efficiency on it, in several different ways; one of them is that people learn to focus their attention firstly in the key-dimensions, meaning, the ones that contribute with the greater variation in the decision result (Shepherd *et al.*, 2003). The mechanisms of information selection also explain how the targeting of economic transactions may affect the appreciation of value. Carmon and Ariely (2000) show that the decision-makers focus their attention on the foreground, namely, the status quo and its characteristics attract more attention and so, have more importance and weight in the decision than other options to choose from.

Implications of Experience in Categorizing the Decision Maker

The Prolonged Exposures to Stimuli That Composes the Experience, Make the Acknowledgment of the Situation and Provide Fluency to Reconstitution

The capacity of grouping several sensorial events and provide categories with significance to new inputs is a fundamental cognitive ability for the adaptive behavior and survival in a dynamic and complex world

(Miller & Cohen, 2001). The decision-making process is not applied to the problem as it is, but instead, to the problem as a subject, consciously or not, it puts itself (Costermans, 2001).

At first, an infinite number of simulators can be developed in the memory in all forms of knowledge, including objects, properties, configurations, events, actions, introspections, etc. A simulator is developed for any experience component that the attention repetitively selects. When the attention is centered repetitively at a kind of object in the experience, a simulator develops it. Similarly, if the attention is focused in a kind of action or in a kind of introspection, simulators should develop them to also represent them (Barsalou, 2005; Harnard, 2005).

The ease or difficulty with which individuals can process new information sets up the fluency of the processing, a term that comprises the perceptual fluency and the conceptual fluency. The fluency of the experience processing may influence a vast range of decisions, including preference judgments, familiarity and truth. The previous exposure of a more prolonged way leads to the development of familiarity in a dominium, with consequent alterations at the information codification. This influence of familiarity of experience in the processing's fluency, origins a reverse conclusion logically unjustified: people deduce from the ease of processing that the material must be familiar. As result, any variable that ease the processing leads to greater perceptions of familiarity, even when the facilitation derives from irrelevant characteristics as embossed figures, long exposure times or of the precedence of semantic or visual cousins (Schwarz, 2005).

The Experience Conforms the Categorization Mechanisms Used Through the Knowledge Developed in the Dominium

There are indications in the literature of the role of the experience in the decision-makers by conditioning the categorization mechanisms used (Cohen & Lefebvre, 2005). These cognitive acts affect the distribution and the interpretation of the information, which are factors that the participants in the decision-making process deal with as externalities and which, if some of these externalities are considered as relevant; the kinds of solutions that are sought and the heuristics by which they are sought (Simon, 1959).

Another key issue refers to how the simulators of abstract concepts are represented. Barsalou (2005) proposed the simulators in order to capture the abstract concepts, generally capture complex multimodal simulations from temporally extended situations, with the simulations of introspective states being central. Rouder and Ratcliff (2006) describe a dynamic path of learning complex stimuli. With sufficient experience, the individuals' categorization is based on copies, independently of the number of stimuli. During the initial phases of learning a dominium, people don't have sufficient knowledge of the characteristics and dimensions relevant of the stimuli in order to store the copies which are immune to oblivion. As consequence, they summarize simple rules about the immediately obvious properties, such as size, color, etc.; which, in the majority of the cases are inadequate. With the experience, the individuals develop the familiarity with the characteristics and dimensions of the dominium. With this acquired knowledge, they can store rich samples that are immune to interferences in a long-term basis. These rich samples serve as a basis to build the category and to intermediate the subsequent categorization of new stimuli. In sum, for complex stimuli, the rules may be initially used, but with the experience, the participants use the copies.

The Experience is One of the Basis that Generates the Formulations of the Mental Representation (Situated Conceptualization)

The mental representation "consists of components derived from prior knowledge and from the contextual cues that depict the situation of the specific task in memory, which an individual uses as a guide for carrying out the task" (Leong, 2003: 10). An individual encodes, usefully, the task that will be carried out and then uses this encoding to actually perform the task. The memory is codified based on past experiences and on the characteristics of the current task (Waxman, 2012). Barsalou (2005) argues that when a situation is repeatedly experienced, the multimodal knowledge accumulates, in the respective simulators, the relevant configurations. Eventually, the situated conceptualization becomes so well established that come to mind, automatically and immediately as a unit, whenever the situation occurs.

Particularly, the human brain of an adult appears to capitalize the images correlations that determine the distinctive character in a scene and learns to detect, categorize and identify the new objects in a flexible way. This adaptive behavior is implemented by plasticity mechanisms dependent on the experience that reorganize the processing in several cortical areas. The learning is implemented through recurrent mechanisms that support the adaptive processing of resources, depending on the context of the tasks and demands (Ashby & Maddox, 2005). This treatment allows the brain combine an ambiguous sensorial input with the prior knowledge, which is fundamental for the better decisions and actions (Waxman, 2012). A situated conceptualization simulates a scenario where the event could occur. Once more, such knowledge is represented as simulations, this time as reconstitutions of specific scenarios.

The Experiences Conform the Situated Conceptualization and are the Basis for the Inferences on the Task

Barsalou (2005) proposed that a complex simulation becomes active through the modalities to implement a situated conceptualization. All the perceptive aspects may be represented as modal simulations in the situated conceptualization. The situated conceptualization about an event probably simulates the actions the agent may have in the situation. According to Harnard (2005), it is likely that the situated conceptualization about an event, includes simulations of introspective states, after all, people experiment particular introspections about the event, the respective situated conceptualization include emotion simulations, evaluations, motivations, cognitive operations, etc.

The processing support provided by the situated conceptualizations is a result of the inference process of pattern conclusion. By entering in a familiar situation and recognize it, a rooted situated conceptualization that represents the situation becomes active (Ashby & Maddox, 2005). The person configuration or relevant event may be perceived, suggesting then, that a particular situation is about to happen.

To Thagard and Toombs (2005), the situated conceptualization that becomes active, constitute a rich source of inference. The conceptualization is essentially a pattern, a complex configuration of multimodal components that represent the situation. When a component of this pattern corresponds the situation, the highest standard becomes active in memory, the left pattern components, still not observed, constitute inferences, namely, suppositions about what could happen next. As the remained components frequently co-occurred with the ones perceived in prior experiences, the other components inference is justified. After a conceptualization receives the activation process, it provides inferences through the pattern conclusion, such as actions that the observer normally conducts, the mental states that are likely to result and so on. The development of such inferences perceived with the simulations, produces inferential forecast.

The Experience Conforms the Perception of the Relative Value in the Selection, Framing and Interpretation of the Information About the Events

Given to the ambiguity of the information basis, the codification processes have selection and interpretation elements, which frequently involve a loss of information. Much of the psychology, from the first psychophysics to the current social cognition, are concerned with the issue of how the physical stimuli are related and interpreted (Waxman, 2012). The experience from the past also play a role in the projection of a future utility for the results. With high level of experience, the decision-makers tend become increasingly susceptible to cognitive traps. In summary, their though tend to become increasingly channeled by their past experiences; such effects can make it harder, for the experienced people, to recognize new variables or to notice that the situation has changed and thus, requires new approaches (Kahneman & Snell, 1992).

The differences in the formulation of a result that leads to its codification as a relative gain or as a relative loss, with the associated assumption that people's value functions for the losses have different form and inclination that their functions of gain value, is an important component of the perspective theory (Kahneman & Tversky, 1979), which allows to describe the choices that violates the expected by the traditional utility theory. An important dimension of the framing literature is the way in which the decisions are conceptualized or "framed", through the organization of individual experiences that may reinforce certain values and beliefs (Tversky & Kahneman, 1981). The underlying premise in the framing research is that the individual conceptual representation of the relevant parameters for the decision-making, determines the decisions, and in a last analysis, the actors' behavior, changing the preferences, and conditioning the expectations.

The feedback has cognitive and motivational effects. Studies suggest that the choice for the heuristics hardly happen in a conscious way, but, when there is suitable feedback in relation to their decision-making experiences, people tend to, unconsciously, adapt their heuristics to dynamic environments according to the ecological rationality. With the increase of the amount of feedback, people adapt the used heuristics to the environment characteristics (Rieskamp & Otto, 2006).

Implications of the Experience in the Decision-Maker's Memory

The Record of the Experiences in the Memory Unconsciously Influences the Decision

Throughout their lives, people live situations, often repeated on their interactions with people, artefacts, social institutions, etc. As result, the knowledge about these repeated situations becomes rooted in the memory, supporting, thus, a skilled performance in front of them (Anderson, 2004). These knowledges can also guide the interactions in new situations that are similar to these familiar situations. Even though the rooted knowledge cannot always provide a perfect adjustment, it cans often fits well enough to provide useful inferences (Rose *et al.*, 2007).

Mechanisms related to memory, as biased encoding and the biased retrieval of information, are used to explain why people are not able to learn the relationship between experience variables. Jacoby *et al.* (1993) highlights that it's important to consider not only the conscious influence of previous events, but also the unconscious one. There is an increasing literature documenting the unconscious influences of the memory on the performance in a variety of tasks. Through the implicit memory, namely, the effects of the previous experience on the task performance, in the absence of any intention or instructions for the memory and without any conscience, seem to be automatically and effortless accessed, by a different set of processes, which, in an explicit, conscious and controlled way, uses the memory (Rakow & Newell, 2010).

The Memory Capacity of an Experience is Influenced by the Memorization of Other Events

The decision-makers may demand the access to the episodic memory in order to obtain information about specific experiences, results or events; or the semantic memory with the abstract knowledge, for instance, the rules abstract from a series of prior experiences or prototypes raised from a series of copies (Purves *et al.*, 2004).

The memory of a certain experience from a person's past is impaired by the occurrence of others. This is an important reason for the forgetfulness (McGuire & Kable, 2012). There are many evidence that the similarity degree between two tasks is of a great importance. However, there are several types of similarities that need to be distinguished. Wickens (1984) concluded on his researches that two tasks interfere one in another as they have the same modality of stimulus, such as, visual or hearing; use the same stages of processing, namely, input, internal processing and output; and count with related memory codes, for instance, verbal or visual.

Whenever a memory of an experience is impaired by experiences that preceded it, the result is called pro-active interference. Whenever the memory of an experience is impaired by following events, the result is called retroactive interference (Guenther, 2002). A variety of experimental paradigms have been used to show theses interferences (McGuire & Kable, 2012).

A set of researches presents the impact in the order of information in the process of memory recovery. The individuals are better at remembering the information presented at the beginning and the end of a document. The phenomenon is presented by Keil & Wilson (1999) under the denomination of primacy effect and recency effect. The primacy reflects the efficiency of the transference of the short-term memory storage items for the long-term one. At the beginning of the information presentation, the memory system has the capability to download from the short-term memory to the long-term one. At the end, with the recency effect, there are the information that have being seen recently and yet were not "destroyed".

The Experiences Conform the Memorization and the Capability of Recovering Information of Related Events

The essential idea of the Record-keeping Theory is that one record of each experience in placed in one kind of storage box. These records may take several forms, including the abstract description or interpretation of events, lists of items and contextual information or images of the perceptive qualities of events (Anderson, 2004). In contrast, the essential idea of a constructivist approach is that the several cognitive systems, for instance, the visual system and the language system are altered by the experiences, but without controlling on each record where the experiences are stored (Rose *et al.*, 2007). The cognitive system is designed to extract the immutable elements or patterns from the experience and observe deviations of the enduring patterns (Guenther, 2002).

Thus, the efficacy of the memory for new found information is improved when is related to the previous knowledge and the experience. The recovery of structures and acquired skills generate integrated structures in the long-term memory mediating the expansion of the working memory of specialists in their specialization dominium. The individuals acquire memory abilities, which combine the characteristics of these two kinds of general mechanisms to meet the recovery and storage demands of the working memory for the tasks of their particular field of performance (Ericsson & Delaney, 1998).

Gigerenzer (1996) suggested the strategy of take-the-best (TTB) as a precise and easy procedure for inferences based on the memory recovery, suggesting that the good inferences may be done by using more diagnostic interpretations distinguishing between two alternatives. Knowledge about diagnosticity depends on the metacognitive insight about the inference of the precision in the past (Rose *et al.*, 2007). TTB presents a good performance, especially when the distribution of cues' validity is highly skewed. However, is not the only heuristic. Simulations show that heuristics that are even simpler than TTB can do very well in the same environments; and other simple heuristics can do as good or better than (Chater et al., 2003) in other environments.

Exams of TTB as a descriptive model of inference based on the memory, suggest that it is not universally used, but it is not rare either, describing something between 20% and 72% of the inferences (Broder & Gaissmaier, 2007). The use of strategy seems to vary adaptive mode to the environment. New models that integrate the TTB are being developed and the use of the complete information over a continuum, defined by the weight given to the comparison of different characteristics, and generalizations that relax the assumption that the decision-makers know the exact weight of the cues (Lee & Cummins, 2004).

The Accessibility to Experience that Comes from Past Events and are Recorded in the Memory, Conforms the Bias in the Processing of that Content

After the acquisition, consolidation and storage, the last memory process is the evocation, through which, one has access to the stored information in order to use it mentally in the cognition and in the emotion or to externalize it through the behavior (Anderson, 2004). In other words, the evocation uses the stored information to create a conscious representation or to execute a learned behavior (Rose *et al.*, 2007).

Schwarz (2005) showed that a recall of an experience provides two different sources of information: the affordable content, which is brought to mind and the accessibility, namely, the ease or difficulty of bringing the experience to mind. These affordable experiences are informative and qualify the content's implications affordable in the decision-making.

In general, the judgments are just coherent with what comes to mind whenever it easily comes to mind. When the recall is experienced as difficult, judgments are opposed to the implications of the retrieved content (Schwarz, 2005). These observations extend the general conclusion that the difficult decisions elicit more conservative choices, in the form of granting the decision, increase in the commitment effect and increase in the status quo bias. Considering that the difficulty was typically manipulated through characteristics from the set of choice on itself, experienced difficulties resulting from other sources have the same effect. The influence of the characteristics of the choice context is presumably mediated by the difficulty of subjective experiences (Schwarz, 2005).

The heuristic of the availability refers to the comparison between events and models, not in terms of similarities, but according to the facility with which they could be imagined and retrieved in the memory. It's admissible that the more accessible events have greater probability of happening. So, the work about the "heuristic f the availability" has shown a connection between the events that people can bring to mind and its high estimative of subjective probability of the future of the event (Tversky & Kahneman, 1973).

Implications of Experience in the Emotion of the Decision Maker

The Experiences Establish the Somatic Markers

There are extensive evidences that the several kinds of emotion frequently influence the judgements and choices made by the individuals. Positive and negative associations from the past, with results of the available choice, contribute for new decisions. Loewenstein & Lerner (2003) classify the emotions according to the moment they manifest during a decision-making process. They distinguish the anticipated emotions and the immediate ones. Anticipated emotions are the individual's believes about the future emotional states that can happen when the results are achieved. Immediate emotions, on the other hand, are really experienced in the decision-making, thereby exerting an effect over the mental processes involved in the choice.

A hypothesis that gain notoriety in this line if the one of the somatic marker. It supports the affective signs, originate from bodily states and acquired through the learning from previous experiences, work as markers on the positivity or negativity in the ongoing experiences (Damásio, 2005). For instance, whenever there is a choice followed by a bad result, an affective reaction becomes associated to this choice. Once the affective reaction is sufficiently well established, the reaction occurs before a choice is made. The anticipation of a bad result before the bad choice to be made, prevents the bad decision and leads at least, to a better choice. Thus, a somatic marker of good and bad options guide and support the decision-making.

According to this theory, the optimal decision-making is not just the result of the rational and cognitive calculation from the gains and losses, but it is, based on the emotional reactions of the previous choices. Essentially, the choice is guided by emotional reactions that skew the decision made. Somatic markers work automatically and mandatorily, influencing the behavior, even before a deliberated intention be generated (Damásio, 2005).

The Perception About the Experiences' Results
Define the Relative Emotional Relevance

The experienced emotions as a decision is made are incorporated as information in the choices. What people consider as relevant, guided by their emotions, depend on their personal experiences and motivations (Zhang, 2008). It's worth to highlight that the emotional relevance does not necessarily imply in common sense and wisdom. Whining and suffers from consequences that cannot be undone and that couldn't possibly be forecasted, are some typical samples of irrational behavior (Yaniv, 2004).

There are also evidences that show emotions immediately experienced or "visceral factors" may have a strong effect on the decisions and behavior in comparison with other more cognitively guided to goals (Lerner & Keltner, 2001). Experienced decision-makers may suffer from "overconfidence", a tendency of super estimate the behavior pattern of a series of events (Shepherd *et al.,* 2003).

The two most studied emotions that serve as relevance function are the regret (or sorrow) and the deception. According to the Theory of Justification of decision, the regret and the disappointment arise from a combination of the results' evaluation; result from the contrafactual comparisons between what was obtained and what could have been obtained and from the feeling of taking a bad decision (Connolly & Zeelenberg, 2002). The comparison process between the result and some pattern is inherent to this view and it is mediated by concepts, so, it's influenced by the categorization mechanisms of the decision-maker. According to the theory of justification of decision, the results that are unjustified or incompatible with a pattern, generate more regret even without knowing if the result itself was good or bad. On the other hand, the more people try to think of counterfactual, the most probable is that they experiment the task as difficult, convincing them more that the obtained result was unavoidable. This logic worth for many cognitive biases, including the planning fallacy, the impact bias, the optimism and related phenomenon (Schwarz, 2005).

The Experience May Not be Somatically Marked if There is an Overload in the Work Memory

The performance of two or more tasks at the same time leads to the sharing of the decision-maker's capacity, comes up against the limitations of human information processing system (Eysenck & Keane, 2002). The researches of Hinson et al. (2002), with a normal population, points out that the performance in the decision-making and the establishment of the somatic markers is dependent on the memory capacity of the available work. They used a game version of Iowa more challenge than the original one, plus secondary tasks to load the working memory. In comparison with the situation without control in terms of working memory load, the participants made poorer choices in conditions of loading of working memory. Besides, the amplitude of the anticipatory response of skin conductance, an index of somatic markers don't appear in conditions of load of the work memory, associated to the poor performance in the game. In sum, by interfering in the work memory, the researchers prevented the development of affective reactions that seem to guide the good decision-making.

Interferences in the working memory executive functions are necessary, to interrupt the game performance and of the somatic markers (Hinson et al., 2002). An intriguing affirmation of the somatic marker hypothesis is that the affective answers that guide the decision-making are a source of influence separated of the purely cognitive factors that depend on the working memory functions.

The Experience with Damages that Influence the Decision-Maker's Perception in Front of the Risk

The influences of past experiences in decisions appear specially in the risks' contexts (Cohen *et al.,* 2010). Two opposing effects may be identified corresponding to the availability bias and the gambler fallacy, in the sense of formulation of Tversky & Kahneman (1973). The availability bias correspond to a super estimation of the probability of an event that recently occurred and imply a behavior that increases the safety after the experience of a situation with damage, this behavior is reduced after a long period without a situation with damage. The opposite occurs with the gambler fallacy effect: individuals underestimate the probability of repetition of an event that they just observed and so, they protect themselves less after a dangerous situation (Cohen *et al.,* 2010).

In decisions from the experience, people tend the search of risk in the loss dominium (for instance, purchase insurance) and the aversion to the risk in the gain dominium (for instance, purchase of lottery tickets). Namely, the rare event seems to be lower than the ponderation (Barron & Leider, 2010).

A more conventional approach suggest that apparently, the behavior of inconsistent risk taking, may, in fact, reflect consistent sensibility to the latent components of the risk taking. Recent cognitive models of individual choices in the decisions from the experience, adopted this approach through the implementation of these factors as two central components of the subjective utility: loss of sensibility and the reduction of sensibility (Ert & Yechiam, 2010). Lerner & Keltner (2001) show that the fear increases risk's estimative as well as the options against it, whilst the anger reduces risk's estimative and increases the search of risky choices.

SOLUTIONS AND RECOMMENDATIONS

Juliusson *et al.* (2005) indicated that past decisions influence the decisions will make in the future. The previous experience may often be useful when the individual prepares his/herself to develop new abilities, but may sometimes be misleading, when encourages the person to super estimates the similarity between what is already known and what is still there to be learned. When something positive results from a decision, people are more likely to decide similarly, given a similar situation. On the other hand, people tend to avoid the repetition of past mistakes (Sagi & Friedland, 2007).

According to the behavioral learning theory, evidences of positive and negative effects of the experience acquisitions were identified. In most cases, when the current activity of a company was too different from its previous actions, the experience had a negative influence over the performance. The best performances seem to be the ones without experiences, which, therefore, didn't make an inadequate generalization mistake; or the ones that have a significant e amount of experience and knew how to accordingly discriminate the activities. In the minority of the cases, when the current activity of a company was similar to its previous actions, the experience in similar activity had a positive influence on the performance (Mckaskill, 2010).

Much of the Judgement Literature and the Decision-Making in differences in the experience contains investigations about the effects of concurrent factors, such as the effect of the description nature of the results by the experimenter on the framing or results' codification (Tversky & Kahneman, 1981). Equally important in the prevision of people's experience with an event, however, are the previous events, particularly the previous experiences of people with equal or similar decisions. The extension of the utility of the previous decision-making experience depends on its relevance for the current decision. The relevance will not be affected just by the similarity degree between the current decision task and the previous decision tasks, but also by the similarity degree of the decision environment. The decision environment consists of several institutional external factors and related with the task that influence the decision's result.

In this scenery, this work adopted as cut, the analysis of the experiences related to decision's object and/or to the context where the decision-maker is inserted. Responding the initial motivation of this research and contributing to the advancement of the body of knowledge on the subject, in the previous sections, it was presented the role of the experience in the decision-making and deeper, which are the implications of the experience in the cognitive process of the decision-maker, as synthesis on Table 1.

Table 1. Relation of the experience's implications in the cognitive process with the roles of the cognition elements in the decision-making. Source: the author.

Role of Decision-Maker's Cognitive Process Elements	Inferences on the Experience Effects on the Decision-Maker's Cognitive Process
Attention as selection, preparation and maintenance: determines the initial perception of the problem	The experiences tend to influence the selective attention, checking perceptions that seem to be precise and fast of known objects and ideas.
	The experiences influence the preparation and the maintenance of the attention.
	The recent experiences tend to be the focus of internal attention, being perceived as more relevant.
	The experiences tend to guide the focus of external attention and influence the sub ponderation of rare events.
Categorization as basis of the recognition of the situation: storing the features and reconstitution	The prolonged exposure to stimuli, which compose the experience, conform the recognition of the situation and provide fluency to reconstitution.
	The experience conforms the used categorization mechanisms, through knowledge developed in the dominium.
Categorization as basis for the situated perception	The experience is one of the basis that generates the mental representation (situated conceptualization).
Categorization as basis of inferences on the problem	The experiences conform the situated conceptualization and are basis for the inferences on the task.
	The experience conforms the perception of the relative value assigned in the selection, framing and interpretation of the information about the events.
Memory as information source	The record of the experiences in the memory unconsciously influences the decision.
Memory as restriction of acquiring information	The memory capacity of an experience is influenced by the memorization of other events.
Memory as basis for quickly perception providing agility to the decision-making process	The experiences conform the memorization and the capacity of information recovery of related events.
	The accessibility to the experience that comes from past events and are recorded in the memory, conform the bias in the processing of this content.
Emotion as source of information	The experiences establish the somatic markers.
	The perception about the result of the experiences defines the relative emotional relevance.
Emotion as attention guiding for relevant aspects of the problem	The experience with damages influence the decision-maker perception facing the risk.
Emotion with speed role, enabling quick decisions whenever there is time pressure.	The experience may not be somatically marked if there is overload in the work memory.

FUTURE RESEARCH DIRECTIONS

In this chapter, it was presented a set of inferences, "controllably" generated, from the bibliographic research, about the effects of the previous experience to the working of the cognitive process of a decision-maker.

Although it has been used a structured bibliographic research method, aiming the identification of all texts relevant to the theme, it's not possible to categorically affirm that all the relevant texts have been selected and analyzed by the author. Additionally, the formulations elaborated as the roles of the cognition elements and the implications of the experience, result from an inductive analysis, contemplating either secondary and tertiary sources as results of field studies and laboratory researches. Thus, there is space for future researches in the treatment of this eventual lacks.

Particularly in the formulation of the experience implications, this research recognized there are degrees of relevance distinct among them. It was not conducted a structured evaluation about them to order the implications that present higher or lower impact during the decision-making process. It's about a topic to be explored, contributing to the improvement of the initial formulation expressed in this chapter.

CONCLUSION

Due to the experience's relevance of the decision-makers in order to make a decision, just like the investigated in this text, one sought in the final considerations, reinforce this aspect and justify the relevance of the contribution of the formulated model towards to the descriptions more adherent to the reality of the made decisions.

By making certain decision, the individual uses his/her own experiences for it. This way, the quality of a decision doesn't depend just on the available information, but also in the way the decision-maker, influenced by his/her previous experiences, perceives, access, understand, categorize and feel this information.

This chapter contributes to the body of knowledge on the theme when identify and describe eleven inferences about the effects of the experience in the decision-maker's cognitive process. These elements interact among themselves, which also determines the way in which the decision-making process occurs. In Table 1, it was presented the relation between the "roles" of attention, categorization, memory and emotion along the decision-making, confirmed by the experiences' effects.

REFERENCES

Allen, P. M., Strathern, M., & Baldwin, J. S. (2010). The Evolutionary Complexity of Social Economic Systems: The Inevitability of Uncertainty and Surprise. In R. R. Mcdaniel & D. J. Driebe (Eds.), *Uncertainty and Surprise in Complex Systems: Questions on Working with the Unexpected* (pp. 31–50). New York, NY: Springer-Verlag. doi:10.1057/rm.2009.15

Anderson, P. (2004). Does experience matter in lending? A process-tracing study on experienced loan officers and novices decision behavior. *Journal of Economic Psychology*, 25(4), 471–492. doi:10.1016/S0167-4870(03)00030-8

Ashby, F. G., & Maddox, W. T. (2005). Human category learning. *Annual Review of Psychology*, 56(1), 149–178. doi:10.1146/annurev.psych.56.091103.070217 PMID:15709932

Barron, G., & Leider, S. (2010). The role of experience in the Gamblers Fallacy. *Journal of Behavioral Decision Making*, 23(1), 117–129. doi:10.1002/bdm.676

Barsalou, L. W. (2005). Situated Conceptualization. In H. Cohen & C. Lefebvre (Eds.), *Handbook of categorization in cognitive science* (pp. 619–650). New York, NY: Elsevier. doi:10.1016/B978-008044612-7/50083-4

Bohanec, M. (2003). *What is Decision Support?* Research Paper. Jozef Stefan Institute.

Bresfelean, V. P., Ghisoiu, N., Lacurezeanu, R., & Sitar-Taut, D. A. (2009). Towards the Development of Decision Support in Academic Environments.*Proceedings of ITI.*

Bondía, J. L. (2002). Notas sobre a experiência e o saber de experiência. *Revista Brasileira de Educação*, *19*(19), 20–28. doi:10.1590/S1413-24782002000100003

Bonner, S. E., & Pennington, N. (1991). Cognitive processes and knowledge as determinants of auditor expertise. *Journal of Accounting Literature*, *10*, 1–50.

Broder, A., & Gaissmaier, W. (2007). Sequential processing of cues in memory-based multiattribute decisions. *Psychonomic Bulletin & Review*, *4*(5), 895–900. doi:10.3758/BF03194118 PMID:18087956

Carmon, Z., & Ariely, D. (2000). Focusing on the forgone: How value can appear so different to buyers and Sellers. *The Journal of Consumer Research*, *27*(3), 360–370. doi:10.1086/317590

Chater, N., Oaksford, M., Nakisa, R., & Redington, M. (2003). Fast, frugal, and rational: How rational norms explain behavior. *Organizational Behavior and Human Decision Processes*, *90*(1), 63–86. doi:10.1016/S0749-5978(02)00508-3

Chib, V. S., Rangel, A., Shimojo, S., & ODoherty, J. P. (2009). Evidence for a common representation of decision values for dissimilar goods in human ventromedial prefrontal cortex. *The Journal of Neuroscience*, *29*(39), 12315–12320. doi:10.1523/JNEUROSCI.2575-09.2009 PMID:19793990

Cho, K. R., & Padmanabhan, P. (2001). The relative importance of old and new decision specific experience in foreign ownership strategies: An exploratory study. *International Business Review*, *10*(6), 645–659. doi:10.1016/S0969-5931(01)00036-1

Cohen, H., & Lefebvre, C. (2005). *Handbook of categorization in cognitive science*. New York, NY: Elsevier.

Cohen, M., Etner, J., & Jeleva, M. (2010). Dynamic Decision Making When Risk Perception Depends on Past Experience. In M. Abdellaoui & J. D. Hey (Eds.), *Advances in Decision Making Under Risk and Uncertaint* (pp. 19–32). New York, NY: Springer-Verlag.

Connolly, T., & Zeelenberg, M. (2002). Regret in decision making. *Current Directions in Psychological Science*, *11*(6), 212–216. doi:10.1111/1467-8721.00203

Costermans, J. (2001). *As actividades cognitivas. Raciocínio, decisão e resolução de problemas*. Coimbra, Portugal: Quarteto.

Damasio, A. (2005). *O erro de Descartes*. São Paulo, Brazil: Companhia das Letras.

Dijksterhuis, A., & Aarts, H. (2010). Goals, Attention, and (Un)Consciousness. *Annual Review of Psychology*, *61*(1), 467–490. doi:10.1146/annurev.psych.093008.100445 PMID:19566422

Ericsson, K. A., & Delaney, P. F. (1998). Working Memory and Expert Performance. In K. Gilhooly (Ed.), *Working Memory And Thinking: Current Issues In Thinking And Reasoning* (pp. 91–112). Hove, UK: Psychology Press. doi:10.4324/9780203346754_chapter_SIX

Ert, E., & Yechiam, E. (2010). Consistent constructs in individuals risk taking in decisions from experience. *Acta Psychologica*, *134*(2), 225–232. doi:10.1016/j.actpsy.2010.02.003 PMID:20223438

Eysenck, M. W., & Keane, M. T. (2002). Attention and Performance Limitations. In D. J. Levitin (Ed.), *Foundations of Cognitive Psychology: Core Readings* (pp. 363–398). Cambridge, MA: The MIT Press.

Fiore, S. M. (2008). Making Time for Memory and Remembering Time in Motivation Theory. In R. Kanfer, G. Chen, & R. D. Pritchard (Eds.), *Work Motivation: Past, Present and Future* (pp. 541–553). New York, NY: Routledge Academic.

Fitzgerald, T., Bach, D., Seymour, B., & Dolan, R. J. (2010). Differentiable neural substrates for learned and described value and risk. *Current Biology*, *20*(20), 1823–1829. doi:10.1016/j.cub.2010.08.048 PMID:20888231

Gigerenzer, G. (1996). On narrow norms and vague heuristics: A rebuttal to Kahneman and Tversky. *Psychological Review*, *103*(3), 592–596. doi:10.1037/0033-295X.103.3.592

Guenther, R. K. (2002). Memory. In D. J. Levitin (Ed.), *Foundations of Cognitive Psychology: Core Readings* (pp. 311–359). Cambridge, MA: The MIT Press.

Harnard, S. (2005). To cognize is to categorize: cognition is categorization. In H. Cohen & C. Lefebvre (Eds.), *Handbook of categorization in cognitive science* (pp. 20–45). New York, NY: Elsevier. doi:10.1016/B978-008044612-7/50056-1

Hertwig, R., Barron, G., Weber, E. U., & Erev, I. (2004). Decisions from experience and the effect of rare events in risky choice. *Psychological Science*, *15*(8), 534–539. doi:10.1111/j.0956-7976.2004.00715.x PMID:15270998

Hinson, J. M., Jameson, T. L., & Whitney, P. (2002). Somatic markers, working memory, and decision making. *Cognitive, Affective & Behavioral Neuroscience*, *2*(4), 341–353. doi:10.3758/CABN.2.4.341 PMID:12641178

Jacoby, L. L., Toth, J. P., & Yonelinas, A. P. (1993). Separating conscious and unconscious influences of memory: Measuring recollection. *Journal of Experimental Psychology. General*, *122*(2), 39–154. doi:10.1037/0096-3445.122.2.139

Jessup, R. K., & ODoherty, J. P. (2010). Decision Neuroscience: Choices of Description and of Experience. *Current Biology*, *20*(20), 881–883. doi:10.1016/j.cub.2010.09.017 PMID:20971429

Jullisson, E. A., Karlsson, N., & Garling, T. (2005). Weighing the past and the future in decision making. *The European Journal of Cognitive Psychology*, *17*(4), 561–575. doi:10.1080/09541440440000159

Kahneman, D. (2003). A perspective on judgment and choice: Mapping bounded rationality. *The American Psychologist*, *58*(9), 697–720. doi:10.1037/0003-066X.58.9.697 PMID:14584987

Kahneman, D., & Snell, J. (1992). Predicting a changing taste: Do people know what they will like? *Journal of Behavioral Decision Making*, *5*(3), 187–200. doi:10.1002/bdm.3960050304

Kahneman, D., & Tversky, A. (1979). Prospect Theory: An Analysis of Decision under Risk. *Econometrica*, *47*(2), 263–292. doi:10.2307/1914185

Keil, F., & Wilson, R. (1999). *The MIT Encyclopedia of the Cognitive Sciences*. Cambridge, MA: The MIT Press.

La Berge, D. (1999). Attention. In B. M. Bly & D. E. Rumelhart (Eds.), *Cognitive Science* (pp. 43–97). New York, NY: Academic Press. doi:10.1016/B978-012601730-4/50004-4

Lee, M. D., & Cummins, T. D. R. (2004). Evidence accumulation in decision making: Unifying the take the best and the rational models. *Psychonomic Bulletin & Review, 11*(2), 343–352. doi:10.3758/BF03196581 PMID:15260204

Leong, S. S. W. (2003). *Does mental representation mediate the roles of knowledge and decision aids in the performance of a task?* (Unpublished doctoral dissertation). University of Utah.

Lerner, J. S., & Keltner, D. (2001). Fear, anger, and risk. *Journal of Personality and Social Psychology, 81*(1), 46–159. doi:10.1037/0022-3514.81.1.146 PMID:11474720

Loewenstein, G., & Lerner, J. S. (2003). The role of affect in decision making. In R. Davidson, K. Scherer, & H. Goldsmith (Eds.), *Handbook of affective science* (pp. 619–642). New York, NY: Oxford University Press.

Mcelroy, T., & Mascari, D. (2007). Temporal framing when is it going to happen? How temporal distance influences processing for risky-choice framing tasks. *Social Cognition, 25*(4), 495–517. doi:10.1521/soco.2007.25.4.495

Mcguire, J. T., & Kable, J. W. (2012). Decision makers calibrate behavioral persistence on the basis of time-interval experience. *Cognition, 124*(2), 216–226. doi:10.1016/j.cognition.2012.03.008 PMID:22533999

Mckaskill, T. (2010). *Ultimate Acquisitions: Unlock high growth potential through smart acquisitions.* Windsor: Breakthrough Publications.

Miller, E. K., & Cohen, J. D. (2001). An integrative theory of prefrontal cortex function. *Annual Review of Neuroscience, 24*(1), 167–202. doi:10.1146/annurev.neuro.24.1.167 PMID:11283309

Penrose, E. T. (1959). *The Theory of the Growth of the Firm.* New York, NY: John Wiley.

Purves, D., Augustine, G. J., Fitzpatrick, D., Katz, L. C., LaMantia, A. S., McNamara, J. O., & Williams, S. M. (2004). Neuroscience (3rd ed.). Sunderland, MA: Sinauer Associates.

Rakow, T., & Newell, B. (2010). Degrees of uncertainty: An overview and framework for research on experience-based choice. *Journal of Behavioral Decision Making, 23*(1), 1–14. doi:10.1002/bdm.681

Rieskamp, J. R., & Otto, P. E. (2006). SSL: A theory of how people learn to select strategies. *Journal of Experimental Psychology. General, 135*(2), 207–236. doi:10.1037/0096-3445.135.2.207 PMID:16719651

Rocha, Z. (2008). A experiência psicanalítica: Seus desafios e vicissitudes, hoje e amanhã. *Ágora. Estudos em Teoria Psicanalítica, 11*(1), 101–116.

Rose, J. M., Rose, A. M., & Mckay, B. (2007). Measurement of knowledge structures acquired through instruction, experience, and decision aid use. *International Journal of Accounting Information Systems, 8*(2), 117–137. doi:10.1016/j.accinf.2007.04.002

Rouder, J. N., & Ratcliff, R. (2006). Comparing exemplar and rule-based theories of categorization. *Current Directions in Psychological Science, 15*(1), 9–13. doi:10.1111/j.0963-7214.2006.00397.x

Sagi, A., & Friedland, N. (2007). The cost of richness: The effect of the size and diversity of decision sets on post-decision regret. *Journal of Personality and Social Psychology, 93*(4), 515–524. doi:10.1037/0022-3514.93.4.515 PMID:17892329

Schwarz, N. (2005). When Thinking Feels Difficult: Meta-Cognitive Experiences in Judgment and Decision Making. *Medical Decision Making, 25*(1), 105–112. doi:10.1177/0272989X04273144 PMID:15673588

Shepherd, D. A., Zacharakis, A., & Baron, R. A. (2003). VCs decision processes: Evidence suggesting more experience may not always be better. *Journal of Business Venturing, 18*(3), 381–401. doi:10.1016/S0883-9026(02)00099-X

Simon, H. A. (1959). Theories of decision-making in economics and behavioral science. *The American Economic Review, 49*, 253–283.

Spiegel, T. (2014). An Overview of Cognition Roles in Decision-Making. In J. Wang (Ed.), *Encyclopedia of Business Analytics and Optimization* (pp. 74–84). Hershey, PA: IGI Global. doi:10.4018/978-1-4666-5202-6.ch008

Spiegel, T. (2011), *O processo cognitivo e a tomada de decisão: articulações necessárias* (Unpublished doctoral dissertation). Rio de Janeiro Federal University, Rio de Janeiro, Brazil.

Thagard, P., & Toombs, E. (2005). Atoms, categorizations and conceptual change. In H. Cohen & C. Lefebvre (Eds.), *Handbook of categorization in cognitive science* (pp. 243–254). New York, NY: Elsevier. doi:10.1016/B978-008044612-7/50065-2

Tversky, A., & Kahneman, D. (1973). Availability: A heuristic for judging frequency and probability. *Cognitive Psychology, 5*(2), 207–232. doi:10.1016/0010-0285(73)90033-9

Tversky, A., & Kahneman, D. (1981). The framing of decisions and the psychology of choice. *Science, 211*(4481), 453–458. doi:10.1126/science.7455683 PMID:7455683

Waxman, S. R. (2012). Social categories are shaped by social experience. *Trends in Cognitive Sciences, 16*(11), 531–532. doi:10.1016/j.tics.2012.09.007 PMID:23026021

Weber, E. U., Shafir, S., & Blais, A. R. (2004). Predicting risk sensitivity in humans and lower animals: Risk as variance or coefficient of variation. *Psychological Review, 111*(2), 430–445. doi:10.1037/0033-295X.111.2.430 PMID:15065916

Whittlesea, B. W. A., Brooks, L. R., & Westcott, C. (1994). After the Learning is over: Factors controlling the selective application of general and particular knowledge. *Journal of Experimental Psychology. Learning, Memory, and Cognition, 20*(2), 259–274. doi:10.1037/0278-7393.20.2.259

Wickens, C. D. (1984). Processing resources in attention. In R. Parasuraman & D. R. Davies (Eds.), *Varieties of attention* (pp. 63–101). London, UK: Academic Press.

Yaniv, I. (2004). Receiving other peoples advice: Influence and benefit. *Organizational Behavior and Human Decision Processes, 93*(1), 1–13. doi:10.1016/j.obhdp.2003.08.002

Zhang, L. (2008). Thinking Styles and Emotions. *The Journal of Psychology, 142*(5), 497–515. doi:10.3200/JRLP.142.5.497-516 PMID:18959222

KEY TERMS AND DEFINITIONS

Attention: Ability of the individual to respond predominantly stimuli that are significant to the detriment of others.

Categorization: Mental operation by which the brain classifies objects and events, comes the ability to group sensory events into meaningful categories.

Cognition: All capture processes of external stimuli through sensory resources and processing, reduction, storage, retrieval and use of these stimuli.

Consciousness: Ability of human beings to get information itself, as well as get other people and objects.

Decision: Deliberate choice of a course of action with the intention of producing a desired result.

Emotion: Mental operations are accompanied by a previous experience, capable of guiding the behavior and conduct physiological adaptations necessary.

Experience: Understood as a result of past events that were lived in a practical way in different situations, either making decisions or observing other people's ones, where the cognition of the human being was confirmed.

Memory: Comprises a number of biological strategies and anatomical substrates; involves a complex mechanism that covers the storage and retrieval of experiences thus is closely associated with learning.

Chapter 6
Strategic Decision Making From the Viewpoint of Systems Thinking:
The Role of Values and Context

Dejana Zlatanović
University of Kragujevac, Serbia

Jelena Nikolić
University of Kragujevac, Serbia

ABSTRACT

Growing complexity and diversity of strategic decisions indicate the need for applying the appropriate holistic tools in strategic decision-making. Thus, the paper deals with the process of strategic decision-making from the viewpoint of systems thinking, with emphasis on the role of values and context in strategic decision-making. The main purpose is to show how systems thinking, through selected systems methodologies, can help decision-makers involve different perceptions and values in the process of strategic decision-making, as well as take into account context in which the strategic decisions are made. Considering the key internal and external factors affecting strategic decision-making (characteristics of decision-makers, organizational characteristics and environmental characteristics), Soft Systems Methodology as interpretive systems methodology and Organizational Cybernetics as functionalist systems methodology have been selected. The way in which they can be combined, aimed at improving effectiveness of strategic decision-making, has been presented.

INTRODUCTION

Strategic decision-making has emerged as one of the most important areas of current management research that has arisen from such research traditions as behavioral decision theory and transaction cost economics (Schwenk, 1995). However, despite a substantial body of literature, it is still widely recognized that our knowledge of strategic decision-making processes is limited and is mostly based on normative or

DOI: 10.4018/978-1-5225-2480-9.ch006

descriptive studies and on assumptions most of which remain untested (Pettigrew, 1990; Rajagopalan, Rasheed, & Datta, 1993). As Eisenhardt and Zbaracki (1992), put it, despite the crucial role of strategic decisions, "the strategy process research has not departed significantly from a stage of being based on mature paradigms and incomplete assumptions"(p. 17). In particular, the need has been recognized for integrative research which explicitly considers the impact of context on strategic decision-making processes (Rajagopalan et al., 1993; Schwenk, 1995).

Furthermore, modern circumstances, resulting in increasing complexity of contemporary business environment, require new creative approaches to strategic decision-making and problem solving. This need is more obvious at strategic level, since managers in contemporary companies are dealing with growing complexity, dynamics and diversity, and do not have appropriate instrumentarium for solving these strategic problems.

Due to ambiguity and uncertainty of strategic problems, strategic decisions, as outcomes of strategic problem solving/strategic-decision process, are unstructured or insufficiently structured. In addition to this, complexity, openness, and novelty can be distinguished as key characteristics of strategic decisions (Babić, 1994, p. 63). In fact, strategic problems and strategic decision-making are characterized by extreme complexity, dynamics, interactivity, diversity, and ambiguity. Therefore, strategic problems in contemporary organizations should be researched as management problem situations, i.e. as a system of real management problems (Rosenhead, 1996; Jackson, 2003, p.18).

Strategic decision-making is a process influenced by different past, present, and future circumstances, and is oriented towards the organization's mission and vision of where it wants to be in the future. Therefore, it consists of a set of activities that top managers and other organizational members undertake from the moment of strategic problem formulation to the moment of its solving. Accordingly, various factors affect the nature and outcome of strategic decision-making. Interdependence, uncertainty, and complexity of these factors complicate the process of making "right" strategic decisions. Therefore, researching these factors becomes a relevant research area, and different researches deals with this topic. In fact, these researches analyze many of different strategic decision-making factors, but the knowledge of how they can be systemically conceptualized and researched is limited. It is a relevant reseach gap, which this paper aims to overcome. The main purpose of the paper is, therefore, to demonstrate how systems thinking and systems methodologies can help decision-makers involve different personal/organizational values and environmental chatracteristics, i.e. to take into account different context in which strategic decisions are making.

Respecting all the above, the paper is structured as follows. First of all, the nature of strategic desicion-making process, as well as the key factors influencing and determining the context of strategic desicion-making process, are analyzed. Since factors affecting the formulation and solving of strategic problems can generally be considered as internal and external, the paper deals with characteristics of decision-makers (personal values, opinions, perceptions or behavioral characteristics of decision-makers), organizational characteristics and values, and environmental characteristics as the key contextual factors. In addition, the process of strategic decision-making is holistically conceptualized and researched. In this regard, and respecting the importance of strategic decisions for companies' survival and development, the analysis of strategic decision-making process in conceptual framework of systems thinking presents a relevant research area. It implies showing the role of values and context in strategic decision-making, and the ways various systems methodologies and their combined use can help decision-makers handle these factors in the process of strategic decision-making.

THE NATURE OF STRATEGIC DECISION-MAKING PROCESS

The main purpose of strategic decision-making is to identify strategic orientation in organizational development, and to create competitive advantage by improving the future strategic position of companies. The key point is that these decisions directly affect nature and success of the firm. One of the main characteristics of strategic decisions is their lack of structure, mainly due to ambiguity and vagueness of strategic problems and strategic decision-making processes (Mintzberg, Raisinghani, & Theoret, 1976). In addition to poor structure, complexity, openness, and novelty can be extracted as the three basic characteristics of strategic decisions (Babić, 1994, p. 64). Therefore, strategic problems in contemporary organizations should be researched as management problem situations, i.e. as a system of complex, interactive, dynamic, and multi-meaning real management problems. Those are undefined or ill-defined real management problems or messes, characterized by the following (Hicks, 2004, p. 18): "they do not have a definitive problem description, each problem is essentially unique, there is no certain way of knowing when you have reached the best solution, they have an infinite number of possible solutions, etc".

Strategic decision-making is incremental and interdependent process, shaped by different influences of past events, present circumstances, and future perspectives (Eisenhardt & Zbaracki, 1992). The process of making strategic decisions involves a set of activities that top managers and members of the organization undertake from the formulation of strategic problems to their solving. These activities include a set of sub-processes, such as problem identification, alternative search and evaluation, and persuasion and negotiation in the process of selection, which take place at different organizational levels, and, to some degree, involve top managers, as well as other members of the organization (Babić, 1994, p. 14). So, this is a proper complex, dynamic, interactive and multi-meaning system. In accordance with the underlying assumptions, nature of the problem to be solved, conditions under which decisions are made, and criteria on the basis of which the best alternative is selected, there are three basic dimensions of the strategic decision-making process: rationality, intuition, and political behavior (Elbanna & Child, 2007).

"Rationality is the reason for doing something and to judge a behaviour as reasonable is to be able to say that the behaviour is understandable within a given frame of reference. Rational processes have long been recognized as a central aspect of strategic decision making and have been intensively subjected to both theoretical and empirical investigation in the literature of decision making" (Elbanna & Child, 2006, p. 434). Starting from this point of view, rational decision-making involves systematic observation and analysis of the environment, evaluation of internal strengths and weaknesses, setting goals, evaluation of alternative courses of action, and development of a comprehensive plan for goal achievement (Tani & Parnell, 2013, p. 94). However, rational decision-making process is difficult to achieve, which is why theory and practice focus much more on subjective, bounded rationality, which, due to the limited knowledge of decision-makers, leads to satisfactory, rather than optimal solutions (Campitelli & Gobet, 2010).

Often, strategic decisions are made not on the basis of careful deliberation, but on the basis of intuitive "gut-feel" (Bresnick & Parnell, 2013, p. 95). Although some authors have argued that intuition has an important role in strategic decision making, there has been little empirical research related to interdependence between intuition and strategic decision-making outcomes. Moreover, one of the basic assumptions about strategic decision-making process, is that rational processes lead to choices that are superior to those coming from intuitive processes (Elbanna & Child, 2007). However, the role of intuition in the strategic decision-making process can be important dimension of strategic outcomes. Furthermore, understanding of intuition can help decision-makers in improving quality decisions. Intuition can be defined as such a feeling or knowledge that cannot be explained. It is based on past experience, knowledge, and values of decision-makers, as well as ethical values and organizational culture (Sikavica, Hunjak, Begičević Ređep, & Hernaus, 2014, p. 257). Intuition is the most important dimension of the strategic decision-making process in situations where decision-makers do not have the relevant information and necessary resources for systematic analysis and evaluation of alternatives, but make a decision based on personal feelings, knowledge, experience, and judgment abilities, usually in a short period of time. This can be reasonable when decision-maker has made similar decisions previously, and has received good timely feedback on their outcomes (Tany & Parnell, 2013, p. 95). Therefore, bias and heuristics in human reasoning result in decisions that deviate from optimal solutions (Bresnick & Parnell, 2013, p. 36). However, the use of heuristics can also have negative consequences and lead to poor problem solution. Thus, identification of "psychological traps" and bias faced by decision-makers should help improving the effectiveness of strategic decision-making. "Cognitive biases are thought process errors that cause a person's beliefs to improperly reflect his or her perceptions" (Howard & Abbas, 2016, p. 351).

Political processes stand for a key dimension of strategic decision-making, when decision-makers have different goals and form a coalition through which they can achieve the determinated goals (El-banna & Child, 2007). The political processes are based on distribution power. Accordingly, the political power of decision makers can be seen as the basis for acquiring the key organizational resources which provide good strategic position of company. Furthermore, political behavior has long been recognized as relevant aspect of decision making and has received considerable attention from researchers (Child & Tsai, 2005). The main characteristic of political processes is the using of negotiating tactics in making decisions, which should lead to a result that is acceptable to various coalitions, but the most powerful coalition can impose its own goals. Strategic decision-making through political processes is completely different from rational decision-making, because it is based on the distribution of power on which the implementation and outcome of applied negotiating tactics depends.

In fact, although various strategic decision-making processes differ from many important aspects, a careful review of these aspects allows us to draw some conclusions. First, analysis of rationality, intuition, and political behavior as the basic dimensions of the strategic decision-making process indicates that there are different factors determining its outcome. Second, interdependence, uncertainty, and complex nature of the factors that affect strategic decision-making complicate the making "right" strategic decisions. Third, given that strategic decision are made in the different context, the nature of process in which strategic decisions are made is influenced by contextual factors. Thus, contextual antecedents factors such as organizational, environmental and decision-makers characteristics significantly influence strategic-decision making process (Rajagopolan et al., 1993).

CONTEXT OF STRATEGIC DECISION-MAKING PROCESS

Many researchers have referred to aspects of contextual influence on strategic decision making process. In order to provide an integrative model, authors propose the following categorization of factors which are expected to influence strategic processes. Although there are different classifications of factors that influence the effectiveness of strategic decision-making, characteristics of decision-makers and organizational characteristics are the most important internal factors, and environmental characteristics are the most important external factors determining the context in which strategic decisions are made. An integration of these contextual domains into a wider framework looks a promising avenue for research.

Such a framework must combine the following basic perspectives: an individual decision perspective by characteristics of decision-makers, organizational context by organizational characteristics, and environmental determinism by environmental characteristics. The following sections briefly discuss the theoretical underpinnings of each perspective, as well as the most important relevant research efforts under each perspective.

Characteristics of Decision-Makers as Personal Values

Research into decision-making cognition suggests that the same contextual input may be interpreted differently by managers (as decision-makers) in different organizations or even within the same organization (Dean & Sharfman, 1993). It has been argued that the perspective decision makers classify and mark decision in the early stages of the decision making process strongly influences effectiveness of the strategic decision-making process as well as the strategic decisions as the organization's responses (Fredrickson, 1985; Mintzberg et al., 1976). In fact, research (e.g. Dean & Sharfman, 1993; Papadakis et al., 1998) on decision-making process recommends that managers in various organizations or even within the same organization may view the same internal or external problem quite differently (Nooraie, 2012). However, our understanding of the impact of decision-makers characteristics on decision-making processes' outcomes is still quite limited. In the other words, existing researches have not yet pointed-out how decision-makers characteristics shape the decision-making processes as a whole. Moreover, the few studies which have been done on the links between manager's characteristics and strategic decision-making process have produced mixed results. According to Papadakis et al. (1998) "our understanding, however, of the impact of decision-makers characteristics on organizational decision-making process is still quite limited" (p. 117).

The most important researched characteristics of decision-makers, which affect the effectiveness of the strategic decision-making process, are demographic and behavioral characteristics (Papadikis et al., 1998; Nooraie, 2011; 2012). Academic education, experience and ages are selected as the most important demographic characteristics. Hitt and Tyler (1991) found that the demographic characteristics of CEOs (i.e., type of academic education) influenced the modes of strategic decision-making process. It is interesting to note that counter arguments have also been arised. According to Hambrick and Mason (1984), level of academic education (but not type of academic education) as well as experience, influence strategic decision-making process. This attitude is supported by the research Nahavandi and Malekzadeh (1993). Furthermore, education and experience as individual characteristics can affect heuristics and mental strategies which decision-makers use. In addition to level of education and experience, decision-makers' ages also influence the mode of strategic decision-making. In fact, ages can shape decision-makers' perspectives on problem formulation and alternatives evaluation (Hitt & Tajler, 1991). According to the defined research topic, the following behavioral characteristics, which determine the manner in which decision-makers perceive and solve certain strategic problems, will be analysed: risk affinity, pursuit of achievement, degree of aggressiveness, and cognitive conflict.

Risk affinity is the psychological feature of the individual, which represents the degree of risk preference and risk aversion of decision-makers (Papadikis et al., 1998). This is one of the main dimensions of personality, which empirical research most often associates with the nature of the strategic decision-making process. The research results of two groups of managers with different degree of risk affinity show that managers with greater risk affinity make decisions quickly and on the basis of less information. It can be concluded that risk affinity is negatively correlated with the application of the model of rational strategic decision-making (Nooraie, 2001).

The need for achievement is an important behavioral feature of decision-makers, which affects the nature of the strategic decision-making process. Initial hypothesis is that decision-makers' need for achievement positively affects the degree of rationality of the strategic decision-making process. Papadakis et al. (1998) and Nooraie (2001) did not confirm such a correlation in their research. Contradictory results point to the need for further research about motivational bias. "Motivational bias is the effect that motivation to have positive attitudes to oneself has on the way a person perceives or acts upon information in the decision process" (Bresnick & Parnell, 2013, p. 44).

Cognitive conflict is a positive force, necessary for effective strategic decision-making, and, thus, should be encouraged. Cognitive conflict arises as a result of differences between decision-makers in the selection of possible options for solving strategic problems (differences in goals and perspectives of decision-makers). In contrast, affective conflict occurs as a result of personal differences that exist between decision-makers (demographic differences, differences in decision-making styles, etc.). In other words, cognitive conflict is related to the problem, and results from the conflict of ideas, while affective conflict is associated with personality. This means that cognitive conflict in the process of making strategic decisions has a positive impact on their quality, while affective conflict, as a form of destructive behavior, negatively affects the quality of decisions, and can block the decision-making process, which is why its consequences are negative (Amason, 1996).

Organizational Characteristics and Values

Research results on the impact of organizational characteristics on the process of strategic decision-making show that organizational structure and power, as well as organizational culture, are the most important internal factors of strategic decision-making.

Although organizational structure can be defined in different ways, the structuring of the organization involves finding answers to two key questions: who should decide and on what (concentration of authority) and who needs to do what in the organization (structuring of activities)? Concentration of authority, as the first question, is analyzed by varying the degree of centralization of decision-making authority. Structuring of activities, as the second question, is resolved through specialization, formalization, and standardization of roles in the organization. This means that organizations are, in accordance with defined structural solutions, to a certain degree centralized, formalized, and complex. Centralization refers to the distribution of decision-making power. The analysis of power distribution shows that centralization leads to amplification of the influence of political processes on strategic decision-making (Bourgeois & Eisenhardt, 1988). Formalization shows the extent to which policies, procedures, and rules are expressed in written documents. The degree of rationality of decision-making processes is positively correlated with the formalization of organizational structure. Complexity is a direct consequence of the division of labor and refers to horizontal, vertical, and spatial differentiation of companies. There is a correlation between the degree of rationality of decision-making processes and the complexity of the organizational structure (Frederickson, 1986). Furthermore, there is a link between the strategic decision-making process and different models of organizational structure. Establishing relations between strategic decision-making models and organizational design is very important, because it leads to increased organizational effectiveness and improves the quality of strategic decision-making process.

Organizational culture is manifested through meanings that people in organizations create in the process of mutual interaction. Therefore, members of the organization in the same or similar way interpret the reality that surrounds them, and act within that reality (Bresnick & Parnell, 2013, p. 26). Organizational culture generally contains meanings of phenomena and events related to life and work in the organization, rarely meanings of phenomena in other contexts. In fact, organizational ideology affects the nature of the decision-making process in several ways: it provides a basis for problem identification, goal setting, and alternative consideration, evaluation, and selection. Depending on the values and norms in the organizational culture, top management chooses the strategy and designs the organizational structure, managers shape the management style, and members of the organization define their motives and needs (Janićijević, 2012). In the process of strategic decision-making, top managers need to take into account the system of values, shared beliefs, symbols, and motives that have developed over time, and make decisions in accordance with them. Cultural values are transmitted from generation to generation through a shared understanding of beliefs, attitudes, meanings and hierarchies. Facing with the problem, decision-makers use cultural values to determine the appropriate course of action or problem solutions. If a person's cultural values encourage characteristics such as honesty and integrity, then this person is more likely to follow ethical decision-making tactics when compared to person who's cultural values do not stress the importance of those charecteristics. In other words, organizational culture implies different models of strategic decision-making and appropriate leadership styles. The leadership style is highly dependent on decision-making process and the role that decision-makers can play (Bresnick & Parnell, 2013, p. 27). Although cultural values play an important role in decision-making, recent research shows that cultural norms and values are not the only criteria to influence behavior. Environmental characteristics also play important role in the strategic decision-making process, since strategic decision analysis cannot be performed in isolation in any organization.

Environmental Characteristics

Starting from different classifications of the most important dimensions of the environment that can be encountered in literature, it can be said that the most important are dynamism, hostility, and uncertainty. In the context of strategic decision the environmental determinism perspective mainly addresses the question of how above mentioned environmental factors (e.g. dynamism, hostility, uncertainty) influence strategic decision making process (Papadikis et al., 1998). Few empirical studies can be found here (e.g. Fredrickson, 1984; Eisenhardt, 1989; Judge & Miller, 1991) and those available seem to have produced contradictory results (Rajagopalan et al., 1997).

Environmental dynamism refers to the degree and speed of change and the degree of unpredictability of the environment, reflected through the uncertainty of customer preferences, production and/or technology, and competitive strategies. Dynamic environment is characterized by a high degree of unpredictability and uncertainty (Miller & Friesen, 1983; Mitchell, Shepherd, & Sharfman, 2011). The most important findings of studies that assessed the impact of environmental dynamism on the process of strategic decision-making (Frederikson & Iaquinto, 1989; Elbanna & Child, 2007) show negative correlation between the degree of rationality in decision-making and performance in an unstable, dynamic environment, while in a stable environment there is a positive correlation. Empirical research has shown that between the application of rational or synoptic decision-making process and company performance there is a positive correlation in a stable environment, while in a dynamic environment, there is negative correlation (Goll & Rasheed, 1997). In a dynamic environment, it is necessary to apply the incremental or adaptive decision-making model (Fredrickson & Iaquinto, 1989). In the same way, Stein (1980) argues that companies operating in highly dynamic environments apply both less extensive search and less explicit analysis of alternatives.

In contrast to these results, Bourgeois (1985), Miler and Friesen (1983), and Bourgeois and Eisenhardt (1988) found that in a highly dynamic environment, successful companies apply rational decision-making models, noting that the higher level of dynamic environment is accompanied by the need to increase the degree of rationality in the process of strategic decision-making. It can be concluded that managers in a dynamic environment must struggle with problems in understanding the nature of strategic problems that arise as a result of incomplete, irrelevant information (Mitchell et al., 2011).

Environmental hostility refers to differences in production programs, distribution channels, competitive tactics, market requirements, and regulations on markets where the company operates (Miller & Friesen, 1983). According to Miller and Friesen (1983) and Papadakis et al. (1998), the degree of environmental hostility is positively correlated with the degree of rationality in strategic decision-making. Furthermore, the results of the study conducted by Nooraie (2011) show that between environmental hostility and rationality in decision-making there is a positive correlation.

However, research results are often contradictory. Nevertheless, the most important findings relating to the impact of hostility, as an environmental dimension, on strategic decision-making process are: a high degree of environmental hostility slows down the adoption of strategic decisions (Baum & Wally, 2003), has a negative impact on the effectiveness of strategic decision-making (Goll & Rasheed, 1997) and the application of the rational model of strategic decision-making (Dean & Sharfman, 1993). It can be generally concluded that a high degree of environmental hostility negatively affects the process of strategic decision-making (Mitchell et al., 2011), leading to quick and hasty decisions that managers make on the basis of simplified information processing and analysis, in order to as soon as possible respond to environmental threats.

In the analysis of strategic decision-making, uncertainty, as environmental characteristics, relates to the possibility of predictability of occurrences in the environment. The degree of environmental uncertainty is negatively correlated with the degree of rationality in decision-making (Dean & Sharfman, 1993; Goll & Rasheed, 1997). However, some studies do not support these findings (Dean & Sharfman, 1996). Although the results of empirical studies in this area are different, based on the analysis of studies on the correlation between rational decision-making and performance, preference may be given to studies based on contingency theory. Starting from the considered factors of strategic decision-making, and in seeking an answer to the question of how to improve strategic decision-making process, an Integrative model of effective strategic decision-making was developed (Figure 1). The presented model combines the most important internal and external factors, possible ways of making strategic decisions, and their impact on the effectiveness of strategic decision-making and quality of strategic decisions.

HOLISTIC INSTRUMENTARIUM FOR SUPPORTING THE EFFECTIVE STRATEGIC DECISION-MAKING

Respecting the nature and factors affecting strategic decision-making, one can conclude that decision-makers need systems thinking as a relevant instrumentarium for dealing with and solving strategic problems. Without systemic thinking, decision-makers might make many oversights due to one-sided behavior (Zlatanović & Mulej, 2015). In conceptual framework of systems thinking, strategic problems

Figure 1. Integrative model of effective strategic decision-making
Source: Authors

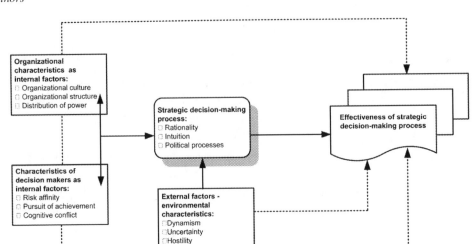

or problem situations are researched in the way that systems ideas are used to enable appropriately arranged thinking about real world problems, i.e. to provide decision-makers with appropriate theoretical and methodological support. Holistic approach to strategic problem solving and strategic decision-making can bring numerous benefits. According to Jackson (2006), the benefits of holism are as follows: using the trans-disciplinary analogies, recognizing the importance of both the structure and the functioning of an organization, as well as their interdependence. In addition, systems thinking provides a basis for the critique of different systems interventions.

Actually, "when we distinguish systems and identify their characteristics, we clearly do so from a particular world-view. Our knowledge is, therefore, always partial" (Jackson, 2006, p. 651). Relying on the considerations presented above, in systemic research and dealing with strategic problems, seen as appropriate management problem situations, there are two basic dimensions (Jackson, 2003, p. 18): system dimension and participant dimension. System dimension explores the complexity of a problem situation. In the context of analyzing the process of strategic decision-making in the conceptual framework of systems thinking, it can be concluded that system dimension makes it possible to explore specific characteristics of the organization and the environment, such as organizational structure, dynamics, uncertainty and hostility of the environment. Another important dimension of problem situations is the participant dimension, which makes it possible to identify the behavioral characteristics of decision-makers.

Based on the above, in solving strategic problems, one can employ the following holistic instrumentarium: systems methodologies for problem situation structuring, systems metaphors and systems paradigms (Petrović, 2013). In the given research context, systems methodologies are particularly important.

Systems Methodologies for Problem Situations Structuring

Systems methodologies can involve, connect, and expose different perceptions of the researched strategic problem, i.e. problem situation, as the basis for generating the consensus in action or facilitating negotiation. In fact, systems methodologies for problem situation structuring can be useful and should be employed if they: accommodate different perspectives, function through interaction and iteration, generate valid problem formulations and action implications (Rosenhead, 1996; Mingers & Rosenhead, 2004). Systems methodologies for problem situations structuring do not only strive to provide for mutual understanding, but also help decision-makers in obtaining the "broader picture" which offers new insights into the problem and possible solutions. So, in the process of structuring the problem situations by systems methodologies, one can interactively (Petrović, 2010, p. 319):

- Name the relevant aspects and issues of the considered strategic problems, and
- Frame the context in which the problems are occured.

Some of the issues dealt by systems methodology include the following (Midgley, Cavana, Brocklesby, Foote, Wood, & Driscoll, 2013): What worldview and which aspects of problem should be included in the analysis and decision-making, and which should be excluded? What are the different problem perspectives and which values and assumptions support them? What interactions within the organization, and those with the relevant environment, lead to desired or undesired results?

Systems methodologies possess the ability to adequately model the problem situation so that participants in a given strategic decision-making process can clearly identify the problems and issues. Each methodology is suitable for a particular type of task and is not universally applicable (Von Winterfeldt & Fasolo, 2009). Because of a large number of different systems methodologies, one possible approach to systems methodology systematization is the System of Systems Methodologies (Jackson & Keys, 1984). Due to the extreme complexity and ambiguity, as the key features of strategic problems and strategic decision-making processes, it is of relevant importance to note that through individual application of systems methodologies, it is almost impossible to provide for a comprehensive study of all aspects of research problems and their relationships. Under such circumstances, it is better to have available the appropriate range of useful, even conflicting methodologies/methods, i.e. it is necessary to explore preconditions, the ways, as well as possibilities and limitations of the combined use of systems methodologies in the process of strategic decision-making.

The essence of multimethodology, i.e. combining systems methodologies, is to employ more than one methodology or parts of methodologies within single intervention. One of the key issues in the combined use of systems methodologies is how one can choose appropriate combination of methodologies in a particular intervention. Therefore, a relevant framework for mapping methodologies is developed. The framework is characterized by the following (Mingers, 2000): multi-dimensionality of the researched problem, represented by three different aspects or worlds – social (including social practices, power relations, conflicts, interests, etc.), personal (including individual beliefs, values, different perceptions and personal rationality, etc.), and material (physical circumstances, alternative physical and structural arrangements, etc.), as well as different activities that should be realized in solving the problem, represented by different phases – appreciation, analysis, assessment, and action.

Respecting the defined research purpose, this framework can help in the selection of appropriate combination of systems methodologies, to support strategic decision-making process. In fact, in analyzing appropriate personal dimensions that determine the strategic decision-making process, i.e. in dealing with appropriate characteristics of decision-makers and values and opinions in the organization, interpretive systems methodologies, such as Soft Systems Methodology, are of relevant importance. SSM mainly contributes to exploring the personal dimension, and is particularly strong for analysis and assessment, although it has some techniques for appreciating the social dimension (Analyses 1, 2, and 3). Furthermore, in the study of material aspects of the problem and dealing with strategic decision-making factors, such as organizational structure and environmental characteristics, functionalist systems methodologies can be of particular importance, such as Organizational Cybernetics and its key methodological tool – Viable System Model (VSM). VSM is seen as relating to material worlds, providing a model of viable organizational structure, and a model that does not address individual participants' views and beliefs. Accordingly, in order to explore the process of making strategic decisions and certain factors that affect it in the conceptual framework of systems thinking, the paper presents a possible way of combining SSM and OC, i.e. VSM.

Briefly About Selected Systems Metodologies

Soft Systems Methodology (SSM), tends to involve different perceptions of reality, facilitating the learning process where different viewpoints are examined and discussed in the way leading to purposeful action and improvement (Jackson, 2003, p. 185). SSM is based on action research. Action research implies that the researchers both observe the researched phenomenon and participate in it. First of all, when researching the problem situation it is necessary to develop relevant models of the situation, i.e., valid ways to represent it. Then appropriate methodologies for problem situations structuring have to be developed. Finally, intervention in the problem situation is essential, i.e., developed models, methodologies, and methods should be applied to the researched problem situation in order to test and further develop it (Zlatanović, 2015).

As a learning cycle based on action research, SSM consists of the following key stages (Checkland, 2000):

1. Finding out about a problem situation through rich pictures and root definitions;
2. Formulating the conceptual models of purposeful activity;
3. Debating the problem situation by comparing conceptual models with reality;
4. Taking action in the situation, i.e. implementing changes leading to the improvement of the problem situation.

The initial expression of the problem situation, as the first phase in the implementation of SSM, is achieved by the construction of the so-called rich picture of a given situation. The aim is to "capture the main entities, structures and viewpoints in the situation, the process going on, the current recognized issues and any potential ones" (Checkland & Poulter, 2010, p. 210). The following analyses are often used to supplement rich pictures, to help in better understanding of the problem situation (Checkland & Poulter, 2010, p. 211):

*   Analysis A_1 refers to the examination of those who need to conduct research, and problem owners.
*   Analysis A_2 explores social roles relevant to the given situation, behavioral norms, values, opinions, meaning that the problem situation is examined as a culture.
*   Finally, analysis A_3 investigates the distribution of power, i.e. examines the problem situation from the standpoint of politics.

Root definitions reflect different perspectives/viewpoints or ways of system's observing, i.e. root definitions can be seen as concise description of the purposeful activity system (relevant system) based on a particular viewpoint. In formulating the root definitions, CATWOE mnemonic was developed (Checkland & Tsouvalis, 1997). In the process of strategic decision-making, it is as follows:

- **C** *(Customers)* – relevant stakeholders involved in a strategic decision-making process;
- **A** *(Actors)* – strategic decision-makers;
- **T** *(Transformation process)* – the process of making strategic decisions: alternative-choice-decision
- **W** *(Weltanschauung)* – world viewpoint that applies to the particular strategic decision, i.e. a set of assumptions that make a decision meaningful
- **O** *(Ownership)* – those who have the power to prevent the adoption of certain strategic decision
- **E** *(Environmental constraints)* – elements outside the system taken as given.

The next stage in SSM application is conceptual models building which represent activities that the system must undertake to be the system named in the root definition (Checkland & Tsouvalis, 1997). The relevant result of the comparison phase is assessing the problem situation from which the possible changes are derived. The changes must meet the following criteria: systemic desirability (derived from the selection of root definitions and conceptual models) and cultural feasibility (given the characteristics of particular situation, i.e. norms, values, experiences of people in the situation) (Checkland, 1996, p. 181). Final stage of SSM application is implementation of these changes.

A key limitation of Soft Systems Methodology, relevant to the given research context, concerns a critique of functionalist systems paradigm representatives. They criticize the neglect of the fact that modern organizations, as complex and dynamic systems, must in their operation take into account that their control and communication systems are adequately designed. The critique of advocates of functionalist systems paradigm is the basis for the combination of SSM with OC.

In contrast to SSM, Organizational Cybernetics (OC) is, through Viable System Model (VSM), focused on exploring the structure and functioning of contemporary enterprises. In order for a system to become viable and develop successfully, organisations must possess high complexity, that is, complexity above certain "complexity barrier". In conceptual framework of Organizational Cybernetics, complexity is measured by variety. Variety is the cybernetic measure of complexity, i.e. the number of potential systems states (Beer, 1994 b, 35).

The Law of Requisite Variety is theoretical core of Organizational Cybernetics and generally reads as follows: "Only variety can destroy variety" (Ashby, 1966, p. 207). If the subject of observation is contemporary organizations, the problem is a great difference in variety between the organization, its environment and the process of managing it. As a rule, environment is much more complex than organization, and the organization is more complex than the process which manages it. In order for the management to control the system and the system to persist in the changeable environment, their varieties must be balanced. The above means that the Law of Requisite Variety must be respected. That further means that the variety of highly variety systems must be decreased and the variety of low variety systems must be increased. This process, defined as variety engineering, can be effective if organizations deal only with the part of the environment causing the threats that the organization must react on in order to survive. This is about so-called residual variety of environment. Analogically, it can be applied to the organization and its management, where residual variety of organization is relevant, i.e. the variety that is not absorbed by the processes of self-organization and self-regulation (Schwaninger, 2000, p. 211; Schwaninger, 2006, p. 15).

Originally developed by Stafford Beer (Beer, 1994a; Beer 1994b; Beer 1994c), VSM contains the five subsystems that represent functions of: implementation (subsystem S_1 or operational elements), coordination (subsystem S_2 which should enable that operational elements function as a whole), control (subsystem S_3 which maintains and allocates recources to operational elements, with addition of the segment $S_{3,}$* representing channels of audit), intelligence (subsystem S_4 which collects information about strategic opportunities, threats, and future directions of the system, as well as information about strenghts and weaknesses of the organization itself) and identity (subsystem S_5 which identifies the purpose of the system) (Brocklesby & Cummings, 1996).

VSM is employed in the (re)designing of organization through the following three relevant subprocesses (Flood, 1995, p. 149): system identification, system diagnosis, and redesign (if it is necessary). Of key importance for the combined use of SSM and OC is the sub-process of diagnosis, which starts with careful analysis of S_1, S_2, S_3, S_4, and S_5 subsystem of the researched system, i.e. organization, and proceeds by the analysis of all information channels, transmitters, and control loops. Accordingly, the following problems can be identified through this process (Peréz Ríos, 2010): S_4 subsystem is missing or, if it does exist, does not work properly; inadequate management style that constrains autonomy of S_1 subsystem; authoritarian S_2 subsystem; uncontrolled growth and activity of some individual parts of the organization; communication channels in the system, as well as those that exist between the system and environment, do not correspond to the information flows, etc.

One of the major disadvantages of the VSM refers to the fact that common values and beliefs are ignored in VSM, and one can conclude that it is much stronger in dealing with complexity, than in dealing with organizational culture (Jackson, 2003, p. 109). This is an important basis for combining VSM with SSM which is focused on the participant dimension.

Combining SSM and OC to Support Strategic Decision-Making

Taking into account the key theoretical and methodological features of the selected systems methodologies, it can be concluded that SSM can help decision-makers to involve different perceptions and understanding of strategic problems, value systems, opinions, which means that, in the process of making strategic decisions, SSM can provide answers to the questions "what": what is the problem, i.e. whether the problem is properly identified, and what needs to be explored in order to identify areas of possible improvement. In contrast, OC focuses on the question "how": how the changes should be implemented to ensure the right solution to a specific strategic problem and improve the process of strategic decision-making. Respecting different possibilities of combining systems methodologies, this paper defines the following approach to combining SSM and OC that implies using VSM in SSM phases of comparison and implementation. This enables involving the different perceptions, value judgments of decision-makers on possible changes, i.e. possible ways of resolving certain strategic problems, as well as characteristics of the organization and the environment.

Starting from an integrative model of effective strategic decision-making, as represented in Figure 1, which includes the role of different values and characteristics of decision-makers, as well as internal and external context in which strategic decisions are made, the corresponding systems approach is defined, which combines SSM and OC. Given that the selected systems methodologies are adequate instrumentarium for capturing the key internal and external factors of strategic decision-making, in Figure 2, strategic decision-making is presented in conceptual framework of these systems methodologies.

As one can see from the Figure 2, the characteristics of decision-makers, as well as values, norms, i.e. organizational culture influence the process of strategic decision-making through the rich pictures and root definitions, as the tools of SSM for representing the strategic problems. In fact, different values, perceptions and perspectives of decision-makers play the most important role in the process of problem identification, as a first stage of strategic decision-making. Since root definitions represents what system should be, one can conclude that root definitions also reflects the ways of improving the problem situation, i.e. alternatives for solving the strategic problem. Conceptual models then involve the set of activities that system should undertake to solve the strategic problems. SSM tools, such as rich pictures, root definitions, and conceptual models are used to perceive the problem situation, i.e. examine strategic problem from different aspects, and identify and present possible ways of solving it.

The next stage in combining SSM and OC is comparing these models with reality, which is done in conceptual framework of VSM. VSM diagnosis enables to identify organizational parts (operational elements), their interdependence, problems in their functioning, the degree of centralization and formalization, organizational connections to environment, etc. In that way, the key characteristics of organizational structure as well as environmental characteristics are taken into account. The procees is proceed by identifying the systemically desirable and culturally feasible changes. In the phase of their implementation, VSM model can also be used in order to enable the efficient implementation of strategic decision.

The two methodologies linked in this way can allow decision-makers to deal with the questions of 'what' and 'how' in one methodology (Kinloch, 2009). Thus, this approach to combining the above sys-

Figure 2. Combining SSM and OC: systems tools to support strategic decision-making
Source: Authors

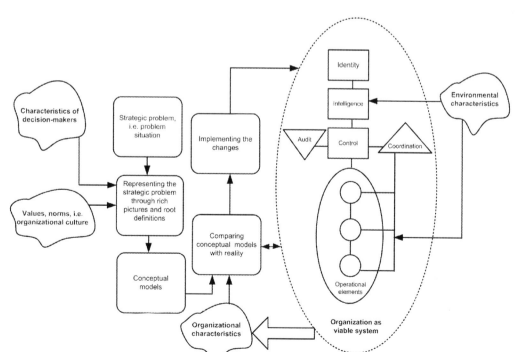

tems methodologies can help in adequate examination of both the system dimension and the participant dimension, i.e. in improving the effectiveness of strategic decision-making through a comprehensive analysis of certain internal and external factors, i.e. environmental characteristics, organizational characteristics, and characteristics of decision-makers. It is important to emphasize that there are another approaches to support strategic decision-making holistically (e.g. Probst & Bassi, 2014).

However, the combined use of the SSM and OC tools cannot help in dealing with problem situations in which there is unequal distribution of power. That is, the combined use of SSM and OC does not allow for the inclusion of power distribution of decision-makers as important organizational characteristics. In this sense, the research needs to include tools of some emancipatory systems approaches, such as Critical Systems Heuristics (Ulrich, 1994) or Team Syntegrity (Beer, 1994d; Pfifner, 2001). In addition, the combined use of SSM and OC, as well as any other systems methodologies from different paradigms, still leaves a number of other relevant issues unresolved, such as paradigmatic incommensurability, cultural, cognitive, and practical constraints (Kotiadis & Mingers, 2006).

PRACTICAL IMPLICATIONS

Good strategic decision-making is based on balancing the current capabilities of the organization, and in the future. "As the environment changes, as demands change, those changes should be anticipated and brought into the strategic debate. Seeing a need for change creates a strategic gap, a gap between what we can currently do, and what we have identified that we need to do in the future (Hoverstadt, 2010, p. 120)".

This can be illustrated by the following problem situation: Management of the company X should make strategic decision which involves introducing a new product in the production. It is a complex-pluralist problem situation that implies different values, perceptions and perspectives of decision-makers as well as high complexity, i.e. it is a system consisted of different interactive subsystems, such as: demands of potential customers, competition, technical and technological dimensions of introducing a new product, organizational aspects, financial aspects, as well as price of a new product, channels of its distribution, its promotion, etc. Combined use of SSM and OC can help decision-makers deal with these relevant aspects of introducing the new product in the production. Firstly, SSM can help involving the different perceptions of decision-makers and reaching accommodation through strategic debate. In fact, if a group of decision-makers and other relvant stakeholders tends to achieve agreed corporate action as a response to identified problem situation they will have to find an accomodation, i.e. to reach a compromise despite different perceptions, values and interests. A compomise may give no member of the group all they personally would look for in action to improve the situation. These stances on change are taken within SSM. In fact, SSM aims to identify both desirable and feasible changes. This recognizes the social context in which any change will sit. But, it is necessary to define the criteria by which a change can be assessed as successful or unsuccessful, namely to examine monitor and control activities in a real situation. OC through VSM can support it. In the case of introducing the new product, the set of activities needs to be examined.

For example, R&D (subsystem S_4 of VSM) need to check with operations (subsystem S_1 of VSM) whether the product can be produced, finance need to be involved over both short term cashflow implications (subsystem S_3 of VSM) and longer term investment planning (subsystem S_4 of VSM). In addition, marketing (subsystem S_4 of VSM) should consult on marketing opportunities for the new product and sales (subsystem S_3 of VSM) about how the new product might disrupt existing sales. New employees might be needed to recruit (subsystem S_4 of VSM), but finance must be taken into account, etc. This is a complex set of interrelated activities that must be implemented in order to enable a viable system, i.e. in order to enable an efficient and adaptable organization. In this way, systemically desirable and culturally feasible changes can be identified which leads to actions improving particular problem situation. VSM can further support efficiently implementation of these actions.

In fact, by combining SSM and VSM creative improvement of managing the problem situations can be enabled. Namely, this will provide enhancing the strategic decision-making process, i.e. the better understanding of strategic problems and the context in which they arise as well as tools to support each step of strategic decision-making process, i.e. identifying the problem, generating the alternatives, evaluating the alternatives and choice of the best alternative.

CONCLUSION

Taking into account the nature and contextual factors of strategic decision-making, the paper has focused on the selection of appropriate systems methodologies and defined the way in which they can be combined, that may be a valid instrumentarium of support to effective strategic decision-making. In accordance with the determined research subject and goal, the starting basis for the selection of SSM lies in its key principles and postulates, according to which systems are understood as subjective constructions of people, while organizations are viewed as cultural entities that govern social relations. This points to the role of different values and opinions of strategic decision-makers, i.e. shows how different values affect the process of making strategic decisions in the conceptual framework of SSM. Respecting the role and importance of the context in which decisions are made, the paper shows how OC, as a relevant functionalist systems methodology, focused on studying the structure and functioning of modern organizations, through VSM model, contributes to the understanding of the context in which strategic decisions are made. In fact, the contribution of the paper is reflected in the identification of the ways in which the combination of the selected systems methodologies can support strategic decision-making process and contribute to the improvement of its effectiveness and the quality of strategic decisions.

However, an important limitation is that the paper has illustrated hypothetical example of combining the above systems methodologies in solving a strategic problem in the company. Applying these combining to enterprises in the Republic of Serbia represents the basis for future research. What is more, taking into account the role and importance of power, as an important factor of strategic decision-making, an important area for future research is the combination of the above systems methodologies with an emancipatory systems methodology, such as Critical Systems Heuristics or Team Syntegrity.

REFERENCES

Amason, A. C. (1996). Distinguishing the effects of functional and dysfunctional conflict on strategic decision making: Resolving a paradox for top management teams. *Academy of Management Journal*, *39*(1), 123–148. doi:10.2307/256633

Ashby, W. R. (1966). *An Introduction to Cybernetics*. New York: John Wiley and Sons, Inc.

Babić, V. (1995). *Strategijsko odlučivanje*. Beograd: Institut za ekonomiku i finansije.

Baum, J. R., & Wally, S. (2003). Strategic decision speed and firm performance. *Strategic Management Journal*, *24*(11), 1107–1129. doi:10.1002/smj.343

Beer, S. (1994a). *Brain of the Firm*. Chichester, UK: John Wiley and Sons.

Beer, S. (1994b). *Diagnosing the System for Organization*. Chichester, UK: John Wiley and Sons.

Beer, S. (1994c). *The Heart of Enterprise*. Chichester, UK: John Wiley and Sons.

Beer, S. (1994d). *Beyond Dispute – The Invention of Team Syntegrity*. Chichester, UK: John Wiley and Sons.

Bourgeois, L. J. (1985). Strategic goals, perceived uncertainty, and economic performance in volatile environments. *Academy of Management Journal*, *28*(3), 548–573. doi:10.2307/256113

Bourgeois, L. J. III, & Eisenhardt, K. M. (1988). Strategic decision processes in high velocity environments: Four cases in the microcomputer industry. *Management Science*, *34*(7), 816–835. doi:10.1287/mnsc.34.7.816

Bresnick, A. T., & Parnell, S. G. (2013). Decision-making challenges. In S. G. Parnell, A. T. Bresnick, N. S. Tani, & E. R. Jonson (Eds.), *Handbook of Decision Analysis* (pp. 22–46). John Wiley & Sons. doi:10.1002/9781118515853.ch2

Brocklesby, J., & Cummings, S. (1996). Designing a Viable Organization Structure. *Long Range Planning*, *29*(1), 49–57. doi:10.1016/0024-6301(95)00065-8

Campitelli, G., & Gobet, F. (2010). Herbert Simons decision-making approach: Investigation of cognitive processes in experts. *Review of General Psychology*, *14*(4), 454–464. doi:10.1037/a0021256

Checkland, P. (1996). *Systems Thinking, Systems Practice*. Chichester, UK: John Wiley and Sons.

Checkland, P., & Poulter, J. (2010). Soft Systems Methodology. In M. Reynolds & S. Holwell (Eds.), *Systems Approaches to Managing Change: A Practical Guide* (pp. 191–242). London: Springer. doi:10.1007/978-1-84882-809-4_5

Checkland, P., & Tsouvalis, C. (1997). Reflecting on SSM: The Link Between Root Definitions and Conceptual Models. *Systems Research and Behavioral Science*, *14*(3), 153–168. doi:10.1002/(SICI)1099-1743(199705/06)14:3<153::AID-SRES134>3.0.CO;2-H

Child, J., & Tsai, T. (2005). The dynamic between firms environmental strategies and institutional constraints in emerging economies: Evidence from China and Taiwan. *Journal of Management Studies*, *42*(1), 95–125. doi:10.1111/j.1467-6486.2005.00490.x

Dean, J. W., & Sharfman, M. P. (1993). Procedural rationality in the strategic decision-making process. *Journal of Management Studies*, *30*(4), 87–610. doi:10.1111/j.1467-6486.1993.tb00317.x

Eisenhardt, K. M., & Zbaracki, M. J. (1992). Strategic decision making. *Strategic Management Journal*, *13*(S2), 17–37. doi:10.1002/smj.4250130904

Elbanna, S., & Child, J. (2007). Influences on strategic decision effectiveness: Development and test of an integrative model. *Strategic Management Journal, 28*(4), 431–453. doi:10.1002/smj.597

Flood, R. L. (1995). *Solving Problem Solving – A Potent force for Effective Management*. Chichester, UK: John Wiley and Sons.

Fredrickson, J. W. (1986). The strategic decision process and organization structure. *Academy of Management Review, 11*(2), 280–297.

Fredrickson, J. W., & Iaquinto, A. L. (1989). Inertia and creeping rationality in strategic decision processes. *Academy of Management Journal, 32*(3), 516–542. doi:10.2307/256433

Goll, I., & Rasheed, A. (1997). Rational decision-making and firm performance: The moderating role of environment. *Strategic Management Journal, 18*(7), 583–591. doi:10.1002/(SICI)1097-0266(199708)18:7<583::AID-SMJ907>3.0.CO;2-Z

Hicks, M. J. (2004). *Problem solving and decision making: Hard, soft and creative approaches*. London: Thomson Learning.

Howard, A. R., & Abbas, E. A. (2016). *Foundation of decision analysis*. Pearson Education Limited.

Howerstadt, P. (2010). The Viable System Model. In M. Reynolds & S. Holwell (Eds.), *Systems Approaches to Managing Change: A Practical Guide* (pp. 191–242). London, UK: Springer. doi:10.1007/978-1-84882-809-4_3

Jackson, M. C. (2003). *Systems Thinking: Creative Holism for Managers*. New York: John Wiley and Sons.

Jackson, M. C. (2006). Creative Holism: A Critical Systems Approach to Complex Problem Situations. *Systems Research and Behavioral Science, 23*(5), 647–657. doi:10.1002/sres.799

Jackson, M. C., & Keys, P. (1984). Towards a System of Systems Methodologies. *The Journal of the Operational Research Society, 35*(6), 473–486. doi:10.1057/jors.1984.101

Janićijević, N. (2012). The influence of organizational culture on organizational preferences towards the choice of organizational change strategy. *Economic Annals, 57*(193), 25–51. doi:10.2298/EKA1293025J

Judge, W. Q., & Miller, A. (1991). Antecedents and outcomes of decision speed in different environmental contexts. *Academy of Management Journal, 34*(2), 449–463. doi:10.2307/256451 PMID:10111313

Kinloch, P., Francis, H., Francis, M., & Taylor, M. (2009). Supporting Crime Detection and Operational Planning with Soft Systems Methodology and Viable Systems Model. *Systems Research and Behavioral Science, 26*(1), 3–14. doi:10.1002/sres.943

Kotiadis, K., & Mingers, J. (2006). Combining PSMs with Hard OR Methods: The Philosophical and Practical Challenges. *The Journal of the Operational Research Society, 57*(7), 856–867. doi:10.1057/palgrave.jors.2602147

Midgley, G., Cavana, R. Y., Brocklesby, J., Foote, J., Wood, D. R., & Driscoll, A. A. (2013). Towards a new framework for evaluating systemic problem structuring methods. *European Journal of Operational Research, 229*(1), 143–154. doi:10.1016/j.ejor.2013.01.047

Miller, D., & Friesen, P. H. (1983). Strategy making and environment: The third link. *Strategic Management Journal, 4*(3), 221–235. doi:10.1002/smj.4250040304

Mingers, J. (2000). Variety Is the Spice of Life: Combining Soft and Hard OR/MS Methods. *International Transactions in Operational Research, 7*(6), 673–691. doi:10.1111/j.1475-3995.2000.tb00224.x

Mingers, J., & Rosenhead, J. (2004). Problem Structuring Methods in Action. *European Journal of Operational Research, 152*(3), 530–554. doi:10.1016/S0377-2217(03)00056-0

Mintzberg, H., Raisinghani, D., & Theoret, A. (1976). The structure of unstructured decision processes. *Administrative Science Quarterly, 21*(2), 246–275. doi:10.2307/2392045

Mitchell, R., Shepherd, D., & Sharfman, M. (2011). Erratic strategic decisions: When and why managers are inconsistent in strategic decision making. *Strategic Management Journal, 32*(7), 683–704. doi:10.1002/smj.905

Nooraie, M. (2008). Decisions magnitude of impact and strategic decision-making process output: The mediating impact of rationality of the decision-making process. *Management Decision, 46*(4), 640–655. doi:10.1108/00251740810865102

Nooraie, M. (2011). Decisions familiarity and strategic decision-making process output: The mediating impact of rationality of the decision-making process.[IJADS]. *International Journal of Applied Decision Sciences, 4*(4), 385–400. doi:10.1504/IJADS.2011.043306

Nooraie, M. (2012). Factors influencing strategic decision-making processes. *International Journal of Academic Research in Business and Social Sciences, 2*(7), 405–429.

Papadakis, V., Lioukas, S., & Chambers, D. (1998). Strategic decision-making processes: The role of management and context. *Strategic Management Journal, 19*(2), 115–147. doi:10.1002/(SICI)1097-0266(199802)19:2<115::AID-SMJ941>3.0.CO;2-5

Pérez Ríos, J. (2010). Models of organizational cybernetics for diagnosis and design. *Kybernetes, 39*(9/10), 1529–1550. doi:10.1108/03684921011081150

Petrović, S. P. (2010). *Sistemsko mišljenje, Sistemske metodologije*. Kragujevac, Srbija: Ekonomski fakultet Univerziteta u Kragujevcu.

Petrović, S. P. (2013). A Holistic Instrumentarium for Creative Managing the Problem Situations. *Teme, 37*(1), 97–116.

Pettigrew, A. M. (1990). Longitudinal field research on change: Theory and practice. *Organization Science, 1*(3), 267–292. doi:10.1287/orsc.1.3.267

Pfifner, M. (2001). Team Syntegrity – Using Cybernetics for Opinion-Forming in Organizations. MOM Malik Management, 5(9), 75-97.

Probst, G., & Bassi, A. (2014). *Tackling Complexity: A Systemic Approach for Decision Makers.* Greenleaf Publishing.

Rajagopalan, N., Rasheed, M. A., & Datta, D. K. (1993). Strategic decision processes: Critical review and future directions. *Journal of Management, 19*(2), 349–384. doi:10.1177/014920639301900207

Rosenhead, J. (1996). Whats the problem? An introduction to problem structuring methods. *Interfaces, 26*(6), 117–131. doi:10.1287/inte.26.6.117

Schwaninger, M. (2000). Managing Complexity – The Path Toward Intelligent Organization. *Systemic Practice and Action Research, 13*(2), 207–241. doi:10.1023/A:1009546721353

Schwaninger, M. (2006). *Intelligent Organizations – Powerful Models for Systemic Management.* Berlin, Germany: Springer.

Schwenk, C. R. (1995). Strategic decision making. *Journal of Management, 21*(3), 471–493. doi:10.1177/014920639502100304

Sikavica, P., Hunjak, T., Begičević Ređep, N., & Hernaus, T. (2014). *Poslovno odlučivanje.* Zagreb: Školska knjiga

Tani, N. S., & Parnell, S. G. (2013). Use the appropriate decision process. In S. G. Parnell, A. T. Bresnick, N. S. Tani, & E. R. Jonson (Eds.), *Handbook of Decision Analysis* (pp. 92–109). John Wiley & Sons. doi:10.1002/9781118515853.ch5

Ulrich, W. (1994). *Critical Heuristics of Social Planning – A New Approach to Practcal Philosophy.* Chichester, UK: John Wiley and Sons.

Von Winterfeldt, D., & Fasolo, B. (2009). Structuring decision problems: A case study and reflections for practitioners. *European Journal of Operational Research, 199*(3), 857–866. doi:10.1016/j.ejor.2009.01.063

Zlatanović, D. (2015). A Holistic Approach to Corporate Social Responsibility as a Prerequisite for Sustainable Development: Empirical Evidence. *Economic Annals, 60*(207), 69–94. doi:10.2298/EKA1507069Z

Zlatanović, D., & Mulej, M. (2015). Soft-systems approaches to knowledge-cum-values management as innovation drivers. *Baltic Journal of Management, 10*(4), 497–518. doi:10.1108/BJM-01-2015-0015

KEY TERMS AND DEFINITIONS

Contextual Factors/Values: Refer to decision maker's personal values and organizational characteristics as well as external environment.

Managing Complexity: The theoretical core of Organizational Cybernetics that is based on The Law of Requisite Variety, according to which the variety of organization and environment must be balanced.

Organizational Cybernetics: A functionalist, i.e. hard systems approach that tends to manage the complexity of problem situation and is focused on researching the problems in structure and operations of organizations.

Soft Systems Methodology: An interpretive, i.e. a soft systems approach to strategic decision-making that tends to involve different personal and organizational values.

Strategic Decision-Making: Consists of a set of activities that top managers and other organizational members undertake from the moment of strategic problem formulation to the moment of its solving.

Strategic Decisions: Outcomes of strategic decision-making process which are unstructured or insufficiently structured. Complexity, openness, and novelty can be distinguished as key characteristics of strategic decisions.

Strategic Problems: Real management problems researched as management problem situations, i.e. as a system of complex, interactive, dynamic and ambiguous real management problems.

Systems Thinking: A relevant scientific instrumentarium, based on principles of General Systems Theory, which uses the systems ideas in order to research and solve complex strategic problems/problem situations.

Variety: The cybernetic measure of complexity, i.e. the number of different systems states.

Chapter 7
Personal Values as a Building Block for Social Responsibility of Higher Education Institutions

Zlatko Nedelko
University of Maribor, Slovenia

Vojko Potocan
University of Maribor, Slovenia

Nikša Alfirević
University of Split, Croatia

ABSTRACT

The purpose of this chapter is to examine the role of personal values for social responsibility (SR) of higher education. Besides the core mission of higher education to create, transfer and preserve knowledge in society, the idea of SR has gained its importance also in institutions of higher education. SR has many drivers, among which personal values are considered as one of the key building blocks for SR. For enhancing SR, higher education institutions should also develop stronger ties with the community. The chapter provides an insight into discussion about community involvement of higher education, into the role of personal values for shaping SR of higher education institutions and explain how personal values can help to enhance community and social involvement of higher education. Findings may be a starting point for re-thinking and/or establishing strategies for achieving higher level of SR in higher education institutions and enhancing the link with the community.

INTRODUCTION

The rising importance of sustainability was in the last decades expressed through various initiatives to preserve the environment for future generations (Dunlap & Mertig, 1990; Elkington, 2004). These initiatives have been used in different names, forms and shapes, like triple bottom line (Elkington, 2004), corporate social responsibility (CSR) (Foote et al., 2010), SR (Blackburn, 2007; Potocan et al., 2013),

DOI: 10.4018/978-1-5225-2480-9.ch007

Agenda 21 (Bullard, 1998), sustainable development (Beckerman, 1994), and sustainability (Clayton & Radcliffe, 1996). We will use terms SR and sustainability interchangeable.

Looking from the perspective of various types of organizations, SR is extensively present and studied in business organizations (Schultz, 2001; Nordlund & Garvill, 2002; Cordano et al., 2011; Cirnu & Kuralt, 2013), while in some other types of organizations, the interest for sustainability is significantly lower. This lack is most clearly seen with lower number of studies in considered field. For instance, one emerging stream is dedicated to the ethics in public administration, focusing on ethical working and behavior of public administration organizations (Bowman & Knox, 2008; Fiorino, 2010; Jelovac et al., 2011; Kovac, 2013; Nedelko & Potocan, 2013). In frame of "non-profit sector", the integration of sustainability into higher education organizations is occurring at an accelerated pace. This is confirmed with plethora of studies about sustainability or SR in higher education (Newman et al., 2004; McNamara, 2010; Gosselin et al., 2013; Figueiró & Raufflet, 2015; Hoover & Harder, 2015).

Various studies in this field emphasized several ways to enhance the SR of higher education institutions. Very commonly are addressed changes in curricula, where the focus in on implementing sustainability and SR principles into the curriculum (Figueiró & Raufflet, 2015) in order to have an impact on rising students' level of SR – i.e. through their perception. For instance, Gosselin et al. (2013) reported, based on three case studies, that curricula were reformed in a way that enable students to learn about behavioral sciences, life sciences, Earth and atmospheric sciences, social sciences, etc., in order to broader their understanding of SR. Figueiró and Raufflet (2015) additionally reported that among 78 papers analyzed, dealing with management education, only 5 papers were dealing with green or sustainable campuses. Warwick (2016) emphasized vital role of students as change agents in the process of heightening SR level of higher education organizations, Wright and Wilton (2012) assigned increasing role to the management of educational institutions. Hoover and Harder (2015) reported about hidden complexity of organizational change for sustainability in higher education, emphasizing for instance, organizational culture, personal characteristics, individual knowledge, etc.. Another promising option to enhance sustainability of higher education is also development of stronger ties between higher education organizations and the community in order to become more socially responsible (Chambers & Gopaul, 2008).

Turning to the most important drivers of SR, in business literature are very frequently emphasized personal values, as an important driver of organizational as well as individual behavior regarding SR (Stern & Dietz, 1994; Karp, 1996; Schultz & Zelezny, 1999). Based on an overview of existing studies, a lot of evidences exist about the importance of personal values for shaping SR of business organizations (Kemmelmeier et al., 2002; Dietz et al., 2005), but on the other hand there is lack of studies clarifying the role of personal values in shaping SR of higher education organizations.

Among plethora of alternatives to enhance sustainability of higher education, the least attention is dedicated to the development of stronger ties between higher education organizations and the community. Turning to the role of stakeholders, the crucial role for increasing sustainability of higher education can be assigned to the various stakeholders of higher education – namely management of educational institutions, teachers, students and society.

Based on above findings about (1) increasing role of sustainability of higher education organizations with enhancing the links with the community, (2) the crucial role of various stakeholders and (3) the key role of personal values for shaping SR behavior, we want to highlight the role of personal values of various stakeholders – i.e. managers and teachers in higher education institutions, students and the values of local community, for improving sustainability of higher education. Values thus have an important role in improving community and social involvement of higher education. In that framework the key question is – which paper tries to answer – how fit (or dissonance) between values of a higher education institution (i.e. management and teachers), students and local community can influence improving sustainability of higher education organizations. The paper will address the issues and controversies in outlined area. Knowing actual state of personal values of various considered stakeholders may be helpful to identify – for instance gaps, fit, dissonance – between values of different groups, and provide a constructive starting point for further discussion.

Based on the above outlined starting points, the chapter has the following structure. First, in terms of background, we outline several selected starting points for understanding sustainability and SR and the role and importance of personal values as an important driver for shaping SR in organizations. Next section will be dedicated to the SR of educational organizations, with special focus on relations between higher education organizations and community. In the discussion we are addressing the role of personal values of various groups, which had been emphasized as one of the most important change agents toward sustainability of higher education institutions. In frame of practical implications we provide some suggestions how to capitalize on cognitions emphasized throughout the chapter. Final part of this chapter is dedicated to the future research directions, as well as some limitations of this paper.

LITERATURE REVIEW

In this section we first address selected cognitions for understanding sustainability and SR, followed by the role of personal values for shaping SR in organizations.

Sustainability and SR

The idea of sustainability can be found under different names and appearance forms in organizational practice, like CSR, SR, corporate sustainability (Baumgartner & Ebner, 2010). Sustainability is a holistic concept, with the central idea that none of the development goals of economic growth, social well-being and a wise use of natural resources, can be reached without considering and effecting the other two (Landrum & Edwards, 2009). John Elkington (2004) developed this notion into the 'triple bottom line' or 'Triple-P (People, Planet, Profit)' concept. Based on the core idea of sustainability, we can define it as striving for balance or harmony between economic sustainability, social sustainability and environmental sustainability.

In terms of sustainability, management in organizations faces a trade-off between pursuing economical, environmental, and societal goals (Agle et al., 1999; Vitell & Hidalgo, 2006; Godos-Diez et al., 2011). Due to the high importance of incorporation of sustainability principles in organizational practices, is in contemporary business environment main question related to the actual state or level of organizational sustainability as well as employee's perception of different sustainability aspects. Employee's perception of SR is important, since employee's at higher managerial positions in organizations importantly influence on organizational directions, thorough developing and implementing different strategies (Ajzen & Fishbein, 1980; Kreitner et al., 2002; Roccas et al., 2002; Smith et al., 2002; Mullins, 2006). For the purpose of this chapter we presuppose that employee's perceptions reflects relatively well in their behavior, since employees' behavior in organizations is driven by plethora of interrelated factors (e.g., stakeholder requirements, shareholders claims, economic conditions, organizational culture, personal values, perceptions, personal situation, etc.) (Hersey & Blanchard, 1977; Agle et al., 1999; Kreitner et al., 2002; Smith et al., 2002; Mullins, 2006).

Sustainability encompasses much more than just balancing profit with people and planet aspects, based on the concepts and standards of sustainability, developed through last decades. According to the findings of different authors a number of key elements or principles of sustainability can be derived, namely (Beckerman, 1994; Clayton & Radcliffe, 1996; Munda, 1997; Dunphy et al., 2000; Hitcock & Willard, 2009; Baumgartner & Ebner, 2010):

- Sustainability is about balancing or harmonizing the social environmental and economic interests. In order to contribute to sustainable development, a company should satisfy all 'three pillars' of sustainability: Social, Environmental and Economic;
- Sustainability is about both short and long term orientation. A sustainable company should consider long-term consequences of their actions, and not only focus on short-term gains;
- Sustainability is about local and global orientation. The increasing globalization of economies affects the geographical area that organizations influence. The behavior and actions of organizations therefore have an effect on economic, social and environmental aspects, both locally and globally; and
- Sustainability is about consuming income, not capital. Sustainability implies that the natural capital remains intact. This means that the extraction of renewable resources should not exceed the rate at which they are renewed, and the absorptive capacity of the environment to assimilate waste, should not be exceeded.

Sustainability is also about personal values and ethics. Sustainable development is inevitably normative concept, reflecting values and ethical considerations of the society. Thus, importance of societal values could reflect national policies; while employees also in their sustainable behavior in organizations. For instance, for those employees, for which the preservation of natural environment is highly important, will give more attention to this issues also in terms of their behavior in organization (Potocan et al., 2013). Part of the change needed for a more sustainable development, will therefore also be the implicit or explicit set of values that project management professionals, business leaders or consumers have and that influence or lead their behavior.

The concept of sustainability has often slightly different meaning to different people (e.g., authors in environmental management, general management, organizational behavior). Authors in management literature often refer to concept of sustainability in terms of social responsibility or CSR. For instance, Certo and Certo (2011) understand CSR as the managerial obligation to take actions that protects and improves both, the welfare of society as whole and the interests of organization. While Schermerhorn (2008) defines CSR as the obligation of organization to serve its own interests and those of society. Based on these examples of understanding CSR, by management authors, it is evident that social and environmental issues are often treated in frame of society, e.g. external organizational environment as a whole. While on the other hand, mainstream of the literature about the sustainability, always emphasize three interrelated underlying aspect of sustainability (Clayton & Radcliffe, 1996; Cancer & Mulej, 2009).

Reviewing the management literature on CSR can show the following evidence:

- With CSR enterprises try to balance the economic, environmental, and social goals of their business (Peet & Hartwick, 2009; Kira & van Eijnatten, 2011).
- CSR helps enterprises match requirements related to: efficiency, technical and commercial quality, flexibility, innovativeness, holism and wholeness of business (Mullins, 2006; Waddock & Bodwell, 2007).
- CSR authors originate their work from environmental paradigm (Dunlap & Van Liere, 1978; Dunlap & Mertig, 1990), and CSR paradigm (Elkington, 2004).
- CSR covers areas of: governance, management and organization, human rights, labor relations, natural environment, fair business practices, consumer issues, and relations to community (Elkington, 2004; Ralston et al., 2011).
- CSR requires values of: accountability, transparency, ethical behavior, respect for stakeholder interests, respect for the rule of law, respect for international norms of behavior, and respect for human rights (Kira & van Eijnatten, 2011).

An overview of acknowledged prior studies about different aspects of sustainability (Axelrod & Lehman, 1993; Stern, 2000; Schultz, 2001; Kemmelmeier et al., 2002) reveals that the majority of previous examinations as well as the measures taken by businesses, focus primarily on the environmental dimension of sustainability and therefore fail to acknowledge the holistic principle of sustainable development (Clayton & Radcliffe, 1996; Ketola, 2008). Several authors (Clayton & Radcliffe, 1996; Elkington, 2004; Potocan et al., 2013) argued, that the socio-cultural, environmental and economic realms are interdependent and the aim of a sustainably managed business should be the optimization of all three.

Personal Values as Drivers of Sustainability

Schwartz and Bilsky (1987) define personal value as concepts or beliefs, referring to desirable behaviours or end states, transcending specific situations. Values are conceptualized as important life goals or standards which serve as guiding principles in a person's life (Rokeach 1973; Schwartz 1994). Research studies about values in frame of management literature and organizational behavior are common, whereas most commonly are values considered based on Hofstede (2001), Schwartz (1992) and Rokeach (1973) cognitions about values. Various studies revealed that managerial and non-managerial staff values represent an important driver of employees behavior in organizations, reflection in their actions (Adler, 1983; Hambrick & Mason, 1984; House et al., 2004; Sosik, 2005; Pastor & Mayo, 2008).

Studies emphasize values as determinants of attitudes and behaviors (Munson & Posner, 1979; Ralston et al., 2014); they used for their consideration different social-psychological paradigms – like values-base theory (Stern & Dietz, 1994). There are many studies available, which consider selected pillars of sustainability, but mainly focusing on one or two out of three key underlying aspects of sustainability. Among studies, which are focusing on one aspect of sustainability, are in the forefront studies, which address natural dimension of sustainability (Karp, 1996; Schultz & Zelezny, 1999; Schultz, 2001; Dietz et al., 2005). Researching solely the economic or social aspect, in the context of sustainability, is rare. Considering the two-aspect studies, those dealing with both environmental and economic aspects of sustainability prevail (Munda, 1997), frequently discussing the justification of sustainability in terms of financial criteria, like return on investments, return on assets (Agle et al., 1999; Agle et al., 2006). Meanwhile, few studies research linkages between social and other aspects of sustainability or all aspects of sustainability (Ciegis et al., 2009; Udo & Jansson, 2009; Potocan et al., 2013).

Research studies in this field primarily confirm the impact of personal values on environmental issues. For instance, Axelrod and Lehman (1993); Dietz et al. (2005) recognized and defined a set of important factors influencing pro-environmental behavior. Meanwhile, Stern (2000) identified several important factors that influence behavior orientation. Schultz and Zelezny (1999) recognized personal values as an important source defining relationships with the environment. The mainstreams of surveys focus primarily on student populations (Schultz & Zelezny, 1999; Cordano et al., 2010), whereas other researchers have used nationwide random samples that have also included employees (Nordlund & Garvill, 2002).

In frame of our discussion about the role of personal values for sustainability of higher education, we are building it on cognitions of Rokeach (1973) and Schwartz and Bilsky (1987). The Schwartz value survey (SVS) (Schwartz, 1992; Schwartz, 2008) includes 56 single values which represent a foundation for building individual and societal level dimensions of values. Based on researching the importance of 56 values in 67 countries, Schwartz proposed a universal structure of personal values valid across cultures. Using 56 single values, ten individual level sub dimensions (motivational types) of values – i.e. groups of values – are created, which are further categorized into two bi-polar high order dimensions, namely openness to change vs. conservation and self-transcendence vs. self-enhancement. Besides those four high order dimensions, another two dimensions, individualism and collectivism, form individualism vs. collectivism dimension.

Based on above starting points about sustainability and sustainability in higher education is an important question – how to achieve higher level of SR of higher education institutions and what is the role of personal values? Literature and organizational practice offers plethora of options to increase sustainability of higher education institutions. One among under-considered alternative in literature and practice is also related to the associations between higher education institutions and community. In line with aims of this chapter, we are next outlining an overview of existing research on higher education social and community involvement.

Higher Education and Social and Community Involvement

It is clearly evident that at the core of higher education institutions are the production, transfer and preservation of knowledge, which is well aligned with the idea of SR and doing good for the society as a whole. However, research suggests that higher education institutions should aim at developing stronger ties with the community by becoming socially responsible (Chambers & Gopaul, 2008). Bringle and Hatcher (1996) pointed out, that "universities have valuable resources that become accessible to the community, while they also have a tradition of serving their communities by strengthening the economic development of the region, addressing educational and health needs of the community, and contributing to the cultural life of the community". Although the idea of community involvement in higher education isn't new, and dates back to the beginning of the 20th century, it is only in the past two decades that the concept has been gaining attention of researchers and academics (Niemi et al., 2000). In that context, community involvement in higher education encompasses: (1) service learning, (2) community-based learning and (3) cross-sectional partnerships (Cadwallader et al., 2013).

Service learning has been defined as "course-based, credit bearing educational experience in which students: (a) participate in an organized service activity that meets identified community needs, (b) reflect on the service activity in such a way as to gain further understanding of course content, a broader appreciation of the discipline and an enhanced sense of civic responsibility" (Bringle & Hatcher, 1996). Similarly, Jerome (2012, p. 60) defined service learning as "an experimental approach to education that involves students in meaningful, real-world activities that can advance social, emotional, career and academic curricula goals while benefiting communities". Research on service-based learning and its impact on the community has mostly been qualitative in nature, and therefore had limited possibilities for producing generalizable results (Henderson et al., 2007). It is only recently that the research began focusing on quantitative studies (Birdwell et al., 2013), aimed at evaluating various outcomes and potential influencing factors. In terms of the outcomes of service-learning activities, two main groups of outcomes have typically been considered, namely: (1) knowledge (i.e. changes in knowledge, and gain of civic skills) and (2) attitudes (i.e. attitude change and dispositions towards public service and civic responsibility). The influencing factors essentially act as moderators of the relationship between service learning and the previously identified groups of outcomes, and may include the educational framework, parental interest, amount of service time, work arrangements, along with social factors such as age or gender (Niemi et al., 2000). Although this study has confirmed existence of a positive link between service learning and learning outcomes, the implementation of service learning has been proven to be a daunting task.

Service learning is a relatively new teaching method in business education, and faculty members are not quite familiar with both the approach and its possible educational outcomes (Seider et al., 2011). Although the method has had good results, it has been found that business students especially are less positive about college courses that incorporate service learning components into the curriculum. Possible reasons that business schools have not adopted this method more widely include the following: (1) students perceive service learning as less attractive than other teaching methods (e.g. case analyses); (2) students prefer courses that develop specific applied skills as well as interaction with industry representatives, (3) students find this method time-consuming because of its requirement that they complete 10–20 hours of volunteer work not directly related to business or marketing; (4) students may not see the relevance of the service learning component, which requires individual reflection and journaling of the learning experience, to their education and (5) faculty tend to choose the path of least resistance given that there is high risk (student rejection or dislike) and little or no reward in terms of promotion and tenure (Cadwallader et al., 2013). To address some of these issues, the authors suggest a „hybrid" model they call community-based learning which embraces the core concepts of service learning, but removes the volunteer work and service-learning reflection.

Finally, we address the importance of cross-sectional partnerships for social and community involvement in higher education. Universities and colleges have increasingly been investing in partnerships with the local communities, as well as by wider society, e.g. by addressing major social problems (Maurrasse, 2002; Murray, 2009). With the community's increasing emphasis on outcomes, evaluation becomes critical to any burgeoning social movement that depends upon external support. The higher education-community partnerships movement is in its early stages despite the deep historical roots of the teaching, research, and service. As suggested by some authors, this movement is highly urban in character and far more centralized than the multiple independently driven efforts of some higher education institutions (Maurrasse, 2002). To be able to evaluate the quality and benefits of community- higher education partnerships, we also draw on the literature in relationship marketing that addresses cooperation (also referred to in the literature as working partnerships) which refers to situations in which parties work together to achieve mutual goals (Anderson & Narus, 1990). In their definition of cooperation, Anderson and Narus (1990) see coordination as a related construct and consider it an integral part of cooperation. In addition, Mohr and Spekman (1994) argue that without coordination, cooperation and planned mutual goals cannot be met. In terms of its measurement, cooperation has been operationalized as reflecting joint responsibilities, concern about the partners' profitability, reciprocity and dedication to mutual goals. See for example measurement scales developed by Cannon and Perreault (1999). We believe these contributions can be especially applicable to the context of community- higher education partnerships. As Maurrasse (2002) concludes, there is a clear tension between the interests of institutions of higher education and those of communities.

While meeting mutual goals and ensuring favorable outcomes on both ends of the community- higher education partnership, many are beginning to realize that institutions of higher education are beginning to gain more mileage out of community partnerships than are communities. Eilam and Trop (2013) reported similar findings when contrasting sustainability agendas, created by communities and educational institutions. These results reveal the potential pitfalls in community- higher education partnerships and relationships, as there is a significant lack of cooperation and coordination between the two partners. This in turn, has several important implications for higher education institutions which have to be considered in the future – from an organizational point of view, it may imply the need for decentralization of program and course curriculum to better fit the higher education and community agenda, but also considers the adaptation of existing teaching methods.

The existing research is mostly fragmented and does not provide an integrative framework for consideration of the previously described tools/approaches. In addition, it does not consider the entire system of relationships with antecedents and other factors influencing higher education involvement. More specifically, some of the core concepts remain under-researched, non-contingent, and overly theoretical with few empirical validations of models that incorporate social and community involvement in higher education. A detailed analysis of the several shortcomings of the existing state of research related to social and community involvement of higher education reveals several important gaps:

- The existing research, analyzing different forms of higher education SR, often exhibits following limitations:
  - Considering many dimensions of higher education social responsibility in parallel, which makes it impossible to operationalize research constructs, as to apply sophisticated quantitative and/or mixed methodology (see Pasque, 2010);
  - Adopting a non-contingent approach by considering individual tools/approaches (such as service learning, or community partnerships) only (see Baxter & Marshall, 2012; Kronick & Cunningham, 2013), instead of developing a comprehensive model of social and community involvement of higher education, that considers both relevant antecedents and outcomes;
  - Limited empirical validation of core concepts, interactions and relations that focuses mostly on qualitative studies at all levels of the educational system. For instance Khalifa (2012) using the ethnographic research methodology; Ishimaru (2013) analyses interviews, observations, and documents; Santamaría (2014), using the case study approach; or restricting its analysis to refer to a single higher education institution, by examination of 'best practices', or specific circumstances – see for instance Gaffikin and Morrissey (2008);
  - Excluding factors at the level of the educational system, or other relevant social factors, or, at least, analysing them on the level of individual practices only (see Moskal & Skokan, 2011; Borrero et al., 2012).
- Research related to improving effectiveness and social relevance of higher education often takes the route of modelling the organizational and/or strategic changes by following the prescriptions of the 'entrepreneurial university' model or other forms of ensuring efficient university-business

linkages (Etzkowitz et al., 2000; D'Este & Patel, 2007). It is believed that the future of universities should not be conceptualized in terms of 'commercialization' and/or 'corporatization' only. At the other hand, the potential of universities to create positive social effects by being socially responsible has been a significant subject of academic research for several decades (Bok, 1982). A framework should be developed, as to balance legitimate interests of higher education stakeholders in the wider society, which has proved to be a useful approach to improving performance of non-profit organizations (Herman & Renz, 1997; Sowa et al., 2004; Balser & McClusky, 2005).It is important to note that this classical approach to assuring effectiveness in the non-profit sector has not yet been applied to the non-profit/public institutions of higher education.

- Existing research does not address the interactions within the educational system and does not refer to a wide range of relevant social factors, in order to develop a systemic model of attaining socially responsible behaviour of higher education institutions, although such approaches have proved as beneficial in the practice of community outreach and engagement programs (Barnes et al., 2009).

On the basis of previous discussion, a conceptual model has been formulated (see Figure 1) that examines the antecedents and consequences of social and community involvement of higher education.

Based on the above model we can define the questions for future research by limiting the inquiry to the topic of higher education social and community involvement, although multiple dimensions of higher education social responsibility have been proposed by a comprehensive framework (Chambers & Gopaul, 2008). Those additional dimensions include: (1) community and social involvement of higher education, (2) epistemological dimension of social responsibility in higher education (as demonstrated by the responsibility for creation, dissemination and critical analysis of knowledge relevant for the society), (3) democratic dimension of social responsibility in higher education (demonstrated by responsibility

Figure 1. Structural elements and hypothesized relationships in the initial model of higher education community and social involvement

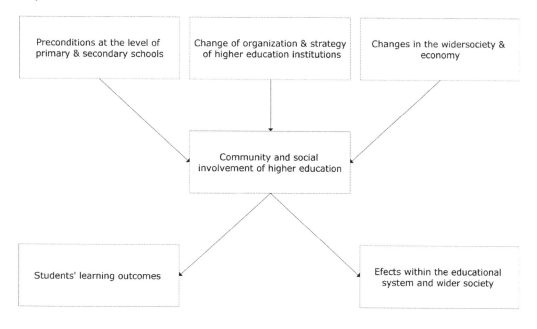

for achievement of democratic/civic values and behavior, securing access to knowledge and education to all relevant social stakeholders) and (4) systemic and organizational preconditions/changes, required for the implementations of previous dimensions.

Coverage of a single dimension ensures that the tangible outputs for the society could be created and serve as foundation for formulation of educational policy and institutional guidelines for socially responsible higher education. These are the community and social involvement of higher education, which will be associated with the analysis of the following systemic and institutional antecedents:

- Preconditions to be achieved by activities and changes at the level of primary and secondary schools,
- Organizational and strategic changes within the institutions of higher education, and
- Changes in the wider society and economy, representing the general trigger for changes of the educational system, its policies and institutions.

In frame of preconditions at the level of primary/secondary schools and the systemic approach we can outline following cognitions. School reform efforts over the last two decades have become increasingly more complex and systemic (Lasky, 2004). Primary „task" of schools is to educate students, in order to acquire knowledge, which should be accompanied by other characteristics, such as responsibility, social skills, empathy, involvement and willingness to contribute to society by planned programs which can provide skill building opportunities for students (Elias et al., 2007). Programs are limited because of insufficient coordination with other components of school operations (Greenberg et al., 2003) and environment. In order for students to use the opportunities provided, educational leaders can use evidence-based resources to help them integrate the development for social and emotional skills (Elias et al., 2007). Demands for coordinated communication and resource distribution across policy domains have increased (Lasky, 2004), which leads to the urgent need for systemic and institutional changes in order to provide better community and social involvement of primary and secondary education, as well as their cooperation with the institutions of higher education.

In primary and secondary education, one of major assumption for social and community involvement is school leaders' perceptions of the importance of school impact on community. It is common that school leaders are encouraged (by the policy makers) to plan, implement, operate and control a range of activities and services with purpose to improve or expand schools' relationships with pupils, families and communities (Peterson & Durrant, 2013). Problem arises when school leaders are „left alone" to deal with systematic changes to achieve better social and community involvement. Often they don't have enough knowledge nor opportunities to learn other than related to their own careers. Without knowledge they can't successfully create solutions to the problems of systemic reforms (Elmore, 2000). Therefore, one of starting points for the further application of SR in higher education is the systemic treatment of relationships among all levels of the educational system, leading to the sustainability of social and community involvement initiatives. This approach is supported by Shriberg (2002), who makes the same point. In this way, existing weaknesses in government policies and educational frameworks will be identified, since they include mostly theoretical (and partly practical) guidelines, but do not offer concrete measures or activities on an operational level.

DISCUSSION

Majority of the texts about sustainability and/or SR of higher education are focused on achieving higher levels of sustainability through curricula development (McDonald, 2004; Eisen & Barlett, 2006; Payne, 2006; Gosselin et al., 2013; Cebrián, 2016; Dmochowski et al., 2016), while there is a lack of focus on the "key stakeholders" that also have an important role in achieving higher level of higher education.

Overview of existing studies (Ceulemans et al., 2015; Figueiró & Raufflet, 2015; Hoover & Harder, 2015; Viegas et al., 2016) reveals that those studies do not focus on employees in higher education institutions, which also play an important role in increasing the level of SR. Another important group of stakeholders – managers, plays an important role in shaping sustainability of higher education. Also the students are not frequently addressed in the studies, even though that they are considered as an important change agent (Warwick, 2016), from the viewpoint of increasing sustainability of higher education institutions. Finally, also the role of community for fostering sustainability of higher education has not received much attention yet (Chambers & Gopaul, 2008).

In that frame personal values of different groups play an important role, while not much attention has been given to the role of values for shaping SR of higher education. For instance, manager's personal values are an important driver of their behavior and can importantly influence behavior and actions regarding sustainability issues in the process of higher education institution management. For instance, managers which consider values targeted toward improving natural and social environment, as very important, may support and focus on actions, which will have more impact on increasing sustainability, than managers, who do not consider outlined values as very important. These can be backed up with findings from business, which suggests that managers, higher importance of "pro-environmental" values is reflected in their actions, which are contribute to the improvement of the sustainability level.

Turning to the next group, we can argue that teachers should be dedicated and highly appreciate SR in order to transfer the core idea of sustainability through learning process and consultative work to the broader audience – i.e. students as well as organizations with which they work.

The role of students for fostering sustainability of higher education has been seldom addressed. For instance, Warwick (2016) emphasized change of students status, which have moved from being mere consumers of higher education to becoming partners in innovation process at higher education institutions. Thus, the academia has recognized the vital role of students as change agents. In that frame, students have unique insight into the current provision of sustainability education, as well as possessing collaborative capacity to invent new learning spaces. Based on these findings – and general under-consideration of students as change agents – there is a need for greater students engagement. In that framework, students personal values play an important role in fostering sustainability of higher education institutions, via active participation in this process.

Social and community involvement are connected with social responsibility, which is dually important: it is a matter of institutions and individuals and can be seen from both a personal and a structural perspective (Dunne & Edwards, 2010). „Improvement" of social and community involvement (among other) should be based on the idea of systemic school development, since schools are integrated, holistic organizations (Prew, 2009). Systemic change of an educational system and policies should be built on the system modeling approach, which focuses on systemic linkages to bring greater knowledge about how the education system works as a whole, and how policy, data, and resources move through the system (Lasky, 2004). In this way, systemic model is seen as a complement of programs and policies that can produce powerful reform by creating reinforcing and synergistic effects (Supovitz & Taylor, 2005).

The current social and academic trends are directed toward perceiving the role of university in the context of a shift from industry-government dyad in the industrial society to a university-industry-government relationship in the knowledge society (Etzkowitz et al., 2000). The potential for innovation and economic development is seen as dependent on universities and their "hybridization", as industry and government start to generate new institutional and social formats for the production, transfer and application of knowledge (Van Looy et al., 2011). William Todorovic et al. (2011) note that governments, industry and funding organizations encourage universities to become more entrepreneurial oriented through increasing the commercialization outcomes of publicly funded research. With less government funding, universities are forced to be more efficient and shift toward a greater commercialization of knowledge. But "this is a grooving concern for higher education's contribution to equity, community development and the public good" (Subotzky, 1999).

It has been clearly evident that the role of personal values of managers, teachers, students and local community in the process of fostering sustainability of higher education has been "under-examined" in the literature. This provides us fertile ground for discussion the role of personal values.

IMPLICATIONS AND RECOMMENDATIONS

Based on the discussion above we can outline several implications and recommendations. First, proposed implications in this paper could serve as an important starting point for management of higher education institutions, for developing future steps in terms of increasing SR. In that frame decisions could capitalize cognitions about the need to take into consideration importance of personal values of different stakeholder groups – like managers, teachers, students and the community, when deciding about future steps regarding sustainability. Accordingly, management in those organizations can build their decisions about future SR actions, based on current importance of values of employees in organization. A comprehensive insight into the state of personal values may offer them a good starting point to start working on achieving higher level of SR in higher education institutions.

Second, knowing the importance of most commonly examined personal values of organizational members, can be helpful for manages in the process of aligning individual and organizational values (Westerman & Cyr, 2004; Vigoda-Gadot & Meiri, 2008; Figueiró & Raufflet, 2015). Hoover and Harder (2015) emphasized that among factors, that influence achieving higher level of sustainability of higher education is at the first place organizational culture, which importantly influence on working in behavior in sustainable manner. With comprehensive research about actual state of values, a possible gap between individual's and organizational values can be identified. Based on the gap, the process of personal – organizational fit can be more holistically conduced. Additionally, based on the presumptions about the role of employees' values of higher education institutions, strategies can be formulated or re-thinked in order to achieve higher level of SR of those organizations. For instance, (McNamara, 2010) emphasized significant correlations between the change strategies and the level of progress achieved on sustainability initiatives. Another important consideration is related to the actual state of values of students' in order to become familiar with current state of values and have an opportunity to identify the gap between actual and desired/needed values, which will reflect SR behavior of students.

Third, emphasized cognitions about the role and importance of personal values of employees in higher education will be helpful to build more comprehensive background for understanding SR of higher education institution, by most influential group of employees – managers of those organizations. For instance, Wright and Wilton (2012) report based on in-depth-interviews with facilities management directors, that they were interested in their university becoming sustainable, and felt universities had a key role in sustainability in society, however not all interviewed managers had a clear idea of what sustainable development and sustainable universities are. For instance, manager's personal values importantly influence choice, design, and execution or performing of leadership style, by management (Barnard, 1938; Schampp, 1978; Egri & Herman, 2000; Sarros & Santora, 2001; Kovač et al., 2004; Pastor & Mayo, 2008; Fein et al., 2011; Nedelko & Mayrhofer, 2012; Cater et al., 2013; Lang et al., 2013). Based on these cognitions we can emphasize that personal values of managers' in higher education institutions will be associated with their behavior and actions in frame of their management process in higher education organizations. In that framework, importance of personal values for managers may have decisive role, when managers are deciding about future actions of higher education institutions regarding sustainability issues. For instance, if managers highly appreciate values that are associated with preservation of natural environment – like care for nature, his/her action will reflect this. For instance, several instances in which managers' values might play an important role are in cases when deciding about investments for reducing needed energy for heating, reducing usage of paper at the institution, implementing content about sustainability in curricula, etc.

Proposed implications in this paper could serve as an important starting point for management of higher education institutions, for developing future steps in terms of increasing SR. In that frame decisions could capitalize cognitions about importance of several selected personal values among employees in higher education institutions. Accordingly, management in those organizations can build their decisions about future SR actions, based on current importance of values of employees in organization or can try to implement programs for realigning the values of individual with desired values of higher education institutions, which will support higher levels of SR.

Values thus have an important role in improving community and social involvement of higher education. In that framework is of crucial importance – how fit (or dissonance) between values of higher education institution (i.e. management and teachers), students and local community can influence improving sustainability.

Based on better alignment of personal values of various stakeholder groups of higher education, many social benefits of socially responsible higher education could be stated, like improving the links between higher education and society, tighter collaboration between society and higher education, improved image of higher education in society. Looking from the perspective of the core mission of higher education – to preserve, transfer and preserve knowledge – the students' learning outcomes seem to be the most significant, as the primary mission of the universities revolves around development of human resources and societies. Learning outcomes can be described in terms of "particular knowledge, skill or behavior that a student is expected to exhibit after a period of study" (WorldBank, 2013). They represent a more realistic and a more genuine measure of the value of education than measures of teaching input (Maher, 2004). Measuring learning outcomes provides information on what particular knowledge, skill or behavior students have gained after instruction is completed. Learning objectives may take different forms, as they might include the academic knowledge, development of personal traits and civic outcomes, including "deep" understanding and implementation of social responsibility. At the fundamental level, students are expected to acquire the learning objectives related to critical thinking and examination of both academic concepts and their environment, as to ensure that, e.g. in case of economic education, they are not turned into "fach idiots - brilliant at esoteric mathematics yet innocent of actual economic life" (Arjo & Colander, 1990). At a "higher" level, the socially responsible higher education is supposed to assure that its participants are able to balance and reconcile different social views and interests, cope with the mounting uncertainties, interpretations of reality, etc. (Svanström et al., 2008, p. 343). It should be established whether the interplay of previously described factors and their mutual relationships leads to the development of relevant learning objectives, which include (Colby & Sullivan, 2009): (1) development of work ethics, (2) personal traits related to the personal and professional integrity, (3) recognizing and implementing contributions to local community and wider society, (4) respecting multiple perspectives and recognizing different interests in professional and social context(s), (5) development and using a complex ethical competence in „real life", based on the four previous dimensions and (6) developing values, which will support sustainability of entire community.

LIMITATIONS AND FUTURE RESEARCH DIRECTION

The main limitation is that this is a theoretical paper, which does not offer an insight into the state of personal values for most influential stakeholders in the process of fostering sustainability of higher education organizations. To empirically examine the role and importance of personal values of key stakeholders in higher education – namely managers, teachers, students and local community a survey instrument should be designed in order to acquire actual state of values of different stakeholders. Based on such research viewpoints of various stakeholder groups about sustainability will be highlighted and will present and important starting point for future actions about fostering links between higher education and society. Another limitation is focusing only on single factors that determine sustainability of organizations, despite several other influential factors have been recognized in practice and in the literature, like policies and strategies of organizations, personal characteristics of CEOs (Godos-Diez et al., 2011), environment in which organizations operate and institutional framework (Ejdys et al., 2016).

Further research of community and social involvement of higher education and the role of personal values of various stakeholder groups, should address following considerations: (1) what is the actual fit and/or dissonance between importance of personal values of various stakeholder groups? (2) how do the models of overall higher education development (such as the 'entrepreneurial university' model) influence the social and community involvement of higher education and their antecedents?; (3) how does social and community involvement of higher education influence the realization of relevant learning and social outcomes?

CONCLUSION

In the centre of this chapter is to examine the role of personal values for fostering sustainability of higher education institution. We addressed this gap in the literature by providing discussion about the role and importance of personal values for SR of higher education institutions, based on fostering links between higher education institutions and community. The topic addressed in this chapter highlights the role of personal values for enhancing sustainability of higher education organizations, via fostering ties between higher education organizations and community. In that frame, the chapter on theoretical level addresses the crucial role of various stakeholders and the key role of personal values for shaping SR behavior, by taking into consideration the role of personal values of various stakeholders – i.e. managers and teachers in higher education institutions, students and the values of local community, for improving sustainability of higher education. By analyzing the actual state of values of various groups of stakeholders, organizations in higher institution can better design their actions in order to foster sustainability in organizations. Certainly, our theoretical discussion still needs to be further developed in the way that actual state of personal values will be examined.

REFERENCES

Adler, N. J. (1983). A typology of management studies involving culture. *Journal of International Business Studies*, *14*(2), 29–47. doi:10.1057/palgrave.jibs.8490517

Agle, B. R., Mitchell, R. K., & Sonnenfeld, J. A. (1999). Who matters to ceos? An investigation of stakeholder attributes and salience, corporate performance, and ceo values. *Academy of Management Journal*, *42*(5), 507–525. doi:10.2307/256973

Agle, B. R., Nagarajan, N. J., Sonnenfeld, J. A., & Srinivasan, D. (2006). Does ceo charisma matter? An empirical analysis of the relationships among organizational performance, environmental uncertainty, and top management team perceptions of ceo charisma. *Academy of Management Journal*, *49*(1), 161–174. doi:10.5465/AMJ.2006.20785800

Ajzen, I., & Fishbein, M. (1980). *Understanding attitudes and predicting social behavior*. Englewood Cliffs, NJ: Prentice-Hall.

Anderson, J. C., & Narus, J. A. (1990). A model of distributor firm and manufacturer firm working partnerships. *Journal of Marketing*, *54*(1), 42–58. doi:10.2307/1252172

Arjo, K., & Colander, D. (1990). *The making of an economist*. Boulder, CO: Westview Press.

Axelrod, L. J., & Lehman, D. R. (1993). Responding to environmental concerns - what factors guide individual action. *Journal of Environmental Psychology*, *13*(2), 149–159. doi:10.1016/S0272-4944(05)80147-1

Balser, D., & McClusky, J. (2005). Managing stakeholder relationships and nonprofit organization effectiveness. *Nonprofit Management & Leadership*, *15*(3), 295–315. doi:10.1002/nml.70

Barnard, C. I. (1938). *Functions of the executive*. Cambridge, MA: Harvard University Press.

Barnes, J. V., Altimare, E. L., Farrell, P. A., Brown, R. E., Burnett, C. R. III, Gamble, L., & Davis, J. (2009). Creating and sustaining authentic partnerships with community in a systemic model. *Journal of Higher Education Outreach & Engagement*, 15.

Baumgartner, R. J., & Ebner, D. (2010). Corporate sustainability strategies: Sustainability profiles and maturity levels. *Sustainable Development*, *18*(2), 76–89. doi:10.1002/sd.447

Baxter, J. E., & Marshall, M. S. (2012). University students and local museums: Developing effective partnerships with oral history, partnerships. *A Journal of Service-Learning & Civic Engagement, 3*(2), 59-77.

Beckerman, W. (1994). Sustainable development - is it a useful concept. *Environmental Values*, *3*(3), 191–209. doi:10.3197/096327194776679700

Birdwell, J., Scott, R., & Horley, E. (2013). Active citizenship, education and service learning. *Education. Citizenship and Social Justice*, *8*(2), 185–199. doi:10.1177/1746197913483683

Blackburn, W. (2007). *The sustainability handbook: The complete management guide to achieving social, economic and environmental responsibility*. London: Earthscan Publications.

Bok, D. C. (1982). *Beyond the ivory tower: Social responsibilities of the modern university*. Boston: Harvard University Press.

Borrero, N., Conner, J., & Mejia, A. (2012). Promoting social justice through service-learning in urban teacher education: The role of student voice, partnerships. *A Journal of Service Learning & Civic Engagement, 3*(1), 1-24.

Bowman, J. S., & Knox, C. C. (2008). Ethics in government: No matter how long and dark the night. *Public Administration Review*, *68*(4), 627–639. doi:10.1111/j.1540-6210.2008.00903.x

Bringle, R. G., & Hatcher, J. A. (1996). Implementing service learning in higher education. *The Journal of Higher Education*, *67*(2), 221–239. doi:10.2307/2943981

Bullard, J. E. (1998). Raising awareness of local agenda 21: The use of internet resources. *Journal of Geography in Higher Education*, *22*(2), 201–210. doi:10.1080/03098269885903

Cadwallader, S., Atwong, C., & Lebard, A. (2013). Proposing community-based learning in the marketing curriculum. *Marketing Education Review*, *23*(2), 137–150. doi:10.2753/MER1052-8008230203

Cancer, V., & Mulej, M. (2009). The multi-criteria assessment of (corporate) social responsibility. In P. Doucek, G. Chroust, & V. Oskrdal (Eds.), *Idimt-2009: System and humans, a complex relationship* (Vol. 29, pp. 207–214). Linz, Austria: Universitatsverlag Rudolf Trauner.

Cannon, J. P., & Perreault, W. D. (1999). Buyer-seller relationships in business markets. *JMR, Journal of Marketing Research*, *36*(4), 439–460. doi:10.2307/3151999

Cater, T., Lang, R., & Szabo, E. (2013). Values and leadership expectations of future managers: Theoretical basis and methodological approach of the globe student project. *Journal for East European Management Studies*, *18*(4), 442–462.

Cebrián, G. (2016). The i3e model for embedding education for sustainability within higher education institutions. *Environmental Education Research*, 1–19. doi:10.1080/13504622.2016.1217395

Certo, S., & Certo, T. (2011). *Modern management concepts and skills*. New York: Prentice Hall.

Ceulemans, K., Molderez, I., & Van Liedekerke, L. (2015). Sustainability reporting in higher education: A comprehensive review of the recent literature and paths for further research. *Journal of Cleaner Production*, *106*, 127–143. doi:10.1016/j.jclepro.2014.09.052

Chambers, T., & Gopaul, B. (2008). Decoding the public good of higher education. *Journal of Higher Education Outreach & Engagement*, 34.

Ciegis, R., Ramanauskiene, J., & Martinkus, B. (2009). The concept of sustainable development and its use for sustainability scenarios. *Inzinerine Ekonomika-Engineering Economics*, (2), 28-37.

Cirnu, C. E., & Kuralt, B. (2013). The impact of employees' personal values on their attitudes toward sustainable development: Cases of slovenia and romania. *Management (Croatia)*, *18*(2), 1–20.

Clayton, T., & Radcliffe, N. (1996). *Sustainability: A systems approach*. London: Routledge.

Colby, A., & Sullivan, W. M. (2009). *Strenghtening of foundations of students' excellence, integrity, and social contribution*. Retrieved from http://www.aacu.org/liberaleducation/le-wi09/documents/LE-WI09_Strengthening.pdf

Cordano, M., Welcomer, S., Scherer, R., Pradenas, L., & Parada, V. (2010). Understanding cultural differences in the antecedents of pro-environmental behavior: A comparative analysis of business students in the united states and chile. *The Journal of Environmental Education*, *41*(4), 224–238. doi:10.1080/00958960903439997

Cordano, M., Welcomer, S., Scherer, R. F., Pradenas, L., & Parada, V. (2011). A cross-cultural assessment of three theories of pro-environmental behavior: A comparison between business students of chile and the united states. *Environment and Behavior*, *43*(5), 634–657. doi:10.1177/0013916510378528

DEste, P., & Patel, P. (2007). University–industry linkages in the uk: What are the factors underlying the variety of interactions with industry? *Research Policy*, *36*(9), 1295–1313. doi:10.1016/j.respol.2007.05.002

Dietz, T., Fitzgerald, A., & Shwom, R. (2005). Environmental values. *Annual Review of Environment and Resources*, *30*(1), 335–372. doi:10.1146/annurev.energy.30.050504.144444

Dmochowski, J. E., Garofalo, D., Fisher, S., Greene, A., & Gambogi, D. (2016). Integrating sustainability across the university curriculum. *International Journal of Sustainability in Higher Education*, *17*(5), 652–670. doi:10.1108/IJSHE-10-2014-0154

Dunlap, R., & Van Liere, K. (1978). The new environmental paradigm: A proposed measuring instrument and preliminary results. *The Journal of Environmental Education*, *9*(1), 10–19. doi:10.1080/00958964.1978.10801875

Dunlap, R. E., & Mertig, A. G. (1990). *American environmentalism: The u.S. Environmental movement, 1970-1990*. Washington, DC: Taylor & Francis.

Dunne, S., & Edwards, J. (2010). International schools as sites of social change. *Journal of Research in International Education*, *9*(1), 24–39. doi:10.1177/1475240909356716

Dunphy, D., Benveniste, J., Griffiths, A., & Sutton, P. (2000). *Sustainability: The corporate challenge of the 21st century*. Crows Nest, IN: Allen & Unwin.

Egri, C. P., & Herman, S. (2000). Leadership in the north american environmental sector: Values, leadership styles, and contexts of environmental leaders and their organizations. *Academy of Management Journal*, *43*(4), 571–604. doi:10.2307/1556356

Eilam, E., & Trop, T. (2013). Evaluating school-community participation in developing a local sustainability agenda. *International Journal of Environmental and Science Education*, *8*(2), 359–380. doi:10.12973/ijese.2013.201a

Eisen, A., & Barlett, P. (2006). The piedmont project: Fostering faculty development toward sustainability. *The Journal of Environmental Education*, *38*(1), 25–36. doi:10.3200/JOEE.38.1.25-36

Ejdys, J., Matuszak-Flejszman, A., Szymanski, M., Ustinovichius, L., Shevchenko, G., & Lulewicz-Sas, A. (2016). Crucial factors for improving the iso 14001 environmental management system. *Journal of Business Economics and Management*, *17*(1), 52–73. doi:10.3846/16111699.2015.1065905

Elias, M. J., Patrikakou, E. N., & Weissberg, R. P. (2007). A competence-based framework for parent—school—community partnerships in secondary schools. *School Psychology International*, *28*(5), 540–554. doi:10.1177/0143034307085657

Elkington, J. (2004). Enter the triple bottom line. In A. Henriques & J. Richardson (Eds.), *The triple bottom line: Does it all add up* (pp. 1–16). London: Earthscan.

Elmore, R. F. (2000). *Building a new structure for school leadership*. Washington, DC: Albert Shanker Institute.

Etzkowitz, H., Webster, A., Gebhardt, C., & Terra, B. R. C. (2000). The future of the university and the university of the future: Evolution of ivory tower to entrepreneurial paradigm. *Research Policy*, *29*(2), 313–330. doi:10.1016/S0048-7333(99)00069-4

Fein, E. C., Vasiliu, C., & Tziner, A. (2011). Individual values and preferred leadership behaviors: A study of romanian managers. *Journal of Applied Social Psychology*, *41*(3), 515–535. doi:10.1111/j.1559-1816.2011.00724.x

Figueiró, P. S., & Raufflet, E. (2015). Sustainability in higher education: A systematic review with focus on management education. *Journal of Cleaner Production*, *106*, 22–33. doi:10.1016/j.jclepro.2015.04.118

Fiorino, D. J. (2010). Sustainability as a conceptual focus for public administration. *Public Administration Review*, *70*, S78–S88. doi:10.1111/j.1540-6210.2010.02249.x

Foote, J., Gaffney, N., & Evans, J. R. (2010). Corporate social responsibility: Implications for performance excellence. *Total Quality Management & Business Excellence*, *21*(8), 799–812. doi:10.1080/14783363.2010.487660

Gaffikin, F., & Morrissey, M. (2008). A new synergy for universities. *Education. Citizenship and Social Justice, 3*(1), 97–116. doi:10.1177/1746197907086721

Godos-Diez, J. L., Fernandez-Gago, R., & Martinez-Campillo, A. (2011). How important are ceos to csr practices? An analysis of the mediating effect of the perceived role of ethics and social responsibility. *Journal of Business Ethics, 98*(4), 531–548. doi:10.1007/s10551-010-0609-8

Gosselin, D., Parnell, R., Smith-Sebasto, N. J., & Vincent, S. (2013). Integration of sustainability in higher education: Three case studies of curricular implementation. *Journal of Environmental Studies and Sciences, 3*(3), 316–330. doi:10.1007/s13412-013-0130-3

Greenberg, M. T., Weissberg, R. P., OBrien, M. U., Zins, J. E., Fredericks, L., Resnik, H., & Elias, M. J. (2003). Enhancing school-based prevention and youth development through coordinated social, emotional, and academic learning. *The American Psychologist, 58*(6-7), 466–474. doi:10.1037/0003-066X.58.6-7.466 PMID:12971193

Hambrick, D. C., & Mason, P. A. (1984). Upper echelons - the organization as a reflection of its top managers. *Academy of Management Review, 9*(2), 193–206.

Henderson, A., Brown, S. D., Pancer, S. M., & Ellis-Hale, K. (2007). Mandated community service in high school and subsequent civic engagement: The case of the double cohort in ontario, canada. *Journal of Youth and Adolescence, 36*(7), 849–860. doi:10.1007/s10964-007-9207-1

Herman, R. D., & Renz, D. O. (1997). Multiple constituencies and the social construction of non-profit organization effectiveness. *Nonprofit and Voluntary Sector Quarterly, 26*(2), 185–206. doi:10.1177/0899764097262006

Hersey, P., & Blanchard, K. H. (1977). *The management of organizational behavior.* Englewood Cliffs, NJ: Prentice Hall.

Hitcock, D., & Willard, M. (2009). *The business guide to sustainability – practical strategies and tools for organizations.* London: Earthscan.

Hofstede, G. (2001). *Culture's consequences. Comparing values, behaviors, institutions, and organizations across nations.* Thousand Oaks, CA: SAGE.

Hoover, E., & Harder, M. K. (2015). What lies beneath the surface? The hidden complexities of organizational change for sustainability in higher education. *Journal of Cleaner Production, 106*, 175–188. doi:10.1016/j.jclepro.2014.01.081

House, R. J., Hanges, P. J., Javidan, M., Dorfman, P. W., & Gupta, V. (2004). *Culture, leadership, and organizations: The globe study of 62 societies.* Thousand Oaks, CA: Sage.

Ishimaru, A. (2013). From heroes to organizers. *Educational Administration Quarterly, 49*(1), 3–51. doi:10.1177/0013161X12448250

Jelovac, D., Van Der Wal, Z., & Jelovac, A. (2011). Business and government ethics in the new and old eu: An empirical account of public-private value congruence in slovenia and the netherlands. *Journal of Business Ethics, 103*(1), 127–141. doi:10.1007/s10551-011-0846-5

Jerome, L. (2012). Service learning and active citizenship education in england. *Education. Citizenship and Social Justice, 7*(1), 59–70. doi:10.1177/1746197911432594

Karp, D. G. (1996). Values and their effect on pro-environmental behavior. *Environment and Behavior, 28*(1), 111–133. doi:10.1177/0013916596281006

Kemmelmeier, M., Krol, G., & Kim, Y. H. (2002). Values, economics, and proenvironmental attitudes in 22 societies. *Cross-Cultural Research, 36*(3), 256–285. doi:10.1177/10697102036003004

Ketola, T. (2008). A holistic corporate responsibility model: Integrating values, discourses and actions. *Journal of Business Ethics, 80*(3), 419–435. doi:10.1007/s10551-007-9428-y

Khalifa, M. (2012). A re-new-ed paradigm in successful urban school leadership. *Educational Administration Quarterly, 48*(3), 424–467. doi:10.1177/0013161X11432922

Kira, M., & van Eijnatten, F. M. (2011). Socially sustainable work organizations: Conceptual contributions and worldviews. *Systems Research and Behavioral Science, 28*(4), 418–421. doi:10.1002/sres.1083

Kovač, J., Mayer, J., & Jesenko, M. (2004). *Stili in značilnosti uspešnega vodenja*. Kranj: Moderna organizacija.

Kovac, P. (2013). Ethics of officials in the context of (slovene) good administration. *NISPAcee Journal of Public Administration and Policy, 5*(1), 23–53.

Kreitner, R., Kinicki, A., & Buelens, M. (2002). *Organizational behavior*. Berkshire, UK: McGraw-Hill.

Kronick, R. F., & Cunningham, R. B. (2013). Service-learning: Some academic and community recommendations. *Journal of Higher Education Outreach & Engagement, 14*.

Landrum, N. E., & Edwards, S. (2009). *Sustainable business: An executive's primer*. New York, NY: Business Expert Press. doi:10.4128/9781606490495

Lang, R., Szabo, E., Catana, G. A., Konecna, Z., & Skalova, P. (2013). Beyond participation? - leadership ideals of future managers from central and east european countries. *Journal for East European Management Studies, 18*(4), 482–511.

Lasky, S. G. (2004). *Toward a policy framework for analyzing educational system effects*. Retrieved from http://www.csos.jhu.edu/crespar/techReports/Report71.pdf

Maher, A. (2004). Learning outcomes in higher education: Implications for curriculum design and student learning. *Journal of Hospitality, Leisure, Sport and Tourism Education, 3*(2), 46–54. doi:10.3794/johlste.32.78

Maurrasse, D. J. (2002). Higher education-community partnerships: Assessing progress in the field. *Nonprofit and Voluntary Sector Quarterly, 31*(1), 131–139. doi:10.1177/0899764002311006

McDonald, G. M. (2004). A case example: Integrating ethics into the academic business curriculum. *Journal of Business Ethics, 54*(4), 371–384. doi:10.1007/s10551-004-1826-9

McNamara, K. H. (2010). Fostering sustainability in higher education: A mixed-methods study of transformative leadership and change strategies. *Environmental Practice, 12*(1), 48–58. doi:10.1017/S1466046609990445

Mohr, J., & Spekman, R. (1994). Characteristics of partnership success: Partnership attributes, communication behavior, and conflict resolution techniques. *Strategic Management Journal, 15*(2), 135–152. doi:10.1002/smj.4250150205

Moskal, B. M., & Skokan, C. K. (2011). Supporting the k-12 classroom through university outreach. *Journal of Higher Education Outreach & Engagement*, 23.

Mullins, L. J. (2006). *Essentials of organisational behavior*. Harlow, UK: Prentice Hall.

Munda, G. (1997). Environmental economics, ecological economics, and the concept of sustainable development. *Environmental Values, 6*(2), 213–233. doi:10.3197/096327197776679158

Munson, J. M., & Posner, B. Z. (1979). Values of engineers and managing engineers. *IEEE Transactions on Engineering Management, 26*(4), 94–100. doi:10.1109/TEM.1979.6447357

Murray, J. (2009). The wider social benefits of higher education: What do we know about them? *Australian Journal of Education, 53*(3), 230–244. doi:10.1177/000494410905300303

Nedelko, Z., & Mayrhofer, W. (2012). *The influence of managerial personal values on leadership style. Management re-imagined*. Paper presented at the 11th World Congress of the International Federation of Scholarly Associations of Management, Limerick, Ireland.

Nedelko, Z., & Potocan, V. (2013). Ethics in public administration: Evidence from slovenia. *Transylvanian Review of Administrative Sciences*, 88-108.

Newman, F., Couturier, L., & Scurry, J. (2004). *The future of higher education*. San Francisco: Jossey-Bass.

Niemi, R. G., Hepburn, M. A., & Chapman, C. (2000). Community service by high school students: A cure for civic ills? *Political Behavior, 22*(1), 45–69. doi:10.1023/A:1006690417623

Nordlund, A. M., & Garvill, J. (2002). Value structures behind proenvironmental behavior. *Environment and Behavior, 34*(6), 740–756. doi:10.1177/001391602237244

Pasque, P. A. (2010). *American higher education, leadership and policy: Critical issues and the public good*. New York: Palgrave Macmillan. doi:10.1057/9780230107755

Pastor, J. C., & Mayo, M. (2008). Transformational leadership among spanish upper echelons: The role of managerial values and goal orientation. *Leadership and Organization Development Journal, 29*(4), 340–358. doi:10.1108/01437730810876140

Payne, P. G. (2006). Environmental education and curriculum theory. *The Journal of Environmental Education, 37*(2), 25–35. doi:10.3200/JOEE.37.2.25-35

Peet, R., & Hartwick, E. (2009). *Theories of development: Contentions, arguments, alternatives*. New York, NY: Guilford Press.

Peterson, A., & Durrant, I. (2013). School leaders perceptions of the impact of extended services on families and communities. *Educational Management Administration & Leadership*, *41*(6), 718–735. doi:10.1177/1741143213494190

Potocan, V., Mulej, M., & Nedelko, Z. (2013). The influence of employees ethical behavior on enterprises social responsibility. *Systemic Practice and Action Research*, *26*(6), 497–511. doi:10.1007/s11213-013-9299-3

Prew, M. (2009). Community involvement in school development. *Educational Management Administration & Leadership*, *37*(6), 824–846. doi:10.1177/1741143209345562

Ralston, D., Egri, C., Furrer, O., Kuo, M.-H., Li, Y., Wangenheim, F., & Weber, M. et al. (2014). Societal-level versus individual-level predictions of ethical behavior: A 48-society study of collectivism and individualism. *Journal of Business Ethics*, *122*(2), 283–306.

Ralston, D. A., Egri, C. P., Reynaud, E., Srinivasan, N., Furrer, O., Brock, D., & Wallace, A. et al. (2011). A twenty-first century assessment of values across the global workforce. *Journal of Business Ethics*, *104*(1), 1–31. doi:10.1007/s10551-011-0835-8

Roccas, S., Sagiv, L., Schwartz, S. H., & Knafo, A. (2002). The big five personality factors and personal values. *Personality and Social Psychology Bulletin*, *28*(6), 789–801. doi:10.1177/0146167202289008

Rokeach, M. (1973). *The nature of human values*. New York: The Free Press.

Santamaría, L. J. (2014). Critical change for the greater good. *Educational Administration Quarterly*, *50*(3), 347–391. doi:10.1177/0013161X13505287

Sarros, J. C., & Santora, J. C. (2001). Leaders and values: A cross-cultural study. *Leadership and Organization Development Journal*, *22*(5), 243–248. doi:10.1108/01437730110397310

Schampp, D. (1978). *A cross-cultural study of multinational companies*. New York: Praeger.

Schermerhorn, J. R. (2008). *Management*. John Wiley & Sons.

Schultz, P. W. (2001). The structure of environmental concern: Concern for self, other people, and the biosphere. *Journal of Environmental Psychology*, *21*(4), 327–339. doi:10.1006/jevp.2001.0227

Schultz, P. W., & Zelezny, L. (1999). Values as predictors of environmental attitudes: Evidence for consistency across 14 countries. *Journal of Environmental Psychology*, *19*(3), 255–265. doi:10.1006/jevp.1999.0129

Schwartz, S. (2008). Personal values and socially significant behavior. *International Journal of Psychology*, *43*(3-4), 168–168.

Schwartz, S. H. (1992). Universals in the content and structure of values - theoretical advances and empirical tests in 20 countries. *Advances in Experimental Social Psychology*, *25*, 1–65. doi:10.1016/S0065-2601(08)60281-6

Schwartz, S. H., & Bilsky, W. (1987). Toward a universal psychological structure of human-values. *Journal of Personality and Social Psychology*, *53*(3), 550–562. doi:10.1037/0022-3514.53.3.550

Seider, S. C., Rabinowicz, S. A., & Gillmor, S. C. (2011). The impact of philosophy and theology service-learning experiences upon the public service motivation of participating college students. *The Journal of Higher Education, 82*(5), 597–628. doi:10.1353/jhe.2011.0031

Shriberg, M. (2002). Institutional assessment tools for sustainability in higher education. *International Journal of Sustainability in Higher Education, 3*(3), 254–270. doi:10.1108/14676370210434714

Smith, P. B., Peterson, M. F., & Schwartz, S. H. (2002). Cultural values, sources of guidance, and their relevance to managerial behavior: A 47-nation study. *Journal of Cross-Cultural Psychology, 33*(2), 188–208. doi:10.1177/0022022102033002005

Sosik, J. J. (2005). The role of personal values in the charismatic leadership of corporate managers: A model and preliminary field study. *The Leadership Quarterly, 16*(2), 221–244. doi:10.1016/j.leaqua.2005.01.002

Sowa, J. E., Selden, S. C., & Sandfort, J. R. (2004). No longer unmeasurable? A multidimensional integrated model of nonprofit organizational effectiveness. *Nonprofit and Voluntary Sector Quarterly, 33*(4), 711–728. doi:10.1177/0899764004269146

Stern, P. C. (2000). Toward a coherent theory of environmentally significant behavior. *The Journal of Social Issues, 56*(3), 407–424. doi:10.1111/0022-4537.00175

Stern, P. C., & Dietz, T. (1994). The value basis of environmental concern. *The Journal of Social Issues, 50*(3), 65–84. doi:10.1111/j.1540-4560.1994.tb02420.x

Subotzky, G. (1999). Alternatives to the entrepreneurial university: New modes of knowledge production in community service programs. *Higher Education, 38*(4), 401–440. doi:10.1023/A:1003714528033

Supovitz, J. A., & Taylor, B. S. (2005). Systemic education evaluation. *The American Journal of Evaluation, 26*(2), 204–230. doi:10.1177/1098214005276286

Svanström, M., Lozano-García, F. J., & Rowe, D. (2008). Learning outcomes for sustainable development in higher education. *International Journal of Sustainability in Higher Education, 9*(3), 339–351. doi:10.1108/14676370810885925

Udo, V. E., & Jansson, P. M. (2009). Bridging the gaps for global sustainable development: A quantitative analysis. *Journal of Environmental Management, 90*(12), 3700–3707. doi:10.1016/j.jenvman.2008.12.020 PMID:19500899

Van Looy, B., Landoni, P., Callaert, J., van Pottelsberghe, B., Sapsalis, E., & Debackere, K. (2011). Entrepreneurial effectiveness of european universities: An empirical assessment of antecedents and trade-offs. *Research Policy, 40*(4), 553–564. doi:10.1016/j.respol.2011.02.001

Viegas, C. V., Bond, A. J., Vaz, C. R., Borchardt, M., Pereira, G. M., Selig, P. M., & Varvakis, G. (2016). Critical attributes of sustainability in higher education: A categorisation from literature review. *Journal of Cleaner Production, 126*, 260–276. doi:10.1016/j.jclepro.2016.02.106

Vigoda-Gadot, E., & Meiri, S. (2008). New public management values and person-organization fit: A socio-psychological approach and empirical examination among public sector personnel. *Public Administration, 86*(1), 111–131. doi:10.1111/j.1467-9299.2007.00703.x

Vitell, S. J., & Hidalgo, E. R. (2006). The impact of corporate ethical values and enforcement of ethical codes on the perceived importance of ethics in business: A comparison of us and spanish managers. *Journal of Business Ethics, 64*(1), 31–43. doi:10.1007/s10551-005-4664-5

Waddock, S., & Bodwell, C. (2007). *Total responsibility management.* Sheffield, UK: Greenleaf Publishing.

Warwick, P. (2016). An integrated leadership model for leading education for sustainability in higher education and the vital role of students as change agents. *Management in Education, 30*(3), 105–111. doi:10.1177/0892020616653463

Westerman, J. W., & Cyr, L. A. (2004). An integrative analysis of person-organization fit theories. *International Journal of Selection and Assessment, 12*(3), 252–261. doi:10.1111/j.0965-075X.2004.279_1.x

William Todorovic, Z., McNaughton, R. B., & Guild, P. (2011). Entre-u: An entrepreneurial orientation scale for universities. *Technovation, 31*(2–3), 128–137. doi:10.1016/j.technovation.2010.10.009

WorldBank. (2013). *Learning outcomes.* Retrieved 15. September 2013, Retrieved from http://go.worldbank.org/GOBJ17VV90

Wright, T. S. A., & Wilton, H. (2012). Facilities management directors conceptualizations of sustainability in higher education. *Journal of Cleaner Production, 31*, 118–125. doi:10.1016/j.jclepro.2012.02.030

KEY TERMS AND DEFINITIONS

Community Involvement: Refers to the links between higher education organizations and community. Higher education institutions have valuable resources that become accessible to the community, while they also have a tradition of serving their communities by strengthening the economic development of the region, addressing educational and health needs of the community, and contributing to the cultural life of the community.

Higher Education Institutions: The core mission of higher education institutions is to create, transfer and preserve knowledge in society.

Personal Values: Are defined as concepts or beliefs, referring to desirable behaviors or end states, transcend specific situations. Values are conceptualized as important life goals or standards which serve as guiding principles in a person's life.

Social Concern: Are actions aimed to actively contribute to the solving society problems and enhancement of the community welfare.

Social Responsibility: About the balance and trade-off between achieving economic, natural and societal aims of an organization.

Sustainability: About the balance or harmony between economic sustainability, social sustainability and environmental sustainability.

Section 3

Chapter 8

Corporate Social Responsibility Values of Managers in Transforming Societies

Rainhart Lang
Chemnitz University of Technology, Germany

Irma Rybnikova
Chemnitz University of Technology, Germany

ABSTRACT

Within the GLOBE project, CEOs from companies in East Germany, Estonia and Romania (N=129) have been interviewed about their value preferences in case of critical management decisions. Furthermore, lower level managers and employees (N=787) filled out questionnaires concerning perceived value preferences of their companies. Drawing on an extended stakeholder approach through focus on managerial values (CSV) and the person-situation concept of Mischel (1973), we particularly focus on country-based contingencies of managerial values coupled with other context factors like managerial position and ownership. The findings show that there are specific country-based combinations of corporate social values in the companies studied, with strategic orientation in East Germany, shareholder focus coupled with a relatively strong religious orientation in Romania and an orientation on shareholders as well as on employees and community in Estonia. Moreover, an interaction between the country effect and organizational factors shaping managerial decisions can be observed.

INTRODUCTION

The term "Corporate Social Responsibility" (CSR) refers to the responsibility vis-à-vis stakeholders as well as the environment of the company (Matten & Moon, 2005; McWilliams & Siegel, 2001). The literature distinguishes between explicit CSR, addressed in the corporate policy, and implicit CSR, namely values, standards and regulations established in the company (Matten & Moon, 2005). The discussion regarding implicit CSR particularly points to the significance of strategic management decisions and the associated individual values of managers, the so called „managerial CSR values" (e.g. Wood, 1991;

DOI: 10.4018/978-1-5225-2480-9.ch008

Waldman et al., 2006). Values, considered as "general beliefs about desirable or undesirable ways of behaving" (Feather, 1994) can be assumed to shape not only individual behaviour but also decisions in organizations. Accordingly, the main research on values focuses either on the individual level of values and their expressions (e.g. Rokeach, 1973; Feather, 1975; Schwartz, 1994) or on conceptualizing values of organizations, e.g. shown by value dimensions of Schein (1992), 'competing values framework' developed by Cameron and Quinn (1999) or Hofstede, Neuijen, Ohayv, & Sanders (1990) six dimensions of organizational practises. Both theoretical concepts are in most cases multidimensional, suggesting the complexity of the value-based landscape. However, the value dimensions referred to and measured are, in their substance, mainly universal(istic), context-free and abstracting from specific organizational issues, such as individualism vs. collectivism dimension (Hofstede et al., 1990). Contrary to those concepts, this article deals with individual values referring to organizational issues, namely individual beliefs about right corporate decisions orientation. We refer to this concept as corporate social responsibility values. Our conceptual approach is based on the assumption that a strong link exist between individual values of corporate managers and practices of corporate social responsibility as observed in companies under consideration. By assuming this relationship, we, first, draw upon the upper echelons theory which states that top managers exert a substantive influence on decisions and practices occurring in organisations (e.g. Hambrick, 2007). According to the upper echelons theory, individual experience, preferences and values of top managers are engraved in any strategic decisions of organizations. Second, empirical basis of our framework is provided by several recent studies which confirm that individual values of managers and corporate social responsibility practices in organizations are strongly linked. For example, Chin and colleagues demonstrate in their study that CEO's political beliefs and ideology has an impact on corporate social responsibility practices of their firms (Chin, Hambrick, & Treviño, 2013). Drawing on these conceptual and empirical considerations, we assume that managerial values represent an important issue of the corporate social responsibility debate in post-socialist contexts too.

From their theoretical conception, individual values can be distinguished in explicit and implicit values, like CSR mentioned above. Whereas implicit values are considered as longstanding preferences and as part of the firm-based or individual beliefs, explicit values are commonly regarded as those articulated by actors if asked for (e.g. Feather, 1994). On the other side, researchers differentiate between real, or lived values, which are expressed in daily action, and espoused values, which are publicly demonstrated and therefore connected with legitimating of actions (Kabanoff & Holt, 1996). Certainly, a clear-cut distinction between implicit and explicit or real and espoused values cannot be made; with the concept of individual implicit CSR values of managers we refer especially to implicit and, thus, rather real values.

The questions of CSR as well as CSR values in Central and East European transformation countries have been addressed only in a few contributions so far. Moreover, the scarce contributions are highly inconsistent. Some authors assume a distinctive short-term economic orientation of the companies, also termed as "East European Capitalism"(Stark, 1996; Grabher & Stark, 1997). Privatized or newly established firms in Central and East European countries have been described as following a short-term economic orientation with a strong focus on shareholders' interests ("Manchester Capitalism"). Contrary to this, other studies have underlined the tendency towards an orientation of managers in transforming societies to common welfare issues and social responsible practices (Pohlmann & Gergs, 1996; Pistrui, Welsch, Pohl, Wintermantel, & Liao, 2003; Koleva, Rodet-Kroichivili, David, & Marasova, 2010). However, empirical evidence from East European transformation countries is still scarce. In contrast to corporate social responsibility practices in companies of Central and Eastern Europe which have been addressed in several studies, e.g. Steurer & Konrad (2009), Kuznetsov, Kuznetsova, & Warren (2009) or

Koleva et al. (2010), corporate social values of managers in these countries have rarely been the subject of empirical research studies up to now. It is still unknown which corporate social values are responsible for shaping managerial strategies in post-Soviet countries or if there are differences between the countries questioned. The following paper therefore addresses the issue of value preferences obtained by top managers and employers in three chosen transformation countries with different national cultures, namely former East Germany[1], Estonia and Romania. The countries represent three transforming societies with clearly distinct cultures which allow a study of the cultural influence. In addition, they also stand for different approaches and stages of political and economic transformation. Similarities can therefore be seen as general features for countries in transformation while differences refer to the culture-specific transformation paths.

The aim of the current study is thus threefold. First, we will compare the main managerial CSR value orientations in three different transformational contexts: East Germany, Romania and Estonia. Our assumption is that different cultural contexts shape specific managerial value orientations. The countries represent by choice quite different cultures, a Germanic culture, a Roman East European culture, and a Baltic-Russian culture. Moreover, the countries also stand for different stages and pathways of the societal transformation.

We furthermore assume that there is an interaction between cultural contexts and organizational settings which have an effect on managerial values as well. Therefore, our second aim is to explore if there are some country-based differences between the holders of hierarchically different management positions (e.g. top level managers vs. lower level managers). And third, we will look at country-based differences between the owner-managers and occupied managers.

THEORETICAL CONSIDERATIONS

Despite the seemingly bursting organizational research on CSR, some authors posit that the antecedents of CRS, such as managerial values or behaviours, have been insufficiently explored up to now (Lindgreen & Swaen, 2010). Whereas recent studies on antecedents and factors of corporate social responsibility focus on multi-level analysis, with individual level which includes values and preferences of managers being one of them (e.g. Athanasopoulou & Selsky, 2015), there is still relatively unknown how prevalent managerial values regarding CSR are, as well as how leader values influence the CSR-practices of their organizations. Since managerial actors are mainly responsible for CSR implementation in organizations, a deeper investigation of managerial values shaping managerial actions (Triandis, 1995) can contribute to a better understanding of the processes through which social responsibility of organizations is realized.

In the contexts of transformation societies, the role of managerial values can be assumed to be more indicative than elsewhere. The settings of instability and insecurity, a lack of established rules and standards are presumed to provide owners and managers of firms more space to act according to their personal values and dispositions (Waldman et al., 2006; Lang, 2008). Instead of strong norms and clear expectations regarding economic behavior, as in established societies, vague rules and norms in transformational countries allow actors a stronger orientation on their personal values and dispositions (Waldman et al., 2006). This argument is basically borrowed from 'person-situation-debate', mainly discussed by Walter Mischel (1973). Mischel assumes that the influence of personality traits on behavior is determined by the extent of the situational 'strength'. Whereas in 'strong situations' there are norms and incentives guiding behavior, the so called 'weak' situation is characterized by a lack of such norms and guidelines. Those situations, Mischel argues, allow for a wide range of individual differences, thus, individual personality traits as well as individual values, as we suppose, play a decisive role for individual behavior. The situation of managers and owners of the companies in transforming societies like those in Central and Eastern Europe can be considered as 'weak' because Soviet norms lack their legitimacy and post-Soviet norms have not yet been established (e.g. Ishekawa, 2005). Accordingly, individual values seem to shape managerial behavior in the context of societal transformation even stronger than in established societies. Thus, an understanding of CSR processes in transforming countries requires a profound investigation of managerial values which underlay strategic decisions in organizations.

Before we turn to our assumptions regarding the prevalence of managerial values in three different transformational countries, we should address the concept of CSR from a value-based perspective as a conceptual background of our study. As many authors state (e.g. Rowley & Berman, 2000; Waldman et al., 2006; Lindgreen & Swaen, 2010), there is still a lack of clarity concerning the definition and the dimensionality of CSR. Recent research shows that CSR should be considered as a multidimensional concept (Waldman et al., 2006). How many and which dimensions the CSR can entail, still remains open. In their international survey, Waldman et al. (2006) disclose three factors contained in CSR: 1) shareholder-orientation, 2) stakeholder-orientation, and 3) community/state welfare-orientation. Unlike the results of Waldman et al. (2006), Lang (2008) demonstrates in his likewise internationally undertaken research that CSR values, measured in accordance with the method applied by Waldman et al. (2006), yield a 5-factors solution.

In agreement with Waldman et al. (2006), one of the factors observed also by Lang (2008) represents *shareholder values* like profit. However, instead of stakeholder orientation and community orientation, four additional factors have been detected here. First there is a *strategy focus* including long-term factors such as product quality, competitiveness, customer satisfaction and consideration of the environment. The second factor is an *employee and community focus* referring to the well-being of the employees and human resource development as well as to the contributions to regional development, public weal and security. The third factor considers *ethical reasons in connection with equal treatment* of female employees and employees from demographic minorities. Finally, as the fourth factor there have been identified *spiritual reasons* for decision-making, such as religious values and belief in supernatural powers. Thus, besides various stakeholder groups, such as financial investors, consumers, employees and community, as declared by the stakeholder-theory, decision-makers in the firms seem to follow rather abstract norms, moral expectations and values prevalent in a local society as well.

Since the simultaneous addressing of all stakeholders and normative expectations through the CSR practices is rather illusory, the question addressed in this paper is which orientations and value preferences prevail in firms of transformational economies. Are value preferences of managers in transforming societies contingent upon the local country and upon the managerial position held by decision makers? Thus, are there differences in CSR values between the countries studied as well as between top managers and lower level managers on the one hand and between owner-managers and occupied managers?

Are Managerial Value Preferences Contingent Upon a Local Country?

Contingency upon a country can be expressed in many ways. Cultural, societal values of the country are one of them. Another kind of country-based contingency explanations is the difference in the so called 'national business systems' (Whitley 1992), where the main focus is on respective specific structural form of capitalist institutions.

There is some evidence showing that national cultural values are an important factor explaining managerial value preferences. The above cited study of Waldman et al. (2006) points to the high correspondence between both national and managerial values. As this paper deals with three countries, East Germany, Estonia and Romania, analyzing different national values (e.g. Heintz 2002; Aycan et al., 2000), it could be assumed that the CSR-oriented value preferences in managerial decisions will be different as well and, thus, country-contingent. Previous findings drawing on national business systems indicate that there are considerable differences between the institutional frameworks in East Germany, Romania and Estonia. Furthermore, those institutional differences are assumed to be reflected by individual value preferences of managers. In the following, we will consider findings from previous studies on cultural as well as institutional frameworks in East Germany, Romania and Estonia and try to hypothesize on what social corporate values managers prefer in each country.

According to former findings drawing on national business systems, the East German capitalism can be assumed to reveal 'social market economy' with a dominance of stakeholder orientation and community focus because of the adaptation of the West German business model (Thielen, 2001). However, Martens & Michailow (2003) disagree with this and show that entrepreneurs and managers in East Germany, especially in smaller enterprises and start-ups demonstrate an orientation close to a 'competitive capitalism' instead of 'social market economy'.

This is partly supported by studies on leadership attitudes and preferred styles by Lindert (1996), Pohlmann & Gergs (1996), Domsch, Harms, & Macke (1998) or Alt & Lang (1998) who found not only some differences to managers from West Germany but also a certain constancy of these differences over time, based on a stable individual value set with strong focus on performance, task orientation, loyalty to the firm, and orientation toward a role model of a leader as a technical expert. The distinctive East German national culture behind the leaders' attitudes characterizes East German managers compared to West Germans as more uncertainty avoidant, more power distant ("pyramid of people"- pattern according to Hofstede, see Lang 1996, p. 16), less masculine and more collectivist (Lang 1996, 2002). Somewhat contrary to this, GLOBE findings on cultural values and leadership expectations in East Germany companies point to striking similarities within the Germanic cluster between West Germany and East Germany with only a few and often non significant differences for middle managers in the above fields. (Brodbeck, Frese, & Javidan, 2002; Brodbeck & Frese, 2007). Thus, some other parallels and resemblances between managers from East and West Germany can be expected as well, for example, strong parallels regarding behavioral norms and values in economic decisions.

Similar contradictory results have been reported from Romanian managers too (Kelemen & Hristov, 1998; Catana, Catana & Finlay, 1999). A recent study by Koleva et al. (2010), for example, contradicts to the assumption of a pure competitive capitalism in East European Countries, including Romania, and indicates that a variety of responsible practices do exists in Romanian organizations as well. This may be rooted in national cultural standards like a high group or family collectivism, as shown within the GLOBE project for CEE countries (Bakacsi, Takacs, Karacsonyi, & Imrek, 2002) and also Romania (Bakacsi et al., 2007).

Moreover, as Catana and Catana (1999) showed in their study, Romanian managers are highly influenced in their behavior by national culture in general, e.g. short term orientation, high uncertainty avoidance, stability orientation instead of risk taking, informal dealing, and importance of family relations and religious values. The last group of values has also been highlighted by Ionescu, Negrusa, & Adam (2003). Contrary, Kelemen (1999) did not see such an influence of religious values but underlined the masculinity of Romanian management and business and viewed an increasing materialism as a results of the introduction of the market economy (see also Lang, Alas, Alt, Catana, & Hartz, 2005). With respect to leadership practices, Lang, Catana, Catana & Steyrer (2008) have shown that Romanian managers compared with their East German and Austrian counterparts, tend to behave more autocratic, directive, decisive and less power sharing, more bureaucratic, more status conscious, but also more team-oriented, human and calm (Lang et al. 2008, p. 126). In another paper on stakeholder relations Brouthers, Gelderman, & Arens (2007) showed differences among managers of private and state enterprises in Romania, with a stronger shareholder orientation of the latter group. Remišová, Lašáková, & Krzykała- Schaefer (2013) analyzed the link between cultural dimensions and CSR related values of future managers, students, from Central and East European countries including Germany and Romania. They found strong links between the cultural profiles of countries and the preference of relevant stakeholder groups and factors in decision processes.

Finally, in the case of Estonia, reliable analyses and empirical evidence on business system are still rare. The literature on the so called 'varieties of capitalism' (Hall & Soskice, 2001) considers the Baltic states in general and Estonia in particular as a precursor of 'liberal market economy' among East European countries (Buchen, 2007). The picture, resulting from the micro-level research on managerial reality in Estonia, shows at least partly contradictory results. On the one hand, the study of Lindert (1996) indicates that Estonian managers mainly share an attitude of Taylorist control over the employees. At the same time, they can be characterized by a smaller power distance than their Baltic neighbor countries' counterparts (Lindert, 1996), whereby differences between hierarchical levels can be assumed as higher level manager tends to be more autocratic. On the other hand, many studies suggest a high social orientation among Estonian managers. For example, the study of Vadi (2005) indicates that collectivism still plays an important role in the Estonian society, and is related to behavior of both employees and managers. Especially the older group of Estonian managers seems to feel more responsible than Western managers for their personnel, for the community, and the Estonian society at large (Nurmi & Üksvärav, 1996). Furthermore, Tuulik and Alas (2005) show that Estonian managers are oriented towards the well-being of the employees, professional growth and development, as well as the well-being of the community and the state. More recently, Alas, Ennulo, & Türnpuu (2006) found that managerial values have changed during the course of transformation. While ethical considerations have been underestimated compared with 'business ideological values` in the immediate transition period, the authors claimed an increasing importance of equality and other ethical values (Alas et al., 2006). Moreover, social values like the importance of employee relations have an increased in the last years. Activities with respect to the community, regional or state welfare were clearly considered as instrumental for business advantages. In addition Kostjuk (2005) found that strategic issues like product quality, orientation to costumers, and employee orientation have been ranked higher in Estonia than in other CEE countries.

Summing up, the existing studies point to considerable differences in national cultures like stronger family collectivism for Romania and partly Estonia compared with Germany, higher uncertainty avoidance for East German manager, a strong power orientation especially for Romanian managers, but also a higher degree of human orientation in CEE countries like Romania, and Estonia. The different stage of transformation may also be influential; the special case of Germany with an early and state supported transformation, a very speedy transformation with the respective risks in Estonia, and much later and slower transition in Romania have also to be taken into account for county variances. Finally, a considerable higher share of minorities for Estonia, with more than 30 per cent mainly Russians, compared with less than 10 per cent in East Germany and Romania, may support an stronger orientation of Estonian managers towards equal treatment.

Thus, based on previous evidence on East Germany, Estonia and Romania we will ask:

Research Question 1: *Are managerial value preferences contingent on the country? Can it be assumed that value preferences of managers from Romania and Estonia show a higher community orientation than in the case of East German managers? Can German and Estonian managers be assumed to have a higher stakeholder-orientation and strategic orientation, while among Romanian managers ethical and spiritual reason may prevail? May a stronger focus on equal treatment of minorities be found for Estonia, compared to the other considered countries?*

Are Managerial Value Preferences Contingent on a Managerial Position?

The question of whether there are any differences between top managers on the one hand and lower level managers on the other hand regarding their value preferences reveals, once again, conflicting positions. Top managers and lower level managers can be assumed to differ in their value preferences. As success and failure of an organization is often attributed to the leaders (Meindl, Ehrlich, & Dukerich, 1985), their main concern is economical performance and viability of organizations. Thus, for top managers shareholder and strategic orientation can be assumed to be of particular relevance, whereas issues of community or equal treatment of employees are of lower importance for them. Unlike top managers, lower level managers can be assumed to attach less importance on shareholder or strategic orientation; they are more concerned with the issues of employees and community. However, the transformational context can lead to a similar state for top managers and lower-level managers, namely a psychologically weak situation with dominating uncertainty and anxiety. In face of this kind of 'collective helplessness' it may be hypothesized that top managers and lower level managers display similar value patterns. It might also be assumed that subordinates share the views of their CEOs and, by doing so, stabilize the values and dispositions of organization (Lang, 2008). Thus, it implies that in the more severe transformational context value preferences of top managers and lower level managers should be more similar. From the three countries studied, Romania could be mainly assumed to still stick in a transition period. In East Germany and Estonia political and societal transformation could be considered as less severe because the most profound reforms past. Our second research question is thus:

Research Question 2: *Do value preferences of top managers and lower level managers show any differences in Romania, East Germany and Estonia?*

The group of top managers in organizations is highly heterogeneous; it contains owners of firms as well as employed top managers. Are there any differences to be expected regarding value preferences between owners-managers and occupied managers? As owners-managers are literally responsible for running an effective business and bear financial risks, their value preferences can be assumed to be mainly directed towards economic targets (Waldman et al., 2006). Thus, owner-managers could be assumed to be more shareholders oriented than occupied managers. On the other hand, it could be argued that owners-managers show high concern for the local community, especially if they are personally associated with the community (e.g. because they grew up here) or if their companies have local history. Furthermore, in accordance with the Resource Dependence Theory (Pfeffer & Salancik, 1978) high orientation towards community concerns by owner-managers could be expected if the business considered depends on community resources, such as employees or local suppliers. However, the arguments mentioned cannot answer the question of whether the community-orientation shown by owner-managers can be expected to be higher than that of occupied managers. Moreover, it still needs to be clarified if the value discrepancies between owner-managers and occupied managers, in case there are any discrepancies, are country-specific. For example, are the differences between the owners and their managers lower in East Germany than in Romania and Estonia? Otherwise, since the legal position of owners and occupied managers is akin in all three transforming societies studied, to the effect that owners in East Germany, Romania and Estonia bear financial risks and occupied managers do not, it could be assumed that there are no country-specific value differences between owners and occupied managers. Our last research questions are thus:

Research Question 3: *Do value preferences of owner-managers and occupied top managers differ in transforming societies? Are these differences country-specific?*

METHODOLOGY

The present study is based on interviews with owners and senior managers as well as questionnaires addressed to lower level managers. The research was conducted between 2001 and 2004 in the frame of the GLOBE CEO project (House, Dorfman, Javidan, Hanges, & Sully de Luque, 2014). The GLOBE CEO project is part of the overall GLOBE research program examining culture and leadership around the world (House, Hanges, Javidan, Dorfman, & Gupta, 2004; Waldman et al., 2006; Chhokar, Brodbeck, & House, 2007, Dorfman, Javidan, Hanges, Dastmalchian, & House, 2012, House et al., 2014). While the focus in phase II of the GLOBE program was aimed at analysing the relationship between cultural values and cultural practices, nationals cultures as well as organizational cultures, on the one hand, and culturally endorsed implicit leadership theories (CLTs) on the other hand (House et al., 2004, Chhokar et al., 2007), phase III of GLOBE was dedicated to the relationship between leadership expectations (CLTs), CEO leadership behaviour and effectiveness (House et al., 2014). A summary of purposes, methods, and samples, design strategies and major results of both phases of the GLOBE research program can be found in House et al. (2014, pp. 96-97). The GLOBE study in phase II was based on survey data from over 17.000 middle managers representing 951 organisations in 62 cultures. In addition, other information gained from interviews, group discussions and media analysis. The mixed-method results for 25 societies can be found in Chhokar et al. (2007).

The results showed a significant influence of cultural values and practices on implicit leadership expectations (CLTs), whereby certain leadership behavioural attributes were found to be universally desirable, like charismatic-transformational or team-oriented behaviours, while others showed culturally specific qualities like participative or autonomous behaviours. The GLOBE study of phase III was based on interviews and questionnaires with more than 1000 CEOs and more than 5000 immediate subordinates of the CEOs from 24 countries. The combined results showed that "Leaders tend to behave in a manner expected within their countries" (House et al., 2014, p. 97). It was also proven that cultural values are not directly influencing leader behaviour but having an indirect effect through culturally endorsed implicit leadership theories.

The analysis in this paper refers to the GLOBE phase III data from Eastern Germany, Estonia and Romania. Altogether, 129 CEOs in around 40 firms were interviewed with respect to their managerial biography, their leadership philosophy, and their activities and strategies for the firm development. The interview included a short survey on, among other things, preferences in critical management decisions. In our study CEOs include founders and/or owners of companies as well as to top managers who were employed by institutional or personal owners. From 129 CEOs interviewed, there were 59 owners and 70 employed top managers. In addition, a number of up to nine lower level managers in each firm were asked to fill out a questionnaire from the GLOBE project with descriptions of perceived leadership behavior, organizational practices, organizational commitment as well as their value preferences for critical respective strategic management decisions. The questionnaire was translated (and re-translated) into Estonian, Romanian and German before. 787 lower level managers and employees filled out the questionnaires.

The East German sample included questionnaires from 40 CEOs and 205 lower level managers, in Estonia 45 questionnaires were filled out by CEOs and 305 by lower level managers. The Romanian sample consists of data provided by 44 CEOs and 277 lower level managers.[2]

The value preferences of managers were measured using the question „ Please indicate how much importance should be assigned to each of the factors listed below when making critical management decisions. "All of the aspects listed were to be answered with a 7-point Likert Scale with (1) – of no importance, to (7) – of most importance: should be considered more important than all other considerations.

The question targeted non-routine, strategic decisions, which consider certain interests groups while ignoring others. The assumption was that these management decisions provoke implicit, underlying value attitudes.

By asking this indirect question we intend to measure implicit values or important, valuable decision-criteria and not so much espoused values. Additionally, we cross-checked the answers to the question on critical management decisions with free comments provided by the respondents in more open interview parts. Nevertheless, it cannot be entirely excluded that our respondents also gave publicly desirable answers or were concerned about the legitimacy of their company by answering the questionnaire.

This kind of measurement of implicit CSR values in some points resembles commonly used value measurements, such as the Value Survey by Rokeach (1973). In the Value Survey by Rokeach respondents are asked to rank two sets of values each containing 18 values; however, the ranking procedure in the Value Survey has frequently been criticized as it doesn't provide information about the absolute importance of each value. In contrast to the Value Survey, the measurement procedure applied in our study provides precisely this kind of information by focusing on values referring to the organizational issues.

In accordance with the above cited study of Lang (2008), 15 aspects were listed which belong to the five factors: strategic focus, shareholder orientation, employee and community issues, equal treatment and religious values.

Besides the factor analysis, we undertook ANOVA and MANOVA tests to compare the group means regarding factor-based added value preferences.

Table 1. Characteristics of the Sample

Parameter	East Germany	Romania	Estonia	Total
Number of Companies Studied	40	44	45	129
Companies up to 100 Employees, %	38	31	43	37
Manufacturing Companies, %	67	55	20	47
Start-ups, %	45	60	39	48
Questionnaires from CEOs	40	44	45	129
Questionnaires from Lower Level Managers	205	277	305	787

RESULTS

As Table 2 shows, our findings point to some universal tendencies between countries as well as to considerable country-specific differences. Managers in all three countries consider *shareholder and strategic orientation* as most important, while *employee and community issues, equal treatment as well as religious orientation* have a secondary relevance. Thus, across all three countries, shareholder orientation, represented by firm profitability and sales volume, and strategic orientation, manifested in the relevance of customer satisfaction, product quality, and long-term competitiveness, are the dominant value orientations underlying critical management decisions in transforming societies. However, some country-based combinations of the dominant values can also be observed here. *Shareholder orientation* seems to dominate in Romania and Estonia, but not in East Germany where *strategic orientation* and *equal treatment and ethical orientation* prevail. In accordance with our assumption, Romanian managers attach a relatively high importance to *religious values*. Furthermore, Romanian and Estonian managers show a relatively high *employee and community orientation*. Interestingly, whereas Romanian manag-

Table 2. Comparison of the Value Dimensions for Countries (Results of ANOVA)

Value Dimensions	East Germany (N=245)	Romania (N=321)	Estonia (N=350)	F-Values	Sign.
Shareholder orientation Mean St. Dev.	 5,70 0,79	 5,92 0,44	 5,62 0,74	2,32	0,10
Strategic orientation Mean St. Dev.	 **6,02** 0,46	 **5,73** 0,43	 **5,44** 0,78	**10,13**	**0,00**
Employee and community orientation Mean St. Dev.	 4,82 0,76	 5,04 0,73	 4,95 0,74	0,93	0,39
Equal treatment and ethical orientation Mean St. Dev.	 **4,43** 1,05	 **2,84** 1,36	 **4,10** 0,90	**23,12**	**0,00**
Religious orientation Mean St. Dev.	 **1,89** 1,07	 **3,19** 0,87	 **1,97** 1,03	**23,12**	**0,00**

ers seem to consider *equal treatment of employees and ethical orientation* the least, Estonian managers attach relatively high importance to these issues.

The results regarding research question 2 are shown in Table 3. Generally speaking, irrespective of the country studied, CEOs as well as lower level managers consider *shareholder and strategic orientation* as most important. However, contrary to our assumption, the value preferences of CEOs and lower level managers show more significant differences in Romania than in Estonia or East Germany. In Romania, the CEOs give significantly more attention to *shareholder orientation* and *strategic orientation* than lower level managers, but lower level managers are significantly more concerned with *equal treatment and ethical orientation* than CEOs. In Estonia, CEOs pay significantly more attention to *strategic orientation* and *employee and community orientation* than lower level managers, while in the sample of East Germany, significant differences between CEOs and lower level managers arise only in terms of *strategic orientation*, with CEOs stressing this value dimension more than their subordinates.

Comparing the values of owner-managers with occupied managers, it becomes apparent that both groups are quite similar. As Table 4 shows, there are barely significant differences between owners and occupied top managers in general. According to the Pillai-Spur statistics, in most cases the effect of the country on value orientations is much more significant than the effect of the ownership or joint effect of ownership and country.. Therefore, the differences in value orientations between the countries are more relevant than between the owners and occupied managers, especially in the case of strategic orientation, equal and ethical treatment of employees or religious orientation. The only case where the interaction of ownership and country seems to have an almost significant impact on value orientation is *equal treatment and ethical orientation*. This effect can mainly be traced back to the results in Romania, where owner-managers show a significant higher concern about *equal treatment and ethical orientation*

Table 3. Comparison of Value Dimensions for CEOs and Lower Level Managers in East Germany, Romania and Estonia (Results of T-Test Per Country)

Value Dimensions	East Germany		Romania		Estonia		Sign. Per Country		
	CEOs	Lower Level Managers	CEOs	Lower Level Managers	CEOs	Lower Level Managers	East Germany	Romania	Estonia
Shareholder Orientation							0,77	*0,05*	0,22
Mean	5,70	5,74	**5,92**	**5,80**	5,62	5,48			
St. Dev.	0,79	0,58	**0,44**	**0,28**	0,74	0,65			
Strategic Orientation							**0,00**	**0,00**	**0,00**
Mean	**6,02**	**5,40**	**5,73**	**5,35**	**5,42**	**5,09**			
St. Dev.	**0,46**	**0,69**	**0,43**	**0,39**	**0,78**	**0,45**			
Employee and Community Orientation							0,53	0,21	*0,03*
Mean	4,82	4,90	5,04	4,93	**4,94**	**4,72**			
St. Dev.	0,76	0,56	0,73	0,54	**0,74**	**0,48**			
Equal Treatment and Ethical Orientation							0,13	**0,00**	0,45
Mean	4,43	4,11	**2,84**	**4,02**	4,10	3,99			
St. Dev.	1,05	0,68	**1,34**	**0,79**	0,90	0,53			
Religious Orientation							0,91	0,49	0,59
Mean	1,89	1,64	3,19	3,28	1,97	1,88			
St. Dev.	1,07	0,64	0,87	0,71	1,03	0,55			

Table 4. Comparison of Value Dimensions for Owner-Managers and Occupied Managers in East Germany, Romania and Estonia (Results of MANOVA)

Value Dimensions	East Germany		Romania		Estonia		Sign. of Effects (Pillai-Spur Statistics)		
	Owner-Managers (N=20)	Occupied Managers (N=17)	Owner-Managers (N=19)	Occupied Managers (N=23)	Owner-Managers (N=17)	Occupied Managers (N=26)	Country	Owner-ship	Country x Ownership
Shareholder Orientation							0,17	0,57	0,25
Mean	5,93	5,53	5,85	5,90	5,62	5,63			
St. Dev.	0,80	0,82	0,37	0,51	0,78	0,76			
Strategic Orientation							**0,00**	0,50	0,11
Mean	5,95	6,10	5,86	5,61	5,31	5,53			
St. Dev.	0,35	0,43	0,38	0,39	0,80	0,66			
Employee and Community Orientation							0,59	0,31	0,32
Mean	4,96	4,76	5,25	4,86	4,87	5,00			
St. Dev.	0,78	0,75	0,66	0,74	0,77	0,75			
Equal Treatment and Ethical Orientation							**0,00**	0,23	*0,08*
Mean	4,56	4,27	3,42	2,36	4,20	4,17			
St. Dev.	1,09	1,03	1,47	1,08	0,86	0,86			
Religious Orientation							**0,00**	0,79	0,51
Mean	1,78	2,12	3,18	3,17	2,09	1,90			
St. Dev.	1,09	1,08	0,79	0,96	1,18	0,95			

than occupied managers. This tendency is also true for the other countries, but the differences here are not so striking. A stronger *shareholder orientation* of owner-managers seems to be a trend only in East Germany; however, this tendency proves to be statistically non-significant.

DISCUSSION

It becomes evident that shareholder values in Central and East European countries play an important role; however, they are inbuilt in each special configurations of a value mix. Despite the confrontation with a fundamental change of the institutional environment, managerial decisions in those countries are not only made in consideration of an increase of profit or cost reduction. Instead, a combination of shareholder values with a strong focus on strategy and employees as well as the community could be observed. Furthermore, value preferences underlying managerial decisions in Central and East European countries seem to be still contingent on the local country, with East German managers stressing strategic and ethical orientation and their Romanian counterparts disregarding employees' equality issues but, like Estonian managers, highly considering shareholder interests and also taking issues of their employees and community into account. Furthermore, when making strategic decisions, Romanian managers, unlike their counterparts in East Germany and Estonia, seem to take religious values into a closer consideration. In line with the notion of "East European capitalism" or "East European Business systems" (Stark, 1996; Grabher & Stark, 1997, Bluhm, 2007), the results showed a still important focus on state and community welfare in Estonia and Romania. But the above mentioned differentiated configurations of value preferences in both countries may also be seen as an indicator of for further studies on differences in CEE Business systems.

Value preferences of managers in transition economies turn out to be contingent on the managerial position as well, however, not in a hypothesized way. Contrary to our assumption, value preferences of the CEOs and lower level managers show more significant differences in Romania than in Estonia or East Germany. The transformational context in Romania seems to polarize hierarchically different positions regarding value preferences by managerial decisions with CEOs stressing more shareholder and strategic orientation and lower level managers in Romania paying more attention to equal treatment and ethics. At the same time, transformational settings seem to equalize the difference between owners and occupied managers as there are barely differences between owners and occupied managers in all three countries regarding their value preferences. A situation of similar psychological weakness seems to lead to a convergence of the value orientations among top managers (owners and occupied managers) and, interestingly, to a divergence between top managers and lower level managers.

Given these findings on CSR values, what implications can be drawn regarding the CSR actions in transforming societies? Arguing that managerial values have both a direct as well as indirect effect, on the strategic choices in firms (Pant & Lachman, 1998) as well as on CSR practices (Agle, Mitchell, & Sonnenfeld, 1999), we can expect that the focus of firms' CSR activities will be slightly different in the countries studied. In East Germany it could be expected that CSR practices will be focused first and foremost on customers or suppliers in order to guarantee a firm's competitiveness, strategic benefits and product quality. Unlikely, Romanian firms can be assumed in their CSR strategy to address especially shareholders, such as banking institutions or other donors, as Romanian CEOs regard shareholder orientation more relevant than lower level managers. Additionally, the relatively high employee and community value orientation as well as religious values point to the fact that CSR practices of Romanian companies also address actors of local community, such as the local government and religious institutions. Finally, Estonian firms can be expected to concentrate their CSR practices on important financial institutions, on customers and supplies in order to attain strategic goals, and also on local governance and politicians.

Differences obtained in value orientations between CEOs and lower level managers or owners and occupied managers' point to the fact that it could be a challenging task to arrange an uniform CSR policy of a firm. It could especially be the case in Romania where CEOs and lower level managers consider the relevance of shareholder orientation, stakeholder orientation and equal treatment and ethical orientation in a different way, whereby CEOs consider the latter point heterogeneously as well: owner-managers regard equal treatment and ethical orientation more relevant than occupied managers.

Several limitations of our study should also be noted. First, we did not measure factual CSR actions of managers. However, as managerial values have shown to be relevant for strategic choice (Pant & Lachman, 1998) as well as CSR practices (Agle et al., 1999), it can be assumed that the CSR-oriented value preferences of managers investigated in the current study are quite valid regarding the de facto practices, be it responsible or non-responsible, on the part of managers. Second, due to our method used to measure CSR-values, the results are possibly biased by the so called 'social desirability'. Using less responsive methods, such as observation of decision making or document-analysis, could potentially earn more valid empirical data. Moreover, the very general question for strategic decision did not refer to special target objects or areas of decision, which may have an influence on the value preferences. Further studies should focus in more detail on this aspect.

MANAGERIAL IMPLICATIONS

The results of our study allow also deriving a number of managerial implications. First of all, the above described differences in the priorities of strategic management decisions of the three countries must be taken into account for successful *international business co-operations*. Partners from abroad should be aware of the agenda of their partners from Estonia, Romania and (East) Germany. Especially for Estonia and Romania, positive effects for a wider community together with short term economic effects seem to be important for the co-operation. Secondly, *stakeholder management* seems to focus on a different set of partners, which also have to take into account when doing business in the respective country.

This includes a special focus on certain aspects of *CSR*, while other aspects are partly neglected or underestimated. Finally, the results are also important for the *selection and preparation of expatriate managers and experts* who are going to work in these countries.

They have to be able to cope with the special value setting in the country, and to handle possible conflicts stemming from different value expectations between home country, sending corporation and local partners.

REFERENCES

Agle, B. R., Mitchell, R. K., & Sonnenfeld, J. A. (1999). Who matters to CEOs? An investigation of stakeholder attributes and salience, corporate performance, and CEO values. *Academy of Management Journal, 42*(3), 507–525. doi:10.2307/256973

Alas, R., Ennulo, J., & Türnpuu, L. (2006). Managerial values in the institutional context. *Journal of Business Ethics, 5*(3), 269–278. doi:10.1007/s10551-005-5494-1

Alt, R., & Lang, R. (1998). Wertorientierungen und Führungsverständnis von Managern in sächsischen Klein- und Mittelunternehmen. In R. Lang (Ed.), Management Executives in the East European Transformation Process (pp. 246-269). München: Hampp.

Athanasopoulou, A., & Selsky, J. W. (2015). The social context of corporate social responsibility: Enriching research with multiple perspectives and multiple levels. *Business & Society, 54*(3), 322–364. doi:10.1177/0007650312449260

Aycan, Z., Kanungo, R. N., Mendonca, M., Yu, K., Deller, J., Stahl, G., & Kurshid, A. (2000). Impact on culture on human resource management practices. A 10-country comparison. *Applied Psychology, 49*(1), 192–221. doi:10.1111/1464-0597.00010

Bakacsi, G., Catana, A., & Catana, D. (2007). *GLOBE Romania: Final report of the results of the GLOBE-Romania project.* Unpublished report.

Bakacsi, G., Takacs, S., Karacsonyi, A., & Imrek, V. (2002). East European Cluster: Tradition and transition. *Journal of World Business, 37*(1), 69–80. doi:10.1016/S1090-9516(01)00075-X

Bluhm, K. (2007). *Experimentierfeld Osteuropa? Deutsche Unternehmen in Polen und der Tschechischen Republik.* Wiesbaden: Gabler.

Brodbeck, F., & Frese, M. (2007). Societal Culture and Leadership in Germany. In J. S. Chokar, F. C. Brodbeck, & R. J. House (Eds.), *Culture and Leadership Across the World: The GLOBE Book of In-Depth Studies of 25 Societies* (pp. 147–214). Mahwah: Lawrence Erlbaum Associates Inc.

Brodbeck, F., Frese, M., & Javidan, M. (2002). Leadership made in Germany: Low on compassion, high on performance. *The Academy of Management Executive, 16*(1), 16–29. doi:10.5465/AME.2002.6640111

Brouthers, K. D., Gelderman, M., & Arens, P. (2007). The Influence of Ownership on Performance: Stakeholder and strategic contingency perspectives. *Schmalenbach Business Review, 59*, 225–242.

Buchen, C. (2007). Estonia and Slovenia as Antipodes. In D. Lane, D., & M. Myant (Eds.), Varieties of capitalism in post-communist countries (pp. 65-89). Basingstoke, UK: Palgrave. doi:10.1057/9780230627574_4

Cameron, K., & Quinn, R. E. (1999). *Diagnosis and changing organizational culture: Based on the competing values framework.* New York: Addison Wesley.

Catana, A., & Catana, D. (1999). Romanian cultural background and its relevance for Cross-Cultural Management. *Journal for East-European Management Studies, 4*(3), 252–258.

Catana, D., Catana, A., & Finlay, J. L. (1999). Managerial resistance to change: Romania's quest for a market economy. *Journal for East European Management Studies, 4*(2), 149–164.

Chhokar, J. S., Brodbeck, F. C., & House, R. J. (Eds.). (2007). *Culture and leadership across the world: The GLOBE book of in-depth studies of 25 societies.* Mahwah, NJ: Sage.

Chin, M. K., Hambrick, D. C., & Treviño, L. K. (2013). Political ideologies of CEOs: The influence of executives values on Corporate Social Responsibilty. *Administrative Science Quarterly, 58*(2), 197–232. doi:10.1177/0001839213486984

Domsch, M. E., Harms, M., & Macke, H. (1998). Selbst- und Fremdbild der Führungsverhaltens von ostdeutschen Führungskräften. In R. Lang (Ed.), Management executives in the East European transformation process (pp. 227-246). München: Hampp.

Dorfman, P., Javidan, M., Hanges, P., Dastmalchian, A., & House, R. (2012). GLOBE: A twenty year journey into the intriguing world of culture and leadership. *Journal of World Business, 47*(4), 504–518. doi:10.1016/j.jwb.2012.01.004

Feather, N. T. (1975). *Values in Eudcation and Society.* New York: Free Press.

Feather, N. T. (1994). Values and Culture. In W.J. Lonner & R.S. Malpass (Eds.), Psychology and Culture (pp. 183-189). Boston: Allyn and Bacon.

Grabher, G., & Stark, D. (1997). *Restructuring Networks in Post-Socialism: Legacies, Linkages and Localities.* New York: Oxford University Press.

Hall, P. A., & Soskice, D. (2001). *Varieties of Capitalism: The institutional foundations of comparative advantage*. New York: Oxford University Press. doi:10.1093/0199247757.001.0001

Hambrick, D. C. (2007). Upper echelons theory: An update. *Academy of Management Review, 32*(2), 334–343. doi:10.5465/AMR.2007.24345254

Heintz, M. (2002). East European Managers and Western Management Theories: An ethnographic approach of Romanian service sector enterprises. *Journal of East European Management Studies, 7*(3), 279–297.

Hofstede, G., Neuijen, B., Ohayv, D. D., & Sanders, G. (1990). Measuring organizational cultures: A qualitative and quantitative study across twenty cases. *Administrative Science Quarterly, 35*(2), 286–316. doi:10.2307/2393392

House, R. J., Dorfman, P. W., Javidan, M., Hanges, P. J., & Sully de Luque, M. (2014). *Strategic Leadership across Cultures. The GLOBE Study of CEO Leadership Behavior and Effectiveness in 24 Countries*. Thousand Oaks, CA: Sage. doi:10.4135/9781506374581

House, R. J., Hanges, P. J., Javidan, M., Dorfman, P., & Gupta, V. (2004). *Culture, Leadership, and Organizations. The GLOBE Study of 62 Societies*. Thousand Oaks, CA: Sage.

Ionescu, G., Negrusa, A. L., & Adam, C. M. (2005). Considerations about business values evolution and the Christian values. In R. Lang (Ed.), The End of Transformation? (pp. 211-220). München: Hampp.

Ishekawa, A. (2005). Social transformation and value differentiation – The Slovak case. In R. Lang (Ed.), The End of Transformation? (pp. 221-232). München: Hampp.

Kabanoff, B., & Holt, J. (1996). Changes in the espoused values of Australian organizations 19861990. *Journal of Organizational Behavior, 17*(3), 201–219. doi:10.1002/(SICI)1099-1379(199605)17:3<201::AID-JOB744>3.0.CO;2-9

Kelemen, M. (1999). Romanian cultural background and its relevance for Cross-cultural management – A Comment. *Journal for East European Management Studies, 4*(3), 259–262.

Kelemen, M., & Hristov, L. (1998). From centrally planned culture to entrepreneurial culture: The example of Bulgarian and Romanian organisations. *Journal for East European Management Studies, 3*(3), 216–226.

Koleva, P., Rodet-Kroichivili, N., David, P., & Marasova, J. (2010). Is corporate social responsibility the privilege of developed market economies? Some evidence from Central and Eastern Europe. *International Journal of Human Resource Management, 21*(2), 274–293. doi:10.1080/09585190903509597

Kostjuk, K. (2005). The thin line between small businesses and big politics. In A. Habisch, J. Jonker, M. Wegner, & R. Schmidpeter (Eds.), *Coporate Social Responsibility Across Europe* (pp. 209–218). Berlin: Springer. doi:10.1007/3-540-26960-6_17

Kuznetsov, A., Kuznetsova, O., & Warren, R. (2009). CSR and the legitimacy of business transition economies: The case of Russia. *Scandinavian Journal of Management, 25*(1), 37–45. doi:10.1016/j.scaman.2008.11.008

Lang, R. (1996). Wandel von Unternehmenskulturen in Ostdeutschland und Osteuropa – Aktuelle Fragen und Problemfelder der Forschung. In R. Lang (Ed.), *Wandel von Unternehmenskulturen in Ostdeutschland und Osteuropa. 2nd Chemnitz East Forum* (pp. 7-22). München: Hampp.

Lang, R. (2002). Wertewandel im ostdeutschen Management. In R. Schmidt, J. Gergs, & M. Pohlmann (Eds.), Managementsoziologie. Themen, Desiderate, Perspektiven (pp. 128-154). München: Hampp.

Lang, R. (2008). Vorwärts zum Shareholder-Kapitalismus? "Corporate social values" von Unternehmern und Managern als Orientierungs- und Wirkungsrahmen bei strategischen Managemententscheidungen in Transformationsgesellschaften. In U. Götze & R. Lang (Eds.), *Strategisches Management zwischen Globalisierung und Regionalisierung* (pp. 177–204). Wiesbaden: Gabler. doi:10.1007/978-3-8349-8067-0_8

Lang, R. (2014). Participative leadership in cross-cultural leadership research: A misconception? In O. Kranz, & T. Steger (Eds.), Zwischen Instrumentalisierung und Bedeutungslosigkeit Mitarbeiter-Partizipation im organisationalen Kontext in Mittel- und Osteuropa (pp. 77-92). München: Hampp.

Lang, R., Alas, R., Alt, R., Catana, D., & Hartz, R. (2005). Leadership in transformation – Between local embeddedness and global challenges. *Journal of Cross-Cultural Competence & Management, 4*, 215–246.

Lang, R., Catana, A., Catana, D., & Steyrer, J. (2008). Impacts of motives and leadership attributes of entrepreneurs and managers on followers commitment in transforming countries – A comparison of Romania, East Germany and Austria. In P. Jurczek & M. Niedobitek (Eds.), *Europäische Forschungsperspektiven – Elemente einer Europawissenschaft 2008* (pp. 109–135). Berlin: Duncker & Humblot.

Lindert, K. (1996). Führungskonzeptionen im Wandel: Eine interkulturelle und intertemporale Studie – Gemeinsamkeiten und Unterschiede west- und osteuropäischer Führungskräfte. In R. Lang (Ed.), *Wandel von Unternehmenskulturen in Ostdeutschland und Osteuropa. 2nd Chemnitz East Forum* (pp. 91-106). München: Hampp.

Lindgreen, A., & Swaen, V. (2010). Corporate Social Responsibility. *International Journal of Management Reviews, 12*(1), 1–7. doi:10.1111/j.1468-2370.2009.00277.x

Martens, B., & Michailow, M. (2003). Konvergenzen und Divergenzen zwischen dem ost- und westdeutschen Management – Ergebnisse einer Befragung von Leitern mittelständischer Industrieunternehmen in Ost- und Westdeutschland. In *SFB 580 – Mitteilungen, Nr. 10*. Jena: Friedrich-Schiller-Universität.

Matten, D., & Moon, J. (2005). A conceptual framework of CSR. In A. Habisch, J. Jonker, M. Wegner, & R. Schmidpeter (Eds.), *Corporate Social Responsibility across Europe* (pp. 335–356). Berlin: Springer.

McWilliams, A., & Siegel, D. (2001). Corporate Social Responsibility: A Theory of the Firm Perspective. *Academy of Management Review, 26*(1), 117–227.

Meindl, J. R., Ehrlich, S. B., & Dukerich, J. M. (1985). The romance of leadership. *Administrative Science Quarterly, 30*(1), 78–102. doi:10.2307/2392813

Mischel, W. (1973). Towards a cognitive social learning reconceptualization of personality. *Psychological Review, 80*(4), 252–283. doi:10.1037/h0035002 PMID:4721473

Nurmi, R., & Üksvärav, R. (1996). Estonian and Finish Management. In R. Lang (Ed.), *Wandel von Unternehmenskulturen in Ostdeutschland und Osteuropa. 2nd Chemnitz East Forum* (pp. 247-256). München: Hampp.

Pant, P. N., & Lachman, R. (1998). Value incongruity and strategic choice. *Journal of Management Studies, 35*(2), 195–212. doi:10.1111/1467-6486.00090

Pfeffer, J., & Salancik, G. R. (1978). *The external control of organizations. A resource dependence perspective.* New York: Harper & Row.

Pistrui, D., Welsch, H. P., Pohl, H. J., Wintermantel, O., & Liao, J. (2003). Entrepreneurship in the New Germany. In D. A. Kirby & A. Watson (Eds.), *Small Firm Development in Developed and Transition Economies: A Reader* (pp. 115–130). Burlington: Ashgate.

Pohlmann, M., & Gergs, H.-J. 1996. Manageriale Eliten im Transformationsprozess. In Management in der ostdeutschen Industrie (pp. 63–98). Opladen: Leske + Budrich.

Remišová, A., & Lašáková, A., & Krzykała-Schaefer, R. (2013). Corporate social responsibility in European countries: The keystones of the concept and intercultural connotations. *Journal for East European Management Studies, 18*(4), 512–543.

Rokeach, M. (1973). *The nature of human values.* New York: Free Press.

Rowley, T., & Berman, S. (2000). A brand new brand of corporate social performance. *Business & Society, 39*(4), 397–418. doi:10.1177/000765030003900404

Sagiv, L., & Schwartz, S. H. (2007). Cultural values in organisations: Insights for Europe. *European Journal of International Management, 1*(3), 176–190. doi:10.1504/EJIM.2007.014692

Schein, V. E. (1992). *Organizational Culture and Leadership* (2nd ed.). San Francisco: Jossey-Bass.

Schwartz, S. H. (1994). Are there universal aspects in the structure and contents of human values? *The Journal of Social Issues, 50*(4), 19–45. doi:10.1111/j.1540-4560.1994.tb01196.x

Stark, D. (1996). Recombinant property in Eastern European Capitalism. *American Journal of Sociology, 101*(4), 993–1027. doi:10.1086/230786

Steurer, R., & Konrad, A. (2009). Business-society relations in Central-Eastern and Western Europe: How those who lead in sustainability reporting bridge the gap in corporate (social) responsibility. *Scandinavian Journal of Management, 25*(1), 23–36. doi:10.1016/j.scaman.2008.11.001

Szabo, E., Reber, G., Weibler, J., Brodbeck, F. C., & Wunderer, R. (2001). Values and behavior orientation in leadership studies: Reflections based on findings in three German-speaking countries. *The Leadership Quarterly, 12*(2), 219–244. doi:10.1016/S1048-9843(01)00070-4

Thielen, K. (2001). Varieties of labour politics in the developed countries. In P. A. Hall & D. Soskice (Eds.), *Varieties of Capitalism: The institutional foundations of comparative advantage* (pp. 71–103). New York: Oxford University Press. doi:10.1093/0199247757.003.0002

Triandis, H. C. (1995). *Individualism and Collectivism.* Boulder, CO: Westview Press.

Tuulik, K., & Alas, R. (2005). The impact of the values of top managers upon their subordinates. In R. Lang (Ed.), The End of Transformation (pp. 439-454). München: Hampp.

Vadi, M. (2005). The relationships between subtypes of collectivism and organizational culture in Estonia. In R. Lang (Ed.), The End of transformation (pp. 267-280). München: Hampp.

Waldman, D. A., de Luque, M. S., Washburn, N., & House, J. R. (2006). Cultural and leadership predictors of Corporate Social Responsibility Values of Top Management: A GLOBE Study of 15 Countries. *Journal of International Business Studies*, *37*(6), 823–837. doi:10.1057/palgrave.jibs.8400230

Whitley, R. (1992). The social structuring of Business Systems. In R. Whitley (Ed.), *European Business Systems: Firms and Markets in their National Contexts* (pp. 5–45). New York: Sage.

Wood, D. J. (1991). Corporate Social Performance revisited. *Academy of Management Review*, *16*(4), 691–718.

KEY TERMS AND DEFINITIONS

Community Orientation: Community orientation describes a pattern of social responsibility values, decision making or behaviour where managers put a strong emphasis on the increase community or state welfare.

Culturally Endorsed Implicit Leadership Theories (CLT): The term refers to expectations good or bad leaders or/and leadership behaviour, which are influenced by specific values of a national or societal culture, contrast to universal expectations about leaders and leadership behaviour.

East European Capitalism: The term describes a specific pattern of institutional and cultural characteristics, which have been developed after the 1990 in post-socialist countries of Central and Eastern Europe as a result of the fundamental societal change. In includes a stronger importance of communitarian values, and relevant networks of actors as well as of the state in the field of the economy.

GLOBE CEO Project: The CEO project is the phase III of the GLOBE project on culture and organizational leadership effectiveness. While the focus in phase II have been on national and organizational culture and its impact on culturally endorsed implicit leadership theories, the CEO project concentrates on the perceived behaviour of CEOs in 24 countries and its impact on Top management team commitment and firm effectiveness.

Managerial Value Preferences: The term refers to rankings of individual values of managers.

National Business Systems: The concept was developed to describe special institutional settings and organization characteristics of countries in the field of economy and business. Comparative analysis has shown that groups of countries can be found who share similar patterns despite of the uniqueness of an institutional pattern for each country.

Robert House: Robert (Bob) House was the main founder of the GLOBE project in the early 1990ties. Moreover, he was one of the leading authors in the field of neo-charismatic leadership.

Shareholder Orientation: Shareholder orientation describes a pattern of social responsibility values, decision making or behaviour where managers are focussing on the increase of shareholder values.

Situational Strength: The concept describes different intensities of the influence of situations or personal traits on the behavior of actors. Strong situations are characterized through the influence norms and incentives guiding the behavior of individuals, while weak situations are characterized by a lack of such norms and guidelines. In the latter case, the behavior is strongly influenced by personal traits and values of the actors.

Stakeholder Orientation: Stakeholder orientation describes a pattern of social responsibility values, decision making or behaviour where managers decide and act by including the interests of various groups of stakeholders like customers, employees etc.

Strategic Decisions: Strategic decisions refer to decisions about main objectives, directions, programs or measures of aimed at the further development of an organization.

ENDNOTES

[1] In the remaining text, we mean by East Germany the region of the *former* East Germany.

[2] We would like to thank Doina and Gheorghe-Alexandru Catana (Babes-Bolyai University Cluj, Romania) as well as Ruth Allas and Krista Tuulik (Estonian Business School, Estonia) for their support by getting empirical data in Estonian and Romanian companies.

Chapter 9

The Importance of Behavior and Personal Values for Managers' Attitudes Towards Innovativeness:
Empirical Evidence From Austria, Poland, and Slovenia

Zlatko Nedelko
University of Maribor, Slovenia

Maciej Brzozowski
Poznan University of Economics and Business, Poland

ABSTRACT

The main purpose of this paper is to examine the impact of prevalent management behavior on management attitudes about creativeness and innovativeness, while also considering the impact of personal values, in three Central European economies, having different development paths, namely Slovenia, Austria, and Poland. Personal values are measured using Schwartz value survey, using openness to change, conservation, self-transcendence and self-enhancement value dimensions. Results reveal that manager's behavior significantly influences on manager's attitudes regarding innovativeness, in all three countries. The impact of personal values on shaping management behavior and manager's attitudes toward innovativeness is significant only in few instances in Austrian sample, while in Slovenia and Poland it is insignificant. Regarding the mediating effect of managers' personal values on the association between management behavior and their creativeness, our results reveal marginal role of personal values.

DOI: 10.4018/978-1-5225-2480-9.ch009

INTRODUCTION

In literature and business practice the important role of creativity in organizations is well acknowledged (Amabile, 1988; DeBono, 1992; Amabile, Conti, Coon, Lazenby, & Herron, 1996; Shalley & Perry-Smith, 2001). Huge proportion of this research focuses on creativity and more broadly on innovations, and explains their roles in organization's success and how creative and/or innovative behavior contributes to the organizational success (Collins & Porras, 2002; Afuah, 2003; Skarzynski & Gibson, 2008). Many studies in this field also offer a lot of evidence about drivers of employee's, person's, organizational or national creativity (Shalley & Perry-Smith, 2001; Nauwelaers & Reid, 2002; Afuah, 2003). However, no deep focus on the role of management behavior in shaping management's or organization creativeness and innovativeness exists. Furthermore, studies in this field are mainly based on practices of well-developed Western economies. Thus, when turning to emerging economies in Central Europe, these issues are becoming way less investigated (Dabic, Potocan, Nedelko, & Morgan, 2013).

In current economic conditions it is often claimed that economies and entities within economies lack creativity and, more generally, innovative thinking and behavior. This issue is way more critical in emerging economies than in well-developed economies (Dyck & Mulej, 1998; Potočan & Mulej, 2007; Dabic et al., 2013). Emerging economies such as former transition economies in Central and Eastern Europe can reduce or even nullify their lag when designing working conditions and a respective behavior grounded in innovative, flexible, and technically modern economy. In order to increase creativity in organizations in emerging economies, an important role is also assigned to management since it must create and also assure suitable conditions for creativeness and innovativeness in organization (i.e., for all organizational employees).

Outdated patterns of management behavior in emerging markets and the legacy of previous collectivistic/socialistic orientations of managers, both of which are still present in transition economies, could have important implications for future development of manager's behavior as well as their creativeness. Since the problems could rest in patterns of behavior it is important to address the possible impact of personal values on shaping management behavior, management innovativeness, and addressing the link between them.

We focus our research on management innovativeness in organizations since management plays a key role, in process of creation and/or assurance of suitable conditions and prerequisites for innovativeness in organization and its employees, especially in emerging markets of Central Europe (Dyck & Mulej, 1998; Potočan & Mulej, 2007).

With this research we want to contribute to the existing cognitions about management behavior, management innovativeness, and the link between them, that is often justified and based on cognitions of well-developed economies (Shalley & Perry-Smith, 2001; Collins & Porras, 2002; Skarzynski & Gibson, 2008), with providing evidence for selected Central Europe economies. Thus, we provide empirical evidence about the association between management behavior and manager's attitudes toward creativeness and innovativeness for one well-developed and two emerging economies in Central Europe. In frame of this link, we also address the role of personal values in shaping innovative behavior, since it is important to determine the impact of outdated behavioral patterns of management from previous system of collectivism/socialism (Nedelko & Mayrhofer, 2012; Nedelko & Potocan, 2013).

Addressing the issues of management attitudes toward creativity is of huge importance in former transition, nowadays emerging economies, since often outdated patterns of behavior are present, which are based on routine and rejection of changes. This issue is not addressed in the case of well-developed economies, since there is no legacy of previous socialistic/collectivistic orientation.

This research empirically tests the association between management behavior and manager's attitudes toward innovativeness, and the influence of personal values on this link. Obtained cognitions importantly complement the abundant literature about innovativeness, with the empirical findings from selected Central Europe economies. Results are reported for three Central Europe Economies with different economic development paths in last two decades; Austria is a well-developed market economy with stable growth, and Slovenia and Poland are former transition economies, adopting different approaches to transitional restructuring and being nowadays considered as emerging economies. Such comparative empirical study, addressing the link between management behavior and its creativity, in considered countries, has not been done yet in relevant literature.

THEORETICAL BACKGROUND AND HYPOTHESES DEVELOPMENT

Innovating has become a key factor for development and/or further success of nowadays organizations (Collins & Porras, 2002; Skarzynski & Gibson, 2008). Due to the high potential of innovations and possible influence on organizational success, a lot of examinations in this field has been done over last two decades, which were primarily focused on identification and definition of key factors of innovativeness or innovative behavior in organizations (Drazin & Schoonhoven, 1996; Slappendel, 1996; Tushman & O'Reilly, 1997; Hurley & Hult, 1998). Among plethora of studies, one stream has pointed out also the role and importance of cultural context and/or personal values of organizational members for shaping and improving innovativeness in organizations (Christiansen, 2000; Afuah, 2003; Lemon & Sahota, 2004; Chesbrough, 2009; Potocan & Nedelko, 2014). An important role in shaping innovative working and behavior of an organization is also attributed to its managers, which are often emphasized an important driver of organizational innovativeness (Amabile et al., 1996; Collins & Porras, 2002; Skarzynski & Gibson, 2008; Nedelko & Potocan, 2013).

Plethora of "soft" and "hard" factors like strategy and goals of organization, stakeholders claims, innovative culture influence innovative behavior (Afuah, 2003; Lester & Piore, 2004; Skarzynski & Gibson, 2008; Chesbrough, 2009), and consequently also innovativeness of managements. According to the cognitions in this field, different starting points (e.g. approaches) to examine management characteristics and its behavior are available, which enable and support its innovativeness (Katz, 2003; Rogers, 2003; Lester & Piore, 2004; Gloor, 2006; Potocan & Nedelko, 2014). Thus, different descriptions exist when considering management characteristics that are associated with its creativeness and innovativeness (Afuah, 2003; Rogers, 2003). Typical characteristic of innovative management are (DeBono, 1992; Amabile et al., 1996; Potočan & Mulej, 2007):

- Management is creative,
- Management accepts and tests new ideas and suggestions also from others (e.g., co-workers, sub-ordinates),
- Management tolerates errors that are consequence of innovative work or behavior,
- Management stimulates organizational learning,
- Management accepts risks,

- Management reduces the importance of formal rules, procedures or standard operating procedures, since they reduce or limit creativeness, and
- Management puts in the forefront method of trial and error.

Management innovativeness is dependent upon a plethora of hard (e.g., organizational goals, stakeholder claims, available resources, etc.) and soft factors (e.g., values, culture, personality, etc.) (Amabile, 1988; Shalley & Perry-Smith, 2001; Collins & Porras, 2002; Skarzynski & Gibson, 2008; Nedelko & Potocan, 2013).

Based on typical characteristics of innovative management and key factors that influence management's innovative behavior, we considered typical characteristics of innovative management as building blocks (or components) of management innovativeness – we used term drivers of management innovativeness. Basic drivers of management innovativeness (e.g. inner middle circle) are outlined in Figure 1.

According to the key drivers of management innovative behavior (i.e. outer circle), we focus on the management characteristics. Thus, a second stream of literature relevant for our research is related to management behavior.

The management literature offers some evidence about the relationship between selected characteristics of management behavior and management innovativeness (DeBono, 1992; Collins & Porras, 2002; Skarzynski & Gibson, 2008; Nedelko & Potocan, 2013).

A plethora of different approaches exist to examine management behavior (Fiedler, 1967; Tannenbaum & Schmidt, 1973; Bass & Avolio, 1990; Yammarino, Dionne, Chun, & Dansereau, 2005; Yukl, 2008).

Figure 1. Basic drivers of management creativeness and innovativeness

For considering management behavior we framed typical behavioral characteristics into continuum ranging from authoritative to democratic behavior (Tannenbaum & Schmidt, 1973), whereas we expanded initial focus of this theory – beyond decision making aspect (Nedelko & Mayrhofer, 2012; Lang, Szabo, Catana, Konecna, & Skalova, 2013).

According to different well-known approaches, we emphasized following typical characteristics of autocratic leaders following, (1) decision making is in the domain of management (Tannenbaum & Schmidt, 1973; Vroom & Yetton, 1973), (2) control process is in the domain of manager/s or superiors (Vroom & Yetton, 1973; Ali, Azim, & Krishnan, 1995), (3) for performing tasks is responsible manger (Yammarino et al., 2005), (4) management has full authority (Hersey & Blanchard, 1969), (5) management relies more on positional power (Daft, 2000), (6) management is oriented especially on achievement of goals (Pastor & Mayo, 2008; Yukl, 2008), and (7) cooperation between management and subordinates is weak, since manager mostly only announces the decisions to subordinates (Tannenbaum & Schmidt, 1973).

On the other hand, typical characteristics of democratic leaders are: (1) leader permits the group to make decisions within defined boundaries (Tannenbaum & Schmidt, 1973), (2) for control processes are responsible also employees, through self-control (Daft, 2000), (3) employees are empowered, and become responsible for their results, while leader has reduced responsibility in terms of performed work, (4) leader delegates some authority to the subordinates (Yukl, 2006), (5) leaders mostly rely on their personal power, charisma, and knowledge (Bass & Avolio, 1990), (6) besides solely focus on goal attainment, leaders also take into consideration employees' needs (Blake & Mouton, 1964), (7) cooperation between management and empowered employees is strong, due to the employees' participation in decision making process and employees' empowerment (Mahsud, Yukl, & Prussia, 2010).

Literature offers us some, mostly theoretical, evidences about (direct) relationship between management behavior and management innovativeness (and its underlying building blocks). In that framework an important stream of literature describes typical behavior of innovative and successful managers and/ or organizations, which emphasizes typical behavior of managers and/or leaders when achieving higher level of innovativeness (DeBono, 1992; Collins & Porras, 2002; Skarzynski & Gibson, 2008; Nedelko & Potocan, 2013). Thus, often are emphasized behavioral characteristics that are closer to the democratic leadership style, than towards autocratic behavior. Frequently mentioned are for instance enthusiasm and willingness to accept ideas of others, willingness to sharing knowledge (Potočan & Mulej, 2007), flexible and non-rigid rules and procedures in organizations, etc. Based on these findings we can outline that the more managers show participative behavior, the higher is their ability to establish and assure a fertile ground for innovations in organizations (Collins & Porras, 2002; Skarzynski & Gibson, 2008).

According to different findings about typical characteristics of management behavior and successful and innovative organizations we can formulate following hypothesis:

H1: *Managers with prevalent democratic behavior will express more positive attitudes toward innovativeness than those with prevalent autocratic behavior.*

In line with the aim of this paper, we dedicate our attention also on the influence of managerial personal values on their behavior and consequently management's innovativeness. These issues are rarely examined and are often blurry, especially in emerging economies, while the link between these concepts is not frequently addressed in the literature.

Personal values can be considered based on many typologies. For our research we used Schwartz's typology of personal values (Schwartz & Bilsky, 1987; Schwartz, 1992) which is often used in empirical researching in management area (Karp, 1996; Ralston et al., 2011). We take into the consideration individual level high-ordered dimensions, which are based on ten dimensions of values, which further based on 56 single values. At this level, Schwartz defines four groups of values. Self-enhancing values emphasize individuals' orientation toward the accomplishment of individual goals, even when the achieving of individual goals potentially occurs at the expense of others. Self-transcending values trigger actions aimed at understanding, appreciation, tolerance, and protection for the welfare of all people and nature. Openness to change emphasizes people's motivation to follow intellectual and emotional interests in unpredictable and uncertain ways. Conservation emphasizes people's motivation to preserve the status quo and conservation provides certainty in relationships with others, institutions, and traditions.

Based on typical innovative behavior and well-known studies from developed market economies, we can outline a few core values that supporting management innovativeness, like freedom, and exciting life, creativity, broad-minded, curiosity, ambitious, choosing own goals, and innovativeness (DeBono, 1992; Amabile et al., 1996; Collins & Porras, 2002; Skarzynski & Gibson, 2008; Nedelko & Potocan, 2013).

In terms of considered four groups of personal values, and in that frame two opposite dimensions; (1) openness to change vs. conservatism; and (2) self-transcendence vs. self-enhancement. Looking from the content viewpoint and prevalent cognitions in the literature, a detailed comparison of the content of typical characteristics of innovative behaviour (and in turn innovativeness of management) and values description, becomes evident that openness to changes vs. conservation values are associated to the innovativeness or innovative behaviour of employees and managers (Hage & Dewar, 1973; Amabile, 1988; Mueller & Thomas, 2000; Rogers, 2003; Lester & Piore, 2004; Conway & Steward, 2009).

On the other hand, other dimension – self-enhancement vs. self-transcendence, is contently related to the management behaviour (Fein, Vasiliu, & Tziner, 2011). Thus, there is a lack of clear indication of relations between this dimension and innovativeness.

According to the well-known cognitions about the influence of managerial personal values on their behavior and manager's innovativeness (Ralston, Gustafson, Cheung, & Terpstra, 1993; Ralston et al., 2011), we formulate one hypothesis and one research question.

H2: Manager's personal values mediate the effect of management behavior on management innovativeness.
RQ1: Is there any relationship between manager's personal values of self-enhancement vs. self-transcendence values and management innovativeness.

METHODS

Sample and Procedure

Sampling was done based on GVIN directory which lists Slovenian organization, Aurelis which lists Austrian organizations, and Kompass directory ("Firmy w Polsce"), which lists Polish organizations. Sampling was done according to the data in NACE classification for all countries involved. We based our calculations on 208 answers from Slovenian managers, 196 Austrian and 201 Poland managers, obtained through years 2012 and 2013.

Answers were obtained using computer assisted telephone interviewing and online surveying. In Slovenia, survey was done using Computer assisted telephone interviewing. We contacted 700 managers at different position in sampled organization via telephone, while 208 answers were obtained, appropriate for our research, resulting in 29.7% response rate. In Austria, an online survey was done. We sent link to the online questionnaire to approximately 2 400 managers at various hierarchical positions in sample organizations. We received 215, while 196 answers were used in analysis, resulting in 8.2% response rate. In Poland as well, an online survey was done. We sent link to online questionnaire to approximately 2000 managers at different managerial levels. We received 262, but 201 answers were appropriate for the research, due to the incompleteness of answers. This resulted in 10.05% response rate.

Demographic characteristics for all three samples are outlined in Table 1.

Measures

Personal Values

Personal values are measured by the Schwartz Value Survey (SVS), a tool with cross-cultural validity (Schwartz, 1992). Respondents in the survey rate each of 56 personal values using a 9-point Likert-type scale, ranging from "opposed to my values" (-1) to "of supreme importance" (7). Our consideration of personal values is focused on individual-level high-order dimensions from Schwartz's values classifica-

Table 1. Demographic Characteristics for Austrian, Slovenian, and Poland sample.

Variable	Austria	Slovenia	Poland
Age	45.66 years	47.02 years	39.01 years
Age – Grouped			
Less Than 35 years	18.4%	20.8%	37.6%
36 – 45 years	28.9%	21.6%	35.6%
46 – 55 years	36.3%	38.6%	23.8%
More than 55 years	16.3%	18.9%	3.0%
Gender			
Male	78.4%	50.2%	42.1%
Female	21.6%	49.8%	57.4%
Education			
Finished Secondary School	37.9%	25.1%	32.6%
Finished Bachelor, Master or Doctorate Degree	62.1%	74.9%	66.8%
Position in Organization			
First-Level Manager	11.5%	7.7%	31.7%
Mid-Level Manager	37.9%	25.1%	35.1%
Upper-Level Manager	50.5%	67.2%	33.2%
Working Experiences	25.24 years	23.31 years	15.44 years
Working Experiences – Grouped			
Less Than 10 years	10.0%	17.0%	31.2%
10 – 20 Years	30.5%	21.6%	43.6%
20 – 30 Years	36.8%	33.2%	22.8%
More Than 30 Years	226.%	28.2%	2.5%
Organization Size			
Fewer than 49 Employees	10.3%	6.9%	47.0%
50 to 249 Employees	42.7%	86.9%	35.1%
More Than 250 Employees	35.7%	6.2%	17.8%

tion and based on a questionnaire adopted from Schwartz's values survey, namely, self-enhancing, self-transcending, openness to change, and conservation values. Those dimensions are aligned as two bi-polar orientations, namely: (1) self-enhancement (power, achievement, hedonism) versus self-transcendence (universalism and benevolence) and (2) openness to change (stimulation and self-direction) versus conservation (tradition, conformity and security) dimensions. Used value dimensions are calculated upon importance of single values for respondents. (Schwartz, 2011).

Management Behavior

Based on exploratory factorial analysis of 15 items aimed to measure management behavior and reliability analyses, eight items accurately and in a reliable manner represent management behavior, framed into leadership continuum (Tannenbaum & Schmidt, 1973; Nedelko & Mayrhofer, 2012) and expanded beyond decision making – participation of employees in decision making process – aspect (Lang et al., 2013). All items were measured using an 8-point Likert-type scale, where the anchor for each item referring to autocratic management behavior (1) and democratic management behavior (8). Those eight items are: (1) for performing work are mostly responsible (1 – manager/s or superior; 8 – employees); (2) decision making in organization is (1 – concentrated only on management; 8 – delegated also to employees), (3) management in organization is focused on (1 – goals/tasks; 8 – employees and their needs); (4) management defines goals/aims/tasks that stimulate (1 – individual work; 8 – group/team work in organization); (5) control process in organization is mainly in domain of (1 – manager/s or superior; 8 – employees); (6) authority (1 – has management; 8 – is delegated to the employees); (7) management in organization rely mainly on (1– positional power; 8 – personal power); and (8) cooperation between management and employees is (1 – weak; 8 – strong).

Based on defined construct – management behavior – we defined two "generic types" of management behavior, namely (1) autocratic behavior and (2) democratic behavior. Cronbach alpha for the construct was .724 and is thus comparable to those in other researches in this area (Sarros & Santora, 2001; Sosik, 2005) and with general research practice (Ho, 2006), due to the exploratory nature of our study. For instance Sarros and Santora (2001) in their study, use transformational-transactional typology, reporting coefficients ranging between .60 and .83. Sosik (2005) in his study of charismatic leadership reports coefficients ranging between .74 and .80.

Management Innovativeness

Management innovativeness is considered in terms of manager's perception, expresses though their attitudes, toward typical innovative behavior, among which is in the forefront creativeness and other factors closely related to the creativeness (Amabile, 1988; Nedelko & Potocan, 2013). In line with previously outlined typical characteristics of management innovativeness, we identified the following set of items in order to examine manager's attitudes towards typical innovative behavior. For measuring management attitudes and/or preferences towards innovativeness, we identified the concept of "management innovativeness", based on prior outlined theoretical and empirical findings about of innovativeness (Amabile, 1988; O'Reilly, Chatham, & Caldwell, 1991; Mumford, Zaccaro, Harding, Jacobs, & Fleishman, 2000; Potočan & Mulej, 2007). In line with proposed framework, five selected items in the construct are measured using a 7-point Likert-type scale, with anchors referring to low level of management innovativeness (1) and high level of management innovativeness (7). Selected items are: (1) manager's stimulation for creativity (1 – not supporting; 7 – supporting); (2) openness of managers to new ideas and other's knowledge (1 – refusing new ideas and other's knowledge; 7 – accepting new ideas and other's knowledge); (3) benevolence to changes (1 – don't support; 7 - support); (4) risk perception (1 – refusing – having aversive attitudes toward risk; 7 – preference – having favorable attitudes toward risk); and (5) innovativeness as a value of managers (1 – low; 7 – high). Cronbach alpha for the construct was .887.

With manager's answers we obtained: (1) the information about how important are single values for them; thus manager's self-perception about importance of each of the values included in the survey (Schwartz, 1992, 2011); and (2) manager's perception about "management behavior" and "their innovativeness"; thus manager's self-assessed behavior and innovativeness is outlined. Adopted approach – self-reporting/ assessment by members of organization, is common in field of business research, especially employees perceptions and/or attitudes regarding their behavior (Egri & Herman, 2000; Ralston et al., 2011).

RESEARCH DESIGN

The impact of typical management behavior, framed into autocratic-democratic continuum, on their perception of their level of innovativeness is controlled with a set of demographic and organizational variables, as well as with the perceived importance of personal values for managers. Proposed research design reflects findings in the literature, which emphasizes important role of personal values in shaping management behavior, as well as influence on level of management innovativeness. Furthermore, suggested relations are examined in Central and East Europe catching up economies (i.e., Slovenia and Poland), while also considering the Western economies context – sample of Austria. Our research agenda is outlined in Figure 2.

For calculations we used SPSS 21. First, we carried out exploratory factorial analysis, followed by the reliability analysis. After new construct computation, we used regression analysis and hierarchical regression analysis in order to examine proposed relations in research model.

Figure 2. Proposed research agenda

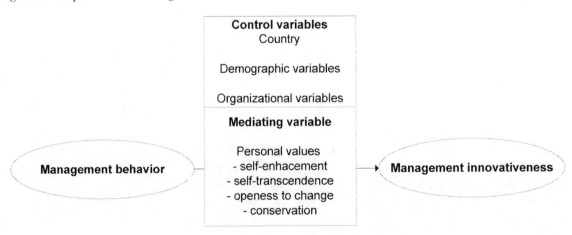

RESULTS

In line with proposed research agenda, we report mean values about management behavior, manager's perception of their innovativeness, and importance of personal values, which are considered as mediating variable. Next are presented results from hierarchical regression analysis. All results are reported for three considered economies. In Table 2 are outlined mean values for variables of interest in the research.

In terms of comparing mean values for single variable in three considered countries, ANOVA results reveal that there are: (1) significant differences in importance of personal values for managers in three compared countries; openness to change values – $F(3,671) = 17.489$, $p < 0.001$, conservation values – $F(3,671) = 39.116$, $p < 0.001$, self-enhancement values – $F(3,671) = 51.611$, $p < 0.001$, and self-transcendence values – $F(3,671) = 59.300$, $p < 0.001$.; (2) significant differences in perceived management behavior among managers, $F(3,655) = 76.849$, $p < 0.001$; and (3) significant differences in perceived innovativeness, – $F(3,655) = 41.900$, $p < 0.001$.

In Table 3 we outlined the impact of personal values on management behavior and manager's perception of their innovativeness, in three considered samples.

Outlined differences in importance of personal values for managers, characteristics of management behavior and perceived level of management innovativeness, as well as the impact of some personal values on management behavior and innovativeness, suggest a deeper examination of the relations between management behavior, management innovativeness and personal values.

In Table 4 we present the impact of management behavior on management's innovative behavior, where demographic and organizational variables were used as control variables.

It is evident that with management behavior we can explain almost one third of variance in management innovativeness, while the impact of demographic and organizational variables on management innovativeness is weak. On the other hand, in Poland example we can explain 16.1% of variance in management innovativeness with management behavior. In Slovenian sample, demographic and organizational variables explain less than 3 percent of management innovativeness. Based on outlined results we support hypothesis 1 for all three considered samples.

Next, we examine the mediating role of personal values on the relationship between management behavior and management innovativeness. We added personal values as mediating variable, keeping all previously introduced control variables as well. Results are summarized in Table 5.

Regarding the mediating effect of managers personal values on the association between management behavior and their innovativeness, our results reveal (only) a marginal role of personal values, in comparison to the impact of management behavior on level of management innovativeness. Results show

Table 2. Mean Values for Variables of Interest in Austria, Slovenia, and Poland.

Variable	Austria	Slovenia	Poland
Openness to Change	4.78	5.21	4.51
Conservation	4.13	5.06	4.35
Self-Enhancement	3.74	4.91	4.25
Self-Transcendence	4.85	5.76	4.60
Management Behavior	4.29	5.09	3.76
Innovative Attitudes	5.37	6.35	4.96

Table 3. The Impact of Personal Values on Management Behavior and Management Innovativeness*

Personal value	Country	Management behavior				Management innovativeness			
		R Square	β	t	Sig.	R Square	β	t	Sig.
Openness to change[a]	SLO	0.143	0.117	1.321	0.188	0.148	0.120	1.327	0.186
	AUT	0.056	0.077	0.815	0.416	0.172	0.181	1.978	0.049
	POL	0.061	0.152	1.493	0.137	0.061	-0.086	-0.870	0.385
Conservation	SLO	0.143	0.026	0.273	0.785	0.148	0.095	0.969	0.334
	AUT	0.056	-0.020	-0.190	0.849	0.172	0.129	1.256	0.211
	POL	0.061	0.085	0.775	0.439	0.061	0.107	1.008	0.315
Self-enhancement	SLO	0.143	-0.073	-0.806	0.421	0.148	-0.016	-0.171	0.865
	AUT	0.056	-0.223	-2.422	0.016	0.172	-0.178	-1.999	0.047
	POL	0.061	-0.090	-0.943	0.347	0.061	-0.011	-0.122	0.903
Self-transcendence	SLO	0.143	0.179	1.868	0.063	0.148	0.156	1.597	0.111
	AUT	0.056	0.020	0.184	0.855	0.172	-0.057	-0.554	0.580
	POL	0.061	-0.159	-1.393	0.165	0.061	0.056	0.505	0.616

*note: when we test the impact of personal values, control variables were gender, age, working experiences, education level, position in organization, organizational size, and industry, as control variables.

[a]for Slovenia the impact is of working experiences (β = 0.379, p = 0.023), position of organization and industry is significant.

Table 4. The Impact of Management Behavior on Management's Innovative Behavior.

	R Square	R Square change[a]	β	t	Sig.
SLO	0.282	0.029	0.533	9.474	0.000
AUT	0.389	0.067	0.517	8.558	0.000
POL	0.253	0.092	0.408	6.408	0.000

[a]R Square change – the change of explained variance in innovative behavior, when introducing control variables (i.e., demographic and organizational variables).

Table 5. The Impact of Management Behavior on Management's Innovative Behavior, Using Personal Values as Mediating Variable.

	R Square	R Square change[a]	β	t	Sig.
SLO[b]	0.344	0.062	0.488	8.565	0.000
AUT[b]	0.413	0.024	0.521	8.503	0.000
POL[b]	0.280	0.027	0.423	6.638	0.000

[a]R Square change – the change of explained variance in innovative behavior, when introducing personal values as mediating variable (we also keeping before introduced demographic and organizational variables).

[b]none of the four groups of values significantly mediates the relation between management behavior and management innovative behavior.

that entry of personal values, significantly contribute to the explanation of management's innovative behavior in all three samples; Slovenia – F(12,246) = 10.748, *p < 0.001*, Austria – F(12,176) = 10.323, *p < 0.001*; Poland – (12,189) = 6.124, *p < 0.001*, as mediating variable, in all three cases . Based on these results we can support hypothesis 2 for all three considered samples.

DISCUSSION

The main purpose of this chapter is to examine the impact of prevalent management behavior on management innovativeness, while also considering the impact of manger's personal values on their innovativeness. Research was done in three Central and East Economies, having different backgrounds and development paths; namely Slovenia, Austria and Poland.

Based on obtained mean values it is evident that management behavior, as perceived by Austrian managers, tends to have more autocratic orientation than behavior of Slovenian and Poland counterparts. More autocratic behavior of Austrian mangers, in comparison to other two economies, is in line with higher relatively higher proportion of typical elements of autocratic management behavior in Germanic culture (Brodbeck et al., 2000; House, Hanges, Javidan, Dorfman, & Gupta, 2004), than for instance in relatively more collectivistic culture, like Slovenia (Lang, Kovač, & Bernik, 2000; Potočan & Mulej, 2007), where historically collectivistic orientation had stronger impact. On the other hand, we can summarized similar for Poland (Kozminski, 2008).

In terms of the impact of management behavior on management innovativeness, for all three considered economies, results indicate that more democratic management behavior is positively related to the higher level of management innovativeness. These findings provide a link between democratic management behavior (Tannenbaum & Schmidt, 1973; Lang et al., 2013), which is more employee oriented and open to the novelties, accepting changes reflecting in innovative behavior (Skarzynski & Gibson, 2008; Adler, 2011; Nedelko & Potocan, 2013). For the considered Western economy it is evident that management behavior plays more important role in shaping management innovative behavior, than in other two catching up economies.

In terms of mediating role of personal values, on the relationship between management behavior and management innovativeness, results show significant impact. Although significant role in mediating relationship between management behavior and its innovativeness, for all three samples, the role of personal values is marginal. Studies that recognized important role of personal values in shaping management innovativeness (Collins & Porras, 2002; Potočan & Mulej, 2007), consider the impact of values isolated of other influencers. In our study, when we considered the impact of behavior and values on management innovativeness, the impact of behavior, is way stronger than that of values.

Openness to change among Polish managers can be explained by the intensity of transition of enterprises in Poland since the collapse of socialistic economy. Only companies that implemented radical process of organizational changes have survived (Kozminski, 2008). It strengthened the conviction of managers that changes, as well as innovation are inevitable. Polish companies are filling the gaps between them and companies from developed economies; the technology gap has almost disappeared but there is still a gap in the quality of management practices (Costigan et al., 2005; Brzozowski, 2001). This gap is being reduced by a dynamic development of managerial education and training in Poland and other post socialist economies (Kozminski, 1996).

Research conducted in companies in Poland indicates the changes in the nature of managerial thinking from traditional strategic thinking (associated with such characteristics as rationality, problem orientation, domination of self-contained roles, focus of intent, dealing with constraints, sequentially, and risk awareness) toward design thinking (associated with growing importance of such characteristics as focus on innovation, celebration of creativity, expectation of wicked problems, solution orientation, domination of interactive skills, using constraints as a source of inspiration, non-linearity, and risk orientation) (Brzozowski, 2014).

The main cognition is that in the current doubtful times, management's innovative behavior is significantly driven by management behavior. A marginal role of personal values in shaping/influencing/predicting management innovativeness could be attributed at least to the following reasons: (1) plethora of "soft" and "hard" factors influence innovative behavior, like strategy and goals of organization, stakeholders claims, innovative culture (Afuah, 2003; Lester & Piore, 2004; Skarzynski & Gibson, 2008; Chesbrough, 2009). Thus each of the influences can explain relatively small proportion of management innovativeness. Thus, looking relatively despite the minor impact, the values can be considered also as an important driver of management innovativeness (in cases where the impact is significant); (2) in terms of people's behavior in organizations, employees personal values are not always in the forefront in comparison to the organizational culture and underlying values, rather their relative importance depend on the level of personal-organizational fit (Westerman & Cyr, 2004; De Clercq, Fontaine, & Anseel, 2008); the higher the level of the fit, more are in the forefront also interests, values, and behavior of individuals, since they are aligned with those of organizations. In this example, the impact of personal values could be higher; (3) in business researching, considering the impact of personal values, authors report about the impact of employee's/manager's personal values on different aspects, like attitudes towards corporate social responsibility, leadership style, innovative thinking (Egri & Herman, 2000; Hemingway, 2005; Ralston et al., 2011; Nedelko & Mayrhofer, 2012), but the impact is mainly considered as weak, although significant; (4) looking also into the cradle of empirical researching of personal values – psychological literature, the common finding is that personal values guides people's behavior (Rokeach, 1973; Schwartz, 1992). This presumption is based on isolating other factors of human behavior, but when taking into consideration also other factors (e.g. big five personality), the impact becomes weaker, and values explanation power reduce. Our results about the influence of personal values show similar tendency.

When comparing the relative importance of personal values, and their dimensions, in Slovenia, Austria and Poland, results need careful interpretation. Different studies considering personal values in considered economies, reveals that importance of personal values for Austrians is relatively lower than for Slovenia and Poland (Ralston et al., 2011). Also our results reflect these findings. Thus, this must be taken into consideration when discussing relative importance of personal values.

IMPLICATIONS AND RECOMMENDATIONS

Findings about stronger influence of management behavior on shaping innovative behavior of management in Western economy heightened the need to re-think existing management practices in catching up economies in order to provide a fertile ground for increasing innovativeness or in general innovative behavior of management.

In catching up economies is often emphasized that management practices still have some elements from past – i.e. from previous socialistic/collectivist regime (e.g. avoiding responsibility, taking care for others). For instance in Slovenia and Poland frequently emphasized are tight control of employees by their superiors, using positional power, and lack of empowerment. In terms of innovative behavior, risk averseness and closeness for ideas and knowledge importantly impede creativeness.

Our findings assigning greater role to the change of management practices and behavior in catching up economies in order to increase innovativeness of management, although in last decade there has been emphasized lack of innovative culture and "outdated personal values", as two primary factors reducing and/or hindering innovativeness in Slovenian organizations (Potočan & Mulej, 2007; Nedelko & Potocan, 2013).

According to this, in case of Slovenia, the focus should be on changing management practices, instead of referring only on lack of innovative culture. But on the other hand findings from western economies show clear link between innovative behavior and openness to change values; this link is not significant in catching up economies.

For instance, these findings give the idea foreign partners what drives management innovativeness in Slovenia and Poland. These findings, could also serve as an important starting point for mainstream topic for discussion at professional meetings/workshops of managers to enlighten this problem and make familiar managers about the impact of management behavior on management's level of innovativeness.

FUTURE RESEARCH DIRECTIONS

For instance, framing the examination of the relationship between management behavior and management innovativeness, in the context of organizational characteristics, would enhance understanding drivers of management innovativeness. Next possible way is to examine the impact tin different economies, in order to define the impact of different economic/social context on management innovativeness.

CONCLUSION

This chapter provides a research approach for researching the impact of management behavior on manager's attitudes toward innovativeness with a mediating role of personal values. Our results can serve as a starting point for enhancing creativity of members of management, which can later have implications for other employees. Thus, in terms of emerging economies, more focus and attention should be dedicated to changing patterns of management behavior, since it strongly influences manager's attitudes toward innovativeness, instead of frequently emphasized personal values and outdated values. These findings are useful for policy makers at the national, business and academic level.

REFERENCES

Adler, N. J. (2011). Leading beautifully: The creative economy and beyond. *Journal of Management Inquiry, 20*(3), 208–221. doi:10.1177/1056492611409292

Afuah, A. (2003). *Innovation management: Strategies, implementation, and profits*. New York: Oxford University Press.

Ali, A. J., Azim, A., & Krishnan, K. D. (1995). Expatriates and host country nationals: Managerial values and decision styles. *Leadership and Organizational Development, 16*(6), 27–34. doi:10.1108/01437739510092252

Amabile, T. M. (1988). A model of creativity and innovation in organization. In B. M. Staw & L. L. Cummings (Eds.), *Research in organizational behavior* (Vol. 10, pp. 123–167). Greenwich, CT: JAI Press.

Amabile, T. M., Conti, R., Coon, H., Lazenby, J., & Herron, M. (1996). Assessing the work environment for creativity. *Academy of Management Journal, 39*(5), 1154–1184. doi:10.2307/256995

Bass, B. M., & Avolio, B. J. (1990). The implications of transactional and transformational leadership for individual, team, and organizational development. *Research in Organizational Change and Development, 4*, 231–272.

Blake, R., & Mouton, J. (1964). *The managerial grid: The key to leadership excellence*. Houston, TX: Gulf Publishing Co.

Brodbeck, F. C., Frese, M., Akerblom, S., Audia, G., Bakacsi, G., Bendova, H., & Wunderer, R. et al. (2000). Cultural variation of leadership prototypes across 22 european countries. *Journal of Occupational and Organizational Psychology, 73*(1), 1–29. doi:10.1348/096317900166859

Brzozowski, M. (2001). Developmental stages of polish companies in the period of transition. In A. Janc (Ed.), *Economy in transition. Problems, ideas, solutions* (pp. 249–257). Poznan: Poznan University of Economics Press.

Brzozowski, M. (2014). The boundaries of management thinking: Design thinking versus strategic thinking. In Within and beyond boundaries of management (pp. 109-120). Warsaw: Warsaw School of Economics Press.

Chesbrough, H. (2009). *Open innovation*. Boston: Harvard Business School Press.

Christiansen, J. A. (2000). *Building the innovative organization: Management systems that encourage innovation*. New York: Palgrave Macmillan. doi:10.1057/9780333977446

Collins, J., & Porras, J. I. (2002). *Built to last: Successful habits of visionary companies*. New York: Harper Collins Publishers.

Conway, S., & Steward, F. (2009). *Managing and shaping innovation*. Oxford, UK: Oxford University Press.

Costigan, R. D., Insinga, R. C., Berman, J. J., Ilter, S. S., Kranas, G., & Kureshov, V. (2005). An Examination of the Relationship of a Western Performance-Management Process to Key Workplace Behaviours in Transition Economies. *Canadian Journal of Administrative Sciences, 22*(3), 255–267. doi:10.1111/j.1936-4490.2005.tb00370.x

Dabic, M., Potocan, V., Nedelko, Z., & Morgan, T. R. (2013). Exploring the use of 25 leading business practices in transitioning market supply chains. *International Journal of Physical Distribution & Logistics Management, 43*(10), 833–851. doi:10.1108/IJPDLM-10-2012-0325

Daft, R. L. (2000). *Management.* Fort Worth, TX: The Dryden Press.

De Clercq, S., Fontaine, J. R. J., & Anseel, F. (2008). In search of a comprehensive value model for assessing supplementary person-organization fit. *The Journal of Psychology, 142*(3), 277–302. doi:10.3200/JRLP.142.3.277-302 PMID:18589938

DeBono, E. (1992). *Serious creativity.* Toronto: HarperCollins.

Drazin, R., & Schoonhoven, C. B. (1996). Community, population, and organization effects on innovation: A multilevel perspective. *Academy of Management Journal, 39*(5), 1065–1083. doi:10.2307/256992

Dyck, R., & Mulej, M. (1998). *Self-transformation of the forgotten four-fifth.* Dubuque, IA: Kendall/Hunt.

Egri, C. P., & Herman, S. (2000). Leadership in the north american environmental sector: Values, leadership styles, and contexts of environmental leaders and their organizations. *Academy of Management Journal, 43*(4), 571–604. doi:10.2307/1556356

Fein, E. C., Vasiliu, C., & Tziner, A. (2011). Individual values and preferred leadership behaviors: A study of romanian managers. *Journal of Applied Social Psychology, 41*(3), 515–535. doi:10.1111/j.1559-1816.2011.00724.x

Fiedler, F. E. (1967). *A theory of leadership effectiveness.* New York: McGraw-Hill Book Co.

Gloor, A. (2006). *Swarm creativity. Competitive advantage through collaborative innovation networks.* Oxford, UK: Oxford University Press. doi:10.1093/acprof:oso/9780195304121.001.0001

Hage, J., & Dewar, R. (1973). Elite values versus organizational structure in predicting innovation. *Administrative Science Quarterly, 18*(3), 279–290. doi:10.2307/2391664

Hemingway, C. A. (2005). Personal values as a catalyst for corporate social entrepreneurship. *Journal of Business Ethics, 60*(3), 233–249. doi:10.1007/s10551-005-0132-5

Hersey, P., & Blanchard, K. H. (1969). Life cycle theory of leadership. *Training and Development Journal, 23*(5), 26–34.

Ho, R. (2006). *Handbook of univariate and multivariate data analysis and interpretation with spss.* Boca Raton, FL: Chapman & Hall/CRC. doi:10.1201/9781420011111

House, R. J., Hanges, P. J., Javidan, M., Dorfman, P. W., & Gupta, V. (2004). *Culture, leadership, and organizations: The globe study of 62 societies.* Thousand Oaks, CA: Sage.

Hurley, R. F., & Hult, G. T. M. (1998). Innovation, market orientation, and organizational learning: An integration and empirical examination. *Journal of Marketing, 62*(3), 42–54. doi:10.2307/1251742

Karp, D. G. (1996). Values and their effect on pro-environmental behavior. *Environment and Behavior, 28*(1), 111–133. doi:10.1177/0013916596281006

Katz, R. (2003). *The human side of managing technological innovation.* Oxford, UK: Oxford University Press.

Kozminski, A. (1996). Management Education in Central and Eastern Europe. In *International Encyclopedia of Business and Management* (Vol. 2, pp. 1123–1129). London: Routledge.

Kozminski, A. (2008). Anatomy of systemic change in polish management in transition. *Communist and Post-Communist Studies, 41*(3), 263–280. doi:10.1016/j.postcomstud.2008.06.006

Lang, R., Kovač, J., & Bernik, M. (2000). *Management v tranzicijskih procesih* [Management in Transition Processes]. Kranj: Moderna organizacija.

Lang, R., Szabo, E., Catana, G. A., Konecna, Z., & Skalova, P. (2013). Beyond participation? - leadership ideals of future managers from central and east European countries. *Journal for East European Management Studies, 18*(4), 482–511.

Lemon, M., & Sahota, P. S. (2004). Organizational culture as a knowledge repository for increased innovative capacity. *Tehnovation, 24*(6), 483–498. doi:10.1016/S0166-4972(02)00102-5

Lester, K., & Piore, M. (2004). *Innovation - the missing dimension.* Cambridge, MA: Harvard Business Press.

Mahsud, R., Yukl, G., & Prussia, G. (2010). Leader empathy, ethical leadership, and relations-oriented behaviors as antecedents of leader-member exchange quality. *Journal of Managerial Psychology, 25*(6), 561–577. doi:10.1108/02683941011056932

Mueller, S. L., & Thomas, A. S. (2000). Culture and entrepreneurial potential: A nine country study of locus of control and innovativeness. *Journal of Business Venturing, 16*(1), 51–75. doi:10.1016/S0883-9026(99)00039-7

Mumford, M. D., Zaccaro, S. J., Harding, F. D., Jacobs, T. O., & Fleishman, E. A. (2000). Leadership skills for a changing world: Solving complex social problems. *The Leadership Quarterly, 11*(1), 11–35. doi:10.1016/S1048-9843(99)00041-7

Nauwelaers, C., & Reid, A. (2002). Learning innovation policy in a market-based context: Process, issues and challenges for eu candidate countries. *Journal of International Relations and Development, 5*(4), 357–379.

Nedelko, Z., & Mayrhofer, W. (2012). *The influence of managerial personal values on leadership style. Management re-imagined.* Paper presented at the 11th World Congress of the International Federation of Scholarly Associations of Management, Limerick, Ireland.

Nedelko, Z., & Potocan, V. (2013). The role of management innovativeness in modern organizations. *Journal of Enterprising Communities, 7*(1), 36–49. doi:10.1108/17506201311315590

OReilly, C. A., Chatham, J. A., & Caldwell, D. F. (1991). People and organizational culture: A profile comparison approach to assessing person-organisation fit. *Academy of Management Journal, 34*(3), 487–516. doi:10.2307/256404

Pastor, J. C., & Mayo, M. (2008). Transformational leadership among spanish upper echelons: The role of managerial values and goal orientation. *Leadership and Organization Development Journal, 29*(4), 340–358. doi:10.1108/01437730810876140

Potočan, V., & Mulej, M. (2007). *Transition into innovative enterprise*. Maribor: Faculty of Economics and Business.

Potocan, V., & Nedelko, Z. (2014). Management innovativeness: A case of slovenian small and medium enterprises. *Transformations in Business & Economics, 13*(1), 41–59.

Ralston, D. A., Egri, C. P., Reynaud, E., Srinivasan, N., Furrer, O., Brock, D., & Wallace, A. et al. (2011). A twenty-first century assessment of values across the global workforce. *Journal of Business Ethics, 104*(1), 1–31. doi:10.1007/s10551-011-0835-8

Ralston, D. A., Gustafson, D. J., Cheung, F. M., & Terpstra, R. H. (1993). Differences in managerial values - a study of united-states, hong-kong and prc managers. *Journal of International Business Studies, 24*(2), 249–275. doi:10.1057/palgrave.jibs.8490232

Rogers, E. (2003). *Diffusion of innovations*. New York: Free Press.

Rokeach, M. (1973). *The nature of human values*. New York: The Free Press.

Sarros, J. C., & Santora, J. C. (2001). Leaders and values: A cross-cultural study. *Leadership and Organization Development Journal, 22*(5), 243–248. doi:10.1108/01437730110397310

Schwartz, S. H. (1992). Universals in the content and structure of values - theoretical advances and empirical tests in 20 countries. *Advances in Experimental Social Psychology, 25*, 1–65. doi:10.1016/S0065-2601(08)60281-6

Schwartz, S. H. (2011). Studying values: Personal adventure, future directions. *Journal of Cross-Cultural Psychology, 42*(2), 307–319. doi:10.1177/0022022110396925

Schwartz, S. H., & Bilsky, W. (1987). Toward a universal psychological structure of human-values. *Journal of Personality and Social Psychology, 53*(3), 550–562. doi:10.1037/0022-3514.53.3.550

Shalley, C. E., & Perry-Smith, J. E. (2001). Effects of social-psychological factors on creative performance: The role of informational and controlling expected evaluation and modeling experience. *Organizational Behavior and Human Decision Processes, 84*(1), 1–22. doi:10.1006/obhd.2000.2918 PMID:11162295

Skarzynski, P., & Gibson, R. (2008). *Innovation to the core*. Boston: Harvard Business Press.

Slappendel, C. (1996). Perspectives on innovation in organizations. *Organization Studies, 17*(1), 107–129. doi:10.1177/017084069601700105

Sosik, J. J. (2005). The role of personal values in the charismatic leadership of corporate managers: A model and preliminary field study. *The Leadership Quarterly, 16*(2), 221–244. doi:10.1016/j.leaqua.2005.01.002

Tannenbaum, R., & Schmidt, W. (1973). How to choose a leadership style. *Harvard Business Review*, *51*(3), 58–67.

Tushman, M. L., & O'Reilly, C. A. (1997). *Winning through innovation: A practical guide to leading organizational change and renewal*. Boston: Harvard Business School Press.

Vroom, V. H., & Yetton, P. W. (1973). *Leadership & decision-making*. Pittsburgh, PA: University of Pittsburgh Press.

Westerman, J. W., & Cyr, L. A. (2004). An integrative analysis of person-organization fit theories. *International Journal of Selection and Assessment*, *12*(3), 252–261. doi:10.1111/j.0965-075X.2004.279_1.x

Yammarino, F. J., Dionne, S. D., Chun, J. U., & Dansereau, F. (2005). Leadership and levels of analysis: A state-of-the-science review. *The Leadership Quarterly*, *16*(6), 879–919. doi:10.1016/j.leaqua.2005.09.002

Yukl, G. (2006). *Leadership in organizations*. Upper Saddle River, NJ: Prentice Hall.

Yukl, G. (2008). How leaders influence organizational effectiveness. *The Leadership Quarterly*, *19*(6), 708–722. doi:10.1016/j.leaqua.2008.09.008

KEY TERMS AND DEFINITIONS

Management Behavior: The study of human behavior in management settings. Management behavior can be perceived as the interface between human behavior and leading the organization, and the organization itself.

Management Innovativeness: Managers' ability to applicate in organizational settings new and improved solutions that meet new requirements, unarticulated needs, or existing market requests. Management innovativeness is dependent upon a plethora of hard (e.g., organizational goals, stakeholder claims, available resources, etc.) and soft factors (e.g., values, culture, personality, etc.).

Managers' Personal Values: Beliefs and guiding principles held by managers regarding both their life in general, but also means and ends that should be identified and implemented in the running of the organization. The individual and organizational dimensions of values are interrelated and they mutually affect each other.

Chapter 10
Different Cultures Different People

Kornélia Lazányi
Obuda University, Hungary

Peter Holicza
Obuda University, Hungary

Kseniia Baimakova
Saint-Petersburg State University of Aerospace Instrumentation, Russia

ABSTRACT

Culture is a scheme of knowledge shared by a relatively large number of people. Hence, it is a collection of explicit as well as implicit patterns of behaviour. It makes the members of the culture feel, think act and react in a certain, predefined way, hence makes their actions predictable. The literature on cultures, especially that of national cultures has focused on cultural differences and on understanding and measuring them for long decades, but in the 21st century the attention has shifted to leveraging benefits of multicultural environments and experiences. Hence, present paper—after providing a short insight into the basic approaches of national cultures—endeavours to analyse Russian and Hungarian culture. We aim to present the similarities and differences of the two cultures, along with tools and methods that are able to lessen these differences and harvest the benefits of them.

INTRODUCTION

Culture is the invisible bond which ties people together. The importance of culture lies in its close association with the ways of thinking and living. Culture is related to the development of our attitude. Our cultural values serve as the founding principles of our life. They shape our thinking, behaviour and personality. Culture is important for a number of reasons because it influences an individual's life in a variety of ways, including values, views, desires, fears and worries. Belonging to a culture can provide individuals with an easy way to connect with others who share the same mindset and values (Chhokar, Brodbeck, House, Mahwah, 2007)

DOI: 10.4018/978-1-5225-2480-9.ch010

Geert Hofstede, a Dutch sociologist who is internationally famous for his intercultural studies, describes culture as the collective mental programming that separates members of one group or category of people from another (Harrison, Yasin, 2015) According to his understanding, culture can be defined as the "body of beliefs, norms, and values shared by a group of people, culture presents the biggest challenge to businesses working internationally", as stated by him "Culture is more often a source of conflict than of synergy".

Culture as an institution has a unique role in the formation of modern states. Culture, forming the «basis» of modern nations, is dynamic, flexible and open to change structure. Culture appears as a semantic network that is woven over again with the change of generations (Malakhov, 2014)

Culture is an important point for international business. It is essential to know what culture is if you wish to operate successfully in an international business setting. It is very important to analyze cultural differences, because they may be the principal cause of failure in international business. It is important for people to realize that a basic understanding of cultural diversity is the key to effective cross-cultural communications (Dumetz, 2012; Kreitner, 2009). In order to understand in what way business partners respond and why certain products do or do not take off in a certain market, attention must be paid to cultural differences.

Present paper endeavors to provide a short overview about relevant literature and analyze the possibilities for creating a much more accepting culture on the basis of the example of Russia and Hungary. The paper also intends to point out potential means and methods and explains the role of the government within all these.

ABOVE THE CULTURES: THE CIVILIZATIONS THEORY

The word civilization comes from the 'civilis' Latin adjective. It referred to a citizen. According to social, religious, legal, financial or political status, views or purposes these citizens gathering into groups (Latin Dictionary). Civilization is "The action or process of civilizing or of being civilized; a developed or advanced state of human society." as the Oxford Dictionary explains (Oxford English Dictionary). Among political scientists, Samuel P. Huntington conducted one of the most comprehensive researches in this field. He defines civilization on the following way: „A civilization is thus the highest cultural grouping of people and the broadest level of cultural identity people have short of that which distinguishes humans from other species. It is defined both by common objective elements, such as language, history, religion, customs, institutions, and by the subjective self-identification of people." (The Post, 1990) Huntington makes difference between countries not in terms of their political and economic development, but the cultural and civilizational affiliation. By these metrics he emphasized the following world regions: Western (Christian), Orthodox (Christian), Islamic, Islamic/Hindu, Hindu, African, Latin American, Sinic (Chinese), Buddhist and Japanese (Huntington, 1993). Focusing on the countries of this research, Hungary belongs to the Western Christian, Russia belongs to the Orthodox Christian civilization.

Based on the civilizations theory, Huntington published his famous concept of the future in the Foreign Affairs, titled "The Clash of Civilizations?". His former student, Francis Fukuyama argued the thesis and presented a different view in The End of History and the Last Man (1992). In respond to that, Huntington expanded his article in the book: The Clash of Civilizations and the Remaking of World Order (1996) (Holicza, 2016a). According to the Huntington's theory, the coming period will be characterized by conflicts erupting as the world's main civilizations reach their breaking points. The conflicts of the future will occur along the cultural lines that are separating civilizations (Huntington, 1993). Huntington's fault lines between civilizations seem to replace the political and ideological boundaries of the Cold War. Europe and the European Higher Education Area (EHEA) are divided between Western Christianity, Orthodox Christianity and the Islam today. Considering the past Balkan wars, the actual Ukrainian situation, the tense relationship between Russia and the NATO, and the multiplying terrorist attacks in Europe, the mentioned theory tends to transform into practice (Holicza, 2016b).

Huntington drew the Eastern Boundary of Western Civilization around Hungary in Central Eastern Europe. Same as Russia, neighbouring countries from the East belong to the Orthodox side on the map of civilizations. In order to confirm or doubt the existence of a fault line, Hofstede's cultural measurements have been applied. "The 6-D analysis (Hofstede) shows approximately 50% difference between Hungary and its neighbours on the Orthodox side. In that sense, the existence of a fault line in Central Eastern Europe is confirmed, but the results are mixed, and based on the mutual cultural values, the fault line near Hungary is bridgeable." (Grachev, 2009) "Even if it is the case of civilizational threats from the east, conflicts are less likely to occur along Western Christian - Orthodox Christian boarders than the Orthodox Christian – Islam that concerns some of the Balkan countries." (Grachev, 2009)

CULTURAL DIFFERENCES THEORIES

Various theories have been developed to classify countries on the basis of their culture's characteristics, so that cultural differences can be identified and measured (Bik, 2010; Blizzard, 2012).

- Edward Hall's background context approach (high-context culture and low-context culture) (for further details see Table 1);
- House et al. and their GLOBE study (power distance), uncertainty avoidance, assertiveness, institutional collectivism, in-group collectivism, future orientation, performance orientation, humane orientation, gender egalitarianism) (for further details see Table 2.)
- Geert Hofstede's dimensions (power distance, individualism versus collectivism, masculinity versus femininity, uncertainty avoidance, perception of time, indulgence) (for further details see Table 3);
- Fons Trompenaars' seven dimensions (universalism versus particularism, individualism versus collectivism, neutral versus emotional, specific versus diffuse, achievement versus ascription, sequential versus synchronic, internal versus external control) (for further details see Table 4);
- Schwartz's cultural value types (power, achievement, hedonism, stimulation (risk and innovation), self-direction, universalism, benevolence, tradition, conformity, security) (For further details see Table 5).

It is interesting to study Russian and Hungarian culture according to these theories, i.e. to describe the features of Russian and Hungarian business cultures and to explore the differences and similarities between them. Underlying this attempt is the wish to identify the cultural features the knowledge of which could be profitably applied to the shaping of the dynamically developing economic and business relations between the two countries.

Table 1. Hall's Cultural Factors

High Context	Low Context
There are numerous contextual elements in a high-context cultures that help people to understand the main rules. As a result, much is taken for granted. This kind of communication can be confusing for person who is not aware of the 'unwritten rules' of the particular culture. Not just the message is important, they are relation oriented.	Very little is taken for granted in the low-context way of communication. In one hand it means that more explanation might be necessary, on the other hand there is less chance for misunderstanding. Explicit messages, little attention for the status of the person, task oriented.
Monochronic Time	**Polychronic Time**
As Hall called: M-Time, it means doing one single thing at a time. It means detailed preparation and planning, as the Western approach calls: time management. As research shows, this kind of organized people tend to have low context way of communication.	People from Polychromic cultures do many things at once. They are committed to people and human relationships, interactions. Their plans are changing easily and often. They tend to have high-context way of communication and tendency to build lifetime relationships. Native Americans have Polychromic culture.
High Territoriality	**Low Territoriality**
People in this culture have greater concern for ownership. They are more territorial and seek to outline the areas that belong to them. They easily start fights with the neighborhood over the land, but the source of conflict can even be the co-worker's piece of paper which overlaps their desk. Many wars have been fought on national and international level over boundaries. It can also extend to material things or anything that is 'mine'. Ownership and security becomes a great issue for people of this "High territoriality" group. They tend to be low-context.	Low or less territoriality people tend also to be high context as they have less ownership of space or land, they are less concerned about boundaries. They share their territory and ownership with little thought. They also have less concern about material stuff and they don't have that developed sense of 'stealing' (it characterizes more the highly territorial people). People with low territoriality tend also to be high context.

Source: Based on Hall (1966) from changingminds.org

Table 2. The Globe Project

HIGH PERFORMANCE ORIENTATION	LOW PERFORMANCE ORIENTATION
Value training and development. Value competitiveness and materialism. View formal feedback as necessary for performance improvement. Value what one does more than who one is. Expect direct, explicit communication.	Value societal and family relationships. Value harmony with the environment. View formal feedback as judgmental and discomfiting. Value who one is more than what one does. Expect indirect, subtle communication.
HIGH UNCERTAINTY AVOIDANCE	**LOW UNCERTAINTY AVOIDANCE**
Use formality in interactions with others. Are orderly and keep meticulous records. Rely on formalized policies and procedures. Take moderate, carefully calculated risks. Show strong resistance to change.	Use informality in interactions with others. Are less orderly and keep fewer records. Rely on informal norms for most matters. Are less calculating when taking risks. Show only moderate resistance to change.
HIGH IN-GROUP COLLECTIVISM	**LOW IN-GROUP COLLECTIVISM**
Duties and obligations are important determinants of social behavior. A strong distinction is made between in-groups and out-groups. People emphasize relatedness with groups. The pace of life is slower. Love is assigned little weight in marriage.	Personal needs and attitudes are important determinants of social behavior. Little distinction is made between in-groups and out-groups. People emphasize rationality in behavior. The pace of life is faster. Love is assigned great weight in marriage.
HIGH POWER DISTANCE	**LOW POWER DISTANCE**
Society is differentiated into classes. Power seen as providing social order. Upward social mobility is limited. Resources available to only a few. Information is localized and hoarded.	Society has a large middle class. Power linked to corruption and coercion. Upward social mobility is common. Resources are available to almost all. Information is widely shared.

continued on next page

Table 2. Continued

HIGH GENDER EGALITARIANISM	LOW GENDER EGALITARIANISM
More women in positions of authority. Less occupational sex segregation. Similar levels of educational attainment for males and females. Afford women a greater decision-making role in community affairs.	Fewer women in positions of authority. More occupational sex segregation. A lower level of female educational attainment, compared to that of males. Afford women little or no decision-making role in community affairs.
HIGH HUMANE ORIENTATION	**LOW HUMANE ORIENTATION**
The interests of others are important. People are motivated primarily by a need for belonging and affiliation. Members of society are responsible for promoting the well-being of others. Child labor is limited by public sanctions. People are urged to be sensitive to all forms of racial discrimination.	One's own self-interest is important. People are motivated primarily by a need for power and material possessions. The state provides social and economic support for individuals' well-being. Child labor is an issue of low importance. People are not sensitive to all forms of racial discrimination.
HIGH INSTITUTIONAL COLLECTIVISM	**LOW INSTITUTIONAL COLLECTIVISM**
Members assume that they are highly interdependent with the organization. Group loyalty is encouraged, even if this undermines the pursuit of individual goals. The society's economic system tends to maximize the interests of collectives. Rewards are driven by seniority, personal needs, and/or within-group equity. Critical decisions are made by groups.	Members assume that they are largely independent of the organization. Pursuit of individual goals is encouraged, even at the expense of group loyalty. The society's economic system tends to maximize the interests of individuals. Rewards are driven very largely by an individuals contribution to task success. Critical decisions are made by individuals
HIGH FUTURE ORIENTATION	**LOW FUTURE ORIENTATION**
Propensity to save now for the future. Emphasize working for long-term success. Organizations tend to be flexible and adaptive. View material success and spiritual fulfillment as an integrated whole.	Propensity to spend now, rather than save. Prefer gratification as soon as possible. Organizations tend to be inflexible and maladaptive. View material success and spiritual fulfillment as separate, requiring trade-offs.
HIGH ASSERTIVENESS	**LOW ASSERTIVENESS**
Value competition, success, and progress. Communicate directly and unambiguously. Try to have control over the environment. Expect subordinates to take initiative. Build trust on basis of calculation.	Value cooperation and warm relationships. Communicate indirectly; try to "save face." Try to be in harmony with the environment. Expect loyalty from subordinate. Build trust on basis of predictability.

Source: Groove (2005a, 2005b) cited from Virkus (2009)

RUSSIA AND HUNGARY ACCORDING TO CULTURAL DIFFERENCES THEORIES

According to Edward Hall's background context approach, Russia and Hungary are both high-context cultures; it means that rules of communication are primarily transmitted through the use of contextual elements (i.e., body language, a person's status, and tone of voice) and are not explicitly stated (Jethu-Ramsoedh, Hendrickx, 2011)

According to GLOBE study both Russia and Hungary are included in Eastern European country cluster (Shi, Wang, 2011; Hoppe, 2007). This means that characteristics which are related to this cluster are the same for all countries in it. Societies belonging to this cluster reflect relatively high scores of

Table 3. Hofstede's Model of Cultural Dimensions

Value Dimension	Value Description	High Score	Low Score
Power Distance Index (PDI)	The degree to which members of a collective expect power to be distributed equally. It does not reflect an objective difference in power distribution, but rather the way people perceive power differences.	Indicates that inequalities of power, social status and wealth have been allowed to grow within the society. These societies do not allow significant upward mobility, citizens are more likely to follow a caste system.	These societies handle citizen's power, social status and wealth more equally, they don't emphasize the differences between the social classes. They offer and demonstrate the opportunity of growth for everyone.
Individualism (IDV)	The degree to which individuals are integrated into groups.	Indicates that individuality and individual rights are paramount within the society. In these societies people are supposed to look after themselves and their direct family only.	In these societies individuals typically have close ties. Collectivist nature reinforces extended groups or families where every member takes responsibility for an other.
Masculinity (MAS)	The distribution of emotional roles between the genders. Masculine cultures' values are competitiveness, assertiveness, materialism, ambition and power, whereas feminine cultures place more value on relationships and quality of life.	It indicates high degree of gender differentiation experiences in the nation. Males are the dominant in the power structure of the society, and females are being controlled, often discriminated in certain aspects.	It means low level of differentiation between males and females. In all aspects of the society, genders are treated equally, without discrimination.
Uncertainty Avoidance Index (UAI)	A society's tolerance for uncertainty and ambiguity. Reflects the extent to which members of a society attempt to cope with anxiety by minimizing uncertainty. People in cultures with high uncertainty avoidance tend to be more emotional. More attention for planning step by step and procedures.	It creates rule-oriented society that play important role to reduce the uncertainty. Nations with low tolerance for uncertainty have the need for laws, rules, regulations, and control.	Indicates the country has less concern about ambiguity and uncertainty and has more tolerance for a variety of opinions. Reflected in a society that is less rule-oriented, more readily accepts change, and takes more and greater
Long-Term Orientation (LTO)	Society of pragmatic virtues oriented to future rewards, in particular perseverance, adapting to changing circumstances vs. of virtues related to the past and the present, such as national pride, respect for tradition and fulfilling social obligations.	It shows the nations' respect for traditions and commitments to long-term values and planning. They tend to support strong work ethic, and expect long-term rewards for the completed duties, work in the present. Business and economics tends to developer slower in these societies.	The nation and its individuals do not reinforce the idea of long-term and traditional orientation. These cultures are more flexible and adoptive for changes that may occur often and rapidly.
Indulgence versus Restraint (IND)	Indulgence stands for a tendency to allow relatively free gratification of basic and natural human desires related to enjoying life and having fun. "a society that controls gratification of needs and regulates it by means of strict social norms."	Cannot easily be motivated with material rewards, to satisfy basic needs and freedom are more important. They enjoy the moment instead of using time to compare with others. Objects are taken to fulfil the original purpose not as status symbols.	Gratification suppressed and regulated. They expect (mostly material) reward for job done well. Status symbols are important such as the phone, laptop, watch, company, etc.

Source: Wendy H. Mason http://www.referenceforbusiness.com/management/Gr-Int/International-Management.html

the societal cultural practices on the dimensions of In-Group Collectivism and Power Distance. Figure 1 shows cultural values in Hungary and Russia.

Thus, there are no cultural differences between Russia and Hungary, according to first two theories. That's why it is more interesting to investigate three other methodological approaches.

According to Geert Hofstede, Russian and Hungarian cultures definitely have differences (Hofstede, Hofstede, Minkov, 2010). Figure 2 shows deep drivers of Russian and Hungarian culture according to 6-D Model.

Table 4. Trompenaars 7 Dimensions of Culture

Dimension	Characteristics
Universalism	Universalism is about finding broad and general rules. To place a high value on laws, rules, and obligations. Focus on formalities rather than relationships. According to Trompenaars, these conditions are present typically in the United States, Canada, UK, Australia, Germany, and Sweden.
Particularism	Particularism is about finding exceptions. To believe that each circumstance, and each relationship, dictates the rules that they live by. Countries that have high particularism are for example: Venezuela, Indonesia, China, South Korea, etc. Their response to a situation may change, they place a greater emphasis on relationships, who's involved.
Individualism	The rights of the individual are in focus. It seeks to let each person grow or fail on their own. To believe in personal freedom and achievement. The United States with high individualist. They believe that everyone takes personal decisions, and they have to take care of themselves, no one else is in charge.
Communitarianism	They think about themselves as part of a group, and believe that the group is more important than the individual, it comes always first, because the group provides help and safety, in return for loyalty. According to Trompenaars, typically communitarian countries include China, Germany, France, Japan, and Singapore.
Specific	They prefer to keep their professional and personal lives separate. As a result, they believe that relationships don't have much of an impact on work objectives, and, although good relationships are important, they believe that people can work together without having a good relationship.
Diffuse	They do not mind if their professional and personal lives overlapping. They believe that meeting socially with co-workers, clients, building good relationship is positive or even essential to profitable and trustworthy business performance and meeting the objectives. They often spend time after working hours with their colleagues or clients.
Neutral	Emotions are held in check, people make a huge effort to control their emotions. Logical reasons influence their decisions and actions far more than their emotions, feelings, and they do not tell and show what they think or how they feel.
Emotional	They do find the way to express their emotions openly and naturally, even spontaneously, either in their personal and professional lives. In these cultures expressing emotion is accepted and welcomed.
Achievement	Achievement cultures are for example Austria, the United States, Israel, Switzerland, Scandinavia or the United Kingdom. Their citizens value performance and functions, reputation, respect and status is based on what a person does.
Ascription	Ascription cultures such as in Venezuela, France, Italy, Japan, Saudi Arabia, Indonesia, and China believe that people should be valued for who they are. In these countries, people's behavior is characterized by their own, or the other party's position, title or power of influence.
Sequential Time	In these cultures people prefer events to happen in the given order. They place a high value on punctuality, and the original planning, schedule. They mention often that the "time is money," and being late - is considered disrespectful and negative reputation. Typical sequential-time culture for example is China and Germany.
Synchronous Time	They follow the changes, go with the flow, take the time to explore alternatives before they execute. Their focus on the relationship represents flexibility and agility. In this group the United States can be mentioned.
Internal Direction	The environment and conditions can be kept in check, they believe that they can control circumstances in order to achieve the exact desired outcome. It effects their personal and professional lives too, how they work with associates, etc.
Outer Direction	External locus of control – their future is determined by fate, even if they work hard, outcomes are independent of them. They believe to be controlled by the nature and external environment, therefore they avoid conflicts in their relationships and at their workplace. They often need and ask for confirmation about their performance.

Source: Mindtools.com, 2017

Power Distance. Russia is a high power distance society, Hungary is the opposite. Power is extremely centralized in Russia, there is the huge discrepancy between the less and the more powerful people, and there are status roles in all areas of business interactions. Hungarian style is the opposite: power is decentralized, hierarchy for convenience only, equal rights, control is disliked and attitude towards managers are informal.

Table 5. Schwartz's Cultural Value Types

Conservatism	They put cultural emphasis on the status quo, ownership of property, solidarity towards the group they identify themselves with. Importance of traditional values and social relationships, collective security.
Intellectual Autonomy	Everyone is a unique, autonomous human being, to express and manage his/her individual views, preferences and also encourage others to do so. They have own (creative) ideas and they are pursuing their own interest toward the desired goal.
Affective Autonomy	The person is an autonomous, bounded entity and finds meaning in his / her own uniqueness, seeking to express own internal attributes (preferences, traits, feelings) and is encouraged to do so. Affective Autonomy promote and protect the individual's independent pursuit of own affectively positive experience (pleasure, exciting life, varied life).
Hierarchy	In a hierarchical system, roles and rights are fixed in order to control interdependencies. People are ranked according to their relative power, importance or status. Requests and decisions go through the chain of command and people have to comply with these regulations to avoid sanctions. The distribution of power is not equal.
Egalitarianism	All people are equal in fundamental worth and deserve freedom, social justice, opportunities, equal treatment across gender, religion, political views, social, or economic life.
Mastery	Stressing the individual and group interests over the classical social and natural norms. Control and change the system to serve own ambition and interests by self-assertion.
Harmony	In harmony the system and the world is accepted in its actual form. Natural and social norms are ruling over the individual interests.

Source: On the Basis of Schwartz (1999) and Smith, Schwartz (1997) Cited from IMO, 2017

Figure 1. Cultural Practices and Values in Hungary and Russia (Hoppe, 2007)

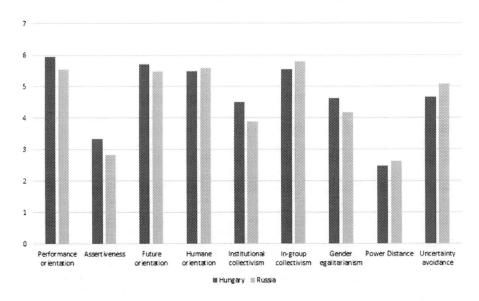

- Individualism versus Collectivism. Russia is collectivist society, and Hungary is individualistic one. Family, friends and not seldom the neighborhood are extremely important in Russia. Relationships need to be personal, authentic and trustful to make any business (Luhmann, 1979; Cook, Hardin, Levi 2005). Hungary has a loosely-knit social framework, people take care of themselves and their immediate families only, the employer/employee relationship is a contract based on mutual advantage.
- Masculinity versus Femininity. Russia is a feminine society, and Hungary is masculine one. Russians at workplace as well as when meeting a stranger rather understate their personal achieve-

Figure 2. Deep Drivers of Russian and Hungarian Culture in 6-D Model (geert-hofstede.com, 2017)

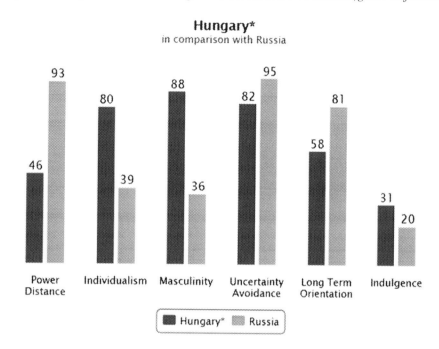

ments, contributions or capacities. They talk modestly about themselves. In Hungary people "live in order to work", managers are expected to be decisive and assertive, the emphasis is on equity, competition, achievement and success.

- Uncertainty Avoidance. Russians feel very much threatened by ambiguous situations; detailed planning and briefing is very common. Russians prefer to have context and background information. Hungary maintains need for rules, time is money for them, people like to be busy and work hard, precision and punctuality are the norm, innovation may be resisted, security is an important element in individual motivation.
- Long Term Orientation. Russia and Hungary are both countries with a pragmatic mindset. People believe that truth depends very much on situation, context and time. They show an ability to adapt traditions easily to changed conditions, a strong propensity to save and invest thriftiness and perseverance in achieving results.
- Indulgence. Russia and Hungary are both restrained cultures. They have a tendency to cynicism and pessimism, do not put much emphasis on leisure time and control the gratification of their desires. People have the perception that their actions are restrained by social norms and feel that indulging themselves is somewhat wrong.

According to Fons Trompenaar, the national cultures of Hungary and Russia can be generally characterized by the following features (Table 6) (Trompenaars, Hampden-Turner, 1997; Hidasi, Lukinykh, 2009).

Thus, it can be said, that according to Trompenaars, Russian and Hungarian cultures definitely have differences almost in all dimensions, except the last one.

According to Schwartz, who emphasized 10 typological value indexes, axiological portrait of the population in Russia and Hungary can be made (Kreitner, 2009). Figure 3 shows the average value

Table 6. Cultural Dimensions of Hungary and Russia

Hungary	Russia
Universalism	Particularism
Individualism	Individualism/Collectivism
Neutral orientation	Affective orientation
Specific orientation	Diffuse orientation
Weak 'achieved status' orientation	Intermediate position in achievement - aspiration parameter
Weak outer orientation	Outer - orientation
Weak future orientation	Weak future orientation

indexes in Russia and Hungary, according to the European Social Survey which is based on Schwartz theory (Schwartz, Schmidt, Davidov, 2004).

As Figure 3 shows, four value indexes of Russian and Hungarian culture are very close to each other (security, tradition, stimulation, universalism), which indicates a significant degree of commonality of these values between Russians and Hungarians. It is worth mentioning that the greatest differences appear in the hedonism and the power. The most significant values for the Russia and Hungary are safety, universalism and benevolence.

DIFFERENT FOREVER?

Since the cultural parameters characteristic of a country can have a serious impact on its economic performance, competitiveness and its everyday business culture practices, the study of these parameters is indispensable for a better understanding of the processes at work. Nonetheless, the analysis of the national cultures is a necessary, but not sufficient part of the process. While we experience an extreme

Figure 3. Typological Value Indexes of Russia and Hungary (Magun, Rudnev, 2008)

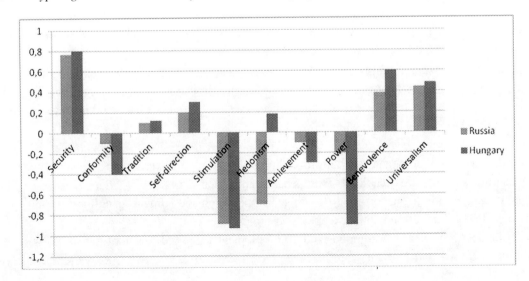

escalation of globalization – thinking in global markets for resources, people and services – we are also witnessing aggressive clash of civilizations, national cultures at the very same time. According to Doney, Cannon and Mullen (1998) trust is inevitable to mitigate the negative effect of cultural differences and to harness the business opportunities embedded in cultural different-ness. On the basis of the World Values Survey (WVS, 2016; Johnson, Mislin, 2012) economic growth is influenced by values and attitudes of the people - by national culture. Zak and Knack (2001) have also pointed out that trust/trusting culture is positively associated with important economic factors, such as growth in per capita income and GDP along with other standard determinants of economic performance. Hence, we have to be aware of the fact that cultural change might be a necessity in case of most national cultures, especially those non-inclusive (Covey, 2006; Knack, Keefer, 1997).

If the situation does not enable development of trust, or the insecurity or the "price" of cessation of insecurity do not explain the need of creation of contractual relations, the individual will decide based on beliefs, ideologies and personal experiences. Interpersonal relationships are formed in the context of cultural, social and other influences and can be defined as strong, deep or close acquaintance or association between two or more individuals. Human beings are social and are shaped by their interactions and experiences with others.

Studies point out three basic implication of trust on our lives: It makes social life predictable, makes it easier for people to cooperate and creates a sense of community (Misztal 1996). A person's dispositional tendency to trust others can be considered a personality trait and one of the strongest predictors of subjective well-being (DeNeve, Cooper 1998). Ability of trust in individuals develops in the early childhood, formed by many psychological and social effects during our lifetime and can be distorted by the individual's perception, beliefs and cultural context as well.

Human beings are different. The difference can be lied in competences, skills, way of perception, information processing, learning, thinking and decision making as well. Perceptual sets of the individuals (also called perceptual expectancy) reflect their own personality traits and has been demonstrated in many social contexts and can be defined as a predisposition to perceive things in certain way (Weiten 2008). Sets can be created by motivation and so can result in individuals describe equivocal things so that they see what they want to see (Coon, Mitterer 2008). For example, people with an aggressive personality are quicker to properly identify aggressive situations or persons (Hardy, Heyes 1999)

However, every country has the opportunity to alter its culture, by exposing it to the effects of other cultures. Despite a lot of differences in Russian and Hungarian cultures (Grachev, 2009; Horváth, Vidra, 2011; Falkné Bánó, 2014; Tompos, 2014; SKFU, 2014), these countries have already cooperation in different spheres (Holicza, Baimakova, 2015). Cooperation in the cultural and humanitarian spheres is one of them. April 15, 2013 between Russian Ministry of Culture and Hungarian Ministry of Social Development a cooperation program for 2013-2015 was signed. In 2015 Hungarian Science and Culture Days were organized in Russia and Russian Science and Culture Days were organized in Hungary, as well as bilateral cultural and tourism forum (RIA news, 2015- Russian Ministry of Culture, 2017; Hungarian state secretariat for culture, 2017).

Besides organizing cultural events, international mobility programs also provide good opportunities for different cultural experiences. After the Tempus Program, the new Erasmus+ Credit Mobility Program became available for Russian universities. It requires close connection and bilateral partnership with another higher education institution in an EU member state. The program helps many students to study outside their own country. They can learn about other cultures and integration, practice languages, develop new relations and friendships without borders that may help them in their future either on professional and personal level. In order to promote international mobility and support participants, Russia has been accepted as full member of the biggest and most developing European student organization: Erasmus Student Network (ESN). Since 2015 the ESN Russia represents itself, growing and involving more and more young people into its international and culturally diverse environment (ESN, 2017). Mobility budgets tend to grow and include extra national and international opportunities, activities in order to support peacemaking by cultural awareness and integration, moreover to contribute to more competitive labour market in the globalising business world.

Considering the international labour market and trade between Russia and Hungary, several complicating conditions occur such as visa obligations, working permit, language barriers and the actual economic sanctions against Russia. Culturally the most diverse international communities are concentrated in the capitals, the biggest cities and the continuously spreading innovation and techno parks, such as the Skolkovo Innovation Center is. These special zones have considerable economic impact on the regions by supporting start-up business, R&D projects, innovative technical solutions and by attracting foreign investments, the flow of foreign labour mobility (Holicza, Baimakova, Lukina, 2016).

What is more on the basis of his extensive research McLaren (2016) indicates that inconsistency of individual and officially stated national culture and values strongly effects the citizens' trust in the regime itself. The discrepancy works as a certain kind of cognitively dissonant situation, where the individual either stands for his/her own values, which leads to escalation of commitment, and hence increased emphasis of own values, or submits his/herself to the values communicated centrally and hence loses authenticity and the inner compass culture should provide for the behavior of the individual.

RECOMMENDATIONS

Owing to the utmost importance of collaboration and mutual acceptance and understanding in the present globalized economy, countries should strive to alter the basic values of their cultures in a way, so that it enables the citizens for inter- and cross-cultural cooperation. However, since culture is the collection of beliefs, values attitudes and even shapes the people's sense of right or wrong, it is very hard to change it. Cultures, as well as their broader spheres civilizations, provide guidance on proper behavior, hence changing culture would cause mass cognitive dissonance (Festinger, 1962, Gawronski, Brannon, 2016). What is more, it is very hard, if possible at all to deliberately change the culture of a country in a centralized manner, without the participation of the people. Such a top down approach would give ground to massive resistance (Janis, 1971; Cross, 2016, Kawulich, Ogletree, Hoff, 2016). Even more so, since belonging to a culture provides individuals an easy way to connect with others who share the same mindset and values, hence the alliances for the old culture and against the changes would easily be formed.

The only way to adjust cultural characteristics of a country to the new expectations of a globalized world is to approach the task with a bottom up approach, which is supported, but not forced by the government. Providing opportunities to get to know people from other cultures, via mobility or cultural, scientific events is a good way to let people see and decide for themselves whether they want a more inclusive culture, a more accepting, a more compassionate and tolerant culture. While providing these chances for change, and supporting them not only by facilitating the change but by providing the moral and social support a culture can change itself radically within a timespan of a generation and create a healthy culture (Arieti, 1976, Dubina, Ramos, Ramos, 2016), which is sustainable in the future, and that can enable the creation of the global melting pot, the "end of history" in a fukuyamaian sense.

Nonetheless, this approach takes the responsibility for change from the central government, as if creating chances and accepting those daring would be all they can do. However, it is important to keep in mind that diverse cultural influences and the coping with them has significant implications for the need of change in primary, secondary, as well as higher education. It is not enough to provide opportunities for mobility, to agitate young people to get to know other people and cultures, the system of education should be able to prepare them for such experiences and provide them with the necessary skills and competences, so that the experience, which should promote acceptance and empathy would not backfire and emphasise the differences in a counterproductive way. Hence, preparing citizens for the acceptance of otherness and the appreciation of diversity should come prior to the opportunity for mobility and has to be initiated by the central government (Smith, Pate, 2016).

CONCLUSION

When comparing cultures of Russia and Hungary, using different theories of cultural differences, the following conclusions can be made. Five theories were analyzed, and according to two theories Russian and Hungarian cultures are the same. Three other theories on the other hand have proved that there are some similarities but more differences in cultures of both countries. The study comes to the conclusion that in spite of relative geographical proximity and shared historical experience the cultural characteristics of the two business cultures set them apart in a number of aspects. These characteristics have to be given due attention in forming and developing business relations.

After thorough consideration Hofstede's theory was taken as the main basis of comparison of two countries that have a shared past, but very different cultural roots, since Hofstede emphasizes that cultural dimensions are only foundation that help to evaluate the specific culture in order to facilitate decision-making. There are also other factors to be considered, such as personal characteristics, family history and personal well-being. In line with his approach the proposed measures can't predict the behavior of individuals, hence it is altered by the individuals' experiences.

The role of the government in decreasing cultural differences, or at least the exclusive nature of them is to create a supportive environment for those eager to get to know other cultures, to foster mobility and to prepare citizens for cross- and inter-cultural experiences.

ACKNOWLEDGMENT

Present paper has been supported through the New National Excellence Program of the Ministry of Human Capacities of Hungary.

REFERENCES

Arieti, S. (1976). *Creativity: The magic synthesis*. Academic Press.

Blizzard, A. (2012). *The Impact of Cultural Distances on the Country Selection Process*. University of Tennessee Honors Thesis Projects.

Changingminds.org. (2017). *Hall's cultural factors*. Retrieved from http://changingminds.org/explanations/ culture/hall_culture.htm

Chhokar, J. S., Brodbeck, F. C., & House, R. J. (2007). *Culture and Leadership Across the World: The GLOBE Book of In-Depth Studies of 25 Societies*. Mahwah, NJ: Lawrence Erlbaum Associates.

Cook, K. S., Hardin, R., & Levi, M. (2005). *Cooperation without trust?* Russell Sage Foundation.

Coon, D., & Mitterer, J. O. (2008, December 29). Introduction to Psychology: Gateways to Mind and Behavior. *Cengage Learning*, 171–172.

Covey, S. M. R. (2006). *The speed of trust: The one thing that changes everything*. Simon and Schuster.

Cross, D. (2016). Globalization and Media's Impact on Cross Cultural Communication: Managing Organizational Change. In Handbook of Research on Effective Communication, Leadership, and Conflict Resolution (pp. 21-41). IGI Global.

DeNeve, K. M., & Cooper, H. (1998). The Happy Personality: A Meta-Analysis of 137 Personality Traits and Subjective Well-Being. *Psychological Bulletin, 124*(2), 197–229. doi:10.1037/0033-2909.124.2.197 PMID:9747186

Doney, P. M., Cannon, J. P., & Mullen, M. R. (1998). Understanding the influence of national culture on the development of trust. *Academy of Management Review, 23*(3), 601–620.

Dubina, I. N., Ramos, S. J., & Ramos, H. (2016). Culture as a Driving Force of Individual and Organizational Behavior. In Creativity, Innovation, and Entrepreneurship Across Cultures (pp. 1-27). Springer New York. doi:10.1007/978-1-4939-3261-0_1

Dumetz, J. (2012). *Cross-cultural management textbook*. Lexington, KY: CreateSpace Independent Publ.

ESN.org. (2017). Retrieved from http://galaxy.esn.org

Falkné Bánó, K. (2014). Identifying Hungarian cultural characteristics in Europe's cultural diversity in The 21st century: a controversial issue [Alkalmazott tudományok I. fóruma: Konferenciakötet]. *Budapesti Gazdasági Főiskola, 2014*, 17–28.

Festinger, L. (1962). *A theory of cognitive dissonance* (Vol. 2). Stanford University Press.

Galaxy Your E. S. N. Gateway. (2017). Retrieved from: http://galaxy.esn.org

Gawronski, B., & Brannon, S. M. (2016). *What is cognitive consistency and why does it matter. Cognitive dissonance: Progress on a pivotal theory in social psychology* (2nd ed.). Washington, DC: American Psychological Association.

Glover, J., Friedman, H., & van Driel, M. (2016). Cultural Dilemmas and Sociocultural Encounters: An Approach for Understanding, Assessing, and Analyzing Culture. In Critical Issues in Cross Cultural Management (pp. 53-60). Springer International Publishing.

Grachev, M.V. (2009). Russia, Culture, and Leadership: Cross-Cultural Comparisons of Managerial Values and Practices. *Problems of Post-Communism*, (1).

Grove. (2005a). *Introduction to the GLOBE Research Project on Leadership Worldwide*. Retrieved from: http://www.grovewell.com/pub-GLOBE-intro.html

Grove. (2005b). *Worldwide Differences in Business Values and Practices: Overview of GLOBE Research Findings*. Retrieved from: http://www.grovewell.com/pub-GLOBE-dimensions.html

Hall, E. T. (1966). *The Hidden Dimension*. New York: Doubleday.

Hardy, M., & Heyes, S. (1999). *Beginning Psychology*. Oxford University Press.

Harrison, L., & Yasin, E. (Eds.). (2015). *Culture Matters in Russia—and Everywhere: Backdrop for the Russia-Ukraine Conflict*. Lexington Books.

Hofstede, G. (2017). Retrieved from: http://geert-hofstede.com/

Hofstede, G., Hofstede, G. J., & Minkov, M. (2010). *Cultures and Organizations. Software of the Mind* (3rd ed.). McGraw-Hill.

Holicza, P. (2016a). Civilizációs Törésvonalak Európában: Magyarország és Szomszédai a Hofstede-Dimenziók Tükrében. *Hadmérnök, 11*(4), 210–215.

Holicza, P. (2016b). *Convergence of Ideas?: Analysing Fukuyama's and Huntington's Concepts of the Future*. In *16th International Scientific Conference Globalization and Its Socio-Economic Consequences* (pp. 663-669). University of Zilina.

Holicza, P., & Baimakova, K. (2015). Innovation potential of Russian and Hungarian young adults. *Actual Problems of Economics and Management, 3*(7), 41-48.

Holicza, P., Baimakova, K., & Lukina, E. (2016). Russian Socio-Economic Development: The Present Situation and Future Directives. In *FIKUSZ '16 Symposium for Young Researchers* (pp. 7-18). Obuda University.

Hoppe, M. H. (2007, September 18). *Culture and Leader Effectiveness: The GLOBE Study*. Retrieved from: http://www.inspireimagineinnovate.com/pdf/globesummary-by-michael-h-hoppe.pdf

Horvath, A., Vidra, Z., & Fox, J. (2011). *Tolerance and cultural diversity discourses in Hungary*. Policy research reports, Central European University Retrieved From: https://www.kcl.ac.uk/sspp/departments/education/web-files2/HorvathA/TC-Diversity-Discourses-in-Hungary.pdf

Hungarian State Secretariat for Culture. (2017). Retrieved from http://www.kormany.hu/hu/emberi-eroforrasok-miniszteriuma/kulturaert-felelos-allamtitkarsag

Huntington, P. S. (1993). The Clash of Civilizations? *Foreign Affairs, 72*(3), 23–24. doi:10.2307/20045621

IMO (Interkulturelle Management- und Organisationsberatung). (2017). *Seven Cultural Orientations and Value Types*. Retrieved from: http://www.imo-international.de/englisch/html/siebenwerte_en.html

Jacobs, A. (2012). *Cross-cultural communication*. Groningen: Noordhoff.

Janis, I. L. (1971). Groupthink. *Psychology Today, 5*(6), 43–46.

Jethu-Ramsoedh, R., & Hendrickx, M. (2011). International business. Noordhoff Uitgevers bv Groningen/Houten, The Netherlands.

Johnson, N. D., & Mislin, A. (2012). How much should we trust the World Values Survey trust question? *Economics Letters*, *116*(2), 210–212. doi:10.1016/j.econlet.2012.02.010

Kawulich, B. B., Ogletree, T. W., & Hoff, D. L. (2016, July). *Cohort Culture: Bonding or Groupthink?* Paper presented at the Fourth European Conference on the Social Sciences.

Knack, S., & Keefer, P. (1997). Does social capital have an economic payoff? A cross-country investigation. *The Quarterly Journal of Economics*, *112*(4), 1251–1288. doi:10.1162/003355300555475

Kreitner, R. (2009). *Management* (11th ed.). Houghton Mifflin Harcourt Publishing Company.

Luhmann, N. (1979). *Trust and Power*. Chichester, UK: John Wiley & Sons.

Lukinykh. (2009). *A comparison of Russian and Hungarian Business Cultures*. Budapesti Gazdasági Főiskola – Magyar tudomany unnepe.

Magun, V., & Rudnev, M. (2008). Zhiznennye tsennosti rossiiskogo naseleniia: skhodstva i otlichiia v sravnenii s drugimi evropeiskimi stranami. Vestnik obshchestvennogo mneniia, (1), 33-58.

Magun, V., & Rudnev, M. (2010). Values of the Russian population: Similarities and differences in comparison with other European countries. *Sociological Research*, *49*(4), 3–57. doi:10.2753/SOR1061-0154490401

Malakhov. V. (2014). Cultural differences and political borders in the era of global migration. *New Literary Review*.

Mason. (2016). *International management*. Retrieved from http://www.referenceforbusiness.com/management/Gr-Int/International-Management.html

McLaren, L. (2016). Immigration, national identity and political trust in European democracies. *Journal of Ethnic and Migration Studies*, 1–21. doi:10.1080/1369183X.2016.1197772

Mindtools.com. (2017). Retrieved from https://www.mindtools.com/pages/article/seven-dimensions.htm

Misztal, B. (1996). *Trust in Modern Societies: The Search for the Bases of Social Order*. Polity Press.

OPG Bik. (2010). *The behavior of assurance professionals: a cross-cultural perspective*. Delft: Eburon. Retrieved from http://www.rug.nl/research/portal/files/13025633/03c3.pdf

RIA news. (2015, February 17). *Межгосударственные отношения РФ и Венгрии*. Retrieved from: https://ria.ru/spravka/20150217/1048123934.html

Russian Ministry of Culture. (2017). Retrieved from http://mkrf.ru/

Schwartz, S. H. (1999). A Theory of Cultural Values and Some Implications for Work. Applied Psychology: An International Review, 48(1), 23-47. doi:10.1111/j.1464-0597.1999.tb00047.x

Schwartz, S. H., Schmidt, P., & Davidov, E. (2004). Values in Europe: A Multiple Group Comparison with 20 Countries Using the European Social Survey 2003.*Sixth International Conference on Social Science Methodology*.

Shi, X., & Wang, J. (2011). Interpreting Hofstede Model and GLOBE Model: Which Way to Go for Cross-Cultural Research? *International Journal of Business and Management*, 6(5), 99. doi:10.5539/ijbm.v6n5p93

SKFU. (2014). *Russia and Hungary are at the crossroads of European history: the almanac* (1st ed.). Stavropol-Kaposvar-Moskva.

Smith, J. O., & Pate, R. N. (2016). Cultures Around the World: A Unique Approach to Youth Cultural Diversity Education. *Journal of Youth Development*, 2(2), 174–179. doi:10.5195/JYD.2007.354

Smith, P. B., & Schwartz, S. H. (1997). Values. Handbook of Cross-Cultural Psychology, 3(2), 77-118.

Storti, C. (1994). *Cross-cultural dialogues: 74 brief encounters with cultural difference*. Yarmouth, ME: Intercultural Press.

The World of Civilizations: The Post-1990. (n.d.). Wayback Machine.

Tompos, A. (2014). Hungarian societal values through business negotiators' practices.*Proceedings of the 14th International Academic Conference*.

Trompenaars, F., & Hampden-Turner, C. (2011). *Riding the waves of culture: Understanding diversity in global business*. Nicholas Brealey Publishing.

Usunier, J., & Lee, J. (2005). *Marketing across cultures*. Harlow, UK: Financial Times/Prentice Hall.

Virkus, S. (2009). *Dimesnions of Culture: Geert Hofstede*. Tallinn University. Retrieved from: http://www.tlu.ee/~sirvir/IKM/Leadership%20Dimensions/globe_project.html

Weiten, W. (2008). *Psychology: Themes and Variations*. Cengage Learning.

World Values Survey. (2017). Retrieved from: http://www.worldvaluessurvey.org/

Zak, P. J., & Knack, S. (2001). Trust and growth. *The Economic Journal*, *111*(470), 295–321. doi:10.1111/1468-0297.00609

KEY TERMS AND DEFINITIONS

Civilization: Is a set of cultural characteristics limited by time and/or place. The result of cultural values manifested in economic, political and religious systems.

Cognitive Dissonance: A state of psychological conflict, which results from incongruous values and attitudes held simultaneously, or discrepancy between an individual's acts and beliefs.

Cultural Differences Theories: Theories developed to classify countries on the basis of their culture's characteristics, hence they create a basis for identifying differences between various cultures.

Culture: A shared set of beliefs, values and patterns of behaviour learned and taught by socialisation. It serves as a guidance for the members of the culture about what is right and wrong, what deeds and interactions shall or shall not be appreciated or punished.

Globalization: A world-wide phenomenon of goods and services losing their local characteristics being sold all around the world fostered by the development of transportation and ICT.

Mobility: Moving of people in physiological, as well as societal sense, it can be characterized as a result by the mixing of social groups, cultures.

Trust: An interpersonal relation, where one of the people involved expects the other to behave in a certain way, while the other has the freedom to act (or not) according to the expectation.

Chapter 11
National Culture and Its Relationship With Innovation and Corruption

Pedro Silva
University of Aveiro, Portugal

António Carrizo Moreira
University of Aveiro, Portugal

ABSTRACT

Innovation is a driver of economic growth, wealth and prosperity. On the other hand, corruption emerges as a worldwide problem responsible for sapping resources, inequality, human suffering and poverty. This study hypothesizes that national culture, measured using Hofstede's six cultural dimensions, have an impact on corruption and innovation, and that highly corrupt nations are less innovative. Data were obtained from Hofstede's, Transparency International, and Global Innovation websites for the year 2012. The findings support the claim that most national culture aspects have an impact on corruption, although their impact on innovation is less measurable. Corruption was found to have a strong and negative effect on innovation. Our results draw attention to the usefulness of Hofstede's six-dimension framework in research and the need for further analysis on how corruption influences innovation through mechanisms other than national culture.

INTRODUCTION

National culture is a set of characteristics, attitudes, norms and values that distinguish members across organizations, institutions or countries (Hofstede, 2001), influencing all aspects of social and individual life. Cultural differences can be one explanation as to why some nations exhibit higher levels of economic development or corruption than others. For example, societies that emphasize freedom and creativity are expected to be more innovative than strictly formalized cultures. Corruption is also expected to be higher in cultures where individuals focus on power rather than on human relationships.

DOI: 10.4018/978-1-5225-2480-9.ch011

Culture is the foundation on which a society is built and has an impact on people's lives. The individual's role in society is likely to influence the decision to create new businesses, to act entrepreneurially and to live within the boundaries of the law. Extant research examining the culture-innovation link is extensive (e.g., Azar & Drogendijk, 2016; Dantas, Moreira, & Valente, 2015; Efrat, 2014; Gaygisiz, 2013; Mihaela, Claudia, & Lucian, 2011; Shane, 1992, 1993; Steel, Rinne, & Fairweather, 2012; Taylor & Wilson, 2012; Turró, Urbano, & Peris-Ortiz, 2013), however, most studies do not use the updated six-dimension of Hofstede's cultural framework (which includes pragmatic versus normative and indulgence versus restraint to the previous power-distance, individualism, masculinity and uncertainty-avoidance dimensions), nor the Global Innovation Index (GII) that captures the multi-dimensional facets of innovation and provide the tools that can assist in tailoring policies to promote long-term output growth, improved productivity, and job growth; instead, the majority of studies carried out to date have used the 'old' four cultural dimensions and traditional measures of innovation (e.g., number of patents or investment in R&D) (e.g., Efrat, 2014). The relationship between national culture and corruption has also been subjected of several studies (e.g., Barr & Serra, 2010; Davis & Ruhe, 2003; Huster, 1999; Sanyal, 2005; Sims, Gong, & Ruppel, 2012; Yeganeh, 2014), nonetheless, extant research lacks the use of complete cultural frameworks and findings are still inconsistent.

Although research supports the relationship between corruption and innovation (e.g., Anokhin & Schulze, 2009; Ulman, 2013), no studies have used the Corruption Perception Index (CPI) and GII simultaneously. As such, the aim of this study is to address the above-mentioned gaps and: (1) model the culture-corruption-innovation relationship, in order to understand how culture influences innovation; (2) to provide additional findings on which cultural variables influence corruption; (3) to measure corruption and innovation using CPI and GII respectively, given they are some of the most up-to-date and comprehensive measures for those variables; and (4) finally, examine the relationships among national culture, corruption and innovation altogether. For that, Hofstede's six cultural dimensions are going to be used to measure culture.

We have structured this book chapter as follows. After this introductory section, the background reviews literature on innovation, national culture, and corruption. The following section presents the theoretical assumptions and the hypotheses. Then, the method section describes the measures, the datasets used and the methodology adopted, followed by the results. Finally, we discuss the results found and present the conclusions.

BACKGROUND

Innovation

Innovation is a driver of economic growth, and prosperity (Turró et al., 2013). In a globalized world of commerce and trade, nations seek the "innovation imperative", in other words, the need to produce successful innovation at individual, business, and national levels, as a way for nations and business to leave their mark in the world (Steel et al., 2012). Several definitions can be found in the literature regarding innovation. Schumpeter (1942) identified three stages when entering a technological market: invention, innovation and adoption. Invention is an act of intellectual creativity, as such, some inventions never go beyond ideas. Innovation occurs when an invention succeeds in the market. Finally, adoption is the acceptance of an innovation by the market. While inventions and innovations occur at the firm or industry levels, adoption happens at the market level. For Frankelius (2009), innovation is something original, new, and important in any field that breaks into a market or society. The OECD (2005) define innovation as the implementation of a new or significantly improved product, a new process, a new marketing method or a new organizational method in business practices or workplace organization.

Innovation can be understood both at micro, meso and macro level. When the unit of analysis is the organization, innovation is understood as following a micro perspective (Dantas & Moreira, 2011; Moreira, 2014). Following this perspective, innovation can be classified into two categories: incremental and radical, in which the former emerges from practice and continuous improvement (Dantas & Moreira, 2011; Moreira, 2014) and the latter emerges when a new product, process or organizational solution is developed and/or introduced onto the market (Carrizo-Moreira & Leonidivna-Karachun 2014).

At a meso level, innovation is intrinsically connected to learning and change (Edquist, 1997) and follows an interdisciplinary perspective involving institutions, socio-economic and political determinants that emphasize and interdependent process in which innovation stems from the interactions of actors (Heindenreich, 2004; Moreira, Carneiro, & Tavares, 2007; Moreira & Vale, 2016).

At a macro level, innovation is analyzed from the national institutional perspective in which industrial dynamics and national perspectives play a key role (Boschma & Martin, 2010). Which this perspective innovation has an impact on economic growth and job creation.

In 2007 the Global Innovation Index (GII) was created by INSEAD, seeking new metrics and approaches to better capture the richness of innovation in society, and go beyond the traditional measures of innovation such as 'the number of research articles' or 'the level of R&D'. This index established itself as a reference among innovation indexes and has evolved into a valuable benchmarking tool (Cornell University, INSEAD, & WIPO, 2013). The Global Innovation Index is based on two sub-indexes: innovation inputs and outputs. The innovation input is made up by five pillars (institutions, human capital and research, infrastructure, market sophistication, and business sophistication) capturing elements related to the regulatory and business contexts. The innovation output is based on two pillars (knowledge and technology outputs, and creative outputs), with a particular focus on the quality of the social and business infrastructure expected to result from innovation, along with the number of patents issued and trademarks granted.

Summing up, innovation is related to the notion that something new has been created and subsequently accepted by the market. Traditionally, this has been measured through the number of patents, R&D, or the amount of scientific articles. The development of GII in 2007 provided a more accurate measurement tool (which has since been improved), often being selected as the indicator of choice for innovation in academic research (e.g., Steel et al., 2012).

National Culture: Hofstede's Cultural Dimensions

Culture can be used to explain what some countries are more developed than others, although, a cultural model that ensures the success of a country does not exist (Mihaela, Claudia, & Lucian, 2011). The same goes for the relationship between culture and corruption, as existent research suggests that national culture has a role in guiding people's behavior (Hofstede, 1997), thus, cultural values justify and guide how social institutions function, i.e., their corruption or anti-corruption behavior (Barr & Serra, 2010). Over recent decades, culture has been one of the main research constructs in several fields such as marketing, business or psychology (Taras, Steel, & Kirkman, 2012). Arguably, one of the primary drivers behind this trend has been Hofstede's work, detailed in his book "Culture's Consequences", which had a profound impact on cross-cultural research (Taras & Steel, 2009). Despite the large amount of definitions of culture, the one presented by Hofstede is certainly among the most used and accepted by scholars. Hofstede (1980, p. 25) defined culture as *"the collective programming of the mind which distinguishes the members of one human group from another"*, thus, the central mechanism of culture is *"a system of societal norms consisting of the value systems (or the mental software) shared by a major group in the population"* (Hofstede, 2001, p. 11). As such, culture is recognized as a set of shared attitudes, values or norms that characterizes a nation or organization and distinguishes it from another.

In his study, Hofstede (1980) analyzed survey data on work-related values obtained over the period 1967-1969 and again over the period 1971-1973 from more than 117 000 IBM employees. His findings revealed four statistically independent dimensions which explained the inter-country variation in the responses to his survey. He labeled those four dimensions as power-distance (PDI), individualism (IDV), masculinity (MAS), and uncertainty-avoidance (UAI). Recently, Hofstede, Hofstede, & Minkov (2010) added two new dimensions to their cultural model: pragmatic versus normative (PRA), and indulgence versus restraint (IVR).

Power-distance is the degree to which less powerful members of society accept that power is distributed unequally, and that some people have more power than others (Hofstede et al., 2010). In societies with a high power to distance index, people accept there is a hierarchical order and that individuals have their place without the need of further justification; however in societies with low power to distance index, people seek to avoid inequalities in the distribution of power and demand justifications for those inequalities (Hofstede et al., 2010). The individualist/collectivist dimension looks at whether people from society focus more on the "I" than on the "we" (Hofstede et al., 2010). In an individualist culture, individuals are expected to care for themselves and their immediate families while under a collectivist culture, individuals expect their relatives or members of a group to look after them (Hofstede et al., 2010). Masculinity/femininity is related to people's orientation towards achievement or relationships, respectively (Hofstede et al., 2010). In a masculine culture, the society rewards achieving success, advancement, power, and money while in a feminine culture, individuals care about cooperation, relationships, modesty, have sympathy for the weak and value the quality of life (Hofstede et al., 2010). Uncertainty-avoidance reflects the degree to which individuals feel threatened or uncomfortable with uncertainty (Hofstede et al., 2010). Strong uncertainty avoidance cultures are usually more pessimistic, more dependent on those in power, more based on rigid codes or beliefs, less willing to introduce change and more intolerant to unorthodox ideas while in weak uncertainty avoidance societies people are more relaxed, more open to new ideas, more tolerant and less stressed regarding the future (Hofstede et al., 2010). The pragmatic versus normative dimension concerns to whether people generically focus on the long term rather than on short term; pragmatic societies focus on the long term and recognize that truth depends on time and context, while normative cultures value the short term, traditions, conventions, and seek for stability (Hofstede et al., 2010). Pragmatic societies deal positively with drawbacks and have a high likelihood to save, invest and persevere to achieve results while normative oriented societies have a strong desire to explain everything and establishing the absolute truth, as well as a need for stability. Normative cultures emphasize traditions and have a small likelihood to save for the future as they are more centered on quick results (Hofstede et al., 2010). Indulgence versus restraint gauges whether emphasis is placed either on indulging in the pleasures of life, or instead, on the suppression of gratification (Hofstede et al., 2010). Indulgent societies allow free gratification of human drives related with life and pleasure, emphasize life control and freedom of expression while restraint cultures suppress the gratification of needs through social norms and control the freedom of expression (Hofstede et al., 2010).

Despite the popularity of Hofstede's cultural dimensions, his work faces some criticism, namely the use of quantitative measures, the fact that data were collected from workers of a particular organization (IBM), and the time separating the two rounds of data collection (Efrat, 2014). In a comparative assessment of multiple cultural frameworks, Magnusson, Wilson, Zdravkovic, Zhou, & Westjohn (2008) found that national culture is more stable than Hofstede himself predicted, furthermore, Hofstede's framework showed stronger convergent validity when compared to other cultural frameworks such as Schwartz' (1994).

Hofstede's cultural dimensions are reliable and one of the most employed in cultural research (e.g., Dantas, et al., 2015; Efrat, 2014; Gaygisiz, 2013; Mihaela et al., 2011; Sims et al., 2012; Taylor & Wilson, 2012), although the six-dimension framework is still relatively underexplored in research (see e.g., Gaygisiz, 2013). Extant research supports that national culture and innovation are related. Steel et al. (2012) approached the culture-innovation relationship evaluating culture through personality. They examined data on the scores of the 'big five' (i.e., neuroticism, extraversion, openness to experience, agreeableness and conscientiousness), finding a strong relationship between openness to experience and innovation.

Analyzing five Hofstede's cultural dimension (power distance, individualism/collectivism, masculinity/femininity, long/short term orientation, and uncertainty avoidance) and entrepreneurship (total entrepreneurial activity, necessity-driven entrepreneurship, and opportunity-driven entrepreneurship) among 44 countries of the GEM database, Dantas et al. (2015) demonstrate that:

- Total entrepreneurial activity (TEA) can be explained by lower levels of power distance and by efficiency-driven economies, and by Latin American and Asian economies. This reflects that the main motivation to start a new business is more stringent in less developed economies as a result of lack of more interesting opportunity-driven options. Clearly, innovation-driven economies are not statistically significant in explaining TEA activity;
- Necessity-driven entrepreneurship can be explained by power distance index and uncertainty avoidance index;
- Opportunity-driven entrepreneurship can be explained by masculinity and uncertainty avoidance index;
- The variations among countries in terms of cultural variables, necessity-driven and opportunity-driven entrepreneurship cannot be explained by innovation-driven economies.

Shane (1992, 1993), using patent statistics and Hofstede's four cultural measures, examined data on 33 countries during four years, finding that societies with high individualism scores are highly inventive. Taylor and Wilson (2012) showed that individualism has a strong and positive effect on both scientific progress and technological innovation (measured using citation-weighted research publications and patents). Efrat (2014) investigated the impact of different cultural aspects on countries' motivation to innovate and to invest in innovation. They found that they demonstrated that investment in innovation is a major facilitator of innovation, and that national culture has a substantial influence on the ability of firms to create and maintain innovation. Gaygisiz (2013) brought together the Hofstede and Schwartz cultural measures, the Worldwide Governance Indicators (WGI) and the Human Development Index (HDI). This author found that the governance, indulgence, harmony, affective and intellectual autonomy, and egalitarianism were positively related to human development, whereas power-distance, embeddedness, and hierarchy were negatively related to human development. While this study uses the six-dimension cultural frameworks and their impact on governance, it does not access innovation directly.

Mihaela et al. (2011) examined the relationship between Hofstede's four cultural dimensions and national competitiveness using the CORREL index, observing that cultural dimensions have an impact on national competitiveness. Specifically, in countries where power-distance is small, individualism predominates, and uncertainty control is low; competitiveness is higher when compared to countries where power-distance is high; collectivism dominates; and uncertainty control is intense. Nevertheless, some countries are competitive through masculinity while others are competitive through femininity, besides individualism, and low power-distance. Azar and Drogendijk (2016) examined the relationships between perceived and objective cultural distance (conceptualized using Hofstede's 1980, 2001 scores for national culture dimensions) with innovation, empirically validating the explanatory power of cultural distance on innovation strategies and firm performance.

Corruption

Corruption is recognized as a serious and worldwide problem affecting societies and the credibility of public institutions and their ambassadors. No country can claim to be completely free of corruption as none achieves a maximum score in the corruption indexes. Corruption is defined as *"the abuse of public power (or public office) for private gain"* (You & Khagram, 2005; p. 137) or the action of private individuals or companies who abuse public resources for private interests (Ulman, 2013). For Anokhin and Schulze (2009), corruption involves behavior that violates the trust in public officials and undermines the foundation on which generalized interpersonal trust relies. Transparency International (TI) measures the perception of corruption in different countries, which it defines as *"the abuse of entrusted power for private gain"*. As such, corruption is related to a loss of trust in the systems serving the public and in taking advantage of them for private interests.

Corruptive practices include bribery, kickbacks, coercion (Sims et al., 2012), baksheesh, pay-offs, gratuities, commercial arrangements, favoritism and nepotism, blackmailing, protection or security money, gifts, under-the-table fees, embezzlement, extortion and fraud (Lindgreen, 2004). These practices undermine fair trade, waste resources, defraud public, increase human suffering (Vogl, 1998), affect growth, increase inequality and poverty, provoke distrust and cause anger (Tanzi & Davoodi, 1998).

The damage caused by corruption has become a growing concern, leading international organizations to develop corruption measures such as the Corruption Perception Index (CPI) of TI (Ko & Samajdar, 2010). The corruption perception index measures the perception of corruption in each country based on surveys of business people or international experts, relying on at least three different sources to assess a country's risk. Critics of corruption indexes insist that the measures do not capture local inhabitant's perceptions of corruption, and that the results would be different when different corruption indexes for different years are used (Ko & Samajdar, 2010). Others argue that the aggregation method is not statistically rigorous (Lambsdorff, 2007) and that perceived corruption is not the same as actual corruption (Montinola & Jackman, 2002). Ko & Samajdar (2010) addressed these issues by testing the reliability and validity of multiple corruption indexes, finding that the international experts' perception of corruption is highly correlated with the local peoples' perceptions of corruption, especially bribery. They also demonstrated that corruption indexes are valid and reliable, being an acceptable tool when the research question is related with the general perception of corruption.

An effective control of corruption can bring several advantages: a higher likelihood that entrepreneurs capture larger portions of the revenues they generate; the stimulation of higher levels of entrepreneurial and innovative activities; and lower investments risk (Anokhin & Schulze, 2009). Existent research conducted in the field supports the idea that corruption affects a country's competitiveness and entrepreneurial activity. Ulman (2013) examined the influence of corruption on competitiveness using regression analysis and index data from The Global Competitiveness Report (GCI) 2012-2013 and the corruption perception index of 2012. She found that countries rated as having low national competitiveness are perceived as more corrupt than more competitive countries; also, innovation-driven countries exhibited a stronger connection between the competitiveness and low levels of corruption than factor-driven countries due to the importance that public institutions image have for economic outcomes.

Anokhin and Schulze (2009) used corruption, economic development, entrepreneurship and innovation to propose that improved control of corruption is related to rising levels of innovation and entrepreneurship. They measured innovation by using the number of patent applications and the rate of realized innovation, finding that the efforts to promote entrepreneurship and innovation within an economy are more productive if complemented with actions designed to control corruption.

Using 2009 data from Global Innovation Index, DiRienzo and Das (2015) explored the impact of corruption and its interactive relationship with economic development, in addition to the effect of three different measures of diversity on country-level innovation. They conclude that although corruption affects negatively innovation activities among countries, the effect is mitigated among wealthier countries, as religious diversity, which was considered a proxy for tolerance, was found to positively contribute to innovation. On the other hand, ethnic diversity weakens innovation activities as ethnically fractionalized groups do not participate in collective and collaborative undertakings.

Sharma and Mitra (2015) concluded that policy impediments are an important cause of bribe payment, as the complexity of the political system and the complex bureaucracy tends to raise the likelihood of firms paying bribes, which dampens firms' performance. They argue that bribe payments support both behaviors: 'grease the wheels' and 'sand the wheels'.

National culture has also shown to have an effect on corruption. However, while most studies support this relationship, the findings on which dimensions influence culture are not consensual. Huster (1999) examined the impact of national wealth, income distribution, government size and four Hofstede's dimensions on country's corruption, finding that wealth, power distance, masculinity and uncertainty avoidance strongly influenced corruption. Their results however do not support the impact of individualism on corruption. Davis and Ruhe (2003) analyzed the relationship between Hofstede's cultural dimensions and country corruption perceptions, providing support for power distance, individualism, masculinity and uncertainty avoidance influence. Sanyal (2005) examined the relationships between the corruption perception index score from 47 countries with economic and cultural variables, finding that bribe was more likely in countries with low income per capita and lower disparities in income distribution; furthermore, among cultural factors, only power distance and masculinity were associated with bribe taking. Yeganeh (2014) conducted an extensive study to investigate the effects of cultural values on corruption using Hofstede's, Schwartz's, and Inglehart's frameworks. Concerning Hofstede's results only, they validated the impact of individualism, power distance and uncertainty avoidance on corrupt behaviors. Clearly, only power distance impact appears to be fully consensual among research. Additionally, the aforementioned studies have resorted only to Hofstede's four cultural dimensions.

Adopting a distinct approach, Barr and Serra (2010) discussed the results obtained by two previous studies on corruption using the corruption perception index and the 'bribery game' (a game based on a sample of individuals originating from 34 countries with markedly different levels of corruption which were presented with a corruption decision). The first study, conducted in 2005, showed that corruption could be predicted among undergraduates by referencing the level of corruption prevailing in their home country. In 2007, using a different sample of individuals, the results showed once again that they could predict which undergraduates would engage in bribery based on the level of corruption prevailing in their home country. They also found that the amount of time spent in the UK was associated with a decline in the predisposition of an individual to engage in bribery within the experiment. The results provided support that country's culture is related with the corruption attitudes of individuals.

Sims et al. (2012) hypothesized that human development restricts corruption and the magnitude of that effect is contingent upon the conditions of national culture. Using regression analysis, data from the corruption perception index, the human development index and Hofstede's four dimensions, Sims et al. (2012) found support for the main effect of human development on corruption, as well as the moderator effect of power distance and individualism on the relationship.

Following a different perspective, Mondlane, Claudio, and Khan (2016), focusing on governance indicators that strongly correlate with corruption, support the idea that corruption in Africa is the result of poor democratic governance enabled by asymmetrical concentration of power in governments, which results in the rise of alliances between elites and corporate interests. They also support that a wider citizen engagement in public governance is necessary to strengthen 'voice and accountability' and to promote 'socially conscious' and transparent leaders.

The results of the aforementioned studies using cultural dimensions, innovation or corruption rely on data which is now outdated (e.g., since the 1990s, countries with low individualism scores such as South Korea, Finland or India have now become highly innovative) and traditionally do not include Hofstede's six cultural measures, or combine them with the most updated innovation or corruption indexes.

Clearly, even though competitiveness and entrepreneurship comprise innovation variables, the relationship between corruption and innovation using specific indexes has received little attention.

Theoretical Assumptions and Hypotheses

The present study is based on three main hypotheses regarding: (1) the effects of national culture on innovation and (2) corruption, and (3) the effect of corruption on innovation. The first and second hypotheses assume that Hofstede's framework represents key aspects of a country's culture, which can determine its orientation towards innovation and corruption, respectively.

In high power-distance cultures, individuals accept there is a hierarchical order, thus, organizations are more rigid and centralized, and decisions are taken by and in order to preserve those in power. Also, in high power-distance countries, inhabitants accept that privileges are held by those in authority and the powerless are less likely to defend their rights and defy power, thus, accepting their inequity and the "legitimacy" of corruption by the powerful. Huster (1999) indicated that in high power distance countries, there is a high level of dependence of subordinates on their superiors on the form of paternalism, which is a system by which superiors provide favors to their subordinates in return for their loyalty. As a result, decisions are not based on merit but on the balance of favors and loyalty. Cohen, Pant, and Sharp (1996) claimed that people in high power distance cultures are more likely to understand questionable business practices as ethical than people in low power distance countries. Davis and Ruhe (2003) indicate that corruption should be higher in high power distance countries due to the lack of trust and cooperation between social groups. Several authors support that high power distance cultures are more corrupt than low power distance cultures (Davis & Ruhe, 2003; Huster, 1999; Sanyal, 2005; Yeganeh, 2014). As such, we expect high power distance cultures to tolerate better corruption practices than low power distance countries.

H$_{1a}$: High power to distance index societies exhibit higher levels of corruption.

In low power-distance countries, organizations are more organic, power decentralized, and with a high level of trust and communication between employees, which should stimulate collaboration and innovation. Davis and Ruhe (2003) argue that in low power distance cultures, the gap between superiors and employees is smaller and titles or status are less important, increasing the harmony and cooperation within the society. Contrariwise, high power distance leads to a hierarchical or organizational structure which tends to be more centralized and inflexible, consequently, decision-making will seek to preserve those in authority (Efrat, 2014). Shane (1992) indicated that in low power distance countries, new organizations are smaller and organic, with high levels of information processing capabilities and communication between superiors and employees. Furthermore, those organizations have control systems based on trust and are power decentralized (Shane, 1992). Ahmed (1998) argues that trust, openness, awards, rewards, autonomy and flexibility can enhance an innovative environment in organizations.

H$_{2a}$: High power to distance index societies exhibit lower levels of innovation.

In collectivist societies, the individuals are subsumed by the group and strive to maintain its harmony. As a result, collectivist societies will not go against the clan or tribe and exhibit weak governance levels. Because the group is deemed as more important to the individuals than the state, these cultures normally display weaker mechanisms for controlling corruption, moreover, individuals may become more risk-prone due the group protection effect, neglecting the consequences of corruption. Yeganeh (2014) argue that in collectivist cultures, the emphasis is set on interpersonal relations, which may lead to favoritism, nepotism and corruption, differently, in individualistic cultures, interpersonal relations are less importance and regulations are often respected. LaPalombara (1994) found that high collectivism is a difficult structural condition to change as persons both in public and private sectors will not hesitate to violate written laws if they are interpreted to run counter to established moral codes. Several authors have found a relationship between Hofstede's collectivism and corruption (Davis & Ruhe, 2003; Yeganeh, 2014).

H$_{1b}$: High individualist societies exhibit lower levels of corruption.

In an individualist culture, individuals are oriented towards the self, their immediate relatives, or the organizations they belong to. These societies focus on personal goals, on fulfilling their individual duties and express their thoughts directly, which should translate into a spirit of mission, and a stronger entrepreneurial orientation and innovation. Hofstede (2001) indicated that high individualist countries have a strong entrepreneurial orientation which in turn stimulates invention and innovation. Additionally, individualism and power distance share some characteristics which should influence innovation. Ahmed (1998) stated an innovative environment is characterized by freedom, trust, awards and rewards and Hofstede (2001) demonstrated a strong correlation between individualism and power distance, i.e., typically, low power distance countries have high individualism scores and vice-versa. Shane (1992) results support the hypothesis that high individualist countries should exhibit higher innovation rates.

H$_{2b}$: High individualist societies exhibit higher levels of innovation.

Masculine societies focus on the ego, the power, money and success, thus, they are expected to display a higher level of corruption based on achievement seeking, as individuals will fight for material resources and be more willing to engage in corrupt behavior. Yeganeh (2014) argues that masculine cultures focus on material possession, performance and ambition, in contrast with feminine cultures emphasize human needs, care and interdependence. Huster (1999) suggested that the focus on material success may lead to a willingness to engage in corrupt behaviors in the hunt of material benefits. Several scholars are supported that higher levels of masculinity and the search for material success to be related with unethical and corrupt behaviors (Davis & Ruhe, 2003; Huster, 1999; Sanyal, 2005).

H$_{1c}$: Masculine societies exhibit higher levels of corruption.

Feminine cultures are characterized by a focus on cooperation, care, and relationships, which should translate into an increased propensity for innovation. Hofstede (2001) indicate that feminine societies exhibit a greater balance between men and women's roles. Efrat (2014) findings revealed that some aspects of innovations are higher in feminine cultures, which may be due to collaboration and networking. Accordingly, feminine societies value relationships as a mean of developing cooperation and well-being through relationships, which in turn help to meet presents goals by creating a favorable environment (Efrat, 2014). Collaborative environments are posed to have a positive impact for creative and inventive processes to occur.

H$_{2c}$: Masculine societies exhibit lower levels of innovation.

High uncertainty avoidance societies are more dependent of those in power and make more use of strict codes. Paradoxically, while high uncertainty avoidance seeks the creation of rules to decrease ambiguity, those very same rules are typically very rigid and not practically observed (Huster, 2000). Davis and Ruhe (2003) indicated that countries which are by natured uncomfortable with uncertainty prefer bureaucratic structures which in turn tend to encourage unethical behaviors. Yeganeh (2014) stated that the abundance of rules and regulations in high uncertainty avoidance societies creates occasions for economic rents and misconducts. Huster (1999) argued that uncertainty avoidance reflects an intolerance for ambiguity, nevertheless, corruption can be perceived as a mechanism to decrease uncertainty but in situations where outcomes are uncertain, corruptive practices lead to a more certain outcome. In high uncertainty avoidance societies its members are also more committed to protect the gains achieved from the status quo, thereby engendering a higher likelihood of engaging in corrupt behaviors. Existing research supports the relationship between uncertainty avoidance and corruption (Davis & Ruhe, 2003; Huster, 1999; Yeganeh, 2014).

H$_{1d}$: High uncertainty-avoidance societies exhibit higher levels of corruption.

Low uncertainty avoidance societies are typically more opened to new ideas, on the other hand, high uncertainty-avoidance cultures are more pessimistic and less willing to introduce changes or unorthodox ideas as these members understand novelties as dangerous. As a consequence, new ideas or innovations are less likely to happen because they can be perceived as dangerous and disturbing the existing order and control. Findings from Shane (1995) support the linkage between low uncertainty avoidance and innovation. Efrat (2014) suggested the rationale that low uncertainty avoidance countries based on a higher open to change, willingness to take risks and abilities prevailing over seniority turn operational in an innovative environment.

H$_{2d}$: High uncertainty-avoidance societies exhibit lower levels of innovation.

The pragmatism versus normative dimension has been related to short term and long term orientation. According to Hofstede et al. (2010), societies with a short-term orientation have a strong concern with the absolute truth, are normative in thinking, have great respect for traditions, and focus on achieving quick results. We have posed that highly strict and conservative societies, averse to change are expected to be more prone to engage in corruptive behaviors. This can be due to the focus on the short-term rather than long-term perspective, which may lead individuals to engage in unethical practices seeking instant rewards.

H$_{1e}$: High pragmatic societies exhibit lower levels of corruption.

In long-term orientated societies, the truth depends on situation, context and time. Thus, long-term orientation is characterized by an ability to adapt traditions to changed conditions, a strong interest in saving and investments, and perseverance in achieving results (Hofstede et al., 2010). Contrariwise, short-term oriented cultures understand societal change with distrust, which in turn can hinder creativity and innovation. Hofstede et al. (2010) argue that long-term oriented cultures are more prone to make efforts in modern education in order to pave the way for the future. We expect pragmatic societies to produce more innovative outputs than normative cultures.

H$_{2e}$: High pragmatic societies exhibit higher levels of innovation.

Restraint cultures suppress the gratification of needs through rigid social norms, and control over freedom of expression, thus, more bureaucratic, closed and normative societies should be associated with higher levels of corruption. Hofstede et al. (2010) indicates that in restrained cultures there is a greater sense of helplessness on the personal destiny. Controlled societies where individuals are conformed with their current situation and lack freedom to comply, may create an environment which allow higher levels of corruption.

H$_{1f}$: High indulgent societies exhibit lower levels of corruption.

Indulgent societies allow people to freely focus on the gratification of human desires associated with the pleasures of life, emphasizing life control, and freedom of expression, which can be expected to lead to more creativity and innovation. Hofstede et al. (2010) state that indulgent cultures place a high importance on freedom of speech and personal control, which may have an impact on the workplace on how willing are employees to voice opinions and provide feedback. As a result, these societies are expected to be more open and collaborative, encouraging networking and cooperation and as a result, innovation.

H$_{2f}$: High indulgent societies exhibit higher levels of innovation.

The third hypothesis is based on the assumption that corruption hampers innovation. Entrepreneurs and investors aim to capture the revenues and profits they generate, thus, in cultures with high levels of corruption, it is more likely that some of the dividends will be lost due to extortion, intellectual protection, fraud or bribery among others, reducing investment attractiveness, entrepreneurship activity and innovation.

H₃: High corruptive societies exhibit lower levels of innovation.

The conceptual model and expected sign of the hypothesized relationships are presented in Figure 1.

METHODS

Values for Hofstede's PDI, IND, MAS, UAI, PRA, and IVR were obtained from Hofstede's Website (2014) for the year 2010 with data ranging from 0-100, with 100 representing the maximum score for each dimension. The Corruption Perception Index scores were gathered from the Transparency International Website (2014) for the year 2012. In the index as published, values range from 0-100 with 0 representing the highest level of corruption and 100 the lowest. Data was reversed by subtracting each CPI score from 100. For this sample, the highest level of corruption was 81 (Venezuela) whilst the minimum was 10 (Denmark, Finland and New Zealand).

The Global Innovation Index is the average of two sub-indexes. The data was retrieved from the Global Innovation Website (2014) for 2012; this index ranges from 0-100 where the higher the score, the higher the innovation. The minimum and maximum values recorded were 23.06 (Pakistan) and 68.24 (Switzerland) respectively.

The sample for this study included data for 61 countries located on five continents (Table 1). The dataset was limited mainly by availability of secondary data on culture. The countries included in this study represent around 76.2% world's population and 90.7% world's Gross Domestic Product in 2012 (The World Databank, 2014).

Figure 1. Conceptual model and expected causal relationships

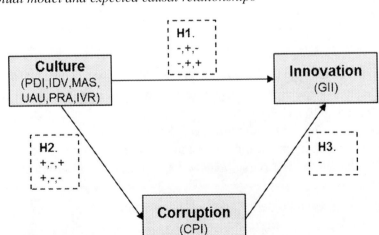

Table 1. Countries included in the sample

Africa: Morocco
Asia: Bangladesh, China, Hong Kong, India, Indonesia, Iran, Japan, South Korea, Malaysia, Pakistan, Philippines, Singapore, Thailand, Vietnam
Europe: Turkey, Greece, Romania, Russia, Serbia, Poland, Bulgaria, Croatia, Slovakia, Lithuania, Italy, Portugal, Hungary, Latvia, Spain, Czech Republic, Slovenia, France, Austria, Belgium, Estonia, Malta, Germany, Norway, Luxembourg, Ireland, Denmark, Netherlands, United Kingdom, Finland, Sweden, Switzerland
Oceania: Australia, New Zealand
North America: Canada, USA
South America: Argentina, Brazil, Chile, Colombia, El Salvador, Mexico, Peru, Trinidad and Tobago, Uruguay, Venezuela

This study uses an approach based on correlations and regressions. Before testing the hypothesis and estimating the model, we examined how innovation and corruption were related with country's wealth. The statistical data analysis of the model was carried out using the partial least squares method structural equation modelling (PLS-SEM) and the SmartPLS 3.0 software. The use of this methodology is justified because this method is robust when testing and validating an exploratory model (Chin, 2010).

RESULTS

As expected, countries with a higher innovation levels display a higher level of wealth, measured by GDP-PC (Gross Domestic Product Per Capita). This reflects the premise that the creation of innovation translates into growth and economic development for the host country (Figure 2). On the other hand, countries with the highest levels of corruption are the ones with the lowest GDP-PC levels; this helps reinforce the notion that corruption prevents a country from retaining its economic profits and prevents a fair distribution of wealth among its population (Figure 3).

We further proceeded to test our hypothesis. Table 2 presents the descriptive statistics and correlation coefficients for the variables examined. Overall, the results support the relationships between national culture on innovation and corruption simultaneously, and that of corruption on innovation. As proposed by the first hypothesis, the cultural dimensions PDI, IDV, UAI and IVR correlate with perceived corruption. As anticipated by the second hypothesis, Hofstede's cultural variables are correlated with the GII. The IDV and PRA cultural dimensions have a strong and positive relationship with the GII, while the link between PDI and UAI towards innovation is negative. The third hypothesis, based on the assumption that corruption and innovation are correlated, is also supported by the data, as the correlation between the CPI and the GII is statistically significant.

The model shown in Figure 4 was evaluated by (a) the sign, magnitude and statistical significance of the parameters of structural relations, and by (b) the explained variance (R^2) of the endogenous variables, following Götz, Liehr-Gobbers, and Krafft (2010) (2010). It is possible to conclude that not all structural relationships have parameters with compatible signal with the hypotheses proposed in the research model. The detailed results can be found in Table 3. The relationship between the power-distance index and innovation is positive and not statistically significant, thus rejecting H_{2a}.

Figure 2. Relationship between GII and GDP PC

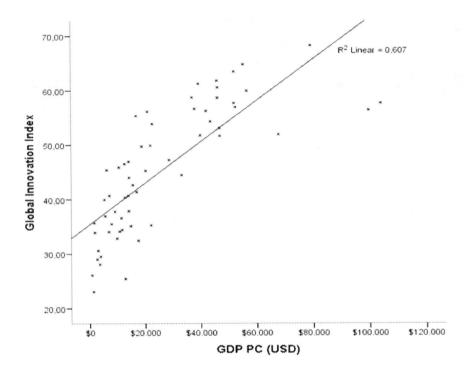

Figure 3. Relationship between CPI and GDP PC

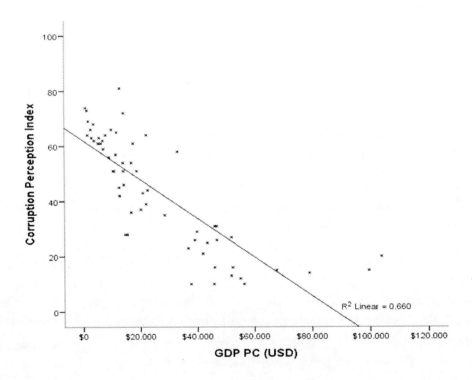

Table 2. Descriptive statistics and correlations

Variable	Mean	Std Dev	GII	CPI	PDI	IDV	MAS	UAI	PRA
GII	45.1	11.7							
CPI	44.0	20.7	-0.894**						
PDI	58.5	20.6	-0.606**	0.656**					
IDV	46.2	23.6	0.663**	-0.650**	-0.662**				
MAS	49.0	20.0	-0.125	0.177	0.152	0.026			
UAI	66.6	22.8	-0.352**	0.289*	0.212	-0.191	0.026		
PRA	49.0	22.4	0.386**	-0.178	0.031	0.131	0.023	-0.031	
IVR	47.5	22.6	0.184	-0.284*	-0.306*	0.160	0.079	-0.067	-0.527**

* $p < .05$

** $p < .01$.

The results also show that all the remaining hypotheses have the sign and magnitude according to the original hypotheses proposed. However, only individualism and uncertainty avoidance indexes have positive statistical significant relationships with innovation, validating H_{2b} and H_{2d} at a 5% significance level.

The analysis between national culture and corruption is somehow different as all the signs and magnitudes are according to what has been proposed in during the hypotheses development process. Moreover, the relationship between power distance, individualism, pragmatism, and indulgence versus restraint indexes show statistical significant relationships with corruption, validating H_{1a}, H_{1b}, H_{1e}, and H_{1f} at a 1% significance level. Although masculinity has a positive statistical significant relationship with corruption at a 5% significance level, uncertainty avoidance index has no statistical relationship with corruption not validating H_{1d}.

Finally, the relationship between corruption and innovation ($\beta = -0.648$), validates H_3 at a 1% significance level.

The direct effect of power distance index on innovation ($\beta = 0.274$) and on corruption ($\beta = 0.286$) are both positive. However, of power distance total effect on innovation is low ($\beta = 0.088$) and not statistically significant. On the other hand, the total effect of all other cultural variables on innovation are statistically significant, being the most important one high individualist cultures with $\beta = 0.510$, followed by programmatic societies with $\beta = 0.409$, and by indulgent societies with $\beta = 0.294$, all of them statistically significant at 1% level.

One can conclude that the more masculine societies are, the more prone to corruption ($\beta = 0.147$) they are, being the total effect of masculine societies less innovative ($\beta = -0.263$). Finally, the relationship between uncertainty-avoidance societies and corruption is not statistically significant; however, one can claim that the total effect of uncertainty avoidance index on innovation is statistically significant at a 5% level and negative ($\beta = 0.215$).

Overall, based on the results found, 62.3% of the variability of corruption can be explained by Hofstede's national cultural influence. As for innovation, 71.8% was explained due to the joint effects of Hofstede's national cultural and corruption.

As shown in Table 4 and Figure 4, H_{1a}, H_{1b}, H_{1c}, H_{1e}, H_{1f}, H_{2b}, H_{2d}, and H_3 are validated.

Table 3. Direct, indirect and total effects

	Direct Effects		Indirect Effects		Total Effects	
	Loadings	t-Values (p-values)	Loadings	Values (p-values)	Loadings	Values (p-values)
CPI → GII	-0.648	6.643 (0.000)			-0.648	6.643 (0.000)
IDV → CPI	-0.352				-0.352	3.078 (0.002)
IDV → GII	0.282	2.013 (0.044)	0.228	3.016 (0.003)	0.510	3.387 (0.001)
IVR → CPI	-0.304	2.783 (0.005)			-0.304	2.783 (0.005)
IVR → GII	0.097	1.351 (0.177)	0.197	2.759 (0.006)	0.294	2.931 (0.003)
MAS → CPI	0.171	2.058 (0.040)			0.171	2.058 (0.040)
MAS → GII	-0.153	1.365 (0.172)	-0.110	2.188 (0.029)	-0.263	2.115 (0.034)
PDI → CPI	0.286	3.077 (0.002)			0.286	3.077 (0.002)
PDI → GII	0.274	1.148 (0.251)	-0.186	2.545 (0.011)	0.088	0.350 (0.726)
PRA → CPI	-0.301	2.917 (0.004)			-0.301	2.917 (0.004)
PRA → GII	0.214	1.878 (0.061)	0.195	2.710 (0.007)	0.409	3.034 (0.002)
UAI → CPI	0.127	1.060 (0.289)			0.127	1.060 (0.289)
UAI → GII	-0.133	2.018 (0.044)	-0.082	1.028 (0.304)	-0.215	2.075 (0.038)

Figure 4. Model relating Hofstede's cultural dimensions on corruption and innovation

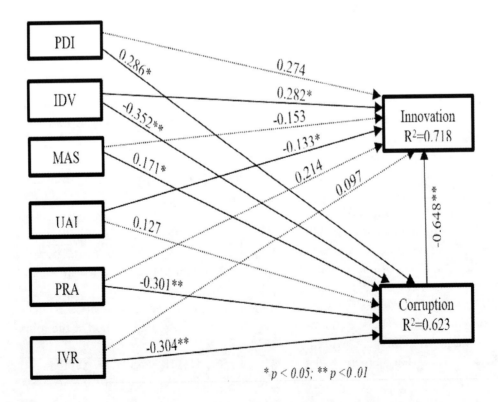

Table 4. Hypotheses validation

Hypothesis and Causal Relations	Results	Hypothesis and Causal Relations	Results
H_{1a}: PDI → CPI	confirmed **	H_{2a}: PDI → GII	not confirmed
H_{1b}: IDV → CPI	confirmed **	H_{2b}: IDV → GII	confirmed *
H_{1c}: MAS → CPI	confirmed *	H_{2c}: MAS → GII	not confirmed
H_{1d}: UAI → CPI	not confirmed	H_{2d}: UAI → GII	confirmed *
H_{1e}: PRA → CPI	confirmed **	H_{2e}: PRA → GII	not confirmed
H_{1f}: IVR → CPI	confirmed **	H_{2f}: IVR → GII	not confirmed

Note: ** p<0,01; *p<0,05

DISCUSSION AND RECOMMENDATIONS

The purpose of this study was to examine the relationship between cultural variables, corruption and innovation. In order to assess those variables, we used Hofstede's six-dimension cultural framework, the corruption perception index and the global innovation index, respectively.

First, Hofstede's cultural dimensions were shown to have an effect on the perception of corruption. Previous studies indicate that a country's culture can partially help explain why some individuals engage in corrupt behavior (Barr & Serra, 2010; Davis & Ruhe, 2003; Huster, 1999; Sanyal, 2005; Yeganeh, 2014). The results obtained complement earlier studies. Power distance is somehow consensual as corruption antecedent and our results corroborate those findings. Clearly, the more hierarchical and power centralized a society is, the higher the corruption perception. Huster (1999) results supported the notion that the cultural profile of a corrupt country is one with a high power distance, masculinity and uncertainty avoidance. Sanyal (2005) showed that power distance and masculinity were significant factors. We obtained a positive impact for both power distance and masculinity. On one hand, corruption seems to be less likely to be challenged on high power distance countries; on the other hand, the pursuit of success that characterizes highly masculine societies seems to trigger corruptive practices.

There is support that collective societies are more corrupt (Davis & Ruhe, 2003; Yeganeh, 2014). We found that more individualistic societies appear to be less corrupt. This might be the result of collectivist societies avoiding disruptive group behaviors, tolerating corruption due to the sense of protection provided by the group, which in turn makes individuals to act more corruptly. According to Yeganeh (2014) collectivist cultures are characterized by the prevalence of interpersonal relationships, hierarchical decision making, unequal distribution of wealth and resources and the importance of tribal ties, as a result, these societies have complex norms rooted in tradition and religion, leading to nepotism, favoritism, bribery and deviance regulations.

Huster (1999), Davis and Ruhe (2003) and Yeganeh (2014) supported uncertainty avoidance impact on corruption. Societies which try to avoid uncertainty are typically more bureaucratic and governed by several rules and procedures. Yeganeh (2014) indicates that cultures with high scores in uncertainty avoidance are more advanced, emphasize rationality and have strong public institutions and education (Yeganeh, 2014). Corruption can be seen as a method to decrease uncertainty, thus, our results demonstrate that societies which deal better with uncertainty are less tempted to obtain predictable outcomes through corruptive practices.

As proposed, our results show that the 'new' Hofstede's cultural dimensions, pragmatism and indulgence, have a strong negative effect on corruption, meaning that, equalitarian societies, which focus on the long term and life pleasure gratification, are perceived as less corrupt than highly normative and suppressive national cultures. The orientation towards the short term seems to be in fact more related with corruptive activities due to rewards seeking. The increase in the number of norms and laws, as well as a resistance to new paradigms, is also linked with higher levels of corruption. This may be the result of individuals in inefficient societies trying to circumvent certain procedures and norms due to unethical behavior of established practices. Furthermore, as in restrained societies individuals are less challenging towards their conditions, they adopt a passive attitude towards corruptive practices.

Second, Hofstede's cultural dimensions were also found to have an impact on innovation. Existent research has shown national culture to be highly related with innovation (Efrat, 2014). Shane (1992, 1993) and Taylor and Wilson (2012) highlighted the importance of the individualism dimension in the development of innovation and scientific progress. This paper supports the direct and total effect of individualism on innovation. In line with Mihaela et al. (2011) and Steel et al. (2012), uncertainty-avoidance was demonstrated to have a direct and total effect on innovation. Although the direct effect was not statistically significant, the total effect of optimistic and positive cultures, which are highly capable of dealing with novelty and uncertainty, on innovation tends to be higher than in orthodox and conservative societies. Moreover, pragmatism was also found to have a positive impact on innovation (i.e., the more future oriented, malleable and resilient a nation is, the higher their innovative drive).

Third, we tested the relationship between corruption and innovation. Existent research shows that innovation is higher when corruption is controlled (Anokhin & Schulze, 2009) and that generally, corruption is related with competitiveness (Ulman, 2013). The results clearly show that the higher the perception of corruption, the less innovative a nation is, thus, corrupt practices hinder the attractiveness of developing and engaging in entrepreneurial and innovative actions, decreasing new developments and the nation's future potential.

CONCLUSION

Several conclusions can be drawn from this study. Of all the variables studied, corruption was the one which had a greater impact on innovation. Highly innovative countries have higher gross domestic product and lower levels of corruption; on the opposite, less innovative countries show higher levels of corruption and consequently have lower levels of wealth. Corruption is a topic of current interest affecting all types of countries, with corruption scandals seen breaking throughout the world on a daily basis. The results show that corruption is highly related to innovation, and at the same time has a strong impact on economic growth. Therefore, corruption emerges as a factor which is well-suited for explaining innovation, and its negative impacts can be explained at two levels. Corrupt countries are less attractive for inventors – there are less prospects of retaining the benefits of an investment and at the same time it is more difficult to carry out entrepreneurial activity due to the necessity of eventually engaging in corrupt activities. From a governance perspective, innovation incentives can be diluted by corruption, preventing them from reaching their targets and thus, stimulating the economy. Cultural dimensions have an impact on corruption and innovation, although, from the six cultural variables examined, only individualism had an impact on both, meaning that culture itself is a weaker predictor of innovation than corruption.

Besides corruption, other factors contribute more for innovation than national culture; nevertheless, the indirect impact of national culture on innovation through corruption should not be neglected.

The results suggest that the more hierarchical, closed and bureaucratic societies are, the more corrupt they become. Several explanations can be presented: first, in highly hierarchical societies, individuals strive to preserve their status quo and, as a consequence, it is harder for powerful individuals to be defied and questioned; second, traditional and conservative societies appear to be more corrupt than free societies, this was expected as this type of society aims to preserve norms and conventions. As a consequence, changing the institutionalized conventions and introducing new developments is harder and might be seen as more disrupting than in more pragmatic societies. Finally, although one could expect highly regulated societies to be less corrupt as there are more control mechanisms, the results show the opposite to be true; the more bureaucratic societies are, the more corrupt they become. If on the one hand, bureaucracy appears to be a substitute for trust, on the other hand, more restrictive countries also have lower levels of freedom of speech or democracy, which not only protect fraudulent activities but foremost, prevent corruption from being reported.

Our results however underline the importance of the new Hofstede dimensions, which have somehow been neglected. Most likely, variables which are a consequence of a country's culture such as the entrepreneurial environment, the country's legal system or labor flexibility, are more important in determining innovation than culture traits themselves.

Although, there is a direct effect of masculinity on corruption, no support was found for the impact of the masculine dimension on innovation. Free societies, where power is distributed equally, with a strong level of perseverance, and which emphasize life's pleasures, gratification, and the development of the "self", are generally less corrupt and more innovative. On the contrary, normative national cultures not only show a lower propensity for innovation, but also a higher level of corruption. Furthermore, the level of corruption poses a serious threat to the innovation levels. Although laws and rules may form the basis for civilized life, in order to develop less corrupt and more innovative societies, government's policies should focus on promoting equality, trust and optimism among individuals using mechanisms other than norms.

There are a number of limitations regarding this research. This study relied on secondary data and the scores concerning Hofstede's cultural variables are not available for all countries, conditioning the study sample to 61 countries. The results show that from the six cultural dimensions examined, only individualism had an effect on both corruption and innovation.

This research does not go beyond looking at national culture to describe how corruption influences innovation. Therefore, future research could look at other mechanisms as well as how innovation and entrepreneurial investments are turned into innovation outputs according to the corruption levels. Also, following the approach of Sims et al. (2012), further research can use several cultural frameworks simultaneously (such as Schwartz or GLOBE) to provide additional insights into the impact of national culture.

This study examined innovation based on the GII only, although, this measure is composed by two sub-indexes based on five and two pillars respectively. Future studies can examine which innovation components are more related to which cultural or corruption variables respectively. Finally, as we used a cross-sectional approach, studies examining cultural, innovation and corruption changes throughout time focusing specifically in rising technological-innovative countries can offer other explanations as to why those countries became more innovative, although they might be restricted to examining four cultural dimensions only.

FUTURE RESEARCH DIRECTIONS

As we resorted to a cross-sectional approach, future studies could address the relationships between cultural dimensions, corruption and innovation using longitudinal data to provide other explanations on the development of those relationships throughout time. Also, culture could be evaluated under various frameworks simultaneously, e.g., Gaygısız (2013) used Hofstede's and Schwartz's, and Yeganeh (2014) used Hofstede's, Schwatz's and Inglehart's frameworks. Other models such as the Global Leadership and Organizational Behavior Effectiveness could also be employed.

Álvarez and Urbano (2011) concluded that the effect of role models in Latin America might be more important for entrepreneurship than originally thought when compared to developed countries. This is most likely due to the successful image entrepreneurs have and the high unemployment rate, which makes entrepreneurship a very attractive alternative. Future studies could complement existing knowledge on innovation and corruption by addressing them from an entrepreneurship perspective, focusing on the role models importance for both corruption and innovation.

Like most cross-cultural studies, our analysis is based on national-level data and does not take into account country-level differences or firm-level specificities. Paunov (2016) found that corruption affected particularly smaller firms but had no impact on foreign and publicly owned firms. Future studies could examine how culture and corruption influence outputs at a firm-level to provide additional findings on whether the examined variables play the same role in national as in an organizational setting. Furthermore, as we have assessed corruption through the CPI, future studies can examine the relationships between culture and the different types of corruption, e.g., passive or active and its modes. Do cultural variables have the same influence on bribery, fraud and extortion and are all these modes harmful for innovation the same way?

REFERENCES

Ahmed, P. (1998). Culture and climate for innovation. *European Journal of Innovation Management, 1*(1), 30–43. doi:10.1108/14601069810199131

Álvarez, C., & Urbano, D. (2011). Environmental factors and entrepreneurial activity in Latin America. *Academia Revista Latinoamericana de Administración, 48,* 126–139.

Anokhin, S., & Schulze, W. S. (2009). Entrepreneurship, innovation, and corruption. *Journal of Business Venturing, 24*(5), 465–476. doi:10.1016/j.jbusvent.2008.06.001

Azar, G., & Drogendijk, R. (2016). Cultural distance, innovation and export performance. *European Business Review, 28*(2), 176–207. doi:10.1108/EBR-06-2015-0065

Barr, A., & Serra, D. (2010). Corruption and culture: An experimental analysis. *Journal of Public Economics, 94*(11-12), 862–869. doi:10.1016/j.jpubeco.2010.07.006

Boschma, R., & Martin, R. (2010). *The handbook of evolutionary economic geography.* Cheltenham, UK: Edward Elgar. doi:10.4337/9781849806497

Carrizo-Moreira, A., & Leonidivna-Karachun, H. (2014). Uma revisão interpretativa sobre o desenvolvimento de novos produtos. *Cuadernos de Administración, 27*(49), 155–182. doi:10.11144/Javeriana. cao27-49.ridn

Chin, W. W. (2010). How to write up and report PLS analyses. In V. Esposito Vinzi, W. Chin, J. Henseler, & H. Wang (Eds.), *Handbook of partial least squares* (pp. 655–688). New York: Springer-Verlag. doi:10.1007/978-3-540-32827-8_29

Cohen, J., Pant, L., & Sharp, D. (1996). A methodological note on cross-cultural accounting ethics research. *The International Journal of Accounting, 31*(1), 55–66. doi:10.1016/S0020-7063(96)90013-8

Cornell University, INSEAD, & WIPO. (2013). The Global innovation index 2013: The local dynamics of innovation. Authors.

Dantas, J. G., & Moreira, A. C. (2011). *O Processo de inovação*. Lisbon: LIDEL.

Dantas, J. G., Moreira, A. C., & Valente, F. M. (2015). Entrepreneurship and national culture: How cultural differences among countries explain entrepreneurial activity. In L. C. Carvalho (Ed.), *Handbook of research on internationalization of entrepreneurial innovation in the global economy* (pp. 1–28). Hershey, PA: IGI Global. doi:10.4018/978-1-4666-8216-0.ch001

Davis, J. H., & Ruhe, J. A. (2003). Perceptions of country corruption: Antecedents and outcomes. *Journal of Business Ethics, 43*(4), 275–288. doi:10.1023/A:1023038901080

DiRienzo, C., & Das, J. (2015). Innovation and role of corruption and diversity: A cross-country study. *International Journal of Cross Cultural Management, 15*(1), 51–72. doi:10.1177/1470595814554790

Edquist, C. (1997). *Systems of innovation: technologies, institutions and organizations*. London: Pinter Publishers.

Efrat, K. (2014). The direct and indirect impact of culture on innovation. *Technovation, 34*(1), 12–20. doi:10.1016/j.technovation.2013.08.003

Frankelius, P. (2009). Questioning two myths in innovation literature. *The Journal of High Technology Management Research, 20*(1), 40–51. doi:10.1016/j.hitech.2009.02.002

Gaygisiz, E. (2013). How are cultural dimensions and governance quality related to socioeconomic development? *Journal of Socio-Economics, 47*, 170–179. doi:10.1016/j.socec.2013.02.012

Global Innovation Website. (2014). *Global innovation index*. Retrieved April 11, 2014, from http://www. globalinnovationindex.org/content.aspx?page=GII-Home

Götz, G., Liehr-Gobbers, K., & Krafft, M. (2010). Evaluation of structural equation models using the partial least squares (PLS) approach. In V. Esposito Vinzi, W. Chin, J. Henseler, & H. Wang (Eds.), *Handbook of partial least squares: Concepts, methods, and applications* (pp. 691–711). Berlin: Springer-Verlag. doi:10.1007/978-3-540-32827-8_30

Hair, J. F., Black, W. C., Babin, B. J., & Anderson, R. E. (2010). *Multivariate data analysis*. Upper Saddle River, NJ: Prentice Hall.

Heidenreich, M. (2004). The dilemmas of regional innovation systems. In P. Cooke, M. Heidenreich, & H. J. Braczyk (Eds.), *Regional innovation systems* (pp. 363–389). London: Routledge.

Hofstede, G. (1980). *Culture's consequences: International differences in work-related values.* Beverly Hills, CA: Sage Publications.

Hofstede, G. (2001). *Culture's consequences: Comparing values, behaviors, institutions and organizations across nations.* Thousand Oaks, CA: Sage Publications.

Hofstede, G. (2014). Retrieved April 11, 2014, from http://www.geerthofstede.nl/dimension-data-matrix

Hofstede, G., Hofstede, G. J., & Minkov, M. (2010). Cultures and organizations: Software of the mind. McGraw-Hill USA.

Husted, B. (2000). The impact of national culture on software piracy. *Journal of Business Ethics, 26*(3), 197–211. doi:10.1023/A:1006250203828

Huster, B. W. (1999). Wealth, culture, and corruption. *Journal of International Business Studies, 30*(2), 339–359. doi:10.1057/palgrave.jibs.8490073

Ko, K., & Samajdar, A. (2010). Evaluation of international corruption indexes: Should we believe them or not? *The Social Science Journal, 47*(3), 508–540. doi:10.1016/j.soscij.2010.03.001

Lambsdorff, J. (2007). The Methodology of the corruption perceptions index 2007. Transparency International (TI) and University of Passau.

LaPalombara, J. (1994). Structural and institutional aspects of corruption. *Social Research, 61*(2), 325–350.

Lindgreen, A. (2004). Corruption and unethical behavior: Report on a set of Danish guidelines. *Journal of Business Ethics, 51*(1), 31–39. doi:10.1023/B:BUSI.0000032388.68389.60

Magnusson, P., Wilson, R. T., Zdravkovic, S., Zhou, J. X., & Westjohn, S. A. (2008). Breaking through the cultural clutter cultural and institutional frameworks. *International Marketing Review, 25*(2), 183–201. doi:10.1108/02651330810866272

Mihaela, H., Claudia, O., & Lucian, B. (2011). Culture and national competitiveness. *African Journal of Business Management, 5*(April), 3056–3062.

Mondlane, H., Claudio, F., & Khan, M. (2016). Remedying Africas self-propelled corruption: The missing link. *Politikon, 43*(3), 345–370. doi:10.1080/02589346.2016.1160859

Montinola, G. R., & Jackman, R. W. (2002). Sources of corruption: A cross-country study. *Sources of Corruption, 32*, 147–170.

Moreira, A. C. (2014). Single minute exchange of die and organizational innovation in seven small and medium-sized firms. In J. L. Carcia-Alcaraz, A. A. Maldonado-Macias, & G. Cortes-Robles (Eds.), *Lean manufacturing in the developing world. Methodology, case studies and trends from Latin America* (pp. 483–499). Springer Verlag. doi:10.1007/978-3-319-04951-9_23

Moreira, A. C., Carneiro, L., & Tavares, M. (2007). Critical technologies for the north of Portugal in 2015: The case of ITCE sectors – information technologies, communications and electronics. *International Journal of Foresight and Innovation Policy, 3*(2), 187–206. doi:10.1504/IJFIP.2007.011624

Moreira, A. C., & Vale, A. A. (2016). Sectoral systems of innovation and nanotechnology. Challenges ahead. In M. Peris-Ortiz, J. Ferreira, L. Farinha, & N. Fernandes (Eds.), *Multiple helix ecosystems for sustainable competitiveness* (pp. 147–168). Heidelberg, Germany: Springer International Publishing Switzerland. doi:10.1007/978-3-319-29677-7_10

OECD. (2005). *Oslo manual: Guidelines for collecting and interpreting innovation data.* Paris: OECD Publications and Eurostat.

Sanyal, R. (2005). Determinants of bribery in international business: The cultural and economic factors. *Journal of Business Ethics, 59*(1), 139–145. doi:10.1007/s10551-005-3406-z

Schumpeter, J. (1942). *Capitalism, socialism and democracy.* London: Allen&Unwin.

Schwartz, S. (1994). Beyond individualism/collectivism: New cultural dimensions of values. In U. Kim, H. C. Triandis, Ç. Kagitçibasi, S.-C. Choi, & G. Yoon (Eds.), *Individualism and collectivism: Theory, method, and applications* (pp. 85–119). Thousand Oaks, CA: Sage Publications.

Shane, S. (1992). Why do some societies invent more than others? *Journal of Business Venturing, 7*(1), 29–46. doi:10.1016/0883-9026(92)90033-N

Shane, S. (1993). Cultural influences on national rates of innovation. *Journal of Business Venturing, 8*(1), 59–73. doi:10.1016/0883-9026(93)90011-S

Shane, S. (1995). Uncertainty avoidance and the preference for innovation championing roles. *Journal of International Business Studies, 26*(1), 47–68. doi:10.1057/palgrave.jibs.8490165

Sharma, C., & Mitra, A. (2015). Corruption, governance and firm performance: Evidence from Indian enterprises. *Journal of Policy Modeling, 37*(5), 835–851. doi:10.1016/j.jpolmod.2015.05.001

Sims, R. L., Gong, B., & Ruppel, C. P. (2012). A contingency theory of corruption: The effect of human development and national culture. *The Social Science Journal, 49*(1), 90–97. doi:10.1016/j.soscij.2011.07.005

Steel, G. D., Rinne, T., & Fairweather, J. (2012). Personality, nations, and innovation: Relationships between personality traits and national innovation scores. *Cross-Cultural Research, 46*(1), 3–30. doi:10.1177/1069397111409124

Tanzi, V., & Davoodi, H. (1998). Roads to nowhere: How corruption in public investment hurts growth. *Economic Issues, 12*, 1–12.

Taras, V., & Steel, P. (2009). Beyond Hofstede: Challenging the ten testaments of cross-cultural research. In C. Nakata (Ed.), *Beyond Hofstede: Culture frameworks for global marketing and management* (pp. 40–61). Chicago, IL: Macmillan/Palgrave. doi:10.1057/9780230240834_3

Taras, V., Steel, P., & Kirkman, B. L. (2012). Improving national cultural indices using a longitudinal meta-analysis of Hofstedes dimensions. *Journal of World Business, 47*(3), 329–341. doi:10.1016/j.jwb.2011.05.001

Taylor, M. Z., & Wilson, S. (2012). Does culture still matter?: The effects of individualism on national innovation rates. *Journal of Business Venturing, 27*(2), 234–247. doi:10.1016/j.jbusvent.2010.10.001

The World Databank. (2014). *World Databank.* Retrieved April 20, 2014, from http://databank.worldbank.org/data/home.aspx

Transparency International Website. (2014). *Corruption perception index.* Retrieved April 11, 2014, from http://www.transparency.org/cpi2012/results

Turró, A., Urbano, D., & Peris-Ortiz, M. (2013). Culture and innovation: The moderating effect of cultural values on corporate entrepreneurship. *Technological Forecasting and Social Change, 88*, 360–369. doi:10.1016/j.techfore.2013.10.004

Ulman, S.-R. (2013). Corruption and national competitiveness in different stages of country development. *Procedia Economics and Finance, 6*(13), 150–160. doi:10.1016/S2212-5671(13)00127-5

Vogl, F. (1998). The Supply side of global bribery. *Finance & Development, 35*(2), 30–33.

Yeganeh, H. (2014). Culture and corruption. *International Journal of Development Issues, 13*(1), 2–24. doi:10.1108/IJDI-04-2013-0038

You, J., & Khagram, S. (2005). A comparative study of inequality and corruption. *American Sociological Review, 70*(February), 36–57.

KEY TERMS AND DEFINITIONS

Corruption Perceptions Index: A score that has been widely used to rank countries regarding how corrupt their public sectors are. Although the index does not capture the individual frustration of this reality, it captures the views of analysts, businesspeople and experts around the world.

Corruption: A form of dishonest or unethical conduct of a person entrusted with a position of authority that misuses public or entrusted power for private interest and personal gain.

Global Innovation Index: Known as GII, it aims to capture the multi-dimensional facets of innovation. It helps to create an environment in which innovation factors are continually evaluated.

Hofstede's Cultural Dimensions Theory: A framework for cross-cultural communication that describes the effects of a society's culture on the values of its members. Hofstede's model is based on six different dimensions: individualism-collectivism; uncertainty avoidance; power distance, masculinity-femininity, long-term orientation, and indulgence versus self-restraint.

Innovation: Can be defined as a new idea or a process of creativity which is taken to, and accepted by the market or society. It is normally viewed as the application of ingenuity to develop new products, processes and devices that meet new requirements or create new needs.

National Culture: A set of norms, behaviors and beliefs shared by the population or the major group within it. There are several models of national culture, however, the most commonly used is Hofstede's that is based on six dimensions that represent independent preferences for one state of affairs over another that distinguish countries (rather than individuals) from each other.

PLS-SEM: A method of structural equations modelling that allows estimating cause-effect relationships with latent variables. It is more oriented towards maximizing the amount of variance explained of the predictive variable than statistical accuracy of the estimates.

Chapter 12
Project Management Culture

Tomasz Kopczynski
Poznan University of Economics and Business, Poland

ABSTRACT

The chapter outlines the importance and influence of organizational culture on contemporary project management in the context of variable and complex environment. The main objective of the study is to show what shapes the culture of project management and how it influences the effectiveness of managing projects in circumstances of the contemporary environment. Individual chapters disclose the essence and importance of organizational culture; besides, attention is brought to factors that form the culture of project management with a specific emphasis on social factors, which play the key role. Based on the results of research carried out in Polish companies, the last part of the chapter presents the influence of organizational culture and forming it factors on effectiveness of project management. It also displays the most important aspects of project management culture that influence the effectiveness of project management in realities of today's environment.

INTRODUCTION

In today's economic reality enterprises are being continually transformed due to constant changes taking place in their environment. These changes develop characteristics of dynamic processes - transformations that fundamentally change the way of enterprise's operation. This fact brings about a natural need of searching for new ways of functioning, which would allow companies to gain a competitive edge. Project management is a commonly used approach that enables realization of business objectives of enterprises in unstable and demanding environment. Keeping up with the competition, growing expectations of customers, significant and fast advance in technology require changes and new ideas and this task is accomplished with use of projects. The environment of project management is also a subject to constant changes, which are more and more often characterized by turbulence, instability and complexity.

Project managers currently have to deal with more and more serious challenges and complexity of projects. This is caused by both quickly changing business environment and the changing character of projects themselves. Many managers work under considerable pressure to finish complicated and uncertain tasks in the shortest time possible, at the same time taking into consideration criteria of cost, quality and

DOI: 10.4018/978-1-5225-2480-9.ch012

end customer's satisfaction. Thus, it can be assumed that a project is a high risk activity where managers have to deal with many types of uncertainties, such as technical, financial, organizational and personal. As a result, a vital necessity to improve project management effectiveness arises. (Hillson, 2002; Ward & Chapman, 2003).

The occurring processes create need for acceleration of actions. Speed of action, enhanced by fast development of information technology, is perceived as one of the key factors that have impact on company's competitive advantage. In enterprises where acceleration becomes particularly important, learning and training of every member of staff is essential; it is based on generation and absorbance of knowledge by organization and intended to improve its effectiveness and contribute to its further development (Maira, 1997). Such phenomena appear mostly thanks to internal knowledge transfer, which occurs predominantly in interdisciplinary teams. The specifics of projects demand and consequently lead to close cooperation between people "representing" different fields of knowledge, while continuous and improved communication and exchange of information enable teams to attain quick results and synergy effects. Besides, complexity is currently a particularly significant aspect as it is a considerable constraint in the decision-making process. At the moment, the complexity level is so high that standard and routine schemes, actions and procedures often do not work properly. In practice results of project teams work often do not meet clients' expectations - they exceed the set time limits and the intended budget, in spite of management techniques use and processes aimed to improve project management effectiveness. Some researches disclose certain limitations of the effectiveness of this approach in business projects environment (Fortune & White, 2006; Raz et al., 2002). It may be caused by the fact that enterprises sometimes act hastily, unaware of the essence and importance of organizational culture for project management. Complexity and variability of contemporary environment are so wide-ranging that it would be very difficult, if possible at all, to characterize them explicitly. Moreover, new elements keep appearing and further complicate the state of the environment. In such settings of the environment, schemes or universal methods of operation may not provide expected results without a proper consideration of the aspect of organizational culture. A large number of studies concentrate on and pay particular attention to the use of tools, techniques, processes and methods of project management (Ahmed et al., 2007). This study, however, focuses on the dimension of culture within project management environment and attempts to disclose the importance of organizational culture for effective project management.

BACKGROUND

Andersen (2008) defines organizational culture as common basic assumptions regarding human aspect, social interactions and perception of the environment kept to in an enterprise. Marguardt (2002) believes that culture is grounded on values, beliefs, rituals and customs, whereas Shein (1990) thinks that organizational culture consists of two layers: perceptible and imperceptible properties. The perceptible outer layer comprises buildings, clothing, regulations, history and myths. The other embraces values, norms and assumptions of organization members. Ajmal & Koskinen (2008) agree with this view saying that culture exists on different levels of organization and manifests itself in virtually all aspects of organizational life.

Andersen (2008) distinguishes organizational culture of the parent organization (enterprise) and the culture within its projects. Wang (2001) defines the culture of project management as a collection of values and benefits that appear in the environment of project management professionals. Du Plessis &

Hoole (2006) note that the majority of authors consider project management culture as a specific type of culture, characteristic for the profession of project management, i.e. a certain kind of subculture within an enterprise. This complies with Cleland (1999) who states that: "each project has a distinct culture reflecting in part a universal culture found in all projects".

Fard et al. (2009) states that in management literature concerning organizational culture (Deal & Kennedy, 1982; Peters & Waterman, 1982; Shein, 1990) culture is commonly understood as a tool that can be utilized by managers to influence and control behaviors and attitudes of people and the organization as a whole to achieve the set goals. Hillson (1997, 1998), Fard et al. (2009) emphasize the operational significance of organizational culture, which can undergo changes and have significant impact on the effectiveness of project management. Organizations should be prepared for the development of organizational culture of project management, which can encourage the use of methods and processes in project environment.

Organizational culture is perceived as an element that influences the morale of the employees, their motivation and commitment, effectiveness and efficiency, quality of work, innovativeness and creativity as well as their attitude to work (Campbell et al. 1999). Cheung et al. (2011), Lynch (2012) postulate that organizational culture can be perceived in terms of commitment, leadership style and the style of decision-making by management. Jones (2013) assumes that organizational culture is a collection of common values and norms which allow for shaping and controlling behavior and relationships between members of the organization and other entities outside. Organizational culture can be seen as a dominant leadership style affecting many areas of an organization and as an instrument to accomplish set objectives (Jones, 2013).

In the context of contemporary challenges that have their roots in the environment, it can be assumed that appropriate organizational culture, which can be a decisive factor in terms of organization's effectiveness and efficiency of organization's functioning, gains extraordinary meaning. Kozminski's (2008) hypothesizes that organization's success depends on its knowledge resources. At the same time this author draws our attention to the fact that ignorance and inanity can be a barrier that effectively blocks and neutralizes positive effects of knowledge. Such behavior is commonly observed in everyday actions of many decision-makers. Huge amounts of information available, its commonness, and ease of obtaining it often lead to behavior characterized by denial and elimination of thinking, which gives way to unoriginal and uncritical acceptance of whatever the environment offers. Therefore, it can be assumed that organization needs, to an ever greater degree, a particular organizational culture, which would foster attitude and behaviors that would allow quick and flexible reaction to the environment's indefiniteness and unpredictability. Conner (1993) points to the fact that there are two ways of shaping organizational cultures: evolutionary and architectonic. The first one takes place when culture is shaped by random events and the second one when managers and leaders actively participate in this process – and this approach deserves a specific attention.

FACTORS SHAPING THE ORGANIZATIONAL CULTURE

In the context of project management it is vital to consider the complexity and variety of factors influencing project management, in particular, two groups of factors: soft and hard. Terms "hard" and "soft" are commonly used both in practice and literature but often in casual and ambiguous meaning. It has to be emphasized that consideration of a balance between these two areas may have key significance for a project (Shenhar & Dvir 1996). Hard factors concern traditional project constraints mainly such as time, costs, resources and quality. Soft factors are identified by Jafaari (2001) as elements of social character (values, relationships, environment) and Thirty (2002) adds to them with elements related to communication within projects. It needs to be emphasized that both groups of factors do not dismiss each other and should be used in complementary way. However, they require different management, attitude and a set of different skills.

In the soft approach people actively co-create the environment in which they work through shaping organizational culture and they concentrate on its refinement with less defined client expectations. As some of the authors underline (Cooke-Davies et al. 2007), in many situations, project's failure is the outcome of social and behavioral factors rather than of technical or organizational problems in projects. Understanding of social processes, which are present in a group and which, to a large extent, shape organizational culture, thus gains importance. The essence of this problem can be found in studies from the behavioral stream area and in particular in studies devoted to organization's betterment. Improving of an organization is in this sense, treated as actions which tend to the betterment of organization's functioning through managing organization's culture, with special attention given to human teams, while utilizing theories and techniques from behavioral sciences. This approach makes an essential aspect in the context of project management culture research as it deals with interactions between people, their evolution and provides a possibility to understand the complexity of social interactions, which consider people and their behavior as one of the key problems of project management (Winter et al. 2006).

The social factor constitutes the essence and sense of organization's being due to potential of creativity, talent, skills, knowledge and motivation, which exist within it (Czerska, 2004). Other elements of building a competitive advantage can be presently considered to be easier to copy than the social system of a company, based on uniqueness of organizational culture and people who shape it. The change of organizational culture concept follows, which causes changes in management methods (Brilman, 2002). It is clearly emphasized by Hamel & Prahalad (1999), who suggest that intellectual leadership is currently an important constituent of competing. Success of leadership is determined by the intellectual capital of enterprise and its competent application (Hamel & Prahalad, 1999). Division of resources into tangible and intangible seems to be essential (Godziszewski, 2001). In the context of the discussed topic, the group of intangible resources is particularly important, and it can be divided into resources the enterprise possesses ownership rights for and which constitute the enterprise's assets (patents, licenses, databases) and another group of intangible resources, such as skills of employees, teams and the whole organization and foremost, broadly understood organizational culture, which cannot be legally protected.

It can be assumed that in today's circumstances, social aspect in its broadest sense constitutes a necessary condition for effective functioning in economic reality. One of the key elements of project management is team work and this is why high leadership competences of the project's manager are of utmost importance. Project manager coordinates the work of all involved departments and organizations and supervises control of costs, schedule and tasks. In reality of today managing projects is a particularly complex task. To complete a project meeting client's expectations requires successful employing of interdisciplinary skills, which include such components of project management as appropriate management style and effective approach to problem solving (Kosieradzki, 2000). The expectations regarding the project manager to a great extent relate to the management style, which has a significant impact on the shape of project management culture and reinforces the feeling of employees' self-esteem.

Social psychology emphasizes the influence of different leadership styles on the effectiveness of project team's functioning. The differences in ways of managing team members are already known from classical theories of Webber and Levin (Mika, 1981). At the same time, research regarding management styles lead to creation of many theories relevant to the subject. These styles depend to a great extend natural predispositions and personality characteristics of managers (Syrek, 1997; Terelak, 2005).

Project specifics and variability of the environment require a leadership style grounded on social sciences and the concept of group dynamics, which concentrates on all team members rather than on the leader alone. It is essential to involve employees in decision-making processes and to pay even greater attention to issues of motivation and interpersonal relations (Tannenbaum & Schmidt, 2007). Management activities require appropriate mechanisms of tasks and responsibilities assignment that take into consideration person's knowledge, skills, experience and personality. The function of management is directly connected with interactions with team members; therefore, it is better performed by extravert leaders open to other people and hence to different opinions and points of view. Taking all this into account, we can conclude that a good project manager should have a well-balanced personality, remarkable flexibility and ability to adapt to changing conditions of the environment.

In the context of these contemplations, we can observe a tendency for changes in leadership style - from traditional management based on orders and control to a new, more flexible approach - which on one hand, requires ability to foresee some events and on the other hand, openness and courage of a leader to delegate powers to others and motivate employees. Project manager performs many functions, binding the whole project, ensuring its completion and arranging for its appropriate dynamics. Functions and tasks of a project manager embrace both planning and organizing, determining the system of communication within the project, constant monitoring of the project, taking responsibility for its completion and for decision-making and, at the same time, dealing with different aspects of leading and encouraging the team, which in turn exerts significant impact on the project team culture. These tasks also comprise motivating and inspiring project team members, solving personal problems and conflicts in the team and optimum use of the team members' potential [Litke, 1995; Lientz & Rea, 1995; Kezsbom & Edward, 2001).

A great diversity of activities performed by a project manager requires special competences, which can be grouped into certain categories: knowledge, skills, experience and personal qualities (Litke, 1995; Kellner, 2000). Hensel and Lomnitz (1987) present a slightly different point of view - they distinguish technical expertise, methodological knowledge and social skills. Creation of an effective project management culture requires from manager a wide range of high level leadership skills. As McCall (1998) points out, many qualities indispensable to reach set targets are related to teamwork, coordination and cooperation with others. Thus, an appropriate set of competences of project manager, whose main task is to achieve the synergy effect with the team, is the necessary condition to be fulfilled to create an effective project team.

As it has already been mentioned, project manager and his leadership competences is an important constituent shaping project management culture. The project team is another, equally important factor. Due to its unique characteristics, teamwork is considered more effective than other forms of organization of work. It is distinctive peculiarities of teamwork, considered its advantages, which make the difference. It should be emphasized that term "team" is often interpreted ambiguously and associated with a group of people assigned for a job (DeMarco & Lister, 2002). It is necessary to clarify the differences of the terms "group" and "team". Relevant literature shows that some authors use these terms interchangeably, treating them as synonyms (Stoner et al. 1992; Stoner et al.1997). They see *group* rather as an informal community, while *team* is a formally approved group. A different approach is suggested by authors who focus their research solely on issues of groups and teams. They point at many differences separating both terms and hold a view that a team is a developing form of a group, characterized by maturity of its organizational culture (Adair, 1987; Antoszkiewicz, 1997; Katzenbach & Smith, 2001). Characteristics of team may include (Klotzl, 1994; Mears & Voehl, 2000; Robbins, 2004):

1. The results of a teamwork are better than the results gained by the same people working in an unintegrated group,
2. A team is focused on objectives to be achieved. These objectives are clearly defined and understandable for every member,
3. Success of the team as a whole entity is preferred. The team members have a feeling of belonging to community. Help and mutual support are favored,
4. Team members possess inner motivation to work and are committed to perform tasks,
5. Roles within team are clear and known to each team member.

Characteristic features of team understood this way are close to the ones (characteristics) of a project team with highly developed organizational culture. Team members concentrate, first of all, on possibilities to improve work methods and processes. They meet systematically to discuss quality problems, to find their causes, suggest solutions and undertake actions to improve the situation (Rothman, 1993). Team members are slanted towards close cooperation and intensified activity. The team delivers results of its work taking into consideration main constraints of the project. In the social dimension, it shows a high level of commitment and is characterized by effective communication and a highly positive attitude towards changes. Building such a team requires team's appropriate structuring, creating good relations and understanding among the team members. The cycle of forming and functioning of a project team is, however, a dynamic process, which undergoes transformations and hardly ever reaches stabilization (table 1.3.5)

The question of whether teams going through different stages of development become more effective is a true dilemma. Some researches indicate that efficiency rises in further, more advanced stages (norming, performing) characterized by better developed organizational culture; however, this correlation is neither direct nor simple. The supposition could be true, but as some authors point out, factors defining

Table 1. The Life Cycle of Project Team (Robbins & DeCenzo, 2002)

Stage	Features
Project Team Forming	The stage of uncertainty and setting objectives, norms and organizational roles of the project. Team members learn the project's specific requirements, its scope and the other members. This stage ends when participants begin to consider themselves team members.
Team Storming	Conflicts within the group. Team members acknowledge the group's existence but test each other and challenge the leader. Emotional conflicts and rivalry for leading roles happen. At this stage, leadership qualities of the project team manager are tested extensively.
Team Norming	This is the stage of stabilization and norming of cooperation between the team members. The feeling of common responsibility for performed tasks develops. Communication, cooperation and coaching become important elements.
Team Performing (Effective Cooperation)	Team members are eager to cooperate and focus on achievement of set objectives. This stage is characterized by permeable communication Channels, mutual trust and understanding. The team is able to self-motivate itself.
Team Expiring (End of Operation)	High effectiveness and efficiency of performing tasks stops being priority for team members. They are concentrated on activities related to the end of team's operation.

team's efficiency is a complex issue (Bragg, 1999; Jewell & Reitz, 1981). Transition from one stage to another does not have to be clear and have distinct boundaries. In some cases, more than one stage of development can take place concurrently. Thus, we should not expect all project teams to go through the same cycle of development. Therefore, it would be safe to assume that team's lifecycle determines a certain type of framework, which helps understand phenomena and processes going on throughout the project team shaping.

Using knowledge of processes in groups, it is possible to distinguish main factors forming project management culture based on effectively working project teams. It would be appropriate to emphasize that individually these factors cannot exert significant impact on the effectiveness of team operation without an appropriate combination of particular elements. It would be extremely difficult to present all factors and determine their influence precisely. Nevertheless, basing on already existing research results, it is possible to focus on the most important factors described in literature, which include the following (Borrelli et al. 1995; Robbins, 2004; Larson & LaFasto, 1989):

1. Leadership. Leader's ability to strengthen and engage people, to define clearly the principles and rules of communication, to take into consideration individual competences and personality types of team members and to adjust the style of management to circumstances.
2. Size of the Team. It is assumed that teams should not include more than 12 persons, while decision-making teams should not be larger 5 members. The size of the team should facilitate communication, cooperation and feeling of responsibility.
3. Skills of team's members can be divided into technical, conceptual, problem-solving and interpersonal.
4. Effective communication. The system of communication and flow of information that extends over all team members, the leader and other key figures in the project.
5. Team's balance. Balancing individualism and team spirit on the basis of mutual trust and respect. Trust stems from the conviction regarding high competences of individual members of the team.
6. Equal commitment. Members of the team are fully devoted to achievement of team's objectives and can be characterized by their willingness to devote much energy and time to achieve it.
7. Organizational roles are assigned adequately with consideration of personalities /personal competences as well as preferences of team members.
8. Responsibility. Team members are responsible both individually and collectively, as a group, for objectives and way of operation of the team and are aware of their individual and collective responsibilities.
9. A fair system of evaluation and rewarding which enables assessment of effectiveness and is based on assessment of individual work contribution of particular members as well as team's performance.

Social aspect is an important condition determining project management culture. Attention is focused on person and his or her behavior in this perspective. Such important role of person in a project is the result of increasing unpredictability and dynamics of projects and their environment, where substantive professional and behavioral competences and attitudes may have key significance. Considering staff members in decision-making processes, attention to different aspects of motivation and human interrelations becomes particularly important. This aspect is dominated by logic oriented to the subject rather than the object of the project. Above all, social values, personal attitudes and interests of project team members are of primary significance; and consequently these create and shape project culture.

THE IMPACT OF ORGANIZATIONAL CULTURE ON THE EFFICIENCY OF PROJECT MANAGEMENT

Efficiency is one of the key concepts in management and due to its interdisciplinary character its definitions vary. Stoner et al. (1997) defines efficiency as a degree of efficacy and effectiveness, i.e. to what extent set objectives are achieve. It is necessary to emphasize the difference in meanings of two terms: effectiveness and efficiency. The former denotes efficacy, usefulness, aim achievement, while the latter means proficiency, productivity, economy defined by expenses to results ratio. It has to be mentioned that concurrent capturing of both approaches allows to state that organization's efficiency increases together with the increase of the degree of aims achievement and decreasing of expenditures incurred. As Shenhar, Shrum, Alon (1994) point out, effectiveness is a notion that concerns the result, considering variables and factors influencing the result. Trocki et al. (2009) offer a little broader definition, postulating that effectiveness of project management is related to answer to the question of whether or not the project realized its aims and achieved the expected results staying within sensible costs, properly managing its resources and its achievement when compared to other projects.

In this context, a broad view of factors determining project management becomes important. The appropriate arrangement as well as relations and dependences between them improve the optimum use of project's key values. It should be noted that it is difficult to define all factors determining efficiency of project management as it depends on many variables, such as environment and project's specifics. It is, however, possible to define the key areas, which can be directly and significantly influenced by decision-makers and the management, and which determine efficiency of project management. Some researches carried out in Poland support supposition of great importance and influence of shaping organizational culture factors on efficiency of project management. The research conducted in Poland by Spalek (2004) establishes the main factors that have impact on efficiency of project management as follows: establishment of a strong position of the project manager (93%), good leadership skills of the project manager (85%), high authority of the project manager (85%), creation of well working and cooperating project team (86%) and support of the project by the enterprise's board (84%). The obtained results of the research clearly show the importance of human aspect and particularly the importance of competences of the project manager.

To evaluate the efficiency of the projects under examination, it was essential to define factors that condition it. This part of the research was conducted in two stages. First, the respondents were asked to list factors that may have a negative impact on project and cause lack of its efficiency in their enterprises. This was an open question and as such it has both benefits and some limitations. On one hand, the participants had an opportunity to speak freely, there were no "imposed" potential answers. On the other hand, however, the lack of the respondents' awareness of existance of certain factors and mentioning only those they notice and understand but not always the most important. To complete and verify answers received through the open question, the respondents were offered a closed list of 22 factors, which according to available in literature results of scientific research can influence effectiveness of project manangement. The participants of the survey evaluated them using a scale from 1 to 5, where 1 means a very slight influence of factor, 2 – insignificant, 3 – medium, 4 – significant and 5 – enormous.

The most frequently specified factors determining lack of efficiency of projects in the open ended question were related to social aspects shaping organizational culture (Figure 1). Respondents most often referred to project team issues, such as improper organization of the team (30.1%), inappropriate selection of team members in terms of their competences (22.0%), low competences of the project leader

Figure 1. Factors influencing the lack of efficiency of projects in the surveyed enterprises (Kopczynski, 2014)

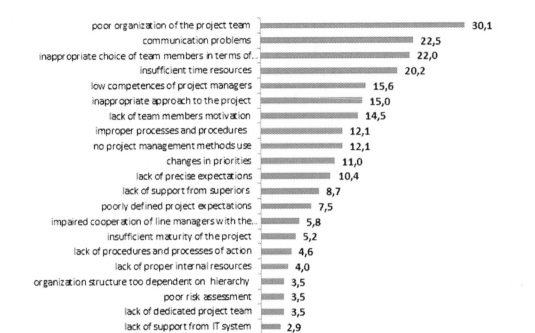

(15.6%) and lack of motivation of the team members (14.5%). More than 20% of responses were linked to communication problems, which is also related to the project team functioning.

As it has been mentioned earlier, the next question concerning the determinants of the project efficiency was a closed question, which to a certain degree, enabled verification of the preceding one (Figure 2).

The results gathered confirm the utmost importance of soft factors related to organizational culture and their influence on the efficiency of project management. Average score of over 4.0 meaning significant or enormous influence on efficiency, were gained by the factors which were often mentioned by the respondents in the open ended question. Those were: the level of project communication (4.28), suitability of knowlegde and technical skills of the project team members (4.14) and the quality of leadership in the project (4.13).

The culture of project management is directly linked to the functioning of the project team. The answers of project managers concerning real and expected presence of organizational culture's factors in a project team, which influence project's efficiency, appea to be quite interesting. The expectations of project managers regarding some attitudes and behaviors of the project team are greater than the extent of their presence in reality. It should be noted that the expectations of respondents concerning being taken into account are at a high or very high level. Special attention needs to be given to those factors which deal with team's creativity and with work based on trust and uninhibited communication. their

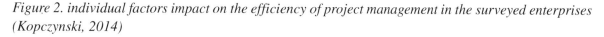

Figure 2. individual factors impact on the efficiency of project management in the surveyed enterprises (Kopczynski, 2014)

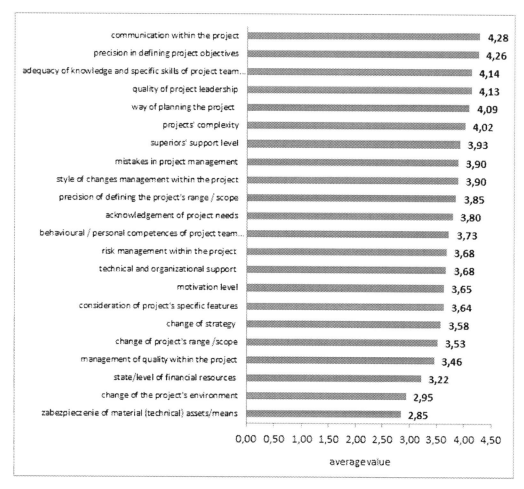

use in researched enterprises was found at an above average level, which can be considered a favourable result, but the expectations are at a higher than significant level.

Conducted empirical research indicates that among factors affecting efficiency of project management, respondents most often pointed to: unfortunate choice of project team members, communication problems in the project team, as well as low competences of project managers and lack of motivation of the members of project team (Figure 3). In Polish enterprises aspects, which have a specific importance in unpredictable, changeable project environment, such as adaptability to changes, team's creativity, continuous learning and developing and teamwork based on trust and unimpaired communication are taken into consideration at a moderate degree. It should be mentioned that the expectations of managerial staff regarding the desirable use of the abovementioned features are high. It can be assumed that on the part of managerial staff there exist a conscious need for a better consideration of these factors, which could be an effect of awareness of new trends in project environment, which is characterized by turbulence, unpredictability and complexity.

Figure 3. Factors of organizational culture in the project team desired by the project managers vs occurring in enterprises (Kopczynski, 2014)

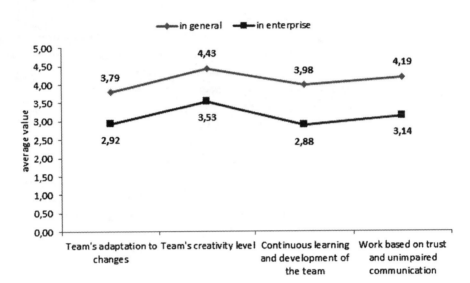

FUTURE RESEARCH DIRECTIONS

The culture of project management becomes an even more important factor influencing the efficiency of project management in this dynamic, turbulent and complex reality. Consideration of this topic in the context of new trends in project management such as agile project management and situational approach may be a good area to study. Furthermore, significance of project management culture within particular branches of industry / business may also be an interesting direction for research. Taking into account the differences between generations widely discussed in literature, examining differences and peculiarities of project management cultures in terms of differences between baby boomers and generations X and Y may be a promising direction for research.

CONCLUSION

Based on the results of conducted study and empirical research we can distinguish the most important aspects of project management culture, which significantly influence efficiency of project management. These include: selection of members and development of team, competences of project manager and team members and processes going on within team.

Individual areas are strongly linked to each other and interdependent. The desirable team processes such as good motivation and commitment of project team members, continuous development and improvement of the team and internal project communication may occur only if team members and the manager possess an appropriate set of competences. Considering the numerous criteria of team members' selection, which exceeds purely substantive professional selection, gains a specific importance. At the same time, behavioral and social criteria also become essential. It is worth paying attention to the increasing role of the project manager who, in new or unusual circumstances, besides managerial competences, should

Table 2. The most important areas of project management culture, which affect the efficiency of project management (Kopczynski, 2014)

Area	Features
Creation and forming of the team	Recruitment and selection of team members according to different criteria: - professional /substantive skills - behavioural - personal
	Forming of project team considering the stages of team evolution, norming and stabilizing it as soon as possible.
Competences	High competences of the project manager and members of the project team: leadership, behavioural and professional qualities.
Processes within the team	Motivation, engagement, inspiration of project team members Team's internal communication (communicating vision, objectives, team members' feedback) Development, learning (coaching, mentoring, co-working) Adaptation to changes Creative processes of action

also have good leadership qualities. It has to be emphasized that the selection of the team members may be the critical element determining efficiency of project management. High and diverse competences of project manager and team members are a vital condition for initiation and appropriate advance of team processes. Good motivation and commitment of project team members derive from their awareness and understanding of their place and the importance of the project. In this case, motivation is mostly natural and is not coerced by any specific external incentives or factors. The same can be said about all other processes going on in a team: communication, development, adapting to changes and creativity. When soft competences are highly developed and there is an appropriate attitude in a team towards work, such processes are initiated naturally and are sustained by the team's culture. They take place because team members are aware of and understand the links between their occurrence and project results; these are not effects of imposed internal procedures. High competences enable desirable processes to begin and the role of project manager is one of a natural leader.

REFERENCES

Adair, J. (2001). *Anatomia biznesu. Budowanie zespołu*. Warszawa: Studio Emka.

Ahmed, A., Kavis, B., & Amornsawadwatana, S. (2007). A review of techniques for risk management in projects, *Benchmarking. International Journal (Toronto, Ont.)*, *14*(1), 22–36.

Ajmal, M. M., & Koskinen, K. U. (2008). Knowledge transfer in project-based organizations: An organizational culture perspective. *Project Management Journal*, *39*(1), 7–15. doi:10.1002/pmj.20031

Andersen, E. S. (2008). *Rethinking Project Management: An Organizational Perspective*. Harlow: Prentice-Hall.

Antoszkiewicz, J. D. (1997). *Firma wobec zagrożeń. Identyfikacja problemów*. Warszawa: Poltext.

Borrelli, G., Cable, J., & Higgs, M. (1995). What makes teams work better? *Team Performance Management*, *1*(3), 23–34. doi:10.1108/13527599510084849

Bragg, T. (1999). *Turn Around an Ineffective Team*. IIE Solutions.

Brilman, J. (2002). *Nowoczesne koncepcje i metody zarzadzania*. Warszawa: PWE.

Campbell, D., Stonehouse, G., & Houston, B. (1999). *Business Strategy an Introduction*. Oxford, UK: Butterworth-Heinemann.

Cheung, S. O., Wong, P. S. P., & Wu, A. W. Y. (2011). Towards an organizational culture framework in construction. *International Journal of Project Management, 29*(1), 33–44. doi:10.1016/j.ijproman.2010.01.014

Cleland, D. (1999). *Project Management: Strategic Design and Implementation*. New York: McGraw-Hill.

Conner, D. R. (1993). *Managing at the Speed of Change*. New York: Villards Books.

Cooke-Davis, T., Cicmil, S. J. K., Crawford, L. H., & Richardson, K. (2007). We're not in Kansas anymore, Toto: Mapping the strange landscape of complexity theory. *Project Management Journal, 38*(2), 50–61.

Czerska, M. (2004). Kadrowe czynniki sukcesu firmy – wyniki badań. In A. Stabryla (Ed.), *Strategie wzrostu produktywności firmy* (p. 124). Krakow: Wydawnictwo Akademii Ekonomicznej w Krakowie.

Deal, T., & Kennedy, A. (1982). *Corporate Culture: The Rites and Rituals of Corporate Life*. London: Penguin Business.

DeMarco, T., & Lister, T. (2002). *Czynnik ludzki. Skuteczne przedsiewziecia i wydajne zespoly*. Warszawa: Wydawnictwo Naukowo – Techniczne.

Du Plessis, Y., & Hoole, C. (2006). An operational project management culture framework. *SA Journal of Human Resource Management, 4*(1), 36–43. doi:10.4102/sajhrm.v4i1.79

Fard, H. D., Rostamy, A. A. A., & Taghiloo, H. (2009). How types of organizational cultures contribute in shaping learning organizations. *Singapore Management Review, 31*(1), 49–61.

Fortune, J., & White, D. (2006). Framing of project critical success factors by a systems model. *International Journal of Project Management, 24*(1), 53–65. doi:10.1016/j.ijproman.2005.07.004

Godziszewski, B. (1999). *Zasobowe uwarunkowania strategii przedsiębiorstwa*. Torun: Wydawnictwo Uniwersytetu Mikolaja Kopernika.

Hamel, G., & Prahalad, C. K. (1999). *Przewaga konkurencyjna jutra. Strategie przejmowania kontroli nad branza i tworzenia rynkow przyszłosci*. Warszawa: Businessman Book.

Hansel, J., & Lomnitz, G. (1987). *Projektleiter-Praxis*. Berlin: Springer Verlag. doi:10.1007/978-3-642-96885-3

Hillson, D. (1997). Towards a risk maturity model. *International Journal of Project & Business Risk Management, 1*(1), 35–45.

Hillson, D. (1998). Project risk management: Future developments. *International Journal of Project & Business Risk Management, 2*(2), 181–195.

Hillson, D. (2002). Extending the risk process to manage opportunities. *International Journal of Project & Business Risk Management, 20*(3), 235–240. doi:10.1016/S0263-7863(01)00074-6

Jaafari, A. (2001). Management of risks, uncertainties and opportunities on projects: Time for a fundamental shift. *International Journal of Project Management, 19*(2), 89–101. doi:10.1016/S0263-7863(99)00047-2

Jewell, L. N., & Reitz, H. J. (1981). *Group Effectiveness in Organizations. Glenview, 1,* 11.

Jones, G. R. (2013). *Organisational Theory, Design, and Change* (7th ed.). London: Pearson.

Katzenbach, J. R., & Smith, D. K. (2001). *Siła zespołów. Wpływ pracy zespolowej na efektywnosc organizacji.* Krakow: Oficyna Wydawnicza, Dom Wydawniczy ABC.

Kellenr, H. (2000). *Projekte konfliktfrei fuhren.* Munchen: Verlag.

Kezsbom, D., & Edward, K. (2001). *The New Dynamic Project Management.* New York: John Wiley & Sons, Inc.

Klotzl, G. (1994). Von der Arbeitsgruppe. *IO Management Zeitschrift, 12*(44).

Kopczynski, T. (2014). *Myslenie systemowe i sieciowe w zarzadzaniu projektami.* Poznan: Wydawnictwo Uniwersytetu Ekonomicznego w Poznaniu.

Kosieradzki, W. (2000, October). *Korzysci z metodyki project management w administracji publicznej,* Paper presented at the Project Management Conference, Profesjonalizm, Stowarzyszenie Project Management Polska, Jelenia Góra.

Kozminski, A. K. (2008). *Koniec swiata menedzerow?* Warszawa: Wydawnictwa Akademickie i Profesjonalne.

Larson, C. E., & La Fasto, M. J. (1989). *Teamwork: What Must Go Right / What Can Go Wrong.* Sage Publications Inc.

Lientz, B., & Rea, K. (1995). *Project Management for the 21th Century.* San Diego, CA: Academic Press.

Litke, H. (1995). *Projektmanagement.* Munchen-Vien: Carl Hanser Verlag.

Lynch, R. (2012). *Strategic Management* (6th ed.). Pearson Prentice Hall.

Maira, A., & Scott-Morgan, P. (1997). *The Accelerating Organization. Embracing the Human Face of Change.* New York: McGraw Hill.

Marguardt, M. J. (2002). *Building the Learning Organization.* New York: McGraw-Hill.

McCall, M. (1987). *High Flyers: Developing the Next Generation of Leaders.* Boston: Harvard Business School Press.

Mears, P., & Voehl, F. (2000). *Tworzenie zespołu. Nauka w sztucznie stworzonym środowisku.* Kludzienko: Centrum Kreowania Liderow Grupa Holdingowa S.A.

Mika, S. (1981). *Psychologia spoleczna.* Warszawa: PWN.

Peters, T. J., & Waterman, R. H. (1982). *In Search of Excellence: Lessons from America's Best-Run Companies*. New York: Harper & Row.

Raz, T., Shenhar, A. J., & Dvir, D. (2002). Risk management, project success, and technological uncertainty. *R & D Management, 32*(2), 101–109. doi:10.1111/1467-9310.00243

Robbins, S. P. (2004). *Zachowania w organizacji*. Warszawa: Polskie Wydawnictwo Ekonomiczne.

Robbins, S. P., & DeCenzo, D. A. (2002). *Podstawy Zarządzania*. Warszawa: PWE.

Rothman, H. (1993). The Power of Powerment. *Nation's Business*.

Shein, E. H. (1990). Organizational culture. *The American Psychologist, 45*(2), 109–119. doi:10.1037/0003-066X.45.2.109

Shenhar, A. J., & Dvir, D. (1996). Toward a typological theory of project management. *Research Policy, 25*.

Shenhav, Y., Shrum, W., & Alon, S. (1994). Goodness concepts in the study of organizations: A longitudinal survey of four leading journals. *Organization Studies, 15*(5), 753–776. doi:10.1177/017084069401500506

Spałek, S. (2004). *Omowienie podstawowych czynnikow wpływających na niepowodzenie przedsiewzięcia*. Paper presented at the Project Management Conference, Profesjonalizm, Stowarzyszenie Project Management Polska, Jelenia Góra.

Stoner, J. A. F., Freeman, R. E., & Gilbert, D. R. (1997). *Kierowanie*. Warszawa: PWE.

Stoner, J. A. F., & Wankel, Ch. (1992). *Kierowanie*. Warszawa: PWE.

Syrek, M. (1997). *Menedzer we wspolczesnym przedsiebiorstwie – sylwetka, kwalifikacje, style zarzadzania*. Katowice: Wydawnictwo WSZM i Jo.

Tannenbaum, R., & Schmidt, W. H. (2007). Jak wybrac styl przywodztwa. *Harvard Business Review Polska, 4*, 131.

Terelak, J. F. (2005). *Psychologia organizacji i zarządzania*. Warszawa: Difin.

Thiry, M. (2002). Combining value and project management into an effective programme management model. *International Journal of Project Management, 20*(3), 221–227. doi:10.1016/S0263-7863(01)00072-2

Trocki, M., Grucza, M., & Ogonek, M. (2009). *Zarzadzanie projektami*. Warszawa: PWE.

Wang, X. (2001). Dimensions and current status of project management culture. *Project Management Journal, 32*(4), 4–17.

Ward, S., & Chapman, C. (2003). Transforming project risk management into project uncertainty management. *International Journal of Project Management, 21*(2), 234–236. doi:10.1016/S0263-7863(01)00080-1

Winter, M., Smith, C., Cooke-Davies, T., & Cicmil, S. (2006). *Rethinking project management—Final report. EPSRC Network 2004–2006*. Retrieved February 10, 2008, from http://www.mace.manchester.ac.uk/project/research/management/rethinkpm/final.htm

KEY TERMS AND DEFINITIONS

Efficiency of Project Management: The achievement of project goals and client satisfaction within the scheduled time, quality and budget.

Hard Factors in Project Management: Project management constraints: time, cost, resources and quality.

Leadership Style: System of methods, techniques and other tools to influence on subordinates.

Organizational Culture: Informal norms and principles formed and accepted by workers in the enterprise.

Project Management Culture: Informal norms and principles accepted in the project team.

Project Team: Group of people directly involved in the implementation of project goals.

Soft Factors in Project Management: Social factors related to behavior, personality traits and attitudes of project team members.

Chapter 13

Role of Masculinity and Uncertainty Avoidance Orientation in the Relationship Between Team Learning Behavior and Self–Efficacy

Ghulam Mustafa
Norwegian University of Science and Technology (NTNU), Norway

Richard Glavee-Geo
Norwegian University of Science and Technology (NTNU), Norway

ABSTRACT

This chapter examines the relationship between team learning behavior and employee work related self- efficacy beliefs and further explores the moderating role of individual difference variables, such as masculinity–femininity and uncertainty avoidance values. The study tested three hypotheses using a sample of employees from a large public organization in Pakistan. The results indicated a significant positive relationship between team learning behavior and employee perceptions of their self-efficacy. Regarding the moderating role of individual differences, the data showed that the link between team learning and self-efficacy was stronger for individuals scoring high (versus low) on masculinity orientation. However, the results revealed no empirical evidence to confirm the hypothesis that employees scoring low on uncertainty avoidance will perceive a stronger relationship between team learning and self-efficacy.

INTRODUCTION

Teams have become a salient feature of today's organizations (Guzzo & Dickson, 1996; Turner, 2014), and a considerable volume of research has accumulated that examines how team work affects group outcomes and how individuals within teams influence group processes and outcomes (Dierdorff & Ellington, 2012; Van den Bossche, Gijselaers, Segers, & Kirschner, 2006). However, a scarce number of

DOI: 10.4018/978-1-5225-2480-9.ch013

studies have examined the impact of groups on their members. Developing a deeper understanding of group effects on individual members is important for several reasons. Despite the growing importance of team-based structures in organizational life (Cohen & Bailey, 1997; Kozlowski & Bell, 2013), a great deal of work in organizations continues to be performed by individuals. For instance, group members may work individually and then bring their efforts together to produce a collective product. Individuals may participate in both collaborative groups and as independent contributors, and they may be assigned to perform work in multiple groups in an organization, either simultaneously or sequentially (Olivera & Straus, 2004). Moreover, team membership is fluid in the sense that members of any given team are often assigned to a new team and thus they are unlikely to stay with a team throughout their career (e.g., Tannenbaum, Mathieu, Salas, & Cohen, 2012). Given the prevalence of both group and individual efforts in organizations, it is important to examine the extent to which members benefit from group activities. A better understanding of how the group level factors and processes influence individual level outcomes may not only benefit the team in which the individual is embedded, but also potential individual and team-based work in the future.

Although the focus of the extant research is on understanding the influence of group level effects and outcomes, there are a few exceptions that have reported positive transfer effects (Brodbeck & Greitemeyer, 2000; Jiang, Jackson, & Colakoglu, 2016; Olivera & Straus, 2004) of group experience on subsequent individual performance. For example, Littlepage, Robison, and Reddington (1997) suggest that group experience improves individual members' task-related skills, and Jiang et al. (2016) recently reported that teams involved in non-routine and interdependent tasks contribute to personal learning of their members. The impact of group experience on individual outcomes has mainly been studied in learning environments (Aguinis & Kraiger, 2009). It has been argued that learning that occurs within work teams goes beyond the teams themselves to include outcomes for individual team members as well (Kozlowski & Bell, 2008). Olivera and Straus (2004) examined the transfer of learning from groups to individuals and found that a group learning climate positively influences personal learning of team members. One of the most widely studied individual-level learning outcomes is self-efficacy (Kraiger, Ford, & Salas, 1993), however, self-efficacy as a core learning outcome has mainly been considered during formal training and development programs (e.g., Colquitt, LePine, & Noe, 2000; Kozlowski et al., 2001). Unfortunately, despite progress in the literature on the effects of workplace learning and training on individuals, we still know relatively little about how teamwork as an informal learning environment contributes to employee self-efficacy. Further, we are aware of only a few studies (e.g., Earley, 1994; Ellington & Dierdorff, 2014) that have considered individual difference variables such as cultural value orientation in the relationship between work place learning and self-efficacy, but again the focus has been on examining relationships in a formal training environment.

The current study takes the existing research a step forward, first, by examining how team learning acts as a social environment in the development of employee self-efficacy, and second, by examining the interactive effects of member's individual cultural values (masculinity–femininity and uncertainty avoidance) and team learning behaviors on individual self-efficacy. Given the earlier assertions that cultural value orientations can influence the frame of reference individuals use when evaluating their work environments (Chao, 2000; Williamson, Burnett, & Bartol, 2009), it is likely that the effect of team learning behaviors on self-efficacy may vary across individual employees based on the strength of their adherence to masculinity–femininity (MAS-FEM) and uncertainty avoidance (UA) values. Drawing on social cognitive theory (Bandura, 1986), we construe team learning activities as a social context that provides opportunities for forming self-efficacy beliefs. And taking an interactionist perspective (Meyer, Irving,

& Allen, 1998), we predict that group learning behaviors create conditions that promote self-efficacy of individual team members, but a person's MAS-FEM and UA values will partly determine his/her use of information provided during such informal training in the development of self-efficacy beliefs. Figure 1 provides a graphic overview of the constructs/factors and their relationships comprising our model.

THEORETICAL BACKGROUND AND HYPOTHESES

Team Learning Behavior

Team learning behaviors are defined as activities by which members of teams seek to acquire, share, refine, or combine task-relevant knowledge through interaction with one another (Argote, Gruenfeld, & Naquin, 1999). It has been argued that such activities involve seeking help and feedback, asking questions, challenging individual or collective assumptions, looking for different perspectives, assessing alternatives, and reflecting on past actions (Edmondson, 2002; Gibson & Vermeulen, 2003). Endomen (1999) argues that team learning is a process that involves behaviors through which greater understanding or improved performance in teams can be achieved.

Self-Efficacy

Self-efficacy refers to an individual's belief in his or her capabilities to successfully accomplish a specific task or set of tasks (Bandura, 1997). Bandura described four broad sources of information involved in the development of self-efficacy: enactive mastery, vicarious experience, verbal persuasion and psychological arousal, with enactive mastery being the most important. It has been argued that the experience of performing a task successfully, witnessing people similar to oneself successfully completing a task, getting verbal encouragement from others about one's potential to master an activity, and one's psychological responses such as moods and emotional states can all impact how a person feels about his/her personal abilities in a particular situation (Bandura, 1997).

Figure 1. Conceptual model

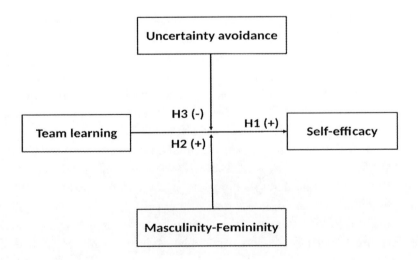

Relationship of Team Learning Behaviors and Self-Efficacy

According to Social Cognitive Theory (Bandura, 1986) environmental factors affect a person's cognitive processes before they can affect a person's behavior. The theory posits two critical cognitive factors: performance expectations and self-efficacy. Environmental factors refer to the social and physical environments. Social environments include interactions in a learning group (Piccoli, Ahmad, & Ives, 2001), and many past studies (e.g., Van Der Vegt & Bunderson, 2005) view team learning behaviors as one aspect of a group's interaction process. Earlier evidence suggests that collaborative learning (Francescato et al., 2006) and social interaction (Johnston, Killion, & Oomen, 2005) act as important antecedents of one's cognitive beliefs.

We predict that team learning behaviors create a social environment that fosters members' self-efficacy beliefs. Our prediction is consistent with research on effects of group interaction and cooperative learning (O'Donnell & Kelly, 1994). Research on cooperative learning suggests the effects of group interaction on individuals through cognitive processes and social factors (O'Donnell & Kelly, 1994). Drawing on cooperative learning perspective, Olivera and Straus (2004) argue that individual knowledge acquisition within group learning environments are influenced by both cognitive and social processes. According to this approach, social interaction promotes the development of individuals' cognitive structures through modeling or when individuals reconcile the differences in their ideas with others (O'Donnell & King, 1999). It has been argued that interaction with others is a vehicle through which a person engages in reflection (Hall, 1996) and one's teammates act as a major source of information and knowledge about task processes, team norms, and roles and relationships in the organization (Jian et al., 2016). Thus, group members represent a point of reference for each other to engage in vicarious learning —an important determinant of self-efficacy.

During group learning activities, group members ask questions and explain their reasoning for solutions as verbal elaboration is said to play an important role in the development and modification of individuals' cognitive structures (O'Donnell & Dansereau, 1992; Teasley, 1997). Research suggests that help seeking and help giving through verbal elaboration contribute to the learning of both the help seeker and giver (Webb, 1992). Group discussions and sharing of information during group interaction facilitate the development of team members' communication and listening skills (Jian et al., 2016). Earlier research posits that environments that encourage self-development by acquiring new skills builds self-esteem and promotes efficacy in approaching work-related problems (Gouillart & Kelly, 1995). Employees who have developed communication and problem-solving skills may feel more competent, and the feeling of competence strengthens an individual's belief that he/she is capable of successfully performing a task (Bandura, 1986).

Team learning may also influence self-efficacy by creating a supportive environment and fostering positive attitudes toward the task. Individuals in a team work interdependently (Manz & Sims, 1993), and such interdependence may lead to frequent interaction and constant exchange of materials and information among team members to complete their tasks (Kirkman & Shapiro, 1997). For individuals who are assigned to a team task, the welfare of the new group tends to take precedence over the welfare of the individual as the team attempts to build a sense of interdependence (Hackman, 1987). Thus, team learning behaviors as one aspect of team interaction is expected to foster participation, interdependence, and diffusion of information throughout the team giving a feeling of cooperative endeavor and psychological empowerment to the team members. Earlier literature suggests that environments that foster psychosocial support engender trust, support and encouragement (Lankau & Scandura, 2002), and such an environment may be conducive for promoting verbal encouragement and for a positive psychological arousal. Team members in a learning group may provide feedback and backup behavior that can lead to individuals becoming more cognizant of their performance (Salas, Sims, & Burke, 2005). Backup behaviors involve providing feedback and coaching to improve performance and to help teammates in performing a task (Marks, Mathieu, & Zaccaro, 2000). Moreover, team work is characterized by cooperation and coordination that leads to increased sharing of information and feedback (Seers, Petty, & Cashman, 1995). Thus, members in a team context, especially in a learning climate, are likely to receive greater amounts of performance feedback, which may in turn foster self-directed reflection on one's own capabilities and performance. According to Bandura (1997) task feedback acts as a source of enactive mastery experiences that serve as indicators of one's capabilities to accomplish a task. Further, a positive learning climate encourages and stimulates the exchange of ideas, information, and knowledge in the organization (Prieto & Revilla, 2006), and increased sharing of knowledge among team members is likely to result in greater chances for vicarious learning (Bandura, 1977).

The above discussion suggests that a team learning environment may contribute to individual members' task related self-efficacy beliefs through information in the form of feedback on performance adequacy, opportunities to emulate each other, persuasive means to build confidence in one's ability to perform the task, and by fostering positive attitudes toward the task. Accordingly, the following hypothesis is proposed:

H1: Learning behavior in teams will be positively associated with employee self-efficacy.

Moderation by Individual Cultural Values

So far, we have argued that team learning behaviors can directly influence self-efficacy, but as we explain next, it is possible that the employee individual level values may bolster or weaken the influence of team learning behaviors on self-efficacy. Past research indicates that individual-level cultural values play an important role in shaping follower reactions to aspects of their work (Earley, 1994; Farh, Hacket, & Liang, 2007; Mustafa & Lines, 2014; Williamson, Burnett, & Bartol, 2009). The results of Earley's (1994) study show that an employee's cultural orientation influences his or her use of training information to form self-efficacy beliefs. This suggests that employee value orientations interact with the attributes of their work environment to shape certain job related outcomes (Meyer et al., 1998). Based on this premise, we suggest that cultural orientation will influence the frame of reference individuals use when evaluating their team environments, thereby shaping self-efficacy.

Two employee characteristics that can influence the relationship between team learning and self-efficacy are MAS– FEM and UA orientation. The MAS– FEM values refer to the extent to which people associate priorities with assertiveness, achievement, and success in contrast with a concern for quality of life and warm and nurturing relationships (Hofstede, 1980). UA describes the extent to which people feel threatened by ambiguous or unknown situations (Hofstede, 1980; Patterson & Smith, 2001). Higher UA is associated with a desire for reduction of ambiguity and a need for predictability, whereas low UA is associated with a propensity to engage in novel and risk taking behavior (Triandis, 1995).

Masculinity-Femininity (MAS-FEM)

The MAS– FEM values reflect the relative strength of one's concern for personal recognition and advancement versus a preference for harmony, collegial ties, and quality of life. People high on masculine orientation tend to place greater value on achievement and advancement in the workplace (Adler, 1997; Hofstede, 1998), and seek conditions that enhance more opportunities for self-development and personal accomplishment (Hofstede, 2001). This suggests that such individuals will strive to improve work performance because of the recognition they may receive. They will need a lot of individual-level cues and information about their capability and will form high efficacy beliefs in a work milieu, such as a team learning context, where they could receive greater amounts of feedback about their actions and potential. Such an environment may foster self-directed reflection on their performance and competence because interdependent tasks, as argued previously, are more likely to prompt team members to seek out information and exchange ideas (Kirkman, Mathieu, Cordery, Rosen, & Kukenberger, 2011). Further, in a team climate teammates are a major source of information and knowledge about task processes, and roles and relationships in the organization (Jian et al., 2016). Members high on masculinity will grasp more opportunities to see other members as a point of reference for themselves. Contrarily, individuals high on feminine values tend to be agreeable, cooperative and friendly in a team and are generally less overwhelmed by the motives of success and accomplishment (Hofstede, 1980). Thus, they will be less sensitive to capture privately referenced information about their own performance in establishing their self-efficacy.

Moreover, team learning activities may offer team members the means to be involved in seeking different perspectives and challenging each other's notions and assumptions. This may be high for employees with more masculine values because such individuals as compared to their counterparts with a feminine orientation, are more verbally assertive, and are less likely to display acquiescent behaviors in the communication process (Johnson, Kulesa, Cho, & Shavitt, 2005). Thus employees high on masculinity are likely to seek and provide feedback on actual task performance. The comparison of information received in the form of feedback to the performance adequacy is argued to enable individuals to identify and eliminate errors, thereby enhancing their self-efficacy beliefs (Shea & Howell, 1999). The above discussion suggests that the beneficial effects of team learning behaviors on self-efficacy are likely to be especially great when employees are high on masculine values. Consequently, we suggest the following:

H2: MAS-FEM orientation moderates the relationship between team learning behavior and self-efficacy, such that the relationship is stronger when individual team members are high on masculine rather feminine orientation.

Uncertainty Avoidance (UA)

As noted earlier, team learning activities may include challenging assumptions, seeking different perspectives, evaluating alternatives, and reflecting on past actions (e.g., Argote et al., 1999). This suggests that team learning activities may provide members with novel or challenging situations and tasks. Novel tasks require members to exchange ideas with other team members (Arrow, McGrath, & Berdahl, 2000) and leverage differing perspectives for creative problem-solving and critical thinking (Pelled, Eisenhardt, & Xin, 1999). Employees who have developed communication and problem-solving skills may feel more competent, and competence has been argued to contribute to efficacy beliefs that one is capable of successfully performing a task (Bandura, 1986). Team learning activities may also involve challenging assignments that motivate members to experiment with new strategies and behaviors to achieve new levels of competence (McCauley, Ruderman, Ohlott, & Morrow, 1994; Taris & Kompier, 2005). Past research suggests that enactive mastery can be experienced when one is able to work on challenging tasks, and to make use of one's competencies. Challenging tasks provide opportunities to apply individual skills and knowledge, thus serving as a source of experiences relevant for self- efficacy (Speier & Frese, 1997).

Given behaviors associated with team learning, it is likely that individuals low on UA orientation would react better to such an environment in the form of greater self-efficacy. People low on UA values tend to place emphasis on new initiatives, show flexibility towards changes and a have proactive and entrepreneurial behavior. This may foster innovative thinking and a high willingness to engage in communicative interaction with each other in the work team. Moreover, low UA is associated with a propensity to engage in risk taking behavior (Triandis, 1995), which may raise their acceptance of novel and challenging situations and tasks. Thus people low on UA tend to favorably view a team context that provide opportunities to work on challenging tasks and may encourage the exploration of new ideas and experimentation with new work procedures in order to meet and exceed performance standards. According to earlier evidence, acquiescent response style in communication tends to be less prevalent for low UA people (Smith, 2004). This suggests that activities associated with team learning such as challenging assumptions and seeking different perspectives that may stimulate knowledge seeking behaviors (Ancona, 1990; Chung & Jackson, 2013) are also likely to be more congruent with low UA values. On the other hand, high UA is associated with a desire for reduction of ambiguity and a need for predictability (Traindis, 1995). People high on UA tend to show little innovative spirit because of their preference for established processes and tested patterns of behavior. Moreover, their strict emphasis on formalized working decreases their motivation to engage in communicative interaction with each other. This suggests that team members low on UA orientation will report higher levels of self-efficacy when they are exposed to team learning activities.

H3: *UA orientation moderates the relationship between team learning behavior and self-efficacy, such that the relationship is stronger when individual team members are low rather than high on UA orientation.*

METHOD

Participants and Procedure

Data for the study were collected from a large public organization in Pakistan. Participants were employees working in different positions, such as supervisors, inspectors, auditors, computer operators and programmers, and clerical staff. At the time of data collection, the organization was undergoing huge structural and procedural changes making the organization suitable for capturing employee learning activities. The participants were randomly recruited from field offices of the organization situated in different cities in the country. Participation was sought on a voluntary basis and involved completing a survey questionnaire designed in English that was manually distributed by the first author. One hundred and sixty employees participated in the survey, while 133 completed the survey. The final number of usable observations was 96.

Measures

All the concepts were measured with items from previously validated scales.

MAS-FEM and UA Orientation

To measure MAS-FEM and UA orientation, Dorfman and Howell's (1988) adapted cultural scale was used. The scale is designed to measure cultural values at the individual level. MAS-FEM was measured with three items, while UA was captured with two items. Participants ranked the items on a scale that ranged from 1 (*strongly disagree*) to 5 (*strongly agree*).

We selected MAS-FEM and UA related items based on certain considerations. We did not include those items that in the perceptions of the respondents could implicitly refer to certain other values and could place those values in a-priori in the MAS-FEM or UA category. For instance, we did not include the item related to use of forcible approach to solving difficult problems to measure masculinity, because respondents by virtue of their being raised in a hierarchical society could classify this item as power distance or autocratic leadership specific. Likewise, we did not include the item 'It is important to closely follow instructions and procedures' to capture UA, because meaning ascribed to this item could again relate to hierarchical distance in the organization.

Team Learning

Team learning was measured with three items from Edmondson's (1996) team learning scale. Responses ranged from 1 (*strongly disagree*) to 7 (*strongly agree*).

Self-Efficacy

Self-efficacy was measured with Riggs, Warka, Babasa, Betancourt, & Hooker's (1994) scale using two items. Responses ranged from 1 (*strongly disagree*) to 6 (*strongly agree*).

ANALYSIS AND FINDINGS

Measures Validation and Data Analysis

The psychometric properties of the measures were assessed by first performing an exploratory factor analysis. The Kaiser-Meyer-Olkin (KMO) measure of sampling adequacy was 0.654 and Bartlett's test of Sphericity was significant at the 0.0001 level, indicating that the data matrix sufficiently correlated to the factor analysis. Further analysis was performed by the use of Partial Least Square (PLS) (Wold, 1975) using the software application SmartPLS (Ringle, Wende and Becker, 2015). SmartPLS is a partial least squares path modeling technique that simultaneously test measurement (relationship between indicators and their constructs or latent variables) and structural model (relationship between constructs). PLS is very useful for model estimation when sample size is small and makes less strict assumptions about the distribution of the data (Chin & Newsted, 1999). The authors' choice of variance based modeling technique such PLS was informed by the small sample size (n=96) and the exploratory nature of this study. PLS also has the capacity to deal with complex models with a high number of constructs, indicators and relationships (Barclay, Thompson, & Higgins. 1995; Hair, Hult, Ringle, & Sarstedt, 2014).

All constructs in this study were operationalized as reflective measures. Thus, the authors assessed the measurement model with respect to individual item reliability, internal consistency and discriminant

Table 1. Loadings, reliability and average variance extracted

Construct	Indicators	M	SD	Loadings#
Self-efficacy CR=0.91 α=0.79 rho_A=0.79 AVE=0.83	There are some tasks required by my job that I cannot do well (SEF1).	4.03	1.49	0.903***
	When my performance is poor it is due to my inability (SEF2).	4.33	1.43	0.916***
Team Learning CR=0.78 α=0.63 rho_A=0.73 AVE=0.56	In our team, people discuss ways to prevent and learn from mistakes (TEL1).	5.89	1.00	0.839***
	We regularly take time to figure out ways to improve our work processes (TEL2).	5.26	1.61	0.468*
	My team frequently coordinates with other teams to meet organizational objectives (TEL3).	5.40	1.47	0.875***
Uncertainty Avoidance CR=0.81 α=0.57 rho_A=0.68 AVE=0.69	It is important to have job requirements and instructions spelled out in detail so that employees always know what they are expected to do (UAV1).	4.64	0.51	0.730*
	Standard operating procedures are helpful to employees on the job (UAV2).	4.46	0.58	0.917**
Masculinity-femininity CR=0.86 α=0.75 rho_A=0.77 AVE=0.66	It is more important for men to have a professional career than women to have a professional career (MAF1).	3.24	1.38	0.858***
	Men usually solve problems with logical analysis; women usually solve problems with intuition (MAF2).	3.43	1.11	0.833***
	It is preferable to have a man in a high level position rather than a woman (MAF3).	3.14	1.37	0.747***

Note: CR = Composite Reliability; α = Cronbach's Alpha; rho_A=Spearman's reliability rho;

AVE = Average Variance Extracted; M = Mean; SD = Standard Deviation

*** $p<0.001$, ** $p<0.01$, * $p<0.05$ (two-tailed)

validity. We used the rule of thumb of accepting items with loadings of 0.707 or more, though loadings of at least 0.5 were acceptable (Barclays et al., 1995). Only one indicator TEL2 present loading below 0.707 (see Table 1). Table 2 shows a correlation matrix of individual items used in the measurement model.

Internal consistency was assessed using Fornell and Larcker's (1981) composite reliability index. The composite reliability index for all constructs exceeded the acceptable value of 0.7 (Hair, Black,

Table 2. Correlation matrix of indicators

	SEF1	SEF2	TEL1	TEL2	TEL3	UAV1	UAV2	MAF1	MAF2	MAF3
SEF1	1.00									
SEF2	.66	1.00								
TEL1	.29	.29	1.00							
TEL2	.05	.12	.19	1.00						
TEL3	.27	.32	.50	.39	1.00					
UAV1	.10	-.01	-.04	-.04	.01	1.00				
UAV2	.10	.03	.22	-,01	.14	.25	1.00			
MAF1	-.26	-.22	.09	.05	.03	-.09	.06	1.00		
MAF2	-.21	-.24	-.10	.03	.12	-.15	.00	.54	1.00	
MAF3	-.16	-.17	-.06	-.17	-.09	.13	.14	.49	.45	1.00

Babin, & Anderson, 2014), with team learning construct presenting the lowest (0.78) and self-efficacy construct the highest (0.91). In terms of Cronbach's alpha and reliability rho, uncertainty avoidance has the minimum value of 0.57 and 0.68 respectively. A value of rho greater than 0.60 is considered the minimum for adequate reliability (Hair, Black, Babin et al., 2014). Discriminant validity indicates the extent to which a given construct is different from other latent constructs. Fornell and Larcker (1981) suggest the use of Average Variance Extracted (AVE) such that a score of 0.5 for the AVE indicates an acceptable level. Average variance extracted by the measures range from 0.56 to 0.83, all above the acceptable value of 0.5 (see Table 1). Further assessment of discriminant validity of the latent variables in the PLS path model was performed using Fornell and Larcker (1981) criterion, which requires that the square root of each latent variable's AVE be greater than the latent variable's correlation with any other construct in the model. Table 3 shows comparison of the square root of the AVE (diagonal values) with the correlations among the constructs. Each variable meets Fornell and Larcker's (1981) criterion in support of discriminant validity. An examination of loadings and cross loadings shows that all constructs were more strongly correlated with their own measures than with any other constructs, suggesting good convergent and discriminant validity.

Common Method Variance

Finally, because the data for all the model's variables came from survey respondents at a point in time, common method variance might influence some of the postulated relations in the PLS path model. Common method bias (CMV) is variance that is attributable to the measurement method rather than to the constructs. This is because the data for all the model variables came from the same respondents at the same time, CMV might influence some of the hypothesized relations in the structural model (Podsakoff, Mackenzie, & Podsakoff, 2003). To minimize common method biases, we used and statistical control test such as Harman's single-factor test. Harman's (1976) single-factor test was used to test for the potential existence of common method bias. Common method variance is assumed present if a single factor emerges from the unrotated factor solution or one factor explains the majority of the variance in the variables (Podsakoff & Organ, 1986).

A one factor solution accounts for only 20.1% of the overall variance, which indicates that common method bias is unlikely to affect the findings of the study. However, it has been suggested that this test suffers from some limitations (Kemery & Dunlap, 1986), hence, we also adopted the marker variable

Table 3. Discriminant Validity Coefficients

	1	2	3	4	5	6
Self-Efficacy (1)	**0.91**					
Masculinity-Femininity (2)	-0.28	**0.81**				
Team Learning x Masculinity-Femininity (3)	0.25	0.05	**1.00**			
Team Learning x Uncertainty Avoidance (4)	0.03	0.08	0.03	**1.00**		
Team Learning (5)	0.36	0.01	0.19	0.01	**0.75**	
Uncertainty Avoidance (6)	0.09	0.01	0.08	-0.10	0.13	**0.83**

Bold Numbers on the Diagonal Shows the Square Root of the AVE
Numbers Below the Diagonal Represent the Construct Correlations

approach (Lindell & Whitney, 2001; Malhotra, Kim, & Patil, 2006). A marker variable is a variable, which is theoretically unrelated to at least one other variable in the study. We used the marker variable to estimate the loadings on every item in the PLS path model and observed each item's loadings on its theoretical construct. We compared the estimated path model relationships with and without the marker. All theorized paths maintain their level of statistical significance. This approach to testing common method variance suggests method variance biases are not likely to confound the interpretations of the results and findings from this study.

Structural Model Estimation

The structural model represents the relationships between constructs or latent variables that were hypothesized in the research model. The structural model consists of twelve latent variables. It includes the ten variables shown in Table 1 plus two latent variables that represent interactions between two other latent variables (team learning x uncertainty avoidance and team learning x masculinity-femininity). The two new constructs which are interaction terms, each have as indicators the product of the standardized indicators relative to the underlying constructs involved in the interaction. The modeling of the interaction term follows the approach of Chin, Marcolin and Newsted (2003) and Coelho and Henseler (2012). The structural model was estimated using Partial Least Squares (PLS) structural equation modeling technique using SmartPLS 3.0 (Ringle et al., 2015).

One of the primary goal of PLS is prediction (Duarte & Rapaso, 2010). Thus, the goodness of a theoretical model is established by the strength of each structural path and the combined predictiveness (R^2) of its exogenous constructs (Chin, 1998). Falk and Miller (1992) suggest that the variance explained or R^2 for endogenous variables should be greater than 0.1. R^2 values of 0.67, 0.33 or 0.19 for endogenous latent variables that are described as substantial, moderate or weak (Chin, 1998; Henseler, Ringle, & Sinkovics, 2009; Hair, Hult, Ringle et al., 2014). The goal of this chapter is not only to understand how team learning acts as a social environment in predicting the development of employee self-efficacy, but also to explore the moderating role of individual level MAS-FEM and UA values on the association between team learning and self-efficacy. The variance explained of the endogenous dependent construct self-efficacy is useful in assessing the model's predictiveness. Assessment of the path coefficients was done by bootstrap analysis in SmartPLS3 to assess the significance of the path coefficients. Table 4 shows the results of the path analysis. The variance inflation factor (VIF), assesses the multicollinearity in terms of the correlation between the predictors in the estimation of regression path coefficients. VIF values above 5 signal problems of multicollinearity (Hair, Hult, Ringle, & Sarstedt, 2014).

Table 4. Path Coefficients, Effect Size and VIF - Dependent Variable Self-Efficacy (n=96; R^2=0.26)

	Path coefficient	t-value#	Effect size	VIF
Team Learning	**0.32**	4.07 ***	0.133	1.050
Uncertainty Avoidance	0.04	0.31 ns	0.002	1.031
Team Learning x Masculinity-Femininity	0.19	2.47 **	0.052	1.044
Team Learning x Uncertainty Avoidance	0.04	0.40 ns	0.003	1.019

Note: # Based on 1000 bootstrapping samples

*** p<0.001 (two-tailed), ** p<0.01 (one-tailed), ns Not Significant

Hypothesis H1 states a positive association between team learning and self-efficacy. Results from the analysis of the dataset finds support for this (β=0.32, p<0.001, two-tailed) with the highest effect size of 0.133 suggesting that team learning is a significant predictor of self-efficacy. Thus, team learning significantly enhances self-efficacy as hypothesized (see Figure 2). Hypothesis H2 states that MAS-FEM orientation moderates the relationship between team learning and self-efficacy, such that the relationship is stronger when individual team members are high on masculine rather feminine orientation. In other words, the association between team learning and self-efficacy will be strengthened at higher levels of masculinity. Our study finds support for H2 (β=0.19, p<0.01, one-tailed). Figure 3 shows the moderating role of MAS-FEM. At higher levels of masculinity (plus one standard deviation above the mean value) team learning leads to increasing levels of self-efficacy more than lower level levels of masculinity. In other words, masculinity enhances the association between team learning and self-efficacy. However, at lower levels of MAS-FEM (shown in Figure 3, minus one standard deviation below the mean value), the effect of team learning on self-efficacy attenuates (increasing at a slower pace shown by the gentle slope compared to the steeper slope +1SD of MAS-FEM). This suggests that at higher levels of femininity, the effect of team learning on self-efficacy increases at a decreasing rate than at a higher level of masculinity. However, our study did not find support for H3 (β=0.04, p>0.05) which states that UA orientation moderates the relationship between team learning and self-efficacy.

DISCUSSION

The purpose of this study was to examine whether team learning behaviors contribute to employee self-efficacy and whether such effects may vary depending upon the extent to which employees espouse masculinity–femininity and UA values. The findings show that learning teams act as immediate social contexts that have the potential to shape employee self-efficacy. Although past studies have found some

Figure 2. Results of the Structural Model

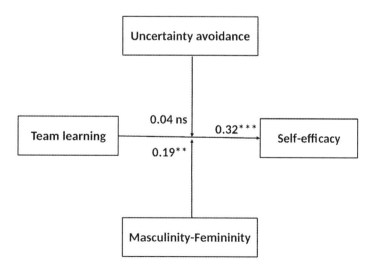

*** p<0.001 (two-tailed), ** p<0.01 (one-tailed), ns not significant

Figure 3. Simple slope: Masculinity-Femininity as Moderator Between the Team Learning Behavior and Self- Efficacy Relationship

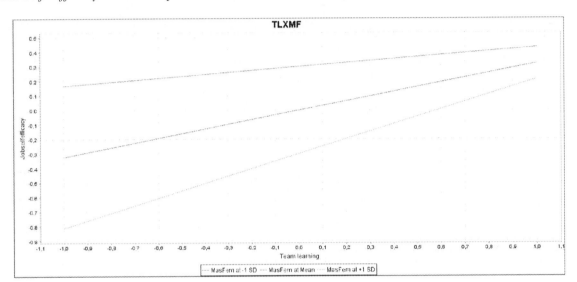

evidence that formal learning programs at the workplace are associated with learning relevant outcomes such as self-efficacy (Earley, 1994), less is known about the consequences of informal team learning activities for the formation of individual efficacy beliefs. We found that employees working in teams characterized by learning activities experience higher levels of self-efficacy, but further analysis revealed that self-efficacy associated with team learning behaviors was constrained by employee personal values of MAS-FEM. The value of the team learning climate for promoting self-efficacy was evident for employees espousing masculine values, but not for employees who endorse feminine values. The findings demonstrate that individual-level differences in MAS-FEM orientation are important pertaining to employees' preference for working in team-based arrangements that potentially offer novel and challenging tasks, and grasping such experiences as rich opportunities to articulate their personal learning and developing cognitive beliefs about their ability to successfully perform work tasks. It is probable that such employees are more adept at benefiting from exchange of information, knowledge, and feedback during collaborative learning processes for self-reflection. The reason why employees with feminine tendencies responded to team learning behaviors with lesser self-efficacy may be that such individuals see empathy, cooperation and modesty in interpersonal interaction as more important than ego goals such as achievement, competition, and assertive behavior (Hofstede, 1980). Thus, it is less likely that they will take an assertive role in team learning activities, will actively seek self- referenced information about their performance, and will emulate high performers as their role models.

The results with respect to the team learning–self-efficacy relationship for members with low UA values do not support our prediction. The probable reason is that despite their proclivity for creativity and innovation, employees low on UA are less sensitive to self-referenced feedback in their interaction with other members during team learning activities. They may actively be involved in seeking and sharing knowledge out of their curiosity to explore new perspectives instead of using that information to judge their own capabilities. It seems that such employees tend to focus more on the exploration of new ideas rather than on their immediate concerns with successfully performing a particular task.

These findings might also be interpreted as a reflection of the cultural characteristics of Pakistan and the context of the study organization. According to Hofstede's findings (1980) Pakistan's rating on the masculinity index shows an equal mix of masculinity and femininity, but many recent studies suggest that people in Pakistan are characterized by masculine values. For example, Shamim and Abbasi (2012) in their study of the cultural value orientations of Pakistani business managers noted that majority of managers in their sample espoused masculine compared to feminine values. Likewise, Routamaa and Hautala's (2008) study suggests that individuals in Pakistan give high importance to work goals such as competence, recognition, success and advancement, which are typical of masculine characteristics. It is thus possible that team learning activities in the study organization may create a learning milieu that better cater to the masculine values. Such activities may involve an active and an assertive role for the individual members, appreciating good performers, setting high achievers as the benchmark, and recognizing and rewarding high performance, which are all expected to be closely associated with masculine values in a learning situation (Jaju, Kwak, & Zinkhan, 2002; Manikutty, Anuradha, & Hansen, 2007).

It is also possible that the organizational context might have some influence on why employees low on UA values reported less of a link between team learning behavior and self-efficacy. Members with low UA prefer new and unknown situations, are more willing to accept uncertainty and do not require or even reject clear structures and regulations (Hofstede, 2001). Such values are likely to be activated when ambiguity prevails. The time when this research was conducted, the organizational change had passed the initiation and implementation stages. This meant that uncertainty and ambiguity regarding structural arrangements and role and relationships were no longer there and the team activities took place in an environment where adherence to the newly implemented regulations and structural arrangements was important. It is therefore possible to speculate that team learning activities in a structured and less ambiguous environment would have offered members with low UA fewer opportunities to form self-efficacy beliefs.

Notwithstanding the above, our findings reaffirm the suggestions of previous research that cultural values can be important factors in explaining differences between employees within the same country (Triandis, 1995; Williamson, Burnett, & Bartol, 2009). It is therefore important to consider variation in individual-level cultural value orientations, in addition to country-level cultural differences, to better understand the role of different value orientations in employees' evaluation of their work environments.

MANAGERIAL IMPLICATIONS

The findings of this study hold some important implications for organizations. The findings suggest that team learning activities are potentially valuable for their contributions to self-efficacy beliefs of employees, organizations can offer developmental opportunities to employees through informal learning activities that naturally occur within teams. Our results suggest that masculine orientation plays an important role in shaping employees' self-efficacy by influencing how they react to team-based learning environments. Organizations interested in increasing their employees' self-efficacy through informal workplace learning activities may benefit from assigning employees to teams based upon cultural orientation. For example, managers may assign individuals with high masculine orientation to teams that have a strong learning focus and where members have the opportunity to receive a lot of self-referenced feedback. Assigning such employees will be beneficial to the type of teams where members may work independently and subsequently combine their efforts, and receive feedback and support in the form of backup behavior for individual work. Such employees may also be suitable for teams in which members work both collaboratively and as independent contributors. The feedback received during collaborative work may act as self-referenced information of capability and competence for independent tasks. Organizations may also want to identify individuals who have a masculine orientation if they are looking for employees who may often be assigned to new teams. The transfer of group effects at individual level may be more pronounced for such individuals leading to high efficacy and performance in the new setting.

LIMITATIONS AND SUGGESTIONS FOR FUTURE RESEARCH

There are several limitations in this study that should be addressed in future research.

First, this study focused only on employees in one organizational context. It is conceivable that the tested relationships differ for different populations. The studied respondents worked in a specific public organization- the country's central revenue organization- that may have a unique organizational culture, and the conclusions are therefore not immediately transferable to completely different organizational settings. For example, the tax officials due to a heavy public mandate may be more prone to an efficiency and performance related scrutiny (Mustafa & Lines, 2012), which might have led to formation of high efficacy beliefs among employees high on masculine orientation when exposed to team learning activities. Future studies may test the generalizability of our findings by broadening the sample size of organizations and extending the research into multiple cultures. Our suggestion is based on the following: the work teams in the study organization may not be fully representative of other professional work teams. This is because all work teams tend to develop distinctive cultures (Levine & Moreland, 1991). The respondents in our sample may share a set of beliefs and values because of their exposure to the same organizational culture that may not be fully comparable to the values and beliefs of employees in other organizations (e.g., Schein, 1996). Pakistan, despite having an overarching national culture is characterized by considerable regional diversity in terms of subcultures (Shamim & Abbasi, 2012) that may contribute to both within country and cross-national variation in organizational culture. Thus, using a sample of respondents representing only one organizational and cultural context does not allow intra and cross-cultural variation in our sample, and our findings do not provide a strong basis to assert that the pattern of employee responses may hold across organizations at national and international level. More conclusive support for whether the team learning behavior leads to high self-efficacy beliefs and whether such relationship is bolstered when employees are high on masculinity values would require testing the proposed relationships in a sample of employees spanning a larger number of organizations and societies.

Second, while we find evidence that team learning behaviors influence individuals' self-efficacy beliefs, the current study does not provide information on the specific mechanisms by which team learning behaviors influence self-efficacy. It is important to understand the mediating processes by which differences are created between employees of masculine and feminine orientations. Third, future research should separately examine the effect of group-based information on self-efficacy for employees with a high feminine orientation, and the effect of individual-referenced information for employees with a masculine orientation to see if group-focused and individual directed information influence individuals with feminine and masculine tendencies respectively. This is in view of the earlier evidence that group-focused information contributes to the self-efficacy of group oriented individuals, while self-referenced information shapes the self-efficacy of people with individualist tendencies (Earley, 1994). Since individuals high on femininity tend to have high affiliation needs, it's likely that they will positively react to group-based information rather than information directed at each individual team member. Finally, future studies may examine how other cultural values may moderate the effect of team learning behaviors on self-efficacy. Assessing the influence of all cultural value dimensions is important because individuals are affected by a complex set of cultural values (Kirkman & Shapiro, 1997). Findings of many cross-cultural management studies reveal that cultural values explain unique variance in outcome variables beyond a single dimension such as individualism-collectivism (Taras, Kirkman, & Steel, 2010).

CONCLUSION

In the present study, we examined how team learning behaviors and employees' cultural values influence self-efficacy. The study shows that it is not only formal training and development programs that shape employee self-efficacy, but learning environments that naturally occur in organizations are also important for such learning outcomes. The results suggest that team learning acts as a workplace milieu for the development of employee self-efficacy beliefs, however, such effects tend to be influenced by the differences in individual level values of MAS-FEM. The study provides support for the earlier assertions that employee individual values interact with workplace attributes to shape employee work outcomes.

REFERENCES

Adler, N. (1997). *International dimensions of organizational behavior*. Cincinnati, OH: South-Western College Publishing.

Aguinis, H., & Kraiger, K. (2009). Benefits of training and development for individuals and teams, organizations, and society. *Annual Review of Psychology*, 60(1), 451–474. doi:10.1146/annurev. psych.60.110707.163505 PMID:18976113

Ancona, D. G. (1990). Outward bound: Strategic for team survival in an organization. *Academy of Management Journal*, 33(2), 334–365. doi:10.2307/256328

Argote, L., Gruenfeld, D., & Naquin, C. (1999). Group learning in organizations. In M. E. Turner (Ed.), *Groups at work: Advances in theory and research* (pp. 369–413). New York: Erlbaum.

Arrow, H., McGrath, J. E., & Berdahl, J. L. (2000). *Small groups as complex systems: Formation, coordination, development, and adaptation*. Thousand Oaks, CA: Sage.

Bandura, A. (1977). *Social learning theory*. Englewood Cliffs, NJ: Prentice Hall.

Bandura, A. (1986). *Social foundations of thought and action: A social cognitive theory*. Englewood Cliffs, NJ: Prentice Hall.

Bandura, A. (1997). *Self-efficacy: The exercise of control*. New York: Freeman.

Barclays, D., Thompson, R., & Higgins, C. (1995). The partial least squares (PLS) approach to causal modeling: Personal computer adoption and use as an illustration. *Technology Studies*, 2(2), 285–309.

Bell, B. S., & Kozlowski, S. W. (2008). Active learning: Effects of core training design elements on self-regulatory processes, learning, and adaptability. *The Journal of Applied Psychology, 93*(2), 296–316. doi:10.1037/0021-9010.93.2.296 PMID:18361633

Brodbeck, F. C., & Greitemeyer, T. (2000). Effects of individual versus mixed individual and group experience in rule induction on group member learning and group performance. *Journal of Experimental Social Psychology, 36*(6), 621–648. doi:10.1006/jesp.2000.1423

Chao, G. T., & Moon, H. (2005). The cultural mosaic: A metatheory for understanding the complexity of culture. *The Journal of Applied Psychology, 90*(6), 1128–1140. doi:10.1037/0021-9010.90.6.1128 PMID:16316269

Chin, W., Marcolin, B. L., & Newsted, P. R. (2003). A Partial Least Squares Latent Variable Modeling Approach for Measuring Interaction Effects: Results from a Monte Carlo Simulation Study and an Electronic-Mail Emotion/Adoption Study. *Information Systems Research, 14*(2), 189–217. doi:10.1287/isre.14.2.189.16018

Chin, W., & Newsted, P. R. (1999), Structural equation modeling analysis with small samples using partial least squares. In R. Hoyle (Eds.), Statistical strategies for small sample research (pp. 307-341). Thousand Oaks, CA: Sage.

Chin, W. W. (1998). The partial least squares approach to structural equation modeling. In G. A. Marcoulides (Ed.), *Modern methods for business research* (pp. 295–336). Lawrence Erlbaum.

Chung, Y., & Jackson, S. E. (2013). The Internal and External Networks of Knowledge-Intensive Teams The Role of Task Routineness. *Journal of Management, 39*(2), 442–468. doi:10.1177/0149206310394186

Coelho, P. S., & Henseler, J. (2012). Creating customer loyalty through service customization. *European Journal of Marketing, 46*(3/4), 331–356. doi:10.1108/03090561211202503

Cohen, S. G., & Bailey, D. E. (1997). What makes teams work: Group effectiveness research from the shop floor to the executive suite. *Journal of Management, 23*(3), 239–290. doi:10.1177/014920639702300303

Colquitt, J. A., LePine, J. A., & Noe, R. A. (2000). Toward an integrative theory of training motivation: A meta-analytic path analysis of 20 years of research. *The Journal of Applied Psychology, 85*(5), 678–707. doi:10.1037/0021-9010.85.5.678 PMID:11055143

Dierdorff, E. C., & Ellington, J. K. (2012). Members matter in team training: Multilevel and longitudinal relationships between goal orientation, self-regulation, and team outcomes. *Personnel Psychology, 65*(3), 661–703. doi:10.1111/j.1744-6570.2012.01255.x

Dorfman, P. W., & Howell, J. P. (1988). Dimensions of national culture and effective leadership patterns: Hofstede revisited. *Advances in International Comparative Management, 3*(1), 127–150.

Duarte, P. A., & Rapaso, M. L. (2010). A PLS model to study brand preference: an application to the mobile phone market. In V. E. Vinzi, W. W. Chin, J. Henseler, & H. Wang (Eds.), *Handbook of partial least squares – concepts, methods and applications* (pp. 449–485). Berlin: Springer. doi:10.1007/978-3-540-32827-8_21

Earley, P. C. (1994). Self or group? Cultural effects of training on self-efficacy and performance. *Administrative Science Quarterly, 39*(1), 89–117. doi:10.2307/2393495

Edmondson, A. (1999). Psychological safety and learning behaviors in work teams. *Administrative Science Quarterly, 44*(2), 350–383. doi:10.2307/2666999

Edmondson, A. C. (1996). *Group and organizational influences on team learning* (Unpublished Doctoral Dissertation). Harvard University, Boston, MA.

Edmondson, A. C. (2002). The local and variegated nature of learning in organizations: A group-level perspective. *Organization Science, 13*(2), 128–146. doi:10.1287/orsc.13.2.128.530

Ellington, J. K., & Dierdorff, E. C. (2014). Individual learning in team training: Self-regulation and team context effects. *Small Group Research, 45*(1), 37–67. doi:10.1177/1046496413511670

Falk, R. F., & Miller, N. B. (1992). *A primer for soft modeling.* The University of Akron Press.

Farh, J. L., Hackett, R. D., & Liang, J. (2007). Individual-level cultural values as moderators of perceived organizational support–employee outcome relationships in China: Comparing the effects of power distance and traditionality. *Academy of Management Journal, 50*(3), 715–729. doi:10.5465/AMJ.2007.25530866

Fornell, C., & Larcker, D. F. (1981). Evaluating structural equation models with unobservable variables and measurement error. *JMR, Journal of Marketing Research, 18*(1), 39–50. doi:10.2307/3151312

Francescato, D., Porcelli, R., Mebane, M., Cuddetta, M., Klobas, J., & Renzi, P. (2006). Evaluation of the efficacy of collaborative learning in face-to-face and computer-supported university contexts. *Computers in Human Behavior, 22*(2), 163–176. doi:10.1016/j.chb.2005.03.001

Gibson, C., & Vermeulen, F. (2003). A healthy divide: Subgroups as a stimulus for team learning behavior. *Administrative Science Quarterly, 48*(2), 202–239. doi:10.2307/3556657

Gouillart, F., & Kelly, J. (1995). *Transforming the Organization.* New York: McGraw-Hill.

Guzzo, R. A., & Dickson, M. W. (1996). Teams in organizations: Recent research on performance and effectiveness. *Annual Review of Psychology, 47*(1), 307–338. doi:10.1146/annurev.psych.47.1.307 PMID:15012484

Hackman, J. R. (1987). The design of work teams. In J. Lorsch (Ed.), *Handbook of organizational behavior* (pp. 315–342). Englewood Cliffs, NJ: Prentice-Hall.

Hair, J. F., Black, W. C., Babin, B. J., & Anderson, R. E. (2014). *Multivariate data analysis* (7th ed.). London: Prentice Hall International.

Hair, J. F., Hult, G. T. M., Ringle, C. M., & Sarstedt, M. (2014). *A primer on partial least squares structural equation modeling (PLS-SEM).* Thousand Oaks, CA: Sage.

Hall, D. T. (1996). Long live the career -A relational approach. In D. Hall et al. (Eds.), *The career is dead -- Long live the career* (pp. 1–14). San Francisco: Jossey-Bass Publishers.

Harman, H. H. (1976). *Modern factor analysis* (3rd ed.). Chicago, IL: University of Chicago Press.

Henseler, J., Ringle, C. M., & Sinkovics, R. R. (2009). The use of partial least squares path modeling in international marketing. *Advances in International Marketing, 20*(1), 277–320.

Hofstede, G. (1980). *Culture's consequences: International differences in work-related values* (Vol. 5). Beverly Hills, CA: Sage.

Hofstede, G. H. (1998). *Masculinity and femininity: The taboo dimension of national cultures*. Thousand Oaks, CA: Sage.

Hofstede, G. H. (2001). *Culture's consequences* (2nd ed.). Thousand Oaks, CA: Sage.

Jaju, A., Kwak, H., & Zinkhan, G. M. (2002). Learning styles of undergraduate business students: A cross-cultural comparison between the US, India, and Korea. *Marketing Education Review, 12*(2), 49–60. doi:10.1080/10528008.2002.11488787

Jiang, Y., Jackson, S. E., & Colakoglu, S. (2016). An empirical examination of personal learning within the context of teams. *Journal of Organizational Behavior, 37*(5), 654–672. doi:10.1002/job.2058

Johnson, T., Kulesa, P., Cho, Y. I., & Shavitt, S. (2005). The relation between culture and response styles evidence from 19 countries. *Journal of Cross-Cultural Psychology, 36*(2), 264–277. doi:10.1177/0022022104272905

Johnston, J., Killion, J., & Oomen, J. (2005). Student satisfaction in the virtual classroom. *The Internet Journal of Allied Health Sciences and Practice, 3*(2), 1–7.

Kemery, E. R., & Dunlap, W. P. (1986). Partialling factor scores does not control method variance: A reply to Podsakoff and Todor. *Journal of Management, 12*(4), 525–530. doi:10.1177/014920638601200407

Kirkman, B. L., Mathieu, J. E., Cordery, J. L., Rosen, B., & Kukenberger, M. (2011). Managing a new collaborative entity in business organizations: Understanding organizational communities of practice effectiveness. *The Journal of Applied Psychology, 96*(6), 1234–1245. doi:10.1037/a0024198 PMID:21688878

Kirkman, B. L., & Shapiro, D. L. (1997). The impact of cultural values on employee resistance to teams: Toward a model of globalized self-managing work team effectiveness. *Academy of Management Review, 22*(3), 730–757.

Kozlowski, S. W., & Bell, B. S. (2013). Work groups and teams in organizations. In N. W. Schmitt, S. Highhouse, & I. B. Weiner (Eds.), Handbook of psychology: Vol. 12. *Industrial and organizational psychology* (pp. 412–469). Hoboken, NJ: Wily.

Kozlowski, S. W., Toney, R. J., Mullins, M. E., Weissbein, D. A., Brown, K. G., & Bell, B. S. (2001). Developing adaptability: A theory for the design of integrated-embedded training systems. *Advances in Human Performance and Cognitive Engineering Research, 1*, 59–124. doi:10.1016/S1479-3601(01)01004-9

Kraiger, K., Ford, J. K., & Salas, E. (1993). Application of cognitive, skill-based, and affective theories of learning outcomes to new methods of training evaluation. *The Journal of Applied Psychology, 78*(2), 311–328. doi:10.1037/0021-9010.78.2.311

Lankau, M. J., & Scandura, T. A. (2002). An investigation of personal learning in mentoring relationships: Content, antecedents, and consequences. *Academy of Management Journal*, *45*(4), 779–790. doi:10.2307/3069311

Levine, J. M., & Moreland, R. L. (1991). Culture and socialization in work groups. In L. Resnick & J. Levine (Eds.), *Perspectives on socially shared cognition* (pp. 257–279). Washington, DC: APA. doi:10.1037/10096-011

Lindell, M. K., & Whitney, D. J. (2001). Accounting for common method variance in cross-sectional research designs. *The Journal of Applied Psychology*, *86*(1), 114–121. doi:10.1037/0021-9010.86.1.114 PMID:11302223

Littlepage, G., Robison, W., & Reddington, K. (1997). Effects of task experience and group experience on group performance, member ability, and recognition of expertise. *Organizational Behavior and Human Decision Processes*, *69*(2), 133–147. doi:10.1006/obhd.1997.2677

Malhotra, N. K., Kim, S. S., & Patil, A. (2006). Common method variance in IS research: A comparison of alternative approaches and reanalysis of past research. *Management Science*, *52*(12), 1865–1883. doi:10.1287/mnsc.1060.0597

Manikutty, S., Anuradha, N. S., & Hansen, K. (2007). Does culture influence learning styles in higher education? *International Journal of Learning and Change*, *2*(1), 70–87. doi:10.1504/IJLC.2007.014896

Manz, C. C., & Sims, H. P. Jr. (1993). *Business without bosses: How self-managing teams are building high performance companies*. New York: Wiley.

Marks, M. A., Mathieu, J. E., & Zaccaro, S. J. (2001). A temporally based framework and taxonomy of team processes. *Academy of Management Review*, *26*(3), 356–376.

McCauley, C. D., Ruderman, M. N., Ohlott, P. J., & Morrow, J. E. (1994). Assessing the developmental components of managerial jobs. *The Journal of Applied Psychology*, *79*(4), 544–560. doi:10.1037/0021-9010.79.4.544

Meyer, J. P., Irving, P. G., & Allen, N. J. (1998). Examination of the combined effects of work values and early work experiences on organizational commitment. *Journal of Organizational Behavior*, *19*(1), 29–52. doi:10.1002/(SICI)1099-1379(199801)19:1<29::AID-JOB818>3.0.CO;2-U

Mustafa, G., & Lines, R. (2012). Paternalism as a predictor of leadership behaviors: A bi-level analysis. *Eurasian Business Review*, *2*(1), 63–92.

Mustafa, G., & Lines, R. (2014). Influence of leadership on job satisfaction: The moderating effects of follower individual-level masculinity–femininity values. *The Journal of Leadership Studies*, *7*(4), 23–39. doi:10.1002/jls.21307

O'Donnell, A. M., & Dansereau, D. F. (1992). Scripted cooperation in student dyads: A method for analyzing and enhancing academic learning and performance. In R. Herz-Lazarowitz & N. Miller (Eds.), *Interaction in cooperative groups: The theoretical anatomy of group learning* (pp. 120–141). New York: Cambridge University Press.

O'Donnell, A. M., & King, A. (Eds.). (1999). *Cognitive perspectives on peer learning*. Mahwah, NJ: Laurence Erlbaum.

ODonnell, A. M., & OKelly, J. (1994). Learning from peers: Beyond the rhetoric of positive results. *Educational Psychology Review*, *6*(4), 321–349. doi:10.1007/BF02213419

Olivera, F., & Straus, S. G. (2004). Group-to-individual transfer of learning cognitive and social factors. *Small Group Research*, *35*(4), 440–465. doi:10.1177/1046496404263765

Patterson, P. G., & Smith, T. (2001). Relationship benefits in service industries: A replication in a Southeast Asian context. *Journal of Services Marketing*, *15*(6), 425–443. doi:10.1108/EUM0000000006098

Pelled, L. H., Eisenhardt, K. M., & Xin, K. R. (1999). Exploring the black box: An analysis of work group diversity, conflict, and performance. *Administrative Science Quarterly*, *44*(1), 1–28. doi:10.2307/2667029

Piccoli, G., Ahmad, R., & Ives, B. (2001). Web-based virtual learning environments: A research framework and a preliminary assessment of effectiveness in basic IT skills training. *MIS Qarterly*, *25*(4), 401–426. doi:10.2307/3250989

Podsakoff, N. P., & Organ, D. W. (1986). Self-reports in organizational research: Problems and prospects. *Journal of Management*, *12*(4), 531–544. doi:10.1177/014920638601200408

Podsakoff, P. M., Mackenzie, S. B., & Podsakoff, N. P. (2003). Common method biases in behavioral research: A critical review of literature and recommended remedies. *The Journal of Applied Psychology*, *88*(5), 879–903. doi:10.1037/0021-9010.88.5.879 PMID:14516251

Prieto, I. M., & Revilla, E. (2006). Assessing the impact of learning capability on business performance: Empirical evidence from Spain. *Management Learning*, *3*(4), 499–522. doi:10.1177/1350507606070222

Riggs, M. L., Warka, J., Babasa, B., Betancourt, R., & Hooker, S. (1994). Development and validation of self-efficacy and outcome expectancy scales for job-related applications. *Educational and Psychological Measurement*, *54*(3), 793–802. doi:10.1177/0013164494054003026

Ringle, C. M., Wende, S., & Becker, J.-M. (2015). *SmartPLS 3*. Bönningstedt: SmartPLS. Retrieved from http://www.smartpls.com

Routamaa, V., & Hautala, T. M. (2008). Understanding Cultural Differences-The Values in a Cross-Cultural Context. *The International Review of Business Research Papers*, *4*(5), 129–137.

Salas, E., Sims, D. E., & Burke, C. S. (2005). Is there a Big Five in teamwork? *Small Group Research*, *36*(5), 555–599. doi:10.1177/1046496405277134

Schein, E. H. (1996). Culture: The missing concept in organization studies. *Administrative Science Quarterly*, *41*(2), 229–240. doi:10.2307/2393715

Seers, A., Petty, M. M., & Cashman, J. F. (1995). Team-member exchange under team and traditional management a naturally occurring quasi-experiment. *Group & Organization Management*, *20*(1), 18–38. doi:10.1177/1059601195201003

Shamim, S., & Abbasi, A. S. (2012). Interethnic Culture Orientation of Business Managers in Pakistan. *Middle-East Journal of Scientific Research*, *12*(5), 632–642.

Shea, C. M., & Howell, J. M. (1999). Charismatic leadership and task feedback: A laboratory study of their effects on self-efficacy and task performance. *The Leadership Quarterly, 10*(3), 375–396. doi:10.1016/S1048-9843(99)00020-X

Smith, P. B. (2004). Acquiescent response bias as an aspect of cultural communication style. *Journal of Cross-Cultural Psychology, 35*(1), 50–61. doi:10.1177/0022022103260380

Speier, C., & Frese, M. (1997). Generalized self-efficacy as a mediator and moderator between control and complexity at work and personal initiative: A longitudinal field study in East Germany. *Human Performance, 10*(2), 171–192. doi:10.1207/s15327043hup1002_7

Tannenbaum, S. I., Mathieu, J. E., Salas, E., & Cohen, D. (2012). Teams are changing: Are research and practice evolving fast enough? *Industrial and Organizational Psychology: Perspectives on Science and Practice, 5*(1), 2–24. doi:10.1111/j.1754-9434.2011.01396.x

Taras, V., Kirkman, B. L., & Steel, P. (2010). Examining the impact of Cultures consequences: A three-decade, multilevel, meta-analytic review of Hofstedes cultural value dimensions. *The Journal of Applied Psychology, 95*(3), 405–439. doi:10.1037/a0018938 PMID:20476824

Taris, T. W., & Kompier, M. A. J. (2005). Job demands, job control, strain and learning behavior: Review and research agenda. In A. S. Antoniou & C. L. Cooper (Eds.), *Research companion to organizational health psychology* (pp. 132–150). Cheltenham, UK: Elgar. doi:10.4337/9781845423308.00015

Teasley, S. D. (1997). Talking about reasoning: How important is the peer in peer collaboration? In L. B. Resnick, R. Saljo, C. Pontecorvo, & B. Burge (Eds.), *Discourse, tools, and reasoning: Essays on situated cognition* (pp. 361–384). Berlin: Springer-Verlag. doi:10.1007/978-3-662-03362-3_16

Triandis, H. C. (1995). *Individualism & collectivism* (Vol. 5). Boulder, CO: Westview Press.

Turner, M. E. (2014). *Groups at work: Theory and research.* Psychology Press.

Van den Bossche, P., Gijselaers, W. H., Segers, M., & Kirschner, P. A. (2006). Social and cognitive factors driving teamwork in collaborative learning environments team learning beliefs and behaviors. *Small Group Research, 37*(5), 490–521. doi:10.1177/1046496406292938

Van Der Vegt, G. S., & Bunderson, J. S. (2005). Learning and performance in multidisciplinary teams: The importance of collective team identification. *Academy of Management Journal, 48*(3), 532–547. doi:10.5465/AMJ.2005.17407918

Webb, N. (1992). Testing a theoretical model of student interaction and learning in small groups. In R. Hertz-Lazarowitz & N. Miller (Eds.), *Interaction in cooperative groups: The theoretical anatomy of group learning* (pp. 102–119). New York: Cambridge University Press.

Williamson, I. O., Burnett, M. F., & Bartol, K. M. (2009). The interactive effect of collectivism and organizational rewards on affective organizational commitment. *Cross Cultural Management: An International Journal, 16*(1), 28–43. doi:10.1108/13527600910930022

Wold, H. (1975). Path models with latent variables: The NIPALS approach. In H. M. Blalock, A. Aganbegian, F. M. Borodkin, R. Boudon, & V. Capecchi (Eds.), *Quantitative sociology: International perspectives on mathematical and statistical modeling* (pp. 307–357). New York: Academic Press. doi:10.1016/B978-0-12-103950-9.50017-4

KEY TERMS AND DEFINITIONS

Exploratory Factor Analysis: This explores the data and provides the researcher with information on how many factors are needed to best represent the data. All measured variables are related to every factor by a factor loading estimate.

Masculinity-Femininity: The MAS– FEM values refer to the extent to which people associate priorities with assertiveness, achievement, and success in contrast with a concern for quality of life and warm and nurturing relationships.

Measurement Model: This is the mapping of measures onto their theoretical constructs. It shows how the measures are related to the theoretical constructs by their loadings.

Self-Efficacy: Self-efficacy refers to an individual's belief in his or her capabilities to successfully accomplish a specific task or set of tasks.

SmartPLS: This is a second generation variance-based structural equation modeling software compared to the covariance-based techniques/softwares such as LISREL, EQS, AMOS, Mplus.

Social Cognitive Theory: Social Cognitive Theory suggests that environment factors influence an individual's behavior through his/her cognitive mechanisms. The theory posits two critical cognitive factors: performance expectations and self-efficacy.

Structural Model: The structural portion of a full structural equation model involves the relations among the latent variables. The primary concern of a full structural model is the evaluation of the extent to which the relations among the latent variables are valid.

Uncertainty Avoidance: UA describes the extent to which people place emphasis on predictability and reduction of ambiguity in contrast with a propensity to engage in novel and risk taking behavior.

Chapter 14
Understanding the Impact of Organisational Culture on Managers' Internal Career Needs

Chi Maher
St. Mary's University Twickenham, UK

ABSTRACT

This chapter explores the influence of organisational culture on managerial internal career needs in small third sector social enterprises. Every organisation develops and maintains a unique culture, which provides guidelines and boundaries for the career management of members of the organisation. The research methodology was designed to allow the collection of data from three case study organisations and 24 operational managers working in these organisations. The qualitative findings of the study add to, and help to explain the inter-play between individual manager's internal career needs and organisational culture. Most importantly the findings suggest that when individual manager's internal career needs are closely supported by organisational culture, it increases their desire to stay with the organisation. The findings make an important contribution in the field of organisational career management.

INTRODUCTION

This chapter seeks to contribute to our understanding of the influence of organisational culture on managerial internal career needs in small third sector social enterprise organisations. Despite changes in career structures in the 21st Century, for example, the growing number of self-employment and contract work, etc. Majority of career still takes place in organisations (Baruch, 2004; Maher, 2016), including small social enterprises (Maher, 2015b). Successive UK government acknowledges the importance of these organisations role in building social capital and developing the social economy (Kendall and Knapp, 1996; Ridley-Duff and Bull 2015).

DOI: 10.4018/978-1-5225-2480-9.ch014

Third sector social enterprise organisations expect commitment and performance from managers to deliver their contractual obligations (Maher, 2015b). They expect managers to deliver projects on time and to budget; with the expected outcomes and benefits to the client group and the community. What organisations do not always realise is that individual managers differ in their career aspirations and career needs (Herriot, 1992; Maher, 2009). Organisational culture can often influence their decision to leave or stay in a particular organisation (Lok and Crawford, 2004). Therefore, the importance of understanding the influence or organisational culture on the internal career needs of managers who manage and develop small social enterprise organisation's activities has increased.

The internal career is conceptualised in terms of an individual's values, motivation and view of their career orientations and decisions between personal and professional life (Ng and Feldman, 2014, Bidwell and Mollick, 2015). It is connected with the individual's goals, aspirations and interests. A key question when considering the internal career is "what do I want from work? (Derr and Laurent, 1989; Ng and Feldman, 2014). This is about the way the individual defines the work they enjoy and cherish. The self-concept that seeks explicit answers from the following questions: 'what are my talents, skills, areas of competence? What are my main motives, drives, goal in life? What are my values: How good do I feel about my job?' (Schein, 1982). Therefore, the internal career will vary between individuals within the same organisation and even those doing the same job (Maher, 2015b).

Studies from the internal career perspective suggest that the individual's internal career needs influence their selection of specific occupations and work settings (Derr and Laurent, 1989; Chompookum and Brooklyn Derr, 2004). These studies contend that organisations whose culture and values do not fulfill an individual's internal career needs; are likely to find that they will be unable to retain these individuals in the long term (Schein, 1990). This may lead to dysfunctional organisational outcomes such as reduced organisational commitment and high turnover (Schein, 1978; Tschopp et al., 2014).

Organisational culture has been widely discussed in terms of its link with, leadership (Block 2003), performance (Ogbonna and Harris 2002) learning (Aksu and Özdemir 2005), empowerment (Beil-Hildebrand, 2002) and corporate governance (Volonté, 2015). Relatively little prior work has explored organisational culture impact on managerial internal career needs in small social enterprises; despite increasing number of research reporting on processes and governance structures of social enterprise organisations (Spear, et al., 2009, iDomenico, et al., 2010). Thus, the exploration of organisational culture in small social enterprises will contribute to our understanding of the organisation norms and beliefs that impacts on managerial internal career needs.

DEFINITIONS OF ORGANISATIONAL CULTURE

Definitions of organisational culture often refer to 'the way we do things around here,' 'the way we think about things round here', or 'the commonly held values and beliefs held within an organisation' (Hudson, 1999). The concept of organisational culture was eluded as early as the Hawthorne studies in 1920's which described work group culture and the influence of the social, physical and psychological environment on workers. However, organisational culture gained momentum in the early 1970's when academics and researchers began to examine the key to organisations thriving in turbulent comparative times. Peters and Waterman (1982) argued that there are a number of common characteristics which are not policies or work practices but rather aspects of organisational culture.

According to Schein (1985) organisational culture is the pattern of shared basic assumptions—invented, discovered, or developed by a given group as it learns to cope with its problems of external adaptation and internal integration—that has worked well enough to be considered valid and, therefore, to be taught to new members as the correct way to perceive, think, and feel in relation to those problems. Schein (1985, 1997) stressed that organisational culture is the key to organisational excellence and therefore, top management play a crucial role in embedding organisational culture.

Cleland (1994) argue that organisational culture are 'shared explicit and implicit agreements among organisational members as to what is important in behavior, as well as attitudes expressed in values, beliefs, standards, and social and management practices'.

Alvesson (2012), presents organisational culture as 'constellation of implicit and emergent symbols, beliefs, values, behavioural norms and ways of working that shape and are shaped by individual and corporate actions and reflect underlying assumptions about social reality'.

These definitional variations are recognised as reflecting underlying differences in author's understanding and interpretation of the concept of organisational culture. What is clear is that, organisational culture is recognised as the hob of organisational life; the philosophies, attitudes, beliefs, behaviours and practices that define an organisation. It also determines how an organisation functions; within a particular sector. The organisational culture may reflect characteristics that differentiate one social enterprise from another, ranging from behavioural norms to models of service delivery.

THE CONCEPT OF SOCIAL ENTERPRISE

Social enterprises are businesses that are set up to improve communities, people's life chances, or the environment. They have explicit social aims and objectives. They undertake trading activities to generate income and profits. They reinvest a significant proportion of their profits to achieve their social activities. Social enterprises are present in almost every sector of the economy, including banking, insurance, agriculture, education and health and social services (NVCO, 2016) The main difference between a social enterprise and a commercial enterprise is that there are a number of individuals that manage a social enterprise on behalf of the community it serves with the interests of the community at the forefront of decision-making. Decisions are not made for individual or shareholders profit (Dart, 2004; Spear & Bidet, 2005).

Since the late 1970s, the concept of social enterprise has achieved policy recognition in many countries. These types of social businesses became more prominent in the United States during the late 1970s and 1980s in response to the economic downturn and major cutbacks in government spending (.Crimmins and Keil (1983) . According to various scholars such as Crimmins and Keil (1983) and Eikenberry and Kluver (2004) third sector organisations saw commercial revenue as a means of replacing government funding. This paved the way for the emergence of social enterprise as a widely accepted concept of addressing social and environmental issues due to a necessity resulting out of state reduction in funding.

Social enterprises in Europe also gained momentum during the economic downturn in the 1970's. As the downturn led to cuts in government budgets across the continent, reducing the states' ability to provide unemployment assistance and job reintegration. In response to the void left by the reduction in government public services funding, several third sector organisations chose to focus their efforts on providing job-training and work-integration programmes which often had social-enterprise, characteristics (Lyon and Sepulveda, 2009). Over the past four decade social enterprises have rapidly expanded and are linked to a range of government agendas particularly in the UK (Office of the Third Sector, 2009). A variety of initiatives introduced to boost the sector included the introduction of the Social Enterprise Unit by the UK Department of Trade and Industry in 2002 who defined social enterprises as:

businesses with primarily social objectives whose surpluses are principally reinvested for that purpose in the business or in the community, rather than being driven by the need to maximise profit for share-holders and owners (DTI, 2002:7).

The DTI definition places a strong emphasis on reinvesting profit back into the business or the community that it serves rather than maxising profits for shareholders and owners. This is fundamentally the UK social enterprise model. Most social enterprises in the UK are part of the third sector, they are non-government organisations with 50 per cent or more of their income raised from income service provision, trading activities, hire of facilities, fees for goods and trading to meet social goals and principally reinvest surpluses in the organisation or community (NVCO, 2008). Social enterprises have been identified as vital to the development and delivery of innovative ways of tackling social and environmental issues which cannot be resolved through private and public sector mechanisms. There is increasing interest in promoting social enterprises and the social and economic impact of these organisations. It has been argued that social enterprises can encourage greater efficiency, as well as an entrepreneurial approach to promote innovation and improve quality of service delivery to communities (Department of Health, 2010; National Audit Office, 2011).

With rapid expansion of small social enterprise organisations, it is timely to examine the impact of this organisation's culture on managerial internal career needs. Particularly, as small social enterprises are seeking to understand how to sustain managerial retention stratagems that are not linked to salaries and pay increments (Coetzee and Schreuder, 2008; Guan et al., 2013, Maher, 2015a). This chapter focuses on exploring to what extent organisational culture influences managerial internal career needs in small social enterprises. The chapter comprises of five sections, which are outlined below:

Section one outlines a brief background of the development of social enterprises, the concept of an internal career and the rationale for investigating the impact of organisational culture on small social enterprise managerial internal career needs.

Section two reviews the literature on organisational culture typologies (Deal and Kennedy (1982), Schein (1985), Handy (1985) and Hofstede et al., (1990)), typologies of organisational culture, and highlighting the contributions they have made in this field of research.

Section three explains the research design, and provides a detailed account of the primary, secondary data collection and analysis. Subsequently, it discusses issues regarding methodological rigor and ethical considerations related to the research.

Section four provides findings from key informants on the impact of organisational culture on managerial internal career needs in organisations.

Section five discusses conclusions and makes recommendation's and suggestions for future research.

LITERATURE REVIEW

For the past number of decades, most academics and researchers studying organisations suggest that the concept of culture is the practices that organisations develop around their handling of people, promoted values and statement of belief (Schein, 2004); for individuals the organisational culture is the glue that binds them to the organisation. Organisational culture is essential in determining managers' commitment to the organisation. The review of organisational culture typologies within this chapter aim to detail an unbiased overview of various organisational culture typologies, highlighting the contributions they have made in this field of research. For instance, Deal and Kennedy's (1982) identified four types of organisational culture: The Tough-Guy Macho culture, The Work Hard/Play Hard Culture, The Bet your Company Culture and The Process Culture.

The Tough-Guy Macho culture is a culture where employees take high risks and receive feedback on their actions. There are high workload and demand from employees but rewards and bonuses are usually very high. In the work hard/play culture employees takes fewer risks and receive fast feedback. They are also required to be highly active and positive most of the time. In the bet your company culture employees takes 'big stakes' decisions but results are known after a very long period of years. The process culture reflects organisations employees' takes no risks, very limited feedback and they are more concerned with how the work is done rather than what is the end result. Deal and Kennedy (2000) argues that most organisations adopt the essential positive characteristics of all four types of culture which helps guarantee top performance.

Schein (1985) suggest three levels of organisational culture. First level includes artifacts or physical attributes such as organisational structure and processes. The second level deals with organisational mission statements, strategies, goals, attitudes, feelings, functioning beliefs throughout the organisation. The third level incorporates elements of culture which are not visible, such as, symbols, ceremonies, stories, slogans, behaviours, dress, unspoken rules that employees are not consciously aware of but may provide explanations why things are done in a particular way in the organisation.

Handy (1985) distinguishes organisational culture by the nature of relationships between the organisation and individuals and the importance of power and hierarchy. Handy (1985) proposed four types of culture namely: 'Power culture', 'Role culture', 'Task culture' and 'Person culture'.

Power culture is like a 'web' that spreads out from the centre to the rest of the organisation (Handy, 1985). The organisation operates within few formalised rules so trust is placed in the leader by employees. In organisations with power culture, performance is judged on results. They can appear tough and abrasive and their successes can be accompanied by low morale and high turnover as individuals fail or opt out of the competitive atmosphere. Working in such organisations requires that employees correctly anticipate what is expected of them from the power holder and perform accordingly. If the organisation leader gets this culture right, it can result in a happy, work environment that in turn can lead to employee's commitment to organisational goals and objectives. Getting it wrong can lead to staff dissatisfaction and sometimes lead to a high employee turnover.

Role cultures are built on detailed organisational structures which are typically tall (not flat) with a long chain of command. A consequence is that decision-making in role cultures can often be very slow and the organisation is less likely to take risks general lack of effort and enthusiasm.

Organisation with a role culture is characterised by strong functional or specialised areas coordinated by a narrow band of senior management at the top and a high degree of formalisation and standardisation; the work of the functional areas and the interactions between them are controlled by rules and procedures defining the job. For employees, the role culture offers security and the opportunity to acquire specialist expertise; performance up to a required standard is rewarded on the appropriate pay scale, and possibly by promotion within the functional or specialist area. Such people will be content in this culture only as senior managers. However, this type of culture is frustrating for ambitious people who are power orientated, want control over their work or are more interested in results than process.

Task culture is job or project-oriented. Individuals find that this culture offers a high degree of autonomy, team working and mutual respect based on ability rather than on status. This culture values creativity and enthusiasm. Most managers, certainly at the middle and junior levels are found to prefer to work in the task culture, with its emphasis on team work, rewards for results and a merging of individual and team objectives. It is most in tune with the current trends of, individual freedom and low status differentials in some small social enterprises (Maher, 2016).

Person culture exists to serve and assist individuals within the organisation without any super-ordinate objectives. In organisations with person cultures, individuals see themselves as unique and superior to the organisation. The individual is the focal point; if there is an organisational structure, it exists only to serve and assist the individuals within it, to further their own personal career interests. Person culture organisations rely on the specialist knowledge of the employees. Person cultures are mostly found in organisations where there is an opportunity for employees to develop their specialist skills; for instance, consultants working in organisations and freelance workers often prefer the person culture. An organisation with a person culture is often a collection of individuals who happen to be working for the same organisation. It is not often that we find an organisation in which the person culture predominated however; there are individuals whose personal preferences are for this type of organisational culture (Lacey Bryant, 1999).

There is a tendency to take Handy's (1985) four cultures as fixed or 'given'. None of the four types of culture can claim to be better or superior than the other; they are each suited to different types of organisations' circumstances. Most organisations tend to adopt a mixture of cultures (Lugosi and Bray, 2008) and in Handy's (1993) view each culture is suited to different types of circumstances, including different types of personal values and career needs.

Hofstede et al. (1990) examined organisational/ corporate cultures from the perspective of practices, i.e. patterns of behaviour and identified dimensions of practices' for organisational cultures ('P' stands for 'practices'), which are described as follows:

P1: Process-oriented versus results-oriented: In process-oriented organisation units cultures individuals perceive themselves as avoiding risks and making only a limited effort in their jobs. In the results-oriented cultures individuals perceive themselves as comfortable in unfamiliar situations, and put in a maximal effort, while each day is felt to bring new challenges.

P2: Employee-oriented versus job-oriented: In employee-oriented cultures individuals feel their personal problems are taken into account that the organisation takes a responsibility for employee welfare, and that important decisions tend to be made by groups or senior management teams. In the job-oriented organisation units individuals experience a strong pressure to complete the job. They perceive the organisation as only interested in the work employees do, not their personal needs.

P3: Parochial versus professional: Members of parochial cultures feel the organisation's norms influence their behaviour at work and outside work. Individuals believe the organisation will always consider their home and work needs. Members of professional cultures consider their private lives their own business; they feel the organisation employs them on the basis of job competence only.

P4: Open system versus closed system: In the open system organisation units' members consider both the organisation and its people open to newcomers. This means that almost anyone would fit into the organisation, and new employees only need a few days to feel integrated. In the closed system organisation units, the organisation and its people fit into the organisation, and new employees need a long time to feel welcomed.

P5: Loose versus tight control: Individuals in loose control organisation units feel that no one thinks of costs, meeting times are flexible, and jokes about the organisation and the job are frequent. Individuals in tight control organisation units describe their work environment as cost-conscious, meeting times are kept punctually, and jokes about the organisation and the job are rare.

P6: Normative versus pragmatic: In normative organisation units individuals correctly follow organisational procedures and business ethics which are more important than results. In the pragmatic organisation units, there is a major emphasis on meeting the customer's needs. Results are more important than correct procedures, and in matters of business ethics, a pragmatic rather than a dogmatic attitude prevails.

The review of organisational culture typologies show that the concept of 'organisational culture' can be viewed as a metaphorical construct (Morgan, 1998) created by psychologists, sociologists and management theorists to provide 'meaning' in the study of organisations. These typologies demonstrate that organisational culture gives organisations a sense of identity which are determined, through the organisation's rituals, beliefs, meanings, values, norms and language. Therefore, typologies of organisational culture tend to classify organisations by a single dominant culture type (unitarist approach) or by the existence of internal sub-cultures within the organisation, a pluralist view point (Van Maanen and Barley, 1985). As a result, typologies of organisational culture may ignore specific contextual and possible 'distinct' cultural attributes of organisations. For instance, small social enterprises do not always adopt a single type of culture. They often have cultures and sub-cultures which are developed from their historical background, mission, governance and values (Hofstede, 1998). Organisational culture can place strong pressure on individuals to change their values. Therefore adopting any typology of organisational culture as a starting point for the research may channel discussions along pre-determined paths. As a result, the study seeks to identify whether any elements of these typologies discussed above are identifiable in small social enterprises.

METHODOLOGY

The research strategy for the study was informed by the purpose of the study, which emphasises an understanding of manager's internal careers within the context of small social enterprises and to answer the research question: Does organisational culture impact on the internal career needs of managers? Also, consideration about the level of knowledge that has been developed in the area of the research was also a contributory factor, in the decision to adopt a case study research strategy (Rowley, 2002; Stake, 2006; Yin.2009; Welch et al., 2010). Yin (2009), points to the technically critical features of the case study strategy, in stating that it is an empirical inquiry that:

Investigates a contemporary phenomenon within its real-life context especially when…the boundaries between phenomenon and context are not clearly evident; and in which multiple sources of evidence are used (p.18).

Yin (2009) affirms that a case study approach is beneficial to an investigation which is seeking to uncover a new area of knowledge. Yin (2009) definition captures the breath and purpose of the study.

The study employed the embedded multi case study design in order to be collect data from various sources: first, documentary evidence and archival data from three case study organisations, second, semi structured interviews with managers (Lee, 1999; Maher, 2013; Bryman and Bell, 2015) and third, fieldnotes data (Ghauri and Gronhaug, 2002, Sachdeva, 2009; Bryman and Bell, 2015). This also allows the author to follow a 'replication' logic approach aims at achieving analytical rather than statistical generalisations (Yin, 2009; Welch et al., 2010). Yin (2009) argues that the generalisability of the embedded multi case study findings will increase with the number of cases included. Furthermore, the investigative approach offered by the case study strategy, facilitates a clearer exposition of organisational culture and provides insights into how organisational rituals and beliefs and norms influences managerial internal career needs in small social enterprises.

A brief profile overview of the three case study organisations that participated in the research is displayed below.

Organisation: Attis

Established in 1998 in the East Midlands region, the organisation provides support to individuals affected by substance use. Their aim is making an impact and making an impact that not only improves the health of the individual, but has a lasting positive impact on the wellbeing of their families, friends and the communities in which they live. People who use their services are not just people with drug and alcohol problems, they are partners, fathers, mothers, sisters, grandmothers, children, brothers, friends, work colleagues and carers.

The organisation structure is arranged as follows: Board of Directors, one Chief Executive Officer, a senior management team, nine project managers, project workers and an administrator.

Organisation: Boreas

Established in 1991 in the South East region, the organisation provides a 'Low Threshold - Harm Reduction' service to individuals who are experiencing problem substance use and their families. Services provided include the provision of an Outreach Service information, advice and individually tailored services to meet the Service User need, aspirations and ambitions. One to one and group sessions are available and a peer mentoring service.

The organisation structure is arranged in to a series of teams led by eight managers. Each time delivers locality based services; and the out of hour helpline delivers online and digital services across the region. These teams are supported by two administrators, Chief Executive Officer, the senior management team and the Board of Directors.

Organisation: Caerus

Established in 1991 in Yorkshire and Humber region, the organisation offers one to one counselling, support, information and advice to individuals and families who are affected by substance use. Free and confidential services are provided includes: identified focused group work sessions, substance awareness raising sessions, peer awareness groups and peer tutor therapy groups. A dynamic social enterprise that work on a locality basis, collaborating with the ex-service recipients and partner agencies in order to access the widest range of resources and create the best opportunities for service users..

The organisation structure is arranged as follows: Board of Directors, one Chief Executive Officer, the senior management team, eight operational managers, project workers and two administrators.

All three organisations were established between 1991 and 2000. This confirms that they have been operating for over 16 years, so they are well established organisations. Organisation Attis operate in the South East region, Organisation 'Y' operate in the East Midlands and Organisation Caerus operate from Yorkshire and Humber region (NVCO, 2011; Social Enterprise UK, 2011, Maher, 2015b).The use of multiple methods of data collection allows for convergence and triangulation of findings (Fick 1979; Bryman 2015).

Data were collected from the following sources:

1. Documentary evidence of the three case study organisations, such as, organisational activities, history, mission statements were examined. Examining these documents was useful to help to ascertain some of the reasons why these managers have chosen to pursue their careers in a particular social enterprise. All documents were collected with the organisation's permission, in their original forms with no modification.

Yin (2009) suggests that (except for studies of preliterate societies) documentary information is likely to be relevant to every research topic. The most important use of documents for this research was to form an overview of the context of the research (Slack and Rowley, 2000; Saunders et al., 2011; Maher, 2013) and to support evidence from other sources such as, information gathered from interviews with operational managers. Examining these organisational documents provided data that the author could not observe (Ghauri and Gronhaug, 2002; Saunders et al., 2011). Information from these documents enabled the author to develop a deeper understanding of the case study organisation's activities (Maher, 2013; Sliverman, 2013).

2. Semi-structured interviews with managers provided evidence of factors that influenced their careers in their respective organisations. The semi-structured interview approach allowed for flexibility with a preference for posing questions so the interview was more like a conversation whilst maintaining focus on issues contained in the interview guide (Healey and Rawlinson, 1994; Smith, 1995). This approach has been considered to be appropriate for the study for the following reasons:
   a. It enabled the study to gain an understanding of managers' experiences and points of view about their career in small social enterprises. In pursuit of answers to the interview questions, such as, what are your career needs? What is your long term career needs? How does your present job fit in with your long term career goal? The author was drawing inferences from answers given by managers during interviews with the aim to produce managers' views of their internal career needs.
   b. It allowed the study to gain an understanding of managers' interpretations of events (such as, organisation beliefs and values) and how these factors affect managerial careers in the sector.

Weber (1949) conceded that "the task of the social scientist is to understand events and explain them through the meanings that the individuals involved attach to their actions" (Weber 1949, in Benton and Crab, 2001, p.80). This implies that people's values and views differ and events are understood by different people differently, therefore, their perceptions are the realities that social science researchers should focus on.

The author sought permission to digitally record all interviews and all participants agreed. All interviews were stored electronically with password protection according to the UK Data Protection Act 2003 guidelines. Assurances regarding individual confidentiality were given and all research notes were available for participants to read if they wished. All ethical principles of beneficence (doing good), non-maleficence (doing no harm), autonomy (respect for self-governance) and justice (treating people equally and fairly) were upheld.

3. Fieldnotes of the physical setting where each interview took place and the development of each interview and ideas which were useful in subsequent interviews. Fieldnotes are an on-going, crucial part of collecting research data. In this research, they took the form of self-reminders about specific events during the interviews (such as participants nodding or smiling) and notes about personal reflections as well as reactions arising from and captured during the interviews. The fieldnotes data include a brief description of the physical setting where each interview took place, nonverbal cues such as postures, facial expressions, gestures, feelings and any type of behaviour or actions that might have affected the interview. The use of multiple sources of evidence allows the author to address a wide range of issues (such as, an organisation's characteristics which are not polices or procedures) that influence manager's internal career needs. The process of combining data from different sources allowed the author to understand how organisational culture, manager's experiences and motives influence their career needs. Yin (2009) affirms that, a study cannot rely on a single data collection method but will need to use multiple sources of evidence. When multiple methods are used, the researcher can place more confidence in the relationships uncovered in the research findings.

Using three sources of data source (documentary evidence, semi-structured interviews and field notes) increases the validity of the findings as the strengths of one approach compensated for the limitations of the other evidence source (Miles and Huberman, 1994; Yin, 2003, 2009). The different sources were used to validate and cross-check the research findings.

The author employed computer-assisted data analysis software (CAQDAS) package NVivo 9 to facilitate the data coding and clustering of themes. Data were imported directly from a word processing package into NVivo 9 simultaneously creating cases with each interview transcript. It provided a disciplined structure to search and analyse data.

The findings of any qualitative research are open to challenges based on questions of reliability and validity. Yin (1994) defines reliability in case studies research as follows:

the objective is to be sure that, if a later investigator followed exactly the same procedure as described by an earlier investigator and conducted the same case study all over again, the later investigator should arrive at the same findings and conclusions. (p.36)

In other words, the reliability of the study is accomplished when another researcher is able to follow the 'audit trail' of the researcher so that comparable conclusions could be achieved, given the same data, similar situations and the researcher's perspective (Yin, 2009). This study was written with a view that allows sufficient detailed information so that the 'audit trail' is adequately maintained. The author has carefully recorded and explained the different stages of the research process.

FINDINGS

The primary objective of the research is to understand the extent to which organisational culture influences social enterprise manager's internal career needs. A significant finding of the study is that organisation culture such as; models of care, support for autonomist and employment opportunity for ex-service recipients, supportive team-work are major organisational culture influencing the internal careers of small social enterprises managers. In addition, senior management laissez-faire attitude to managerial internal career needs were identified as an unspoken organisational culture impacting managerial internal career needs. Each of these factors is discussed below.

Organisation Models of Care

Models of Care (MoC) are a multifaceted concept, which broadly defines the way an organisation services are delivered to service users. It can be applied to support services or client's case management. An organisation's MoC could include services such as, extended therapy sessions, sports activities, training and employment skills and self-efficacy groups for clients. These services are provided according to the service recipients' needs and pace of recovery (Wardle, 2013). Some managers stated that they have chosen to pursue their careers in their present organisation due to the organisation's specific MoC.

The model of care here is to meet clients' individual needs. That's rewarding for me. Sometimes within the client's treatment plan the client long term needs are not really addressed in the statutory sector. So it has conflict for me. So for me the organisation's models of care are important. I prefer focusing on meeting client's individual needs rather than being bound by [funder's] requirements (Participant 4).

I knew about the organisation because I did some training here before and I liked what they do here. I liked their models of care for clients ... the inclusion of family needs when developing client's care packages. (Participant 6)

These organisations' MoC are based on therapeutic and on-going psychosocial support that allows service recipients to have a choice of treatment and to have personalised treatment programmes for each individual depending on their needs and circumstances at point of contact with the organisation. The above evidence suggests that the organisation's MoC appeal to managers' who desire the freedom from funders' stringently enforced regulations. These managers enjoy the freedom to develop services using their own initiative to put in place services based on service recipients' needs. They also expressed their responsibility for their client's recovery process (by offering long-term support services) which they want to implement without interference from the funders. They adopted a person-centered approach ('recovery is an individual journey') to client care management and service delivery; which are linked to the organisation's own culture of MoC. The results of the research suggest that MoC does differ between the case study organisations and that an organisation's specific MoC is an influencing factor on manager's developing their careers in these organisations.

Support for Autonomist

Several managers reported that the organisation's culture of supporting managers' autonomy to use their own initiative in developing and managing projects was one of the main reasons they are attracted to work in their respective organisations. Job role autonomy enhances performance through the increased scope it gives managers to use their knowledge, skills and abilities. This raises motivation, thereby enhancing managerial retention. Several of the study participants focus on the intrinsic content of the work. They tend to build their work performance around flexibility and independence of judgment.

I applied for this job when I was working at the County Council. There they [the County Council] are governed by so many red tapes. But when you are here [in this organisation] you are independent. Although you have rules they [the organisation] see a different side the real side of people not the statistics as such. They see first and foremost the person [the client] who needs help not the numbers. You then are given the freedom to tailor services to meet the needs of services users. That gives me job satisfaction ..." (Participant: 14)

I like the flexibility of planning client services. This is important for our clients. Our services are client-led. We need to be there for the clients not put up barriers to suit ourselves. I like the freedom and independence I have to decide how to tailor services to meet client needs without interference from my boss or funders. (Participant: 16)

I have the freedom here to offer the number of counselling sessions in relation to the client's needs. The freedom to choose how we work with clients not having to tick boxes as required by the [Funder] but to provide counselling sessions to suit the needs of the client. (Participant, 2)

These managers were primarily driven by the need to have the flexibility within an organisation to use their own initiatives to develop client's services. These views were expressed in the context of autonomy derived from having the freedom to develop client-centered services. These managers have the desire to develop and manage projects without direct intervention by line-managers or funding agencies.

This finding supports previous third sector career research that suggests that the sector managers often seek to work in small organisations due to the autonomy of the job role and the freedom to design and develop services (Onyx and Maclean, 1996; Alatrista and Arrowsmith, 2004; Cunningham, 2010; Maher, 2015b). These opportunities have not been found to be readily available in large bureaucratic organisations, where managerial roles are often structured in a pyramid top-down chain of command with limited flexibility for individual managers to re-design services without a long consultation process (Flynn, 2007; Radnor, 2010; Osborne et al., 2013).

Employment Opportunities for Ex- Service-Recipients

The culture of organisations providing employment and managerial opportunities for ex-service recipients was identified as an organisational culture influencing several managers' decision to pursue their managerial careers in a small social enterprise; that supported their recovery process and provided employment opportunities (Wardle, 2013). Previous authors have drawn attention to the benefits of providing ex-service recipients with employment opportunities within social care organisations (which includes third sector social enterprises) (Hoad, 2002, Neuberger, 2008; Hardill and Dwyer, 2011). The evidence suggests that it helps ex-service recipients to develop self-confidence and social networks (Lowe et al., 2007; Redman, 2012; Wardle, 2013).The fieldwork evidence suggests that the culture of providing employment opportunities for ex-service recipients within small social enterprises enabled several individuals to pursue their managerial careers in these organisations.

I started here volunteering as an ex-client. The organisation is very supportive ... they are 150% behind me. They have given me a chance to make something of my life. (Participant: 15)

I love it here. They [the organisation] gave me my life back. I've come a long way. It just gives me great pleasure knowing I can do this, manage this project, and help people in the same situation I was before. This is meaningful; this is meaningful to me anyhow. I took so much out of the system for so long, I'd like to put something back in. (Participant: 22)

The fieldwork evidence suggest that organisations that have a culture of providing employment opportunities for individuals who have been service-recipients can potentially be a catalyst in these individual's decision to pursue managerial career in these organisations . The benefits of supporting ex-service recipients who wants to pursue their careers within the organisation that has helped them in their recovery process, is that these individuals are often committed to the organisation (Hardill and Dwyer, 2011; Wardle, 2013) and wants to stay developing their careers with the organisation (Mold, 2006; Wardle, 2013), this in turn helps these organisations to retain managers in the long term.

Supportive Team-Work

Teamwork has been promoted as an important means of enhancing organisational productivity and achieving positive outcomes. A central argument for linking teamwork to organisational productivity is that it gives employees a sense of empowerment, by increasing the control they can exercise over their work (Steyn and Steyn, 2009; Reeves, Lewin, Espin, and Zwarenstein, 2011). Supportive team work enables team members to promote a wider sense of ownership work towards common goals when approaching their everyday tasks. This creates a strong team dynamic that supports small social enterprises to achieve their mission and collectively toward achieving the company's objectives.

Several managers stated that working in a supportive team and acceptance within the team and confirmation that their views are taken into consideration within the organisation's team decision making processes offers them a sense of belonging.

We work well together ... we share understanding of the purpose of our work. I like being part of a team. It gives me gives a sense of belonging. (Participant: 15)

I like the solace of knowing my team members ... very supportive. (Participant: 22)

I had some bad experiences in the past; I was in the private sector ... there it was everyman for himself. Here there's good team work. I enjoy working with my colleagues ... the team .I get on with everyone here... it's a joy to come to work. (Participant: 24)

These managers view of a supportive organisational culture is linked to being part of a team, being valued and working in an organisation where they felt their contributions are valued and needed in a supportive team environment. Managers who feel their work is valued are likely to feel more committed to their organisations and more satisfied with their jobs (Gallie, Zhou, Felstead and Green, 2012).

Laissez-Faire Attitude to Managerial Career Needs

Some study participants felt that the culture of senior management unwillingness to taken an interest in their internal career needs is very disheartening. They referred to this as Laissez-faire attitude to managerial career needs (senior management gives the least possible guidance and support to managers on how to achieve their career needs within the organisation setting) . They reported that management provides little or no interest in their career goals and values. Laissez-faire is less than ideal when a manager is new to the organisation and lack knowledge of the organisation's culture that he/she needs to understand in order to make decisions about how to pursue their internal career needs and how it fits with the organisation's objectives.

There is a very laissez-faire attitude to our career needs here. It all about targets, targets and meeting more targets. (Participant: 22)

Very little understanding of my career needs here ... never discussed. There is a lack of understanding of our [manager's] career needs. This is a major obstacle between us and senior management. (Participant: 5)

The above evidence suggests a sense of weary resignation and disappointment with some senior management lack of interest in managerial career needs. When managers sense that senior management are disinterested in their internal career needs, these managers may naturally become less focused on the quality of their work, increase their intension to leave and eventually reduce their level of commitment.

RECOMMENDATIONS

The importance of understanding, harnessing, managing and maintaining an appropriate culture in organisations cannot be underestimated in terms of its impact on managerial internal career needs. Developing appropriate measures which addresses how organisational culture supports managerial internal career needs, is an organisational issue.

However, embedding effective and supportive management culture that supports the career needs of managers falls within the remit of the Board of Directors and senior management teams of these organisations.

FUTURE RESEARCH

Organisational culture in small social enterprises hold signification potential as future research area to further explore its impact on small organisations in other sectors will provide opportunity for insightful 'cross-case synthesis' (Yin, 2009).

There is clearly a need to expand the research to take account not only of managers views but to capture different levels of staff perception within the organisation, of the influence of organisational culture on their internal career needs, including the senior management team. Inclusion of the senior management team views are also critical if we are to begin to understand the ways in which organisational culture influences senior management views of their internal career needs and their attitude towards internal career needs of those they manage.

Other areas of high potential value for organisations should be a study that examines how employees can become more effectively 'logged into' an organisation's culture. What is the value of investments in helping employees to build up their knowledge of the organisational culture? What investments are required to improve senior management understanding of employee's internal career needs?

CONCLUSION

The chapter's findings provide important insight how organisational culture is not simply a way of highlighting organisational structures and processes. It also provides insight into how organisational culture impact on managerial internal career needs in small social enterprises. There is evidence that the case study organisations adopted characteristics of Schein (1985) typology of organisational culture such as organisational mission statements, attitudes, functioning beliefs and values of managerial career needs.

Also there were evidence of Handy (1985) role culture and task culture. Managers provided evidence of how the organisation culture enabled them to achieve their internal career needs by the flexibility and autonomy the organisation allows for them to use their own initiatives to develop client's services. In addition, there were evidence of Hofstede et al., (1990) employee-orientation and open system culture in two of the case study organisations.

However, there were limited evidence of Handy's (1985) person culture, Deal and Kennedy's (1982) The Tough-Guy Macho culture, The Work Hard/Play Hard Culture, The Bet your Company Culture and The Process Culture and Hofstede et al., (1990) close system and loose versus tight control culture.

Specific contextual organisational cultural issues such as, the culture of supportive team work, organisation's MOC, consultation by the organisation before decisions are taken in teams and employment opportunities for ex-service recipients as an organisational culture were highlighted to be abetting managers internal career needs. The study suggests that it is important to understand organisational culture that not only increases experience such as autonomy, but also enhance the effectiveness of the job role.

The research also identified one particular organisational culture that managers found unsupportive of their internal career needs. Senior management laissez-faire attitude to managers' internal career needs. The study participants prefer senior management understanding of their career needs and to provide an environment that supports them.

Cross-case observations derived from the findings suggests that the case study organisations can be viewed as exhibiting elements of Schein (1985) and Handy (1985) organisational culture. These is also evidence of Hofstede et al., (1990) employee-orientated, job-orientated and open system organisational culture; with limited evidence of Deal and Kennedy's (1982) typologies of organisational culture.

In closing, the research findings have to be tempered by the limitations of the study. First, this study limited its focus to only one country (the UK). There may be a question of whether the research findings are specific to the UK or if they are more universal. Due to limited empirical research that have examined the influence of organisational culture on small social enterprises manager's internal career needs; the chapter findings are likely to have wider relevance and applicability, particularly in small social enterprises in other countries.

REFERENCES

Alvesson, M. (2012). Understanding organizational culture. *Safe Journal, 20*(4), 422–441.

Baruch, Y. (2004). Transforming careers: from linear to multidirectional career paths: organizational and individual perspectives. *Career Development International, 9*(1), 58–73. doi:10.1108/13620430410518147

Benton, T., & Craib, I. (2001). *Philosophy of social science: Philosophical issues in social thought (traditions in social theory)*. Academic Press.

Bidwell, M., & Mollick, E. (2015). Shifts and ladders: Comparing the role of internal and external mobility in managerial careers. *Organization Science, 26*(6), 1629–1645. doi:10.1287/orsc.2015.1003

Block, L. (2003). The leadership-culture connection: An exploratory investigation. *Leadership and Organization Development Journal, 24*(6), 318–334. doi:10.1108/01437730310494293

Bryman, A. (2015). *Social research methods*. Oxford University Press.

Chompookum, D., & Brooklyn Derr, C. (2004). The effects of internal career orientations on organizational citizenship behavior in Thailand. *Career Development International, 9*(4), 406–423. doi:10.1108/13620430410544355

Coetzee & Schreuder. (2008). *A multi-cultural investigation of students' career anchors at a South African higher education institution*. Academic Press.

Crimmins, J. C., & Keil, M. (1983). *Enterprise in the nonprofit sector*. Americans for the Arts.

Dart, R. (2004). The legitimacy of social enterprise. *Nonprofit Management & Leadership, 14*(4), 411–424. doi:10.1002/nml.43

Deal, T. E., & Kennedy, A. A. (1982). *Corporate cultures reading*. Addison-Wesley.

Deal, T. E., & Kennedy, A. A. (2000). *Corporate cultures: The rites and rituals of corporate life*. Da Capo Press.

Deal, T. E., Kennedy, A. A., & Peregrina, R. L. (1985). *Culturas corporativas: ritos y rituales de la vida organizacinal*. Fondo Educativo Interamericano.

DH. (2005). *Health reform in England: Update and next steps*. London: DH.

DH. (2007). *Third sector mapping*. London: DH.

DH. (2008). *World class commissioning: Vision*. London: DH.

DH (Department of Health). (1998). *Modernising Social Services - Promoting Independence, Improving Protection, Raising Standards*. London: The Stationary Office.

Eikenberry, A. M., & Kluver, J. D. (2004). The marketization of the nonprofit sector: Civil society at risk? *Public Administration Review, 64*(2), 132–140. doi:10.1111/j.1540-6210.2004.00355.x

Gallie, D., Zhou, Y., Felstead, A., & Green, F. (2012). Teamwork, skill development and employee welfare. *British Journal of Industrial Relations, 50*(1), 23–46. doi:10.1111/j.1467-8543.2010.00787.x

Ghauri, P., & Gronhaug, K. (2002). *Research Methods in Business Studies: A Practical Guide* (2nd ed.). London: Sage.

Handy, C. (1993). *Understanding organisations*. Penguin.

Harris, B. (2010). Voluntary action and the state in historical perspective. *Voluntary Sector Review, 1*(1), 25–40. doi:10.1332/204080510X496993

Healey, M. J., & Rawlinson, M. B. (1994). Interviewing techniques in business and management research. In V. J. Wass & P. E. Wells (Eds.), *Principles and Practice in* (pp. 123–146). Aldershot, UK: Business and Management Research.

Herriot, P. (1992). The career management challenge: Balancing individual and organizational needs. *Sage (Atlanta, Ga.)*.

Hofstede, G. (1998). Identifying organizational subcultures: An empirical approach. *Journal of Management Studies, 35*(1), 1–12. doi:10.1111/1467-6486.00081

Hofstede, G. (2001). *Culture's Consequences: Comparing Values, Behaviors, Institutions and Organizations across Nations*. Thousand Oaks, CA: Sage.

Hofstede, G., Neuijen, B., Ohayv, D. D., & Sanders, G. (1990). Measuring Organizational Cultures: A Qualitative and Quantitative Study across Twenty Cases. *Administrative Science Quarterly, 35*(2), 286–316. doi:10.2307/2393392

Lacey Bryant, S. (1999). Information services for primary care: The organizational culture of General Practice and the information needs of partnerships and Primary Care Groups. *Health Libraries Review, 16*(3), 157–165. doi:10.1046/j.1365-2532.1999.00223.x PMID:10620850

Lok, P., & Crawford, J. (2004). The effect of organisational culture and leadership style on job satisfaction and organisational commitment: A cross-national comparison. *Journal of Management Development, 23*(4), 321–338. doi:10.1108/02621710410529785

Lugosi, P., & Bray, J. (2008). Tour guiding, organisational culture and learning: Lessons from an entrepreneurial company. *International Journal of Tourism Research, 10*(5), 467–479. doi:10.1002/jtr.681

Lyon, F., & Sepulveda, L. (2009). Mapping social enterprise: Past approaches, challenges and future direction. *Social Enterprise Journal, 5*(1), 83–94. doi:10.1108/17508610910956426

Maher, C. (2009). Managing Career Development in the Not for Profit Sector. Business Leadership Review, 6(4).

Maher, C. (2013). A Qualitative Case Study Approach to Understanding Third Sector Managers' Career Orientations. Work Based Learning e-Journal International, 3(2).

Maher, C. (2015a). Social Enterprise Manager's Career Path Preferences. *International Journal of Globalisation and Small Business, 7*(1).

Maher, C. (2015b). *Public Policies Impact on Third Sector Social Enterprises in UK Regions.* IGI Global.

Maher, C. (2016). Career anchors of social enterprise managers in the UK – an empirical analysis, *J. International Business and Entrepreneurship Development, 9*(4), 398–416. doi:10.1504/JIBED.2016.080019

Miles, M. B., & Huberman, A. M. (1994). *Qualitative Data Analysis* (2nd ed.). Thousand Oak, CA: Sage.

Mold, A. (2006). The welfare branch of the alternative society? The work of drug organisations Release, 19671978. *20 Century British History, 17*(1), 50–73. doi:10.1093/tcbh/hwi064

Ng, T. W., & Feldman, D. C. (2014). Subjective career success: A meta-analytic review. *Journal of Vocational Behavior, 85*(2), 169–179. doi:10.1016/j.jvb.2014.06.001

NVCO. (2008). *The UK Civil Society Almanac.* London: NVCO Publications.

NVCO. (2009). *The UK Civil Society Almanac.* London: NVCO Publications.

NVCO. (2010). *The UK Civil Society Almanac.* London: NVCO Publication.

NVCO. (2016). *The UK Civil Society Almanac.* London: NVCO Publication.

Ogbonna, E., & Harris, L. C. (2002). Managing organisational culture: Insights from the hospitality industry. *Human Resource Management Journal, 12*(1), 33–53. doi:10.1111/j.1748-8583.2002.tb00056.x

Peters, T. J., & Waterman, R. H. (1982). *Search of Excellence.* New York: Harper and Row.

Reeves, S., Lewin, S., Espin, S., & Zwarenstein, M. (2011). *Interprofessional teamwork for health and social care* (Vol. 8). John Wiley & Sons.

Ridley-Duff, R., & Bull, M. (2015). Understanding social enterprise: Theory and practice. *Sage (Atlanta, Ga.).*

Rowley, J. (2002). Using case studies in research. *Management Research News, 25*(2), 16 – 27.

Saunders, M., Lewis, P., & Thornhill, A. (2011). *Research Methods for Business Students.* Harlow: Pearson Education Ltd.

Schein, E. H. (1978). *Career dynamics: Matching individual and organizational needs* (Vol. 6834). Addison Wesley Publishing Company.

Schein, E. H. (1982). *What to observe in a group: Reading book for human relations training*. Bethel, ME: NTL Institute.

Schein, E. H. (1985). Defining organizational culture. *Classics of Organization Theory, 3*, 490-502.

Smith, J. A. (1995). Semi-structured interviewing and qualitative analysis. In Rethinking Methods of Psychology. Sage. doi:10.4135/9781446221792.n2

Spear, R., & Bidet, E. (2005). Social enterprise for work integration in 12 European countries: A descriptive analysis. *Annals of Public and Cooperative Economics, 76*(2), 195–231. doi:10.1111/j.1370-4788.2005.00276.x

Stake, R. E. (2006). *Multiple case studies analysis*. New York: The Guildford press.

Steyn, E., & Steyn, T. F. J. (2009). The challenge to incorporate teamwork as a managerial competency: The case of mainstream South African newsrooms. *Journal of Media Business Studies, 6*(2), 47–65. doi:10.1080/16522354.2009.11073484

Tschopp, C., Grote, G., & Gerber, M. (2014). How career orientation shapes the job satisfaction–turnover intention link. *Journal of Organizational Behavior, 35*(2), 151–171. doi:10.1002/job.1857

Volonté, C. (2015). Culture and corporate governance: The influence of language and religion in Switzerland. *Management International Review, 55*(1), 77–118. doi:10.1007/s11575-014-0216-5

Wardle, I. (2013). The Drug Treatment Workforce: Lifeline Project. Academic Press.

Welch, C., Piekkari, R., Plakoyiannaki, E., & Paavilainen-Mäntymäki, E. (2010). Theorising from case studies: Towards a pluralist future for international business research. *Journal of International Business Studies, 42*(5), 740–762. doi:10.1057/jibs.2010.55

Yin, R. K. (2009). Case Study Research Design and Methods (4th ed.). Sage.

ADDITIONAL READING

Akin Aksu, A., & Özdemir, B. (2005). *Individual learning and organization culture in learning organizations: five star hotels in Antalya region of Turkey*. Managerial Auditing.

Babbie, E. (2007) The practice of social research (11ed). Belmont: Thomson

Beil-Hildebrand, M. B. (2002). Theorising culture and culture in context: Institutional excellence and control. *Nursing Inquiry, 9*(4), 257–274. doi:10.1046/j.1440-1800.2002.00156.x PMID:12460421

Cabinet Office. (2010). *The Compact*. London: Cabinet Office.

Cabinet Office. (2010). *National Survey of Third Sector Organisations (2010)*. Office for Civil Society.

Cabinet Office. (2011) Cabinet Office Website, 'Big Society', www.cabinetoffice.gov.uk/bigsociety

Creswell, J. W. (2013). *Research design: Qualitative, quantitative, and mixed methods approaches*. Sage publications.

Deakin, N. (2001). *In search of civil society*. Palgrave Macmillan.

Department for Business. Innovation & Skills. 2010. Local Growth: Rearising Every Place's Potential. Cm7961. London: TSO.

Di Domenico, M., Haugh, H., & Tracey, P. (2010). Social bricolage: Theorizing social value creation in social enterprises. *Entrepreneurship theory and practice, 34(4), 681-703.*

Evans, G. (2000). Measure for measure: Evaluating performance and the arts organisation. *Studies in Cultures, Organizations and Societies*, 6(2), 243–266. doi:10.1080/10245280008523549

Flick, U. (2009). *An introduction to Qualitative Research*. London: Sage.

Funding Commission. (2010). *Funding the Future: A ten-year framework for civil society*. London: NVCO.

Gardiner, B., Martin, R., Sunley, P., & Tyler, P. (2013). Spatially Unbalanced Growth in the British Economy. *Journal of Economic Geography*, *13*(6), 889–928. doi:10.1093/jeg/lbt003

Gibbs, G. R. (2007). *Analysing Qualitative Data*. London: Sage. doi:10.4135/9781849208574

Gomm, R., Hamersley, M., & Foster, P. (2008). *Case study method*. London: Sage.

Hamnett, C. (2011). The Reshaping of the British Welfare System and Its Implications for Geography and Geographers. *Progress in Human Geography*, *35*(2), 147–152. doi:10.1177/0309132510394121

Hynes, B. (2009) Growing the social enterprise – issues and challenges, *Social Ent Kendall, J., & Knapp, M. R. J. (1996). The voluntary sector in the UK Eerprise* Journal, vol. 5, no. 2, pp. 114-125.

Lyon, F., & Sepulveda, L. (2012). Social Enterprise Support Policies: distinctions and challenges. In R. Blackburn & M. Schaper (Eds.), *Government, SMEs and Entrepreneurship. Development: Policy, Practice and Challenges*. Farnham: Gower.

Martin, J. (Ed.), *Organizational Culture* (pp. 31–53). Newbury Park, Cal.: Sage.

Mason, C., Kirkbride, J., & Bryde, D. (2007). From stakeholders to institutions: The changing face of social enterprise governance theory. *Management Decision*, *45*(2), 284–301. doi:10.1108/00251740710727296

Miles, M.B. & Huberman, A.M. (1985) Analysing qualitative data: a source book for new methods. Beverly Hills. CA: sage.

Mold, A. (2012). From the alternative society to the Big Society? Voluntary organisations and drug services in Britain, 1960s2010s. *Voluntary Sector Review*, *3*(1), 51–66. doi:10.1332/204080512X632728

Mold, A., & Berridge, V. (2010). *Voluntary action and illegal drugs: Health and society in Britain since the 1960's*. Basingstoke: Palgrave Macmillan. doi:10.1057/9780230274693

Office of the Third Sector (OTS). (2009) National Survey of Third Sector Organisations: Further information on Social Enterprises in the NSTSO, Cabinet Office, http://www.nstso.com/GetFile. aspx?Guid=4bc541d7-4ac3-4429-a405- available at: www. third sector. co. UK (accessed 1 January 2015041352ca9226 Silverman, D. (2013) *Doing qualitative research: A practical handbook*. SAGE Publications Limited.

Social Enterprise Coalition. (2010). *State of Social Enterprise*. London: Social Enterprise Coalition.

KEY TERMS AND DEFINITIONS

Career Management: The combination of structured planning and the active self-management of one's own professional career development through a partnership between organisation and the employee.

Career: An occupation, profession or all the roles you undertake throughout your life, including education, training, paid and unpaid work.

Internal Career: An individual's values, motivation, goals, aspirations and interest and view of their career orientations and decisions between personal and professional life.

Manager: A person responsible for managing, controlling or administering tasks or a certain subset of a company or group of staff.

Organisational Culture: A system of shared assumptions collective values, beliefs and principles of organizational members and management style, and national culture;, which governs how people behave in organisation.

Social Capital: Refers to the underlying networks, norms and social ownership structures that bind stakeholders together in pursuit of a common (social) purpose.

Social Enterprises: Enterprises that trade to meet social/environmental goals (Department of Trade and Industry, 2002).

The Third Sector: Includes a very diverse range of organisations comprising non-governmental and non-profit-making organisations or associations, including charities, voluntary and community groups, cooperatives and mutual benefits societies.

Section 4

Chapter 15

The Flexibility of the Workplace and Working Time:
Analysis of Employees' Preferences in Poland

Beata Skowron-Mielnik
Poznan University of Economics and Business, Poland

Grzegorz Wojtkowiak
Poznan University of Economics and Business, Poland

ABSTRACT

Organisations are more and more interested in ensuring flexibility of working time and space for their employees. This approach is enforced both by labour market volatility and company strategic plans, e.g. relocation. However, employers begin to realise that employees' flexibility is limited. While the reasons behind it might be objective (lack of legal regulations, commuting expenses), in some cases it is the employees' personal views that stand in the way. In such situation the company is much more limited in its attempts to offer a greater flexibility to its workforce. The research problem that arises here is as follows: is it possible to define the characteristics and situations in which employees are willing to accept flexible conditions of working time and space? Therefore, the aim of the study is to indicate how to increase work flexibility on the side of employees. The study focuses on four areas, i.e. changing the place of residence due to work, frequent business trips, long commuting and flexible work arrangements.

INTRODUCTION

"For employers, workforce flexibility refers to the ability to use labour in a more adaptable and variable way. For employees, flexibility refers particularly to the degree of choice available in their work arrangements" (Blyton & Jenkins, 2007, p. 74). While work flexibility can bring tangible benefits to the both parties, the diversity of available solutions and interests has put employers in a rather less comfortable situation. They are forced to adjust their working patterns not only to their business needs (e.g.

DOI: 10.4018/978-1-5225-2480-9.ch015

flexibility of production processes or customer requirements), but also to the needs of their workforce. In turn, employees analyse the available work arrangements from their own perspective, typically in terms of work-life balance (Bailyn, Drago, & Kochan, 2001). It is considered to be one of the key EVP (Employee Value Proposition) elements in building up employees' commitment to their organisation, so welcomed by employers (Aon, 2015; Aon, 2016; Gallup, 2013).

Companies cannot afford not to take into account employees' preferences, particularly in the so-called employee's labour market, as the Polish market has been known to be called these days. As cyclical labour market research in Poland shows, the employment rate has continued to grow while the working age population has been dropping (NBP, 2016). The unemployment rate has fallen below its historical low in 2008 and currently amounts to 6.3%, reflecting both a high demand for labour and a decreasing labour supply. This drop is partially compensated by increased market participation among the youngest and oldest populations of employees; however, the rising participation cannot offset the demographic decline in the number of working people (ageing society). Employers are aware of this change – 77% of the studied entities believe that the Polish labour market is shifting towards employee's domination (HRM Partners, 2015). Consequently, it is more and more difficult to recruit candidates, whose expectations are rising also in terms of work organisation. This refers particularly to talents and those representing younger generations of employees, who pay more and more attention to working conditions, including working time and place of work (Gibson, Greenwood, & Murphy, 2009; Weyland, 2011). At the same time, studies conducted in Poland reveal that the Generation Y employees value work stability and job security, which makes them less keen on having as high a degree of flexibility as their peers in other European countries and the US (Kmiotek, 2015).

In view of the above, a question arises: is it possible to draw conclusions about preferences of job applicants or employees regarding work flexibility, based on demographic characteristics and competence? With these features in mind, is it possible to select people whose preferences are consistent with the employer's needs or to offer them a solution acceptable to them? Can a workforce be recruited whose flexibility profile complies with that of the company, as enforced by the character of its business operations? The article tries to define the characteristics and situations in which employees agree to flexible conditions in terms of working time and space.

The authors deliberately did not consider legal aspects of flexibility in their analysis due to the variety of legislations of different countries around the world.

BACKGROUND

Organisational flexibility is a concept which has been defined and discussed by management science and in managerial practice for many years, with H.I. Ansoff (1965), H.W. Volberd (1997), Sushil (2001) and R.C. Pathak (2005) as its researchers (in: Osbert-Pociecha, 2011, pp. 136-137). It is a multifaceted term which refers to a variety of issues and solutions, differently approached by entrepreneurs, employees and governmental institutions, often used ideologically to reflect the views and understanding of the value of flexibility (Zeytinoglu, Cooke, & Mann, 2009). The diversity of the concept of flexibility makes it difficult to operationalise actions aimed at its promotion and determine the management methods and tools used in practice to achieve flexibility; its development is, however, one of the basic dimensions of the newly emerging paradigm of organisational management (Volberda, 1998, p. 13), next to securing effectiveness and quality. Due to the duality of its nature, flexibility is an equivocal term – it is associated both with changes and with stability that comes afterwards, only to be disturbed again and modified even further. As a feature of the organisation, flexibility is to ensure a smooth and the quickest possible transition through changes in between the consecutive periods of stability. The organisation may therefore be recognised as flexible not because of its ability to bring about changes but its ability to incorporate changes, which should occur spontaneously, by itself, without the need for major organisational operations. Approach to change is crucial here (is it provoked or managed), together with the source of resources (external or internal) which are necessary to ensure adequate flexibility, as discussed by H.I. Ansoff, D.J. Eppink or H.W. Volberd and others, in their concepts of flexibility.

Definition dilemmas arise in connection with labour flexibility recognised as flexible resources and as the basis for the flexibility of the organisation as a whole (Karuppan, 2004). As a feature of the organisation it takes into account the variability of external conditions and needs of the organisation and its employees, and describes labour development which is as much innovative, non-standard and deregulated, as it is adaptable and unstable (Thomas, 2009, p.13). The object it refers to is also diversified, as the category of flexibility is applied to work, labour market, employment, human capital and human resources. Out of various classifications of labour flexibility (Beardwell & Holden, 2001; Garsten, 2008; Grudney & Sarvutyte, 2007; Krol, 2014; Martinez-Sanchez, Vela-Jimenez, Perez-Perez, & de-Luis-Carnicer, 2008; Schief, 2010), two seem to be essential, i.e. that of space and type. The former denotes external flexibility which covers developments occurring in the labour market and between the organisation and the labour market, including recruitment of new employees and dismissal of those whose services are no longer required, and internal flexibility focused on changes of working conditions within the organisation. These two dimensions of flexibility are also respectively called macro- and microeconomic flexibility, with the first one interpreted as a way of ensuring the balance in the external labour market, and the second as the organisation's adaptability in labour resources management. The both types of flexibility cannot be separated, as they depend on and influence each other, i.e. a rise in the micro-scale flexibility will result in an increased macro-scale flexibility; similarly, it would be difficult to develop internal flexibility without taking external flexibility into account.

In terms of macro- and microeconomic flexibility, another classification may be proposed which focuses on what is to be made more flexible: number of employees, forms of employment and working time (numerical or quantitative); tasks/responsibilities, competence, working place, occupational and spatial mobility (functional or qualitative); or remuneration and labour costs (financial or payroll flexibility). Some authors (Grudney & Sarvutyte, 2007; Eamets & Masso, 2004) indicate that some of these flexibilities exist only in the macro, while others only in the micro terms. In fact, all of them may be found in the internal and external dimension, and all of them have a different effect on each other. For example, flexitime may be applied as a specific solution in a company, but it is at the same time regulated by the labour law as a macroeconomic phenomenon; on the other hand, the introduction of flexible forms of employment, e.g. contracts of mandate, is reflected in the flexibility of labour costs. Macroeconomic flexibility may be described as institutional, represented in formal regulations (labour regulations on working time, telework, pay). Microeconomic flexibility is organisational in its nature, as exemplified by the respective solutions implemented by organisations (flexible working hours, remote, part-time or temporary work, self-employment). The diversity of solutions proposed by organisations is reflected in numerous studies conducted in the recent years (Brown, Wong, & McNamara, 2009; Eurofound, 2016; Houseman, 2001; WorldatWork, 2015). Specific proposals depend on a number of exogenous (phenomena at the level of the economy) and endogenous (phenomena at the level of the organisation) conditions (Anxo & O'Reilly, 2000; Krol, 2014), which to a bigger or smaller extent force or encourage companies to make changes in their models of work. The conditions result from the organisation's internal and external environment, and are generated by a number of legal, economic, technological and social factors. The last group of factors encompasses employees' individual characteristics and preferences that have an increasing impact on work organisation and which determine benefits for the both parties to the employment relationship (Eurofound, 2015; Zeytinoglu, 2005).

Zeytinoglu, Cooke, and Mann (2009) point to two most recent streams of literature devoted to flexibility. One discusses flexibility as demand-driven, i.e. a strategic initiative of employers to enhance business requirements of the firm. The other analyses flexibility as supply-driven, where employees have the ability to influence decisions about the nature of their work and where they, particularly women, can demand flexible work schedules to ensure a greater work-life balance. "Flexibility is about an employee and an employer making changes to when, where and how a person will work to better meet individual and business needs. Flexibility enables both individual and business needs to be met through making changes to the time (when), location (where) and manner (how) in which an employee works. Flexibility should be mutually beneficial to both the employer and employee and result in superior outcomes" (Aequus Partners, 2010). "A meta-analysis by Baltes, Briggs, Huff, Wright, and Neuman (1999) found that flexible work schedules had positive effects on both job satisfaction and satisfaction with work schedule. In a study of the 'virtual office', Callentine's (1995) participants attributed an increase in job satisfaction to increased flexibility in the location and timing of their work. Teleworkers in Quaid and Lagerberg's 1992 study (cited in Standen, Daniels, & Lamond, 1999) also reported higher levels of job satisfaction. In their 2007 meta-analysis, Gajendran and Harrison found that telework was associated with increased job satisfaction and reduced intentions to turnover, with these relationships partially mediated by lower levels of work-life conflict" (Beauregard & Henry, 2009).

In view of the above, the following research problem may be formed: when deciding about work organisation, to what extent is the organisation limited by its employees' needs? If flexible work arrangements are to motivate employees, they cannot be imposed purely for business reasons. However, if flexibility is necessary in order to ensure competitiveness, meet hard technological conditions or customer requirements, the company has to find employees willing to accept the solutions it offers. Organisations may find it easier if they know which characteristics to look for and objectively verify either in a recruitment process or workforce analysis. Given the development prospects for the Polish labour market (deepening labour shortages), key groups of employees include women, young people entering the labour market, people over 50, and, regardless of age and sex, people with higher education and a high potential for personal growth (NBP, 2016). Increased participation of women and people over 50 may result in an employment growth in organisations, while young people and those with higher education can have a positive effect on the amount and quality of work, thus compensating for quantitative shortages. Each of these groups is associated with a positive attitude towards work flexibility (Kmiotek 2015; Zeytinoglu, 2005; Zeytinoglu, 2009): women due to family responsibilities, older people may no longer have those but they are limited by health issues, young people are on the pursuit of diverse and constantly changing interests and seek professional development, while the well-educated and talented perceive flexibility as a privilege and compensation for their competence. However, as studies from the UK and Greece show, employees' attitude to flexible work arrangements is not always so positive and it depends on sex, place of work and previous opportunity to work in a flexible environment (with seniority and age as important factors) (Giannikis & Miahail, 2011; Sullivan & Smithson, 2007).

Based on the study results presented below, an attempt was made to evaluate the attitude of the Polish labour market to selected forms of working time and space flexibility, with respect to demographic characteristics and competence of the respondents.

FLEXIBILITY OF WORKING TIME AND SPACE IN THE LIGHT OF AN EMPIRICAL STUDY IN POLAND

Methodology

The data was collected by the means of the Paper and Pencil Interviews (PAPI) carried out in the period of July-August 2015 on a sample of 160 people – the structure of the sample is presented in Table 1.

With such structure the sample is not representative. The main selection criterion was the respondents' availability and consent to providing information. Consequently, the analysis of the responses cannot be used for forming general conclusions about the whole population. Obtained in a sample survey, the responses allow for some observations to be made only as an example which may be subject to a further in-depth research. For this reason, what was carried out was in fact an analysis of the structure of the responses without an in-depth statistical analysis.

The study focused on spatial mobility and flexibility of working time, based on the assumption that the both are strongly interconnected. Spatial mobility affects the time devoted to work, typically by extending it without any temporal or financial compensation offered in return (working overtime).The time available to the employee to organise their life outside work is limited, which affects their level of commitment and satisfaction.

Table 1. Structure of the Sample

Category		Persons in the sample (%)
Sex	Male	34.38%
	Female	65.00%
Age (years)	20-29	45.63%
	30-40	23.75%
	40-55	20.63%
	>55	10.00%
Years of work experience/ seniority	<3	23.75%
	4-9	25.63%
	10-20	17.50%
	>20	29.38%
Education	Primary and vocational	1.88%
	Secondary	23.75%
	Higher: BA degree	33.75%
	Higher: MA degree	40.63%

The following were adopted as potentially different for the respondents and thus relevant to the subject of the study: demographic characteristics (sex and age) and competence (education and seniority, i.e. years of work experience). In terms of education it was assumed that higher education offers more opportunities to decide about working conditions; organisational talents are also mainly people with a solid formal education. For this reason, only the respondents with at least secondary education were included in the analysis. Those who described their education as primary (graduates of primary school or lower secondary school, in Polish: *gimnazjum*) and vocational (graduates of vocational school) constituted a small percentage of the sample and were therefore not taken into consideration.

All the respondents were professionally active before and/or at the time of filling out the questionnaire and had work experience allowing them to realistically assess the options offered in questions (verified against their seniority). The questionnaire included projection questions in which the respondents had to refer to hypothetical situations reflecting four aspects of labour flexibility: changing the place of residence due to work, business trips, commuting to work and organisation of working time. The first three are related to spatial and the last one to temporal flexibility. The results of the study are presented in these four categories.

Changing the Place of Residence Due to Work

In its most radical version, spatial flexibility or mobility, involves changing the place of residence due to the change of employer or job relocation. The survey outlines a situation which may occur both when the employer is changed and when the employer remains the same while the place of work changes. The respondents had to answer the following question:

If my employer offers me a relocation package (equivalent of the 6-month salary), will I be willing to move 300 km away from the current place of residence?

The amount of the relocation package was estimated as an offset between an attractive offer and potential removal expenses. The distance between the previous and new place of work was calculated to exclude daily commuting from the current place of residence (given the average transport conditions in Poland), with the option of weekend returns.

In total, the answer of 34% of the respondents was positive. Surprisingly, this percentage was slightly higher among women (36% compared to 33% of men; Figure 1). The difference in responses was negligible; however, the optional mobility was rather expected to be higher among men, as men are traditionally less obliged to perform house work and family duties which require daily presence at home.

The analysis of responses by age revealed that the older the respondents, the less willing they were to relocate; although those aged over 55 were already slightly more open to this idea.

The analysis of the structure of seniority in the group which responded positively showed clearly that people with the shortest professional experience were the most willing to accept the change (Figure 2). In the other seniority groups the situation was almost identical, with most respondents rejecting the offer. Professional experience seems therefore to contribute to a negative opinion about changing the place of residence due to work or results in significantly bigger demands in this respect.

The analysis carried out with respect to education reveals significant differences. Those with the BA degree were most keen on consenting to moving (approx. 46%). This is mainly due to transition period in their professional life: people at this stage are typically still in the process of learning (which they

Figure 1. Decision about relocation with respect to demographic characteristics

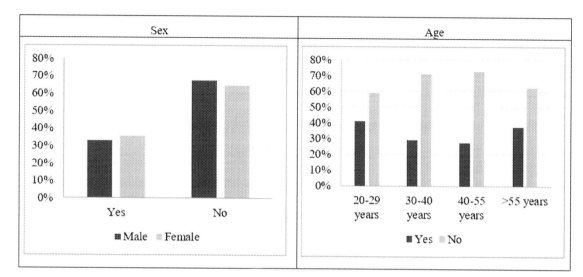

Figure 2. Decision about relocation with respect to competence

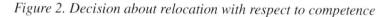

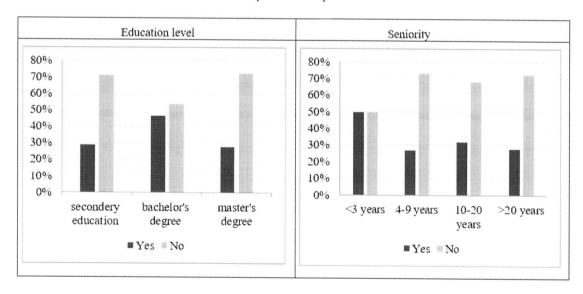

later continue as MA studies), have a shorter work experience, are younger, and consequently, their family or life situation is different. Given the current generational changes in the approach to work, this group is most open to change and most mobile in its search for an optimal place of work. In most cases people with the MA degree have already completed their formal education and, sometimes even straight after graduation, they seek stability, want a dream/target job, have a greater sense of the significance of their competence, and are thus more ready to reject the proposal of moving, perceiving it rather as destabilising their life, even if it means professional development for them. Similarly, those with secondary education will also see themselves as people with completed formal education (based on the respondents' declared seniority) and already formed competence and skills, and will rather expect their work to be stable and predictable.

Business Trips

Another question was about business trips which involve staying away from home. While it might be typical for certain jobs, such as salespeople, technicians, construction workers or consultants, it does not have to be a rule limited to specific sectors. For example, a construction company may operate exclusively in the local market and thus require no travelling on business; on the other hand, some jobs, although traditionally perceived as stationary, may require frequent business trips due to the specificity of the company operations. When choosing a profession, a career path and eventually a particular job, every employee considers their own preferences and acknowledges the fact that sometimes they will have to go away from home (e.g. to attend a training). Meanwhile, their job description, market demands or employer's expectations might change, in which case the ability to accept new conditions may be critical to boost their motivation and keep the job.

The following statement was presented to the respondents who had to choose one of the options:

As part of my job, I accept being away from home (as % of nights spent at work between working days per year): none at all, up to 10%, up to 25%, up to 50%, up to 70%.

The analysis of the distribution of the responses confirms what was assumed, i.e. a low mobility of the studied employees. Respectively, 31% and 34% of the respondents were not willing or agreed to spending approx. 10% of nights away from home as part of their job, 23% accepted spending every fourth night away from home, while less than 10% agreed to half of nights and less than 2% approved being away from home almost permanently (70% of nights per year).

The distribution by sex also reflects the general assumption (Figure 3). Among women, 41% would not accept staying away from home at all (compared to 13% of men), while 30% would agree to 10% of nights (compared to 40% of men). Extending the number of multi-day business trips was accepted by far fewer women than men; the longer the trips, the fewer respondents agreed to them.

Figure 3. Approval for business trips with respect to demographic characteristics

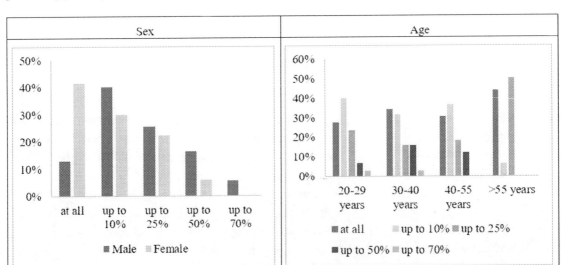

The structure of the responses by the respondents' age was relatively stable in all the groups: there was generally no consent to the longest business trips, while staying away from home for up to 10% of nights per year was approved. The older the respondents, the less willing they were to accept longer trips, with the longest option marked only in the first two age groups (up to 40 years of age). Compared to other age groups, the first one (20-29 years of age) declared a greater acceptance of shorter trips and a smaller one (10% of the respondents) of travels for over 25% of nights; in this group, however, work takes a different place among life priorities. The responses of those aged over 55 are the most interesting and homogenous; these respondents did not agree to the longest business trips at all and accepted trips for 10% of nights only to a small extent, while their approval for staying away from home for 25% of nights was the biggest.

Similar characteristics are revealed in the analysis of the responses with respect to seniority (Figure 4). The first two seniority groups (in total, up to 9 years of work experience) were most willing to spend up to 10% of nights away from home, with a similar percentage in each group objecting to making such sacrifice for work (approx. ¼ of the respondents). In the third seniority group (10-20 years of work experience), the percentage of those against such solution was the highest (46%). The group of 4-9 years of working experience was the only one in which the longest trip option (up to 70% of nights away from home) was at all accepted. The last group with the longest seniority turned out to be the most polarised; the percentage of the respondents who did not accept any overnight trips and those who agreed to trips of up to 10% and 25% of nights was similar. At the level of 9%, the acceptance of trips taking up to 50% of nights per year was also similar to the other groups.

The analysis of the results with respect to education suggests that people with the BA degree were the most open group to the idea of working away from home; in this group the percentage of those who did not accept this option at all was the smallest, while that of those who agreed to trips of up to 10% and 25% of nights was the biggest. The groups with secondary and higher education seem to be the least flexible or the most demanding in this respect, i.e. they were characterised by a high refusal to be

Figure 4. Approval for business trips with respect to competence

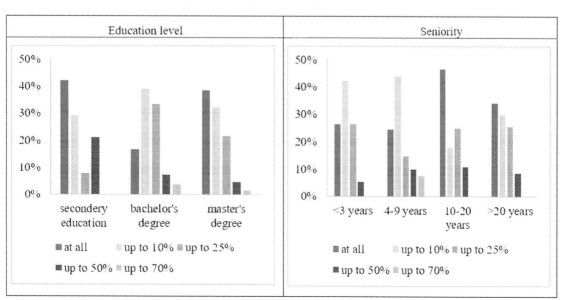

away from home at night and a low acceptance of working away from home for more than 10% of nights (except for the respondents with secondary education whose acceptance of working for up to 50% of nights was relatively high, while they were totally against the option of 70% of nights).

Commuting to Work

One of the responsibilities carried out directly at the expense of the employee's private life is regular commuting to work. Travel expenses depend on the means of transport and travel allowance offered (or not) by the employer (e.g. transport organised by the employer free of charge). However, time spent on commuting can truly affect the level of satisfaction with the workplace. Not everyone has the possibility to choose such work in which the commuting time would not exceed 30 minutes (one way), i.e. the time adopted by the authors as a standard value accepted by most employees under the Polish conditions. In many cases a change of the employer's seat may significantly affect the organisation of employees' private life; the distance of a few kilometres can add extra 30 minutes to the regular commuting time.

The organisation of private life connected with leisure time activities, children's education and/or spouse's work may be crucial to the logistics of commuting; unattractive commuting options or changes in this area may affect the employee's decision about their work. It is worth adding that the standard maximum time of 1 hour per day already represents as much as 12.5% of the working time.

In view of that, the respondents were asked the following:

As part of my job, I accept commuting to work which takes up to 30 minutes, up to 60 minutes or up to 90 minutes one way.

The analysis of the responses reveals that in general 30 minutes turned out to be the upper limit for 58% of the respondents, 60 minutes for 40% of the respondents, while only 3% accepted commuting for up to 90 minutes. Consequently, no further analysis of this question was necessary, whereas any future studies might consider adding the intermediate category of 45 minutes. The analysis of distribution by sex is consistent with the previous assumptions: 63% of women accepted commuting for only up to 30 minutes, compared to 47% of men (Figure 5).

In terms of age, the distribution of preferences is similar in all the groups up to 55 years of age, with small differences for the generally prevalent time of up to 30 minutes. The age groups of 40-55 and over 55 did not mark the longest commuting time of up to 90 minutes, probably for family (the former) and biological (the latter) reasons, such as health and physical condition. The group of the oldest respondents was strongly in favour of the shortest time of commuting (over 70%), with just over 20% of them accepting the commuting time of up to 60 minutes.

The analysis of the responses with respect to the seniority (Figure 6) also shows a fairly similar distribution of preferences in every seniority group: 50-60% chose the shortest time of commuting, 30-40% opted for 1 hour, while approx. 5% of the respondents (except for those with the longest work experience who did not mark this option at all) –1.5 hours. The group with the shortest work experience was also the most balanced in terms of its preferences, i.e. commuting for 30 minutes was as good as commuting for 60 minutes.

Figure 5. Approval for commuting to work with respect to demographic characteristics

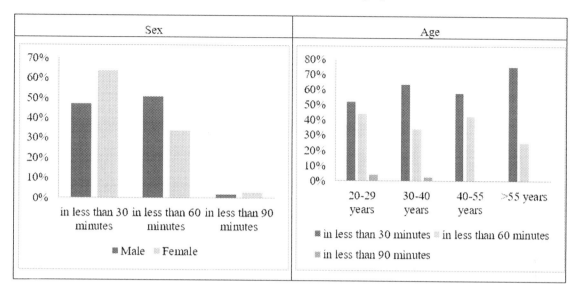

Figure 6. Approval for commuting to work with respect to competence

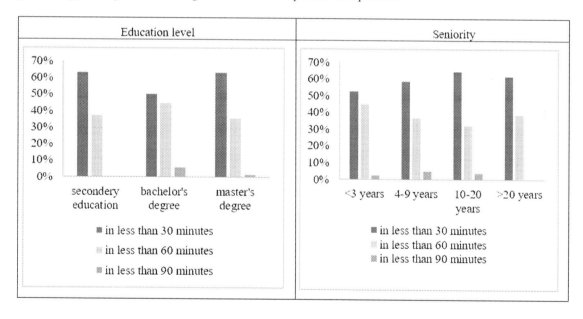

It is more difficult to explain the discrepancy between the responses with respect to the respondents' education. The results for the groups with secondary and higher education are nearly identical; the only difference being that those with secondary education did not mark the longest time of commuting at all, while this option was accepted by 2% of the people with higher education. The respondents with the BA degree more willingly agreed to longer commuting (60 and 90 minutes), which can be linked to the respondents' age and the, already mentioned, transition period in their professional life (education still in progress).

Organisation of Working Time

Undoubtedly, flexibility of working time has the largest effect on the organisation of private life. The range of solutions available to employers is truly significant. They primarily include different working time arrangements and calculation, but also business phone calls and e-mails outside of the working hours, being at the employer's disposal even during holidays, overtime (not always correctly settled), or business trips interfering with private life (as discussed above). Naturally, flexitime is a solution that can be beneficial for the both parties. It allows the employer to reduce payments for overtime and adjust working hours to the actual requirements, while the employee may enjoy a longer weekend without taking a day off, start late or leave work early, or take brakes at work. Of course, for these solutions to be well-organised and to ensure mutual benefits for both the employee and the employer, clear rules have to be agreed in terms of planning and adjusting working hours, whereby the both parties need to respect each other's interests. This cannot be guaranteed with rules and regulations, and can only be verified in practice. Therefore, when interpreting the responses it is necessary to pay attention to the respondents' individual experience with managers representing their employers.

The study focused on the formal aspects of working time, i.e. those that determine how it is paid for and which in practice have the biggest effect on employees' private time, making it difficult for them to plan their life outside work.

The respondents had to consider the following situation:

Choose one of the two following work arrangements:

1. *Work starts at 8 am and ends at 4 pm, you need to take a day off to deal with any personal matters at this time, overtime paid in full.*
2. *Flexible working hours, overtime compensated only by taking time off on other days, unpredictability of working time (hours and days changing depending on the needs of customers and business partners).*

The distribution analysis of the preference of the fixed (option 1) or flexible (option 2) working time revealed that as many as 60% of the respondents opted for the traditional organisation of working time, with 68% of them being female (Figure 7). In the group of men, only 44% selected the fixed working hours. The traditional perception of male and female roles seems to be reflected in the decisions regarding the preferred working time arrangements.

The analysis of the responses with respect to age produced interesting results: among those up to 55 years of age, preferences for the both working time arrangements were rather balanced, with the acceptance of flexitime growing slowly but steadily. In contrast, a radical change was observed in the group over 55 years of age, in which only 6% marked option 2, compared to 94% of those in favour of option 1.

The analysis with respect to the respondents' seniority reveals a very balanced distribution of the responses, with the preference for the traditional, fixed work arrangements (approx. 60%) and a slightly higher than in the other groups level of acceptance of flexitime among those with the working experience of 4-9 years.

Figure 7. Approval for working time arrangements with respect to demographic characteristics

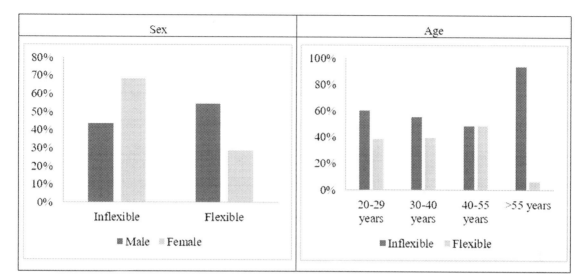

Figure 8. Approval for commuting to work with respect to competence

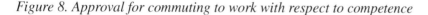

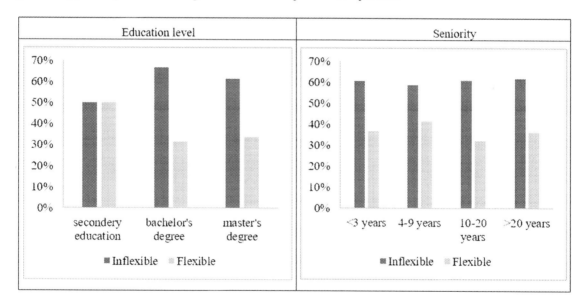

With regard to education, respondents with higher education (both with the BA and MA degrees) had similar preferences, with 60% of them in favour of fixed working time. Those with secondary education accepted the both options to the same extent. This may be the result of their previous experience with different work arrangements and acceptance of different solutions due to the situation in the labour market. People with the BA degree may require a greater stability, as they need to continue their education, while those with the MA may be more interested in being able to combine their professional and private life in a more predictable way.

SOLUTIONS AND RECOMMENDATIONS

The results presented in the article come from a pilot study. Naturally, it is impossible to develop a universal profile of a flexible employee using only this data. However, based on the analysis of the respondents' social characteristics, a general hypothesis may be formed that contemporary Polish employees are rather reluctant to relocate because of their job. Similarly, they will not be very keen on too long business trips and commuting to work, which may generally point to the importance of work-life balance in their assessment of work arrangements.

In terms of sex, a similar proportion of women and men accept or do not accept (majority) changing the place of residence due to work. The same applies to business trips; the longer the stay away from home, the fewer respondents, particularly women, agreed to it. Not much changes in commuting to work, either. Most women accept the travel time of up to 30 minutes, men are equally fine with commuting for up to 60 minutes, while none of the sexes approved of longer commuting. In terms of work arrangements, women definitely opted for fixed working hours, in contrast to men. In the light of these analyses, a flexible employee would therefore be male.

In terms of age, young employees and those who are about to finish their professional career were more flexible about moving. The approval for business trips was also the biggest in the youngest group. On the other hand, the oldest respondents were more willing to agree to multi-day business trips rather than longer commuting time. This group, however, did not accept flexible working time at all. The results may be linked to the family and life situation of the respondents. People under 30 and over 55 years of age tend to have fewer non-negotiable family responsibilities, as they typically do not yet have a family of their own or their children are adult and do not require constant care anymore. Moreover, a greater mobility among younger employees may be explained by their search for an optimal model of work and professional development, and under Polish conditions, also fear of unemployment. In Poland, unemployment affects primarily young people. In Q1 of 2016, the unemployment rate among people aged 15-24 was 19.6%, compared to 16.1% in Q3 of 2008 (the lowest) and 46.5% in Q1 of 2003 (the highest). At the end of the quarter in which the study was carried out, i.e. Q3 of 2015, people aged 25-34 constituted the largest group among the unemployed (449,200), accounting for 28.1% of the total number of the unemployed. People aged 24 and younger accounted for 14.6% of the total unemployment rate. The percentage of the registered unemployed aged 35-44 was 21.6%, 45-54 – 18.1%, and over 55 – 17.6% (Central Statistical Office of Poland, 2016). It is therefore difficult to clearly identify the preferences based on age; every age group is flexible in certain categories, while it is not in others.

The analysis of the results with respect to education points to people with the BA degree as the most likely to take up work which involves moving, business trips and commuting. However, this group is the least willing to work flexitime, which makes it similar to the preferences of people with the MA degree. The latter group seems to be the least keen on flexible work arrangements, possibly because of their competence, which allows them to demand stable working conditions, and life outside work which is becoming more stable too. In the light of these analyses, the most flexible employee would therefore have the BA degree and, under Polish conditions, would typically be a young person, preferably still a student.

Seniority, understood as years of work experience, was the last category considered in the study. Approval for changing the place of residence was the biggest among those with the shortest work experience, while business trips were not accepted primarily by the employees with 10-20 years of experience, which could be the effect of their family situation. Seniority turned out to be practically irrelevant in case of commuting and working time arrangements – in the respective groups the responses were almost the same, with the approval for the shortest commuting time and fixed working hours. A flexible employee would therefore rather have a short work experience.

Based on these conclusions, it may be noticed that the career stage, focus on professional development and family situation have a significant effect on preferences regarding the organisation of work. This means that relatively competent people who develop their career and have families are not very willing to work under spatially and temporally unstable conditions. They see flexibility as something rather negative because it disrupts the predictability of their professional activity and private life, and may additionally have a negative impact on how their career path is perceived in the future (flexible solutions as offered to "worse" employees).

FUTURE RESEARCH DIRECTIONS

The analysis leads to the conclusion that according to Polish employees there is a category of "good" and "bad" work flexibility. Unfortunately, no clear criteria exist for what is considered to be a good or bad proposal in this respect. However, this should be an important recommendation for employers to implement such flexibility solutions which do not interfere too much with employees' private life, e.g. teleworking, home office or remote communication between branches. As many as 60% of the respondents preferred fixed solutions in terms of time directly spent at work, with a significant diversification of the responses with respect to age, sex and education, which – if interpreted as a solid and fixed conclusion – would require the implementation of extremely individualised work arrangements. While definitely welcomed by employees, such approach would not be possible in many organisations due to objective limitations (technological regime, contractors' requirements, and need for supervision). However, the diversity of preferences shows that sticking rigidly to one uniform type of work arrangement, regardless if flexible or fixed, is also not beneficial for the organisation, primarily due to the poor effect it may have on the employer's image and reputation.

A number of conclusions is difficult to interpret – particularly those regarding the analysis of the impact of seniority or education on flexibility. The interpretation of the results should be complemented with a wider social research including generational differences, with the primary focus on the position of work on young people's priority list and on the question whether the value of work changes with age or is characteristic of the given generation. Next to its scientific significance, this information may be crucial for employers in the future organisational planning and human resources management. The future studies should also address the topic of job security depending on the employee's position in the labour market, also to explore how it affects the employee's agreement to working conditions and flexibility, both formal and informal. Another interesting aspect is the question of work flexibility limits, i.e. to what extent and how the organisation can make work more flexible without it having a negative social impact (e.g. refusal to work under such conditions).

The difficulty with the interpretation of the conclusions also points to the need for collecting more extensive information on the social aspects of the respondents' life (e.g. their professional function, current form of employment, financial status or family situation).

CONCLUSION

In the chapter, a microeconomic point of view was adopted, with the study focused mainly on employees' spatial mobility and flexibility of working time perceived as a social factor affecting the organisation of work. The observations presented in the chapter may be applied in companies – in operational management of human resources in terms of selecting and retaining employees, and in strategic management of human resources in terms of demographic changes and competence shift in the workforce. They point to the need to analyse the preferences of employees and job applicants in order to have the work organisation adjusted also to them. Even though it deals with the topic already explored for some time, the study shows that further in-depth research is needed in this respect, addressing also new aspects of work flexibility.

REFERENCES

Aequus Partners. (2010). *Workplace flexibility: Advice, training, research*. Retrieved on October 6, from http://www.workplaceflexibility.com.au/index.htm

Anxo, D., & O'Reilly, J. (2000). Working time regimes and transitions in comparative perspective. In J. O'Reilly, I. Cebrién, & M. Lallement (Eds.), *Working time changes: Social integration through transitional labour markets*. Cheltenham, UK: Edward Elgar Publishing. doi:10.4337/9781781952788.00013

Aon Hewitt. (2015). *Trends in Global Employee Engagement*. Retrieved from http://www.aon.com/attachments/human-capital-consulting/2015-Trends-in-Global-Employee-Engagement-Report.pdf

Aon Hewitt. (2016). *Trends in Global Employee Engagement*. Retrieved from http://www.aon.com/poland/attachments/hr/meh/2016-Trends-in-Global-Employee-Engagement.pdf

Bailyn, L., Drago, R., & Kochan, T. (2001). *Integrating Work and Family Life: A Holistic Approach*. Report for Alfread P. Sloan Foundation Work-Family Policy Network.

Beardwell, I., & Holden, L. (2001). *Human Resource Management*. Edinburgh, UK: Pearson Education.

Beauregard, T. A., & Henry, L. C. (2009). Making the link between work-life balance practices and organizational performance. *Human Resource Management Review, 19*(1), 9–22. doi:10.1016/j.hrmr.2008.09.001

Blyton, P., & Jenkins, J. (2007). *Key Concepts in Work*. Los Angeles, CA: SAGE Publications Ltd. doi:10.4135/9781446215814

Brown, M., Wong, M., & McNamara, T. (2009). Flexible work options in state agencies. State Issue Brief No. 01. Chestnut Hill, MA: The Sloan Center on Aging and Work at Boston College. Retrieved from http://www.bc.edu/content/dam/files/research_sites/agingandwork/pdf/publications/SIB01_ Flex.pdf

Eamets, R., & Masso, J. (2004). *Labour Market Flexibility and Employment Protection Regulation in the Baltic States*. IZA Discussion Paper Series, 1147.

Eurofound. (2015). *First findings: Sixth European Working Conditions Survey*. Retrieved from https://www.eurofound.europa.eu/publications/resume/2015/working-conditions/first-findings-sixth-european-working-conditions-survey-resume

Eurofound. (2016). *Working time developments in the 21st century: Work duration and its regulation in the EU*. Publications Office of the European Union.

Gallup. (2013). *State of global workplace. Employee engagement insights for business leaders worldwide*. Retrieved from http://www.gallup.com/services/178517/state-global-workplace.aspx

Garsten, C. (2008). *Workplace Vagabonds. Carter and Community in Changing Worlds of Work*. Palgrave Macmillan. doi:10.1057/9780230227460

Giannikis, S. K., & Miahail, D. M. (2011). Flexible work arrangements in Greece: A study of employment perceptions. *International Journal of Human Resource Management, 22*(2), 417–432. doi:10.10 80/09585192.2011.540163

Gibson, J. W., Greenwood, R. A., & Murphy, E. F. Jr. (2009). Generational differences in the workplace: Personal values, behaviors, and popular beliefs. *Journal of Diversity Management, 4*(3), 1–7. doi:10.19030/jdm.v4i3.4959

Grudney, D., & Sarvutyte, M. (2007). Conceptualizing the Determinants of Labour Market Flexibility: the UE Perspective. In D. Kopycińska (Ed.), *Flexibility of Labour Market. Monograph No 7" in the series Economics and Competition Policy*. Szczecin: Wydawnictwo Uniwersytetu Szczecinskiego.

GUS. (2016). Bezrobocie rejestrowane. I kwartał 2016 r. Warsaw: GUS.

Houseman, S. N. (2001). Why Employers Use Flexible Staffing Arrangements: Evidence from an Establishment Survey. *Industrial & Labor Relations Review, 55*(1), 149–170. doi:10.1177/001979390105500109

HRM Partners. (2015). *Prognoza HR 2016: Koniec rynku pracodawcy?* Retrieved from http://www.hrmpartners.pl/docs/raporty/raport-z-badania-prognoza-hr-2016-hrm-partners.pdf

Karuppan, C. M. (2004). Strategies to foster labor flexibility. *International Journal of Productivity and Performance Management, 53*(6), 532–547. doi:10.1108/17410400410556192

Kmiotek, K. (2015). The Generation Y approach to flexibility of employment. *The Journal of American Academy of Business, 20*(2), 72–80.

Krol, M. (2014). *Elastyczność zatrudnienia w organizacji*. Warsaw: CeDeWu.

Martinez-Sanchez, A., Vela-Jimenez, M.J., Perez-Perez, M., & de-Luis-Carnicer, P. (2008). Workplace flexibility and innovation. The moderator effect of intra-organizational cooperation. *Personal Review, 37*(6).

NBP. (2016). *Kwartalny raport o rynku pracy w I kw. 2016 r.* Retrieved from http://www.nbp.pl/publikacje/rynek_pracy/rynek_pracy_2016_1kw.pdf

Osbert-Pociecha, G. (2011). *Zdolnosc do zmian jako sila sprawcza elastycznosci organizacji*. Wroclaw: Wydawnictwo Uniwersytetu Ekonomicznego we Wroclawiu.

Schief, S. (2010). Does location master? An empirical investigation of flexibility patterns in foreign and domestic companies in five European countries. *International Journal of Human Resource Management, 21*(1-3).

Sullivan, C., & Smithson, J. (2007). Perspectives of homeworkers and their partners on working flexibility and gender equity. *Journal of Human Resources Management, 3*(3), 448–461. doi:10.1080/09585190601167797

Thomas, M. P. (2009). *Regulating Felxibility. The Political Economy of Employment Standards*. Montreal: McGill-Queen's University Press.

Volberda, H. W. (1998). *Building the Flexibility Firm. How to Remain Competitive*. New York: Oxford University Press.

Weyland, A. (2011). Engagement and talent management of Gen Y. *Industrial and Commercial Training, 43*(7), 439–445. doi:10.1108/00197851111171863

WorldatWork. (2015). *Trends in Workplace Flexibility. A report by WorldatWork, underwritten by FlexJobs*. Retrieved from https://www.worldatwork.org/waw/adimLink?id=79123

Zeytinoglu, I. U. (Ed.). (2005). Flexibility in Workplaces: Effects on Workers, Work Environment and the Unions. Geneva: IIRA/ILO.

Zeytinoglu, I. U., Cooke, G. B., & Mann, S. L. (2009). Flexibility: Whose Choice Is It Anyway? *Relations Industrielles. Industrial Relations, 64*(3), 555–574. doi:10.7202/038873ar

KEY TERMS AND DEFINITIONS

Commuting: To regularly travel from home to work and back, with all its implications (travel time, financial and organisational implications).

Flexible Working Time: Ability of both the employer and employee to modify working hours (e.g. flexitime, part-time, job sharing, compressed workweek).

Formal Flexibility: A policy officially approved by human resources or any other official policy which implements and regulates flexible work arrangements.

Informal Flexibility: A policy or practice that is not official or specified in writing but which in fact allows flexibility at work.

Mobile Working: To perform work remotely, in different locations, e.g. in the office, at home, at the customer's seat, also during commuting and business trips.

Organisation of Working Time: To regulate the length and schedule of the employee's working time (number of hours and work schedule).

Relocation: A permanent change of the location of the place of work.

Work-Life Balance: Ability to combine the professional and private life in a smooth, conflict-free way.

Workplace Flexibility: To modify and adjust the working conditions to the needs of the employer and employee.

Chapter 16
Interface Between Stress and Labour Productivity

Ilona Skačkauskienė
Vilnius Gediminas Technical University, Lithuania

Rasa Pališkienė
Vilnius Gediminas Technical University, Lithuania

ABSTRACT

The main purpose of this article is to examine the relationship between the stress and labour productivity. It is recognized that high stress levels make a negative impact on the job productivity results – the incidents or errors occur because of stressful situations in the working environment. After performing the analysis of stress models, it can be stated, that stress could be assessed as a process, i.e. researches are oriented more on the person, or as the situation, i.e. researches are oriented on the causes of stress in the working environment. The metaanalysis of stress factors allow us to identificate the main causes of stress at work, whose at least partial elimination is essential for every organization to increase the productivity of employee. Analysis of the content of factors that cause stress showed that these factors can be classified into the individual and situational. The labour productivity of employees can be seen as a result of stress management, and interface among stress and job productivity are modelling.

INTRODUCTION

Global economic changes in the world and the competitive dynamic environment are raising more claim for working person, are influencing his opportunities of career, for all living areas. Modern life can be described as an uncertainty and a world of chaos, in which the economy isn't built on land, money or natural resources, but intellectual capital.

Nowadays the organizations are searching specialists, who are working productively, capable independently to accept decisions, oriented into the permanent learning and perfection, when the learning is becoming no episodic experience, but the permanent part of life. In the modern society has been formed the attitude, that it is important to have job for every person, because there are means to keep for self-respect. Although job can indulge difficulties and stress (permanent routine of work, uninspir-

DOI: 10.4018/978-1-5225-2480-9.ch016

ing monotonous tasks, control and obedience for leaders, inappropriate work conditions, lack of self-expression, psychological discomfort, tension, rush and etc.), it is considered the element, which defines personality of human.

One mostly and one the oldest analysing areas of activity of working person is interface of work environment and work accomplishment. Work environment is understandable as time and space limited totality of factors, which determines welfare of members of work process by physical, mental, spiritual, intellectual, emotional and social point of views, as well an employee's personality becoming, his health. Today is awared increasingly, that people, who are satisfied with their work and work effectively, need not only to ensure safety, but they need conditions of job for their well-being, also.

The International Labour Organization emphasizes, that well-being at work is a basic factor of seeking to determine a long-term effectiveness of organizations. Workers' mental health and well-being is a fundamental labour productivity resource (European Comission, 2008).

In this article are examing a concept of stress, stress management models, which are based on measuring stress levels, after analysing stress and productivity factors, are modeling stress and productivity interaction. The aim of the article is to represent interface, after purification of the concept of stress and job productivity. The research is based on the comparative analysis scientific literature, abstraction, synthesis and mathematical modeling.

LITERATURE REVIEW

Organizations, in order to maximize the utility, are looking for ways on how to manage the work of employees' productivity. First of all, we define the concept of labour productivity. Pichardo (1990, 1995), Williams (2002) state that the definition of productivity is multifaceted because the different members of disciplines state the productivity differently. Engineers understand the productivity as how the yield of the system divided by the input to the system. Thus, the productivity of this case is the operation of the system's performance efficiency. Economists understand the productivity of the entire organization or organizational unit of output, divided by the cost of the particular production, which is made when both production and consumption are measured in the monetary value. Managers widely perceived productivity. In this case, the productivity of the organization covers all aspects which are important for the functioning of the organization. It includes not only the efficiency, but also the quality of the result, the division of labour, the absenteeism, the turnover of employee, the satisfaction of the customer. Everything that causes the organization to function better is related to the productivity of labour (Williams 2002).

In order to reveal the concept of labour productivity, it is important to note, that the affirmation may vary depending on whether the company or the productivity of employee are analysing. The productivity of employee can be seen as the actions and behavior, which are controling by the same individual and are contributing to the organization's objectives (Rotundo, Sackett 2002; Côté, Miners 2006). Grant (2008) the labour productivity defines as the employee's behavioral performance, which contributes to the organization's objectives.

This article focuses on employee productivity and stress, as the largest impact on labour productivity analysis of factors, and labour productivity is considered as working efficiency, which, as shown by research shows, is directly influenced by stress. A favorable working environment, stress is one of the most grueling events staff (Elfering et al. 2006; Kaklauskas et al. 2011, 2013; Leung et al. 2012). The workers with high work motivation more easy overcome the dificulties of work environment, stress. The economists Stoner, Freeman, Gilbert (2000), provide the motivation of the company substantial role in providing, that motivation also helps managers effectively lead an organization, if managers know what motivates employees to work productively, they can create a supportive work environment, adjust the optimum working tasks, including encouraging employees to work more productively. Employees can be motivated in different ways, but scientists (Venkatesan et al. 2009, Yisa et al. 2000) say that will not be easy to raise the motivation of employees to work more productively, when there is a strong motivation to reduce stress and posing factors. The long-term effects of the above factors increases the possibility of illness and absenteeism, dissatisfaction with work and for these reasons, the decline in labor productivity, and the stress level increases. According to Edelmann (1993), a person throughout his life on average spends 100 000 hours at work, so it is important for employers to create working environment in which employees do not have high stress (Bamber, 2006).

WHAT IS JOB STRESS?

Stress is considered one of the biggest problems of modern civilization. Selye, who is the author of stress theory, called stress certain body reactions (physiological, harmonic, psychological, behavioral, and so on.). According to this author, stress is the nonspecific response to any request made to him. This is a non-specific response to the stimulus (stressor). The same stimulus is interpreted differently by different employees, and only from the human affects the stress they cause stress and possible consequences. Some workers, stress and heavy workload quite a challenge, test yourself and, if you manage to perform the work in a shorter period of time, it is more productive, it raises the workers' self-esteem and gives a sense of satisfaction with their own. However, too much stress, too long a time may be harmful factors. When stress for a short period, the price of a small, but prolonged uncontrollable stressors can adversely affect the health of workers (Myers, 2000, 2001), and at the same time, reduce labor productivity. Stress, as a harmful work environment factor among many professions, especially in the highest chain operators, industry, business and production managers, teachers, doctors.

Stress have an important position in relation to the productivity of human resources. Work stress faced by labours is associated with decreased job performance, increased work absenteeism and prone to accidents. Similarly, if many of the workers in organizations or companies experience work stress, work productivity and health of the organization will be disturbed (Collins, 1993).

Science research (Sauter 1990; Elisburg 1995; Benach 2007; Alavinia 2009; Kaklauskas 2011, 2012, 2013; Cheng 2013; Bureš, Stropkova 2014) show, that the greatest impact on productivity makes the appropriate work physical and psychological environment, character of work and experienced stress, as well.

It is recognized that high stress makes negative impact on the results, as if incidents or errors occur for stressful situations in the working environment, it is necessary to compensate or restore incurred costs, because of the increase of the cost of production (Dollard, Neser 2013).

Job stress can be defined (Barrick 2002; DeGroote 2013) as the harmful physical and emotional responses that occur when the requirements of the job do not match the capabilities, resources, or needs of the worker.

Job stress can lead to poor health and even injury. The concept of job stress is often confused with challenge, but these concepts are not the same. Challenge energizes us psychologically and physically, and it motivates us to learn new skills and master our jobs. When a challenge is met, we feel relaxed and satisfied. Thus, challenge is an important ingredient for healthy and productive work. The importance of challenge in our work lives is probably what people are referring to when they say "a little bit of stress is good for you".

Some employers assume that stressful working conditions are a necessary evil - that companies must turn up the pressure on workers and set aside health concerns to remain productive and profitable in today's economy. But research findings challenge this belief. Studies show that stressful working conditions are actually associated with increased absenteeism, tardiness, and intentions by workers to quit their jobs - all of which have a negative effect on the bottom line.

The National Institute for Occupational Safety and Health (hereinafter – NIOSH) research has identified organizational characteristics associated with both healthy, low-stress work and high levels of productivity (Figure 1).

Examples of these characteristics include the following:

- Recognition of employees for good work performance;
- Opportunities for career development;
- An organizational culture that values the individual worker;
- Management actions are consistent with organizational values.

In the past 20 years, many studies have looked at the relationship between job stress and a variety of ailments. Mood and sleep disturbances, upset stomach and headache, and disturbed relationships with family and friends are examples of stress-related problems that are quick to develop and are commonly seen in these studies. These early signs of job stress are usually easy to recognize. But the effects of job stress on chronic diseases are more difficult to see because chronic diseases take a long time to develop and can be influenced by many factors other than stress.

Figure 1. Model of Job Stress (NIOSH 2016)

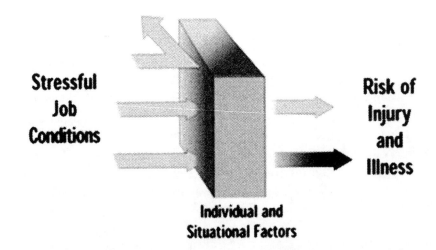

STRESS THEORY AND MODELS

One of the most widely applied the stress theory in the researches is Lazarus stress theory of understanding. According to Lazarus (1984) assertion, more important is how a person perceives and evaluates this event, but not the stressful event. The subjective perception and evaluation are mediators between the stressor and response of person.

Another theoretical stress model, which is applicable, is work stress theory and following it, Karasek represents the Job, Demand and Control Model. There are analysing two aspects of the work situation: work requirements (requirements of the task, workload, deadlines, role conflict) and job control (so-called freedom of decision, or – autonomy, discretion). These two variables relationship lead to different employee well-being, herewith and labour productivity (Figure 2).

According to literature, can be found a variety of stress theories and models, the analysis is presented in the Table 1.

After performing the analysis of stress models, it can be said, that the authors of the models (Lazarus 1984, Siegrist 2002, Matesson and Ivancevich 1979) assess stress as process and oriented more to the person. The other authors of the models such as Karasek (1979), Bakker, Demerouti (2007) and Kerr (2001) more emphasize the situation, for example there are researching the causes of stress in the working environment. Many scientists assessed stress at work by selecting one or more factors, for example Karasek (1979) analyzed the job requirements and control, Siegrist (2002) – the effort - reward balance, Lazarus (1975) - the perceived control.

Figure 2. Job Demand Control Model (Karasek, 2010)

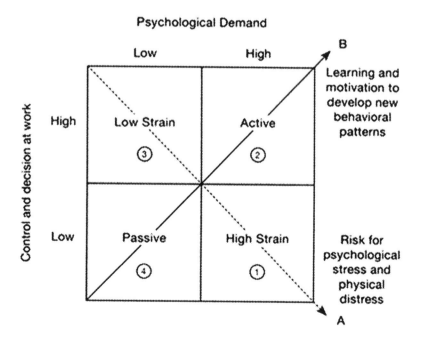

Table 1. Stress models and theories characteristics

Authors, year	Models of Stress	Description of Stress's Model
Yerkes, Dodson (1908)	Inverted U model	There is revealed U-shaped dependence on emotional stress strength and productivity of activity. According to this model, when excitement is intensifying from low to average, the quality of performed activity is improving. However, when the excitement is becoming strong, the quality is falling.
Hardy (1996)	CatastropheTheory	In the state of stress can be distinguished cognitive (thought), somatic (physiological) and self-confidence aspects, which effect is not cumulative, but interactive. Physiological excitation is not the isolated reaction, but on the contrary - depends on the cognitive excitement (thoughts, which cause excitement).
Kerr (2001)	Reversal Theory	The most important factor that may explain the link between stress and operating activity is how a person appreciates his status. Otherwise, if feeling stress (excitement) is assessed as positive, it helps to perform the activity better. However, if pressure) is assessed as negative, excitement will grow and the results will be wrong. So, in order to succeed, a person should see the positive sides of his status.
Spielberger (1972)	Anxiety State Model. State Trait Anxiety Inventory	The Anxiety state model states, that the individuals with stronger anxiety feature shows more intensive anxiety reactions than those with a less pronounced anxiety feature.
Hanin (1977)	Individual Zones of Optimal Functioning	Every person is characterized by the individual optimal level of excitement. Anxiety, stress (or pressure) level can fluctuate from very low to very high, depending on the individual character.
Bandura (1986)	Model of Self-Regulatory Conduct	In the context of self-regulation The emotional reactions (stress, fear and etc.) is seen as the source of information. The emotions can inform about the reinforcement changes, caused by the negative impact of the external environment of disturbed self-regulation process. In the theory identifies three processes: self-monitoring, self-assessment and self-reinforcement.
Lazarus (1975)	Cognitive Transactional Stress Model	The same stressful event may affect different people because of their differences of cognitive performance and motivation. There are distinguished the main intermediate variables between the organism and environment: the cognitive assessment of the situation and stress coping process. The cognitive assessment determines the nature and intensity of stressful event, which was caused by the reaction.
Holmes and Rahe (1967)	Life Events Model	There is interpreted the rise of different stress levels. There is focused on the individual people's reactions to life events as to potential stressors.
Clark and Wells (1995)	Cognitive Model Of Social Anxiety	There is emphasized the importance of cognitive factors in assessing the social situations. The model reveals the beliefs of a person, who feels the reality, which doesn't comply social anxiety (stress) for his behavior in public, which with social sufferers personal beliefs on their behavior in public. A person has the selective guiding focus on the negative aspects of the situation and the positive aspects are omitted.
Karasek (1979)	Model Of Stress Management At Work	There are two determinants, which cause stress at work: job requirements and job control.
Bakker and Demeruoti (2007)	Job Requirements - Resource Model	There are based on that the working conditions cause stress, when there are lack of labour resources.
Matesson ir Ivancevich (1989)	Stress At Work Model	There are covered the whole range of potential stressors and emphasized that stress is a phenomenon of individual perception. There is analyzing the relationship between stress at work and heart diseases.
Siegrist (2002)	Transactional Model	There are emphasized the cognitive processes and emotional reactions (anxiety, stress and etc.), which do influence to an individual and environment.

RESEARCH OF STRESS FACTORS

Work stress is not only caused by one factor alone, but stress can occur due to the incorporation of multiple causes at once. According to Luthans (2006), it is stated that there are several factors causing stress, namely:

1. Extra organization stressors. They come from outside the organization. These stressors can occur in an opened organization, that is the state of the external environment affecting the organization, for instance social and technological changes, globalization, family and others;
2. Organizational stressors. They come from the organization where the labours work. These stressors focus more on policy or organization regulations causing excessive pressure on the labours;
3. Group stressors. They come from working groups that interact every day with the labours, e.g. co-workers or supervisors or the direct supervisors of the labours;
4. Individual stressors. They are derived from individuals within the organization.

Labour productivity due to the employees feeling. There are distinguished emotions and stress as one of the main factors of the labour productivity (Pekrun et al. 2007; Kaklauskas et al. 2011, 2012, 2013). Emotions can initiate, terminate or disrupt the processing of information and achievement of results at work or block the activity of employee, who meets with negative emotions. Emotions have the influence on process of employees' learning and concentration of attention (Pekrun et al. 2007). Boredom, anger, dissatisfaction, aimless haste and anxiety are the emotional factors, which can degrade a person and reduce his labour productivity. Anxiety, stress and emotional frustrations are three repeated causes of fatigue (Carnegie 2004). Brill (1946) states that people, who work the sedentary jobs, mostly are tired because of the psychological and emotional factors. Another factor, which has the influence on the labour productivity – stress. Leung et al. (2010, 2012) distinquished five organizational stressors: inadequate remuneration, inadequate safety equipment, lack of training, the lack of goals and poor physical environment. Also, the authors distinguish two types of stress, emotional and physical, which has negative impact on the results of work (see Figure 3). Emotional stress reduces motivation, concentration of attention and self-preservation, causing fear and increases the number of accidents at work (Alexander, Klein 2001, Elfering et al. 2006, Leung et al. 2010), generally affects the emotions of person. So, the occurrence of negative emotions can be called as consequence of stress. Meanwhile, the physical stress helps to react to stressful situation. However, the long-term physical stress has persistent phenomenon such as diseases, pain, skin problems and etc. (Leung et al. 2012). Both too high and too low level of stress causes the negative impact (Alexander, Klein, 2001; Elfering et al., 2006; Leung et al., 2010).

Scientists (Vearing, Mak 2007, Hu 2011, Lingard 2012, Boschman 2013, Mellor 2011, Manzoor 2012) performed a lot of stress tests to find out the causes of stress at work. It was found that the main causes of stress at work are significant results consuming work, job scarcity of resources, inadequate work organization, instability, lack of prospects, work-family conflict, working lack of control, lack of social support in the workplace, inadequate remuneration, relations at workplace (Table 2).

The researches of stress factors show the main causes of stress at work, witch at least partial elimination is essential for every organization to increase the productivity of employee. The problems, which arise at work, cause stress, which consequences respond to company's quality and results, eventually to economy. Stress of employees and its consequences were analyzed in the scientific research of stress at American Institute of Stress (The American Institute of stress, 2011).

Figure 3. Relations between organizational stressors, stress and safety for workers (Leung et al. 2012)

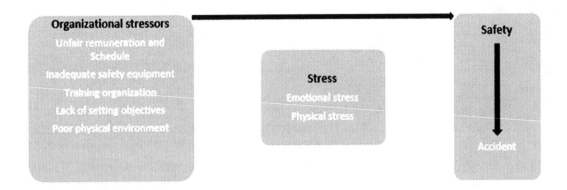

Table 2. Factors influencing stress

Factors	Authors
High score consuming work, job scarcity, menstrual ailments	Hu *et al.* 2011, Lingard *et al.* 2012, Boschman *et al.* 2013, Mellor *et al.* 2011, Manzoor *et al.* 2012
Improper work organization, instability, the lack of prospects	Chan *et al.* 2000, Lingard *et al.* 2012, Manzoor *et al.* 2012, Boschman *et al.* 2013, Leung *et al.* 2012
Work-family conflict	Chan *et al.* 2000, Lingard *et al.* 2012, Manzoor *et al.* 2012
Lack of social support in the workplace	Chan *et al.* 2000, Boschman *et al.* 2013, Manzoor *et al.* 2012
Improper reward	Leung *et al.* 2012, Vearing and Mak 2007
Relationships in the workplace	Leung *et al.* 2012, Chan *et al.* 2000

The obtained results showed, that:

- 65% of workers said that workplace stress had caused difficulties and more than 10 percent described these as having major effects;
- 10% said they work in an atmosphere where physical violence has occurred because of job stress and in this group, 42% report that yelling and other verbal abuse is common; these as having major effects;
- 29% had yelled at co-workers because of workplace stress, 14% said they work where machinery or equipment has been damaged because of workplace rage and 2% admitted that they had actually personally struck someone;
- 19% or almost one in five respondents had quit a previous position because of job stress and nearly one in four have been driven to tears because of workplace stress;
- 62% routinely find that they end the day with work-related neck pain, 44% reported stressed-out eyes, 38% complained of hurting hands and 34% reported difficulty in sleeping because they were too stressed-out;
- 12% had called in sick because of job stress.

Over half said they often spend 12-hour days on work related duties and an equal number frequently skip lunch because of the stress of job demands. Stress tests showed that even 25% view their jobs as the number one stressor in their lives. It was also found that:

- 29% of workers felt quite a bit or extremely stressed at work;
- 26% of workers said they were "often or very often burned out or stressed by their work;
- 80% of workers feel stress on the job, nearly half say they need help in learning how to manage stress and 42% say their coworkers need such help;
- 14% of respondents had felt like striking a coworker in the past year, but didn't;
- 25% have felt like screaming or shouting because of job stress, 10% are concerned about an individual at work they fear could become violent;
- 9% are aware of an assault or violent act in their workplace and 18% had experienced some sort of threat or verbal intimidation in the past year.

Safe working environment related to how the managers assesses the worker's psychological health, profit and productivity and take into account the workers' psychological state (Dollard, Neser 2013). Employees,who often place in the awkward position, seek to reduce their liabilities, activity at work. The psychosocial safe working environment is the factor of enhancing productivity, therefore the leadership has to forsee the strategic objectives how to prevent the stressful situations and to respond appropriately to them. The level of labour productivity is associated with stress - stress has the greatest negative impact on employee's productivity. Therefore, the organization is very important to identify and assess the causes of stress at work and to reduce them in order to increase labour productivity levels.

To improve productivity, the main attention should be paid on controlling of the factors of work environment (Profiles Research Institute, 2010). There is distinguished the factors, which cause stress and the greatest impact on labour productivity:

- Excessive workload or physical hazards;
- Workers' ability to control their job quantity and quality;
- Perception of staff functions performed;
- Relationships, including issues such as harassment and violence;
- Colleagues and managers support;
- Personnel training, training.

Issues of coping is dealing with the context of psychophysiological research, cognitive psychology and psychoanalytic theory, because of that are designed for a variety of coping definitions. Lazarus (1993), the creator of coping concept suggested the direction of coping researches is the main, so often coping studies are based on the scientist. Lazarus stress coping describes as constantly changing cognitive, emotional and behavioral efforts fighting with specific external and / or internal requirements, that makes it difficult or above the employee's capabilities.

The main features of personnel stress (emotional, cognitive, physiological and behavioral) can be reduced, when managers properly organize the work process and regulate the work relations correctly. Also, the workers themselves can manage stress and work productivity. Therefore, it is recommended for managers to organize staff training in stress management, which provides psychological knowledge and practical coping skills.

MODELING OF LABOUR PRODUCTIVITY AND STRESS INTERACTION

In order, effectively to manage stress and determine its impact on productivity, it is appropriate to form the factors, which are characterizing an exhaustive list of the indicators. In such way it would be created preconditions for the comprehensive assessment of stress. At the end, the stressor must be:

1. To classify into groups, which in turn submitted without duplicates indicators are described in detail stress;
2. Defined indicators could be explored.

The groups of stress factors. Stress is considered as the emotional and physical aspects of the employee's reaction to the stressors. The reaction to the stressors varies according to the individual characteristics of the worker and the working environment pressure. It should be noted, that the employee's individual characteristics (for example, the problem of scale perception, self-esteem), and the operating environment pressure (for example, labour requirements, control) is the stress causing factors that affect employee productivity at one and the same time. Analysis of factors, which cause stress showed that these factors can be classified into the individual and situational. The individual factors are related to the personal characteristics, but the situational factors are related to the working conditions of the organization and the organizational environment.

So, the individual factors of stress – the stressors, which originated from the person's (employee's) beliefs, his evaluation of conduct. The situational factors of stress are the environment of organization and the stressors, which were caused by the working conditions.

Both individual and situational factors affect the employee and have influence to labour productivity. These factors associated examination makes full disclosure of stress influence on productivity. So, the labour productivity of employee's can be seen as a result of stress management:

$$P=f(S_i; S_t) \tag{1}$$

There are P – labour productivity; S – stress, i – individual stress's factors; t – situational stress's factors.

Indicators group consists of assumptions comprehensive evaluation of a stress factor and get a summary quantitative assessment of this factor. It is calculated from the values of the indicators according to their relevance. Groups quantitative indicator values can easily be calculated analytically, qualitative indicators applicable to determine the values of expert assessment methods based on the chosen methodology and assessment scale (e.g., Relative unit, points). It is appropriate to determine the amplitude of factors fluctuation, because there are requesting negligible quantity of the factors, which cause stress, but the factors can be expressed in relative dimensions. For comparability of quantitative and qualitative indicators values must be normalized, using the methods, which are recommended in the literature. Significance of indicators to determine the recommended application in practice proven, widely applicable methods. For example, different areas of applied expert evaluation method in 1980 Saaty (1993) created widespread *AHP* method.

Classifying indicators into groups clearly establishes their mutual relations and influence on the final assessment. Each element of the indicator, respectively, of the individual (*i*), situational (*t*) is calculated using the following formulas:

$$i = \sum_{j=1}^{n} \omega_j I_j; \tag{2}$$

$$t = \sum_{l=1}^{k} \omega_l T_l; \tag{3}$$

There are I – the individual factors of the contents of revealing indicators ($j = 1, ..., n$) values; T – situational factors group content revealing indicators ($l = 1, ..., k$) values; ω – the significance of the relevant indicator.

The application possibilities. Stress characterizing factors - individual and situational - the system operated estimating their content describing indicators. The evaluation of the factors or indicators characterizing the content of the order is not important, but it is necessary to consistently perform the factor rating. The proposed complex of stress assessment of the content enables to carry out monitoring work-related stress and during certain changes to make reasoned decisions. The proposed system of indicators allows the coherent and comprehensive evaluation of stress, based on proposals to improve the management of stress, thereby purposefully act in the productivity of employee.

Provided grouping of indicators allows to study the certain stress factor and get generalized quantitative evaluation. This is particularly useful in the analysis of labour productivity, setting the certain stress factor changes of the direction, the impact of labour productivity.

RECOMMENDATIONS

To effectively manage stress, it is necessary to identify the factors and their significance to the final result. Firstly, the set of individual and situational factors should be formed. According to this set and taken into consideration the specification of the case, the most important stress factors of an organization should be picked out and the finite casebook of stress factors should be formed. Attention should be paid to the volatile circumstances, and the set of individual and situational factors must be revised and actualized in this case. Secondly, the stress factors might have a different impact on the final result. In order to evaluate the stress objectively, the significance of separate stress factors and also the group of factors (individual and situational) should be measured. In this case it is recommended to use the multicriteria methods created to identify the aforementioned significance. The evaluation of the factors or indicators characterizing the content of the order is not important, it does not affect the final result. Finally, when the factors, which cause stress, are identified, the finite casebook of them is formed, the values and the significances of the indicators are evaluated, then can the systematic monitoring of the job stress be carried out.

CONCLUSION

Scientists, exploring stress as one of the most important factors, which do influence to the employee's labour productivity and the results of organization activity, value it as a process, affect the employee or the situation of working environment, and focus attention on factors realation and reaction. Done analysis of stress factors allows to state that the main factors of stress are work, which requires high results, job scarcity, menstrual ailments, inadequate work organization, instability, lack of prospects, work-family conflict, lack of work control, lack of social support in the workplace, inadequate remuneration, relations between the workplace. Labour productivity can be seen as a result of stress management, but in order to model management of stress, it is necessary to distinguish the essential components of stress. To this, the factors, causing stress originally, are classified into two groups: 1) individual (stressors, arising from the person's (employee's) beliefs, his evaluation of conduct); 2) situational (environment of organization and stressors, which are caused with the relevant working conditions). Control of these factors creates the preconditions for increasing productivity, improving the organization's results of performance. Further researches should be focus on the formation of finite casebook and determine the importance. The results of studies allow to scientists to suggest the tools of stress management and it would be the assumption for practitioners (employers and employees) to take the effective tools of stress management.

REFERENCES

СаатиТ. Л. (1993). *Принятие решений. Метод анализа иерархий* (пер. с англ.). Москва: Радио и связъ.

Alavinia, S. M., Van den Berg, T. I. J., Van Duivenbooden, C., Elders, L. A. M., & Burdorf, A. (2009). Impact of work-related factors, lifestyle, and work ability on sickness absence among Dutch construction workers. *Scandinavian Journal of Work, Environment & Health*, 35(5), 325–333. doi:10.5271/sjweh.1340 PMID:19554244

Alexander, D. A., & Klein, S. (2001). Impact of accident and emer-gency work on mental health and emotional well-being. *The British Journal of Psychiatry*, 178, 76–81. doi:10.1192/bjp.178.1.76 PMID:11136215

Bakker, A. B., Demerouti, E., & Verbeke, W. (2004, Spring). Using the Job Demands-Resources Model to Predict Burnout and Performance. *Human Resource Management*, 43(1), 83–104. doi:10.1002/hrm.20004

Bandura, A. (2001). Social cognitive theory: An agentic perspective. *Annual Review of Psychology*, 52(1), 1–26. doi:10.1146/annurev.psych.52.1.1 PMID:11148297

Barrick, M. R. (2005). Yes, personality matters: Moving on to more important matters. *Human Performance*, 18(4), 359–372. doi:10.1207/s15327043hup1804_3

Barrick, M. R., Steward, G. L., & Piotrowski, M. (2002). Personality and job performance: Test of the mediating effects of mo-tivation among sales representatives. *The Journal of Applied Psychology*, 87(1), 43–51. doi:10.1037/0021-9010.87.1.43 PMID:11916215

Benach, J., Muntaner, C., & Santana, V. (2007). *Employment conditions and health inequalities*. Employment Conditions Knowledge Network. Final Report of WHO Commission on Social Determinants of Health.

Boschman, J. S., Van der Molen, H. F., Sluiter, J. K., & Frings-Dresen, M. H. W. (2013). Psychosocial work environment and mental health among construction workers. *Applied Ergonomics*, 44(5), 748–755. doi:10.1016/j.apergo.2013.01.004 PMID:23380530

Bureš, V., & Stropková, A. (2014). Labour Productivity and Possibilities of its Extension by Knowledge Management Aspects. *Procedia: Social and Behavioral Sciences, 109*, 1088–1093.

Carnegie, D. (2004). *How to stop worrying and start living.* New York: Pocket Books.

Chan, K. B., Lai, G., Ko, Y. C., & Boey, K. W. (2000). Work stress among six professional groups: The Singapore experience. *Social Science & Medicine, 50*(10), 1415–1432. doi:10.1016/S0277-9536(99)00397-4 PMID:10741577

Cheng, T., Teizer, J., Migliaccio, G. C., & Gatti, U. C. (2013). Automated task-level productivity analysis through fusion of real time location sensors and workers thoracic posture data. *Automation in Construction, 29*, 24–39. doi:10.1016/j.autcon.2012.08.003

Cheng, T., Venugopal, M., Teizer, J., & Vela, P. A. (2011). Performance evaluation of ultra wideband technology for construction resource location tracking in harsh environments. *Automation in Construction, 20*(8), 1173–1184. doi:10.1016/j.autcon.2011.05.001

Clark, D. M., & Wells, A. (1995). A Cognitive Model of Social Phobia. In R. G. Heimberg, M. R. Liebowitz, D. A. Hope, & F. R. Schneier (Eds.), Social phobia, diagnosis, assessment and treatment. The Guilford Press.

Collins, K. M. (1993). Stress and departures from the public accounting profession: A study of gender differences. *Accounting Horizons*, (March), 29–38.

DeGroote, S. E., & Marx, T. G. (2013). The impact of IT on supply chain agility and firm performance: An empirical investigation. *International Journal of Information Management, 33*(6), 909–916. doi:10.1016/j.ijinfomgt.2013.09.001

Dollard, M. F., & Neser, D. Y. (2013). Worker health is good for the economy: Union density and psychosocial safety climate as determinants of country differences in worker health and productivity in 31 European countries. *Social Science & Medicine, 92*, 114–123. doi:10.1016/j.socscimed.2013.04.028 PMID:23849285

Elfering, A., Semmer, N. K., & Grebner, S. (2006). Work stress and patient safety: Observer-rated work stressors as predictors of characteristics of safety-related events reported by young nurses. *Ergonomics, 49*(5), 457–469. doi:10.1080/00140130600568451 PMID:16717004

Elisburg, D. (1995). Workplace stress: legal developments, economic pressures, and violence. In Workers' Compensation Year Book. Horsham, PA: LRP Publications.

European Commission. Slovenian EU Presidency, WHO Regional Office for Europe. (2008). *European Pact for Mental Health and Well-being.* Brussels: European Commission. Available: http://ec.europa.eu/health/mental_health/docs/mhpact_en.pdf

Hanin, Y. L. (1997). Emotions and athletic performance: Individual zones of optimal functioning model. *European Yearbook of Sport Psychology, 1*, 29–72.

Hardy, L. (1996). Testing the predictions of the cusp catastrophe model of anxiety and performance. *The Sport Psychologist, 10*(2), 140–156. doi:10.1123/tsp.10.2.140

Holmes, D. S., & Rahe, R. (1967). Holmes – Rahe Cife chantes seal. *Journal of Psychosomatic Research*, 215–218.

Hu, Q., Schaufeli, W. B., & Taris, T. W. (2011). The Job Demands–Resources model: An analysis of additive and joint effects of demands and resources. *Journal of Vocational Behavior, 79*(1), 181–190. doi:10.1016/j.jvb.2010.12.009

Kain, J., & Jex, S. (2010). Karasek's (1979) job demands-control model: A summary of current issues and recommendations for future research. In New Developments in Theoretical and Conceptual Approaches to Job Stress (Research in Occupational Stress and Well-being, Volume 8). Emerald Group Publishing Limited.

Kaklauskas, A., Zavadskas, E. K., Pruskus, V., Vlasenko, A., Bartkienė, L., Pališkienė, R., & Tamulevičius, G. et al. (2011). Recommended biometric stress management system. *Expert systems with applications Oxford: Elsevier Science Ltd., 38*(5), 14011–14025.

Kaklauskas, A., Zavadskas, E. K., Seniut, M., Dzemyda, G., Stankevič, V., Šimkevičius, Č., . . . Gribniak, V. (2011). Web-based biometric computer mouse advisory system to analyze a user's emotions and work productivity. Engineering Applications of Artificial Intelligence, 24(6), 928-945.

Kaklauskas, A., Zavadskas, E. K., Seniut, M., Stankevic, V., Raistenskis, J., Simkevicius, C., . . . Cerkauskiene, R. (2013). Recommender system to analyze student's academic performance. Expert Systems With Applications, 40(15), 6150-6165.

Kerr, J. H. (2001). *Counseling Athletes: Applying Reversal Theory*. London: Routledge.

Lazarus, R. S. (1993). From psychological stress to the emotions: A History of Changing Outlooks. *Annual Review of Psychology, 44*(1), 1–22. doi:10.1146/annurev.ps.44.020193.000245 PMID:8434890

Lazarus, R. S., & Folkman, S. (1984). *Stress, appraisal and coping*. New York: Springer publishing Company.

Leung, M. Y., Chan, I. Y., & Yu, J. (2012). Preventing construction worker injury incidents through the management of personal stress and organizational stressors. *Accident; Analysis and Prevention, 48*(1), 156–166. doi:10.1016/j.aap.2011.03.017 PMID:22664679

Leung, M. Y., Chan, Y. S., & Yuen, K. W. (2010). Impacts of stressors and stress on the injury incidents of construction workers in Hong Kong. *Journal of Construction Engineering and Management, 136*(10), 1093–1103. doi:10.1061/(ASCE)CO.1943-7862.0000216

Leung, M. Y., Chan, Y. S., & Yuen, K. W. (2010). Impacts of stressors and stress on the injury incidents of construction workers in Hong Kong. *Journal of Construction Engineering and Management, 136*(10), 1093–1103. doi:10.1061/(ASCE)CO.1943-7862.0000216

Lingard, H., Francis, V., & Turner, M. (2012). Work–life strategies in the Australian construction industry: Implementation issues in a dynamic project-based work environment. *International Journal of Project Management, 30*(3), 282–295. doi:10.1016/j.ijproman.2011.08.002

Lingard, H., Francis, V., & Turner, M. (2012). Work–life strategies in the Australian construction industry: Implementation issues in a dynamic project-based work environment. *International Journal of Project Management, 30*(3), 282–295. doi:10.1016/j.ijproman.2011.08.002

Luthans, F. (2006). *Organisational Behaviour* (10th Indonesian Edition). Yogyakarta: Penerbit Andi.

Manzoor, A., Awan, H., & Mariam, S. (2012). Investigating the impact of work stress on job performance: A study on textile sector of Faisalabad. *Asian Journal of Business and Management Sciences, 2*(1), 20–28.

Manzoor, A., Awan, H., & Mariam, S. (2012). Investigating the impact of work stress on job performance: A study on textile sector of Faisalabad. *Asian Journal of Business and Management Sciences, 2*(1), 20–28.

Matteson, M. T., & Ivancevich, J. M. (1979). Organizational Stressors and Heart Disease: A Research Model. *Academy of Management Review, 4*(3), 347–357.

Matteson, M. T., & Ivancevich, J. M. (1979). Organizational Stressors and Heart Disease: A Research Model. *Academy of Management Review, 4*(3), 347–357.

Mellor, N., Mackay, C., Packham, C., Jones, R., Palferman, D., Webster, S., & Kelly, P. (2011). Management Standards and work-related stress in Great Britain: Progress on their implementation. *Safety Science, 49*(7), 1040–1046. doi:10.1016/j.ssci.2011.01.010

Mellor, N., Mackay, C., Packham, C., Jones, R., Palferman, D., Webster, S., & Kelly, P. (2011). Management Standards and work-related stress in Great Britain: Progress on their implementation. *Safety Science, 49*(7), 1040–1046. doi:10.1016/j.ssci.2011.01.010

Myers, D. G. (2000). Hope and happiness. In J. Gillham (Ed.), *The science of optimism and hope*. Radnor, PA: Templeton Foundation Press.

Myers, D. G. (2001). *Political and economic theory meet social psychology. (Review of Robert E. Lane's The loss of happiness in market democracies.)*. Contemporary Psychology.

Pekrun, R., Frenzel, A. C., Goetz, T., & Perry, R. P. (2007). *The control-value theory of achievement emotions: an integrative approach to emotions in education. In Emotion in Education* (pp. 13–36). Burlington, MA: Elsevier. doi:10.1016/B978-012372545-5/50003-4

Profiles Research Institut. (2010). *Streso darbe valdymas*. Available: http://www.profilesinternational.lt/upload/infofiles/streso_darbe_valdymas.pdf

Sauter, S. L., Murphy, L. R., & Hurrell, J. Jr. (1990). Prevention of work-related psychological disorders. *The American Psychologist, 45*(10), 1146–1158. doi:10.1037/0003-066X.45.10.1146 PMID:2252233

Siegrist, J. (2002). Reducing social inequalities in health: Work-related strategies. *Scandinavian Journal of Public Health, 30*(59 suppl), 49–53. doi:10.1177/14034948020300030801 PMID:12227965

Spielberger, C. D. (1972). *Anxiety: current trends in theory and research* (Vol. 1). New York: Academic Press.

Stoner, J. A. F., Freeman, R. E., & Gilbert, D. R. (2000). *Vadyba*. Kaunas: poligrafija ir informatika.

The American Institute of Stress. (2011). Retrieved from http://www.stress.org/about/

U.S. Department of Health and Human Services. (n.d.). *Public Health Service Centers for Disease Control and Prevention National Institute for Occupational Safety and Health.* Retrieved from https://www.cdc.gov/niosh/docs/99-101/

Yerkes, R. M., & Dodson, J. D. (1908). The Relation of Strength of Stimulus to Rapidity of Habit-Formation. *The Journal of Comparative Neurology and Psychology, 18*(5), 459–482. doi:10.1002/cne.920180503

ADDITIONAL READING

Chain, D. W. (2002). Stress, Self-Efficacy, Social Support, and Psychological Distress Among Prospective Chinese Teachers in Hong Kong. *Educational Psychology, 22*(5).

Chaplain, R. P. (1995). Stress and job satisfaction: A study of English primary school teachers. *Educational Psychology, 15*(4), 473–489. doi:10.1080/0144341950150409

Côté, S., & Miners, C. T. H. (2006). Emotional Intelligence, Cognitive Intelligence, and Job Performance. *Administrative Science Quarterly, 51*, 1–28.

Dantzer, R. (2001). Stress, emotions and health: Where do we stand? *Social Sciences Information. Information Sur les Sciences Sociales, 40*(1), 61–78. doi:10.1177/053901801040001004

Dryson, E. W., Scragg, R. K., Metcalf, P. A., & Baker, J. R. (1996). Stress at work: An evaluation of occupational stressors as reported by a multi-cultural New Zealand workforce. *Int. J. Occup. Health, 2*(1), 18–25. doi:10.1179/oeh.1996.2.1.18 PMID:9933861

Grant, A. M. (2008). The Significance of Task Significance: Job Performance Effects, Relational Mechanisms, and Boundary Conditions. *The Journal of Applied Psychology, 93*(1), 108–124. doi:10.1037/0021-9010.93.1.108 PMID:18211139

Hunter, L., & Thatcher, S. M. (2007). Feeling the heat: Effects of stress, commitment, and job experience on job performance. *Academy of Management Journal, 50*(4), 953–968. doi:10.5465/AMJ.2007.26279227

Le Fevre, M., Matheny, J., & Kolt, G. S. (2006). Eustress, distress and their interpretation in primary and secondary occupational stress management interventions: Wich way first? *Journal of Managerial Psychology, 21*(6), 547–565. doi:10.1108/02683940610684391

Murphy, L. R. (1995). Managing job stress: An employee assistance/human resource management partnership. *Personnel Review, 24*(1), 41–50. doi:10.1108/00483489510079075

Narayanan, L., Manon, S., & Spector, P. E. (1999). Stress in the Workplace: A Comparison of Gender and Occupations. *Journal of Organizational Behavior, 20*(1), 63–73. doi:10.1002/(SICI)1099-1379(199901)20:1<63::AID-JOB873>3.0.CO;2-J

Newman, J. D., & Beehr, T. (1979). Personal and Organizational Strategies for handling Job Stress: A review of Research and Opinion. *Personnel Psychology, 32*(1), 1–43. doi:10.1111/j.1744-6570.1979.tb00467.x

Rossi, A. M., Perrewe, P. L., & Sauter, S. L. (Eds.). (2006). *Stress and quality working life*. International Stress Management Association.

Rotundo, M., & Sackett, P. R. (2002). The relative importance of task, citizenship and counterproductive performance to Global rating of job performance: A policy-capturing approach. *The Journal of Applied Psychology, 87*(1), 66–80. doi:10.1037/0021-9010.87.1.66 PMID:11916217

Sharma, M., & Kaur, G. (2011). Workplace empowerment and organizational effectiveness: An empirical investigation of Indian bankine sector. *Academy of Banking Studies Journal, 10*(2), 105–120.

Smith, L. A., Roman, A., Dollard, M. F., Winefield, A. H., & Siegrist, J. (2005). Effortreward imbalance at work: The effects of work stress on anger and cardiovascular disease symptoms in a community sample. *Stress and Health, 21*(2), 113–128. doi:10.1002/smi.1045

Spector, P. E., Yang, L., & Che, H. (2008). Job stress and well-being: An examination from the view of person–environment fit. *Journal of Occupational and Organizational Psychology, 81*(3), 567–587. doi:10.1348/096317907X243324

Stacciarini, J. M. R., & Troccoli, B. T. (2003). Occupational stress and constructive thinking: Health and job satisfaction. *Journal of Advanced Nursing, 46*(5), 480–487. doi:10.1111/j.1365-2648.2004.03022.x PMID:15139936

Stanton, J. M., Balzer, W. K., Smith, P. C., Parra, L. F., & Ironson, G. (2001). A general measurement of work stress: The stress in general scale. *Educational and Psychological Measurement, 61*(5), 866–888. doi:10.1177/00131640121971455

Van der Hek, H., & Plomp, H. N. (1997). Occupational stress management programmes: A practical overview of published effect studies. *Occupational Medicine, 47*(3), 133–141. doi:10.1093/occmed/47.3.133 PMID:9156467

Whitfied, G. B. (2007). ASK EOS: EmployeeMotivation. http://www.expat.or.id/business/employeemotivational.html

Williams, G. C., Grow, V. M., Freedman, Z., Ryan, R. M., & Deci, E. L. (1996). Motivational predictors of weight loss and weight-loss maintenance. *Journal of Personality and Social Psychology, 70*(1), 115–126. doi:10.1037/0022-3514.70.1.115 PMID:8558405

Williams, R. S. (2002). *Managing employee performance: design and implementation in organizations*. Cengage Learning EMEA.

KEY TERMS AND DEFINITIONS

Efficiency in the Economic Sense: Means that things should be done in an economic way considering that resources are scarce. Efficiency therefore implies doing the right things in a rightful manner.

Efficiency: Doing things right.

Individual Factors of Stress: The stressors, which originated from the person's (employee's) beliefs, his evaluation of conduct.

Productivity: Refers to the conversion level of inputs into outputs. A process that can produce more output using less inputs is more proactive. Productivity = Output / Input.

Situational Factors of Stress: The environment of organization and the stressors, which were caused by the working conditions.

Stress Coping Strategies: Different strategies taken to avoid or deal with the problem. Job stress is considered as the emotional and physical aspects of the employee's reaction to stressors.

Stress: The process by which we evaluate and respond to the specific threat or challenge of presenting events - stressors.

Working Conditions: The nature of work, work and leisure time and other circumstances, which are having the direct impact on the employee' well-being, efficiency, safety and health.

Working Environment: The area, which is surrounding the workplace, where the employee can be affected with the factors of harmful and dangerous risk.

Chapter 17
Leadership Behavior Predictor of Employees' Job Satisfaction and Psychological Health

Mateja Lorber
University of Maribor, Slovenia

Sonja Treven
University of Maribor, Slovenia

Damijan Mumel
University of Maribor, Slovenia

ABSTRACT

Research about relationship between the leadership behavior and the psychological health is still limited. The effect of job dissatisfaction on health is important not only from medical but also from the economic perspective. The association between leadership behavior, job satisfaction and psychological health in nursing was tested. 640 hospital nurses from surgery and internal medicine departments in Slovenian hospitals participated. Data analysis was carried out by using SPSS, 20.0. The transformational leadership style, leaders' characteristics, job satisfaction predicted better psychological health. More frequent exposure to stress and the lack of stress management was associated with poor psychological health. Job satisfaction is at a medium level. The results indicated that 85% of employees in nursing had good psychological health. The psychological health of employees does not affect only on individual, but also on the quality and effectiveness. It is important to monitor employees' job satisfaction and take care for health by providing a healthy work environment.

DOI: 10.4018/978-1-5225-2480-9.ch017

INTRODUCTION

Hospitals play an important role in the health care system. They are health care institutions that have an organized medical and other professional staff, and deliver medical, nursing and related services 24 hours per day, 7 days per week. Hospitals offer a varying range of acute, convalescent and terminal care using diagnostic and curative services in response to acute and chronic conditions, arising from diseases as well as injuries and genetic anomalies (WHO, 2016a).

The importance of effective leadership in health care was exposed (Carney, 2006; Greenfield, 2007; Sutherland & Dodd, 2008). Leadership in nursing is pivotal because nurses represent the most extensive discipline in health care, they are also the main working group in hospitals and play a vital role in the caring system of every country (Marquis & Huston, 2009; Roussel, Swansburg, & Swansburg, 2009; Sullivan & Garland, 2010; WHO, 2013). The nurses' job assignment as health team members is very important, they must to preserve and promote the quality of care to a standard level (Mohammmadi et al., 2011), but there is a problem because the average age of nurses in developed countries increasing (WHO, 2013). Nursing is a profession that involves interaction with different people (patients, their families, other nurses, doctors and various specialists), emotional and physical work in a very challeng-ing environment (Purcell, Kutash, & Cobb, 2011; Scheick, 2011) and heavy load (Aiken et al., 2001). According to the progress and development, working conditions are constantly changing, including strategies for increasing productivity and reducing costs and maintaining quality of care (Aiken, Clarke, Sloane, Sochalski, & Silber, 2002). Nursing is an emotional and physical strenuous job, and studies show that work in health care poses a major risk for the occurrence of stress, anxiety and depression (Gershon et al., 2007). Aiken et al. (2002) also noted that nurses in hospitals with a higher ratio patient to nurse, more likely to experience burnout and job dissatisfaction, what can lead to different symptoms or illness (Aiken et al., 2001; Miller & McGoven, 2000; West, Tan, Habermann, Sloan, & Shanafelt, 2009). Burnout is associated with psychological disorders, physical illness, decrease work productiv-ity and an increase work absence (Ahola et al., 2008). Chronic work stress and burnout in nursing are related to consequences for psychological and physical symptoms (Melamed, Shirom, Toker, Berliner, & Shapira, 2006; Tsutsumi, Kayaba, Tsutsumi, & Igarashi, 2001). The field of work, as well as age, education (Schulz et al., 2009) and gender (Bauer et al., 2006) play an important role of nurses' burnout.

BACKGROUND

Psychological Health

Psychological health is an integral and essential part of health. Some people say psychological health as "mental health" or "emotional health" or "prosperity", but is just as important as good physical health (Mental Health Foundation, 2016). The WHO (2016b) states: "Health is a state of complete physical, mental and social well-being and not merely the absence of disease or infirmity." An important implica-tion of this definition is that mental health is more than just the absence of mental disorder or disability. Mental or psychological health is a state of well being in which the individual realizes his own abilities, can cope with the normal stresses of life, can work productively and is able to contribute to the com-munity. On the other hand, psychological health is defined as the absence of symptoms related with depression and anxiety, including the ability to concentrate and irritability in the last few weeks (WHO,

2001). Psychological health is the successful performance of mental function, resulting in activities, fulfilling relationships with other people, and providing the ability to adapt to change and cope with adversity (National Alliance of Mental Illness, 2011). Multiple social, psychological, and biological factors determine the level of psychological health of a person at any point of time. Poor psychological health associated with rapid social change, stressful work conditions, discrimination, social exclusion, unhealthy lifestyle, risks of violence, physical ill-health and human rights violations (WHO, 2016b).

Psychological health is a significant element of social needs (Zandi, Sayari, Ebadi, & Sanaisanasab, 2011). Good psychological health is a sense of well-being, confidence and self-esteem and enables us, to fully enjoy and appreciate other people day-to-day life in our environment. When we are psychological healthy, we can form positive relationships, use our abilities to reach potential and deal with our life's challenges (Mental Health Commission, 2010). Mental Health Foundation (2016) noted that good psychological health is characterised by a person's ability to fulfil a number of key functions and activities, including with the ability to learn, to feel, to express and to manage a range of positive and negative emotions, the ability to form and maintain good relationships with others and the ability to cope with and manage change and uncertainty. Jenkins & Elliot (2004) noted that research of psychological health at work growing in the recent years.

Women have almost to 40% more likely to develop mental disorders than men (Ball, 2013; Gaidos, 2016; Thorpe, 2015; WHO, 2016c). Ball (2013) and WHO (2016c) also noted that women more likely to have depression and anxiety than men. Anxiety and depressive disorders are known as mental disorders (Gärtner, Nieuwehuijsn, Dijk, & Sluiter, 2010). Avoiding anxiety and depression is one of the most essential necessities of human beings (Ryan & Deci, 2000), but anxiety and depression are the most common psychological problems of health personnel (Zandi et al., 2011). Nursing is an emotionally and physically demanding occupation and researches indicated that work in nursing entails high risks of experiencing stress, anxiety and depression (Gershon et al., 2007). Mental disorders may result from a variety of workplace, organisational and individual factors (Healy, & McKay, 2003; Hover-Kramer, Mabbett, & Shames, 1996). These factors include working environments where nurses have lack autonomy and discretion, and where is limited the access to support and learning (Purdy, Spence Laschinger, Finegan, Ker, & Olivera, 2010); where occur high levels of emotional exhaustion and burnout (Vahey, Aiken, Sloane, Clarke, & Vargas, 2004); where nurses frequently experience workplace stress (Brunero, Cowan, & Fairbrother, 2008; Chang et al., 2007), high workloads and low reward (Jasper et al., 2012), and where rotational shift patterns result in poor sleep (Lin et al., 2012). The nature of peer relationships in work environments experienced by nurses can also contribute to negative mental health symptoms (Way & MacNeil 2006).

Mental disorders have strongly associated with productivity in nursing (Letvak, Ruhm, & Gupta, 2012), absenteeism and presenteeism (Warren et al., 2011); poor work performance, reduced productivity, workplace errors, decreased quality of patient care and low levels of patient satisfaction (Gärtner, Neiuweinhuijsen, Dijk, & Sluiter, 2012). Physical and psychological health of nurses is in direct relation with providing of patient care. A healthy workplace can result in prevention of depression, anxiety and stress and lead to promotion of satisfaction and efficiency of employees. Also, Laschinger, Finegan, & Shamian (2001) and Laschinger, Almost, Purdy, & Kim (2004) noted that empowering work environments is associated with positive health outcomes. Nursing is a profession, which requiring a high degree of commitment and involvement.

Leadership Behavior

The achievement of organizational goals largely depends of the leadership behavior which is related with the number of employees and organizational variables (Malik, 2013). Mosadegh Rad (2003) presented the leadership behavior, as a set of characteristics, attitudes, and skills used by a leader in different situations, depending on individual and organizational values. Daft (2005) defined the leadership behavior as a relationship between leaders and co-workers. Different dimensions of the leadership behavior have been developed, and the researchers still continue to discover what contributes to the success of leadership. Leadership behavior depending of leadership style, leaders' personal characteristics and emotions.

Theories of management is often described with different classifications based on personality and behavior, and were used to determine the characteristics and behaviors of an effective way management (Muchinsky, 2006; Spector, 2006). Management style is a construct related to the number of employees and organizational variables. Many theories and leadership styles have been developed, and different leadership styles show how to keep nurses in hospitals (Huber, 2006). Huber et al. (2000) explain that the leadership style as a combination of tasks and behaviors that influence employees to achieve objectives. Goethals, Sorenson, & Burns (2004) noted that the transaction leadership based on the theory that employees are motivated by rewards and discipline, but transformation leadership style focus on the team-building, motivation and participation of the employees at various levels of the organization. Transformational leadership style is based on the active role played by leaders to promote the motivation and objectives in the context of employees, but business management style is based on the mutual exchange between the leader and co-workers (Burns, 2010, p. 425). Leadership style laissez-faire is the style in which the leader gives little or no direction or control, and prefers to make its own decision. Changes occur rarely and improving quality is usually low. Laissez-faire leadership style is used mostly new and inexperienced leaders or those at the end of his career (Goethals et al, 2004; Skogstad, et al., 2007). Already Kouzes and Posner (1997) noted that there is no best leadership style; but leaders must choose the method of management and leadership according to the situations and circumstances. All kind of leadership style has advantages and disadvantages (Goethals et al, 2004; Marquis and Huston, 2009).

The leadership style associated with the leaders' personality (Brown & Reilly, 2009), leaders' emotional intelligence (Barling, Kelloway, & Slater., 2000; Downey, Papageorgiou, & Stough, 2006; Vrba, 2007), stress and burnout (Gill, Flaschner, & Shacha, 2006; Kanste, Kyngas, & Nikkila, 2007; Zopiatis & Constanti, 2010), job satisfaction (Cummings et al, 2008; Failla, & Stichler, 2008; Mancheno-Smoak, Endres, Potak, & Athanasaw, 2009; Sellgren, Ekwall, & Tomson, 2008), psychological health (Faragher, Cass, & Cooper, 2005; Lambert, lampert, & Ito, 2004; Skogstad et al., 2007), and well-being (Arnold et al., 2007; Kuoppala, Lamminpää, Liira, & Vainio, 2008; Nielsen, Randall, Yarker, & Brenner, 2008; Skakon, Bielsen, Borg, & Guzman, 2010).

Leadership style, used by individual leader depend of the personal characteristics of leader. Leadership style that leader will be adopted in its own way, is selected according to the knowledge, experience and skills from leader's past. Leaders can work easier and more efficient if they aware their own actions and decisions, and they know, why in a particular situation, act on a distinctive way. Leaders' characteristics are those, which have a significant impact on leaders' achievements and success in a conflict resolution and perform tasks (Musek & Pečjak 2001). Because of that the leadership behavior also depends on the personal characteristics of each individual leader.

According to the research different researchers highlighted different characteristics that leaders should have for successful leadership. Leadership-Toolbox (2008) presents six relevant characteristics of a successful leadership, like empathy, consistency, honesty, communication, flexibility, and beliefs. Holden Leadership Center (2009) noted that every leader should have responsibility, flexibility, good communication skills, trusting, enthusiasm, creativity, openness to change, interests for feedback, and delegating. Prive (2012) noted that honesty, delegating, good communication, sense of humor, confidence, dedication, positive attitude, creativity, intuition, and the ability to inspire are the most important leaders' characteristics for success. Economy (2014) presents that the characteristics of successful leaders are: awareness, assertiveness, empathy, responsibility, trust, optimism, honesty, and inspiration, but Javitch (2014) exposes only team skills, communication skills, interpersonal skills, and ambition. Lorber & Skela Savič (2011) found that leaders and employees in nursing in Slovenian hospitals from twenty-five characteristics of successful leaders highlighted next ten characteristics: honesty, organizational skills, teamwork, decisiveness, reliability, objectivity, responsibility, communication skills, self-confidence, and ambition.

Emotions in Western societies, have been so far regarded as irrational and dysfunctional factors (Muchinsky, 2000). Barsade (2002) demonstrated the important implications of emotions in work teams. Sy, Côté, & Saavedra (2005) found that leaders' emotions can also affect the mood and performance of their employees. Emotions are fundamental for nursing practice (Brunton, Mark, 2005; Bulmer-Smith, Profetto-McGrath, & Cummings, 2009). Researchers (Bulmer-Smith et al., 2009; Obholzer, 2005; Waddington & Fletcher, 2005) noted that emotional labor and increasing workloads effect on health of employees. Emotions play an important role in nursing probably because nursing requires not only technical expertise, but also psychologically oriented care and knowledge of self and others (Landa & López-Zafra, 2010).

Emotional intelligence also plays an important role on an individual and group behavior and performance in the workplace (Goleman, Boyatzis, & McKee, 2002; Law, Wong, & Song, 2004; Sy & Côté, 2004; Wong & Law, 2002). Some researchers (Clarke, 2010; Harms & Crede, 2010; Kerr, Garvin, Heaton, & Boyle, 2006; Lorber, 2015; Riggio & Reichard, 2008) found that emotional intelligence is an important ability of leaders for successful leadership. Lorber (2015) found that leaders' emotional intelligence was positively correlated with leaders' quality of communication, teamwork at the hospital unit, interpersonal relationships at the hospital unit, conflict solving, and quality of care. Segal and Smith (2014) noted that emotional intelligence affects on work performance, physical health, psychological health, and relationships. Employees in health care institutions, in which have leaders with highly developed emotional intelligence have better psychological health, are more satisfied, and have better quality of healthcare (Goleman & Boyatzis, 2008). Emotional intelligence affects on job satisfaction (Gűleryűz, Güney, Aydin, & Asan, 2008), organizational commitment (Gűleryűz et al., 2008), well-being (Karimi, Leggat, Donohue, Farrell, & Couper, 2014) and reduced stress (Cummings, Hayduk, & Estabrooks, 2005; Karimi et al., 2014)

Job Satisfaction

Each person has their own views of work. Working environment effect on the employees, at their level of performance and also on their satisfaction, well-being and health. Work has effect on satisfaction, well-being and health of the individual, because it provides income and means to broader social progress. Because of that job satisfaction is define in many different ways. The most widely accepted theory of job satisfaction was proposed by Locke (1976), who defined job satisfaction as "a pleasurable or positive emotional state resulting from the appraisal of one's job or job experiences". Business Dictionary (2016) define job satisfaction as satisfaction that arising out of interplay interaction of positive and negative feelings of employees towards his or her work. Already Lu, While, & Bariball (2005) noted that job satisfaction related to beliefs and emotions that individuals have about their work.

It is known that the organizations that satisfied employees are more productive than those with unhappy employees (Hellriegel & Slocum, 2007). Researchers (Al-Hussami, 2008Aron, 2015; Koy, Yunibhand, Angsuroch, & Fisher 2015; Mrayyan, 2006), showed that a higher level of job satisfaction in health care, it also increases the organizational commitment of employees and the quality of patient care. The level of satisfaction also plays an important role in staffing levels as their level of health and also at the organizational level and employee productivity (Faragher et al., 2005). Studies (Faragher et al, 2005Kudielka et al, 2005, Marklund, Bolin, & von Essen 2008; Nadinloyi, Sadeghi, & Hajloo 2013; Thorsteinsson, Brown, & Richards, 2014) have also shown a link between psychological health and job satisfaction of employees. Psychological health and job satisfaction are the key elements of sick leaves and also the crucial reasons for leaving an organization (Coomber & Barriball, 2007). Nurses' poor psychological health is more likely to lead to problems of patients and also the quantity and quality of patient care will be reduced (Michie & Williams, 2002). Physical and psychological health of nurses is in direct relation with the providing of care, therefore a healthy workplace results the prevention of depression, anxiety and stress among nurses and lead to promotion of satisfaction and efficiency (Taghinejad, Suhrabi, Kikhvani, Jaafarpour, & Azadi, 2014). Nurses have higher than normal rates of physical illness, mortality, and psychiatric admissions (Kirkcaldy & Martin, 2000) according to the profession that they work in.

According to the literature review we can see the importance of effective leadership and healthy working environment for employees. Working environment, together with the leadership have a significant impact on employee health and well-being. Moreover, the behavior of the leadership can have positive or negative implications for the psychological health of employees. According to that the aim of the present study was to examine the level of psychological health and job satisfaction, and to find the differences between leaders and other employees in health care according to the level of job satisfaction and psychological health.

On this basis, three hypotheses were formed:

1. Increased use of the transformational leadership style associated with improved psychological health.
2. Well, expressed leaders' characteristics associated with improved psychological health.
3. Job dissatisfaction associated with decreased psychological health.

Testing the hypotheses provides a protection of psychological health of nurses, on which affect the leaders' behavior (leadership style, leaders' characteristics, leaders' emotional intelligence) nurses' characteristics (age, years in nursing, work position, presence of chronic disease, the level of stress), and job satisfaction. We also compared the level of psychological health between leaders and other employees in nursing. The analysis was exploratory, as we know that there is no research to guide the specific hypothesis relating to these two specific work positions. As described above, there is strong evidence indicating a link between the workplace, job satisfaction, and psychological health.

METHODS

Participants and Procedure

The Institute of Public Health of the Republic of Slovenia lists 12 state hospitals with the departments of internal medicine and surgery. The current study included 8 of them. As the research instrument was used a questionnaire of closed type questions. The questionnaires were distributed in the morning shift by the author and by the research coordinator in the participating hospitals. The sample consisted of 1100 nurses (the response rate was 58%), which voluntarily participated in a survey of eight Slovenian hospitals with internal medicine and surgery department. Data of 640 Slovenian nurses from the current study contributed to answering different research questions. First, we received a written permission for the study from the National Medical Ethics Committee of the Republic of Slovenia (No.157/09/13) and from all the participating hospitals. The researchers randomly selected 1100 hospital nurses from eight Slovenian hospitals; all Slovenian regions were included. 85 questionnaires were sent to middle- and unit-level nurse leaders and 1015 questionnaires to other nursing employees. Nurse leaders were not selected randomly; the questionnaires were sent only to those who occupied a leading position in a department or unit which means the purposive sampling was used. 1100 hospital nurses received an application for participation, instructions, guarantee of anonymity, and an envelope with a stamp and researcher's address for returning the questionnaire.

Instruments

In the study, the questionnaire was used which included:

- Demographic and other characteristics of nurses like age, gender, years in nursing, education level, work position, the presence of chronic diseases, frequency of coping with stress in the workplace, and managing stress.
- Multifactorial Leadership Questionnaire (Bass & Avolio, 1994) contains 21 items of leadership style, measured leaders' expression of transformational, transactional and laissez-faire leadership style. The leaders self-assessed their leadership style, while other employees assessed leadership style of their direct leaders. Leadership style assessed on the 6-point Likert scale ranging from 1 (strongly disagree) to 6 (strongly agree).
- Ten leaders' characteristics (Lorber & Skela Savič, 2011). The leaders self-assessed their personal characteristics, while other employees assessed personal characteristics of their direct leaders. Leaders' characteristics assessed on the 6-point Likert scale ranging from 1 (strongly disagree) to 6 (strongly agree).
- Emotional Intelligence Questionnaire developed by Petrides & Furnham (2001). The leaders self-assessed their emotional intelligence, while other employees assessed leaders' emotional intelligence of their direct leaders. Both assessments were made on the 6-point Likert scale ranging from 1 (strongly disagree) to 6 (strongly agree).
- Job satisfaction measured with a 15-item satisfaction questionnaire prepared by Warr; Cook, & Wall (1979). The respondents were asked to assess their job satisfaction on a 6-point scale from 1 (extremely dissatisfied) to 6 (extremely satisfied).

- General Health Questionnaire (GHQ) (a 12-item version) was used for self-perceived psychological health (Goldberg & Williams, 1988). The items were scored on a four-point Likert-type scale from 0 (more than usual) to 3 (much less than usual). The sum of scores creates an overall image of psychological health. Higher scores indicated more positive (better) psychological health.

Data analysis was carried out by using the statistical software package SPSS, 20.0. P-values equal or lower than 0.05 were considered statistically significant. Exploratory factor analysis was performed on 21 items of the leadership style. The principal component analysis and principal axis factoring concluded three factors, representing the transformational, transactional and laissez-faire leadership style. For further analysis by mean scores represent only the transformational (Cronbach's α was 0.960) and transactional (Cronbach's α was 0.937) leadership as indicators. The exploratory factor analysis on 16 items of emotional intelligence concluded four factors: self-identifying of emotions; identifying others' emotions; use of emotions, and emotion regulation. For further analysis, the mean of the items was used as a score sum to represent the emotional intelligence ability as an indicator (Cronbach's α was 0.974). Exploratory factor analysis on 15 items of job satisfaction concluded two factors, internal and external job satisfaction. For further analysis, the mean of the items was used as a score sum to represent the aspects of job satisfaction as an indicator (Cronbach's α was 0.943). The exploratory factor analysis of 12 items of psychological health concluded three factors, social dysfunction, anxiety and insomnia, and loss of confidence. For further analysis, the mean of the items was used as a score sum to represent the psychological health as an indicator (Cronbach's α was 0.812). Cronbach's alpha coefficient exceeded 0.8 or more in all cases.

Data Analysis

The descriptive statistics, and multiple regression analysis were used to determine the effect of independent variables (transformational leadership, transactional leadership, leaders' characteristics, leaders' emotional intelligence, and job satisfaction) on the depended variable (psychological health). Because we were also interested in differences in the self-assessment of the psychological health according to the presence of chronic diseases, the exposure frequency to stress, coping with stress, level of education, and years of employment in nursing, the One-way ANOVA and Mann Whitney test were used. A *p*-value of <0.05 was considered to be statistically significant.

Sample Description

The study included 640 employees in nursing from eight Slovenian hospitals. 346 (54%) of them were employed in surgery departments and 294 (46%) of them were employed in internal medicine departments. 75 (12%) of them were nurse leaders and 565 (88%) of them were other employees in nursing. There were 87 (14%) men and 553 (86%) women. 24% of participants were less than 30 years old, 64% of them were between 30 and 50 years of age and 12% of them were older than 50 years. On average, leaders spent 8.6 years (from 0.5 to 32 years) in the leading positions. 40 (6%) of them had less than 5 years of experience in nursing, 134 (21%) of them had 5 to 10 years of experience, 218 (34%) of them had 11 to 20 years of experience, 128 (20%) of them had 21 to 30 years of experience and 120 (19%) of them had more than 31 years of experience in nursing.

RESULTS

473 (74%) respondents do not have any chronic diseases, 163 (26%) have one or more chronic diseases. 194 (30%) respondents are always exposed to stress at the workplace, 334 (52%) respondents are often exposed to stress, 109 (17%) of them are sometimes exposed to stress and only 1 (0.2%) respondent is never exposed to stress at the workplace. 525 (82%) respondents are managing stress, but 113 (18%) respondents do not manage stress at the workplace. Figure 1 presents the studied variables.

The average value of expressed transformational and transactional leadership style, personal characteristics, and emotional intelligence are at the middle level (from 3.42 to 4.36 from 6). The level of job satisfaction of employees in nursing is also at the middle level ($\bar{x}$ =3.17; s=1.755). 47% (301) respondents are satisfied with their job but 15% (96) respondents have poor psychological health. We found a statistically significant difference in the level of job satisfaction (Z=-6.640; p<0.001) and psychological health (Z=-2.219; p=0.026) according to their job position.

To test the influence of the leadership behavior and characteristics on job satisfaction of employees in nursing, a multiple linear regression was performed. Demographic and other nurses' characteristics (gender, age, level of education, job position and years of employment), transformational leadership style, transactional leadership style, leaders' characteristics, and leaders' emotional intelligence were entered into the model as independent variables. Job satisfaction was a dependent variable. The regression analysis revealed that 48% of nurses' job satisfaction could be statistically predicted from independent variables, as presented in Figure 2.

To test the influence of leadership behavior, nurses' characteristics, and job satisfaction on nurses' psychological health, a multiple linear regression was performed. Demographic and other nurses' characteristics (gender, age, level of education, job position and years of employment), transformational and transactional leadership style, leaders' characteristics, leaders' emotional intelligence, and job satisfaction were entered into the model as independent variables. Psychological health was a dependent variable. The results revealed that 41% of nurses' psychological health could be statistically predicted from independent variables, as presented in Figure 3.

We also have found statistically significant differences in psychological health according to the level of education (F=1.994; p=0.002), years in nursing (F=1.576; p=0.031), exposure to stress (F=8.727; p<0.001) and managing stress (F=1.610, p=0.025). We have seen statistically significantly better psychological health in those with higher levels of education, those who have been employed in nursing for several years, those who are exposed to stress less often, and those who are managing stress well. We

Figure 1. Indicators and descriptive variables in the research

Variables	disagree/ dissatisfaction / poor health	agree/ satisfaction / good health	x̄	s
Transformational leadership	339(54%)	289(46%)	3.77	1.354
Transactional leadership	297(47%)	330(53%)	3.63	1.414
Leaders' characteristics	288(46%)	343(54%)	4.36	1.397
Leaders' emotional intelligence	333(52%)	306(48%)	3.42	1.823
Job satisfaction	339(53%)	301(47%)	3.14	1.755
Psychological health	96(15%)	544(85%)	17.1	4.595

Note: x̄=average value; s=standard deviation

Figure 2. Regression results for the prediction of job satisfaction

Variables	B	S.E.	β	t	p-value
Gender	0.009	0.042	0.006	0.206	0.837
Age in years	-0.005	0.004	-0.001	-0.007	0.994
Years in nursing	-0.001	0.004	-0.003	-0.034	0.973
Level of education	0.003	0.014	0.007	0.213	0.831
Job position	0.093	0.062	0.058	1.113	0.078
Transformational leadership	0.072	0.022	0.197	3.501	**0.001**
Transactional leadership	-0.083	0.022	-0.236	-1.102	**0.046**
Leaders' characteristics	0.167	0.048	0.167	3.484	**0.002**
Leaders' emotional intelligence	0.162	0.091	0.179	2.117	**0.034**
Adjusted R^2=0.483; F=141.389; p<0.001					

Note: B=unstandardizired regression coefficient; S.E.=standard error; β=standardized regression coefficient; t=t-value of t-statistic; p=p-value of significance; R^2=coefficient of determination

Figure 3. Regression results for the prediction of psychological health

Variables	B	S.E.	β	t	p-value
Gender	0.624	0.429	0.048	1.456	0.146
Age in years	-0.007	0.041	-0.014	-0.173	0.863
Years in nursing	-0.016	0.038	-0.035	-0.416	0.678
Level of education	0.238	0.146	0.058	1.633	0.103
Job position	0.378	0.573	0.025	1.003	0.092
Transformational leadership	1.919	0.217	0.564	8.851	**<0.001**
Transactional leadership	-1.805	0.216	-0.186	-2.336	**0.028**
Leaders' characteristics	1.011	0.471	0.109	2.147	**0.032**
Leaders' emotional intelligence	1.976	0.619	0.214	3.181	**0.003**
Job satisfaction	2.162	0.395	0.234	5.477	**<0.001**
Adjusted R^2=0.413; F=107.811; p<0.001					

Note: B=unstandardizired regression coefficient; S.E.=standard error; β=standardized regression coefficient; t=t-value of t-statistic; p=p-value of significance; R^2=coefficient of determination

also found that nurses with one or more chronic disease were poor psychological health than those with no chronic disease (Z=-3.062; p=0.002).

DISCUSSION

Mean scores for psychological health demonstrated that Slovenian nurses in this sample had high level of psychological health. The findings indicated that only 15% of employees in nursing were had poor psychological health. This finding is more encouraging according to the previous studies, like Calnan, Wainwright, Forsthye, Wall, & Almond. (2001) which indicate that nearly a quarter of the respondents were suffering from mental distress, and studies (Lavoie-Tremblay et al., 2008; Nakata et al., 2004; Suzuki et al., 2004) which indicated that about one third of employees have poor psychological health. In the research were found that psychological health was positively correlated with years of employment in nursing, higher level of education, absence of chronic diseases, lower presence of stress at the workplace, and good managing stress. Also, Chang et al. (2006) found higher psychological health scores relating to more years worked at the unit, and lower psychological health where are lack of support, lack of self-controlling and higher workload. Differences in psychological health according to the working position can be explained with varying degrees of autonomy, duties, and decision-making process.

In Slovenian hospitals the level of nurses' job satisfaction is at the medium level. Some other researchers (Burke, Koyincu, & Fiksenbaum, 2010; Golbasi, Kelleci, & Dogan, 2008; Gurkova, Harokova, Džuka, & Žiakova, 2014; Jaafarpour & Khani, 2012; Lorber & Skela Savič, 2012) also found that the nurses' job satisfaction is at the medium level. Higher level of job satisfaction positively correlated with psychological health. It means that employees with a higher level of job satisfaction tended to have better psychological health than those who with a low level of job satisfaction. Also some other studies have found a close link between psychological health and job satisfaction (Bennett, Plint, & Clifford, 2005; Evans et al., 2006; Faragher et al. 2005; Janyam, 2009; Nadinloyi et al. 2013). Findings of contemporary and some past researches suggest, that the level of job satisfaction has an important impact on general, and also psychological health of employees.

Better expressed leaders' characteristics, also emotional intelligence have an impact on both job satisfaction and psychological health. Behavior of leaders through leaders' characteristics have an important effect on well-being, health, satisfaction, and effectiveness (Janssen & Van Yperen, 2004; Lorber & Skela Savič, 2012; Sarin & McDermoll, 2003; Skakon et al., 2010; Upenieks, 2003a; Upenieks, 2003b). Some studies (Chiva & Alegre, 2008; Clarke, 2010; Kafetsios & Zampetakis, 2007; Kerr et al., 2006; Mittal & Sindhu, 2012; Naidu, 2014; Rosete & Ciarrochi, 2005) described the importance of emotional intelligence in the context of organizational leadership and job satisfaction.

Based on the six independent variables, the multiple regression analysis indicated that the transformational leadership style had a significant impact on the job satisfaction and also on the psychological health. Most researchers also found the impact of the transformational leadership style on job satisfaction (Al-Hussami, 2008; Cummings et al., 2008; Larrabee et al., 2003; Leach, 2005; Mosadegh Rad & Yarmohammadian, 2006: Nielsen, Yarker, Randall, & Munir, 2009, Sellgren et al., 2008), but just a few (Nielsen et al., 2008; Salanova, Lorenre, Chambel, & Martinez., 2011) of them found an impact of the transformational leadership style on psychological health. Also Kuoppala et al. (2008) in the meta-analysis found a few of prospective studies about the association between leadership style and employees' health. Salanova et al. (2011) noted that the transformational leadership style can help to create a more positive and psychologically healthy work environment.

A leadership style, leaders' characteristics, and leaders' emotional intelligence reflecting the leaders' behavior and have an important effect on nurses' job satisfaction and psychological health. Our results provide a support to previous studies about the importance of nurses' satisfaction and psychological health for the organizational effectiveness and performance. Cyhlarova, McCulloch, McGuffin, & Wykes (2010) and Goetzel, Ozminkowski, Sederer, & Mark (2002) noted that psychological distress is a major cause of absence from work, reduction in productivity, and staff turnover. Employers should take care of employees' psychological health because psychological health affects not only employees' well-being and health, but also on the organizational effectiveness. We agree with Grawitch, Trares, & Kohler (2007) that for every organization, it is important to meet the needs of employees, and to recognize the positive and negative effects on job satisfaction and health.

The studied topic provides opportunities for further research. The research could be conducted in all healthcare institutions in Slovenia. For management it is important to monitor job satisfaction and well-being of all employees every year or two. Further work is also required to determine which particular dimensions of workplace the most influence on employees' job satisfaction and psychological health. The employers will benefit from such information as they can then develop strategies to increase job satisfaction and psychological health of employees.

Study Limitations

The study has some limitations. We have studied the influence of some predictors on psychological health. For research instrument were used a multiple choice closed-ended questions, which limited to a list of answers from which the respondents were allowed to choose. The researcher was not always available during the research. The respondents did not get any help in the case that they did not understand items, and also no additional explanations were provided if they maybe need it. Among the limitations is also incomplete responding for some of the scales, which reduced the effective sample size for some analyses.

Solutions and Recommendations

Better collaboration and consultation between leaders and other employees in healthcare is the basis to achieve higher level of job satisfaction better psychological health of employees in all nonprofit organization, not only in the health care institutions. The leadership style is important factor, that employees are satisfied, committed, stay at workplace and are in good health. Leaders in healthcare would benefit from initiatives, if they had better preparation on the leader role. Leaders have to learn and also explore about the improvement of leadership style. Leaders have to take care about their health, because only healthy leaders can take care for health of their employees. When establishing the level of job satisfaction and health, we have to focus on what the employees feel about their work, about personal relationships at the workplace and on the way how leaders influence on the employees.

For leaders and employees, it is important that workplace health promotion encompasses employers, their employees, and society to improve health and well-being of all people at work. It includes improving the way of work, improving the working environment, encouraging employees to get involved in healthy activities, and encouraging personal development. For the health care institutions, it is an important goal to become healthy organizations that would take care of the health of all employees.

CONCLUSION

The work has an essential impact on people's health because of the risk factors at the workplace, that can have consequences like health problems related with work. In a constantly changing health system, hospitals will have to recognize the importance of satisfied and healthy employees. Psychological health has effects on individuals, and also on quality and effectiveness of health care institutions. It is important that employer monitors employees' job satisfaction and take care for employees' health. That is the only way that organizations are adapt to an individual and to achieve greater efficiency, and better quality.

Employees in health care institutions will be more satisfied and will have better health if they get a good example and an appropriate support by the leaders.

The implications of these findings suggest that leaders in nursing have an important role in the promotion of job satisfaction and health among nurses, since nurses also play an important role for the patients' satisfaction and safety care. A leader can improve employees' satisfaction, when he/she determines the factors of job satisfaction for each individual employee, incorporates other employees as equal co-workers, and also promotes a positive work climate and healthy work environment. Our research suggests health benefits for employees in nursing by creating a healthy environment, and encouraging better interpersonal relationship by preparing and training leaders in nursing. Health in the workplace can be improved by modifying work environment. Thus, a holistic approach is needed for the promotion of health, and incorporating individual and work factors.

REFERENCES

Ahola, K., Kivimaki, M., Honkonen, T., Virtanen, M., Koskinen, S., Vahtera, J., & Lönnqvist, J. (2008). Occupational burnout and medically certified sickness absence: A population-based study of Finnish employees. *Journal of Psychosomatic Research, 64*(2), 185–193. doi:10.1016/j.jpsychores.2007.06.022 PMID:18222132

Aiken, L. H., Clarke, S. P., Sloane, D. M., Sochalski, J., & Silber, J. H. (2002). Hospital nurse staffing and patient mortality, nurse burnout, and job dissatisfaction. *Journal of the American Medical Association, 288*(16), 1987–1993. doi:10.1001/jama.288.16.1987 PMID:12387650

Aiken, L. H., Clarke, S. P., Sloane, D. M., Sochalski, J. A., Busse, R., Clarke, H., & Shamian, J. et al. (2001). Nurses reports on hospital care in five countries. *Health Affairs, 20*(3), 43–53. doi:10.1377/hlthaff.20.3.43 PMID:11585181

Al-Hussami, M. (2008). A study of nurses' job satisfaction: The relationship to organizational commitment, perceived organizational support, transactional leadership, transformational leadership, and level of education. *European Journal of Scientific Research, 22*(2), 286–295.

Arnold, K. A., Turner, N., Barling, J., Kelloway, E. K., & Mckee, M. C. (2007). Transformational leadership and psychological well-being: The mediating role of meaningful work. *Journal of Occupational Health Psychology, 12*(3), 193–203. doi:10.1037/1076-8998.12.3.193 PMID:17638487

Aron, S. (2015). *Relationship between nurses' job satisfaction and quality of healthcare they deliver.* Minnesota State University, Mankato. Retreived April 13, 2015 from cornerstone.lib.mnsu.edu/cgi/viewcontent.cgi?article

Ball, J. (2013). Mental health. *The Guardian.* Retrieved 29, July 2016 from: https://www.theguardian.com/society/2013/may/22/women-men-mental-illness-study

Barling, J., Kelloway, E. K., & Slater, F. (2000). TL and emotional intelligence: An exploratory study. *Leadership and Organization Development Journal, 21*(3), 157–161. doi:10.1108/01437730010325040

Barsade, S. G. (2002). The ripple effect: Emotional contagion and its influence on group behavior. *Administrative Science Quarterly, 47*(4), 644–675. doi:10.2307/3094912

Bass, B., & Avolio, B. (1994). Developing transformational leadership: 1992 and beyond. *Journal of European Industrial Training, 14*(5), 21–27.

Bauer, J., Stamm, A., Virnich, K., Wissing, K., Müller, U., Wirsching, M., & Schaarschmidt, U. (2006). Correlation between burnout syndrome and psychological and psychosomatic symptoms among teachers. *International Archives of Occupational and Environmental Health, 79*(3), 199–204. doi:10.1007/s00420-005-0050-y PMID:16258752

Bennett, S., Plint, A., & Clifford, T. J. (2005). Burnout, psychological morbidity, job satisfaction, and stress: A survey of Canadian hospital based child protection professionals. *Archives of Disease in Childhood, 90*(11), 1112–1116. doi:10.1136/adc.2003.048462 PMID:16243862

Brown, F. W., & Reilly, M. D. (2009). The Myers-Briggs type indicator and transformational leadership. *Journal of Management Development, 28*(10), 916–932. doi:10.1108/02621710911000677

Brunero, S., Cowan, D., & Fairbrother, G. (2008). Reducing emotional distress in nurses using cognitive behavioural therapy: A preliminary program evaluation. *Japan Journal of Nursing Science, 5*(2), 109–115. doi:10.1111/j.1742-7924.2008.00102.x

Brunton, M. (2005). Emotion in health care: The cost of caring. *Journal of Health Organization and Management, 19*(4/5), 340–354. doi:10.1108/14777260510615387 PMID:16206918

Bulmer-Smith, S. K., Profetto-McGrath, J., & Cummings, G. G. (2009). Emotional intelligence and nursing: An integrative literature review. *International Journal of Nursing Studies, 46*(2), 162–136. PMID:19596323

Burke, R. J., Koyincu, M., & Fiksenbaum, L. (2010). Burnout, work satisfaction and psychological well-being among nurses in Turkish hospitals. *Europe's Journal of Psychology, 1*, 63–81.

Burns, J. M. (2010). *Leadership*. New York, NY: Harper Collins Publishers.

Calnan, M., Wainwright, D., Forsythe, M., Wall, B., & Almond, S. (2001). Mental health and stress in the workplace: The case of general practice in the UK. *Social Science & Medicine, 52*(4), 499–507. doi:10.1016/S0277-9536(00)00155-6 PMID:11206648

Carney, M. (2006). *Health service management: Consensus, culture and the middle manager.* Cork, Ireland: Oak Tree Press.

Chang, E. M., Bidewell, J. W., Huntington, A. D., Daly, J., Johnson, A., Wilson, H., & Lambert, C. E. et al. (2007). A survey of role stress, coping and health in Australian and New Zealand hospital nurses. *International Journal of Nursing Studies, 44*(8), 1354–1362. doi:10.1016/j.ijnurstu.2006.06.003 PMID:16901488

Chang, E. M., Daly, J., Hancock, K., Bidewell, J. W., Johnson, A., Lambert, V. A., & Lambert, C. E. (2006). The relationships among workplace stressors, coping methods, demographic characteristics, and health in Australian nurses. *Journal of Professional Nursing, 22*(1), 30–38. doi:10.1016/j.profnurs.2005.12.002 PMID:16459287

Chiva, R., & Alegre, J. (2008). Emotional intelligence and job satisfaction: The role of organizational learning capability. *Personnel Review, 37*(6), 680–701. doi:10.1108/00483480810906900

Clarke, N. (2010). Emotional intelligence and its relationship to transformational leadership and key project manager competences. *Project Management Journal, 41*(2), 5–20. doi:10.1002/pmj.20162

Coomber, B., & Barriball, L. K. (2007). Impact of job satisfaction components on intent to leave and turnover for hospital-based nurses: A review of the research literature. *International Journal of Nursing Studies, 44*(2), 297–314. doi:10.1016/j.ijnurstu.2006.02.004 PMID:16631760

Cummings, G., Hayduk, L., & Estabrooks, C. (2005). Mitigating the impact of hospital restructuring on nurses: The responsibility of emotionally intelligent leadership. *Nursing Research, 54*(1), 2–12. doi:10.1097/00006199-200501000-00002 PMID:15695934

Cummings, G. G., Olson, K., Hayduk, L., Bakker, D., Fitch, M., Green, E., & Conlon, M. et al. (2008). The relationship between nursing leadership and nurses job satisfaction in Canadian oncology work environments. *Journal of Nursing Management, 15*(6), 508–518. doi:10.1111/j.1365-2834.2008.00897.x PMID:18558921

Cyhlarova, E., McCulloch, A., McGuffin, P., & Wykes, T. (2010). *Economic Burden of Mental Illness Cannot be Tackled Without Research Investment.* London, UK: Mental Health Foundation.

Daft, R. L. (2005). *The Leadership Experience* (3rd ed.). Vancouver, Canada: Thomson-Southwestern.

Downey, L. A., Papageorgiou, V., & Stough, C. (2006). Examining the relationship between leadership, emotional intelligence and intuition in senior female managers. *Leadership and Organization Development Journal, 27*(4), 250–264. doi:10.1108/01437730610666019

Economy, P. (2014). *The 9 Traits that define great leadership.* Retrieved 20 July, 206 from: www.inc.com/peter-economy/the-9-traits-that-define-great-leadership.html

Evans, S., Huxley, P., Gately, C., Webber, M., Mears, A., Pajak, S., Medina, J., Kendall, T., & Katona, C. (2006). Mental health, burnout and job satisfaction among mental health social workers in England and Wales. *British Journal of Psychiatry, 188*, 75-80.

Failla, K., & Stichler, J. (2008). Manager and staff perceptions of the manager's leadership style. *Journal of Advanced Nursing, 38*(11), 480–487. PMID:18997553

Faragher, E. B., Cass, M., & Cooper, C. I. (2005). The relationship between job satisfaction and health: A meta-analysis. *Occupational and Environmental Medicine, 62*(2), 105–112. doi:10.1136/oem.2002.006734 PMID:15657192

Gaidos, S. (2016). His stress is not like her stress: Scientists puzzle over why men and women react differently to pressure. *Magazine of Society for Science & the Public, 189*(2), 18.

Gärtner, F. R., Nieuwenhuijsen, K., Dijk, F. J. H., & Sluiter, J. K. (2010). The impact of common mental disorders on the work functioning of nurses and allied health professionals: A systematic review. *International Journal of Nursing Studies, 47*(8), 1047–1061. doi:10.1016/j.ijnurstu.2010.03.013 PMID:20444449

Gärtner, F. R., Nieuwenhuijsen, K., Dijk, F. J. H., & Sluiter, J. K. (2012). Impaired work functioning due to common mental disorders in nurses and allied health professionals: The Nurses Work Functioning Questionnaire. *International Archives of Occupational and Environmental Health, 85*(2), 125–138. doi:10.1007/s00420-011-0649-0 PMID:21626312

Gershon, R., Stone, P., Zeltser, M., Faucett, J., MacDavitt, K., & Chou, S. (2007). Organisational climate and nurse health outcomes in the united states: A systematic review. *Industrial Health, 45*(5), 622–636. doi:10.2486/indhealth.45.622 PMID:18057805

Gill, A. S., Flaschner, A. B., & Shacha, M. (2006). Mitigating stress and burnout by implementing transformational leadership. *International Journal of Contemporary Hospitality Management, 18*(6), 469–481. doi:10.1108/09596110610681511

Goethals, G., Sorenson, G., & Burns, J. (2004). *Encyclopedia of leadership*. Thousand Oaks, CA: SAGE Publications. doi:10.4135/9781412952392

Goetzel, R. Z., Ozminkowski, R. J., Sederer, L. I., & Mark, T. L. (2002). The business case for quality mental health services: Why employers should care about the mental health and well-being of their employees. *Journal of Occupational and Environmental Medicine, 44*(4), 320–330. doi:10.1097/00043764-200204000-00012 PMID:11977418

Golbasi, Z., Kelleci, M., & Dogan, S. (2008). Relationship between coping strategies, individual characteristics and job satisfaction in a sample of hospital nurses: Cross-section questionnaire survey. *International Journal of Nursing Studies, 45*(12), 1800–1806. doi:10.1016/j.ijnurstu.2008.06.009 PMID:18703192

Goldberg, D., & Williams, P. (1988). *A user's guide to the General Health Questionnaire*. Windsor, UK: NFER-Nelson.

Goleman, D., & Boyatzis, R. (2008). Social intelligence and the biology of leadership. *Harvard Business Review*. Retreived April 25, 2015: http://hbr.org/2008/09/social-intelligence-and-the-biology-of-leadership/ar/1

Goleman, D., Boyatzis, R., & McKee, A. (2002). *Primal leadership*. Boston, MA: Harvard Business School Press.

Grawitch, M. J., Trares, S., & Kohler, J. M. (2007). Healthy workplace practices and employee outcomes. *International Journal of Stress Management, 14*(3), 275–293. doi:10.1037/1072-5245.14.3.275

Greenfield, D. (2007). The enactment of dynamic leadership. *Leadership in Health Services, 20*(3), 159–168. doi:10.1108/17511870710764014 PMID:20690461

Güleryüz, G., Güney, S., Aydın, E. M., & Aşan, O. (2008). The mediating effect of job satisfaction between emotional intelligence and organisational commitment of nurses: A questionnaire survey. *International Journal of Nursing Studies, 45*(11), 1625–1635. doi:10.1016/j.ijnurstu.2008.02.004 PMID:18394625

Gurkova, E., Harokova, S., Džuka, J., & Žiakova, K. (2014). Job satisfaction and subjective well-being among Czech nurses. *International Journal of Nursing Practice, 20*(2), 194–203. doi:10.1111/ijn.12133 PMID:24713016

Harms, P. D., & Crede, M. (2010). Emotional Intelligence and Transformational and Transactional Leadership: A Meta-Analysis. *Journal of Leadership & Organizational Studies, 17*(1), 5–17. doi:10.1177/1548051809350894

Healy, C. M., & McKay, M. F. (2000). Nursing stress: The effects of coping strategies and job satisfaction in a sample of Australian Nurses. *Journal of Advanced Nursing, 31*(3), 681–688. doi:10.1046/j.1365-2648.2000.01323.x PMID:10718888

Hellriegel, D., & Slocum, J. W. (2007). *Organizational behavior* (11th ed.). Mason, OH: Thomson South-Western.

Holden Leadership Center. (2009). *Leadership*. University of Oregon. Retrieved 19 July, 2016 from: http://leadership.uoregon.edu/

Hover-Kramer, D., Mabbett, P., & Shames, K. H. (1996). Vitality for caregivers. *Holistic Nursing Practice, 10*(2), 38–48. doi:10.1097/00004650-199601000-00006 PMID:8550689

Huber, D. L. (2006). *Leadership and nursing care management* (3rd ed.). Philadelphia, PA: Elsevier Inc.

Huber, D. L., Maas, M., McCloskey, J., Scherb, C. A., Goode, C. J., & Watson, C. (2000). Evaluating nursing administration instruments. *The Journal of Nursing Administration, 30*(5), 251–272. doi:10.1097/00005110-200005000-00006 PMID:10823178

Jaafarpour, M., & Khani, A. (2012). Evaluation of the Nurses' Job Satisfaction, and Its Association with Their Moral Sensitivities and Well-being. *Journal of Clinical and Diagnostic Research, 6*(10), 1761–1764. PMID:23373046

Janssen, O., & Van Yperen, N. W. (2004). Employees Goal Orientations, the Quality of Leader-Member Exchange, and the Outcomes of Job Performance and Job Satisfaction. *Academy of Management Journal, 47*(3), 368–384. doi:10.2307/20159587

Janyam, K. (2009). The Influence of Job Satisfaction on Mental Health of Factory Workers. *The Internet Journal of Mental Health, 7*(1). Retreived July 18, 2016 from: http://ispub.com/IJMH/7/1/9829

Jasper, S., Stephan, M., Al-Khalaf, H., Rennekampff, H. O., Vogt, P., & Mirastschijski, U. (2012). Too little appreciation for great expenditure? Workload and resources in ICUs. *International Archives of Occupational and Environmental Health, 85*(7), 753–761. doi:10.1007/s00420-011-0721-9 PMID:22086785

Javitch, D. G. (2014). 10 Qualities of superior leaders. *Enterpreneur*. Retrieved 20 July, 206 from: www.enterpreneur.com/article/204248

Jenkins, R., & Elliott, P. (2004). Stressors, burnout and social support: Nurses in acute mental health settings. *Journal of Advanced Nursing, 48*(6), 622–631. doi:10.1111/j.1365-2648.2004.03240.x PMID:15548253

Kafetsios, K., & Zampetakis, L. (2008). Emotional intelligence and job satisfaction: Testing the mediatory role of positive and negative affect at work. *Personality and Individual Differences, 44*(3), 712–722. doi:10.1016/j.paid.2007.10.004

Kanste, O., Kyngas, H., & Nikkila, J. (2007). The relationship between multidimensional leadership and burnout among nursing staff. *Journal of Nursing Management, 15*(7), 731–739. doi:10.1111/j.1365-2934.2006.00741.x PMID:17897150

Karimi, L., Leggat, S. G., Donohue, L., Farrell, G., & Couper, G. E. (2014). Emotional rescue: The role of emotional intelligence and emotional labour on well-being and job-stress among community nurses. *Journal of Advanced Nursing, 70*(1), 176–186. doi:10.1111/jan.12185 PMID:23763612

Kerr, R., Garvin, J., Heaton, N., & Boyle, E. (2006). Emotional intelligence and leadership effectiveness. *Leadership and Organization Development Journal, 27*(4), 265–279. doi:10.1108/01437730610666028

Kirkcaldy, B. D., & Martin, T. (2000). Job stress and satisfaction among nurses: Individual differences. *Stress Medicine, 16*(2), 77–89. doi:10.1002/(SICI)1099-1700(200003)16:2<77::AID-SMI835>3.0.CO;2-Z

Kouzes, J. M., & Posner, B. Z. (1997). *Leadership practices inventory—Industrial contributor (LPI–IC). Observer response sheet.* San Francisco, CA: Jossey Bass/Pfeiffer.

Koy, V., Yunibhand, J., Angsuroch, Y., & Fisher, M. L. (2015). Relationship between nursing care quality, nurse staffing, nurse job satisfaction, nurse practice environment, and burnout: Literature review. *International Journal of Research in Medical Sciences, 3*(8), 1825–1831. doi:10.18203/2320-6012. ijrms20150288

Kudielka, B. M., Hanebuth, D., von Känel, R., Gander, M. L., Grande, G., & Fischer, J. E. (2005). Health-related quality of life measured by the SF12 in working populations: Associations with psychosocial work characteristics. *Journal of Occupational Health Psychology, 10*(4), 429–440. doi:10.1037/1076-8998.10.4.429 PMID:16248690

Kuoppala, J., Lamminpää, A., Liira, J., & Vainio, H. (2008). Leadership, job well-being, and health effects—A systematic review and a meta-analysis. *Journal of Occupational and Environmental Medicine, 50*(8), 904–915. doi:10.1097/JOM.0b013e31817e918d PMID:18695449

Lambert, V. A., Lambert, C. E., & Ito, M. (2004). Workplace stressors, ways of coping and demographic characteristics as predictors of physical and mental health of Japanese hospital nurses. *International Journal of Nursing Studies, 41*(1), 85–97. doi:10.1016/S0020-7489(03)00080-4 PMID:14670398

Landa, J., & López-Zafra, E. (2010). The Impact of Emotional Intelligence on Nursing: An Overview. *Psychology (Savannah, Ga.), 1*(1), 50–58.

Larrabee, J. H., Janney, M. A., Ostrow, C. L., Withrow, M. L., Hobbs, G. R. Jr, & Burant, C. M. (2003). Predictors of registered nurse job satisfaction and intention to leave. *The Journal of Nursing Administration, 33*(5), 271–283. doi:10.1097/00005110-200305000-00003 PMID:12792282

Laschinger, H. K. S., Almost, J., Purdy, N., & Kim, J. (2004). Predictors of nurse managers health in Canadian restructured healthcare settings. *Canadian Journal of Nursing Leadership, 17*(4), 88–105. doi:10.12927/cjnl.2004.17020 PMID:15656251

Laschinger, H. K. S., Finegan, J., & Shamian, J. (2001). Promoting nurses' health: Effect of empowerment on job strain and work satisfaction. *Nursing Economics, 19*(2), 42–52.

Lavoie-Tremblay, M., Wright, D., Desforges, N., Gelinas, C., Marchionni, C., & Drevniok, U. (2008). Creating a Healthy Workplace for New-Generation Nurses. *Journal of Nursing Scholarship, 40*(3), 290–297. doi:10.1111/j.1547-5069.2008.00240.x PMID:18840214

Law, K. S., Wong, C., & Song, L. J. (2004). The construct and criterion validity of emotional intelligence and its potential utility for management studies. *The Journal of Applied Psychology, 89*(3), 483–496. doi:10.1037/0021-9010.89.3.483 PMID:15161407

Leach, L. S. (2005). Nurse executive transformational leadership and organizational commitment. *The Journal of Nursing Administration, 35*(5), 228–237. doi:10.1097/00005110-200505000-00006 PMID:15891486

Leadership-Toolbox. (2008*). The Characteristic of Leadership - 7 Important Traits.* Retrieved 22 July, 2016 from: http://www.leadership-toolbox.com/characteristic-of-leadership.html

Letvak, S. A., Ruhm, C. J., & Gupta, S. N. (2012). Nurses presenteeism and its effects on self-reported quality of care and costs. *The American Journal of Nursing, 112*(2), 30–38. doi:10.1097/01. NAJ.0000411176.15696.f9 PMID:22261652

Lin, P. C., Chen, C. H., Pan, S. M., Pan, C. H., Chen, C. J., Chen, Y. M., & Wu, M. T. et al. (2012). Atypical work schedules are associated with poor sleep quality and mental health in Taiwan female nurses. *International Archives of Occupational and Environmental Health, 85*(8), 877–884. doi:10.1007/ s00420-011-0730-8 PMID:22207296

Locke, E. A. (1976). The nature and causes of job satisfaction. In M. D. Dunnette (Ed.), *Handbook of industrial and organizational psychology* (pp. 1297–1349). Chicago, IL: Rand McNally.

Lorber, M. (2015). Emotional intelligence – A key ability for leaders in nursing. In L. Zysberg & S. Raz (Eds.), *Emotional intelligence: Current evidence from psychological, educational and organizational perspectives* (pp. 277–292). New York, NY: Nova Science Publishers.

Lorber, M., & Skela-Savič, B. (2011). Perceptions of managerial competencies, style, and characteristics among professionals in nursing. *Croatian Medical Journal, 52*(2), 198–204. doi:10.3325/cmj.2011.52.198 PMID:21495203

Lorber, M., & Skela-Savič, B. (2012). Job satisfaction of nurses in Slovenian hospitals. *Croatian Medical Journal, 53*(3), 263–270. doi:10.3325/cmj.2012.53.263 PMID:22661140

Lu, H., While, K., & Bariball, K. (2005). Job satisfaction among nurses: A literature review. *International Journal of Nursing Studies, 42*(2), 211–227. doi:10.1016/j.ijnurstu.2004.09.003 PMID:15680619

Malik, S. H. (2013). Relationship between Leader Behaviors and Employees' Job Satisfaction: A Path-Goal Approach. *Pakistan Journal of Commerce and Social Sciences, 7*(1), 209–222.

Mancheno-Smoak, L., Endres, G., Potak, R., & Athanasaw, Y. (2009). The individual cultural values and job satisfaction of the transformational leader. *Organization Development Journal, 27*(3), 9–21.

Mark, A. (2005). Organizing emotions in health care. *Journal of Health Organization and Management, 19*(4-5), 277–289. doi:10.1108/14777260510615332 PMID:16206913

Marklund, S., Bolin, M., & von Essen, J. (2008). Can Individual Health Differences Be Explained by Workplace Characteristics? — A Multilevel Analysis. *Social Science & Medicine, 66*(3), 650–662. doi:10.1016/j.socscimed.2007.09.008 PMID:17996347

Marquis, B. L., & Huston, C. J. (2009). *Leadership Roles and Management Functions in Nursing: Theory and Application* (6th ed.). Philadelphia, PA: Wolters/Kluwer/Lippincott Williams and Wilkins.

Melamed, S., Shirom, A., Toker, S., Berliner, S., & Shapira, I. (2006). Burnout and risk of cardiovascular disease: Evidence, possible causal paths, and promising research directions. *Psychological Bulletin, 132*(3), 327–353. doi:10.1037/0033-2909.132.3.327 PMID:16719565

Mental Health Commission. (2010). *What is mental health?* Retrieved 22 July, 2016 from: http://www.mentalhealth.wa.gov.au/mental_illness_and_health/mh_whatis.aspx

Mental Health Foundation. (2016). *About mental health.* Retrieved 22 July, 2016 from: https://www.mentalhealth.org.uk/your-mental-health/about-mental-health/what-mental-health

Michie, S., & Williams, S. (2003). Reducing work related psychological ill health and sickness absence: A systematic literature review. *Occupational and Environmental Medicine, 60*(1), 6–9. doi:10.1136/oem.60.1.3 PMID:12499449

Miller, N. M., & McGowen, R. K. (2000). The painful truth: Physicians are not invincible. *Southern Medical Journal, 93*(10), 966–973. doi:10.1097/00007611-200093100-00004 PMID:11147478

Mittal, V., & Sindhu, E. (2012). Emotional Intelligence & Leadership. *Global Journal of Management and Business Research, 12*(16), 35–38.

Mohammadi, A., Sarhanggi, F., Ebadi, A., Daneshmandi, M., Reiisifar, A., Amiri, F., & Hajamini, Z. (2011). Relationship between psychological problems and quality of work life of Intensive Care Units Nurses. *Iranian Journal of Critical Care Nursing, 4*(3), 135–140.

Mosadegh Rad, A. M. (2003). The role of participative management (suggestion system) in hospital effectiveness and efficiency. *Research in Medical Sciences, 8*(3), 85–89.

Mosadegh Rad, A. M., & Yarmohammadian, M. H. (2006). A study of relationship between managers leadership style and employees job satisfaction. *Leadership in Health Services, 19*(2), 11–28. doi:10.1108/13660750610665008 PMID:16875105

Mrayyan, M. T. (2006). Jordanian nurses job satisfaction, patients satisfaction and quality of nursing care. *International Nursing Review, 53*(3), 224–230. doi:10.1111/j.1466-7657.2006.00439.x PMID:16879186

Muchinsky, P. M. (2000). Emotions in the workplace: The neglect of organizational behavior. *Journal of Organizational Behavior, 21*(7), 801–805. doi:10.1002/1099-1379(200011)21:7<801::AID-JOB999>3.0.CO;2-A

Muchinsky, P. M. (2006). *Psychology Applied to Work: An Introduction to Industrial and Organisational Psychology* (8th ed.). Belmont, CA: Thompson/Wadsworth.

Musek, J., & Pečjak, V. (2001). *Psihologija*. Ljubljana, Slovenia: Educy.

Nadinloyi, K. B., Sadeghi, H., & Hajloo, N. (2013). Relationship Between Job Satisfaction and Employees Mental Health. *Procedia: Social and Behavioral Sciences, 84*, 293–297. doi:10.1016/j.sbspro.2013.06.554

Naidu, N. G. (2014). Emotional intelligence in leadership. *International Journal of Entrepreneurship & Business Environment Perspectives, 3*(1). Retrieved from http://pezzottaitejournals.net/index.php/IJEBEP/article/view/1115

Nakata, A., Haratani, T., Takahashi, M., Kawakami, N., Arito, H., Kobayashi, F., & Araki, S. (2004). Job stress, social support and prevalence of insomnia in a population of Japanese daytime workers. *Social Science & Medicine, 59*(8), 1719–1730. doi:10.1016/j.socscimed.2004.02.002 PMID:15279928

National Alliance of Mental Illness. (2011). *Mental health*. Retrieved 22 July, 2016 from: http://www.nami.org/ mental+health&searchmode

Nielsen, K., Randall, R., Yarker, J., & Brenner, S. O. (2008). The efects of transformational leadership on followers perceived work characteristics and psychological well-being: A longitudinal study. *Work and Stress, 22*(1), 16–32. doi:10.1080/02678370801979430

Nielsen, K., Yarker, J., Randall, R., & Munir, F. (2009). The mediating effects of team and self-efficacy on the relationship between transformational leadership, and job satisfaction and psychological well-being in healthcare professionals: A cross-sectional questionnaire survey. *International Journal of Nursing Studies, 46*(9), 1236–1244. doi:10.1016/j.ijnurstu.2009.03.001 PMID:19345946

Obholzer, A. (2005). The impact of setting and agency. *Journal of Health Organization and Management, 19*(4/5), 297–303. doi:10.1108/14777260510615350 PMID:16206915

Petrides, K. V., & Furnham, A. (2001). Trait emotional intelligence: Psychometric investigation with reference to established trait taxonomies. *European Journal of Personality, 15*(6), 425–448. doi:10.1002/per.416

Prive, T. (2012). Top 10 Qualities that make a great leader. *Forbes*. Retrieved 20 Julx, 206 from: www.forbes.com/sites/tanyprive/2012/12/19/top_10_qualities_that_make_a_great_leader/

Purcel, S. Y., Kutash, M., & Cobb, S. (2011). The relationship between nurses stress and nurse staffing factors in a hospital setting. *Journal of Nursing Management, 19*(6), 714–720. doi:10.1111/j.1365-2834.2011.01262.x PMID:21899624

Purdy, N., Spence Laschinger, H. K., Finegan, J., Kerr, M., & Olivera, F. (2010). Effects of work environments on nurse and patient outcomes. *Journal of Nursing Management, 18*(8), 901–913. doi:10.1111/j.1365-2834.2010.01172.x PMID:21073564

Riggio, E. R., & Reichard, R. J. (2008). The emotional and social intelligences of effective leadership: An emotional and social skill approach. *Journal of Managerial Psychology, 23*(2), 169–185. doi:10.1108/02683940810850808

Rosete, D., & Ciarrochi, J. (2005). Emotional intelligence and its relationship to workplace performance outcomes of leadership effectiveness. *Leadership and Organization Development Journal, 26*(5), 388–399. doi:10.1108/01437730510607871

Roussel, L., Swansburg, R. C., & Swansburg, R. J. (2009). *Management and leadership for nurse administrators* (5th ed.). Sudbury, MA: Jones and Bartlett Publishers.

Ryan, R. M., & Deci, E. L. (2000). The darker and brighter sides of human existence: Basic psychological needs as a unifying concept. *Psychological Inquiry, 11*(4), 319–338. doi:10.1207/S15327965PLI1104_03

Salanova, M., Lorente, L., Chambel, M. J., & Martínez, I. M. (2011). Linking transformational leadership to nurses extra-role performance: The mediating role of self-efficacy and work engagement. *Journal of Advanced Nursing, 67*(10), 2256–2266. doi:10.1111/j.1365-2648.2011.05652.x PMID:21535088

Sarin, S., & McDermoll, C. (2003). The Effect of Team Leader Characteristics on Learning, Knowledge Application, and Performance of Cross-Functional New Product Development Teams. *Decision Sciences, 34*(4), 707–739. doi:10.1111/j.1540-5414.2003.02350.x

Scheick, D. M. (2011). Developing self-aware mindfulness to manage countertransference in the nurse-client relationship: An evaluation and developmental study. *Journal of Professional Nursing, 27*(2), 114–223. doi:10.1016/j.profnurs.2010.10.005 PMID:21420044

Schulz, M., Damkroger, A., Heins, C., Wehlitz, L., Löhr, M., Driessen, M., & Wingenfeld, K. et al. (2009). Effort-reward imbalance and burnout among German nurses in medical compared with psychiatric hospital settings. *Journal of Psychiatric and Mental Health Nursing, 16*(3), 225–233. doi:10.1111/j.1365-2850.2008.01355.x PMID:19291150

Segal, J., & Smith, M. (2014). *Emotional intelligence: Key skills for raising emotional intelligence.* Retreived May 12, 2015 from: http://www.helpguide.org/mental/eq5_raising_emotional_intelligence.htm

Sellgren, S. F., Ekvall, G., & Tomson, G. (2008). Leadership behaviour of nurse managers in relation to job satisfaction and work climate. *Journal of Nursing Management, 16*(5), 578–587. doi:10.1111/j.1365-2934.2007.00837.x PMID:18558928

Skakon, J., Nielsen, K., Borg, V., & Guzman, J. (2010). Are leaders' well-being, behaviours and style associated with the affective well-being of their employees? A systematic review of three decades of research. *Work & Stress: An International Journal of Work, Health & Organisations, 24*(2), 17–139.

Skogstad, A., Einarsen, S., Torsheim, T., Schanke Aasland, M. S., & Hetland, H. (2007). The Destructiveness of Laissez-Faire Leadership Behavior. *Journal of Occupational Health Psychology, 12*(1), 80–92. doi:10.1037/1076-8998.12.1.80 PMID:17257068

Spector, P. E. (2006). *Industrial and Organisational Psychology: Research and Practice* (4th ed.). John Wiley & Sons.

Sullivan, E. J., & Garland, G. (2010). *Practical leadership and management in nursing.* Harlow: Pearson Education Limited.

Sutherland, A. M., & Dodd, F. (2008). NHS Lanarkshires leadership development programs impact on clinical practice. *International Journal of Health Care Quality Assurance, 21*(6), 569–584. doi:10.1108/09526860810900727 PMID:19055267

Suzuki, K., Ohida, T., Kaneita, Y., Yokoyama, E., Miyake, T., Harano, S., & Uchiyama, M. et al. (2004). Mental Health Status, Shift Work, and Occupational Accidents among Hospital Nurses in Japan. *Journal of Occupational Health, 46*(6), 448–454. doi:10.1539/joh.46.448 PMID:15613767

Sy, T., & Côté, S. (2004). Emotional intelligence: A key ability to succeed in the matrix organization. *Journal of Management Development, 23*(5), 437–455. doi:10.1108/02621710410537056

Sy, T., Côté, S., & Saavedra, R. (2005). The contagious leader: Impact of the leaders mood on the mood of group members, group affective tone, and group processes. *The Journal of Applied Psychology, 90*(2), 295–305. doi:10.1037/0021-9010.90.2.295 PMID:15769239

Taghinejad, H., Suhrabi, Z., Kikhavani, S., Jaafarpour, M., & Azadi, A. (2014). Occupational Mental Health: A Study of Work-Related Mental Health among Clinical Nurses. *Journal of Clinical & Diagnostic Research, 8*(9), WC01–WC03. PMID:25386506

Thorpe, J. R. (2015). Do women suffer mental illness more than men? 8 factors behind the gender imbalance in treatment. *Bustle*. Rerieved 28 July, 2016 from: http://www.bustle.com/articles/83245-do-women-suffer-mental-illness-more-than-men-8-factors-behind-the-gender-imbalance-in-treatment

Thorsteinsson, R. B., Brown, R. F., & Richards, C. (2014). The Relationship between Work-Stress, Psychological Stress and Staff Health and Work Outcomes in Office Workers. *Psychology (Savannah, Ga.), 5*, 1301–1311.

Tsutsumi, A., Kayaba, K., Tsutsumi, K., & Igarashi, M. (2001). Association between job strain and prevalence of hypertension: a cross sectional analysis in a Japanese working population with a wide range of occupations: the Jichi Medical School cohort study. *Occupational and Environmental Medicine, 58*(6), 367–373. doi:10.1136/oem.58.6.367 PMID:11351051

Upenieks, V. V. (2003a). The Interrelationship of Organizational Characteristics of Magnet Hospitals, Nursing Leadership, and Nursing Job Satisfaction. *Health Care Management (Philadelphia, Pa.), 22*(2), 83–98. PMID:12785545

Upenieks, V. V. (2003b). Nurse Leaders Perceptions of What Compromises Successful Leadership in Todays Acute Inpatient Environment. *Nursing Administration Quarterly, 27*(2), 140–152. doi:10.1097/00006216-200304000-00008 PMID:12765106

Vahey, D., Aiken, L., Sloane, D., Clarke, S., & Vargas, D. (2004). Nurse burnout and patient satisfaction. *Medical Care, 42*(2), 1157–1166. PMID:14734943

Vrba, M. (2007). Emotional intelligence skills and leadership behavior in a sample of South Africa. *Management Dynamics*. Retrieved 22 July, 2016 from https://www.questia.com/library/journal/1P3-1357960571/emotional-intelligence-skills-and-leadership-behaviour

Waddington, K., & Fletcher, C. (2005). Gossip and emotion in nursing and health-care organizations. *Journal of Health Organization and Management, 19*(4/5), 378–394. doi:10.1108/14777260510615404 PMID:16206920

Warr, P. B., Cook, J., & Wall, T. (1979). Scales for the measurement of some work attitudes and aspects of psychological wellbeing. *Journal of Occupational Psychology, 52*(2), 129–148. doi:10.1111/j.2044-8325.1979.tb00448.x

Warren, C., White-Means, S., Wicks, M., Chang, C., Gourley, D., & Rice, M. (2011). Cost burden of the presnteeism health outcome: Diverse workforce of nurses and pharmacists. *Journal of Occupational and Environmental Medicine, 53*(1), 90–99. doi:10.1097/JOM.0b013e3182028d38 PMID:21187792

Way, M., & MacNeil, M. (2006). Organizational characteristics and their effect on health. *Nursing Economics, 24*(2), 67–77. PMID:16676749

West, C. P., Tan, A. D., Habermann, T. M., Sloan, J. A., & Shanafelt, T. D. (2009). Association of resident fatigue and distress with perceived medical errors. *Journal of the American Medical Association, 302*(12), 1294–1300. doi:10.1001/jama.2009.1389 PMID:19773564

WHO. (2001). *World health report. Mental disorders affect one in four people*. Retrieved 21 July, 2016 from at: http://www.who.int/whr/2001/media_centre/press_release/en/

WHO. (2013). *WHO Nursing and midwifery progress report 2008-2012*. Retrieved 20 July, 2016 from: http://www.who.int/hrh/nursing_midwifery/progress_report/en/

WHO. (2016a). *Hospitals*. Health Topics. Retrieved 20 July, 2016 from: http://www.who.int/topics/hospitals/en/

WHO. (2016b).*Mental health: strengthening our response*. Media centre. Retrieved 20 July, 2016 from: http://www.who.int/mediacentre/factsheets/fs220/en/

WHO. (2016c). *Gender and women's mental health*. Gender disparities and mental health: The Facts. Retreived 28 July, 2016 from: http://www.who.int/mental_health/prevention/genderwomen/en/

Wong, C., & Law, K. (2002). The effects of leader and follower emotional intelligence on performance and attitude. *The Leadership Quarterly, 13*(3), 243–274. doi:10.1016/S1048-9843(02)00099-1

Zandi, A., Sayari, R., Ebadi, A., & Sanainasab, H. (2011). Abundance of depression, anxiety and stress in militant Nurses. *Iranian Journal of Military Medicine, 13*(2), 103–138.

Zopiatis, A., & Constanti, P. (2010). Leadership styles and burnout: Is there an association? *International Journal of Contemporary Hospitality Management, 22*(3), 300–320. doi:10.1108/09596111011035927

KEY TERMS AND DEFINITIONS

Employee: A person who works full-time or part-time acording to the contract of employment and has their rights and duties to do a specific job. An employee has their own skills, knowledge, experience and contribution for the employer.

Leader: A person on a dominant position. Leader lead a group of people in a given area, and he / she able to control and influence on the group, in achieving the objectives. A good leader is person of strong character which inspires confidence in people, and from them bring out the best qualities.

Nursing: An integral part of health care system and focused on patients, families and communities during health and disease, with the aim to achieve the highest possible level of health. Nursing includes the promotion of health, prevention of illness and the care of ill, disabled and dying people.

Psychological Health: An integral part of the general health of the individual and is also a source of well-being. This is much more than the absence of mental illness. The concept of positive mental health consist of individual internal psychological state, such as happiness, satisfaction, self-esteem, daily operations, the ability to control their own lives, and cope with challenges and problems.

Chapter 18
Empathy and Leadership From the Organizational Perspective

Nira Shalev
The Open University, Israel

ABSTRACT

The purpose of the chapter is to review the developments in the field of leadership and the concept of empathy, and to examine possible interrelation between empathy and leadership. This chapter describes the complexity of the concept of empathy according to different authors, and refers to the psychological aspects in an attempt to connect this category with organizational behavior. Further, the chapter describes developments in the field of leadership in an attempt to focus on the contribution of the identified approaches to the relations between the leader and the employee. Finally, the chapter describes a perspective that combines chosen elements of empathy and leadership theories.

INTRODUCTION

Over the years, empathy has been identified primarily as the domain of members of the therapy professions: social workers, psychologists, and educational counselors. Kohut (1977) saw empathy as an instrument for the collection of data on the client's internal world. From his perspective, empathy is borrowed introspection, or, in other words, the attempt of one person to live the internal life of another person, with a preservation of the attitude of an objective observer. It is difficult to find a sweeping definition of empathy agreed upon by all researchers. From this perspective, it is possible to agree upon a number of characteristics of empathy. For example, empathy addresses the emotions, thoughts, and behaviors of two sides. Empathy is a dynamic, multidimensional, and circular process. There are a number of layers in the process of empathy, comprised of emotions, thoughts, and behaviors and this is not 'all or nothing'; the person may be found in one layer and from the processes that he experienced, may move between the different layers (Kaniel, 2013).

The components of empathy have been studied by various researchers (Davis, 1983; Eisenberg & Fabes, 1990). The conditions under which empathy can develop have crystallized from this research, as well as the differentiations between the components that support empathy and the components that

DOI: 10.4018/978-1-5225-2480-9.ch018

prevent it. In addition, the importance of empathy in improving interpersonal mediation has come to be understood (Goleman, 2008). Currently, it is possible to discern research studies that examine relations between empathy and organizational aspects (Holt & Marques, 2012). In recent decades, its components have been researched (Eisenberg, 2000; Shamay-Tsoory, Aharon-Peretz, & Perry, 2009) and attempts have been made to define empathy (Hoffman, 2000), describe its contribution in the organizational context (Davis, 1983), and identify its importance in the treatment process (Freud, 1918).

The field of leadership is continuously developing because of the considerable and still accumulating body of research on types of leadership, theories for the examination of leadership, the influence of leadership on organizational effectiveness, and the attempts to research the leadership factors perceived as having great influence on the behavior of followers (Burns, 1978; Bass & Avolio, 1994; Popper, 2007). In recent decades the phenomenon of leadership has become a broad platform for research. Many research studies are collected in handbooks of leadership around the world. In-depth research studies examine the components of leadership (Amit et al., 2011). It is enough to look at the quantity of books and research studies and the keyword 'leadership' in the websites of libraries to discover that there is an abundance of research material in this field. Leadership has been researched from both the psychological perspective (Yukl, 1989; Popper, 2007) and the organizational perspective, in an attempt to link leadership and organizational effectiveness (Burns, 1978; Bass & Avolio, 1994).

This chapter examines new directions in the concept of empathy and leadership theory. Relevant literature is synthesized to provide a holistic picture of current knowledge of the topic, highlighting meanings, principles, prerequisites, process and consequences. The purpose of this chapter is to bring concepts of leadership and empathy together. The author intended to expose the two concepts and try to relate them, establishing a conceptual bridge between leadership and empathy. The specific aim of the chapter is to review the different aspects of the concept of empathy, in an attempt to position them within the organizational context.

THE CONCEPT OF EMPATHY

The word 'empathy' originates from the Greek word 'empathiea', which means feeling other persons' reactions and entering their world (Campbell and Babrow 2004). The term 'empathy' has been used in many ways in different disciplines: psychology, philosophy, treatment, and organizational behavior.

The broadest generally accepted definition is that empathy is a state of emotional arousal that stems from apprehension and comprehension of another's affective state (Eisenberg 1987). From this definition of empathy, points of overlap can be found in interpersonal relationships that are based on understanding the emotional state of others, and being willing to help and to provide care.

The place of empathy in the psychological literature is central and significant. Many psychologists have worked to understand empathy. Sigmund Freud (1918), who developed the theory of psychoanalysis, saw empathy as a way of understanding and identifying the internal processes that occur in others. In his opinion, empathy is based on the single mechanism through which it is possible to adopt a position towards others. The empathic process is an intuitive process based on the controlled use of the mechanism of projection in which the person attributes to another person the feelings, drives, and desires he experiences himself. This process is not intentional but unconscious, so that the person experiences in actuality that the other person experienced these drives. Empathy is essential, and Freud emphasizes this as a condition of the creation of the treatment relationship based on relations of closeness between the therapist and the client. Freud (1918) explained that we must educate the client not to be similar to us but to be free and to realize his nature. He emphasized the role of the psychoanalyst: as the surgeon needs to keep calm, promising greater help to the client, the psychoanalyst needs to develop 'calm' to protect against possible deviation in the empathic process.

Kohut (1977) defined empathy as introspection borrowed from one person's attempt to experience another person's internal life when he maintains the position of an objective observer. In other words, Kohut saw empathy as a tool that helps in the collection of data on the client's internal world. Empathy defines the field of therapeutic inquiry. According to Kohut, empathy constitutes the sole means of understanding the other person and recognizing his internal world. The person attempts to understand the other from the other person's world, as a subject, instead of looking at him from the outside and analyzing and evaluating him as an object. He believes that the investigation of the client's internal world through outside observation will lead to distortions in the perception of the other person, and therefore when the client does not display an empathic perception, he does not see the patient's perspective and is not found in the field of psychological investigation.

According to Carl Rogers (1969), empathy means perceiving the internal frame of reference of another with accuracy, with the emotional components and meanings which pertain thereto, as if they are conditions. Rogers maintained that there are three essential conditions in relations among people. The first condition is congruence, the connection and suitability between the internal feeling and the presentation towards the outside. The second condition is acceptance, accepting the other person unconditionally. Can I always promise in all my contacts with people an attitude of warmth, concern, and respect? This condition promises the growth of authenticity and the absence of judgment. The third condition is empathy understanding, the attempt to understand the other person's world without prejudice. Rogers clarified that this is the most central and most significant learning. In the understanding of the other person, it is possible to change. The person may change and this change threatens the person.

Seligman (2005), who developed positive psychology, described empathy as the ability to see the good points of the other person even if they conflict with own immediate desires and needs of the moment. The approach of Seligman and those who followed him presents the difference in the psychological approaches that tend to perceive the 'self' at the expense of the other person.

Table 1 summarizes the psychological approaches toward empathy and its contribution to an organization's working life.

The reference to philosophy in the concept of empathy is undertaken in a few ways. Some philosophers adopt a certain position regarding the concept of empathy to explain this category. Other philosophers perceive empathy as a significant and important component of human's life. The latest recognizable philosophical approaches towards empathy have been presented by Noddings (2003), and Davis (2007).

The ethics of concern and caring described by Noddings (2003) is based on the fundamental assumption that an ethical life is not distinct from everyday life. At the basis of this perception is the fundamental assumption that in all relationships there are two sides, divided into the caring side and the cared for side. This is not based on principles but rather on concern and caring without the need for moral effort. This process is natural, with the use of love, sympathy, compassion, and attention. The ethics of concern and caring are composed of four components: (1) dialogue, (2) example, (3) practice, and (4) confirmation. The dialogue conveys to the other person open and true concern that encompasses total acceptance and appreciation. Through the dialogue it is possible to learn about the other person, and to evaluate the influences of individuals' attempts to be caring. These relations require two sides. Firstly, the caring person asks a basic question, such as: what is happening with you? The question derives from

Table 1. Empathy and its organizational perspective according to alternative psychological theories

Author	Definition of empathy	The role of empathy in an organization
Freud	Empathy is a way of the understanding and identifying the internal processes that occur in another person	Maintaining emotional distance between people, supporting the human right to be protected
Kohut	Empathy as introspection borrowed from one person's attempt to experience another person's internal life when he maintains the position of an objective observer	Empathy as a helper in collecting data on a person's world
Rogers	Empathy means to perceive the internal frame of reference of another with accuracy and with emotional components and meanings which pertain thereto, as if they are conditions.	Empathy as one of three basic conditions to establish proper relations among organization's members. The remaining two conditions are congruence and acceptance.
Seligman	Empathy is the ability to see the good points of the other person even if they conflict with my immediate desires and needs.	To cultivate and practice empathy in conflict management as a way to achieve a common understanding and acceptance on organization basic values and objectives.

a placing of attention to the other side, the person who is cared for. The caring person listens out of acceptance, openness, and unlimited attention based on empathy. This empathy leads the person who is cared for to feel the open attention focused on him. The second component, modeling, constitutes the personal example of the person showing empathy towards the other person. It is necessary to show in our behavior the meaning of concern, and to demonstrate the empathy in relations with the other person. As far as practice is concerned, it is necessary to allow the person to attempt actions of help, support, and volunteering so as to develop the caring and thus to cultivate and promote the abilities for caring and concern. For confirmation, it is necessary to discover the good in other people, and when the good is confirmed, its development is encouraged.

Davis (2007) reviewed the phenomenon of empathy and saw it as a multidimensional phenomenon, having both cognitive and emotional dimensions simultaneously. Davis's broad definition of empathy is that it is a set of constructs that connect the responses of one individual to the experiences of another.

In contrast to previous research studies, which differentiated between the cognitive dimension and the emotional dimension of empathy (Hoffman 1984; Eisenberg & Strayer 1987; Batson 1991), Davis proposed four elements that connect the person's experiences and the other person's experiences and that may constitute the prototype for the understanding of empathy (Figure 1).

In his model, Davis organizes antecedents, processes, intrapersonal outcomes, and interpersonal outcomes as a set of activities that occur at different points in time and have a cause-effect relationship to each other. Antecedents are related to all later parts of the model. Next are processes, which influence intrapersonal and interpersonal outcomes. Intrapersonal outcomes have an impact on interpersonal outcomes (Hakansson, 2003).

Figure 1. The Empathy Model of Davis. Adopted from (Davis, 2007, p.444)

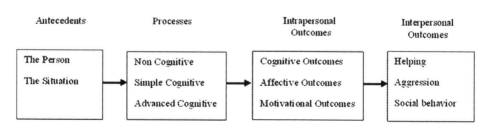

LEADERSHIP THEORIES

James Burns (1978) claimed that *"while the leadership is the most widely studied phenomenon at the same time it's the less understood."* From the dawn of history, leadership has intrigued readers and researchers. Research on leadership has addressed the topic using many different approaches and disciplines such us psychology, sociology, philosophy, management and political sciences. The knowledge base of leadership is constantly increasing and has produced a plethora of alternative and competing models. This part of the chapter is tries to offer a basic overview of chosen examples of the most popular and fundamental theories of leadership.

The earliest basic theory, the trait theory, also called the 'Great Man' theory or the dispositional theory, is based on the research study of Terman (1904). At its center is the perception that there are certain traits that cause the person to be perceived as a leader. These traits give the person a feeling that he is good and select among the group members. A leader, according to this perception, is an intelligent person, with self-confidence and with a sense of responsibility. From the external perspective, a leader is gifted with impressive appearance, height, tone of speech, and reasonable body weight. This approach does not allow the person who is lacking these traits to become a leader. Research studies found it difficult to find a person who possessed all the required traits. In addition, this theory has been criticized for not taking into consideration the conditions under which the leader operates (Bourantas & Agapitou, 2016).

The second approach to leadership, the behavioral approach, put the emphasis on the leader behavior, trying to answer the question "what the leader has to do and how?" The question is approached through setting up roles and styles that determine the effective leadership behavior (Minrzberg, 1994; Quinn et al. 2007). Behaviors, unlike traits, can be learned so it followed that individuals trained in appropriate leadership behaviors would be able to lead more effectively. The more advanced version of behavioral approach is situational leadership theory (also contingency theory), trying to interpret the most effective leadership style in a given situation. According to Hersey and Blanchard (1993) there is no optimal leadership style that can be characterized as 'the best'. Leaders can positively influence the performances and satisfaction of their subordinates by examining two dimensions of leadership behavior: reference to task and reference to people. Those two dimensions indicate four basic situations and appropriate styles of leadership: (1) telling, (2) selling, (3) delegating, and (4) participating. The four styles of leadership are different in three main ways, including: (1) the scope of the direction that the leader provides, (2) the scope of the support and encouragement that the leader provides, (3) the scope of the involvement of the followers in the decision making processes. A general conclusion of situational leadership theories is that a good leader should be able to adapt her or his leadership style to the goals or objectives to be accomplished.

The third example of the most recognizable leadership models is the model of growth and renewal in the organization developed by Adizes (1999). Adizes suggests that the fundamental role of management for any team or organization, can be defined by just four basic roles. If organization's leaders can develop these four roles, then the organization will be successful over the short as well as the long term:

- **The Purposeful Role:** The manager needs to cause the organization to be purposeful in a short period of time. The manager needs to define the organizational goal. The manager needs to understand who his clients are and what their needs are. The manager needs to fulfill the goal for which the organization was established and to achieve the results to which it is committed.

- **The Administrative Role:** The manager needs to assimilate methods of planning and efficiency in the organization. It is necessary to supervise and to examine that the desired activities are being completed effectively and in the right order.
- **The Entrepreneurial Role:** The manager needs to predict events in the long-term and to plan the responses to these events. This role drives the organization to successfully adapt to change. It's focused on creating new opportunities or responding to threats.
- **The Integrative Role:** Managers should offer the organization an organizational culture, values, and vision so as to create mutual trust and respect. The integrative role concentrates on the development of a consistent team that makes the organization efficient.

The fourth example of the fundamental leadership theories is the Full Range Model of Bass and Avolio (1994). This theory assumes that it is possible to divide all the behaviors of the leader into three categories, or three types of leadership:

- *Laissez-faire leadership* causes the leader to avoid taking responsibility and making decisions. In a laissez-faire leadership style, a manager may be given a leader position without providing leadership, which leaves subordinates to fend for themselves. The degree of manager's impact on the work processes and the staff behavior is marginal. This leads to employees having a free choice in deciding plans and methods.
- *Transactional leadership* focuses on the use of rewards and punishments in order to achieve obedience from subordinates. Transactional leaders rather try to preserve the *status quo*, than aiming for progress. Transactional leadership is an exchange activity based on the fulfillment of contractual requirements and is typically exemplified as setting objectives and controlling outcomes (Antonakis et al., 2003).
- *Transformational leadership* is based on four components: idealized influence, inspirational motivation, intellectual simulation, and individualized consideration (Bourantas & Agapitou, 2016). Transformational leaders facilitate organizational change by creating a vision, motivating people through example, supporting a culture of intellectual stimulation, and providing support and development to individual organization's members (Shatzer et al., 2013). Transformational leaders are proactive, raise subordinates' awareness for supreme collective interests, and help employees achieve extraordinary goals (Antonakis et al., 2003).

The following table (Table 2) summarizes described leadership theories with reference to the leader's position, attitude towards the employee, and points of criticism on the theory.

INTERRELATIONS BETWEEN LEADERSHIP AND EMPATHY

This part of the chapter presents a proposal for a perspective that attempts to connect leadership (using the perspective of transformational leadership) and empathy (applying the model of Davis), trying to find out whether empathy might facilitate the perception of the leader among his workers.

Leadership involves significant emotional processes that constitute a part of the social influence that the leader has on the members of the group following him. These processes are based on the leader's personality traits, such as honesty, trustworthiness, sensitivity, and empathy. Because of these traits,

Table 2. The leadership theories

Leadership Model	Basic Assumptions	Employee's Attitude	Leader's Position	Examples of Criticism
The Trait Theory	The leader possesses extraordinary innate ability or a unique background that makes him different in a positive sense from other group members. Leadership is an overall quality. A person who has it would be a leader at any time, under any circumstances, and in any place.	The employee is not being discussed.	Focusing on leaders' qualities and traits.	This model does not consider a variety of options depending on existing conditions. This model does not examine the leader's influence on the followers.
Situational Leadership	There are two dimensions to address leadership behavior: reference to the task and treatment of people. It is necessary to adjust the leadership style according to the degree of the employees' maturity.	Focus on employee readiness expressed by the employee's degree of knowledge and experience, organizational commitment, personal responsibility, and extent of motivation.	An effective leader is endowed with situational sensitivity and adapts to the conditions and situation, or acts to adjust to the situation and context.	Several studies do not support the basic recommendations offered by situational leadership theory (Vecchio, 1987; Fernandez & Vecchio, 1997)
The Model of Growth and Renewal in the Organization	Examining the behaviors in the organization according to the life cycle. The fundamental role of management for any team or organization can be defined by just four basic roles.	There is no strong reference to the relationship between the leader and the employee.	Leaders should concentrate on covering all of the identified basic managers' roles.	It's difficult to expect that each manager will be able to cover all basic roles. Those four roles should be provided by all organizational leaders as a group.
The Full Range of Leadership Model	It is possible to divide all the leader's behaviors into three categories.	Emphasis on the ability of leaders to motivate their employees, demonstration of efforts and performance are beyond personal feasibility	Leaders are the ones that lead regular people do extraordinary work. Leader's behavior reflects the different styles of leadership.	The leader influences employees, but employees also influence the leader. This aspect is absent in this model.

the leader can motivate others to act. It is possible to identify and assess other people in the employee-employer relations. As West-Burnham (2002) explains:

If leadership appears as the shift of people from response to commitment, from agreement to action, and from completion of tasks to perfect involvement, then the interpersonal ability is the essential mediator. It is impossible to form a model of leadership without interpersonal intelligence as a key element and if leadership is perceived as the motivation of people from obedience to commitment, from acceptance to active agreement, from completion of tasks to involvement.

Interpersonal intelligence is one of the types of intelligence defined by Gardner (1983) in the theory of multiple intelligences. This ability is required in the therapy professions (psychologist, social worker) but its advantage is also apparent in the role of teaching and the role of management based on personal interactions. Reinforcement of this direction can be found in research studies that have examined the phenomenon of leadership in recent years. These research studies found that the followers ascribe considerable importance to three main factors in the leader: self-confidence, optimism about the future, and the leader's ability to display personal references and to develop and cultivate the followers (Amit et al., 2006). Therefore, it is possible to clearly see that beyond administrative abilities, the employee wants to meet a leader in an organization who sees a person with desires and needs and a partner for success, a leader that presents an organizational vision in which every individual has a part. Thus, the employee perceives the leader as a response to the most basic human needs.

Goleman (2008), in his book *Social Intelligence,* explains the importance of social intelligence, which is composed of social awareness, including empathy, attention, and empathic accuracy. The second component, social skills, includes the ability to hold interactions even without the verbal element, the ability to present ourselves in the best way, and the ability to evince true concern for the needs of others and to act accordingly. The innovation in this approach is that this intelligence can be learned and practiced through emphasizing the importance of the improvement of social skills. This can ensure the existence of a more tolerant and better society.

The leader is examined and is required to lead his organization and to emphasize the human component. Of the theories of leadership described in this article, the model that best fits is the Full Range Model of Bass and Avolio (1994). The transformational leadership style and the pattern of behavior of individual reference are characterized by special attention to the developmental needs of every person through instruction and mentoring. Human reference is expressed in developed human relations that let the worker in the organization feel a relationship, belonging, and security. A leader of this type gives every worker as many opportunities as possible for learning and gives them a supportive environment that enables them to try things without fear of making mistakes. The leader acts from a caring and attentive perspective. The workers receive personal treatment, which may reduce their level of frustration and competitiveness and increase their willingness to cooperate. It is possible to see in this pattern of leadership a connection to the factor of empathy and management of emotions. It is possible to link the transformational leadership style with the model of imitation and identification, in which the leader displays power, self-confidence, consistency, and task persistence. It is possible to also link it to the first component, self-confidence. This leader will not hesitate in taking responsibility and will refrain from the use of power to achieve his goals.

When the relations in the organization are effective, the leader is perceived as a good leader, who can influence positively his followers (Argabright et al., 2014). In this research the influence of leadership is examined through a program that strengthens and develops emotional intelligence (EQ). The research results found a relationship between the development of emotional intelligence and the improvement of leadership abilities. Another research study conducted over three years on the connection between leadership and empathy found that the integration of empathy in leadership is important (Holt & Marques 2012). In addition, the study found that although empathy is based on cognitive structures, it is possible and even desirable to teach it and to practice it, even within the framework of the educational system.

Davis' model of empathy (2007), which presents empathy as a multidimensional phenomenon, as presented in the chapter, may support the development of empathy among leaders. The author will attempt to connect this model and leadership with an attempt to respond to the question of whether it is possible to develop and teach the use of empathy.

In the first stage, antecedents, there are basic data about the person. These data include the person's basic traits: degree of maturity, structure of the personality, insights, experiences, and learning history, the degree of sense of identification of the person who had a certain experience, the degree of feeling of pain/sorrow for a person who had a difficult experience. Davis' starting point assumes that every person can be empathic, aside from unusual situations where there is an organic problem, such as autism or sociopathy. However, every person is different based on the components of biology-heredity, which produces a different degree of empathy based on personality characteristics, learning, history, and degree of maturity. This difference explains the differentiation between people in their empathic ability. This stage gives the person the starting point for the use of empathy in his life. The initial stage of the model also indicates the importance of contextual conditions that may determine individual traits in the process of empathy development. This element can relate to the Full Range Model (Bass & Avolio, 1994). A transformational leader from the behavior pattern of individual reference is identified as a leader who enables his workers to respond to the needs of his development and attempts to provide his workers with an environment that has instruction, mentoring, and support. This leader's reliance on his personality characteristics may contribute to his functioning as a transformational leader.

The second stage is processes. These are the processes that lead to empathy in the other person. There are three main patterns that are differentiated through the ranking of the cognitive effort and sophistication required for their implementation. In each one of the three patterns, there can be cognitive elements and emotional elements. The first pattern is non-cognitive, processes that are based on the empathic result. An infant who hears the crying of another infant responds to this crying. In other words, before there is a task of education, a person, by his nature is empathic; otherwise there is no explanation as to why an infant responds to another infant's crying. The second pattern is simply cognitive. In this pattern the person is helped by cognitive processes: memory and understanding of a case where a person sees another person after his home has burned down and this causes a person to remember a similar situation that happened to him. It is possible to see cognitive and emotional dimensions simultaneously in this pattern. The third pattern is advanced cognitive. In this pattern the language constitutes a significant factor for the development of empathy. The person will feel empathy even without physical appearance; just from hearing the situation the person will feel empathy for another person from reference to words that remind the person of his past and that connect him to it. A person receives a message and from the words feels empathy for the person who sent it. The words express and recall his past and convey and connect him to the feeling of empathy. The manager who learns and internalizes the meaning of empathy may develop and use empathy through the construction of the relations in his organization. In the attempt to find common ground between leadership and empathy, we can find a common denominator with transformational leadership (Bass & Avolio, 1994), which by nature shapes and creates commitment and leads workers to self-fulfillment. The transformational leader with a pattern of behavior employing a model of imitation and identification creates a value-based and moral vision shared by the entire organization. The leader and his workers create a language that establishes the organizational culture.

The third stage is intrapersonal outcomes. Outcomes are divided into three categories: cognitive outcomes, affective outcomes, and motivational outcomes. Cognitive outcomes are primarily the recognition and precise assessment of the thoughts and emotions of another person. When I feel empathy for another person, I can understand and assess the other person's ways of thinking and feelings. When a person takes another person's point of view, the result is frequently that the other person's goals represent that person's goals. There is correspondence in the mental representations between one person and the other person. A common basis can be found with the Full Range Model (Bass & Avolio, 1994) with the transformational leader displaying a behavior pattern of intellectual challenge. This leader acts out of the attempt to see a problem from a number of possible viewpoints. This leader sees the worker who thinks differently to be an opportunity and a source of openness, innovation, and creativity.

Affective outcomes are emotional experiences of identification and emotional distress. A person has emotional experiences and the other person feels identification or acts from an emotional experience he receives from the person. The range of emotions may include the person feeling excitement following the emotion he receives from another person. However, it is possible that the person will feel emotional distress from the feeling of empathy he receives from the other person. It is possible to find a common basis with the Full Range Model (Bass & Avolio, 1994. The transformational leader with a pattern of behavior employing the model of imitation and identification is characterized by power, self-confidence, and perseverance in the task. The followers feel a sense of identification with the leader and aspire to imitate his ways of acting.

Motivational outcomes are the result of affective outcomes. In this category the person acts in another way and even understands the other person out of the desire to continue to cooperate. A person's motivation is to understand the other person. Davis (1983) believed that at the basis of this category is the feeling of forgiveness, which is what leads the person to attempt to understand the other and sometimes also to act and bring about a change from the same feeling.

The fourth stage is interpersonal outcomes. These outcomes can be subsumed by three categories: helping behavior, aggression, and a more general category of social behavior. This stage is characterized by an overt behavioral act by the empathizing individual. Helping behavior is one straightforward way that an empathically created affect can lead to helping. If seeing another in distress leads observers to experience a parallel effect and if that effect is experienced as unpleasant, then helping might result in simply reducing this undesirable stage. The role of empathy in reducing aggressive behavior has not received the same degree of research attention as the empathy-helping link, but has been shown, nonetheless, to regulate systematic hostile or aggressive behaviors. There are at least two primary mechanisms by which empathy can regulate hostile or aggressive behaviors. The first is the observers' emotional responses to the distress of others lessening their likelihood of aggressing against those others. The second mechanism is through the process of perspective taking: that is, adopting the point of view of the person who acts in a potentially provocative way might lead to a more tolerant perception of that person's actions, which can consequently reduce the likelihood that retaliation will occur. Social behavior based on the idea that social intercourse is significantly influenced by the capacity for empathy is certainly not new. Other people commonly have needs, desires, and goals that differ from our own and because the attainment of their goals is frequently incompatible with ours, a powerful tendency toward conflict is inherent in all social life, resulting in high levels of conflict and disagreement. Empathic concern is positively and substantially related to a considerate style and personal distress is more weakly and generally negatively associated with such a style.

FUTURE RESEARCH DIRECTIONS

Future directions of research that arise from this chapter are the development of approaches for implementation and development of leadership that combine empathy. As arising from the article, the importance of empathy among workers is considerable and hence, the possibility of developing human leadership at the basis of empathy. More specifically, in the processes of the training of the new manager, it is possible to include research and tools for the development and cultivation of empathy.

In addition, there is room to examine the influence of the manager's personal traits as predicting his perception by his workers as a transformational leader. A manager is characterized by his organizational activity, but it is possible that there is influence on the leader's traits and their influence on the followers.

There is also room to increase the depth of the research and to examine the extent to which personal traits and personality characteristics may play a part in the leader's mode of functioning. More precisely, the leader's traits can predict the way in which the worker perceives the leader.

In addition, it is possible to examine the influence of culture on leadership styles. It is possible that the field of leadership is complex and is influenced by the culture in which it operates. Hence, certain values are perceived as best, as opposed to other values. Leadership does not occur in a void; it is a part of the state, of society, and of the culture in which it acts. Therefore, it is possible to see that in every place the perspective of the leader's activity is composed from the researcher's outlook.

CONCLUSION

This chapter attempts to examine the relation between the concept of empathy and theories of leadership. Over the past one hundred years, it is possible to see trends of approaches and theories of leadership that from different perspectives saw the worker as having needs and not only productive aspects. The field of leadership ranges from a traditional perception, at the basis of which leadership is equivalent to a role or responsibility and relies on a perception that positions the leadership in a process of the creation of influence and leadership as a factor that intentionally influences and is applied by one person or a group of people on other people (Yukl, 1995) through the perception that sees leadership to be a phenomenon that emphasizes the influence of leadership in the human interactions that occur in the organization, with the goal to improve and to build organizational processes in the best possible way (Bass & Avolio, 1994).

Regarding the first research question, as an answer to the question of whether it is possible to develop and learn the use of empathy, it is possible on the basis of social intelligence of Goleman (2008), which presents social intelligence from both components: social awareness and social skills. The second component, social skills, can be developed and trained and thus can be improved. At the basis of social skills there is the understanding and knowledge of verbal and nonverbal social interactions. The ability to train and cultivate a young manager will benefit the development of this component. According to Peter Drucker's model of leadership (1999), leadership is fundamental thinking about the organization's tasks, the definition of objectives, the determination of priorities, and the formation of standards for performance. Leadership is responsibility and not privilege. Purposeful leaders see their subordinates as true partners in success. They surround themselves with excellent and ambitious people. They know that the supreme task is to create people with vision. Drucker sees the leader as a personal example, because of his diligence, his aspirations to better performances, and his respectful attitude towards his workers. The leader is patient and transparent and furthers the processes in the organization. In addition, on the basis of the multidimensional model of empathy it is possible to discern aspects that can be revealed to the young manager and that can help him in the improvement and cultivation of empathy. The model begins with the stage of antecedents, which assumes that every person can be empathic. The recognition of the model, in its components, can contribute to the crystallization of a perception of leadership that supports and promotes empathy.

Regarding the second research question, as an answer to the question of whether there is room for the leader to use empathy, it is possible to see the contribution of empathy on the basis of research studies. Holt and Marques (2011), who show in their research study the importance of empathy in leadership activity, propose in their recommendations to teach empathy so as to benefit and improve the organization. A research study that examined what the significant factors in the leader are found that the followers ascribe great importance to three main factors in the leader: self-confidence, optimism regarding the future, and the leader's ability to display personal references to develop and cultivate followers (Amit et al., 2006). The necessity for empathy in the leader's toolkit may contribute and constitute an aid.

As an answer to the third research question, organizational commitment is defined as a strong belief in the organization's goals and values, with the willingness to invest considerable effort into the organization and to be a part of it for the long-term (Manheim & Papo, 2000). In the definition of organizational commitment, there is the distinction between three dimensions:

1. Organizational commitment from response – The person chooses to remain in the organization from interest-based considerations.
2. Organizational commitment from identification – The person does not want to disappoint his peers in the organization and therefore he will perform his tasks and meet the company's expectations. Loyalty is based on a social need and not on the organization's goals.
3. Organizational commitment from internalization – The person feels very committed. He feels that his values are identical to the organization's values and he believes in what the organization represents. This type of commitment is the strongest of the three types.

Empathy is defined as the person's awareness and emotional development towards another person. The broadest definition generally accepted is that empathy is a state of emotional arousal that stems from apprehension and comprehension of another's affective state (Eisenberg 1987). Hence, if a manager acts with empathy towards his workers, then it is more likely that his workers will develop organizational commitment from internalization. The worker will feel that he is expressed in his values and beliefs and because of the empathy towards him he will succeed in strengthening his organizational belonging. According to Bass and Avolio (1994), the transformational leader is a person who raises the awareness and the expectations of his workers to achievements and causes them to search for an answer to higher needs and to work hard for goals that deviate from the personal interest. This leader is helped by empathy, truly listens to his people, and gives them a considerable degree of autonomy through the encouragement of their personal development.

REFERENCES

Adizes, I. (1999). *Managing Corporate Lifecycles. Adizes Institute.*

Amit, K., Lisak, A., Popper, M., & Gal, R. (2007). Motivation To Lead (MTL) – Research on the Motives for Undertaking Leadership Roles. *Military Psychology, 19*(3), 137–160. doi:10.1080/08995600701386317

Amit, K., Popper, M., Gal, R., Mishkal Sinai, M., & Lisak, A. (2006). The Potential to Lead: The Difference between "Leaders" and "Non-leaders".[Hebrew]. *Megamot, 44*(2), 277–296.

Antonakis, J., Avolio, B. J., & Sivasubramaniam, N. (2003). Context and leadership: An examination of the nine-factor full-range leadership theory using the Multifactor Leadership Questionnaire. *The Leadership Quarterly, 14*(3), 261–295. doi:10.1016/S1048-9843(03)00030-4

Argabright, K. J., King, J., Cochran, G. R., & Chen, C. Y. (2014). Evaluation of the Leadership Institute: A Program to Build Individual and Organizational Capacity through Emotional Intelligence. *Journal of Extension, 52*(1).

Avolio, B. J., Bass, B. M., & Jung, D. I. (1999). Reexamining the Components of Transformational and Transactional Leadership Using the Multifactor Leadership Questionnaire. *Journal of Occupational and Organizational Psychology, 72*(4), 441–462. doi:10.1348/096317999166789

Bass, B. M., & Avolio, B. J. (1994). *Improving Organizational Effectiveness through Transformational Leadership.* Thousand Oaks, CA: Sage Pub.

Batson, C. D. (1991). *The Altruism Question: Toward a Social-Psychological Answer.* Hillsdale, NJ: Lawrence Erlbaum Associates.

Blanchard, K. (2007). *Leading at Higher Level Blanchard on Leadership and Creating High Performing Organizations.* Prentice Hall.

Bourantas, D., & Agapitou, V. (2016). *Leadership Meta-Competencies. Discovering Hidden Virtues.* London: Routledge.

Burns, J. M. G. (1978). *Leadership.* New York: Harper & Row.

Bush, T. (2015). Understanding instructional leadership. *Educational Management Administration & Leadership, 43*(4), 487–489. doi:10.1177/1741143215577035

Campbell, R. G., & Babrow, A. S. (2004). The Role of Empathy in Responses to Persuasive Risk Communication: Overcoming Resistance to HIV Prevention Messages. *Health Communication, 16*(2), 159–182. doi:10.1207/S15327027HC1602_2 PMID:15090283

Davis, M. H. (1983). Measuring Individual Differences in Empathy: Evidence for a Multidimensional Approach. *Journal of Personality and Social Psychology, 44*(1), 113–136. doi:10.1037/0022-3514.44.1.113

Davis, M. H. (2007). Empathy. In *Handbook of the Sociology of Emotions* (pp. 443–466). New York: Springer.

De Vignemont, F., & Singer, T. (2006). The Empathic Brain: How, When, and Why? *Trends in Cognitive Sciences, 10*(10), 435–441. doi:10.1016/j.tics.2006.08.008 PMID:16949331

Decety, J., & Jackson, P. L. (2006). The Functional Architecture of Human Empathy. *Behavioral and Cognitive Neuroscience Reviews, 3*(2), 71–100. doi:10.1177/1534582304267187 PMID:15537986

Decety, J., & Meyer, M. (2008). From Emotion Resonance to Empathic Understanding: A Social Developmental Neuroscience Account. *Development and Psychopathology, 20*(04), 1053–1080. doi:10.1017/S0954579408000503 PMID:18838031

Drucker, P.F., (1999). *Management challenges for 21st century.* New York: Harper.

Eisenberg, N. (2000). Emotion, Regulation, and Moral Development. *Annual Review of Psychology, 51*(1), 665–697. doi:10.1146/annurev.psych.51.1.665 PMID:10751984

Eisenberg, N., & Fabes, R. A. (1990). Empathy: Conceptualization, Measurement and relation to Prosocial Behavior. *Motivation and Emotion, 14*(2), 131–149. doi:10.1007/BF00991640

Eisenberg, N., & Strayer, J. (1987). *Empathy and its Development*. New York: University of Cambridge.

Eyal, O., & Roth, G. (2011). Principals leadership and teachers motivation: Self-determination theory analysis. *Journal of Educational Administration, 49*(3), 256–275. doi:10.1108/09578231111129055

Fernandez, C. F., & Vecchio, R. P. (1997). Situational leadership theory revisited: A test of an across-jobs perspective. *The Leadership Quarterly, 8*(1), 67–84. doi:10.1016/S1048-9843(97)90031-X

Freud, S. (1918). Psychoanalytic Treatment. Tel Aviv: Am Oved.

Gallese, V. (2007). *Before and Below Theory of Mind: Embodied Simulation and the Neural Correlates of Social Cognition*. Retrieved from http://www.ncbi.nlm.nih.gov/pmc/articles/PMC2346524/?report=classic

Gardner, H. (1983). *Frames of Mind*. New York: Basic Books.

Gerdes, K. E. (2014). Empathy, Sympathy and Pity: 21st Century Definitions and Implications for Practice and Research. *Journal of Social Service Research, 3*(37), 230–241.

Goleman, D. (1997). *Emotional Intelligence*. New York: Bantam Books.

Goleman, D. (2008). Social Intelligence: The Biology of Leadership. *Harvard Business Review*, (September), 1–8. PMID:18777666

Gregoire, M. B., & Arendt, S. W. (2014). Leadership: Reflections over the Past 100 Years. *Journal of the Academy of Nutrition and Dietetics, 114*(5), S10–S19. doi:10.1016/j.jand.2014.02.023 PMID:24725519

Hakansson, J. (2003). *Exploring the phenomenon of empathy* (Doctoral dissertation). Department of Psychology, Stockholm University.

Harris, A. (2004). Distributed Leadership and School Improvement: Leading or Misleading? *Educational Management Administration & Leadership, 32*(1), 11–24. doi:10.1177/1741143204039297

Heathcote, J. M. (2006). *Predicting Fair Behaviour: Using Empathy to Understand a Manager's Procedural and Interaction Justice* (PHD dissertation). University of Western Ontario.

Hersey, P., & Blanchard, K. H. (1993). Management of Organizational behavior utilizing human resources. Academic Press.

Hoffman, M. (2000). *Empathy and Moral Development*. New York: Cambridge University Press. doi:10.1017/CBO9780511805851

Hoffman, M. L. (1984). Interaction of affect and Cognition in Empathy. In C. E. Izard, J. Kagan, & R. B. Zajonc (Eds.), *Emotions, Cognitions, and Behavior* (pp. 103–131). Cambridge, UK: Cambridge University Press.

Holt, S., & Marques, J. (2012). Empathy in Leadership: Appropriate or Misplaced? An Empirical Study on a Topic that Is Asking for Attention. *Journal of Business Ethics, 105*(1), 95–105. doi:10.1007/s10551-011-0951-5

Kaniel, S. (2013). *Empathy in Education – Education with Love*. Tel-Aviv: Mofet.

Kohut, H. (1977). *The Restoration of the Self*. New York: International Universities Press.

Krznaric, R. (2014). *Empathy Why It Matters and How To Get It*. New York: Penguin Group.

Mill, J. S. (2006). *On Liberty*. Jerusalem: Shalem Publisher.

Mintzberg, H. (1994). *The Rise and Fall of Strategic Planning*. New York: The Free Press.

Noddings, N. (2003). *Caring*. University of California Press.

Noddings, N. (2016). *Philosophy of Education*. New York: Westview Press.

Poland, W. S. (2007). The Limits of Empathy. *The American Imago, 64*(1), 87–93. doi:10.1353/aim.2007.0017

Popper, M. (2007). Transformational Leadership: A Psychological View. Tel Aviv: Tel Aviv University Press. (in Hebrew)

Popper, M. (2013). Leaders Perceived as Distant and Close. Some Implications for Psychological Theory on Leadership. *The Leadership Quarterly, 24*(1), 1–8. doi:10.1016/j.leaqua.2012.06.008

Quinn, R. E., Faerman, S. R., Thompson, M. P., & McGrath, M. (2007). *Becoming a Master Manager: A Competency Framework*. John Wiley & Sons.

Rogers, C.R. (1959). A Therapy, Personality and Interpersonal Relationships, As Developed in Client – Centered. *Psychology: A Study of Science, 3*, 184-256.

Rogers, C. R. (1969). *Freedom to Learn*. Center for Studies of the Person La Joller.

Seligman, M. E. P., Steen, T. A., Park, N., & Peterson, C. (2005). Positive Psychology Progress: Empirical Validation of Interventions. *The American Psychologist, 60*(5), 410–421. doi:10.1037/0003-066X.60.5.410 PMID:16045394

Shamay-Tsoory, S. G., Aharon-Peretz, J., & Perry, D. (2009). Two Systems for Empathy: A Double Dissociation between Emotional and Cognitive Empathy in Inferior Frontal Gyrus versus Ventromedial Prefrontal Lesions. *Brain, 132*(3), 617–627. doi:10.1093/brain/awn279 PMID:18971202

Shatzer, R., Caldarella, P., Hallam, P., & Brown, B. (2014). Comparing the effects of instructional and transformational leadership on student achievement: Implications for practice. *Educational Management Administration & Leadership, 42*(4), 445–459. doi:10.1177/1741143213502192

Stets, J. E., & Turner, J. H. (2007). *Handbook of the Sociology of Emotions*. New York: Springer.

Terman, L. M. (1904). A Preliminary Study of the Psychology of Leadership. In *Handbook of leadership Research: A Survey of Theory and Research*. Riverside, N.Y.: Free Press.

Vecchio, R. P. (1987). Situational Leadership Theory: An examination of a prescriptive theory. *The Journal of Applied Psychology, 72*(3), 444–451. doi:10.1037/0021-9010.72.3.444

West-Burnham, J. (2002). *Leading and Managing for High Performance*. Australia Principals Center Ltd.

Yalom, D. Y. (2002). *The Gift of Therapy*. Kinneret, Israel: Hebrew.

Young, A. (2010). *Empathy, Cruelty, the Origins of the Social Brain*. Paper presented at Interacting Mind Workshop, Aarhus, Denmark.

Yukl, G. (1989). *Leadership in Organizations*. Prentice-Hall.

Yukl, G., & Mahsud, R. (2010). Why flexible and adaptive leadership is essential? *Consulting Psychology Journal: Practice and Research, 62*(2), 81–93. doi:10.1037/a0019835

KEY TERMS AND DEFINITIONS

Empathy: A state of emotional arousal that stems from apprehension and comprehension of another's affective state (Eisenberg, 1987).

Leadership: The process of influencing others to understand and agree about what needs to be done and how to do it, and the process of facilitating individual and collective efforts to accomplish shared objectives (Yukl, 2010).

Transformational Leadership: A process where leaders and their followers raise one another to higher levels of morality and motivation (Burns, 1978).

Chapter 19
Cyberloafing:
An Emerging Online Counter-Productive Work Behaviour

J-Ho Siew Ching
Universiti Sains Malaysia, Malaysia

Ramayah Thurasamy
Universiti Sains Malaysia, Malaysia

ABSTRACT

Technology has pervaded our daily lives more than ever. The use of technology has become a tool to achieve competitive advantage by firms. The pervasive use of technology also has its drawbacks. Employees who cannot recognise the limits between work and leisure may have taken this opportunity to utilise companies' Internet access while at work by surfing non-work related websites to satisfy their own needs. This behaviour is known as Cyberloafing and it is thought to contribute to failures of organisations. This study introduces cyberloafing as one of the counter-productive work behaviour at the workplace. It consists of an introduction to cyberloafing, counter-productive work behaviour, and some reviews on cyberloafing research. Overall, the study provides the reader with a better understanding of cyberloafing.

INTRODUCTION

In this 21st Century, the convergence between telecommunication and computers provides the world with unlimited access to information technology via an internet connection. Almost every workplace and organisation is managed by a computer programming system, adopts wireless devices for better productivity and provides faster communication around the world. ICT are widely used in many sectors such as business, manufacturing, wholesale trade, telecommunication and computer related services. It covers enterprises, households, private as well as public sectors. The use of ICT indirectly impacts economic and social developments around the world as ICT engage in most workplaces.

A research done by Miniwatts Marketing Group regarding the Internet world statistic estimated that there are 3,566,321,015 world internet users from a total world population of 7,340,093,980 until 30th

DOI: 10.4018/978-1-5225-2480-9.ch019

of June, 2016 (Miniwatts Marketing Group, 2016). The number of internet users has increased from 3,366,260,056 to 3,566,321,015, just between short periods of time ranging from the last statistic summary of 30th November, 2015. Asia secured first place for the highest number of internet users worldwide with 49.5%, followed by Europe with 17.2%, Lat Am with 10.5%, Africa with 9.4%, North America with 9.0%, the Middle East with 3.6%, and Australia with 0.8%.

Another Asian independent telecommunications research and consultancy company i.e. Buddecomm also carried out a research on technologies which covered 35 countries in North, South, South East, and Central Asia. In the reports, the global technology usage has grown rapidly not only through the use of computers as the main telecommunications tools but also other devices such as mobile phones or smartphones, handsets, touchscreen tablets in sales and marketing department, as well as organisational operating systems (Paul Budde Communication Pty Ltd, 2016).

Although the Internet is used as a telecommunications tool in organisations, some employees are involved in social networking sites besides the official website. A study conducted by the Pew Research Center reported that majority of the Internet users accessed news from social media platforms, with 52% were Twitter users while 47% were Facebook users (Pew Research Center, 2016). The ease of accesing informaton and communicating via the internet has somewhat believed to reduce the users' stress level For example, employees surf the internet as the means of taking break from work, reducing stress and entertainment at work. Yet this action became a conscious attempt to motivate their own needs without noticing that their action has actually caused a disturbance to their work. This is called cyberloafing i.e. involving in personal Internet use during working hours (Garrett & Danziger, 2008).

BACKGROUND

Cyberloafing is personal use of the Internet by employees while at work for non-work-related purposes (Jia & Jia, 2015; Al-shuaibi, Subramaniam, & Mohd Shamsudin, 2014; Blanchard & Henle, 2008; Liberman, Seidman, McKenna, & Buffardi, 2011; Weatherbee, 2010). Related activities of cyberloafing include sending and receiving emails or messaging, browsing the Internet for information or news, watching online movies using YouTube, and online shopping (Liberman et al., 2011; Weatherbee, 2010). In some cases, some employees even browse through famous social networking sites (SNSs) such as Facebook, Twitter, and YouTube for the sake of seeking friends, chatting with a friend, or updating their daily lifestyle activities on their own blogs (Kim, Sohn, & Choi, 2011).

Numeruous cyberloafing related studies has been carried out. Different terminologies were used to the refer the same phenomenon. These include personal web usage (PWU) (Garrett & Danziger, 2008; Kim & Byrne, 2011; Mahatanankoon, Anandarajan, & Igbaria, 2004), cyber deviance (Al-shuaibi et al., 2014; Blanchard & Henle, 2008), cyberslacking (O'Neill, Hambley, & Chatellier, 2014), cyberbludging, internet deviance, online loafing, internet addiction, and internet dependency (Celik, 2014; Kim & Byrne, 2011). As identified by Blanchard and Henle (2008), cyberloafing is divided into minor and serious cyberloafing. Minor cyberloafing is surfing a network which involves sending and receiving personal emails at work and doing online shopping. Meanwhile, surfing a network which highlights organisational legal liabilities is categorised as serious cyberloafing.

Only a hanful of studies in various countries emphasized that users actually admitted to the fact that surfing the Internet decreases their own productivity (Bortolani & Favretto, 2009) as cyberloafing distracts the employees from completing their task or work, lowers their performance and reduces their productivity (Al-shuaibi et al., 2014; Lim & Chen, 2012). A survey administered in Americaby using Websense.com found that American employees spent on average 24% of their working hours on cyber-loafing activities per day (Lim & Chen, 2012). Another study which carried out by Ramayah (2010) in one of the companies in Malaysia, showed that the employees spent on average 25% of their daily work time to access materials for personal use. Evidently, cyberloafing lead to lost of producivity in a oganization (Celik, 2014; Melnick, 2014; Yılmaz, Yilmaz, Öztürk, Sezer, & Karademir, 2015) apart from increasing the risk of getting viruses or spyware, and finally contribute to the waste of IT resources (Moody & Siponen, 2013).

A REVIEW OF STUDIES RELATING TO CYBERLOAFING

Who are Those Involved in Cyberloafing?

Some of the demographic variables are found related to cyberloafing although some of the research may use them as control variables. Gender is the most common construct of biological differences between men and women dedicated to their different behaviours. Males' involvement in cyberloafing has been found to be greater than their female counterparts (Akbulut, Dursun, Dönmez, & Şahin, 2016; Askew et al., 2014; Baturay & Toker, 2015; Garrett & Danziger, 2008; Lim & Chen, 2012; Yılmaz et al., 2015; Yogun, 2015). In contrast to these studies, a report on social media usage revealed incomparable percentage between the two genders, in which 68% are female users and 62% are males (Pew Research Center, 2016). This might indicate that the behaviour of cyberloafing between male and female users differs and depends on a specific activity and not all employees cyberloaf for social media usage. The amount of time they spend on cyberloafing at the workplace might also be different.

In terms of age factor, young adults whose age are between 18 to 29 years old, are most likely to use the Internet for social networking in comparison to users aged above 65 (Pew Research Center, 2016). Nevertheless, users age 65 and above have increased in percentage i.e. from 2% in 2005 to 35% in 2016. These findings actually show the positive side of the Internet where the changing in information technology era leads to changes of behaviour in the Internet usage, no matter how young or old the users are. However, the setback of such changes is the Internet addiction habits that leads to cyberloafing. In other words, the users surf the Internet for own personal usage rather than take responsibility for their work. Cyberloafing was found to be negatively correlated with age (Andreassen, Torsheim, & Pallesen, 2014; Vitak, Crouse, & LaRose, 2011). Interestingly, however, younger workers were found positively related to cyberloafing compared to older workers (Garrett & Danziger, 2008).

Nowadays, cyberloafing activities exist not only in the private sector but in government sector as well. Employees of higher status, earnings, or educational levels are significantly related to cyberloafing when compared to those of lower status (Çınar & Karcıoğlu, 2015; Garrett & Danziger, 2008). This indicates that those with higher positions such as managers or supervisors are easily involved in cyberloafing in comparison to their subordinates. They are driven by the belief that the Internet is a source of personal work innovation. Besides searching and sending information or reports, they do think that surfing the Internet for personal purposes at the same time is not a serious problem (Garrett & Danziger, 2008). This is in line with the report that reveals 76% of the users who surf social media sites are at least college or graduate degrees (Pew Research Center, 2016) as well as of higher educational level (Andreassen et al., 2014).

Cyberloafing as Counter-Productive Work Behavior

In the past, numerous research were done to study workplace behaviour. Some of the behaviours might be harmful while others were less harmful. In the 1940s, the researchers were more likely to emphasis on white collar crimes or criminal behaviours in occupation (Sharma & Singh, 2015). Since then, researchers have continued their studies on behaviour which is known as workplace deviant behaviour (Mishra & Pandey, 2014). Among the behaviours are lying, spreading rumors, absenteeism, dishonesty, aggression, and stealing among employees (Norsilan, Omar, & Ahmad, 2014).

Additionally, Robinson and Bennett (1995), as well as Mishra and Pandey (2014), defined workplace deviance as voluntary and unethical behaviour that is in violation of the organisation, its members, or both. Thus, this behaviour may harm the organisation, its members, or both (Robinson & Bennett, 1995; Norsilan et al., 2014). In worst case scenario, it can also cause organisation failure (Mishra & Pandey, 2014; Sharma & Singh, 2015). Similarly, this 'workplace deviant' term does share the same literature and meaning as 'counter-productive work behaviour' (CWB) (Norsilan et al., 2014) to indicate the employees' behaviour which are unacceptable and wrong (Ramayah, 2010).

Samnani et al. (2014) described CWB as employees' behaviour engaging in physical or verbal aggression and other forms of interpersonal mistreatment, which can be described as harmful. It can also result in deviance in production (Liberman et al., 2011), for example, theft, fraud, and vandalism towards the organisation, as well as violence, harassment, and discrimination against other individuals (Pecker & Fine, 2015). To maintain a better environment and organisational behaviour, there are numerous studies on CWB in organisations which adopt a number of methods to minimise such incidence as this behaviour is the result of weak security controls, job dissatisfaction, job stress, and abusive management (Pecker & Fine, 2015).

According to Robinson and Bennett (1995), workplace deviance can be divided into four categories. Which include production deviance, property deviance, political deviance, and personal aggression. Cyberloafing is identified as production deviance (Bortolani & Favretto, 2009; Robinson & Bennett, 1995) where employees may easily waste their time to surf the internet without leaving their desks for non-work-related purposes. This behaviour actually demonstrates an act of wasting company resources. Furthermore, using the company computers to shop online during working hours is against the work ethics (Alshuaibi, Mohd Shamsudin, & Alshuaibi, 2015) which can be considered a CWB.

Activities Related to Cyberloafing

A lots of studies have been carried out by researchers around the world regarding ICT issues over the years. Besides the statistics presented by the Miniwatts Marketing Group, there are a few more groups or portals that also report on ICT issues. Apart from using the Internet as the main telecommunication tool for business, it can also be used as a social media platform for social purposes. Among many websites, currently, Facebook tops the most popular social network, which has at least 1.59 billion monthly active users (The Statistics Portal, 2016). This is followed by WhatsApp with 1,000 billion users, Facebook Messenger with 900 billion users, QQ with 853 billion users, and WeChat with 697 Billion users. All these applications can be connected to smart phones and provides easy access over the device. Users uses social media as a plaform of communicating and socializing with others, and a person whom did not use social media are considered outdated among their peers.

Similarly, the Brandwatch company has also executed a study which shows Facebook as the most popular social media website with 1.65 billion users, followed by Youtube with over 1 billion users, WhatsApp with 900 million users, Weibo with 600 million users, Instagram with 400 million users, and Google+ with 300 million users (Smith, 2016). Subsequently, there are 40 million active small business pages on Facebook, but only 2 million of those businesses pay for advertising. At the same time, there are 65.8% of the United States of America companies that use Twitter for marketing purposes. In addition, famous search engines such as Google processes 100 billion searches a month with an average of 40,000 search queries every second. Interestingly, more than half of Google searches come from smartphones. Also, there are 3.25 billion hours of videos being watched each month by YouTube users all around the world, and more than half are viewed via smartphones. Furthermore, 1 million new active mobile social users are added every day. However, considering a normal employee who works 8 hours a day, fully utilising his or her working hours with job-related stuff, no such amount of users as mentioned by the statistics of those studies can be true, unless they are actually cyberloafing.

A study has shown that 79% of the respondents had their smartphones placed near to them for easy connection and productivity (Cooper, 2013). On the other hand, 93% of the business sector adopt social media as a business strategy because it is the most common way to do budget marketing. This strategy saves cost and efficient. Out of all the websites, 1 million websites have integrated Facebook, 80% of Facebook users enjoy connectivity on social media i.e. Facebook, and 23% of the users check their Facebook accounts 5 times or more every day. In light of this evidence, Facebook is one of the social media websites that generates 30% of mobile usage, which has increased 7% from the year of 2012. Moreover, 25% of the smartphone users aged 18 until 44 years old claimed that they could hardly recall the last time their smartphones were not next to them. It can clearly be concluded from this situation that the growing number of smartphone usage needs to be given attention. This may reveal that some of the users actually indulge in cyberloafing via smartphones aside from computers or laptops for personal usage. Among the expected activities are personal messaging or browsing through social media sites while doing actual marketing strategy activities.

Currently, individuals all over the world are actually adapting new ways of communicating to fulfil their needs. A total of 91% American adults own a cell phone or mobile phone for daily usage instead of using normal phone calls (Pew Research Center, 2016). Among the popular activities performed via their cellphones are 81% sending or receiving text messages, 60% accessing the Internet, 52% sending or receiving emails, 50% downloading applications (apps), 49% getting directions or information, and 48% listening to music. If all these activities are actually performed during working hours, cyberloafing activities are not performed solely on computers or laptops, but also via mobile phones that can be easily taken anywhere and whenever the users need them.

BBC News did broadcast some issues related to ICTs. Some employees argued that employers should embrace Facebook to accomplished business goal, and allowing workers to use SSNs freely and flexibility (BBC NEWS, 2008b). These employees felt banning Facebook is wrong and inhibit their social life such as develop stronger relationships among friends and colleagues. Another articles showed that India is grew together with latest ICT technologies especially mobile internet to put together their citizens so that they are not far left behind (BBC NEWS, 2008a). Recently, there are reported news on the ICT related misbehaviour by employees which cause loses to the organizations. Indeed, younger generation employees whom grew up with technologies are attached to their devices cannot left their device far behind. In order to cope with such problems, some organizations support their employees by looking at what the younger generation can do as physical and virtual space is needed to explore more creative idea besides networking online.

Cyberloafing as Organization Culture

As defined by Yusof (2014), "*culture is a set of rules and behavior patterns that an individual learns, not inherited at birth*" (p. 49), and "*organizational culture is to develop commitment among members of the organizations*" (p. 51). Each workplace and organisation have their own norms, values, or working patterns that are developed after a period of adaptation time. Employees behave according to their commitment, loyalty, and beliefs in the combined manner of the group and individual within the same organisation in order to get things done accordingly. They may change their behaviour patterns to stay away from creating problems or trouble to the organisation.

Every organisation has accepted the changes especially when computers were introduced to replace typewriters at workplace. Training are provided to the employess to ensure they are able to keep up with the trend and innovation at the work place. Human resources department has to provide appropriate training to all employees regarding awareness of technological usage (Bortolani & Favretto, 2009). Somehow, some of the behaviours may lead to positive changes while some may result in negative ways without realising it. For example, when computers were introduced to replace typewriters in office, employees fear of losing their job. Instead of resisting to change, they learnt to use computers. Their habits changed together with their behaviour too. This is the positive side of work culture although the changes might be quite hard especially for elderly staffs whose computer and technological skills might not be up to date.

However, the changes may not be the same for young and energetic, or freshly graduated employees whose computer skills may be advanced in comparison to their supervisors'. An employee may come on time to their office every morning, but they may not be really keen to delve into their actual work stuff. A research done by Kidwell (2010) shows that an employee's work routine might begin with switching on his or her computer early morning to check emails and followed by reading news online. Some might continue with doing online personal stuff for example paying bills online or updating Facebook page or blog. For them, looking up some news updates online or simple chatting would only take a couple of seconds and are no big deal. Without realising, they might take for granted a couple of seconds, a couple of minutes or even a couple of hours and these are still considered as cyberloafing.

Organizational culture (OC) also being defined as "Values, norms, and practices influence employee behavior, while practices are found the most direct levers for changing behaviors" (Richards, 2010, pp23). When most employees shared same beliefs system or some behavior that physically used to while in the organization, it slowly become the culture of that organization. This culture explained why people behave the same way in the same organizational and some good cultures that implement actually prove to success over time. OC can be differentiated by two types which known as implicit and explicit components. Examples of Implicit components are assumptions or idea which shared together in their social surrounding; while explicit components included norms or practices (example: dressing code, working hours time period), patterns and behavior (Richards, 2010). Thus, cyberloafing can be considered as one of the implicit components as different individual has different assumptions either it can be accepted or not in the organizations.

Meanwhile, Jiang and Tsohou (2014) emphasized that capability of ICTs and devices in workplace increasing the blurred boundary between work and non-work. In addition, personal web usage (PWU) may lead to three different ideas, which include the antecedents, impacts and regulating policies. For antecedents, PWU is one of the channels for employees to perform positive behavior as use of ICT can improve creativity and ability of employees towards their task; for impacts, PWU might have both positive and negative impacts in different circumstances; lastly, regulating policies should be proposed in different circumstances as some security policies that fixed might have bad impression or behavior in that organization cultural.

Although it is rare to impresses both positive and negative impacts of PWU in organization, however, duality of PWU may results different impacts (Jiang & Tsohou, 2014). Instrumental is the positive side of using device at work place. Devices such as tablets and smart phones are actually basic facilities for personal purposes during working hours. Employees need to know their boundary between work and non-work to maintain work and home balance. Meanwhile, expressive is the negative side of PWU as over activities on non-work related stuffs may give negative impact on organizations especially productivity and information security. For example, some employees might engage in PWU just for a short mental break by surfing news or social networking sites (SNSs); or some employess even spents more times on surfing to express their negative affections towards some injustice or role problems given by their employers. Thus, PWU is not an issue if both approaches and duality of PWU being studies carefully by determined job characteristics and organizational culture.

Variables Correlated to Cyberloafing

With regards to factors that lead to cyberloafing, Mishra and Pandey (2014) evaluated three different factors that determine workplace deviance, which include personality-related factors, organisational-related factors, and work-related factors. Negative affectivity, conscientiousness, agreeableness, and emotional intelligence demonstrate personality-related factors; organisational climate, organisational justice, and organisational support are pointed out as organisational-related factors; work stress and powerlessness are recognised as work-related factors. In between, job satisfaction was found mediating these three factors which influence a variety of workplace deviance.

Job satisfaction might be a term that cannot be observed from an individual's surrounding. It can only be felt by the individual himself or herself. Job satisfaction is defined as "emotions creating positive and satisfaction at the end of job" (Celik, 2014: p.174). As further discussed by Celik (2014), he mentioned that an individual requires positive attitude to gain high satisfaction while negative attitude for low satisfaction. If employees cannot fulfill expectations on job area properly, the job satisfaction will decrease and it has a direct link to cyberloafing at work (Al-shuaibi et al., 2014; Celik, 2014). Employees actually respond to the situation they face as a form of interaction between persons and situations, as claimed by the social exchange theory. Despite this connection, some employees who cyberloaf may have gone through unsatisfactory job experiences causing them to behave unwisely such as cyberloafing (Chun & Bock, 2006). Additionally, married employees were found to enjoy and gain job satisfaction more than single employees. They, however, indulged in cyberloafing more than single employees (Celik, 2014).

In terms of personality, the five inventory was applied. Studies found that extraversion (Andreassen et al., 2014; Jia & Jia, 2015), neuroticism (Andreassen et al., 2014; O'Neill et al., 2014), and openness (Jia & Jia, 2015) were positively related to cyberloafing whereas emotional stability and conscientiousness were negatively related (Andreassen et al., 2014). Agreeableness, on the contrary, was found unrelated to cyberloafing (Andreassen et al., 2014; Jia & Jia, 2015). This inventory is widely used by most organisations to identify workers' personality in enhancing their job satisfaction. Some organisations even use it as one of the personality tests for the pre-interview in order to find out the type of personality the future employee may have. The test is to determine whether he or she is suitable for the work being offered. Other variables or studies regarding cyberloafing issues are shown in Table 1.

Table 1. Summary of Studies Regarding Cyberloafing Issues

Researchers	Independent Variable	Moderator	Dependent Variable
(Chun & Bock, 2006)	Cyberloafing attitude and Subjective norms	Job satisfaction	Cyberloafing intention
(Lee, Lee, & Kim, 2007)	Individual's attitude and Subjective norm	-	Cyberloafing behavior
(Wang, Tian, & Shen, 2013)	Perceived Internet Use Policy and Perceived Electronic Monitoring	Self-esteem Job Satisfaction	Cyberloafing intention
(Moody & Siponen, 2013)	Habit, affect, role, and self-concept	-	Cyberloafing behavior
(Betts, Setterstrom, Pearson, & Totty, 2014)	Facilitating conditions	-	Cyberloafing behavior
(Celik, 2014)	Job satisfaction	-	Cyberloafing behavior
(Zhang, Zhao, Liu, Xu, & Hui, 2015)	Dampening effect.	Self-control	Cyberloafing behavior

Theories Related to Cyberloafing

When going back to basics, every human behaviour is said to actually linked to the individual's needs of fulfilment towards self-satisfaction. Different individual has different needs and requirements. Abraham Maslow, the most famous behavioural psychologist, has drawn a pyramid highlighting individual needs which is known as Maslow's hierarchy of needs. The model is divided into five stages. The lowest stage indicates the basic needs (physiological needs and safety needs), psychological needs (belongingness and love needs, esteem needs), and finally self-fulfilment (self-actualisation). Individuals must satisfy lower needs before achieving the higher level growth needs of self-actualisation.

As an employee in this technological era, the individual is actually fulfilling the last stage of needs, which aims for achieving one's full potential by doing creative activities. Surfing the Internet at the office during working hours is an individual's requirement of needs that he or she may not notice. Surfing a website that is related to work is considered as self-achievement. However, without realising, when the time spent and the usage of the Internet are increasing, which includes surfing for non-work related stuff in order to fulfill social needs, the behaviour is considered as cyberloafing (Kim & Byrne, 2011). As an illustration, an employee may spend time browsing social media sites such as Facebook or personal blog to update status after submitting his or her job report by electronic mail (email).

Good behaviour is important to enhance the quality of services, and negative behaviour can be linked to an organisation's failure (Mishra & Pandey, 2014). Such situation can be explained via technology acceptance model (TAM) by Davis in 1989. This model categorised two types of motivators: the extrinsic motivators and intrinsic motivators, aside from other variables that may affect perceived ease of use, perceived usefulness, social influence, playfulness, facilitation conditions, and trust. In this model, individual that often uses the internet may improve job characteristics that linked to job satisfaction and productivity; however, cyberloafing behaviour may increas when there is no sanctions and workload is low between the employees (Henle & Blanchard, 2005). Employees that do not have much work tend to spend their time cyberloafing just to pass the time. Worst still when cyberloafing becomes one of the organisations' culture, whereby their ways of behaving adapted into the environment and become a norm. This can also mean that whoever that does not commit cyberloafing may get left behind, being isolated or boycotted by others.

Lately, many studies on cyberloafing issues were explained using the theory of planned behaviour (TPB) by Aizen in 1991 (Askew et al., 2014; Lee et al., 2007) and theory of interpersonal behaviour (TIB) by Triandis in 1977 (Betts et al., 2014; Chun & Bock, 2006; Moody & Siponen, 2013). To date, TIB is the best theory in exploring cyberloafing issues in working situations. TIB was tested and extended by Triandis. As a result, the new theory expanded TPB and theory of reasoned action (TRA) by Fishbein and Ajzen in 1975. Added up to the model of TIB are affective variables or constructs (emotional response) and social factors which lead to behavioural intentions (Moody & Siponen, 2013). Besides that, habits and facilitating conditions function as a moderator between behavioural intention and actual behaviour. Askew et al. (2014) pointed out that ability to hide cyberloafing activities suggests a non-harmful way to reduce cyberloafing. When it is linked with lower intention, cyberloafing can be decreased. Similarly, there is a direct relationship between facilitating conditions and cyberloafing behaviour, instead of functioning as the moderator (Betts et al., 2014).

FUTURE RESEARCH DIRECTIONS

Among the constant dispute related to internet misusage at work, many organisations have practised some prevention measures to avoid cyberloafing activities from getting worse. Some business companies in Jordan have installed software tools to block certain websites (Alshuaibi et al., 2015). The Ministry of National Education has blocks the most popular social networking sites in Turkey so that neither students nor teachers can access it at schools (Baturay & Toker, 2015). In fact, most USA companies apply employee privacy and protection (EPP) solutions, employee Internet management (EIM) solutions, and secure web gateways (SWGs) as their monitoring systems (Melnick, 2014). Moreover, some organisations take extreme measures like banning the use of cell phones in the office during work hours due to its high potential effects on customer service (Kidwell, 2010).

For some organisations, monitoring systems might not the best way to prevent cyberloafing activities as these can indicate the improper operation of the organisation systems (Lee et al., 2007), give negative impact on the organisational climate (Bortolani & Favretto, 2009) besides create mistrust among the employees (Kidwell, 2010). Nonetheless, a study on monitoring issues was executed. It revealed that electronic monitoring is only effective for employees who have high level of job satisfaction (Wang et al., 2013). Furthermore, the policy of Internet uses at the workplace is only effective for employees who have high level of self-esteem. Interestingly, employees that belonged to organisations in which the working environment promotes restricted computer use policies are less occupied with cyberloafing activities (Garrett & Danziger, 2008). Consequently, monitoring issue needs further study especially in different countries be it in the government sector or the private sector.

Although, everyone thinks that they need a break from hardwork. Employees should manage their conditions wisely in terms of balance and flexibility, such as limiting their surfing for own stuff strictly during lunch hours so that working hours are not wasted with cyberloafing activities that can decrease productivity. Balancing between some personal web usage and work may be acceptable with company Internet use policy to motivate employees to become more productive during working hours. This is because loafing during allowable breaks will not affect productivity (Duhita & Daellenbach, 2015). Proper cyberloafing policies should be developed by organisations to cope with these issues (Blanchard & Henle, 2008). The policies should clearly explain the level of acceptance of Internet usage and how the Internet usage is monitored. Unresolved issues can be linked to CWB if the policies are not in place thus cannot change cyberloafing behaviour. Thus, cybeloafing should be further be studies to see its' terms usage, time spent, content, objectives and pattern to further understand its' impact while differentiate among differ organization culture and country (Jiang & Tsohou, 2014).

On the other hand, American Time Use Survey (ATUS) investigated thousands of Americans daily activities and found out that 82% of the workers worked at the office while 24% worked from home (Cooper, 2013). Among the employees who worked from home include varied professions such as the management, business, financial and others. This may suggest that the Internet may not be 100% linked to a negative work environment, but also positive in bringing some professions to continue working from home for better productivity due to accessibility. The Internet seems to widen the capabilities of world-wide electronic communication network and its flexibility (Garrett & Danziger, 2008). Further studies to seek whether individuals who work from home experience cyberloafing or whether they indulge more of it compared to those working in offices can be included in this field.

Looking back at the studies done by a different researcher in Table 1, little study has used moderator variable to further discuss cyberloafing issues. In some essential studies, supervisor cyber incivility is positively related to burnout and turnover intentions (Giumetti, McKibben, Hatfield, Schroeder, & Kowalski, 2012), burnout as moderator between high performance work system and CWB (Gulzar, Moon, Attiq, & Azam, 2014); and workload causing cyberloafing activity (Henle & Blanchard, 2008; Lee et al., 2007). Current working lifestyle are different than earlier decades, increasing peer pressure and high workloads may influence how organizational performance being achieved. Perhaps, the level of workload, stress, or burnout can be considered of use as moderators in future studies. In addition, ICT truly offers the opportunity for economic growth and receives attention from both private and government sectors. Consequently, general ICT usage as well as how ICT operates the business can be considered to be looked into in connection to cyberloafing issues.

CONCLUSION

Working individual spends most of their time in the office apart from communiting to work, sleep and spending time with their loved ones. Individual experiences, social factors, psychological factors and personal intention affect ones' activities and behaviour in daily life. Cyberloafing might be an unacceptable behaviour committed by employees who try to get some relief from boredom and work stress in this technological era of the information system. Thus, a good behaviour is important to enhance the quality of services that may lead to job efficiency and effectiveness. However, either cyberloafing is acceptable or unacceptable, employees can combine work and leisure in daily working activities or not, it is actually decided by employers of the organization. Organization with supervision or certain level restrictions via Internet usage policy in general usage of ICT, proper job characteristics and better environment of organizational culture is needed for efficiency in work life nowadays.

REFERENCES

Akbulut, Y., Dursun, Ö. Ö., Dönmez, O., & Şahin, Y. L. (2016). In search of a measure to investigate cyberloafing in educational settings. *Computers in Human Behavior*, *55*, 616–625. doi:10.1016/j.chb.2015.11.002

Al-shuaibi, A. S. I., Subramaniam, C., & Mohd Shamsudin, F. (2014). The Mediating Influence of Job Satisfaction on the Relationship between HR practices and Cyber deviance. *Journal of Marketing and Management*, 5(1), 105–119. doi:10.1017/jmo.2014.50

Alshuaibi, A. S. I., Mohd Shamsudin, F., & Alshuaibi, M. S. I. (2015). Internet misuse at work in Jordan: Challenges and implications. In *Proceedings of the 3rd convention of the world association of business schools (WAiBS) 2015: Enhancing Productivity and sustainability* (pp. 68–78). Universiti Utara Malaysia. Retrieved from http://3rd.waibs.org/images/Proceedingsof3rdWAiBS2015.pdf#page=68

Andreassen, C. S., Torsheim, T., & Pallesen, S. (2014). Predictors of use of social network sites at work - a specific type of cyberloafing. *Journal of Computer-Mediated Communication*, 19(4), 906–921. doi:10.1111/jcc4.12085

Askew, K., Buckner, J. E., Taing, M. U., Ilie, A., Bauer, J. A., & Coovert, M. D. (2014). Explaining cyberloafing: The role of the theory of planned behavior. *Computers in Human Behavior*, 36, 510–519. doi:10.1016/j.chb.2014.04.006

Baturay, M. H., & Toker, S. (2015). An investigation of the impact of demographics on cyberloafing from an educational setting angle. *Computers in Human Behavior*, 50, 358–366. doi:10.1016/j.chb.2015.03.081

BBC News. (2008a). *Social networking sites*. Retrieved from http://news.bbc.co.uk/2/hi/business/7410600.stm

BBC News. (2008b, October 29). *Bosses should embrace Facebook*. Retrieved from http://news.bbc.co.uk/2/hi/business/7695716.stm

Betts, T. K., Setterstrom, A. J., Pearson, J. M., & Totty, S. (2014). Explaining cyberloafing through a theoretical integration of Theory of Interpersonal Behavior and Theory of Organizational Justice. *Journal of Organizational and End User Computing*, 26(4), 23–42. doi:10.4018/joeuc.2014100102

Blanchard, A. L., & Henle, C. A. (2008). Correlates of different forms of cyberloafing: The role of norms and external locus of control. *Computers in Human Behavior*, 24(3), 1067–1084. doi:10.1016/j.chb.2007.03.008

Bortolani, E., & Favretto, G. (2009). Organizational aspects of cyberloafing. In *Human Aspects of Technology* (pp. 2923–2928). IGI Global.

Celik, N. (2014). Job satisfaction's impact on cyberloafing: An university example. *10th International Academic Conference*, 171–181.

Chun, Z. Y., & Bock, G.-W. (2006). Why employees do non-work-related computing: An investigation of factors affecting NWRC in a workplace. In Pacific Asia Conference on Information Systems (pp. 1259–1273). PACIS. Retrieved from http://aisel.aisnet.org/pacis2006/79

Çınar, O., & Karcıoğlu, F. (2015). The relationship between cyber loafing and organizational citizenship behavior: A survey study in Erzurum/Turkey. *Procedia: Social and Behavioral Sciences*, 207, 444–453. doi:10.1016/j.sbspro.2015.10.114

Cooper, B. B. (2013). *10 Surprising social media statistics that will make you rethink your social strategy*. Retrieved June 7, 2016, from http://www.fastcompany.com/3021749/worksmart/

Duhita, S., & Daellenbach, U. (2015). Is loafing at work necessarily detrimental? In Centre for Labour, Employment and Work. Victoria University of Wellington.

Garrett, R. K., & Danziger, J. N. (2008). Disaffection or expected outcomes: Understanding personal internet use during work. *Journal of Computer-Mediated Communication*, *13*(4), 937–958. doi:10.1111/j.1083-6101.2008.00425.x

Giumetti, G. W., McKibben, E. S., Hatfield, A. L., Schroeder, A. N., & Kowalski, R. M. (2012). Cyber incivility @ work: The new age of interpersonal deviance. *Cyberpsychology, Behavior, and Social Networking*, *15*(3), 148–154. doi:10.1089/cyber.2011.0336 PMID:22304404

Gulzar, S., Moon, M. A., Attiq, S., & Azam, R. I. (2014). The darker side of high performance work systems: Examining employee psychological outcomes and counterproductive work behavior. *Pakistan Journal of Commerce and Social Sciences*, *8*(3), 715–732.

Henle, C. A., & Blanchard, A. L. (2008). Cyberloafing as a coping method: Relationship between work stressors, sanctions, and cyberloafing.*Proceedings of the Annual Meeting of the Academy of Management*.

Jia, R., & Jia, H. H. (2015). An individual trait-based investigation of employee cyberloafing. *Journal of Information Technology Management*, *26*(1), 58–71.

Jiang, H., & Tsohou, A. (2014). The dual nature of personal web usage in workplace: Impacts, antecedents and regulating policies.*Twenty Second European Conference on Information Systems*, 1–16.

Kidwell, R. E. (2010). Loafing in the 21st century: Enhanced opportunities-and remedies-for withholding job effort in the new workplace. *Business Horizons*, *53*(6), 543–552. doi:10.1016/j.bushor.2010.06.001

Kim, S. J., & Byrne, S. (2011). Conceptualizing personal web usage in work contexts: A preliminary framework. *Computers in Human Behavior*, *27*(6), 2271–2283. doi:10.1016/j.chb.2011.07.006

Kim, Y., Sohn, D., & Choi, S. M. (2011). Cultural difference in motivations for using social network sites: A comparative study of American and Korean college students. *Computers in Human Behavior*, *27*(1), 365–372. doi:10.1016/j.chb.2010.08.015

Lee, Y., Lee, Z., & Kim, Y. (2007). Understanding personal web usage in organizations. *Journal of Organizational Computing and Electronic Commerce*, *17*(1), 75–99. doi:10.1080/10919390701291067

Liberman, B., Seidman, G., McKenna, K. Y. A., & Buffardi, L. E. (2011). Employee job attitudes and organizational characteristics as predictors of cyberloafing. *Computers in Human Behavior*, *27*(6), 2192–2199. doi:10.1016/j.chb.2011.06.015

Lim, V. K. G., & Chen, D. J. Q. (2012). Cyberloafing at the workplace: Gain or drain on work? *Behaviour & Information Technology*, *31*(4), 343–353. doi:10.1080/01449290903353054

Mahatanankoon, P., Anandarajan, M., & Igbaria, M. (2004). Development of a measure of personal web usage in the workplace. *Cyberpsychology & Behavior*, *7*(1), 93–104. doi:10.1089/109493104322820165 PMID:15006174

Melnick, D. (2014). Employee internet access in the workplace: Unleashing the power of the employee to protect the organization. In *Compliance & Ethics Professional* (pp. 33–38). The Society of Corporate Compliance and Ethics. Retrieved from www.corporatecompliance.org

Miniwatts Marketing Group. (2016). *Internet users in the world by regions June 2016*. Retrieved November 7, 2016, from http://www.internetworldstats.com/stats.htm

Mishra, M., & Pandey, S. (2014). A theoretical model on the determinants of workplace deviance among employees in the public service organizations of India. *International Journal of Business Behavior*, *2*(3), 1321–1337.

Moody, G. D., & Siponen, M. (2013). Using the theory of interpersonal behavior to explain non-work-related personal use of the Internet at work. *Information & Management*, *50*(6), 322–335. doi:10.1016/j.im.2013.04.005

Norsilan, I. N., Omar, Z., & Ahmad, A. (2014). Workplace deviantbehaviour: A review of typology of workplace deviantbehaviour. *Middle-East Journal of Scientific Research*, *19*, 34–38. doi:10.5829/idosi.mejsr.2014.19.icmrp.6

ONeill, T. A., Hambley, L., & Chatellier, G. S. (2014). Cyberslacking, engagement, and personality in distributed work environments. *Computers in Human Behavior*, *40*, 152–160. doi:10.1016/j.chb.2014.08.005

Paul Budde Communication Pty Ltd. (2016). *Global mobile devices market - smartphones, handsets, phablets and tablets*. Retrieved July 1, 2016, from http://www.budde.com.au/Research/Global-Mobile-Devices-Market-Smartphones-Handsets-Phablets-and-Tablets.html

Pecker, G., & Fine, S. (2015). Using exit surveys to assess counterproductive work behaviors: A case study. *Psychological Reports*, *116*(1), 89–96. doi:10.2466/01.PR0.116k16w4 PMID:25650640

Pew Research Center. (2016). *Social media usage: 2005-2015*. Retrieved July 1, 2016, from http://www.pewinternet.org/2015/10/08/social-networking-usage-2005-2015/

Ramayah, T. (2010). Personal web usage and work inefficiency. *Business Strategy Series*, *11*(5), 295–301. doi:10.1108/17515631011080704

Richards, J. (2010). The employee and the Internet age : A reflection, map and research agenda.*28th International Labour Process Conference*, 1–23.

Robinson, S. L., & Bennett, R. J. (1995). A typology of deviant workplace behaviors: A multidimensional scaling study. *Academy of Management Journal*, *38*(2), 555–572. doi:10.2307/256693

Samnani, A.-K., Salamon, S. D., & Singh, P. (2014). Negative affect and counterproductive workplace behavior: The moderating role of moral disengagement and gender. *Journal of Business Ethics*, *119*(2), 235–244. doi:10.1007/s10551-013-1635-0

Sharma, N., & Singh, V. K. (2015). Differential association and imitation as moderators of workplace deviance. In *Twelfth AIMS International Conference on Management* (pp. 2515–2520). Retrieved from http://papers.ssrn.com/sol3/papers.cfm?abstract_id=2548091

Smith, K. (2016). *Marketing: 96 amazing social media statistics and facts for 2016*. Retrieved July 19, 2016, from https://www.brandwatch.com/2016/03/96-amazing-social-media-statistics-and-facts-for-2016/

The Statistics Portal. (2016). *Leading social networks worldwide as of April 2016, ranked by number of active users (in millions)*. Retrieved July 19, 2016, from http://www.statista.com/statistics/272014/global-social-networks-ranked-by-number-of-users/

Vitak, J., Crouse, J., & LaRose, R. (2011). Personal Internet use at work: Understanding cyberslacking. *Computers in Human Behavior*, *27*(5), 1751–1759. doi:10.1016/j.chb.2011.03.002

Wang, J., Tian, J., & Shen, Z. (2013). The effects and moderators of cyber-loafing controls: An empirical study of Chinese public servants. *Information Technology Management*, *14*(4), 269–282. doi:10.1007/s10799-013-0164-y

Weatherbee, T. G. (2010). Counterproductive use of technology at work: Information & communications technologies and cyberdeviancy. *Human Resource Management Review*, *20*(1), 35–44. doi:10.1016/j.hrmr.2009.03.012

Yılmaz, F. G. K., Yilmaz, R., Öztürk, H. T., Sezer, B., & Karademir, T. (2015). Cyberloafing as a barrier to the successful integration of information and communication technologies into teaching and learning environments. *Computers in Human Behavior*, *45*, 290–298. doi:10.1016/j.chb.2014.12.023

Yogun, A. E. (2015). Cyberloafing and innovative work behavior among banking sector employees. *International Journal of Business and Management Review*, *3*(10), 61–71.

Yusof, A. A. (2014). *The human side of human resource management*. Kedah, Malaysia: UUM Press.

Zhang, H., Zhao, H., Liu, J., Xu, Y., & Hui, L. (2015). The dampening effect of employees' future orientation on cyberloafing behaviors: The mediating role of self-control. *Frontiers in Psychology*, 1–18. doi:10.3389/fp??g.2015.01482 PMID:26483735

KEY TERMS AND DEFINITIONS

Cyberloafing: The behaviour of misusing the Internet for personal use during working hours for non-work related purposes.

Counterproductive Work Behaviour (CWB): Behaviour that goes against the legal benefit of an organisation.

Email: Electronic message or mail sent via Internet networks.

Employee: An individual who is hired by the organisation to perform specific duties or services.

Facebook: One of the social media websites.

Internet: Communication network to connect and exchange information worldwide via servers.

Information and Communications Technology (ICT): Is an integration of information regarding technology and telecommunication device (telephones, computers and other devices that store, transmit, and manipulate information).

Job Satisfaction: A level of satisfaction in the job area and may differ according to individuals.

Personality: Individual differences in terms of attitudes, social relationships, and habits.

Smartphone: A portable phone which has features like personal computer operating system, pocket-sized, which can be used to make phone calls, make an appointment calendar, use a digital camera, access the Internet and run third-party software components ("apps").

Compilation of References

A Survey of China: A Tangled Web. (2000). Retrieved 4 December, 2016, from http://www.economist.com/node/299613

Acs, Z. J., & Audretsch, D. B. (2008). Innovation in large and small firms: An empirical analysis. *The American Economic Review, 78*(4), 678–690.

Adair, J. (2001). *Anatomia biznesu. Budowanie zespołu*. Warszawa: Studio Emka.

Adizes, I. (1999). *Managing Corporate Lifecycles. Adizes Institute*.

Adler, N. (1997). *International dimensions of organizational behavior*. Cincinnati, OH: South-Western College Publishing.

Adler, N. J. (1983). A typology of management studies involving culture. *Journal of International Business Studies, 14*(2), 29–47. doi:10.1057/palgrave.jibs.8490517

Adler, N. J. (2011). Leading beautifully: The creative economy and beyond. *Journal of Management Inquiry, 20*(3), 208–221. doi:10.1177/1056492611409292

Adler, P. S., & Kwon, S. W. (2002). Social capital: Prospects for a new concept. *Academy of Management Review, 27*(1), 17–40.

Aequus Partners. (2010). *Workplace flexibility: Advice, training, research*. Retrieved on October 6, from http://www.workplaceflexibility.com.au/index.htm

Afuah, A. (2003). *Innovation management: Strategies, implementation, and profits*. New York: Oxford University Press.

Agle, B. R., Mitchell, R. K., & Sonnenfeld, J. A. (1999). Who matters to ceos? An investigation of stakeholder attributes and salience, corporate performance, and ceo values. *Academy of Management Journal, 42*(5), 507–525. doi:10.2307/256973

Agle, B. R., Nagarajan, N. J., Sonnenfeld, J. A., & Srinivasan, D. (2006). Does ceo charisma matter? An empirical analysis of the relationships among organizational performance, environmental uncertainty, and top management team perceptions of ceo charisma. *Academy of Management Journal, 49*(1), 161–174. doi:10.5465/AMJ.2006.20785800

Aguinis, H., & Kraiger, K. (2009). Benefits of training and development for individuals and teams, organizations, and society. *Annual Review of Psychology, 60*(1), 451–474. doi:10.1146/annurev.psych.60.110707.163505 PMID:18976113

Ahmadi, S. A. A., Salamzadeh, Y., Daraei, M., & Akbari, J. (2012). Relationship between organizational culture and strategy implementation: Typologies and dimensions. *Global Business and Management Research: An International Journal, 4*(3/4), 286–299.

Ahmed, A., Kavis, B., & Amornsawadwatana, S. (2007). A review of techniques for risk management in projects, *Benchmarking. International Journal (Toronto, Ont.), 14*(1), 22–36.

Ahmed, P. (1998). Culture and climate for innovation. *European Journal of Innovation Management, 1*(1), 30–43. doi:10.1108/14601069810199131

Ahola, K., Kivimaki, M., Honkonen, T., Virtanen, M., Koskinen, S., Vahtera, J., & Lönnqvist, J. (2008). Occupational burnout and medically certified sickness absence: A population-based study of Finnish employees. *Journal of Psychosomatic Research, 64*(2), 185–193. doi:10.1016/j.jpsychores.2007.06.022 PMID:18222132

Aiken, L. H., Clarke, S. P., Sloane, D. M., Sochalski, J. A., Busse, R., Clarke, H., & Shamian, J. et al. (2001). Nurses reports on hospital care in five countries. *Health Affairs, 20*(3), 43–53. doi:10.1377/hlthaff.20.3.43 PMID:11585181

Aiken, L. H., Clarke, S. P., Sloane, D. M., Sochalski, J., & Silber, J. H. (2002). Hospital nurse staffing and patient mortality, nurse burnout, and job dissatisfaction. *Journal of the American Medical Association, 288*(16), 1987–1993. doi:10.1001/jama.288.16.1987 PMID:12387650

Ajmal, M. M., & Koskinen, K. U. (2008). Knowledge transfer in project-based organizations: An organizational culture perspective. *Project Management Journal, 39*(1), 7–15. doi:10.1002/pmj.20031

Ajzen, I., & Fishbein, M. (1980). *Understanding attitudes and predicting social behavior.* Englewood Cliffs, NJ: Prentice-Hall.

Akbulut, Y., Dursun, Ö. Ö., Dönmez, O., & Şahin, Y. L. (2016). In search of a measure to investigate cyberloafing in educational settings. *Computers in Human Behavior, 55,* 616–625. doi:10.1016/j.chb.2015.11.002

Alas, R., Ennulo, J., & Türnpuu, L. (2006). Managerial values in the institutional context. *Journal of Business Ethics, 5*(3), 269–278. doi:10.1007/s10551-005-5494-1

Alavinia, S. M., Van den Berg, T. I. J., Van Duivenbooden, C., Elders, L. A. M., & Burdorf, A. (2009). Impact of work-related factors, lifestyle, and work ability on sickness absence among Dutch construction workers. *Scandinavian Journal of Work, Environment & Health, 35*(5), 325–333. doi:10.5271/sjweh.1340 PMID:19554244

Alexander, D. A., & Klein, S. (2001). Impact of accident and emer-gency work on mental health and emotional well-being. *The British Journal of Psychiatry, 178,* 76–81. doi:10.1192/bjp.178.1.76 PMID:11136215

Al-Hussami, M. (2008). A study of nurses' job satisfaction: The relationship to organizational commitment, perceived organizational support, transactional leadership, transformational leadership, and level of education. *European Journal of Scientific Research, 22*(2), 286–295.

Ali, A. J., Azim, A., & Krishnan, K. D. (1995). Expatriates and host country nationals: Managerial values and decision styles. *Leadership and Organizational Development, 16*(6), 27–34. doi:10.1108/01437739510092252

Allen, P. M., Strathern, M., & Baldwin, J. S. (2010). The Evolutionary Complexity of Social Economic Systems: The Inevitability of Uncertainty and Surprise. In R. R. Mcdaniel & D. J. Driebe (Eds.), *Uncertainty and Surprise in Complex Systems: Questions on Working with the Unexpected* (pp. 31–50). New York, NY: Springer-Verlag. doi:10.1057/rm.2009.15

Allport, G. W. (1937). *Personality: A psychological interpretation.* New York: Holt, Rinehart, & Winston.

Alshuaibi, A. S. I., Mohd Shamsudin, F., & Alshuaibi, M. S. I. (2015). Internet misuse at work in Jordan: Challenges and implications. In *Proceedings of the 3rd convention of the world association of business schools (WAiBS) 2015: Enhancing Productivity and sustainability* (pp. 68–78). Universiti Utara Malaysia. Retrieved from http://3rd.waibs.org/images/Proceedingsof3rdWAiBS2015.pdf#page=68

Al-shuaibi, A. S. I., Subramaniam, C., & Mohd Shamsudin, F. (2014). The Mediating Influence of Job Satisfaction on the Relationship between HR practices and Cyber deviance. *Journal of Marketing and Management, 5*(1), 105–119. doi:10.1017/jmo.2014.50

al-Suwaidi, M. (2008). *When an Arab executive says "yes": Identifying different collectivistic values that influence the Arabian decision-making process. (MSc).* University of Pennsylvania.

Alt, R., & Lang, R. (1998). Wertorientierungen und Führungsverständnis von Managern in sächsischen Klein- und Mittelunternehmen. In R. Lang (Ed.), Management Executives in the East European Transformation Process (pp. 246-269). München: Hampp.

Álvarez, C., & Urbano, D. (2011). Environmental factors and entrepreneurial activity in Latin America. *Academia Revista Latinoamericana de Administración, 48,* 126–139.

Alvesson, M. (2012). Understanding organizational culture. *Safe Journal, 20*(4), 422–441.

Amabile, T. M. (1988). A model of creativity and innovation in organization. In B. M. Staw & L. L. Cummings (Eds.), *Research in organizational behavior* (Vol. 10, pp. 123–167). Greenwich, CT: JAI Press.

Amabile, T. M., Conti, R., Coon, H., Lazenby, J., & Herron, M. (1996). Assessing the work environment for creativity. *Academy of Management Journal, 39*(5), 1154–1184. doi:10.2307/256995

Amason, A. C. (1996). Distinguishing the effects of functional and dysfunctional conflict on strategic decision making: Resolving a paradox for top management teams. *Academy of Management Journal, 39*(1), 123–148. doi:10.2307/256633

Amit, K., Lisak, A., Popper, M., & Gal, R. (2007). Motivation To Lead (MTL) – Research on the Motives for Undertaking Leadership Roles. *Military Psychology, 19*(3), 137–160. doi:10.1080/08995600701386317

Amit, K., Popper, M., Gal, R., Mishkal Sinai, M., & Lisak, A. (2006). The Potential to Lead: The Difference between "Leaders" and "Non-leaders".[Hebrew]. *Megamot, 44*(2), 277–296.

Ancona, D. G. (1990). Outward bound: Strategic for team survival in an organization. *Academy of Management Journal, 33*(2), 334–365. doi:10.2307/256328

Andersen, E. S. (2008). *Rethinking Project Management: An Organizational Perspective.* Harlow: Prentice-Hall.

Anderson, J. C., & Narus, J. A. (1990). A model of distributor firm and manufacturer firm working partnerships. *Journal of Marketing, 54*(1), 42–58. doi:10.2307/1252172

Anderson, P. (2004). Does experience matter in lending? A process-tracing study on experienced loan officers and novices decision behavior. *Journal of Economic Psychology, 25*(4), 471–492. doi:10.1016/S0167-4870(03)00030-8

Andreassen, C. S., Torsheim, T., & Pallesen, S. (2014). Predictors of use of social network sites at work - a specific type of cyberloafing. *Journal of Computer-Mediated Communication, 19*(4), 906–921. doi:10.1111/jcc4.12085

Anokhin, S., & Schulze, W. S. (2009). Entrepreneurship, innovation, and corruption. *Journal of Business Venturing, 24*(5), 465–476. doi:10.1016/j.jbusvent.2008.06.001

Antonakis, J., Avolio, B. J., & Sivasubramaniam, N. (2003). Context and leadership: An examination of the nine-factor full-range leadership theory using the Multifactor Leadership Questionnaire. *The Leadership Quarterly, 14*(3), 261–295. doi:10.1016/S1048-9843(03)00030-4

Antoszkiewicz, J. D. (1997). *Firma wobec zagrożeń. Identyfikacja problemów.* Warszawa: Poltext.

Anxo, D., & O'Reilly, J. (2000). Working time regimes and transitions in comparative perspective. In J. O'Reilly, I. Cebrién, & M. Lallement (Eds.), *Working time changes: Social integration through transitional labour markets.* Cheltenham, UK: Edward Elgar Publishing. doi:10.4337/9781781952788.00013

Aon Hewitt. (2015). *Trends in Global Employee Engagement*. Retrieved from http://www.aon.com/attachments/human-capital-consulting/2015-Trends-in-Global-Employee-Engagement-Report.pdf

Aon Hewitt. (2016). *Trends in Global Employee Engagement*. Retrieved from http://www.aon.com/poland/attachments/hr/meh/2016-Trends-in-Global-Employee-Engagement.pdf

Ardichvili, A., & Kuchinke, K. P. (2002). Leadership styles and cultural values among managers and subordinates: A comparative study of four countries of the former Soviet Union, Germany, and the US. *Human Resource Development International*, 5(1), 99–117. doi:10.1080/13678860110046225

Argabright, K. J., King, J., Cochran, G. R., & Chen, C. Y. (2014). Evaluation of the Leadership Institute: A Program to Build Individual and Organizational Capacity through Emotional Intelligence. *Journal of Extension*, 52(1).

Argote, L., Gruenfeld, D., & Naquin, C. (1999). Group learning in organizations. In M. E. Turner (Ed.), *Groups at work: Advances in theory and research* (pp. 369–413). New York: Erlbaum.

Arieti, S. (1976). *Creativity: The magic synthesis*. Academic Press.

Arjo, K., & Colander, D. (1990). *The making of an economist*. Boulder, CO: Westview Press.

Arnold, K. A., Turner, N., Barling, J., Kelloway, E. K., & Mckee, M. C. (2007). Transformational leadership and psychological well-being: The mediating role of meaningful work. *Journal of Occupational Health Psychology*, 12(3), 193–203. doi:10.1037/1076-8998.12.3.193 PMID:17638487

Aron, S. (2015). *Relationship between nurses' job satisfaction and quality of healthcare they deliver*. Minnesota State University, Mankato. Retreived April 13, 2015 from cornerstone.lib.mnsu.edu/cgi/viewcontent.cgi?article

Aronson, E., & Wieczorkowska, G. (2001). *Kontrola naszych myśli i uczuć*. Warsaw: Wyd. Jacek Santorski & Co.

Arrow, H., McGrath, J. E., & Berdahl, J. L. (2000). *Small groups as complex systems: Formation, coordination, development, and adaptation*. Thousand Oaks, CA: Sage.

Ashby, F. G., & Maddox, W. T. (2005). Human category learning. *Annual Review of Psychology*, 56(1), 149–178. doi:10.1146/annurev.psych.56.091103.070217 PMID:15709932

Ashby, W. R. (1966). *An Introduction to Cybernetics*. New York: John Wiley and Sons, Inc.

Askew, K., Buckner, J. E., Taing, M. U., Ilie, A., Bauer, J. A., & Coovert, M. D. (2014). Explaining cyberloafing: The role of the theory of planned behavior. *Computers in Human Behavior*, 36, 510–519. doi:10.1016/j.chb.2014.04.006

Athanasopoulou, A., & Selsky, J. W. (2015). The social context of corporate social responsibility: Enriching research with multiple perspectives and multiple levels. *Business & Society*, 54(3), 322–364. doi:10.1177/0007650312449260

Avolio, B. J., Bass, B. M., & Jung, D. I. (1999). Re-examining the components of transformational and transactional leadership using the Multifactor Leadership. *Journal of Occupational and Organizational Psychology*, 72(4), 441–462. doi:10.1348/096317999166789

Axelrod, L. J., & Lehman, D. R. (1993). Responding to environmental concerns - what factors guide individual action. *Journal of Environmental Psychology*, 13(2), 149–159. doi:10.1016/S0272-4944(05)80147-1

Aycan, Z., Kanungo, R. N., Mendonca, M., Yu, K., Deller, J., Stahl, G., & Kurshid, A. (2000). Impact on culture on human resource management practices. A 10-country comparison. *Applied Psychology*, 49(1), 192–221. doi:10.1111/1464-0597.00010

Azar, G., & Drogendijk, R. (2016). Cultural distance, innovation and export performance. *European Business Review, 28*(2), 176–207. doi:10.1108/EBR-06-2015-0065

Babić, V. (1995). *Strategijsko odlučivanje*. Beograd: Institut za ekonomiku i finansije.

Baecker, D. (2003). *Organisation und Management*. Frankfurt am Main: Suhrkamp Verlag.

Bailyn, L., Drago, R., & Kochan, T. (2001). *Integrating Work and Family Life: A Holistic Approach*. Report for Alfread P. Sloan Foundation Work-Family Policy Network.

Bakacsi, G., Catana, A., & Catana, D. (2007). *GLOBE Romania: Final report of the results of the GLOBE-Romania project*. Unpublished report.

Bakacsi, G., Takacs, S., Karacsonyi, A., & Imrek, V. (2002). East European Cluster: Tradition and transition. *Journal of World Business, 37*(1), 69–80. doi:10.1016/S1090-9516(01)00075-X

Bakker, A. B., Demerouti, E., & Verbeke, W. (2004, Spring). Using the Job Demands-Resources Model to Predict Burnout and Performance. *Human Resource Management, 43*(1), 83–104. doi:10.1002/hrm.20004

Ball, J. (2013). Mental health. *The Guardian*. Retrieved 29, July 2016 from: https://www.theguardian.com/society/2013/may/22/women-men-mental-illness-study

Balser, D., & McClusky, J. (2005). Managing stakeholder relationships and nonprofit organization effectiveness. *Nonprofit Management & Leadership, 15*(3), 295–315. doi:10.1002/nml.70

Balz, U., & Arlinghaus, O. (Eds.). (2007). Praxisbuch Mergers & Akquisition. Von der strategischen Überlegung zur erfolgreichen Integration. Landsberg am Lech: mi-Fachverlag.

Bandura, A. (1977). *Social learning theory*. Englewood Cliffs, NJ: Prentice Hall.

Bandura, A. (1986). *Social foundations of thought and action: A social cognitive theory*. Englewood Cliffs, NJ: Prentice Hall.

Bandura, A. (1997). *Self-efficacy: The exercise of control*. New York: Freeman.

Bandura, A. (2001). Social cognitive theory: An agentic perspective. *Annual Review of Psychology, 52*(1), 1–26. doi:10.1146/annurev.psych.52.1.1 PMID:11148297

Barbian, J. (2002). Short Shelf Life. *Training (New York, N.Y.), 25*(6).

Barclays, D., Thompson, R., & Higgins, C. (1995). The partial least squares (PLS) approach to causal modeling: Personal computer adoption and use as an illustration. *Technology Studies, 2*(2), 285–309.

Barling, J., Kelloway, E. K., & Slater, F. (2000). TL and emotional intelligence: An exploratory study. *Leadership and Organization Development Journal, 21*(3), 157–161. doi:10.1108/01437730010325040

Barnard, C. I. (1938). *Functions of the executive*. Cambridge, MA: Harvard University Press.

Barnathan, J., Crock, S., Einhorn, B., Engardio, P., Roberts, D., & Borrus, A. (1996). Rethinking China. *Business Week, 4*, 13-20.

Barnes, J. V., Altimare, E. L., Farrell, P. A., Brown, R. E., Burnett, C. R. III, Gamble, L., & Davis, J. (2009). Creating and sustaining authentic partnerships with community in a systemic model. *Journal of Higher Education Outreach & Engagement, 15*.

Barr, A., & Serra, D. (2010). Corruption and culture: An experimental analysis. *Journal of Public Economics*, *94*(11-12), 862–869. doi:10.1016/j.jpubeco.2010.07.006

Barrick, M. R. (2005). Yes, personality matters: Moving on to more important matters. *Human Performance*, *18*(4), 359–372. doi:10.1207/s15327043hup1804_3

Barrick, M. R., Steward, G. L., & Piotrowski, M. (2002). Personality and job performance: Test of the mediating effects of mo-tivation among sales representatives. *The Journal of Applied Psychology*, *87*(1), 43–51. doi:10.1037/0021-9010.87.1.43 PMID:11916215

Barron, G., & Leider, S. (2010). The role of experience in the Gamblers Fallacy. *Journal of Behavioral Decision Making*, *23*(1), 117–129. doi:10.1002/bdm.676

Barsade, S. G. (2002). The ripple effect: Emotional contagion and its influence on group behavior. *Administrative Science Quarterly*, *47*(4), 644–675. doi:10.2307/3094912

Barsalou, L. W. (2005). Situated Conceptualization. In H. Cohen & C. Lefebvre (Eds.), *Handbook of categorization in cognitive science* (pp. 619–650). New York, NY: Elsevier. doi:10.1016/B978-008044612-7/50083-4

Baruch, Y. (2004). Transforming careers: from linear to multidirectional career paths: organizational and individual perspectives. *Career Development International*, *9*(1), 58–73. doi:10.1108/13620430410518147

Bass, B. M. (1997). Does the transactional–transformational leadership paradigm transcend organizational and national boundaries? *The American Psychologist*, *52*(2), 130–139. doi:10.1037/0003-066X.52.2.130

Bass, B. M., & Avolio, B. J. (1990). The implications of transactional and transformational leadership for individual, team, and organizational development. *Research in Organizational Change and Development*, *4*, 231–272.

Bass, B. M., & Avolio, B. J. (1994). *Improving Organizational Effectiveness through Transformational Leadership*. Thousand Oaks, CA: Sage Pub.

Bass, B., & Avolio, B. (1994). Developing transformational leadership: 1992 and beyond. *Journal of European Industrial Training*, *14*(5), 21–27.

Bates, K. A., Amundson, S. D., Schroeder, R. G., & Morris, W. T. (1995). The crucial interrelationship between manufacturing strategy and organizational culture. *Management Science*, *41*(10), 1565–1580. doi:10.1287/mnsc.41.10.1565

Batson, C. D. (1991). *The Altruism Question: Toward a Social-Psychological Answer*. Hillsdale, NJ: Lawrence Erlbaum Associates.

Baturay, M. H., & Toker, S. (2015). An investigation of the impact of demographics on cyberloafing from an educational setting angle. *Computers in Human Behavior*, *50*, 358–366. doi:10.1016/j.chb.2015.03.081

Bauer, J., Stamm, A., Virnich, K., Wissing, K., Müller, U., Wirsching, M., & Schaarschmidt, U. (2006). Correlation between burnout syndrome and psychological and psychosomatic symptoms among teachers. *International Archives of Occupational and Environmental Health*, *79*(3), 199–204. doi:10.1007/s00420-005-0050-y PMID:16258752

Baumgartner, R. J., & Ebner, D. (2010). Corporate sustainability strategies: Sustainability profiles and maturity levels. *Sustainable Development*, *18*(2), 76–89. doi:10.1002/sd.447

Baum, J. R., & Wally, S. (2003). Strategic decision speed and firm performance. *Strategic Management Journal*, *24*(11), 1107–1129. doi:10.1002/smj.343

Baxter, J. E., & Marshall, M. S. (2012). University students and local museums: Developing effective partnerships with oral history, partnerships. *A Journal of Service-Learning & Civic Engagement*, *3*(2), 59-77.

BBC News. (2008a). *Social networking sites*. Retrieved from http://news.bbc.co.uk/2/hi/business/7410600.stm

BBC News. (2008b, October 29). *Bosses should embrace Facebook*. Retrieved from http://news.bbc.co.uk/2/hi/business/7695716.stm

Beardwell, I., & Holden, L. (2001). *Human Resource Management*. Edinburgh, UK: Pearson Education.

Beauregard, T. A., & Henry, L. C. (2009). Making the link between work-life balance practices and organizational performance. *Human Resource Management Review*, *19*(1), 9–22. doi:10.1016/j.hrmr.2008.09.001

Beckerman, W. (1994). Sustainable development - is it a useful concept. *Environmental Values*, *3*(3), 191–209. doi:10.3197/096327194776679700

Bedford, O., & Hwang, S. L. (2013). Building relationships for business in Taiwanese hostess clubs: The psychological and social processes of guanxi development. *Gender, Work and Organization*, *20*(3), 297–310. doi:10.1111/j.1468-0432.2011.00576.x

Beer, S. (1994a). *Brain of the Firm*. Chichester, UK: John Wiley and Sons.

Beer, S. (1994b). *Diagnosing the System for Organization*. Chichester, UK: John Wiley and Sons.

Beer, S. (1994c). *The Heart of Enterprise*. Chichester, UK: John Wiley and Sons.

Beer, S. (1994d). *Beyond Dispute – The Invention of Team Syntegrity*. Chichester, UK: John Wiley and Sons.

Bell, B. S., & Kozlowski, S. W. (2008). Active learning: Effects of core training design elements on self-regulatory processes, learning, and adaptability. *The Journal of Applied Psychology*, *93*(2), 296–316. doi:10.1037/0021-9010.93.2.296 PMID:18361633

Benach, J., Muntaner, C., & Santana, V. (2007). *Employment conditions and health inequalities*. Employment Conditions Knowledge Network. Final Report of WHO Commission on Social Determinants of Health.

Bennett, S., Plint, A., & Clifford, T. J. (2005). Burnout, psychological morbidity, job satisfaction, and stress: A survey of Canadian hospital based child protection professionals. *Archives of Disease in Childhood*, *90*(11), 1112–1116. doi:10.1136/adc.2003.048462 PMID:16243862

Benton, T., & Craib, I. (2001). *Philosophy of social science: Philosophical issues in social thought (traditions in social theory)*. Academic Press.

Berger, R., Silbiger, A., Herstein, R., & Barnes, B. R. (2015). Analyzing business-to-business relationships in an Arab context. *Journal of World Business*, *50*(3), 454–464. doi:10.1016/j.jwb.2014.08.004

Betts, T. K., Setterstrom, A. J., Pearson, J. M., & Totty, S. (2014). Explaining cyberloafing through a theoretical integration of Theory of Interpersonal Behavior and Theory of Organizational Justice. *Journal of Organizational and End User Computing*, *26*(4), 23–42. doi:10.4018/joeuc.2014100102

Bidwell, M., & Mollick, E. (2015). Shifts and ladders: Comparing the role of internal and external mobility in managerial careers. *Organization Science*, *26*(6), 1629–1645. doi:10.1287/orsc.2015.1003

Bielski, M. (1992). *Organziacje. Istota, struktury, procesy*. Lodz: Wydawnictwo Uniwersytetu Lodzkiego.

Bierema, L. L. (2016). Womens Leadership Troubling Notions of the Ideal (Male) Leader. *Advances in Developing Human Resources*, *18*(2), 119–136. doi:10.1177/1523422316641398

Birdwell, J., Scott, R., & Horley, E. (2013). Active citizenship, education and service learning. *Education. Citizenship and Social Justice*, *8*(2), 185–199. doi:10.1177/1746197913483683

Blackburn, W. (2007). *The sustainability handbook: The complete management guide to achieving social, economic and environmental responsibility*. London: Earthscan Publications.

Blake, R. R., Mouton, J. S., & Bidwell, A. C. (1962). *Managerial grid*. Advanced Management-Office Executive.

Blake, R., & Mouton, J. (1964). *The managerial grid: The key to leadership excellence*. Houston, TX: Gulf Publishing Co.

Blanchard, A. L., & Henle, C. A. (2008). Correlates of different forms of cyberloafing: The role of norms and external locus of control. *Computers in Human Behavior*, *24*(3), 1067–1084. doi:10.1016/j.chb.2007.03.008

Blanchard, K. (2007). *Leading at Higher Level Blanchard on Leadership and Creating High Performing Organizations*. Prentice Hall.

Blanchard, K. (2010). *Leading at a Higher Level*. Pearson Education LTD.

Blanchard, K., & O'Connor, M. (1997). *Managing By Values*. San Francisco, CA: Berrett-Kochler Publishers, Inc.

Blizzard, A. (2012). *The Impact of Cultural Distances on the Country Selection Process*. University of Tennessee Honors Thesis Projects.

Block, L. (2003). The leadership-culture connection: An exploratory investigation. *Leadership and Organization Development Journal*, *24*(6), 318–334. doi:10.1108/01437730310494293

Bluhm, K. (2007). *Experimentierfeld Osteuropa? Deutsche Unternehmen in Polen und der Tschechischen Republik*. Wiesbaden: Gabler.

Blyton, P., & Jenkins, J. (2007). *Key Concepts in Work*. Los Angeles, CA: SAGE Publications Ltd. doi:10.4135/9781446215814

Bohanec, M. (2003). *What is Decision Support?* Research Paper. Jozef Stefan Institute.

Bok, D. C. (1982). *Beyond the ivory tower: Social responsibilities of the modern university*. Boston: Harvard University Press.

Bondía, J. L. (2002). Notas sobre a experiência e o saber de experiência. *Revista Brasileira de Educação*, *19*(19), 20–28. doi:10.1590/S1413-24782002000100003

Bond, M. H., & Hwang, S. (2008). *The psychology of the Chinese people*. New York: Oxford University Press.

Bonner, S. E., & Pennington, N. (1991). Cognitive processes and knowledge as determinants of auditor expertise. *Journal of Accounting Literature*, *10*, 1–50.

Borrelli, G., Cable, J., & Higgs, M. (1995). What makes teams work better? *Team Performance Management*, *1*(3), 23–34. doi:10.1108/13527599510084849

Borrero, N., Conner, J., & Mejia, A. (2012). Promoting social justice through service-learning in urban teacher education: The role of student voice, partnerships. *A Journal of Service Learning & Civic Engagement, 3*(1), 1-24.

Bortolani, E., & Favretto, G. (2009). Organizational aspects of cyberloafing. In *Human Aspects of Technology* (pp. 2923–2928). IGI Global.

Boschman, J. S., Van der Molen, H. F., Sluiter, J. K., & Frings-Dresen, M. H. W. (2013). Psychosocial work environment and mental health among construction workers. *Applied Ergonomics*, *44*(5), 748–755. doi:10.1016/j.apergo.2013.01.004 PMID:23380530

Boschma, R., & Martin, R. (2010). *The handbook of evolutionary economic geography*. Cheltenham, UK: Edward Elgar. doi:10.4337/9781849806497

Boss, F., & Mitterer, G. (2014). *Einführung in das systemische Management*. Heidelberg: Carl-Auer Verlag.

Bourantas, D., & Agapitou, V. (2016). *Leadership Meta-Competencies. Discovering Hidden Virtues*. London: Routledge.

Bourgeois, L. J. (1985). Strategic goals, perceived uncertainty, and economic performance in volatile environments. *Academy of Management Journal*, *28*(3), 548–573. doi:10.2307/256113

Bourgeois, L. J. III, & Eisenhardt, K. M. (1988). Strategic decision processes in high velocity environments: Four cases in the microcomputer industry. *Management Science*, *34*(7), 816–835. doi:10.1287/mnsc.34.7.816

Bowers, K. S. (1973). Situationism in psychology-- Analysis and a critique. *Psychological Review*, *80*, 307–336.

Bowman, J. S., & Knox, C. C. (2008). Ethics in government: No matter how long and dark the night. *Public Administration Review*, *68*(4), 627–639. doi:10.1111/j.1540-6210.2008.00903.x

Braendle, U. C., Gasser, T., & Noll, J. (2005). Corporate governance in China—is economic growth potential hindered by guanxi? *Business and Society Review*, *110*(4), 389–405. doi:10.1111/j.0045-3609.2005.00022.x

Bragg, T. (1999). *Turn Around an Ineffective Team*. IIE Solutions.

Branderburger, A. M., & Nalebuff, B. J. (1996). *Co-opetition*. New York: Currency Doubleday.

Bresfelean, V. P., Ghisoiu, N., Lacurezeanu, R., & Sitar-Taut, D. A. (2009). Towards the Development of Decision Support in Academic Environments.*Proceedings of ITI*.

Bresnick, A. T., & Parnell, S. G. (2013). Decision-making challenges. In S. G. Parnell, A. T. Bresnick, N. S. Tani, & E. R. Jonson (Eds.), *Handbook of Decision Analysis* (pp. 22–46). John Wiley & Sons. doi:10.1002/9781118515853.ch2

Brewster, C. (1995). Effective expatriate training. In J. Selmer (Ed.), *Expatriate management: New ideas for international business* (pp. 57–72). Westport, CT: Quorum.

Brilman, J. (2002). *Nowoczesne koncepcje i metody zarzadzania*. Warszawa: PWE.

Bringle, R. G., & Hatcher, J. A. (1996). Implementing service learning in higher education. *The Journal of Higher Education*, *67*(2), 221–239. doi:10.2307/2943981

Brocklesby, J., & Cummings, S. (1996). Designing a Viable Organization Structure. *Long Range Planning*, *29*(1), 49–57. doi:10.1016/0024-6301(95)00065-8

Brodbeck, F. C., Frese, M., Akerblom, S., Audia, G., Bakacsi, G., Bendova, H., & Wunderer, R. et al. (2000). Cultural variation of leadership prototypes across 22 european countries. *Journal of Occupational and Organizational Psychology*, *73*(1), 1–29. doi:10.1348/096317900166859

Brodbeck, F. C., & Greitemeyer, T. (2000). Effects of individual versus mixed individual and group experience in rule induction on group member learning and group performance. *Journal of Experimental Social Psychology*, *36*(6), 621–648. doi:10.1006/jesp.2000.1423

Brodbeck, F., & Frese, M. (2007). Societal Culture and Leadership in Germany. In J. S. Chokar, F. C. Brodbeck, & R. J. House (Eds.), *Culture and Leadership Across the World: The GLOBE Book of In-Depth Studies of 25 Societies* (pp. 147–214). Mahwah: Lawrence Erlbaum Associates Inc.

Brodbeck, F., Frese, M., & Javidan, M. (2002). Leadership made in Germany: Low on compassion, high on performance. *The Academy of Management Executive*, *16*(1), 16–29. doi:10.5465/AME.2002.6640111

Broder, A., & Gaissmaier, W. (2007). Sequential processing of cues in memory-based multiattribute decisions. *Psychonomic Bulletin & Review*, *4*(5), 895–900. doi:10.3758/BF03194118 PMID:18087956

Broodryk, J. (2006b). *Ubuntu: African Life Coping Skills: Theory and Practice.* Presented at the CCEAM, Lefkosia Nicosia, Cyprus.

Broodryk, J. (2006a). *Ubuntu: life coping skills from Africa.* Randburg: Knowledge Resources.

Brouthers, K. D., Gelderman, M., & Arens, P. (2007). The Influence of Ownership on Performance: Stakeholder and strategic contingency perspectives. *Schmalenbach Business Review, 59,* 225–242.

Brown, M., Wong, M., & McNamara, T. (2009). Flexible work options in state agencies. State Issue Brief No. 01. Chestnut Hill, MA: The Sloan Center on Aging and Work at Boston College. Retrieved from http://www.bc.edu/content/dam/files/research_sites/agingandwork/pdf/publications/SIB01_ Flex.pdf

Brown, F. W., & Reilly, M. D. (2009). The Myers-Briggs type indicator and transformational leadership. *Journal of Management Development, 28*(10), 916–932. doi:10.1108/02621710911000677

Bruner, C. H. (1993). *The Heinemann book of African women's writing.* London: Heinemann.

Brunero, S., Cowan, D., & Fairbrother, G. (2008). Reducing emotional distress in nurses using cognitive behavioural therapy: A preliminary program evaluation. *Japan Journal of Nursing Science, 5*(2), 109–115. doi:10.1111/j.1742-7924.2008.00102.x

Brunton, M. (2005). Emotion in health care: The cost of caring. *Journal of Health Organization and Management, 19*(4/5), 340–354. doi:10.1108/14777260510615387 PMID:16206918

Bryman, A. (2015). *Social research methods.* Oxford University Press.

Brzozowski, M. (2014). The boundaries of management thinking: Design thinking versus strategic thinking. In Within and beyond boundaries of management (pp. 109-120). Warsaw: Warsaw School of Economics Press.

Brzozowski, M. (2001). Developmental stages of polish companies in the period of transition. In A. Janc (Ed.), *Economy in transition. Problems, ideas, solutions* (pp. 249–257). Poznan: Poznan University of Economics Press.

Buchen, C. (2007). Estonia and Slovenia as Antipodes. In D. Lane, D., & M. Myant (Eds.), Varieties of capitalism in post-communist countries (pp. 65-89). Basingstoke, UK: Palgrave. doi:10.1057/9780230627574_4

Buchhorn, E., & Schmalholz, C. G. (2005). (in press). Ciezka dola nowicjusza. *Manager Magazin.*

Bullard, J. E. (1998). Raising awareness of local agenda 21: The use of internet resources. *Journal of Geography in Higher Education, 22*(2), 201–210. doi:10.1080/03098269885903

Bulmer-Smith, S. K., Profetto-McGrath, J., & Cummings, G. G. (2009). Emotional intelligence and nursing: An integrative literature review. *International Journal of Nursing Studies, 46*(2), 162–136. PMID:19596323

Bureš, V., & Stropková, A. (2014). Labour Productivity and Possibilities of its Extension by Knowledge Management Aspects. *Procedia: Social and Behavioral Sciences, 109,* 1088–1093.

Burke, R. J., Koyincu, M., & Fiksenbaum, L. (2010). Burnout, work satisfaction and psychological well-being among nurses in Turkish hospitals. *Europe's Journal of Psychology, 1,* 63–81.

Burns, J. M. (2010). *Leadership.* New York, NY: Harper Collins Publishers.

Burns, T., & Stalker, G. M. (1961). *The Management of Innovation.* London: Travistock Publications.

Burt, R. S. (1992). *Structural holes: the social structure of competition.* Cambridge, MA: Harvard University Press.

Bush, T. (2015). Understanding instructional leadership. *Educational Management Administration & Leadership*, *43*(4), 487–489. doi:10.1177/1741143215577035

Cable, D. M., & Edwards, J. R. (2004). Complementary and Supplementary Fit: A Theoretical and Empirical Integration. *The Journal of Applied Psychology*, *10*, 822–834.

Cadwallader, S., Atwong, C., & Lebard, A. (2013). Proposing community-based learning in the marketing curriculum. *Marketing Education Review*, *23*(2), 137–150. doi:10.2753/MER1052-8008230203

Callahan, J. L. (2010). Constructing a manuscript: Distinguishing integrative literature reviews and conceptual and theory articles. *Human Resource Development Review*, *9*(3), 300–304. doi:10.1177/1534484310371492

Calnan, M., Wainwright, D., Forsythe, M., Wall, B., & Almond, S. (2001). Mental health and stress in the workplace: The case of general practice in the UK. *Social Science & Medicine*, *52*(4), 499–507. doi:10.1016/S0277-9536(00)00155-6 PMID:11206648

Cameron, K., & Quinn, R. E. (1999). *Diagnosis and changing organizational culture: Based on the competing values framework*. New York: Addison Wesley.

Campbell, D., Stonehouse, G., & Houston, B. (1999). *Business Strategy an Introduction*. Oxford, UK: Butterworth-Heinemann.

Campbell, R. G., & Babrow, A. S. (2004). The Role of Empathy in Responses to Persuasive Risk Communication: Overcoming Resistance to HIV Prevention Messages. *Health Communication*, *16*(2), 159–182. doi:10.1207/S15327027HC1602_2 PMID:15090283

Campitelli, G., & Gobet, F. (2010). Herbert Simons decision-making approach: Investigation of cognitive processes in experts. *Review of General Psychology*, *14*(4), 454–464. doi:10.1037/a0021256

Cancer, V., & Mulej, M. (2009). The multi-criteria assessment of (corporate) social responsibility. In P. Doucek, G. Chroust, & V. Oskrdal (Eds.), *Idimt-2009: System and humans, a complex relationship* (Vol. 29, pp. 207–214). Linz, Austria: Universitatsverlag Rudolf Trauner.

Cannon, J. P., & Perreault, W. D. (1999). Buyer-seller relationships in business markets. *JMR, Journal of Marketing Research*, *36*(4), 439–460. doi:10.2307/3151999

Carley, K. M., & Lin, Z. (2007). Organizational decision making and error in a dynamic task environment. *The Journal of Mathematical Sociology*, *100*(1), 720–749.

Carmon, Z., & Ariely, D. (2000). Focusing on the forgone: How value can appear so different to buyers and Sellers. *The Journal of Consumer Research*, *27*(3), 360–370. doi:10.1086/317590

Carnegie, D. (2004). *How to stop worrying and start living*. New York: Pocket Books.

Carney, M. (2006). *Health service management: Consensus, culture and the middle manager*. Cork, Ireland: Oak Tree Press.

Carrizo-Moreira, A., & Leonidivna-Karachun, H. (2014). Uma revisão interpretativa sobre o desenvolvimento de novos produtos. *Cuadernos de Administración*, *27*(49), 155–182. doi:10.11144/Javeriana.cao27-49.ridn

Catana, A., & Catana, D. (1999). Romanian cultural background and its relevance for Cross-Cultural Management. *Journal for East-European Management Studies*, *4*(3), 252–258.

Catana, D., Catana, A., & Finlay, J. L. (1999). Managerial resistance to change: Romania's quest for a market economy. *Journal for East European Management Studies*, *4*(2), 149–164.

Cater, T., Lang, R., & Szabo, E. (2013). Values and leadership expectations of future managers: Theoretical basis and methodological approach of the globe student project. *Journal for East European Management Studies, 18*(4), 442–462.

Cebrián, G. (2016). The i3e model for embedding education for sustainability within higher education institutions. *Environmental Education Research*, 1–19. doi:10.1080/13504622.2016.1217395

Celik, N. (2014). Job satisfaction's impact on cyberloafing: An university example. *10th International Academic Conference*, 171–181.

Certo, S., & Certo, T. (2011). *Modern management concepts and skills*. New York: Prentice Hall.

Ceulemans, K., Molderez, I., & Van Liedekerke, L. (2015). Sustainability reporting in higher education: A comprehensive review of the recent literature and paths for further research. *Journal of Cleaner Production, 106*, 127–143. doi:10.1016/j.jclepro.2014.09.052

Chambers, T., & Gopaul, B. (2008). Decoding the public good of higher education. *Journal of Higher Education Outreach & Engagement*, 34.

Chang, E. M., Bidewell, J. W., Huntington, A. D., Daly, J., Johnson, A., Wilson, H., & Lambert, C. E. et al. (2007). A survey of role stress, coping and health in Australian and New Zealand hospital nurses. *International Journal of Nursing Studies, 44*(8), 1354–1362. doi:10.1016/j.ijnurstu.2006.06.003 PMID:16901488

Chang, E. M., Daly, J., Hancock, K., Bidewell, J. W., Johnson, A., Lambert, V. A., & Lambert, C. E. (2006). The relationships among workplace stressors, coping methods, demographic characteristics, and health in Australian nurses. *Journal of Professional Nursing, 22*(1), 30–38. doi:10.1016/j.profnurs.2005.12.002 PMID:16459287

Changingminds.org. (2017). *Hall's cultural factors*. Retrieved from http://changingminds.org/explanations/ culture/ hall_culture.htm

Chang, M., & Harrington, J. E. Jr. (2005). Discovery and diffusion of knowledge in an endogenous social network. *American Journal of Sociology, 110*(1), 937–976. doi:10.1086/426555

Chan, K. B., Lai, G., Ko, Y. C., & Boey, K. W. (2000). Work stress among six professional groups: The Singapore experience. *Social Science & Medicine, 50*(10), 1415–1432. doi:10.1016/S0277-9536(99)00397-4 PMID:10741577

Chao, G. T., & Moon, H. (2005). The cultural mosaic: A metatheory for understanding the complexity of culture. *The Journal of Applied Psychology, 90*(6), 1128–1140. doi:10.1037/0021-9010.90.6.1128 PMID:16316269

Chater, N., Oaksford, M., Nakisa, R., & Redington, M. (2003). Fast, frugal, and rational: How rational norms explain behavior. *Organizational Behavior and Human Decision Processes, 90*(1), 63–86. doi:10.1016/S0749-5978(02)00508-3

Checkland, P. (1996). *Systems Thinking, Systems Practice*. Chichester, UK: John Wiley and Sons.

Checkland, P., & Poulter, J. (2010). Soft Systems Methodology. In M. Reynolds & S. Holwell (Eds.), *Systems Approaches to Managing Change: A Practical Guide* (pp. 191–242). London: Springer. doi:10.1007/978-1-84882-809-4_5

Checkland, P., & Tsouvalis, C. (1997). Reflecting on SSM: The Link Between Root Definitions and Conceptual Models. *Systems Research and Behavioral Science, 14*(3), 153–168. doi:10.1002/(SICI)1099-1743(199705/06)14:3<153::AID-SRES134>3.0.CO;2-H

Chen, C., Chen, X., & Huang, S. (2013). Chinese Guanxi: An integrative review and new directions for future research. *Management and Organization Review, 9*(1), 167–207. doi:10.1111/more.12010

Cheng, B. S., Chou, L. F., Wu, T. Y., Huang, M. P., & Farh, J. L. (2004). Paternalistic leadership and subordinate responses: Establishing a leadership model in Chinese organizations. *Asian Journal of Social Psychology*, *7*(1), 89–117. doi:10.1111/j.1467-839X.2004.00137.x

Cheng, T., Teizer, J., Migliaccio, G. C., & Gatti, U. C. (2013). Automated task-level productivity analysis through fusion of real time location sensors and workers thoracic posture data. *Automation in Construction*, *29*, 24–39. doi:10.1016/j. autcon.2012.08.003

Cheng, T., Venugopal, M., Teizer, J., & Vela, P. A. (2011). Performance evaluation of ultra wideband technology for construction resource location tracking in harsh environments. *Automation in Construction*, *20*(8), 1173–1184. doi:10.1016/j.autcon.2011.05.001

Chen, X.-P., & Chen, C. C. (2004). On the intricacies of the Chinese guanxi: A process model of guanxi development. *Asia Pacific Journal of Management*, *21*(3), 305–324. doi:10.1023/B:APJM.0000036465.19102.d5

Chen, Y. F., & Tjosvold, D. (2006). Participative leadership by American and Chinese managers in China: The role of relationships. *Journal of Management Studies*, *43*(8), 1727–1752. doi:10.1111/j.1467-6486.2006.00657.x

Chesbrough, H. (2009). *Open innovation*. Boston: Harvard Business School Press.

Cheung, M. F., Wu, W.-P., Chan, A. K., & Wong, M. M. (2009). Supervisor–subordinate guanxi and employee work outcomes: The mediating role of job satisfaction. *Journal of Business Ethics*, *88*(1), 77–89. doi:10.1007/s10551-008-9830-0

Cheung, S. O., Wong, P. S. P., & Wu, A. W. Y. (2011). Towards an organizational culture framework in construction. *International Journal of Project Management*, *29*(1), 33–44. doi:10.1016/j.ijproman.2010.01.014

Chhokar, J. S., Brodbeck, F. C., & House, R. J. (2007). *Culture and Leadership Across the World: The GLOBE Book of In-Depth Studies of 25 Societies*. Mahwah, NJ: Lawrence Erlbaum Associates.

Chhokar, J. S., Brodbeck, F. C., & House, R. J. (Eds.). (2007). *Culture and leadership across the world: The GLOBE book of in-depth studies of 25 societies*. Mahwah, NJ: Sage.

Chib, V. S., Rangel, A., Shimojo, S., & ODoherty, J. P. (2009). Evidence for a common representation of decision values for dissimilar goods in human ventromedial prefrontal cortex. *The Journal of Neuroscience*, *29*(39), 12315–12320. doi:10.1523/JNEUROSCI.2575-09.2009 PMID:19793990

Child, J., & Tsai, T. (2005). The dynamic between firms environmental strategies and institutional constraints in emerging economies: Evidence from China and Taiwan. *Journal of Management Studies*, *42*(1), 95–125. doi:10.1111/j.1467-6486.2005.00490.x

Chin, W., & Newsted, P. R. (1999), Structural equation modeling analysis with small samples using partial least squares. In R. Hoyle (Eds.), Statistical strategies for small sample research (pp. 307-341). Thousand Oaks, CA: Sage.

Chin, M. K., Hambrick, D. C., & Treviño, L. K. (2013). Political ideologies of CEOs: The influence of executives values on Corporate Social Responsibilty. *Administrative Science Quarterly*, *58*(2), 197–232. doi:10.1177/0001839213486984

Chin, W. W. (1998). The partial least squares approach to structural equation modeling. In G. A. Marcoulides (Ed.), *Modern methods for business research* (pp. 295–336). Lawrence Erlbaum.

Chin, W. W. (2010). How to write up and report PLS analyses. In V. Esposito Vinzi, W. Chin, J. Henseler, & H. Wang (Eds.), *Handbook of partial least squares* (pp. 655–688). New York: Springer-Verlag. doi:10.1007/978-3-540-32827-8_29

Chin, W., Marcolin, B. L., & Newsted, P. R. (2003). A Partial Least Squares Latent Variable Modeling Approach for Measuring Interaction Effects: Results from a Monte Carlo Simulation Study and an Electronic-Mail Emotion/Adoption Study. *Information Systems Research*, *14*(2), 189–217. doi:10.1287/isre.14.2.189.16018

Chiva, R., & Alegre, J. (2008). Emotional intelligence and job satisfaction: The role of organizational learning capability. *Personnel Review*, *37*(6), 680–701. doi:10.1108/00483480810906900

Cho, K. R., & Padmanabhan, P. (2001). The relative importance of old and new decision specific experience in foreign ownership strategies: An exploratory study. *International Business Review*, *10*(6), 645–659. doi:10.1016/S0969-5931(01)00036-1

Chompookum, D., & Brooklyn Derr, C. (2004). The effects of internal career orientations on organizational citizenship behavior in Thailand. *Career Development International*, *9*(4), 406–423. doi:10.1108/13620430410544355

Christiansen, J. A. (2000). *Building the innovative organization: Management systems that encourage innovation*. New York: Palgrave Macmillan. doi:10.1057/9780333977446

Chun, Z. Y., & Bock, G.-W. (2006). Why employees do non-work-related computing: An investigation of factors affecting NWRC in a workplace. In Pacific Asia Conference on Information Systems (pp. 1259–1273). PACIS. Retrieved from http://aisel.aisnet.org/pacis2006/79

Chung, Y., & Jackson, S. E. (2013). The Internal and External Networks of Knowledge-Intensive Teams The Role of Task Routineness. *Journal of Management*, *39*(2), 442–468. doi:10.1177/0149206310394186

Ciegis, R., Ramanauskiene, J., & Martinkus, B. (2009). The concept of sustainable development and its use for sustainability scenarios. *Inzinerine Ekonomika-Engineering Economics*, (2), 28-37.

Çınar, O., & Karcıoğlu, F. (2015). The relationship between cyber loafing and organizational citizenship behavior: A survey study in Erzurum/Turkey. *Procedia: Social and Behavioral Sciences*, *207*, 444–453. doi:10.1016/j.sbspro.2015.10.114

Cirnu, C. E., & Kuralt, B. (2013). The impact of employees' personal values on their attitudes toward sustainable development: Cases of slovenia and romania. *Management (Croatia)*, *18*(2), 1–20.

Civelek, M. E., Cemberci, M., & Asci, M. S. (2015). Conceptual Approach to the Organizational Trust Building in Commitment Perspective. *Doğuş Üniversitesi Dergisi*, *16*(2), 217–226.

Clark, D. M., & Wells, A. (1995). A Cognitive Model of Social Phobia. In R. G. Heimberg, M. R. Liebowitz, D. A. Hope, & F. R. Schneier (Eds.), Social phobia, diagnosis, assessment and treatment. The Guilford Press.

Clarke, N. (2010). Emotional intelligence and its relationship to transformational leadership and key project manager competences. *Project Management Journal*, *41*(2), 5–20. doi:10.1002/pmj.20162

Clayton, T., & Radcliffe, N. (1996). *Sustainability: A systems approach*. London: Routledge.

Cleland, D. (1999). *Project Management: Strategic Design and Implementation*. New York: McGraw-Hill.

Coelho, P. S., & Henseler, J. (2012). Creating customer loyalty through service customization. *European Journal of Marketing*, *46*(3/4), 331–356. doi:10.1108/03090561211202503

Coetzee & Schreuder. (2008). *A multi-cultural investigation of students' career anchors at a South African higher education institution*. Academic Press.

Cohen, H., & Lefebvre, C. (2005). *Handbook of categorization in cognitive science*. New York, NY: Elsevier.

Cohen, J., Pant, L., & Sharp, D. (1996). A methodological note on cross-cultural accounting ethics research. *The International Journal of Accounting, 31*(1), 55–66. doi:10.1016/S0020-7063(96)90013-8

Cohen, M., Etner, J., & Jeleva, M. (2010). Dynamic Decision Making When Risk Perception Depends on Past Experience. In M. Abdellaoui & J. D. Hey (Eds.), *Advances in Decision Making Under Risk and Uncertaint* (pp. 19–32). New York, NY: Springer-Verlag.

Cohen, S. G., & Bailey, D. E. (1997). What makes teams work: Group effectiveness research from the shop floor to the executive suite. *Journal of Management, 23*(3), 239–290. doi:10.1177/014920639702300303

Cohen, W. M., & Klepper, S. (2006). A reprise of size and R & D. *The Economic Journal, 106*(1), 925–951.

Colby, A., & Sullivan, W. M. (2009). *Strenghtening of foundations of students´ excellence, integrity, and social contribution.* Retrieved from http://www.aacu.org/liberaleducation/le-wi09/documents/LE-WI09_Strengthening.pdf

Coleman, J. S. (1988). Social capital in the creation of human capital. *American Journal of Sociology, 94*, S95-S120.

Collins, J. (2005). Level 5 leadership: The triumph of humility and fierce resolve. *Harvard Business Review*. PMID:11189464

Collins, J. C., & Porras, J. I. (2002). *Built to last. Successful Habits of Visionary Companies.* New York: HarperCollins Publishers Inc.

Collins, J., & Porras, J. I. (2002). *Built to last: Successful habits of visionary companies.* New York: Harper Collins Publishers.

Collins, K. M. (1993). Stress and departures from the public accounting profession: A study of gender differences. *Accounting Horizons*, (March), 29–38.

Colquitt, J. A., LePine, J. A., & Noe, R. A. (2000). Toward an integrative theory of training motivation: A meta-analytic path analysis of 20 years of research. *The Journal of Applied Psychology, 85*(5), 678–707. doi:10.1037/0021-9010.85.5.678 PMID:11055143

Conner, D. R. (1993). *Managing at the Speed of Change.* New York: Villards Books.

Connolly, T., & Zeelenberg, M. (2002). Regret in decision making. *Current Directions in Psychological Science, 11*(6), 212–216. doi:10.1111/1467-8721.00203

Conway, S., & Steward, F. (2009). *Managing and shaping innovation.* Oxford, UK: Oxford University Press.

Cooke-Davis, T., Cicmil, S. J. K., Crawford, L. H., & Richardson, K. (2007). We're not in Kansas anymore, Toto: Mapping the strange landscape of complexity theory. *Project Management Journal, 38*(2), 50–61.

Cook, K. S., Hardin, R., & Levi, M. (2005). *Cooperation without trust?* Russell Sage Foundation.

Coomber, B., & Barriball, L. K. (2007). Impact of job satisfaction components on intent to leave and turnover for hospital-based nurses: A review of the research literature. *International Journal of Nursing Studies, 44*(2), 297–314. doi:10.1016/j.ijnurstu.2006.02.004 PMID:16631760

Coon, D., & Mitterer, J. O. (2008, December 29). Introduction to Psychology: Gateways to Mind and Behavior. *Cengage Learning*, 171–172.

Cooper, B. B. (2013). *10 Surprising social media statistics that will make you rethink your social strategy.* Retrieved June 7, 2016, from http://www.fastcompany.com/3021749/worksmart/

Cordano, M., Welcomer, S., Scherer, R. F., Pradenas, L., & Parada, V. (2011). A cross-cultural assessment of three theories of pro-environmental behavior: A comparison between business students of chile and the united states. *Environment and Behavior*, *43*(5), 634–657. doi:10.1177/0013916510378528

Cordano, M., Welcomer, S., Scherer, R., Pradenas, L., & Parada, V. (2010). Understanding cultural differences in the antecedents of pro-environmental behavior: A comparative analysis of business students in the united states and chile. *The Journal of Environmental Education*, *41*(4), 224–238. doi:10.1080/00958960903439997

Cornell University, INSEAD, & WIPO. (2013). The Global innovation index 2013: The local dynamics of innovation. Authors.

Costermans, J. (2001). *As actividades cognitivas. Raciocínio, decisão e resolução de problemas*. Coimbra, Portugal: Quarteto.

Costigan, R. D., Insinga, R. C., Berman, J. J., Ilter, S. S., Kranas, G., & Kureshov, V. (2005). An Examination of the Relationship of a Western Performance-Management Process to Key Workplace Behaviours in Transition Economies. *Canadian Journal of Administrative Sciences*, *22*(3), 255–267. doi:10.1111/j.1936-4490.2005.tb00370.x

Covey, S. M. R. (2006). *The speed of trust: The one thing that changes everything*. Simon and Schuster.

Crimmins, J. C., & Keil, M. (1983). *Enterprise in the nonprofit sector*. Americans for the Arts.

Cross, D. (2016). Globalization and Media's Impact on Cross Cultural Communication: Managing Organizational Change. In Handbook of Research on Effective Communication, Leadership, and Conflict Resolution (pp. 21-41). IGI Global.

Cummings, G. G., Olson, K., Hayduk, L., Bakker, D., Fitch, M., Green, E., & Conlon, M. et al. (2008). The relationship between nursing leadership and nurses job satisfaction in Canadian oncology work environments. *Journal of Nursing Management*, *15*(6), 508–518. doi:10.1111/j.1365-2834.2008.00897.x PMID:18558921

Cummings, G., Hayduk, L., & Estabrooks, C. (2005). Mitigating the impact of hospital restructuring on nurses: The responsibility of emotionally intelligent leadership. *Nursing Research*, *54*(1), 2–12. doi:10.1097/00006199-200501000-00002 PMID:15695934

Cunningham, R., & Sarayrah, Y. K. (1993). *Wasta: The hidden force in Middle Eastern society*. Westport, CT: Praeger.

Cyhlarova, E., McCulloch, A., McGuffin, P., & Wykes, T. (2010). *Economic Burden of Mental Illness Cannot be Tackled Without Research Investment*. London, UK: Mental Health Foundation.

Czarnecki, J. (2011). *Architektura korporacji. Analiza teoretyczna i metodologiczna*. Lodz: Wydawnictwo Uniwersytetu Lodzkiego.

Czerska, M. (2004). Kadrowe czynniki sukcesu firmy – wyniki badań. In A. Stabryla (Ed.), *Strategie wzrostu produktywności firmy* (p. 124). Krakow: Wydawnictwo Akademii Ekonomicznej w Krakowie.

Dabic, M., Potocan, V., Nedelko, Z., & Morgan, T. R. (2013). Exploring the use of 25 leading business practices in transitioning market supply chains. *International Journal of Physical Distribution & Logistics Management*, *43*(10), 833–851. doi:10.1108/IJPDLM-10-2012-0325

Daft, R. L. (2005). *The Leadership Experience* (3rd ed.). Vancouver, Canada: Thomson-Southwestern.

Damasio, A. (2005). *O erro de Descartes*. São Paulo, Brazil: Companhia das Letras.

Dantas, J. G., & Moreira, A. C. (2011). *O Processo de inovação*. Lisbon: LIDEL.

Dantas, J. G., Moreira, A. C., & Valente, F. M. (2015). Entrepreneurship and national culture: How cultural differences among countries explain entrepreneurial activity. In L. C. Carvalho (Ed.), *Handbook of research on internationalization of entrepreneurial innovation in the global economy* (pp. 1–28). Hershey, PA: IGI Global. doi:10.4018/978-1-4666-8216-0.ch001

Dart, R. (2004). The legitimacy of social enterprise. *Nonprofit Management & Leadership*, *14*(4), 411–424. doi:10.1002/nml.43

Davis, J. H., & Ruhe, J. A. (2003). Perceptions of country corruption: Antecedents and outcomes. *Journal of Business Ethics*, *43*(4), 275–288. doi:10.1023/A:1023038901080

Davis, M. H. (1983). Measuring Individual Differences in Empathy: Evidence for a Multidimensional Approach. *Journal of Personality and Social Psychology*, *44*(1), 113–136. doi:10.1037/0022-3514.44.1.113

Davis, M. H. (2007). Empathy. In *Handbook of the Sociology of Emotions* (pp. 443–466). New York: Springer.

De Clercq, S., Fontaine, J. R. J., & Anseel, F. (2008). In search of a comprehensive value model for assessing supplementary person-organization fit. *The Journal of Psychology*, *142*(3), 277–302. doi:10.3200/JRLP.142.3.277-302 PMID:18589938

De Vignemont, F., & Singer, T. (2006). The Empathic Brain: How, When, and Why? *Trends in Cognitive Sciences*, *10*(10), 435–441. doi:10.1016/j.tics.2006.08.008 PMID:16949331

Deal, T. E., & Kennedy, A. A. (1982). *Corporate cultures reading*. Addison-Wesley.

Deal, T. E., & Kennedy, A. A. (2000). *Corporate cultures: The rites and rituals of corporate life*. Da Capo Press.

Deal, T. E., Kennedy, A. A., & Peregrina, R. L. (1985). *Culturas corporativas: ritos y rituales de la vida organizacinal*. Fondo Educativo Interamericano.

Deal, T., & Kennedy, A. (1982). *Corporate Culture: The Rites and Rituals of Corporate Life*. London: Penguin Business.

Deal, T., & Kennedy, A. (1988). *Corporate Cultures. The Rites and Rituals of Corporate life*. London: Penguin Books.

Dean, J. W., & Sharfman, M. P. (1993). Procedural rationality in the strategic decision-making process. *Journal of Management Studies*, *30*(4), 87–610. doi:10.1111/j.1467-6486.1993.tb00317.x

DeBono, E. (1992). *Serious creativity*. Toronto: HarperCollins.

Decety, J., & Jackson, P. L. (2006). The Functional Architecture of Human Empathy. *Behavioral and Cognitive Neuroscience Reviews*, *3*(2), 71–100. doi:10.1177/1534582304267187 PMID:15537986

Decety, J., & Meyer, M. (2008). From Emotion Resonance to Empathic Understanding: A Social Developmental Neuroscience Account. *Development and Psychopathology*, *20*(04), 1053–1080. doi:10.1017/S0954579408000503 PMID:18838031

DeGroote, S. E., & Marx, T. G. (2013). The impact of IT on supply chain agility and firm performance: An empirical investigation. *International Journal of Information Management*, *33*(6), 909–916. doi:10.1016/j.ijinfomgt.2013.09.001

DeMarco, T., & Lister, T. (2002). *Czynnik ludzki. Skuteczne przedsiewziecia i wydajne zespoly*. Warszawa: Wydawnictwo Naukowo – Techniczne.

DeNeve, K. M., & Cooper, H. (1998). The Happy Personality: A Meta-Analysis of 137 Personality Traits and Subjective Well-Being. *Psychological Bulletin*, *124*(2), 197–229. doi:10.1037/0033-2909.124.2.197 PMID:9747186

Denison, D. R., & Mishra, A. K. (2015). Toward a theory of organizational culture and effectiveness. *Organization Science*, *6*(2), 204–223. doi:10.1287/orsc.6.2.204

DEste, P., & Patel, P. (2007). University–industry linkages in the uk: What are the factors underlying the variety of interactions with industry? *Research Policy*, *36*(9), 1295–1313. doi:10.1016/j.respol.2007.05.002

DH (Department of Health). (1998). *Modernising Social Services - Promoting Independence, Improving Protection, Raising Standards*. London: The Stationary Office.

DH. (2005). *Health reform in England: Update and next steps*. London: DH.

DH. (2007). *Third sector mapping*. London: DH.

DH. (2008). *World class commissioning: Vision*. London: DH.

Dierdorff, E. C., & Ellington, J. K. (2012). Members matter in team training: Multilevel and longitudinal relationships between goal orientation, self-regulation, and team outcomes. *Personnel Psychology*, *65*(3), 661–703. doi:10.1111/j.1744-6570.2012.01255.x

Dietz, T., Fitzgerald, A., & Shwom, R. (2005). Environmental values. *Annual Review of Environment and Resources*, *30*(1), 335–372. doi:10.1146/annurev.energy.30.050504.144444

Dijksterhuis, A., & Aarts, H. (2010). Goals, Attention, and (Un)Consciousness. *Annual Review of Psychology*, *61*(1), 467–490. doi:10.1146/annurev.psych.093008.100445 PMID:19566422

DiRienzo, C., & Das, J. (2015). Innovation and role of corruption and diversity: A cross-country study. *International Journal of Cross Cultural Management*, *15*(1), 51–72. doi:10.1177/1470595814554790

Dmochowski, J. E., Garofalo, D., Fisher, S., Greene, A., & Gambogi, D. (2016). Integrating sustainability across the university curriculum. *International Journal of Sustainability in Higher Education*, *17*(5), 652–670. doi:10.1108/IJSHE-10-2014-0154

Dolan, S. L., & Garcia, S. (2002). Managing by values: Cultural redesign for strategic organizational change at the dawn of the twenty-first century. *Journal of Management Development*, *21*(2), 101–117. doi:10.1108/02621710210417411

Dollard, M. F., & Neser, D. Y. (2013). Worker health is good for the economy: Union density and psychosocial safety climate as determinants of country differences in worker health and productivity in 31 European countries. *Social Science & Medicine*, *92*, 114–123. doi:10.1016/j.socscimed.2013.04.028 PMID:23849285

Domsch, M. E., Harms, M., & Macke, H. (1998). Selbst- und Fremdbild der Führungsverhaltens von ostdeutschen Führungskräften. In R. Lang (Ed.), Management executives in the East European transformation process (pp. 227-246). München: Hampp.

Doney, P. M., Cannon, J. P., & Mullen, M. R. (1998). Understanding the influence of national culture on the development of trust. *Academy of Management Review*, *23*(3), 601–620.

Dorfman, P. W., & Howell, J. P. (1988). Dimensions of national culture and effective leadership patterns: Hofstede revisited. *Advances in International Comparative Management*, *3*(1), 127–150.

Dorfman, P., Javidan, M., Hanges, P., Dastmalchian, A., & House, R. (2012). GLOBE: A twenty year journey into the intriguing world of culture and leadership. *Journal of World Business*, *47*(4), 504–518. doi:10.1016/j.jwb.2012.01.004

Downey, L. A., Papageorgiou, V., & Stough, C. (2006). Examining the relationship between leadership, emotional intelligence and intuition in senior female managers. *Leadership and Organization Development Journal*, *27*(4), 250–264. doi:10.1108/01437730610666019

Drazin, R., & Schoonhoven, C. B. (1996). Community, population, and organization effects on innovation: A multilevel perspective. *Academy of Management Journal*, *39*(5), 1065–1083. doi:10.2307/256992

Drucker, P.F., (1999). *Management challenges for 21st century.* New York: Harper.

Du Plessis, Y., & Hoole, C. (2006). An operational project management culture framework. *SA Journal of Human Resource Management, 4*(1), 36–43. doi:10.4102/sajhrm.v4i1.79

Duarte, P. A., & Rapaso, M. L. (2010). A PLS model to study brand preference: an application to the mobile phone market. In V. E. Vinzi, W. W. Chin, J. Henseler, & H. Wang (Eds.), *Handbook of partial least squares – concepts, methods and applications* (pp. 449–485). Berlin: Springer. doi:10.1007/978-3-540-32827-8_21

Dubina, I. N., Ramos, S. J., & Ramos, H. (2016). Culture as a Driving Force of Individual and Organizational Behavior. In Creativity, Innovation, and Entrepreneurship Across Cultures (pp. 1-27). Springer New York. doi:10.1007/978-1-4939-3261-0_1

Duhita, S., & Daellenbach, U. (2015). Is loafing at work necessarily detrimental? In Centre for Labour, Employment and Work. Victoria University of Wellington.

Dumetz, J. (2012). *Cross-cultural management textbook.* Lexington, KY: CreateSpace Independent Publ.

Dunlap, R. E., & Mertig, A. G. (1990). *American environmentalism: The u.S. Environmental movement, 1970-1990.* Washington, DC: Taylor & Francis.

Dunlap, R., & Van Liere, K. (1978). The new environmental paradigm: A proposed measuring instrument and preliminary results. *The Journal of Environmental Education, 9*(1), 10–19. doi:10.1080/00958964.1978.10801875

Dunne, S., & Edwards, J. (2010). International schools as sites of social change. *Journal of Research in International Education, 9*(1), 24–39. doi:10.1177/1475240909356716

Dunphy, D., Benveniste, J., Griffiths, A., & Sutton, P. (2000). *Sustainability: The corporate challenge of the 21st century.* Crows Nest, IN: Allen & Unwin.

Dyck, R., & Mulej, M. (1998). *Self-transformation of the forgotten four-fifth.* Dubuque, IA: Kendall/Hunt.

Eamets, R., & Masso, J. (2004). *Labour Market Flexibility and Employment Protection Regulation in the Baltic States.* IZA Discussion Paper Series, 1147.

Earley, P. C. (1994). Self or group? Cultural effects of training on self-efficacy and performance. *Administrative Science Quarterly, 39*(1), 89–117. doi:10.2307/2393495

Economy, P. (2014). *The 9 Traits that define great leadership.* Retrieved 20 July, 206 from: www.inc.com/peter-economy/the-9-traits-that-define-great-leadership.html

Edmondson, A. C. (1996). *Group and organizational influences on team learning* (Unpublished Doctoral Dissertation). Harvard University, Boston, MA.

Edmondson, A. (1999). Psychological safety and learning behaviors in work teams. *Administrative Science Quarterly, 44*(2), 350–383. doi:10.2307/2666999

Edmondson, A. C. (2002). The local and variegated nature of learning in organizations: A group-level perspective. *Organization Science, 13*(2), 128–146. doi:10.1287/orsc.13.2.128.530

Edquist, C. (1997). *Systems of innovation: technologies, institutions and organizations.* London: Pinter Publishers.

Efrat, K. (2014). The direct and indirect impact of culture on innovation. *Technovation, 34*(1), 12–20. doi:10.1016/j.technovation.2013.08.003

Egejuru, P. (Ed.). (1980). *Towards African literary independence: a dialogue with contemporary African writers.* Westport, CT: Greenwood Press.

Egri, C. P., & Herman, S. (2000). Leadership in the north american environmental sector: Values, leadership styles, and contexts of environmental leaders and their organizations. *Academy of Management Journal, 43*(4), 571–604. doi:10.2307/1556356

Eikenberry, A. M., & Kluver, J. D. (2004). The marketization of the nonprofit sector: Civil society at risk? *Public Administration Review, 64*(2), 132–140. doi:10.1111/j.1540-6210.2004.00355.x

Eilam, E., & Trop, T. (2013). Evaluating school-community participation in developing a local sustainability agenda. *International Journal of Environmental and Science Education, 8*(2), 359–380. doi:10.12973/ijese.2013.201a

Eisen, A., & Barlett, P. (2006). The piedmont project: Fostering faculty development toward sustainability. *The Journal of Environmental Education, 38*(1), 25–36. doi:10.3200/JOEE.38.1.25-36

Eisenberg, N. (2000). Emotion, Regulation, and Moral Development. *Annual Review of Psychology, 51*(1), 665–697. doi:10.1146/annurev.psych.51.1.665 PMID:10751984

Eisenberg, N., & Fabes, R. A. (1990). Empathy: Conceptualization, Measurement and relation to Prosocial Behavior. *Motivation and Emotion, 14*(2), 131–149. doi:10.1007/BF00991640

Eisenberg, N., & Strayer, J. (1987). *Empathy and its Development.* New York: University of Cambridge.

Eisenhardt, K. M., & Zbaracki, M. J. (1992). Strategic decision making. *Strategic Management Journal, 13*(S2), 17–37. doi:10.1002/smj.4250130904

Ejdys, J., Matuszak-Flejszman, A., Szymanski, M., Ustinovichius, L., Shevchenko, G., & Lulewicz-Sas, A. (2016). Crucial factors for improving the iso 14001 environmental management system. *Journal of Business Economics and Management, 17*(1), 52–73. doi:10.3846/16111699.2015.1065905

Elbanna, S., & Child, J. (2007). Influences on strategic decision effectiveness: Development and test of an integrative model. *Strategic Management Journal, 28*(4), 431–453. doi:10.1002/smj.597

Elfering, A., Semmer, N. K., & Grebner, S. (2006). Work stress and patient safety: Observer-rated work stressors as predictors of characteristics of safety-related events reported by young nurses. *Ergonomics, 49*(5), 457–469. doi:10.1080/00140130600568451 PMID:16717004

Elias, M. J., Patrikakou, E. N., & Weissberg, R. P. (2007). A competence-based framework for parent—school—community partnerships in secondary schools. *School Psychology International, 28*(5), 540–554. doi:10.1177/0143034307085657

Elisburg, D. (1995). Workplace stress: legal developments, economic pressures, and violence. In Workers' Compensation Year Book. Horsham, PA: LRP Publications.

Elkington, J. (2004). Enter the triple bottom line. In A. Henriques & J. Richardson (Eds.), *The triple bottom line: Does it all add up* (pp. 1–16). London: Earthscan.

Ellington, J. K., & Dierdorff, E. C. (2014). Individual learning in team training: Self-regulation and team context effects. *Small Group Research, 45*(1), 37–67. doi:10.1177/1046496413511670

Elmore, R. F. (2000). *Building a new structure for school leadership.* Washington, DC: Albert Shanker Institute.

Ericsson, K. A., & Delaney, P. F. (1998). Working Memory and Expert Performance. In K. Gilhooly (Ed.), *Working Memory And Thinking: Current Issues In Thinking And Reasoning* (pp. 91–112). Hove, UK: Psychology Press. doi:10.4324/9780203346754_chapter_SIX

Ert, E., & Yechiam, E. (2010). Consistent constructs in individuals risk taking in decisions from experience. *Acta Psychologica, 134*(2), 225–232. doi:10.1016/j.actpsy.2010.02.003 PMID:20223438

ESN.org. (2017). Retrieved from http://galaxy.esn.org

Etzkowitz, H., Webster, A., Gebhardt, C., & Terra, B. R. C. (2000). The future of the university and the university of the future: Evolution of ivory tower to entrepreneurial paradigm. *Research Policy, 29*(2), 313–330. doi:10.1016/S0048-7333(99)00069-4

Eurofound. (2015). *First findings: Sixth European Working Conditions Survey*. Retrieved from https://www.eurofound.europa.eu/publications/resume/2015/working-conditions/first-findings-sixth-european-working-conditions-survey-resume

Eurofound. (2016). *Working time developments in the 21st century: Work duration and its regulation in the EU*. Publications Office of the European Union.

European Commission. Slovenian EU Presidency, WHO Regional Office for Europe. (2008). *European Pact for Mental Health and Well-being*. Brussels: European Commission. Available: http://ec.europa.eu/health/mental_health/docs/mhpact_en.pdf

Evans, S., Huxley, P., Gately, C., Webber, M., Mears, A., Pajak, S., Medina, J., Kendall, T., & Katona, C. (2006). Mental health, burnout and job satisfaction among mental health social workers in England and Wales. *British Journal of Psychiatry, 188*, 75-80.

Eyal, O., & Roth, G. (2011). Principals leadership and teachers motivation: Self-determination theory analysis. *Journal of Educational Administration, 49*(3), 256–275. doi:10.1108/09578231111129055

Eysenck, M. W., & Keane, M. T. (2002). Attention and Performance Limitations. In D. J. Levitin (Ed.), *Foundations of Cognitive Psychology: Core Readings* (pp. 363–398). Cambridge, MA: The MIT Press.

Fagiolo, G., Paul, W., & Moneta, A. (2007). A critical guide to empirical validation of agent-based models in economics: Methodologies, procedures, and open problems. *Computational Economics, 30*(3), 195–226. doi:10.1007/s10614-007-9104-4

Failla, K., & Stichler, J. (2008). Manager and staff perceptions of the manager's leadership style. *Journal of Advanced Nursing, 38*(11), 480–487. PMID:18997553

Falkné Bánó, K. (2014). Identifying Hungarian cultural characteristics in Europe's cultural diversity in The 21st century: a controversial issue [Alkalmazott tudományok I. fóruma: Konferenciakötet]. *Budapesti Gazdasági Főiskola, 2014*, 17–28.

Falk, R. F., & Miller, N. B. (1992). *A primer for soft modeling*. The University of Akron Press.

Faragher, E. B., Cass, M., & Cooper, C. I. (2005). The relationship between job satisfaction and health: A meta-analysis. *Occupational and Environmental Medicine, 62*(2), 105–112. doi:10.1136/oem.2002.006734 PMID:15657192

Fard, H. D., Rostamy, A. A. A., & Taghiloo, H. (2009). How types of organizational cultures contribute in shaping learning organizations. *Singapore Management Review, 31*(1), 49–61.

Farh, J. L., Hackett, R. D., & Liang, J. (2007). Individual-level cultural values as moderators of perceived organizational support–employee outcome relationships in China: Comparing the effects of power distance and traditionality. *Academy of Management Journal, 50*(3), 715–729. doi:10.5465/AMJ.2007.25530866

Feather, N. T. (1994). Values and Culture. In W.J. Lonner & R.S. Malpass (Eds.), Psychology and Culture (pp. 183-189). Boston: Allyn and Bacon.

Feather, N. T. (1975). *Values in Eudcation and Society*. New York: Free Press.

Fein, E. C., Vasiliu, C., & Tziner, A. (2011). Individual values and preferred leadership behaviors: A study of romanian managers. *Journal of Applied Social Psychology*, *41*(3), 515–535. doi:10.1111/j.1559-1816.2011.00724.x

Fernandez, C. F., & Vecchio, R. P. (1997). Situational leadership theory revisited: A test of an across-jobs perspective. *The Leadership Quarterly*, *8*(1), 67–84. doi:10.1016/S1048-9843(97)90031-X

Festinger, L. (1957). *A Theory of Cognitive Dissonance*. Stanford, CA: Stanford University Press.

Festinger, L. (1962). *A theory of cognitive dissonance* (Vol. 2). Stanford University Press.

Fiedler, F. E. (1967). *A theory of leadership effectiveness*. New York: McGraw-Hill Book Co.

Figueiró, P. S., & Raufflet, E. (2015). Sustainability in higher education: A systematic review with focus on management education. *Journal of Cleaner Production*, *106*, 22–33. doi:10.1016/j.jclepro.2015.04.118

Fink, G., Holden, N., Karsten, L., & Illa, H. (2005). Ubuntu as a key African management concept: Contextual background and practical insights for knowledge application. *Journal of Managerial Psychology*, *20*(7), 607–620. doi:10.1108/02683940510623416

Fiore, S. M. (2008). Making Time for Memory and Remembering Time in Motivation Theory. In R. Kanfer, G. Chen, & R. D. Pritchard (Eds.), *Work Motivation: Past, Present and Future* (pp. 541–553). New York, NY: Routledge Academic.

Fiorino, D. J. (2010). Sustainability as a conceptual focus for public administration. *Public Administration Review*, *70*, S78–S88. doi:10.1111/j.1540-6210.2010.02249.x

Fitzgerald, T., Bach, D., Seymour, B., & Dolan, R. J. (2010). Differentiable neural substrates for learned and described value and risk. *Current Biology*, *20*(20), 1823–1829. doi:10.1016/j.cub.2010.08.048 PMID:20888231

Flood, R. L. (1995). *Solving Problem Solving – A Potent force for Effective Management*. Chichester, UK: John Wiley and Sons.

Foote, J., Gaffney, N., & Evans, J. R. (2010). Corporate social responsibility: Implications for performance excellence. *Total Quality Management & Business Excellence*, *21*(8), 799–812. doi:10.1080/14783363.2010.487660

Fornell, C., & Larcker, D. F. (1981). Evaluating structural equation models with unobservable variables and measurement error. *JMR, Journal of Marketing Research*, *18*(1), 39–50. doi:10.2307/3151312

Fortune, J., & White, D. (2006). Framing of project critical success factors by a systems model. *International Journal of Project Management*, *24*(1), 53–65. doi:10.1016/j.ijproman.2005.07.004

Francescato, D., Porcelli, R., Mebane, M., Cuddetta, M., Klobas, J., & Renzi, P. (2006). Evaluation of the efficacy of collaborative learning in face-to-face and computer-supported university contexts. *Computers in Human Behavior*, *22*(2), 163–176. doi:10.1016/j.chb.2005.03.001

Frankelius, P. (2009). Questioning two myths in innovation literature. *The Journal of High Technology Management Research*, *20*(1), 40–51. doi:10.1016/j.hitech.2009.02.002

Fredrickson, J. W. (1986). The strategic decision process and organization structure. *Academy of Management Review*, *11*(2), 280–297.

Fredrickson, J. W., & Iaquinto, A. L. (1989). Inertia and creeping rationality in strategic decision processes. *Academy of Management Journal*, *32*(3), 516–542. doi:10.2307/256433

Freud, S. (1918). Psychoanalytic Treatment. Tel Aviv: Am Oved.

Gade, C. B. (2011). The historical development of the written discourses on ubuntu. *South African Journal of Philosophy, 30*(3), 303–329. doi:10.4314/sajpem.v30i3.69578

Gaffikin, F., & Morrissey, M. (2008). A new synergy for universities. *Education. Citizenship and Social Justice, 3*(1), 97–116. doi:10.1177/1746197907086721

Gaidos, S. (2016). His stress is not like her stress: Scientists puzzle over why men and women react differently to pressure. *Magazine of Society for Science & the Public, 189*(2), 18.

Galaxy Your E. S. N. Gateway. (2017). Retrieved from: http://galaxy.esn.org

Gallese, V. (2007). *Before and Below Theory of Mind: Embodied Simulation and the Neural Correlates of Social Cognition.* Retrieved from http://www.ncbi.nlm.nih.gov/pmc/articles/PMC2346524/?report=classic

Gallie, D., Zhou, Y., Felstead, A., & Green, F. (2012). Teamwork, skill development and employee welfare. *British Journal of Industrial Relations, 50*(1), 23–46. doi:10.1111/j.1467-8543.2010.00787.x

Gallup. (2013). *State of global workplace. Employee engagement insights for business leaders worldwide.* Retrieved from http://www.gallup.com/services/178517/state-global-workplace.aspx

Gardner, H. (1983). *Frames of Mind.* New York: Basic Books.

Garrett, R. K., & Danziger, J. N. (2008). Disaffection or expected outcomes: Understanding personal internet use during work. *Journal of Computer-Mediated Communication, 13*(4), 937–958. doi:10.1111/j.1083-6101.2008.00425.x

Garsten, C. (2008). *Workplace Vagabonds. Carter and Community in Changing Worlds of Work.* Palgrave Macmillan. doi:10.1057/9780230227460

Gärtner, F. R., Nieuwenhuijsen, K., Dijk, F. J. H., & Sluiter, J. K. (2010). The impact of common mental disorders on the work functioning of nurses and allied health professionals: A systematic review. *International Journal of Nursing Studies, 47*(8), 1047–1061. doi:10.1016/j.ijnurstu.2010.03.013 PMID:20444449

Gärtner, F. R., Nieuwenhuijsen, K., Dijk, F. J. H., & Sluiter, J. K. (2012). Impaired work functioning due to common mental disorders in nurses and allied health professionals: The Nurses Work Functioning Questionnaire. *International Archives of Occupational and Environmental Health, 85*(2), 125–138. doi:10.1007/s00420-011-0649-0 PMID:21626312

Gathogo, J. (2008). African philosophy as expressed in the concepts of hospitality and ubuntu. *Journal of Theology for Southern Africa, 130*(March), 39–53.

Gawronski, B., & Brannon, S. M. (2016). *What is cognitive consistency and why does it matter. Cognitive dissonance: Progress on a pivotal theory in social psychology* (2nd ed.). Washington, DC: American Psychological Association.

Gaygisiz, E. (2013). How are cultural dimensions and governance quality related to socioeconomic development? *Journal of Socio-Economics, 47*, 170–179. doi:10.1016/j.socec.2013.02.012

Gerdes, K. E. (2014). Empathy, Sympathy and Pity: 21st Century Definitions and Implications for Practice and Research. *Journal of Social Service Research, 3*(37), 230–241.

Gershon, R., Stone, P., Zeltser, M., Faucett, J., MacDavitt, K., & Chou, S. (2007). Organisational climate and nurse health outcomes in the united states: A systematic review. *Industrial Health, 45*(5), 622–636. doi:10.2486/indhealth.45.622 PMID:18057805

Ghauri, P., & Gronhaug, K. (2002). *Research Methods in Business Studies: A Practical Guide* (2nd ed.). London: Sage.

Giannikis, S. K., & Miahail, D. M. (2011). Flexible work arrangements in Greece: A study of employment perceptions. *International Journal of Human Resource Management, 22*(2), 417–432. doi:10.1080/09585192.2011.540163

Gibson, C., & Vermeulen, F. (2003). A healthy divide: Subgroups as a stimulus for team learning behavior. *Administrative Science Quarterly, 48*(2), 202–239. doi:10.2307/3556657

Gibson, J. W., Greenwood, R. A., & Murphy, E. F. Jr. (2009). Generational differences in the workplace: Personal values, behaviors, and popular beliefs. *Journal of Diversity Management, 4*(3), 1–7. doi:10.19030/jdm.v4i3.4959

Gigerenzer, G. (1996). On narrow norms and vague heuristics: A rebuttal to Kahneman and Tversky. *Psychological Review, 103*(3), 592–596. doi:10.1037/0033-295X.103.3.592

Gill, A. S., Flaschner, A. B., & Shacha, M. (2006). Mitigating stress and burnout by implementing transformational leadership. *International Journal of Contemporary Hospitality Management, 18*(6), 469–481. doi:10.1108/09596110610681511

Giumetti, G. W., McKibben, E. S., Hatfield, A. L., Schroeder, A. N., & Kowalski, R. M. (2012). Cyber incivility @ work: The new age of interpersonal deviance. *Cyberpsychology, Behavior, and Social Networking, 15*(3), 148–154. doi:10.1089/cyber.2011.0336 PMID:22304404

Global Innovation Website. (2014). *Global innovation index.* Retrieved April 11, 2014, from http://www.globalinnovationindex.org/content.aspx?page=GII-Home

GLOBE. (2016). *Global Leadership & Organizational Behavior Effectiveness: Overview.* Retrieved 4 December, 2016, from http://globeproject.com/studies

Gloor, A. (2006). *Swarm creativity. Competitive advantage through collaborative innovation networks.* Oxford, UK: Oxford University Press. doi:10.1093/acprof:oso/9780195304121.001.0001

Glover, J., Friedman, H., & van Driel, M. (2016). Cultural Dilemmas and Sociocultural Encounters: An Approach for Understanding, Assessing, and Analyzing Culture. In Critical Issues in Cross Cultural Management (pp. 53-60). Springer International Publishing.

Godos-Diez, J. L., Fernandez-Gago, R., & Martinez-Campillo, A. (2011). How important are ceos to csr practices? An analysis of the mediating effect of the perceived role of ethics and social responsibility. *Journal of Business Ethics, 98*(4), 531–548. doi:10.1007/s10551-010-0609-8

Godziszewski, B. (1999). *Zasobowe uwarunkowania strategii przedsiębiorstwa.* Torun: Wydawnictwo Uniwersytetu Mikolaja Kopernika.

Goethals, G., Sorenson, G., & Burns, J. (2004). *Encyclopedia of leadership.* Thousand Oaks, CA: SAGE Publications. doi:10.4135/9781412952392

Goetzel, R. Z., Ozminkowski, R. J., Sederer, L. I., & Mark, T. L. (2002). The business case for quality mental health services: Why employers should care about the mental health and well-being of their employees. *Journal of Occupational and Environmental Medicine, 44*(4), 320–330. doi:10.1097/00043764-200204000-00012 PMID:11977418

Golbasi, Z., Kelleci, M., & Dogan, S. (2008). Relationship between coping strategies, individual characteristics and job satisfaction in a sample of hospital nurses: Cross-section questionnaire survey. *International Journal of Nursing Studies, 45*(12), 1800–1806. doi:10.1016/j.ijnurstu.2008.06.009 PMID:18703192

Goldberg, D., & Williams, P. (1988). *A user's guide to the General Health Questionnaire.* Windsor, UK: NFER-Nelson.

Goleman, D., & Boyatzis, R. (2008). Social intelligence and the biology of leadership. *Harvard Business Review.* Retreived April 25, 2015: http://hbr.org/2008/09/social-intelligence-and-the-biology-of-leadership/ar/1

Goleman, D. (1997). *Emotional Intelligence*. New York: Bantam Books.

Goleman, D. (2008). Social Intelligence: The Biology of Leadership. *Harvard Business Review*, (September), 1–8. PMID:18777666

Goleman, D., Boyatzis, R., & McKee, A. (2002). *Primal leadership*. Boston, MA: Harvard Business School Press.

Goll, I., & Rasheed, A. (1997). Rational decision-making and firm performance: The moderating role of environment. *Strategic Management Journal*, *18*(7), 583–591. doi:10.1002/(SICI)1097-0266(199708)18:7<583::AID-SMJ907>3.0.CO;2-Z

Gosselin, D., Parnell, R., Smith-Sebasto, N. J., & Vincent, S. (2013). Integration of sustainability in higher education: Three case studies of curricular implementation. *Journal of Environmental Studies and Sciences*, *3*(3), 316–330. doi:10.1007/s13412-013-0130-3

Götz, G., Liehr-Gobbers, K., & Krafft, M. (2010). Evaluation of structural equation models using the partial least squares (PLS) approach. In V. Esposito Vinzi, W. Chin, J. Henseler, & H. Wang (Eds.), *Handbook of partial least squares: Concepts, methods, and applications* (pp. 691–711). Berlin: Springer-Verlag. doi:10.1007/978-3-540-32827-8_30

Gouillart, F., & Kelly, J. (1995). *Transforming the Organization*. New York: McGraw-Hill.

Grabher, G., & Stark, D. (1997). *Restructuring Networks in Post-Socialism: Legacies, Linkages and Localities*. New York: Oxford University Press.

Grachev, M.V. (2009). Russia, Culture, and Leadership: Cross-Cultural Comparisons of Managerial Values and Practices. *Problems of Post-Communism*, (1).

Granovetter, M. S. (1973). The strength of weak ties. *American Journal of Sociology*, *78*(6), 1360–1380. doi:10.1086/225469

Grawitch, M. J., Trares, S., & Kohler, J. M. (2007). Healthy workplace practices and employee outcomes. *International Journal of Stress Management*, *14*(3), 275–293. doi:10.1037/1072-5245.14.3.275

Greenberg, M. T., Weissberg, R. P., OBrien, M. U., Zins, J. E., Fredericks, L., Resnik, H., & Elias, M. J. (2003). Enhancing school-based prevention and youth development through coordinated social, emotional, and academic learning. *The American Psychologist*, *58*(6-7), 466–474. doi:10.1037/0003-066X.58.6-7.466 PMID:12971193

Greenfield, D. (2007). The enactment of dynamic leadership. *Leadership in Health Services*, *20*(3), 159–168. doi:10.1108/17511870710764014 PMID:20690461

Gregoire, M. B., & Arendt, S. W. (2014). Leadership: Reflections over the Past 100 Years. *Journal of the Academy of Nutrition and Dietetics*, *114*(5), S10–S19. doi:10.1016/j.jand.2014.02.023 PMID:24725519

Grove. (2005a). *Introduction to the GLOBE Research Project on Leadership Worldwide*. Retrieved from: http://www.grovewell.com/pub-GLOBE-intro.html

Grove. (2005b). *Worldwide Differences in Business Values and Practices: Overview of GLOBE Research Findings*. Retrieved from: http://www.grovewell.com/pub-GLOBE-dimensions.html

Grudney, D., & Sarvutyte, M. (2007). Conceptualizing the Determinants of Labour Market Flexibility: the UE Perspective. In D. Kopycińska (Ed.), *Flexibility of Labour Market. Monograph No 7" in the series Economics and Competition Policy*. Szczecin: Wydawnictwo Uniwersytetu Szczecinskiego.

Guenther, R. K. (2002). Memory. In D. J. Levitin (Ed.), *Foundations of Cognitive Psychology: Core Readings* (pp. 311–359). Cambridge, MA: The MIT Press.

Güleryüz, G., Güney, S., Aydın, E. M., & Aşan, O. (2008). The mediating effect of job satisfaction between emotional intelligence and organisational commitment of nurses: A questionnaire survey. *International Journal of Nursing Studies, 45*(11), 1625–1635. doi:10.1016/j.ijnurstu.2008.02.004 PMID:18394625

Gulzar, S., Moon, M. A., Attiq, S., & Azam, R. I. (2014). The darker side of high performance work systems: Examining employee psychological outcomes and counterproductive work behavior. *Pakistan Journal of Commerce and Social Sciences, 8*(3), 715–732.

Gupta, B. (2011). A comparative study of organizational strategy and culture across industry. *Benchmarking: An International Journal, 18*(4), 510–528. doi:10.1108/14635771111147614

Gurkova, E., Harokova, S., Džuka, J., & Žiakova, K. (2014). Job satisfaction and subjective well-being among Czech nurses. *International Journal of Nursing Practice, 20*(2), 194–203. doi:10.1111/ijn.12133 PMID:24713016

GUS. (2016). Bezrobocie rejestrowane. I kwartał 2016 r. Warsaw: GUS.

Guthrie, D. (1999). Producing Guanxi: Sentiment, Self, and Subculture in a North China Village. *The China Quarterly, 158*, 509–510. doi:10.1017/S0305741000006044

Guzzo, R. A., & Dickson, M. W. (1996). Teams in organizations: Recent research on performance and effectiveness. *Annual Review of Psychology, 47*(1), 307–338. doi:10.1146/annurev.psych.47.1.307 PMID:15012484

Hackman, J. R. (1987). The design of work teams. In J. Lorsch (Ed.), *Handbook of organizational behavior* (pp. 315–342). Englewood Cliffs, NJ: Prentice-Hall.

Hage, J., & Dewar, R. (1973). Elite values versus organizational structure in predicting innovation. *Administrative Science Quarterly, 18*(3), 279–290. doi:10.2307/2391664

Hair, J. F., Black, W. C., Babin, B. J., & Anderson, R. E. (2010). *Multivariate data analysis*. Upper Saddle River, NJ: Prentice Hall.

Hair, J. F., Hult, G. T. M., Ringle, C. M., & Sarstedt, M. (2014). *A primer on partial least squares structural equation modeling (PLS-SEM)*. Thousand Oaks, CA: Sage.

Hakansson, J. (2003). *Exploring the phenomenon of empathy* (Doctoral dissertation). Department of Psychology, Stockholm University.

Hall, E. (1959). The Silent Language. New York: Garden City.

Hall, D. T. (1996). Long live the career -A relational approach. In D. Hall et al. (Eds.), *The career is dead -- Long live the career* (pp. 1–14). San Francisco: Jossey-Bass Publishers.

Hall, E. T. (1966). *The Hidden Dimension*. New York: Doubleday.

Hall, P. A., & Soskice, D. (2001). *Varieties of Capitalism: The institutional foundations of comparative advantage*. New York: Oxford University Press. doi:10.1093/0199247757.001.0001

Hambrick, D. C. (2007). Upper echelons theory: An update. *Academy of Management Review, 32*(2), 334–343. doi:10.5465/AMR.2007.24345254

Hambrick, D. C., & Mason, P. A. (1984). Upper echelons - the organization as a reflection of its top managers. *Academy of Management Review, 9*(2), 193–206.

Hamel, G., & Prahalad, C. K. (1999). *Przewaga konkurencyjna jutra. Strategie przejmowania kontroli nad branza i tworzenia rynkow przyszłosci*. Warszawa: Businessman Book.

Hampden-Turner, Ch., & Trompenaars, A. (2000). *Siedem kultur kapitalizmu*. Krakow: Oficyna Ekonomiczna.

Handy, C. (1993). *Understanding organisations*. Penguin.

Handy, Ch. (2002). *The Age of Unreason*. London: Random House Group Ltd.

Hanin, Y. L. (1997). Emotions and athletic performance: Individual zones of optimal functioning model. *European Yearbook of Sport Psychology, 1*, 29–72.

Hansel, J., & Lomnitz, G. (1987). *Projektleiter-Praxis*. Berlin: Springer Verlag. doi:10.1007/978-3-642-96885-3

Hardy, M., & Heyes, S. (1999). *Beginning Psychology*. Oxford University Press.

Hardy, L. (1996). Testing the predictions of the cusp catastrophe model of anxiety and performance. *The Sport Psychologist, 10*(2), 140–156. doi:10.1123/tsp.10.2.140

Harman, H. H. (1976). *Modern factor analysis* (3rd ed.). Chicago, IL: University of Chicago Press.

Harms, P. D., & Crede, M. (2010). Emotional Intelligence and Transformational and Transactional Leadership: A Meta-Analysis. *Journal of Leadership & Organizational Studies, 17*(1), 5–17. doi:10.1177/1548051809350894

Harnard, S. (2005). To cognize is to categorize: cognition is categorization. In H. Cohen & C. Lefebvre (Eds.), *Handbook of categorization in cognitive science* (pp. 20–45). New York, NY: Elsevier. doi:10.1016/B978-008044612-7/50056-1

Harrington, J. E. (2008). The social selection of flexible and rigid agents. *The American Economic Review, 88*(1), 63–82.

Harris, A. (2004). Distributed Leadership and School Improvement: Leading or Misleading? *Educational Management Administration & Leadership, 32*(1), 11–24. doi:10.1177/1741143204039297

Harris, B. (2010). Voluntary action and the state in historical perspective. *Voluntary Sector Review, 1*(1), 25–40. doi:10.1332/204080510X496993

Harrison, L., & Yasin, E. (Eds.). (2015). *Culture Matters in Russia—and Everywhere: Backdrop for the Russia-Ukraine Conflict*. Lexington Books.

Healey, M. J., & Rawlinson, M. B. (1994). Interviewing techniques in business and management research. In V. J. Wass & P. E. Wells (Eds.), *Principles and Practice in* (pp. 123–146). Aldershot, UK: Business and Management Research.

Healy, C. M., & McKay, M. F. (2000). Nursing stress: The effects of coping strategies and job satisfaction in a sample of Australian Nurses. *Journal of Advanced Nursing, 31*(3), 681–688. doi:10.1046/j.1365-2648.2000.01323.x PMID:10718888

Heathcote, J. M. (2006). *Predicting Fair Behaviour: Using Empathy to Understand a Manager's Procedural and Interaction Justice* (PHD dissertation). University of Western Ontario.

Heidenreich, M. (2004). The dilemmas of regional innovation systems. In P. Cooke, M. Heidenreich, & H. J. Braczyk (Eds.), *Regional innovation systems* (pp. 363–389). London: Routledge.

Heintz, M. (2002). East European Managers and Western Management Theories: An ethnographic approach of Romanian service sector enterprises. *Journal of East European Management Studies, 7*(3), 279–297.

Hemingway, C. A. (2005). Personal values as a catalyst for corporate social entrepreneurship. *Journal of Business Ethics, 60*(3), 233–249. doi:10.1007/s10551-005-0132-5

Henderson, A., Brown, S. D., Pancer, S. M., & Ellis-Hale, K. (2007). Mandated community service in high school and subsequent civic engagement: The case of the double cohort in ontario, canada. *Journal of Youth and Adolescence, 36*(7), 849–860. doi:10.1007/s10964-007-9207-1

Henle, C. A., & Blanchard, A. L. (2008). Cyberloafing as a coping method: Relationship between work stressors, sanctions, and cyberloafing.*Proceedings of the Annual Meeting of the Academy of Management.*

Henseler, J., Ringle, C. M., & Sinkovics, R. R. (2009). The use of partial least squares path modeling in international marketing. *Advances in International Marketing, 20*(1), 277–320.

Herman, R. D., & Renz, D. O. (1997). Multiple constituencies and the social construction of nonprofit organization effectiveness. *Nonprofit and Voluntary Sector Quarterly, 26*(2), 185–206. doi:10.1177/0899764097262006

Herriot, P. (1992). The career management challenge: Balancing individual and organizational needs. *Sage (Atlanta, Ga.).*

Hersey, P., & Blanchard, K. H. (1993). Management of Organizational behavior utilizing human resources. Academic Press.

Hersey, P., & Blanchard, K. H. (1969). Life cycle theory of leadership. *Training and Development Journal, 23*(5), 26–34.

Hersey, P., & Blanchard, K. H. (1977). *The management of organizational behavior.* Englewood Cliffs, NJ: Prentice Hall.

Hertwig, R., Barron, G., Weber, E. U., & Erev, I. (2004). Decisions from experience and the effect of rare events in risky choice. *Psychological Science, 15*(8), 534–539. doi:10.1111/j.0956-7976.2004.00715.x PMID:15270998

Hicks, M. J. (2004). *Problem solving and decision making: Hard, soft and creative approaches.* London: Thomson Learning.

Hillson, D. (1997). Towards a risk maturity model. *International Journal of Project & Business Risk Management, 1*(1), 35–45.

Hillson, D. (1998). Project risk management: Future developments. *International Journal of Project & Business Risk Management, 2*(2), 181–195.

Hillson, D. (2002). Extending the risk process to manage opportunities. *International Journal of Project & Business Risk Management, 20*(3), 235–240. doi:10.1016/S0263-7863(01)00074-6

Hinson, J. M., Jameson, T. L., & Whitney, P. (2002). Somatic markers, working memory, and decision making. *Cognitive, Affective & Behavioral Neuroscience, 2*(4), 341–353. doi:10.3758/CABN.2.4.341 PMID:12641178

Hitcock, D., & Willard, M. (2009). *The business guide to sustainability – practical strategies and tools for organizations.* London: Earthscan.

Hoffman, M. (2000). *Empathy and Moral Development.* New York: Cambridge University Press. doi:10.1017/CBO9780511805851

Hoffman, M. L. (1984). Interaction of affect and Cognition in Empathy. In C. E. Izard, J. Kagan, & R. B. Zajonc (Eds.), *Emotions, Cognitions, and Behavior* (pp. 103–131). Cambridge, UK: Cambridge University Press.

Hofstede, G. (2011). Dimensionalizing cultures: The Hofstede model in context. *Online Readings in Psychology and Culture, 2*(1).

Hofstede, G. (2014). Retrieved April 11, 2014, from http://www.geerthofstede.nl/dimension-data-matrix

Hofstede, G. (2017). Retrieved from: http://geert-hofstede.com/

Hofstede, G., Hofstede, G. J., & Minkov, M. (2010). Cultures and organizations: Software of the mind. McGraw-Hill USA.

Hofstede, G. (1980). *Culture's consequences: International differences in work-related values.* Beverly Hills, CA: Sage Publications.

Hofstede, G. (1980). *Culture's consequences: international differences in work-related values.* Beverly Hills, CA: Sage.

Hofstede, G. (1993). Cultural constraints in management theories. In J. Wren (Ed.), *The leader's companion* (pp. 253–270). New York: Free Press.

Hofstede, G. (1998). Identifying organizational subcultures: An empirical approach. *Journal of Management Studies, 35*(1), 1–12. doi:10.1111/1467-6486.00081

Hofstede, G. (2001). *Culture's consequences. Comparing values, behaviors, institutions, and organizations across nations.* Thousand Oaks, CA: SAGE.

Hofstede, G. (2001). *Culture's consequences: Comparing values, behaviors, institutions and organizations across nations.* Thousand Oaks, CA: Sage Publications.

Hofstede, G. (2001). *Culture's Consequences: Comparing Values, Behaviors, Institutions and Organizations across Nations.* Thousand Oaks, CA: Sage.

Hofstede, G. H. (1998). *Masculinity and femininity: The taboo dimension of national cultures.* Thousand Oaks, CA: Sage.

Hofstede, G. H. (2001). *Culture's consequences* (2nd ed.). Thousand Oaks, CA: Sage.

Hofstede, G., Hofstede, G. J., & Minkov, M. (2010). *Cultures and Organizations. Software of the Mind* (3rd ed.). McGraw-Hill.

Hofstede, G., Neuijen, B., Ohayv, D. D., & Sanders, G. (1990). Measuring organizational cultures: A qualitative and quantitative study across twenty cases. *Administrative Science Quarterly, 35*(2), 286–316. doi:10.2307/2393392

Holden Leadership Center. (2009). *Leadership.* University of Oregon. Retrieved 19 July, 2016 from: http://leadership.uoregon.edu/

Holicza, P. (2016b). *Convergence of Ideas?: Analysing Fukuyama's and Huntington's Concepts of the Future.* In *16th International Scientific Conference Globalization and Its Socio-Economic Consequences* (pp. 663-669). University of Zilina.

Holicza, P., & Baimakova, K. (2015). Innovation potential of Russian and Hungarian young adults. *Actual Problems of Economics and Management, 3*(7), 41-48.

Holicza, P., Baimakova, K., & Lukina, E. (2016). Russian Socio-Economic Development: The Present Situation and Future Directives. In *FIKUSZ '16 Symposium for Young Researchers* (pp. 7-18). Obuda University.

Holicza, P. (2016a). Civilizációs Törésvonalak Európában: Magyarország és Szomszédai a Hofstede-Dimenziók Tükrében. *Hadmérnök, 11*(4), 210–215.

Holmes, D. S., & Rahe, R. (1967). Holmes – Rahe Cife chantes seal. *Journal of Psychosomatic Research*, 215–218.

Holt, S., & Marques, J. (2012). Empathy in Leadership: Appropriate or Misplaced? An Empirical Study on a Topic that Is Asking for Attention. *Journal of Business Ethics, 105*(1), 95–105. doi:10.1007/s10551-011-0951-5

Hong, J., & Engeström, Y. (2004). Changing principles of communication between Chinese managers and workers Confucian authority chains and guanxi as social networking. *Management Communication Quarterly, 17*(4), 552–585. doi:10.1177/0893318903262266

Honneger, J. (2008). *Vernetztes Denken und Handeln in der Praxis. Mit Netmapping und Erfolgslogik schrittweise von der Vision zur Aktion. Komplexität verstehen –Ziele erreichen-Hebel wirksam nutzen.* Zürich: Versus Verlag.

Hoover, E., & Harder, M. K. (2015). What lies beneath the surface? The hidden complexities of organizational change for sustainability in higher education. *Journal of Cleaner Production, 106*, 175–188. doi:10.1016/j.jclepro.2014.01.081

Hoppe, M. H. (2007, September 18). *Culture and Leader Effectiveness: The GLOBE Study*. Retrieved from: http://www.inspireimagineinnovate.com/pdf/globesummary-by-michael-h-hoppe.pdf

Ho, R. (2006). *Handbook of univariate and multivariate data analysis and interpretation with spss*. Boca Raton, FL: Chapman & Hall/CRC. doi:10.1201/9781420011111

Horvath, A., Vidra, Z., & Fox, J. (2011). *Tolerance and cultural diversity discourses in Hungary*. Policy research reports, Central European University Retrieved From: https://www.kcl.ac.uk/sspp/departments/education/web-files2/HorvathA/TC-Diversity-Discourses-in-Hungary.pdf

House, R. J., Wright, N. S., & Aditya, R. N. (1997). *Cross-cultural research on organizational leadership: A critical analysis and a proposed theory*. Academic Press.

Houseman, S. N. (2001). Why Employers Use Flexible Staffing Arrangements: Evidence from an Establishment Survey. *Industrial & Labor Relations Review*, *55*(1), 149–170. doi:10.1177/001979390105500109

House, R. J., Dorfman, P. W., Javidan, M., Hanges, P. J., & Sully de Luque, M. (2014). *Strategic Leadership across Cultures. The GLOBE Study of CEO Leadership Behavior and Effectiveness in 24 Countries*. Thousand Oaks, CA: Sage. doi:10.4135/9781506374581

House, R. J., Hanges, P. J., Javidan, M., Dorfman, P. W., & Gupta, V. (2004). *Culture, leadership, and organizations: The globe study of 62 societies*. Thousand Oaks, CA: Sage.

House, R. J., Hanges, P. J., Javidan, M., Dorfman, P., & Gupta, V. (2004). *Culture, Leadership, and Organizations. The GLOBE Study of 62 Societies*. Thousand Oaks, CA: Sage.

Hover-Kramer, D., Mabbett, P., & Shames, K. H. (1996). Vitality for caregivers. *Holistic Nursing Practice*, *10*(2), 38–48. doi:10.1097/00004650-199601000-00006 PMID:8550689

Howard, A. R., & Abbas, E. A. (2016). *Foundation of decision analysis*. Pearson Education Limited.

Howerstadt, P. (2010). The Viable System Model. In M. Reynolds & S. Holwell (Eds.), *Systems Approaches to Managing Change: A Practical Guide* (pp. 191–242). London, UK: Springer. doi:10.1007/978-1-84882-809-4_3

HRM Partners. (2015). *Prognoza HR 2016: Koniec rynku pracodawcy?* Retrieved from http://www.hrmpartners.pl/docs/raporty/raport-z-badania-prognoza-hr-2016-hrm-partners.pdf

Huber, D. L. (2006). *Leadership and nursing care management* (3rd ed.). Philadelphia, PA: Elsevier Inc.

Huber, D. L., Maas, M., McCloskey, J., Scherb, C. A., Goode, C. J., & Watson, C. (2000). Evaluating nursing administration instruments. *The Journal of Nursing Administration*, *30*(5), 251–272. doi:10.1097/00005110-200005000-00006 PMID:10823178

Hui, C., & Graen, G. (1998). Guanxi and professional leadership in contemporary Sino-American joint ventures in mainland China. *The Leadership Quarterly*, *8*(4), 451–465. doi:10.1016/S1048-9843(97)90024-2

Hungarian State Secretariat for Culture. (2017). Retrieved from http://www.kormany.hu/hu/emberi-eroforrasok-miniszteriuma/kulturaert-felelos-allamtitkarsag

Huntington, P. S. (1993). The Clash of Civilizations? *Foreign Affairs*, *72*(3), 23–24. doi:10.2307/20045621

Hu, Q., Schaufeli, W. B., & Taris, T. W. (2011). The Job Demands–Resources model: An analysis of additive and joint effects of demands and resources. *Journal of Vocational Behavior*, *79*(1), 181–190. doi:10.1016/j.jvb.2010.12.009

Hurley, R. F., & Hult, G. T. M. (1998). Innovation, market orientation, and organizational learning: An integration and empirical examination. *Journal of Marketing, 62*(3), 42–54. doi:10.2307/1251742

Husted, B. (2000). The impact of national culture on software piracy. *Journal of Business Ethics, 26*(3), 197–211. doi:10.1023/A:1006250203828

Huster, B. W. (1999). Wealth, culture, and corruption. *Journal of International Business Studies, 30*(2), 339–359. doi:10.1057/palgrave.jibs.8490073

Hutchings, K., & Weir, D. (2006). Guanxi and wasta: A comparison. *Thunderbird International Business Review, 48*(1), 141–156. doi:10.1002/tie.20090

Hwang, D. B., Golemon, P. L., Chen, Y., Wang, T.-S., & Hung, W.-S. (2009). Guanxi and business ethics in Confucian society today: An empirical case study in Taiwan. *Journal of Business Ethics, 89*(2), 235–250. doi:10.1007/s10551-008-9996-5

IMO (Interkulturelle Management- und Organisationsberatung). (2017). *Seven Cultural Orientations and Value Types.* Retrieved from: http://www.imo-international.de/englisch/html/siebenwerte_en.html

Ionescu, G., Negrusa, A. L., & Adam, C. M. (2005). Considerations about business values evolution and the Christian values. In R. Lang (Ed.), The End of Transformation? (pp. 211-220). München: Hampp.

Isaac, R. J. (2012). *African Humanism: A Pragmatic Prescription For Fostering Social Justice And Political Agency.* Philadelphia, PA: Temple University.

Ishekawa, A. (2005). Social transformation and value differentiation – The Slovak case. In R. Lang (Ed.), The End of Transformation? (pp. 221-232). München: Hampp.

Ishimaru, A. (2013). From heroes to organizers. *Educational Administration Quarterly, 49*(1), 3–51. doi:10.1177/0013161X12448250

Jaafari, A. (2001). Management of risks, uncertainties and opportunities on projects: Time for a fundamental shift. *International Journal of Project Management, 19*(2), 89–101. doi:10.1016/S0263-7863(99)00047-2

Jaafarpour, M., & Khani, A. (2012). Evaluation of the Nurses' Job Satisfaction, and Its Association with Their Moral Sensitivities and Well-being. *Journal of Clinical and Diagnostic Research, 6*(10), 1761–1764. PMID:23373046

Jackson, M. C. (2003). *Systems Thinking: Creative Holism for Managers.* New York: John Wiley and Sons.

Jackson, M. C. (2006). Creative Holism: A Critical Systems Approach to Complex Problem Situations. *Systems Research and Behavioral Science, 23*(5), 647–657. doi:10.1002/sres.799

Jackson, M. C., & Keys, P. (1984). Towards a System of Systems Methodologies. *The Journal of the Operational Research Society, 35*(6), 473–486. doi:10.1057/jors.1984.101

Jacobs, A. (2012). *Cross-cultural communication.* Groningen: Noordhoff.

Jacoby, L. L., Toth, J. P., & Yonelinas, A. P. (1993). Separating conscious and unconscious influences of memory: Measuring recollection. *Journal of Experimental Psychology. General, 122*(2), 39–154. doi:10.1037/0096-3445.122.2.139

Jaju, A., Kwak, H., & Zinkhan, G. M. (2002). Learning styles of undergraduate business students: A cross-cultural comparison between the US, India, and Korea. *Marketing Education Review, 12*(2), 49–60. doi:10.1080/10528008.2002.11488787

Janićijević, N. (2012). The influence of organizational culture on organizational preferences towards the choice of organizational change strategy. *Economic Annals, 57*(193), 25–51. doi:10.2298/EKA1293025J

Janis, I. L. (1971). Groupthink. *Psychology Today, 5*(6), 43–46.

Janssen, O., & Van Yperen, N. W. (2004). Employees Goal Orientations, the Quality of Leader-Member Exchange, and the Outcomes of Job Performance and Job Satisfaction. *Academy of Management Journal, 47*(3), 368–384. doi:10.2307/20159587

Janyam, K. (2009). The Influence of Job Satisfaction on Mental Health of Factory Workers. *The Internet Journal of Mental Health, 7*(1). Retreived July 18, 2016 from: http://ispub.com/IJMH/7/1/9829

Jasper, S., Stephan, M., Al-Khalaf, H., Rennekampff, H. O., Vogt, P., & Mirastschijski, U. (2012). Too little appreciation for great expenditure? Workload and resources in ICUs. *International Archives of Occupational and Environmental Health, 85*(7), 753–761. doi:10.1007/s00420-011-0721-9 PMID:22086785

Javitch, D. G. (2014). 10 Qualities of superior leaders. *Enterpreneur.* Retrieved 20 July, 206 from: www.enterpreneur.com/article/204248

Jelovac, D., Van Der Wal, Z., & Jelovac, A. (2011). Business and government ethics in the new and old eu: An empirical account of public-private value congruence in slovenia and the netherlands. *Journal of Business Ethics, 103*(1), 127–141. doi:10.1007/s10551-011-0846-5

Jenkins, R., & Elliott, P. (2004). Stressors, burnout and social support: Nurses in acute mental health settings. *Journal of Advanced Nursing, 48*(6), 622–631. doi:10.1111/j.1365-2648.2004.03240.x PMID:15548253

Jerome, L. (2012). Service learning and active citizenship education in england. *Education. Citizenship and Social Justice, 7*(1), 59–70. doi:10.1177/1746197911432594

Jessup, R. K., & ODoherty, J. P. (2010). Decision Neuroscience: Choices of Description and of Experience. *Current Biology, 20*(20), 881–883. doi:10.1016/j.cub.2010.09.017 PMID:20971429

Jethu-Ramsoedh, R., & Hendrickx, M. (2011). International business. Noordhoff Uitgevers bv Groningen/Houten, The Netherlands.

Jewell, L. N., & Reitz, H. J. (1981). *Group Effectiveness in Organizations. Glenview, 1,* 11.

Jiang, H., & Tsohou, A. (2014). The dual nature of personal web usage in workplace: Impacts, antecedents and regulating policies. *Twenty Second European Conference on Information Systems,* 1–16.

Jiang, Y., Jackson, S. E., & Colakoglu, S. (2016). An empirical examination of personal learning within the context of teams. *Journal of Organizational Behavior, 37*(5), 654–672. doi:10.1002/job.2058

Jia, R., & Jia, H. H. (2015). An individual trait-based investigation of employee cyberloafing. *Journal of Information Technology Management, 26*(1), 58–71.

Johnson, N. D., & Mislin, A. (2012). How much should we trust the World Values Survey trust question? *Economics Letters, 116*(2), 210–212. doi:10.1016/j.econlet.2012.02.010

Johnson, T., Kulesa, P., Cho, Y. I., & Shavitt, S. (2005). The relation between culture and response styles evidence from 19 countries. *Journal of Cross-Cultural Psychology, 36*(2), 264–277. doi:10.1177/0022022104272905

Johnston, J., Killion, J., & Oomen, J. (2005). Student satisfaction in the virtual classroom. *The Internet Journal of Allied Health Sciences and Practice, 3*(2), 1–7.

Jones, G. R. (2013). *Organisational Theory, Design, and Change* (7th ed.). London: Pearson.

Judge, W. Q., & Miller, A. (1991). Antecedents and outcomes of decision speed in different environmental contexts. *Academy of Management Journal, 34*(2), 449–463. doi:10.2307/256451 PMID:10111313

Jullisson, E. A., Karlsson, N., & Garling, T. (2005). Weighing the past and the future in decision making. *The European Journal of Cognitive Psychology, 17*(4), 561–575. doi:10.1080/09541440440000159

Jung, C. G. (1971). Psychological types (4th ed.). Princeton, NJ: Princeton University Press.

Kabanoff, B., & Holt, J. (1996). Changes in the espoused values of Austrailian organizations 19861990. *Journal of Organizational Behavior, 17*(3), 201–219. doi:10.1002/(SICI)1099-1379(199605)17:3<201::AID-JOB744>3.0.CO;2-9

Kabasakal, H., & Bodur, M. (2002). Arabic cluster: A bridge between East and West. *Journal of World Business, 37*(1), 40–54. doi:10.1016/S1090-9516(01)00073-6

Kafetsios, K., & Zampetakis, L. (2008). Emotional intelligence and job satisfaction: Testing the mediatory role of positive and negative affect at work. *Personality and Individual Differences, 44*(3), 712–722. doi:10.1016/j.paid.2007.10.004

Kahneman, D. (2003). A perspective on judgment and choice: Mapping bounded rationality. *The American Psychologist, 58*(9), 697–720. doi:10.1037/0003-066X.58.9.697 PMID:14584987

Kahneman, D., & Snell, J. (1992). Predicting a changing taste: Do people know what they will like? *Journal of Behavioral Decision Making, 5*(3), 187–200. doi:10.1002/bdm.3960050304

Kahneman, D., & Tversky, A. (1979). Prospect Theory: An Analysis of Decision under Risk. *Econometrica, 47*(2), 263–292. doi:10.2307/1914185

Kain, J., & Jex, S. (2010). Karasek's (1979) job demands-control model: A summary of current issues and recommendations for future research. In New Developments in Theoretical and Conceptual Approaches to Job Stress (Research in Occupational Stress and Well-being, Volume 8). Emerald Group Publishing Limited.

Kaklauskas, A., Zavadskas, E. K., Seniut, M., Dzemyda, G., Stankevič, V., Šimkevičius, Č., . . . Gribniak, V. (2011). Web-based biometric computer mouse advisory system to analyze a user's emotions and work productivity. Engineering Applications of Artificial Intelligence, 24(6), 928-945.

Kaklauskas, A., Zavadskas, E. K., Seniut, M., Stankevic, V., Raistenskis, J., Simkevicius, C., . . . Cerkauskiene, R. (2013). Recommender system to analyze student's academic performance. Expert Systems With Applications, 40(15), 6150-6165.

Kaklauskas, A., Zavadskas, E. K., Pruskus, V., Vlasenko, A., Bartkienė, L., Pališkienė, R., & Tamulevičius, G. et al. (2011). Recommended biometric stress management system. *Expert systems with applications Oxford: Elsevier Science Ltd., 38*(5), 14011–14025.

Kaniel, S. (2013). *Empathy in Education – Education with Love.* Tel-Aviv: Mofet.

Kanste, O., Kyngas, H., & Nikkila, J. (2007). The relationship between multidimensional leadership and burnout among nursing staff. *Journal of Nursing Management, 15*(7), 731–739. doi:10.1111/j.1365-2934.2006.00741.x PMID:17897150

Karimi, L., Leggat, S. G., Donohue, L., Farrell, G., & Couper, G. E. (2014). Emotional rescue: The role of emotional intelligence and emotional labour on well-being and job-stress among community nurses. *Journal of Advanced Nursing, 70*(1), 176–186. doi:10.1111/jan.12185 PMID:23763612

Karp, D. G. (1996). Values and their effect on pro-environmental behavior. *Environment and Behavior, 28*(1), 111–133. doi:10.1177/0013916596281006

Karsten, L., & Illa, H. (2001). Ubuntu as a management concept. *Quest, 15*(1-2), 111–134.

Karuppan, C. M. (2004). Strategies to foster labor flexibility. *International Journal of Productivity and Performance Management, 53*(6), 532–547. doi:10.1108/17410400410556192

Katzenbach, J. R., & Smith, D. K. (2001). *Siła zespołów. Wplyw pracy zespolowej na efektywnosc organizacji.* Krakow: Oficyna Wydawnicza, Dom Wydawniczy ABC.

Katz, R. (2003). *The human side of managing technological innovation.* Oxford, UK: Oxford University Press.

Kawulich, B. B., Ogletree, T. W., & Hoff, D. L. (2016, July). *Cohort Culture: Bonding or Groupthink?* Paper presented at the Fourth European Conference on the Social Sciences.

Keil, F., & Wilson, R. (1999). *The MIT Encyclopedia of the Cognitive Sciences.* Cambridge, MA: The MIT Press.

Kelemen, M. (1999). Romanian cultural background and its relevance for Cross-cultural management – A Comment. *Journal for East European Management Studies, 4*(3), 259–262.

Kelemen, M., & Hristov, L. (1998). From centrally planned culture to entrepreneurial culture: The example of Bulgarian and Romanian organisations. *Journal for East European Management Studies, 3*(3), 216–226.

Kellenr, H. (2000). *Projekte konfliktfrei fuhren.* Munchen: Verlag.

Kemery, E. R., & Dunlap, W. P. (1986). Partialling factor scores does not control method variance: A reply to Podsakoff and Todor. *Journal of Management, 12*(4), 525–530. doi:10.1177/014920638601200407

Kemmelmeier, M., Krol, G., & Kim, Y. H. (2002). Values, economics, and proenvironmental attitudes in 22 societies. *Cross-Cultural Research, 36*(3), 256–285. doi:10.1177/10697102036003004

Kerr, J. H. (2001). *Counseling Athletes: Applying Reversal Theory.* London: Routledge.

Kerr, R., Garvin, J., Heaton, N., & Boyle, E. (2006). Emotional intelligence and leadership effectiveness. *Leadership and Organization Development Journal, 27*(4), 265–279. doi:10.1108/01437730610666028

Ketola, T. (2008). A holistic corporate responsibility model: Integrating values, discourses and actions. *Journal of Business Ethics, 80*(3), 419–435. doi:10.1007/s10551-007-9428-y

Kezsbom, D., & Edward, K. (2001). *The New Dynamic Project Management.* New York: John Wiley & Sons, Inc.

Khalifa, M. (2012). A re-new-ed paradigm in successful urban school leadership. *Educational Administration Quarterly, 48*(3), 424–467. doi:10.1177/0013161X11432922

Khoza, R. J. (2006). *Let Africa lead: African transformational leadership for 21st century business.* Johannesburg: Vezubuntu.

Kidwell, R. E. (2010). Loafing in the 21st century: Enhanced opportunities-and remedies-for withholding job effort in the new workplace. *Business Horizons, 53*(6), 543–552. doi:10.1016/j.bushor.2010.06.001

Kieser, A., & Ebers, M. (2014). *Organisationstheorien.* Stuttgart: Kohlhammer Verlag.

Kihlstrom, J. F. (2013). The person-situation interaction. In D. E. Carlston (Ed.), *The Oxford Handbook of Social Cognition.* Oxford Library of Psychology. doi:10.1093/oxfordhb/9780199730018.013.0038

Kim, S. J., & Byrne, S. (2011). Conceptualizing personal web usage in work contexts: A preliminary framework. *Computers in Human Behavior, 27*(6), 2271–2283. doi:10.1016/j.chb.2011.07.006

Kim, Y., Sohn, D., & Choi, S. M. (2011). Cultural difference in motivations for using social network sites: A comparative study of American and Korean college students. *Computers in Human Behavior, 27*(1), 365–372. doi:10.1016/j.chb.2010.08.015

Kinloch, P., Francis, H., Francis, M., & Taylor, M. (2009). Supporting Crime Detection and Operational Planning with Soft Systems Methodology and Viable Systems Model. *Systems Research and Behavioral Science, 26*(1), 3–14. doi:10.1002/sres.943

Kinnicki, W., & Williams, B. K. (2011). *Management. A Practical Introduction.* New York: McGraw-Hill.

Kira, M., & van Eijnatten, F. M. (2011). Socially sustainable work organizations: Conceptual contributions and worldviews. *Systems Research and Behavioral Science, 28*(4), 418–421. doi:10.1002/sres.1083

Kirkcaldy, B. D., & Martin, T. (2000). Job stress and satisfaction among nurses: Individual differences. *Stress Medicine, 16*(2), 77–89. doi:10.1002/(SICI)1099-1700(200003)16:2<77::AID-SMI835>3.0.CO;2-Z

Kirkman, B. L., Mathieu, J. E., Cordery, J. L., Rosen, B., & Kukenberger, M. (2011). Managing a new collaborative entity in business organizations: Understanding organizational communities of practice effectiveness. *The Journal of Applied Psychology, 96*(6), 1234–1245. doi:10.1037/a0024198 PMID:21688878

Kirkman, B. L., & Shapiro, D. L. (1997). The impact of cultural values on employee resistance to teams: Toward a model of globalized self-managing work team effectiveness. *Academy of Management Review, 22*(3), 730–757.

Klotzl, G. (1994). Von der Arbeitsgruppe. *IO Management Zeitschrift, 12*(44).

Kmiotek, K. (2015). The Generation Y approach to flexibility of employment. *The Journal of American Academy of Business, 20*(2), 72–80.

Knack, S., & Keefer, P. (1997). Does social capital have an economic payoff? A cross-country investigation. *The Quarterly Journal of Economics, 112*(4), 1251–1288. doi:10.1162/003355300555475

Kohut, H. (1977). *The Restoration of the Self.* New York: International Universities Press.

Ko, K., & Samajdar, A. (2010). Evaluation of international corruption indexes: Should we believe them or not? *The Social Science Journal, 47*(3), 508–540. doi:10.1016/j.soscij.2010.03.001

Koleva, P., Rodet-Kroichivili, N., David, P., & Marasova, J. (2010). Is corporate social responsibility the privilege of developed market economies? Some evidence from Central and Eastern Europe. *International Journal of Human Resource Management, 21*(2), 274–293. doi:10.1080/09585190903509597

Kopczynski, T. (2014). *Myslenie systemowe i sieciowe w zarzadzaniu projektami.* Poznan: Wydawnictwo Uniwersytetu Ekonomicznego w Poznaniu.

Korte, R. (2010). First, get to know them: A relational view of organizational socialization. *Human Resource Development International, 13*(1), 27–43. doi:10.1080/13678861003588984

Korte, R., & Lin, S. (2013). Getting on board: Organizational socialization and the contribution of social capital. *Human Relations, 66*(3), 407–428. doi:10.1177/0018726712461927

Kosieradzki, W. (2000, October). *Korzysci z metodyki project management w administracji publicznej,* Paper presented at the Project Management Conference, Profesjonalizm, Stowarzyszenie Project Management Polska, Jelenia Góra.

Kostjuk, K. (2005). The thin line between small businesses and big politics. In A. Habisch, J. Jonker, M. Wegner, & R. Schmidpeter (Eds.), *Coporate Social Responsibility Across Europe* (pp. 209–218). Berlin: Springer. doi:10.1007/3-540-26960-6_17

Kotiadis, K., & Mingers, J. (2006). Combining PSMs with Hard OR Methods: The Philosophical and Practical Challenges. *The Journal of the Operational Research Society, 57*(7), 856–867. doi:10.1057/palgrave.jors.2602147

Kouzes, J. M., & Posner, B. Z. (1997). *Leadership practices inventory—Industrial contributor (LPI–IC). Observer response sheet*. San Francisco, CA: Jossey Bass/Pfeiffer.

Kovač, J., Mayer, J., & Jesenko, M. (2004). *Stili in značilnosti uspešnega vodenja*. Kranj: Moderna organizacija.

Kovac, P. (2013). Ethics of officials in the context of (slovene) good administration. *NISPAcee Journal of Public Administration and Policy, 5*(1), 23–53.

Koy, V., Yunibhand, J., Angsuroch, Y., & Fisher, M. L. (2015). Relationship between nursing care quality, nurse staffing, nurse job satisfaction, nurse practice environment, and burnout: Literature review. *International Journal of Research in Medical Sciences, 3*(8), 1825–1831. doi:10.18203/2320-6012.ijrms20150288

Kozlowski, S. W., & Bell, B. S. (2013). Work groups and teams in organizations. In N. W. Schmitt, S. Highhouse, & I. B. Weiner (Eds.), Handbook of psychology: Vol. 12. *Industrial and organizational psychology* (pp. 412–469). Hoboken, NJ: Wily.

Kozlowski, S. W., Toney, R. J., Mullins, M. E., Weissbein, D. A., Brown, K. G., & Bell, B. S. (2001). Developing adaptability: A theory for the design of integrated-embedded training systems. *Advances in Human Performance and Cognitive Engineering Research, 1*, 59–124. doi:10.1016/S1479-3601(01)01004-9

Kozminski, A. (1996). Management Education in Central and Eastern Europe. In *International Encyclopedia of Business and Management* (Vol. 2, pp. 1123–1129). London: Routledge.

Kozminski, A. (2008). Anatomy of systemic change in polish management in transition. *Communist and Post-Communist Studies, 41*(3), 263–280. doi:10.1016/j.postcomstud.2008.06.006

Kozminski, A. K. (2008). *Koniec swiata menedzerow?* Warszawa: Wydawnictwa Akademickie i Profesjonalne.

Kraiger, K., Ford, J. K., & Salas, E. (1993). Application of cognitive, skill-based, and affective theories of learning outcomes to new methods of training evaluation. *The Journal of Applied Psychology, 78*(2), 311–328. doi:10.1037/0021-9010.78.2.311

Kreitner, R., Kinicki, A., & Buelens, M. (2002). *Organizational behavior*. Berkshire, UK: McGraw-Hill.

Kreuter, M. W., & Lezin, N. (2002). Social capital theory: implications for community-based health promotion. In R. diClemente, R. Crosby, & M. Kegler (Eds.), *Emerging theories in health promotion practice and research: Strategies for improving public health* (pp. 228–254). San Francisco, CA: Jossey-Bass.

Krol, M. (2014). *Elastyczność zatrudnienia w organizacji*. Warsaw: CeDeWu.

Kronick, R. F., & Cunningham, R. B. (2013). Service-learning: Some academic and community recommendations. *Journal of Higher Education Outreach & Engagement, 14.*

Kropf, A., & Newbury-Smith, T. C. (2016). Wasta as a form of social capital: an institutional perspective. In M. A. Ramady (Ed.), *The Political Economy of Wasta: Use and Abuse of Social Capital Networking* (pp. 3–22). New York: Springer International. doi:10.1007/978-3-319-22201-1_1

Krznaric, R. (2014). *Empathy Why It Matters and How To Get It*. New York: Penguin Group.

Kuchinke, K. P. (1999). Leadership and culture: Work-related values and leadership styles among one companys US and German telecommunication employees. *Human Resource Development Quarterly, 10*(2), 135–154. doi:10.1002/hrdq.3920100205

Kudielka, B. M., Hanebuth, D., von Känel, R., Gander, M. L., Grande, G., & Fischer, J. E. (2005). Health-related quality of life measured by the SF12 in working populations: Associations with psychosocial work characteristics. *Journal of Occupational Health Psychology*, *10*(4), 429–440. doi:10.1037/1076-8998.10.4.429 PMID:16248690

Kuoppala, J., Lamminpää, A., Liira, J., & Vainio, H. (2008). Leadership, job well-being, and health effects—A systematic review and a meta-analysis. *Journal of Occupational and Environmental Medicine*, *50*(8), 904–915. doi:10.1097/JOM.0b013e31817e918d PMID:18695449

Kushner, J. (2009). *Wangari Maathai: Righteous leader of environmental and social change*. Presented at the Adult Education Research Conference, Chicago, IL. Retrieved from http://newprairiepress.org/cgi/viewcontent.cgi?article=3780&context=aerc

Kuznetsov, A., Kuznetsova, O., & Warren, R. (2009). CSR and the legitimacy of business transition economies: The case of Russia. *Scandinavian Journal of Management*, *25*(1), 37–45. doi:10.1016/j.scaman.2008.11.008

La Berge, D. (1999). Attention. In B. M. Bly & D. E. Rumelhart (Eds.), *Cognitive Science* (pp. 43–97). New York, NY: Academic Press. doi:10.1016/B978-012601730-4/50004-4

Lacey Bryant, S. (1999). Information services for primary care: The organizational culture of General Practice and the information needs of partnerships and Primary Care Groups. *Health Libraries Review*, *16*(3), 157–165. doi:10.1046/j.1365-2532.1999.00223.x PMID:10620850

Lackner, H. (2016). Wasta: Is it such a bad thing? An anthropological perspective. In M. A. Ramady (Ed.), *The Political Economy of Wasta: Use and Abuse of Social Capital Networking* (pp. 33–46). New York: Springer International. doi:10.1007/978-3-319-22201-1_3

Lambert, E. G., Paoline, E. A., & Hogan, N. L. (2006). Impact of centralization and formalization on satisfaction and commitment. *Criminal Justice Studies*, *19*(1), 23–44. doi:10.1080/14786010600615967

Lambert, V. A., Lambert, C. E., & Ito, M. (2004). Workplace stressors, ways of coping and demographic characteristics as predictors of physical and mental health of Japanese hospital nurses. *International Journal of Nursing Studies*, *41*(1), 85–97. doi:10.1016/S0020-7489(03)00080-4 PMID:14670398

Lambsdorff, J. (2007). The Methodology of the corruption perceptions index 2007. Transparency International (TI) and University of Passau.

Landa, J., & López-Zafra, E. (2010). The Impact of Emotional Intelligence on Nursing: An Overview. *Psychology (Savannah, Ga.)*, *1*(1), 50–58.

Landau, D. (2007). *Unternehmenskultur und Organisationsberatung. Über Umgang mit Werten und Veränderungsprozessen*. Heidelberg: Carl-Auer Verlag.

Landrum, N. E., & Edwards, S. (2009). *Sustainable business: An executive's primer*. New York, NY: Business Expert Press. doi:10.4128/9781606490495

Lang, R. (1996). Wandel von Unternehmenskulturen in Ostdeutschland und Osteuropa – Aktuelle Fragen und Problemfelder der Forschung. In R. Lang (Ed.), *Wandel von Unternehmenskulturen in Ostdeutschland und Osteuropa. 2nd Chemnitz East Forum* (pp. 7-22). München: Hampp.

Lang, R. (2002). Wertewandel im ostdeutschen Management. In R. Schmidt, J. Gergs, & M. Pohlmann (Eds.), Managementsoziologie. Themen, Desiderate, Perspektiven (pp. 128-154). München: Hampp.

Lang, R. (2014). Participative leadership in cross-cultural leadership research: A misconception? In O. Kranz, & T. Steger (Eds.), Zwischen Instrumentalisierung und Bedeutungslosigkeit Mitarbeiter-Partizipation im organisationalen Kontext in Mittel- und Osteuropa (pp. 77-92). München: Hampp.

Lang, R., Kovač, J., & Bernik, M. (2000). *Management v tranzicijskih procesih* [management in transition processes]. Kranj: Moderna organizacija.

Lang, R., Kovač, J., & Bernik, M. (2000). *Management v tranzicijskih procesih* [Management in Transition Processes]. Kranj: Moderna organizacija.

Lang, R. (2008). Vorwärts zum Shareholder-Kapitalismus? "Corporate social values" von Unternehmern und Managern als Orientierungs- und Wirkungsrahmen bei strategischen Managementenscheidungen in Transformationsgesellschaften. In U. Götze & R. Lang (Eds.), *Strategisches Management zwischen Globalisierung und Regionalisierung* (pp. 177–204). Wiesbaden: Gabler. doi:10.1007/978-3-8349-8067-0_8

Lang, R., Alas, R., Alt, R., Catana, D., & Hartz, R. (2005). Leadership in transformation – Between local embeddedness and global challenges. *Journal of Cross-Cultural Competence & Management, 4*, 215–246.

Lang, R., Catana, A., Catana, D., & Steyrer, J. (2008). Impacts of motives and leadership attributes of entrepreneurs and managers on followers commitment in transforming countries – A comparison of Romania, East Germany and Austria. In P. Jurczek & M. Niedobitek (Eds.), *Europäische Forschungsperspektiven – Elemente einer Europawissenschaft 2008* (pp. 109–135). Berlin: Duncker & Humblot.

Lang, R., Szabo, E., Catana, G. A., Konecna, Z., & Skalova, P. (2013). Beyond participation? - leadership ideals of future managers from central and east european countries. *Journal for East European Management Studies, 18*(4), 482–511.

Lang, R., Szabo, E., Catana, G. A., Konecna, Z., & Skalova, P. (2013). Beyond participation? - leadership ideals of future managers from central and east European countries. *Journal for East European Management Studies, 18*(4), 482–511.

Lankau, M. J., & Scandura, T. A. (2002). An investigation of personal learning in mentoring relationships: Content, antecedents, and consequences. *Academy of Management Journal, 45*(4), 779–790. doi:10.2307/3069311

LaPalombara, J. (1994). Structural and institutional aspects of corruption. *Social Research, 61*(2), 325–350.

Larrabee, J. H., Janney, M. A., Ostrow, C. L., Withrow, M. L., Hobbs, G. R. Jr, & Burant, C. M. (2003). Predictors of registered nurse job satisfaction and intention to leave. *The Journal of Nursing Administration, 33*(5), 271–283. doi:10.1097/00005110-200305000-00003 PMID:12792282

Larson, C. E., & La Fasto, M. J. (1989). *Teamwork: What Must Go Right / What Can Go Wrong.* Sage Publications Inc.

Laschinger, H. K. S., Almost, J., Purdy, N., & Kim, J. (2004). Predictors of nurse managers health in Canadian re-structured healthcare settings. *Canadian Journal of Nursing Leadership, 17*(4), 88–105. doi:10.12927/cjnl.2004.17020 PMID:15656251

Laschinger, H. K. S., Finegan, J., & Shamian, J. (2001). Promoting nurses' health: Effect of empowerment on job strain and work satisfaction. *Nursing Economics, 19*(2), 42–52.

Lasky, S. G. (2004). *Toward a policy framework for analyzing educational system effects.* Retrieved from http://www.csos.jhu.edu/crespar/techReports/Report71.pdf

Lavoie-Tremblay, M., Wright, D., Desforges, N., Gelinas, C., Marchionni, C., & Drevniok, U. (2008). Creating a Healthy Workplace for New-Generation Nurses. *Journal of Nursing Scholarship, 40*(3), 290–297. doi:10.1111/j.1547-5069.2008.00240.x PMID:18840214

Law, K. S., Wong, C.-S., Wang, D., & Wang, L. (2000). Effect of supervisor–subordinate guanxi on supervisory decisions in China: An empirical investigation. *International Journal of Human Resource Management, 11*(4), 751–765. doi:10.1080/09585190050075105

Law, K. S., Wong, C., & Song, L. J. (2004). The construct and criterion validity of emotional intelligence and its potential utility for management studies. *The Journal of Applied Psychology, 89*(3), 483–496. doi:10.1037/0021-9010.89.3.483 PMID:15161407

Lazarus, R. S. (1993). From psychological stress to the emotions: A History of Changing Outlooks. *Annual Review of Psychology, 44*(1), 1–22. doi:10.1146/annurev.ps.44.020193.000245 PMID:8434890

Lazarus, R. S., & Folkman, S. (1984). *Stress, appraisal and coping*. New York: Springer publishing Company.

Le Grange, L. (2012). Ubuntu, ukama and the healing of nature, self and society. *Educational Philosophy and Theory, 44*(sup2s2), 56–67. doi:10.1111/j.1469-5812.2011.00795.x

Leach, L. S. (2005). Nurse executive transformational leadership and organizational commitment. *The Journal of Nursing Administration, 35*(5), 228–237. doi:10.1097/00005110-200505000-00006 PMID:15891486

Leadership-Toolbox. (2008*). The Characteristic of Leadership - 7 Important Traits*. Retrieved 22 July, 2016 from: http://www.leadership-toolbox.com/characteristic-of-leadership.html

Lee, J. (2008). Effects of leadership and leader-member exchange on innovativeness. *Journal of Managerial Psychology, 23*(6), 670–687. doi:10.1108/02683940810894747

Lee, M. D., & Cummins, T. D. R. (2004). Evidence accumulation in decision making: Unifying the take the best and the rational models. *Psychonomic Bulletin & Review, 11*(2), 343–352. doi:10.3758/BF03196581 PMID:15260204

Lee, Y., Lee, Z., & Kim, Y. (2007). Understanding personal web usage in organizations. *Journal of Organizational Computing and Electronic Commerce, 17*(1), 75–99. doi:10.1080/10919390701291067

Lemon, M., & Sahota, P. S. (2004). Organizational culture as a knowledge repository for increased innovative capacity. *Tehnovation, 24*(6), 483–498. doi:10.1016/S0166-4972(02)00102-5

Leong, S. S. W. (2003). *Does mental representation mediate the roles of knowledge and decision aids in the performance of a task?* (Unpublished doctoral dissertation). University of Utah.

Lerner, J. S., & Keltner, D. (2001). Fear, anger, and risk. *Journal of Personality and Social Psychology, 81*(1), 46–159. doi:10.1037/0022-3514.81.1.146 PMID:11474720

Lester, K., & Piore, M. (2004). *Innovation - the missing dimension*. Cambridge, MA: Harvard Business Press.

Letvak, S. A., Ruhm, C. J., & Gupta, S. N. (2012). Nurses presenteeism and its effects on self-reported quality of care and costs. *The American Journal of Nursing, 112*(2), 30–38. doi:10.1097/01.NAJ.0000411176.15696.f9 PMID:22261652

Leung, M. Y., Chan, I. Y., & Yu, J. (2012). Preventing construction worker injury incidents through the management of personal stress and organizational stressors. *Accident; Analysis and Prevention, 48*(1), 156–166. doi:10.1016/j.aap.2011.03.017 PMID:22664679

Leung, M. Y., Chan, Y. S., & Yuen, K. W. (2010). Impacts of stressors and stress on the injury incidents of construction workers in Hong Kong. *Journal of Construction Engineering and Management, 136*(10), 1093–1103. doi:10.1061/(ASCE)CO.1943-7862.0000216

Levine, J. M., & Moreland, R. L. (1991). Culture and socialization in work groups. In L. Resnick & J. Levine (Eds.), *Perspectives on socially shared cognition* (pp. 257–279). Washington, DC: APA. doi:10.1037/10096-011

Lewin, K. (1946/1951). Behavior and development as a function of the total situation. In K. Lewin (Ed.), *Field theory in social science* (pp. 239–240). New York: Harper & Ro. doi:10.1037/10756-016

Liberman, B., Seidman, G., McKenna, K. Y. A., & Buffardi, L. E. (2011). Employee job attitudes and organizational characteristics as predictors of cyberloafing. *Computers in Human Behavior, 27*(6), 2192–2199. doi:10.1016/j.chb.2011.06.015

Lientz, B., & Rea, K. (1995). *Project Management for the 21th Century*. San Diego, CA: Academic Press.

Lim, V. K. G., & Chen, D. J. Q. (2012). Cyberloafing at the workplace: Gain or drain on work? *Behaviour & Information Technology, 31*(4), 343–353. doi:10.1080/01449290903353054

Lindell, M. K., & Whitney, D. J. (2001). Accounting for common method variance in cross-sectional research designs. *The Journal of Applied Psychology, 86*(1), 114–121. doi:10.1037/0021-9010.86.1.114 PMID:11302223

Lindert, K. (1996). Führungskonzeptionen im Wandel: Eine interkulturelle und intertemporale Studie – Gemeinsamkeiten und Unterschiede west- und osteuropäischer Führungskräfte. In R. Lang (Ed.), *Wandel von Unternehmenskulturen in Ostdeutschland und Osteuropa. 2nd Chemnitz East Forum* (pp. 91-106). München: Hampp.

Lindgreen, A. (2004). Corruption and unethical behavior: Report on a set of Danish guidelines. *Journal of Business Ethics, 51*(1), 31–39. doi:10.1023/B:BUSI.0000032388.68389.60

Lindgreen, A., & Swaen, V. (2010). Corporate Social Responsibility. *International Journal of Management Reviews, 12*(1), 1–7. doi:10.1111/j.1468-2370.2009.00277.x

Lingard, H., Francis, V., & Turner, M. (2012). Work–life strategies in the Australian construction industry: Implementation issues in a dynamic project-based work environment. *International Journal of Project Management, 30*(3), 282–295. doi:10.1016/j.ijproman.2011.08.002

Lin, L.-H. (2011). Cultural and organizational antecedents of guanxi: The Chinese cases. *Journal of Business Ethics, 99*(3), 441–451. doi:10.1007/s10551-010-0662-3

Lin, N. (1999). Social networks and status attainment. *Annual Review of Sociology, 25*(1), 467–487. doi:10.1146/annurev.soc.25.1.467

Lin, P. C., Chen, C. H., Pan, S. M., Pan, C. H., Chen, C. J., Chen, Y. M., & Wu, M. T. et al. (2012). Atypical work schedules are associated with poor sleep quality and mental health in Taiwan female nurses. *International Archives of Occupational and Environmental Health, 85*(8), 877–884. doi:10.1007/s00420-011-0730-8 PMID:22207296

Litke, H. (1995). *Projektmanagement*. Munchen-Vien: Carl Hanser Verlag.

Littlepage, G., Robison, W., & Reddington, K. (1997). Effects of task experience and group experience on group performance, member ability, and recognition of expertise. *Organizational Behavior and Human Decision Processes, 69*(2), 133–147. doi:10.1006/obhd.1997.2677

Locke, E. A. (1976). The nature and causes of job satisfaction. In M. D. Dunnette (Ed.), *Handbook of industrial and organizational psychology* (pp. 1297–1349). Chicago, IL: Rand McNally.

Loewe, M., Blume, J., & Speer, J. (2008). How favoritism affects the business climate: Empirical evidence from Jordan. *The Middle East Journal, 62*(2), 259–276. doi:10.3751/62.2.14

Loewenstein, G., & Lerner, J. S. (2003). The role of affect in decision making. In R. Davidson, K. Scherer, & H. Goldsmith (Eds.), *Handbook of affective science* (pp. 619–642). New York, NY: Oxford University Press.

Lok, P., & Crawford, J. (2004). The effect of organisational culture and leadership style on job satisfaction and organisational commitment: A cross-national comparison. *Journal of Management Development, 23*(4), 321–338. doi:10.1108/02621710410529785

Lorber, M. (2015). Emotional intelligence – A key ability for leaders in nursing. In L. Zysberg & S. Raz (Eds.), *Emotional intelligence: Current evidence from psychological, educational and organizational perspectives* (pp. 277–292). New York, NY: Nova Science Publishers.

Lorber, M., & Skela-Savič, B. (2011). Perceptions of managerial competencies, style, and characteristics among professionals in nursing. *Croatian Medical Journal, 52*(2), 198–204. doi:10.3325/cmj.2011.52.198 PMID:21495203

Lorber, M., & Skela-Savič, B. (2012). Job satisfaction of nurses in Slovenian hospitals. *Croatian Medical Journal, 53*(3), 263–270. doi:10.3325/cmj.2012.53.263 PMID:22661140

Lugosi, P., & Bray, J. (2008). Tour guiding, organisational culture and learning: Lessons from an entrepreneurial company. *International Journal of Tourism Research, 10*(5), 467–479. doi:10.1002/jtr.681

Lu, H., While, K., & Bariball, K. (2005). Job satisfaction among nurses: A literature review. *International Journal of Nursing Studies, 42*(2), 211–227. doi:10.1016/j.ijnurstu.2004.09.003 PMID:15680619

Luhmann, N. (1973). *Vertrauen. Ein Mechanismus der Reduktion sozialer Komplexität.* Stuttgart: Enke Verlag.

Luhmann, N. (1979). *Trust and Power.* Chichester, UK: John Wiley & Sons.

Luhmann, N. (1984). *Soziale Systeme. Grundriss einer allgemeinen Theorie.* Frankfurt am Main: Suhrkamp Verlag.

Luhmann, N. (2000). *Organisation und Entscheidung.* Wiesbaden: Westdeutscher Verlag. doi:10.1007/978-3-322-97093-0

Lukinykh. (2009). *A comparison of Russian and Hungarian Business Cultures.* Budapesti Gazdasági Főiskola – Magyar tudomany unnepe.

Luthans, F. (2006). *Organisational Behaviour* (10th Indonesian Edition). Yogyakarta: Penerbit Andi.

Lynch, R. (2012). *Strategic Management* (6th ed.). Pearson Prentice Hall.

Lyon, F., & Sepulveda, L. (2009). Mapping social enterprise: Past approaches, challenges and future direction. *Social Enterprise Journal, 5*(1), 83–94. doi:10.1108/17508610910956426

Maathai, W. (2006). *Unbowed: a memoir.* New York: Alfred A. Knopf.

Magnusson, P., Wilson, R. T., Zdravkovic, S., Zhou, J. X., & Westjohn, S. A. (2008). Breaking through the cultural clutter cultural and institutional frameworks. *International Marketing Review, 25*(2), 183–201. doi:10.1108/02651330810866272

Magun, V., & Rudnev, M. (2008). Zhiznennye tsennosti rossiiskogo naseleniia: skhodstva i otlichiia v sravnenii s drugimi evropeiskimi stranami. Vestnik obshchestvennogo mneniia, (1), 33-58.

Magun, V., & Rudnev, M. (2010). Values of the Russian population: Similarities and differences in comparison with other European countries. *Sociological Research, 49*(4), 3–57. doi:10.2753/SOR1061-0154490401

Mahatanankoon, P., Anandarajan, M., & Igbaria, M. (2004). Development of a measure of personal web usage in the workplace. *Cyberpsychology & Behavior, 7*(1), 93–104. doi:10.1089/109493104322820165 PMID:15006174

Maher, C. (2009). Managing Career Development in the Not for Profit Sector. Business Leadership Review, 6(4).

Maher, C. (2013). A Qualitative Case Study Approach to Understanding Third Sector Managers' Career Orientations. Work Based Learning e-Journal International, 3(2).

Maher, A. (2004). Learning outcomes in higher education: Implications for curriculum design and student learning. *Journal of Hospitality, Leisure, Sport and Tourism Education, 3*(2), 46–54. doi:10.3794/johlste.32.78

Maher, C. (2015a). Social Enterprise Manager's Career Path Preferences. *International Journal of Globalisation and Small Business, 7*(1).

Maher, C. (2015b). *Public Policies Impact on Third Sector Social Enterprises in UK Regions.* IGI Global.

Maher, C. (2016). Career anchors of social enterprise managers in the UK – an empirical analysis, *J. International Business and Entrepreneurship Development, 9*(4), 398–416. doi:10.1504/JIBED.2016.080019

Mahsud, R., Yukl, G., & Prussia, G. (2010). Leader empathy, ethical leadership, and relations-oriented behaviors as antecedents of leader-member exchange quality. *Journal of Managerial Psychology, 25*(6), 561–577. doi:10.1108/02683941011056932

Maira, A., & Scott-Morgan, P. (1997). *The Accelerating Organization. Embracing the Human Face of Change.* New York: McGraw Hill.

Makowska, S. (2016). *Adaptacja nowo zatrudnionych pracownikow a ich zaangazowanie w prace* (unpublished master's thesis). University of Lodz, Poland.

Malakhov. V. (2014). Cultural differences and political borders in the era of global migration. *New Literary Review.*

Malhotra, N. K., Kim, S. S., & Patil, A. (2006). Common method variance in IS research: A comparison of alternative approaches and reanalysis of past research. *Management Science, 52*(12), 1865–1883. doi:10.1287/mnsc.1060.0597

Malik, F. (2014). *Führen, leisten, leben. Wirksames Management für eine neue Welt.* Frankfurt, New York: Campus Verlag.

Malik, F. (2014). *Wenn Grenzen keine sind. Management und Bergsteigen.* Frankfurt am Main: Campus Verlag.

Malik, S. H. (2013). Relationship between Leader Behaviors and Employees' Job Satisfaction: A Path-Goal Approach. *Pakistan Journal of Commerce and Social Sciences, 7*(1), 209–222.

Mancheno-Smoak, L., Endres, G., Potak, R., & Athanasaw, Y. (2009). The individual cultural values and job satisfaction of the transformational leader. *Organization Development Journal, 27*(3), 9–21.

Mangaliso, M. P. (2001). Building competitive advantage from ubuntu: Management lessons from South Africa. *The Academy of Management Executive, 15*(3), 23–33. doi:10.5465/AME.2001.5229453

Manikutty, S., Anuradha, N. S., & Hansen, K. (2007). Does culture influence learning styles in higher education? *International Journal of Learning and Change, 2*(1), 70–87. doi:10.1504/IJLC.2007.014896

Mansfield, E. (2013). Composition of R & D expenditures: Relationship to size of firm, concentration and innovative output. *The Review of Economics and Statistics, 63*(1), 610–615.

Manz, C. C., & Sims, H. P. Jr. (1993). *Business without bosses: How self-managing teams are building high performance companies.* New York: Wiley.

Manzoor, A., Awan, H., & Mariam, S. (2012). Investigating the impact of work stress on job performance: A study on textile sector of Faisalabad. *Asian Journal of Business and Management Sciences, 2*(1), 20–28.

March, J. G. (2011). Exploration and exploitation in organizational learning. *Organization Science, 2*(1), 71–87. doi:10.1287/orsc.2.1.71

Marguardt, M. J. (2002). *Building the Learning Organization.* New York: McGraw-Hill.

Mark, A. (2005). Organizing emotions in health care. *Journal of Health Organization and Management, 19*(4-5), 277–289. doi:10.1108/14777260510615332 PMID:16206913

Marklund, S., Bolin, M., & von Essen, J. (2008). Can Individual Health Differences Be Explained by Workplace Characteristics? — A Multilevel Analysis. *Social Science & Medicine, 66*(3), 650–662. doi:10.1016/j.socscimed.2007.09.008 PMID:17996347

Marks, M. A., Mathieu, J. E., & Zaccaro, S. J. (2001). A temporally based framework and taxonomy of team processes. *Academy of Management Review, 26*(3), 356–376.

Marks, S. C. (2000). Ubuntu, Spirit of Africa: Example for the World. In S. C. Marks (Ed.), *Watching the wind: conflict resolution during South Africa's transition to democracy* (pp. 181–190). Washington, DC: United States Institute of Peace Press.

Marktanner, M., & Wilson, M. (2016). The economic cost of Wasta in the Arab world: an empirical approach. In M. A. Ramady (Ed.), *The Political Economy of Wasta: Use and Abuse of Social Capital Networking* (pp. 79–95). New York: Springer International. doi:10.1007/978-3-319-22201-1_6

Marquis, B. L., & Huston, C. J. (2009). *Leadership Roles and Management Functions in Nursing: Theory and Application* (6th ed.). Philadelphia, PA: Wolters/Kluwer/Lippincott Williams and Wilkins.

Martens, B., & Michailow, M. (2003). Konvergenzen und Divergenzen zwischen dem ost- und westdeutschen Management – Ergebnisse einer Befragung von Leitern mittelständischer Industrieunternehmen in Ost- und Westdeutschland. In *SFB 580 – Mitteilungen, Nr. 10*. Jena: Friedrich-Schiller-Universität.

Martinez-Sanchez, A., Vela-Jimenez, M.J., Perez-Perez, M., & de-Luis-Carnicer, P. (2008). Workplace flexibility and innovation. The moderator effect of intra-organizational cooperation. *Personal Review, 37*(6).

Mason. (2016). *International management*. Retrieved from http://www.referenceforbusiness.com/management/Gr-Int/International-Management.html

Matten, D., & Moon, J. (2005). A conceptual framework of CSR. In A. Habisch, J. Jonker, M. Wegner, & R. Schmidpeter (Eds.), *Corporate Social Responsibility across Europe* (pp. 335–356). Berlin: Springer.

Matteson, M. T., & Ivancevich, J. M. (1979). Organizational Stressors and Heart Disease: A Research Model. *Academy of Management Review, 4*(3), 347–357.

Matthews, G., Deary, I. J., & Whiteman, M. C. (2003). *Personality Traits*. Cambridge, UK: Cambridge University Press. doi:10.1017/CBO9780511812736

Maturana, H. (1982). *Erkennen Die Organisation und Verkörperung von Wirklichkeit*. Braunschweig: Vieweg.

Maurrasse, D. J. (2002). Higher education-community partnerships: Assessing progress in the field. *Nonprofit and Voluntary Sector Quarterly, 31*(1), 131–139. doi:10.1177/0899764002311006

Mbigi, L., & Maree, J. (2005). *Ubuntu: The spirit of African transformation management*. Randburg: Knowledge Resources.

McCall, M. (1987). *High Flyers: Developing the Next Generation of Leaders*. Boston: Harvard Business School Press.

McCauley, C. D., Ruderman, M. N., Ohlott, P. J., & Morrow, J. E. (1994). Assessing the developmental components of managerial jobs. *The Journal of Applied Psychology, 79*(4), 544–560. doi:10.1037/0021-9010.79.4.544

McDonald, G. M. (2004). A case example: Integrating ethics into the academic business curriculum. *Journal of Business Ethics, 54*(4), 371–384. doi:10.1007/s10551-004-1826-9

Mcelroy, T., & Mascari, D. (2007). Temporal framing when is it going to happen? How temporal distance influences processing for risky-choice framing tasks. *Social Cognition, 25*(4), 495–517. doi:10.1521/soco.2007.25.4.495

McGee-Cooper, A., & Trammell, D. (2002). From Hero-as-Leader to Servant-as-Leader. In Focus on Leadership. Servant Leadership for the 21st Century, (p. 143). New York: John Wiley & Sons, Inc.

McGregor, D. (1960). Theory X and theory Y. *Organization Theory*, 358-374.

Mcguire, J. T., & Kable, J. W. (2012). Decision makers calibrate behavioral persistence on the basis of time-interval experience. *Cognition, 124*(2), 216–226. doi:10.1016/j.cognition.2012.03.008 PMID:22533999

Mckaskill, T. (2010). *Ultimate Acquisitions: Unlock high growth potential through smart acquisitions*. Windsor: Breakthrough Publications.

McLaren, L. (2016). Immigration, national identity and political trust in European democracies. *Journal of Ethnic and Migration Studies*, 1–21. doi:10.1080/1369183X.2016.1197772

McLean, G. N. (2005). *Organization Development: Principles, Processes, Performance*. San Francisco: Berrett-Koehler Publishers.

McNamara, K. H. (2010). Fostering sustainability in higher education: A mixed-methods study of transformative leadership and change strategies. *Environmental Practice, 12*(1), 48–58. doi:10.1017/S1466046609990445

McWilliams, A., & Siegel, D. (2001). Corporate Social Responsibility: A Theory of the Firm Perspective. *Academy of Management Review, 26*(1), 117–227.

Meadows, D. (2010). *Die Grenzen des Denkens. Wie wir sie mit Systemen erkennen und überwinden können*. München: Oekom Publishers.

Mears, P., & Voehl, F. (2000). *Tworzenie zespołu. Nauka w sztucznie stworzonym środowisku*. Kludzienko: Centrum Kreowania Liderow Grupa Holdingowa S.A.

Meindl, J. R., Ehrlich, S. B., & Dukerich, J. M. (1985). The romance of leadership. *Administrative Science Quarterly, 30*(1), 78–102. doi:10.2307/2392813

Melamed, S., Shirom, A., Toker, S., Berliner, S., & Shapira, I. (2006). Burnout and risk of cardiovascular disease: Evidence, possible causal paths, and promising research directions. *Psychological Bulletin, 132*(3), 327–353. doi:10.1037/0033-2909.132.3.327 PMID:16719565

Mellor, N., Mackay, C., Packham, C., Jones, R., Palferman, D., Webster, S., & Kelly, P. (2011). Management Standards and work-related stress in Great Britain: Progress on their implementation. *Safety Science, 49*(7), 1040–1046. doi:10.1016/j.ssci.2011.01.010

Melnick, D. (2014). Employee internet access in the workplace: Unleashing the power of the employee to protect the organization. In *Compliance & Ethics Professional* (pp. 33–38). The Society of Corporate Compliance and Ethics. Retrieved from www.corporatecompliance.org

Menkiti, I. A. (1984). Person and community in African traditional thought. *African Philosophy: An Introduction, 3*, 171-182.

Mental Health Commission. (2010). *What is mental health?* Retrieved 22 July, 2016 from: http://www.mentalhealth.wa.gov.au/mental_illness_and_health/mh_whatis.aspx

Mental Health Foundation. (2016). *About mental health*. Retrieved 22 July, 2016 from: https://www.mentalhealth.org.uk/your-mental-health/about-mental-health/what-mental-health

Meyer, J. P., Irving, P. G., & Allen, N. J. (1998). Examination of the combined effects of work values and early work experiences on organizational commitment. *Journal of Organizational Behavior*, *19*(1), 29–52. doi:10.1002/(SICI)1099-1379(199801)19:1<29::AID-JOB818>3.0.CO;2-U

Michie, S., & Williams, S. (2003). Reducing work related psychological ill health and sickness absence: A systematic literature review. *Occupational and Environmental Medicine*, *60*(1), 6–9. doi:10.1136/oem.60.1.3 PMID:12499449

Midgley, G., Cavana, R. Y., Brocklesby, J., Foote, J., Wood, D. R., & Driscoll, A. A. (2013). Towards a new framework for evaluating systemic problem structuring methods. *European Journal of Operational Research*, *229*(1), 143–154. doi:10.1016/j.ejor.2013.01.047

Mihaela, H., Claudia, O., & Lucian, B. (2011). Culture and national competitiveness. *African Journal of Business Management*, *5*(April), 3056–3062.

Mika, S. (1981). *Psychologia spoleczna*. Warszawa: PWN.

Miles, M. B., & Huberman, A. M. (1994). *Qualitative Data Analysis* (2nd ed.). Thousand Oak, CA: Sage.

Miller, D., & Friesen, P. H. (1983). Strategy making and environment: The third link. *Strategic Management Journal*, *4*(3), 221–235. doi:10.1002/smj.4250040304

Miller, E. K., & Cohen, J. D. (2001). An integrative theory of prefrontal cortex function. *Annual Review of Neuroscience*, *24*(1), 167–202. doi:10.1146/annurev.neuro.24.1.167 PMID:11283309

Miller, N. M., & McGowen, R. K. (2000). The painful truth: Physicians are not invincible. *Southern Medical Journal*, *93*(10), 966–973. doi:10.1097/00007611-200093100-00004 PMID:11147478

Mill, J. S. (2006). *On Liberty*. Jerusalem: Shalem Publisher.

Mindtools.com. (2017). Retrieved from https://www.mindtools.com/pages/article/seven-dimensions.htm

Mingers, J. (2000). Variety Is the Spice of Life: Combining Soft and Hard OR/MS Methods. *International Transactions in Operational Research*, *7*(6), 673–691. doi:10.1111/j.1475-3995.2000.tb00224.x

Mingers, J., & Rosenhead, J. (2004). Problem Structuring Methods in Action. *European Journal of Operational Research*, *152*(3), 530–554. doi:10.1016/S0377-2217(03)00056-0

Miniwatts Marketing Group. (2016). *Internet users in the world by regions June 2016*. Retrieved November 7, 2016, from http://www.internetworldstats.com/stats.htm

Mintzberg, H. (1994). The fall and rise of strategic-planning. *Harvard Business Review*, *72*(1), 107–114.

Mintzberg, H. (1994). *The Rise and Fall of Strategic Planning*. New York: The Free Press.

Mintzberg, H., Raisinghani, D., & Theoret, A. (1976). The structure of unstructured decision processes. *Administrative Science Quarterly*, *21*(2), 246–275. doi:10.2307/2392045

Mischel, W. (1973). Towards a cognitive social learning reconceptualization of personality. *Psychological Review*, *80*(4), 252–283. doi:10.1037/h0035002 PMID:4721473

Mishra, M., & Pandey, S. (2014). A theoretical model on the determinants of workplace deviance among employees in the public service organizations of India. *International Journal of Business Behavior*, *2*(3), 1321–1337.

Misztal, B. (1996). *Trust in Modern Societies: The Search for the Bases of Social Order*. Polity Press.

Mitchell, R., Shepherd, D., & Sharfman, M. (2011). Erratic strategic decisions: When and why managers are inconsistent in strategic decision making. *Strategic Management Journal, 32*(7), 683–704. doi:10.1002/smj.905

Mittal, V., & Sindhu, E. (2012). Emotional Intelligence & Leadership. *Global Journal of Management and Business Research, 12*(16), 35–38.

Mohammadi, A., Sarhanggi, F., Ebadi, A., Daneshmandi, M., Reiisifar, A., Amiri, F., & Hajamini, Z. (2011). Relationship between psychological problems and quality of work life of Intensive Care Units Nurses. *Iranian Journal of Critical Care Nursing, 4*(3), 135–140.

Mohr, J., & Spekman, R. (1994). Characteristics of partnership success: Partnership attributes, communication behavior, and conflict resolution techniques. *Strategic Management Journal, 15*(2), 135–152. doi:10.1002/smj.4250150205

Mold, A. (2006). The welfare branch of the alternative society? The work of drug organisations Release, 19671978. *20 Century British History, 17*(1), 50–73. doi:10.1093/tcbh/hwi064

Mondlane, H., Claudio, F., & Khan, M. (2016). Remedying Africas self-propelled corruption: The missing link. *Politikon, 43*(3), 345–370. doi:10.1080/02589346.2016.1160859

Montinola, G. R., & Jackman, R. W. (2002). Sources of corruption: A cross-country study. *Sources of Corruption, 32,* 147–170.

Moody, G. D., & Siponen, M. (2013). Using the theory of interpersonal behavior to explain non-work-related personal use of the Internet at work. *Information & Management, 50*(6), 322–335. doi:10.1016/j.im.2013.04.005

Moreira, A. C. (2014). Single minute exchange of die and organizational innovation in seven small and medium-sized firms. In J. L. Carcia-Alcaraz, A. A. Maldonado-Macias, & G. Cortes-Robles (Eds.), *Lean manufacturing in the developing world. Methodology, case studies and trends from Latin America* (pp. 483–499). Springer Verlag. doi:10.1007/978-3-319-04951-9_23

Moreira, A. C., Carneiro, L., & Tavares, M. (2007). Critical technologies for the north of Portugal in 2015: The case of ITCE sectors – information technologies, communications and electronics. *International Journal of Foresight and Innovation Policy, 3*(2), 187–206. doi:10.1504/IJFIP.2007.011624

Moreira, A. C., & Vale, A. A. (2016). Sectoral systems of innovation and nanotechnology. Challenges ahead. In M. Peris-Ortiz, J. Ferreira, L. Farinha, & N. Fernandes (Eds.), *Multiple helix ecosystems for sustainable competitiveness* (pp. 147–168). Heidelberg, Germany: Springer International Publishing Switzerland. doi:10.1007/978-3-319-29677-7_10

Mosadegh Rad, A. M. (2003). The role of participative management (suggestion system) in hospital effectiveness and efficiency. *Research in Medical Sciences, 8*(3), 85–89.

Mosadegh Rad, A. M., & Yarmohammadian, M. H. (2006). A study of relationship between managers leadership style and employees job satisfaction. *Leadership in Health Services, 19*(2), 11–28. doi:10.1108/13660750610665008 PMID:16875105

Moskal, B. M., & Skokan, C. K. (2011). Supporting the k-12 classroom through university outreach. *Journal of Higher Education Outreach & Engagement, 23.*

Mrayyan, M. T. (2006). Jordanian nurses job satisfaction, patients satisfaction and quality of nursing care. *International Nursing Review, 53*(3), 224–230. doi:10.1111/j.1466-7657.2006.00439.x PMID:16879186

Muchinsky, P. M. (2000). Emotions in the workplace: The neglect of organizational behavior. *Journal of Organizational Behavior, 21*(7), 801–805. doi:10.1002/1099-1379(200011)21:7<801::AID-JOB999>3.0.CO;2-A

Muchinsky, P. M. (2006). *Psychology Applied to Work: An Introduction to Industrial and Organisational Psychology* (8th ed.). Belmont, CA: Thompson/Wadsworth.

Mueller, S. L., & Thomas, A. S. (2000). Culture and entrepreneurial potential: A nine country study of locus of control and innovativeness. *Journal of Business Venturing*, *16*(1), 51–75. doi:10.1016/S0883-9026(99)00039-7

Mullins, L. J. (2006). *Essentials of organisational behavior*. Harlow, UK: Prentice Hall.

Mumford, M. D., Zaccaro, S. J., Harding, F. D., Jacobs, T. O., & Fleishman, E. A. (2000). Leadership skills for a changing world: Solving complex social problems. *The Leadership Quarterly*, *11*(1), 11–35. doi:10.1016/S1048-9843(99)00041-7

Munda, G. (1997). Environmental economics, ecological economics, and the concept of sustainable development. *Environmental Values*, *6*(2), 213–233. doi:10.3197/096327197776679158

Munson, J. M., & Posner, B. Z. (1979). Values of engineers and managing engineers. *IEEE Transactions on Engineering Management*, *26*(4), 94–100. doi:10.1109/TEM.1979.6447357

Murithi, T. (2006). Practical peacemaking wisdom from Africa: Reflections on Ubuntu. *The Journal of Pan African Studies*, *1*(4), 25–34.

Murray, J. (2009). The wider social benefits of higher education: What do we know about them? *Australian Journal of Education*, *53*(3), 230–244. doi:10.1177/000494410905300303

Musek, J., & Pečjak, V. (2001). *Psihologija*. Ljubljana, Slovenia: Educy.

Mustafa, G., & Lines, R. (2012). Paternalism as a predictor of leadership behaviors: A bi-level analysis. *Eurasian Business Review*, *2*(1), 63–92.

Mustafa, G., & Lines, R. (2014). Influence of leadership on job satisfaction: The moderating effects of follower individual-level masculinity–femininity values. *The Journal of Leadership Studies*, *7*(4), 23–39. doi:10.1002/jls.21307

Myers, D. G. (2000). Hope and happiness. In J. Gillham (Ed.), *The science of optimism and hope*. Radnor, PA: Templeton Foundation Press.

Myers, D. G. (2001). *Political and economic theory meet social psychology. (Review of Robert E. Lane's The loss of happiness in market democracies.).* Contemporary Psychology.

Nadinloyi, K. B., Sadeghi, H., & Hajloo, N. (2013). Relationship Between Job Satisfaction and Employees Mental Health. *Procedia: Social and Behavioral Sciences*, *84*, 293–297. doi:10.1016/j.sbspro.2013.06.554

Nafukho, F. M. (2006). Ubuntu worldview: A traditional African view of adult learning in the workplace. *Advances in Developing Human Resources*, *8*(3), 408–415. doi:10.1177/1523422306288434

Naidu, N. G. (2014). Emotional intelligence in leadership. *International Journal of Entrepreneurship & Business Environment Perspectives*, *3*(1). Retrieved from http://pezzottaitejournals.net/index.php/IJEBEP/article/view/1115

Nakata, A., Haratani, T., Takahashi, M., Kawakami, N., Arito, H., Kobayashi, F., & Araki, S. (2004). Job stress, social support and prevalence of insomnia in a population of Japanese daytime workers. *Social Science & Medicine*, *59*(8), 1719–1730. doi:10.1016/j.socscimed.2004.02.002 PMID:15279928

Nakata, C., & Sivakumar, K. (2006). National culture and new product development: An integrative review. *Journal of Marketing*, *60*(1), 61–72. doi:10.2307/1251888

National Alliance of Mental Illness. (2011). *Mental health*. Retrieved 22 July, 2016 from: http://www.nami.org/mental+health&searchmode

Nauwelaers, C., & Reid, A. (2002). Learning innovation policy in a market-based context: Process, issues and challenges for eu candidate countries. *Journal of International Relations and Development*, *5*(4), 357–379.

NBP. (2016). *Kwartalny raport o rynku pracy w I kw. 2016 r.* Retrieved from http://www.nbp.pl/publikacje/rynek_pracy/rynek_pracy_2016_1kw.pdf

Nedelko, Z., & Mayrhofer, W. (2012). *The influence of managerial personal values on leadership style. Management re-imagined.* Paper presented at the 11th World Congress of the International Federation of Scholarly Associations of Management, Limerick, Ireland.

Nedelko, Z., & Potocan, V. (2013). Ethics in public administration: Evidence from slovenia. *Transylvanian Review of Administrative Sciences*, 88-108.

Nedelko, Z., & Potocan, V. (2013). The role of management innovativeness in modern organizations. *Journal of Enterprising Communities*, *7*(1), 36–49. doi:10.1108/17506201311315590

Newman, F., Couturier, L., & Scurry, J. (2004). *The future of higher education.* San Francisco: Jossey-Bass.

Ng, T. W., & Feldman, D. C. (2014). Subjective career success: A meta-analytic review. *Journal of Vocational Behavior*, *85*(2), 169–179. doi:10.1016/j.jvb.2014.06.001

Ngunjiri, F. W. (2016). I Am Because We Are Exploring Womens Leadership Under Ubuntu Worldview. *Advances in Developing Human Resources*, *18*(2), 223–242. doi:10.1177/1523422316641416

Nica, E. (2013a). Ethical Challenges of Integrating Local Leadership in the Global Mindset. *Journal of Self-Governance and Management Economics*, *1*(3), 32–37.

Nica, E. (2013b). The importance of leadership development within higher education. *Contemporary Readings in Law and Social Justice*, *5*(2), 189–194.

Nielsen, K., Randall, R., Yarker, J., & Brenner, S. O. (2008). The efects of transformational leadership on followers perceived work characteristics and psychological well-being: A longitudinal study. *Work and Stress*, *22*(1), 16–32. doi:10.1080/02678370801979430

Nielsen, K., Yarker, J., Randall, R., & Munir, F. (2009). The mediating effects of team and self-efficacy on the relationship between transformational leadership, and job satisfaction and psychological well-being in healthcare professionals: A cross-sectional questionnaire survey. *International Journal of Nursing Studies*, *46*(9), 1236–1244. doi:10.1016/j.ijnurstu.2009.03.001 PMID:19345946

Niemi, R. G., Hepburn, M. A., & Chapman, C. (2000). Community service by high school students: A cure for civic ills? *Political Behavior*, *22*(1), 45–69. doi:10.1023/A:1006690417623

Noddings, N. (2003). *Caring.* University of California Press.

Noddings, N. (2016). *Philosophy of Education.* New York: Westview Press.

Nooraie, M. (2008). Decisions magnitude of impact and strategic decision-making process output: The mediating impact of rationality of the decision-making process. *Management Decision*, *46*(4), 640–655. doi:10.1108/00251740810865102

Nooraie, M. (2011). Decisions familiarity and strategic decision-making process output: The mediating impact of rationality of the decision-making process.[IJADS]. *International Journal of Applied Decision Sciences*, *4*(4), 385–400. doi:10.1504/IJADS.2011.043306

Nooraie, M. (2012). Factors influencing strategic decision-making processes. *International Journal of Academic Research in Business and Social Sciences*, *2*(7), 405–429.

Nordlund, A. M., & Garvill, J. (2002). Value structures behind proenvironmental behavior. *Environment and Behavior*, *34*(6), 740–756. doi:10.1177/001391602237244

Norsilan, I. N., Omar, Z., & Ahmad, A. (2014). Workplace deviantbehaviour: A review of typology of workplace deviantbehaviour. *Middle-East Journal of Scientific Research*, *19*, 34–38. doi:10.5829/idosi.mejsr.2014.19.icmrp.6

Nurmi, R., & Üksvärav, R. (1996). Estonian and Finish Management. In R. Lang (Ed.), *Wandel von Unternehmenskulturen in Ostdeutschland und Osteuropa. 2nd Chemnitz East Forum* (pp. 247-256). München: Hampp.

NVCO. (2008). *The UK Civil Society Almanac*. London: NVCO Publications.

O'Connor, J., & McDermott. (1998). *Die Lösung lauert überall. Systemisches Denken verstehen&nutzen.* Kiechzarten bei Freiburg: VAK Velag.

O'Donnell, A. M., & Dansereau, D. F. (1992). Scripted cooperation in student dyads: A method for analyzing and enhancing academic learning and performance. In R. Herz-Lazarowitz & N. Miller (Eds.), *Interaction in cooperative groups: The theoretical anatomy of group learning* (pp. 120–141). New York: Cambridge University Press.

O'Donnell, A. M., & King, A. (Eds.). (1999). *Cognitive perspectives on peer learning*. Mahwah, NJ: Laurence Erlbaum.

O'Reilly, C. A., & Chatman, J. A. (2006). Culture as social control: Corporations, culture and commitment. *Research in Organizational Behavior*, *18*(1), 157–200.

O'Reilly, C. A., Chatman, J., & Caldwell, D. F. (2014). People and organizational culture: A profile comparison approach to assessing person-organization fit. *Academy of Management Journal*, *34*(1), 487–516.

Obholzer, A. (2005). The impact of setting and agency. *Journal of Health Organization and Management*, *19*(4/5), 297–303. doi:10.1108/14777260510615350 PMID:16206915

ODonnell, A. M., & OKelly, J. (1994). Learning from peers: Beyond the rhetoric of positive results. *Educational Psychology Review*, *6*(4), 321–349. doi:10.1007/BF02213419

OECD. (2005). *Oslo manual: Guidelines for collecting and interpreting innovation data*. Paris: OECD Publications and Eurostat.

Ogbonna, E., & Harris, L. C. (2002). Managing organisational culture: Insights from the hospitality industry. *Human Resource Management Journal*, *12*(1), 33–53. doi:10.1111/j.1748-8583.2002.tb00056.x

Olivera, F., & Straus, S. G. (2004). Group-to-individual transfer of learning cognitive and social factors. *Small Group Research*, *35*(4), 440–465. doi:10.1177/1046496404263765

ONeill, T. A., Hambley, L., & Chatellier, G. S. (2014). Cyberslacking, engagement, and personality in distributed work environments. *Computers in Human Behavior*, *40*, 152–160. doi:10.1016/j.chb.2014.08.005

OPG Bik. (2010). *The behavior of assurance professionals: a cross-cultural perspective*. Delft: Eburon. Retrieved from http://www.rug.nl/research/portal/files/13025633/03c3.pdf

OReilly, C. A., Chatham, J. A., & Caldwell, D. F. (1991). People and organizational culture: A profile comparison approach to assessing person-organisation fit. *Academy of Management Journal*, *34*(3), 487–516. doi:10.2307/256404

Osbert-Pociecha, G. (2011). *Zdolnosc do zmian jako sila sprawcza elastycznosci organizacji*. Wroclaw: Wydawnictwo Uniwersytetu Ekonomicznego we Wroclawiu.

Pant, P. N., & Lachman, R. (1998). Value incongruity and strategic choice. *Journal of Management Studies*, *35*(2), 195–212. doi:10.1111/1467-6486.00090

Papadakis, V., Lioukas, S., & Chambers, D. (1998). Strategic decision-making processes: The role of management and context. *Strategic Management Journal, 19*(2), 115–147. doi:10.1002/(SICI)1097-0266(199802)19:2<115::AID-SMJ941>3.0.CO;2-5

Pasque, P. A. (2010). *American higher education, leadership and policy: Critical issues and the public good*. New York: Palgrave Macmillan. doi:10.1057/9780230107755

Pastor, J. C., & Mayo, M. (2008). Transformational leadership among spanish upper echelons: The role of managerial values and goal orientation. *Leadership and Organization Development Journal, 29*(4), 340–358. doi:10.1108/01437730810876140

Patterson, P. G., & Smith, T. (2001). Relationship benefits in service industries: A replication in a Southeast Asian context. *Journal of Services Marketing, 15*(6), 425–443. doi:10.1108/EUM0000000006098

Paul Budde Communication Pty Ltd. (2016). *Global mobile devices market - smartphones, handsets, phablets and tablets*. Retrieved July 1, 2016, from http://www.budde.com.au/Research/Global-Mobile-Devices-Market-Smartphones-Handsets-Phablets-and-Tablets.html

Payne, P. G. (2006). Environmental education and curriculum theory. *The Journal of Environmental Education, 37*(2), 25–35. doi:10.3200/JOEE.37.2.25-35

Pearce, J. A. II, & Robinson, R. B. Jr. (2000). Cultivating guanxi as a foreign investor strategy. *Business Horizons, 43*(1), 31–38. doi:10.1016/S0007-6813(00)87385-1

Pecker, G., & Fine, S. (2015). Using exit surveys to assess counterproductive work behaviors: A case study. *Psychological Reports, 116*(1), 89–96. doi:10.2466/01.PR0.116k16w4 PMID:25650640

Peet, R., & Hartwick, E. (2009). *Theories of development: Contentions, arguments, alternatives*. New York, NY: Guilford Press.

Pekrun, R., Frenzel, A. C., Goetz, T., & Perry, R. P. (2007). *The control-value theory of achievement emotions: an integrative approach to emotions in education. In Emotion in Education* (pp. 13–36). Burlington, MA: Elsevier. doi:10.1016/B978-012372545-5/50003-4

Pelled, L. H., Eisenhardt, K. M., & Xin, K. R. (1999). Exploring the black box: An analysis of work group diversity, conflict, and performance. *Administrative Science Quarterly, 44*(1), 1–28. doi:10.2307/2667029

Penrose, E. T. (1959). *The Theory of the Growth of the Firm*. New York, NY: John Wiley.

Pérez Ríos, J. (2010). Models of organizational cybernetics for diagnosis and design. *Kybernetes, 39*(9/10), 1529–1550. doi:10.1108/03684921011081150

Peterson, A., & Durrant, I. (2013). School leaders perceptions of the impact of extended services on families and communities. *Educational Management Administration & Leadership, 41*(6), 718–735. doi:10.1177/1741143213494190

Peters, T. J., & Waterman, R. H. (1982). *In Search of Excellence: Lessons from America's Best-Run Companies*. New York: Harper & Row.

Peters, T. J., & Waterman, R. H. (1982). *Search of Excellence*. New York: Harper and Row.

Petrides, K. V., & Furnham, A. (2001). Trait emotional intelligence: Psychometric investigation with reference to established trait taxonomies. *European Journal of Personality, 15*(6), 425–448. doi:10.1002/per.416

Petrović, S. P. (2010). *Sistemsko mišljenje, Sistemske metodologije*. Kragujevac, Srbija: Ekonomski fakultet Univerziteta u Kragujevcu.

Petrović, S. P. (2013). A Holistic Instrumentarium for Creative Managing the Problem Situations. *Teme*, *37*(1), 97–116.

Pettigrew, A. M. (1990). Longitudinal field research on change: Theory and practice. *Organization Science*, *1*(3), 267–292. doi:10.1287/orsc.1.3.267

Pew Research Center. (2016). *Social media usage: 2005-2015*. Retrieved July 1, 2016, from http://www.pewinternet.org/2015/10/08/social-networking-usage-2005-2015/

Pfeffer, J., & Salancik, G. R. (1978). *The external control of organizations. A resource dependence perspective*. New York: Harper & Row.

Pfifner, M. (2001). Team Syntegrity – Using Cybernetics for Opinion-Forming in Organizations. MOM Malik Management, 5(9), 75-97.

Piccoli, G., Ahmad, R., & Ives, B. (2001). Web-based virtual learning environments: A research framework and a preliminary assessment of effectiveness in basic IT skills training. *MIS Qarterly*, *25*(4), 401–426. doi:10.2307/3250989

Pistrui, D., Welsch, H. P., Pohl, H. J., Wintermantel, O., & Liao, J. (2003). Entrepreneurship in the New Germany. In D. A. Kirby & A. Watson (Eds.), *Small Firm Development in Developed and Transition Economies: A Reader* (pp. 115–130). Burlington: Ashgate.

Podsakoff, N. P., & Organ, D. W. (1986). Self-reports in organizational research: Problems and prospects. *Journal of Management*, *12*(4), 531–544. doi:10.1177/014920638601200408

Podsakoff, P. M., Mackenzie, S. B., & Podsakoff, N. P. (2003). Common method biases in behavioral research: A critical review of literature and recommended remedies. *The Journal of Applied Psychology*, *88*(5), 879–903. doi:10.1037/0021-9010.88.5.879 PMID:14516251

Pohlmann, M., & Gergs, H.-J. 1996. Manageriale Eliten im Transformationsprozess. In Management in der ostdeutschen Industrie (pp. 63–98). Opladen: Leske + Budrich.

Poland, W. S. (2007). The Limits of Empathy. *The American Imago*, *64*(1), 87–93. doi:10.1353/aim.2007.0017

Popper, M. (2007). Transformational Leadership: A Psychological View. Tel Aviv: Tel Aviv University Press. (in Hebrew)

Popper, M. (2013). Leaders Perceived as Distant and Close. Some Implications for Psychological Theory on Leadership. *The Leadership Quarterly*, *24*(1), 1–8. doi:10.1016/j.leaqua.2012.06.008

Portes, A. (2000). Social capital: Its origins and applications in modern sociology. In E. Lesser (Ed.), *Knowledge and Social Capital* (pp. 43–67). Boston: Butterworth-Heinemann. doi:10.1016/B978-0-7506-7222-1.50006-4

Potočan, V., & Mulej, M. (2007). *Transition into innovative enterprise*. Maribor: Faculty of Economics and Business.

Potocan, V., Mulej, M., & Nedelko, Z. (2013). The influence of employees ethical behavior on enterprises social responsibility. *Systemic Practice and Action Research*, *26*(6), 497–511. doi:10.1007/s11213-013-9299-3

Potocan, V., & Nedelko, Z. (2014). Management innovativeness: A case of slovenian small and medium enterprises. *Transformations in Business & Economics*, *13*(1), 41–59.

Prew, M. (2009). Community involvement in school development. *Educational Management Administration & Leadership*, *37*(6), 824–846. doi:10.1177/1741143209345562

Prieto, I. M., & Revilla, E. (2006). Assessing the impact of learning capability on business performance: Empirical evidence from Spain. *Management Learning*, *3*(4), 499–522. doi:10.1177/1350507606070222

Prive, T. (2012). Top 10 Qualities that make a great leader. *Forbes*. Retrieved 20 Julx, 206 from: www.forbes.com/sites/tanyprive/2012/12/19/top_10_qualities_that_make_a_great_leader/

Probst, G., & Bassi, A. (2014). *Tackling Complexity: A Systemic Approach for Decision Makers*. Greenleaf Publishing.

Probst, G., & Gomez, P. (1997). *Die Praxis des ganzheitlichen Problemlösens. Vernetz denken, unternehmerisch handeln, persönlich überzeugen*. Bern: Gabler Verlag.

Profiles Research Institut. (2010). *Streso darbe valdymas*. Available: http://www.profilesinternational.lt/upload/infofiles/streso_darbe_valdymas.pdf

Purcel, S. Y., Kutash, M., & Cobb, S. (2011). The relationship between nurses stress and nurse staffing factors in a hospital setting. *Journal of Nursing Management, 19*(6), 714–720. doi:10.1111/j.1365-2834.2011.01262.x PMID:21899624

Purdy, N., Spence Laschinger, H. K., Finegan, J., Kerr, M., & Olivera, F. (2010). Effects of work environments on nurse and patient outcomes. *Journal of Nursing Management, 18*(8), 901–913. doi:10.1111/j.1365-2834.2010.01172.x PMID:21073564

Purves, D., Augustine, G. J., Fitzpatrick, D., Katz, L. C., LaMantia, A. S., McNamara, J. O., & Williams, S. M. (2004). Neuroscience (3rd ed.). Sunderland, MA: Sinauer Associates.

Putnam, R. D. (1995). Bowling alone: Americas declining social capital. *Journal of Democracy, 6*(1), 65–78. doi:10.1353/jod.1995.0002

Quinn, R. E., Faerman, S. R., Thompson, M. P., & McGrath, M. (2007). *Becoming a Master Manager: A Competency Framework*. John Wiley & Sons.

Rai, G. S. (1983). Reducing bureaucratic inflexibility. *The Social Service Review, 57*(1), 44–58. doi:10.1086/644071

Rai, G. S. (2013). Job Satisfaction Among Long-Term Care Staff: Bureaucracy Isnt Always Bad. *Administration in Social Work, 37*(1), 90–99. doi:10.1080/03643107.2012.657750

Rajagopalan, N., Rasheed, M. A., & Datta, D. K. (1993). Strategic decision processes: Critical review and future directions. *Journal of Management, 19*(2), 349–384. doi:10.1177/014920639301900207

Rakow, T., & Newell, B. (2010). Degrees of uncertainty: An overview and framework for research on experience-based choice. *Journal of Behavioral Decision Making, 23*(1), 1–14. doi:10.1002/bdm.681

Ralston, D. A., Egri, C. P., Reynaud, E., Srinivasan, N., Furrer, O., Brock, D., & Wallace, A. et al. (2011). A twenty-first century assessment of values across the global workforce. *Journal of Business Ethics, 104*(1), 1–31. doi:10.1007/s10551-011-0835-8

Ralston, D. A., Gustafson, D. J., Cheung, F. M., & Terpstra, R. H. (1993). Differences in managerial values - a study of united-states, hong-kong and prc managers. *Journal of International Business Studies, 24*(2), 249–275. doi:10.1057/palgrave.jibs.8490232

Ralston, D., Egri, C., Furrer, O., Kuo, M.-H., Li, Y., Wangenheim, F., & Weber, M. et al. (2014). Societal-level versus individual-level predictions of ethical behavior: A 48-society study of collectivism and individualism. *Journal of Business Ethics, 122*(2), 283–306.

Ramayah, T. (2010). Personal web usage and work inefficiency. *Business Strategy Series, 11*(5), 295–301. doi:10.1108/17515631011080704

Rametsehoa, M. (1999). *A cultural diversity model for corporate South Africa. (Business Administration MBA)*. Johannesburg: Technikon Witwatersrand.

Ravasi, D., & Schultz, M. (2006). Responding to organizational identity threats: Exploring the role of organizational culture. *Academy of Management Journal*, *49*(1), 433–458. doi:10.5465/AMJ.2006.21794663

Raz, T., Shenhar, A. J., & Dvir, D. (2002). Risk management, project success, and technological uncertainty. *R & D Management*, *32*(2), 101–109. doi:10.1111/1467-9310.00243

Reeves, S., Lewin, S., Espin, S., & Zwarenstein, M. (2011). *Interprofessional teamwork for health and social care* (Vol. 8). John Wiley & Sons.

Remišová, A., & Lašáková, A., & Krzykała-Schaefer, R. (2013). Corporate social responsibility in European countries: The keystones of the concept and intercultural connotations. *Journal for East European Management Studies*, *18*(4), 512–543.

RIA news. (2015, February 17). *Межгосударственные отношения РФ и Венгрии*. Retrieved from: https://ria.ru/spravka/20150217/1048123934.html

Richards, J. (2010). The employee and the Internet age : A reflection, map and research agenda.*28th International Labour Process Conference*, 1–23.

Ridley-Duff, R., & Bull, M. (2015). Understanding social enterprise: Theory and practice. *Sage (Atlanta, Ga.).*

Rieskamp, J. R., & Otto, P. E. (2006). SSL: A theory of how people learn to select strategies. *Journal of Experimental Psychology. General*, *135*(2), 207–236. doi:10.1037/0096-3445.135.2.207 PMID:16719651

Riggio, E. R., & Reichard, R. J. (2008). The emotional and social intelligences of effective leadership: An emotional and social skill approach. *Journal of Managerial Psychology*, *23*(2), 169–185. doi:10.1108/02683940810850808

Riggs, M. L., Warka, J., Babasa, B., Betancourt, R., & Hooker, S. (1994). Development and validation of self-efficacy and outcome expectancy scales for job-related applications. *Educational and Psychological Measurement*, *54*(3), 793–802. doi:10.1177/0013164494054003026

Ringle, C. M., Wende, S., & Becker, J.-M. (2015). *SmartPLS 3*. Bönningstedt: SmartPLS. Retrieved from http://www.smartpls.com

Robbins, S. P. (2004). *Zachowania w organizacji*. Warszawa: Polskie Wydawnictwo Ekonomiczne.

Robbins, S. P., & DeCenzo, D. A. (2002). *Podstawy Zarządzania*. Warszawa: PWE.

Robinson, S. L., & Bennett, R. J. (1995). A typology of deviant workplace behaviors: A multidimensional scaling study. *Academy of Management Journal*, *38*(2), 555–572. doi:10.2307/256693

Roccas, S., Sagiv, L., Schwartz, S. H., & Knafo, A. (2002). The big five personality factors and personal values. *Personality and Social Psychology Bulletin*, *28*(6), 789–801. doi:10.1177/0146167202289008

Rocha, Z. (2008). A experiência psicanalítica: Seus desafios e vicissitudes, hoje e amanhã. *Ágora. Estudos em Teoria Psicanalítica*, *11*(1), 101–116.

Rogers, C.R. (1959). A Therapy, Personality and Interpersonal Relationships, As Developed in Client – Centered. *Psychology: A Study of Science, 3*, 184-256.

Rogers, C. R. (1969). *Freedom to Learn*. Center for Studies of the Person La Joller.

Rogers, E. (2003). *Diffusion of innovations*. New York: Free Press.

Rokeach, M. (1973). *The nature of human values*. New York: The Free Press.

Ronen, S., & Shenkar, O. (1985). Clustering countries on attitudinal dimensions: A review and synthesis. *Academy of Management Review, 10*(3), 435–454.

Rose, J. M., Rose, A. M., & Mckay, B. (2007). Measurement of knowledge structures acquired through instruction, experience, and decision aid use. *International Journal of Accounting Information Systems, 8*(2), 117–137. doi:10.1016/j.accinf.2007.04.002

Rosenhead, J. (1996). Whats the problem? An introduction to problem structuring methods. *Interfaces, 26*(6), 117–131. doi:10.1287/inte.26.6.117

Rosete, D., & Ciarrochi, J. (2005). Emotional intelligence and its relationship to workplace performance outcomes of leadership effectiveness. *Leadership and Organization Development Journal, 26*(5), 388–399. doi:10.1108/01437730510607871

Rothman, H. (1993). The Power of Powerment. *Nation's Business.*

Rouder, J. N., & Ratcliff, R. (2006). Comparing exemplar and rule-based theories of categorization. *Current Directions in Psychological Science, 15*(1), 9–13. doi:10.1111/j.0963-7214.2006.00397.x

Roussel, L., Swansburg, R. C., & Swansburg, R. J. (2009). *Management and leadership for nurse administrators* (5th ed.). Sudbury, MA: Jones and Bartlett Publishers.

Routamaa, V., & Hautala, T. M. (2008). Understanding Cultural Differences-The Values in a Cross-Cultural Context. *The International Review of Business Research Papers, 4*(5), 129–137.

Rowley, J. (2002). Using case studies in research. *Management Research News, 25*(2), 16 – 27.

Rowley, T., & Berman, S. (2000). A brand new brand of corporate social performance. *Business & Society, 39*(4), 397–418. doi:10.1177/000765030003900404

Russian Ministry of Culture. (2017). Retrieved from http://mkrf.ru/

Ryan, R. M., & Deci, E. L. (2000). The darker and brighter sides of human existence: Basic psychological needs as a unifying concept. *Psychological Inquiry, 11*(4), 319–338. doi:10.1207/S15327965PLI1104_03

Sagi, A., & Friedland, N. (2007). The cost of richness: The effect of the size and diversity of decision sets on post-decision regret. *Journal of Personality and Social Psychology, 93*(4), 515–524. doi:10.1037/0022-3514.93.4.515 PMID:17892329

Sagiv, L., & Schwartz, S. H. (2007). Cultural values in organisations: Insights for Europe. *European Journal of International Management, 1*(3), 176–190. doi:10.1504/EJIM.2007.014692

Salanova, M., Lorente, L., Chambel, M. J., & Martínez, I. M. (2011). Linking transformational leadership to nurses extra-role performance: The mediating role of self-efficacy and work engagement. *Journal of Advanced Nursing, 67*(10), 2256–2266. doi:10.1111/j.1365-2648.2011.05652.x PMID:21535088

Salas, E., Sims, D. E., & Burke, C. S. (2005). Is there a Big Five in teamwork? *Small Group Research, 36*(5), 555–599. doi:10.1177/1046496405277134

Samnani, A.-K., Salamon, S. D., & Singh, P. (2014). Negative affect and counterproductive workplace behavior: The moderating role of moral disengagement and gender. *Journal of Business Ethics, 119*(2), 235–244. doi:10.1007/s10551-013-1635-0

Santamaría, L. J. (2014). Critical change for the greater good. *Educational Administration Quarterly, 50*(3), 347–391. doi:10.1177/0013161X13505287

Sanyal, R. (2005). Determinants of bribery in international business: The cultural and economic factors. *Journal of Business Ethics*, *59*(1), 139–145. doi:10.1007/s10551-005-3406-z

Sarin, S., & McDermoll, C. (2003). The Effect of Team Leader Characteristics on Learning, Knowledge Application, and Performance of Cross-Functional New Product Development Teams. *Decision Sciences*, *34*(4), 707–739. doi:10.1111/j.1540-5414.2003.02350.x

Sarros, J. C., & Santora, J. C. (2001). Leaders and values: A cross-cultural study. *Leadership and Organization Development Journal*, *22*(5), 243–248. doi:10.1108/01437730110397310

Saunders, M., Lewis, P., & Thornhill, A. (2011). *Research Methods for Business Students*. Harlow: Pearson Education Ltd.

Sauter, S. L., Murphy, L. R., & Hurrell, J. Jr. (1990). Prevention of work-related psychological disorders. *The American Psychologist*, *45*(10), 1146–1158. doi:10.1037/0003-066X.45.10.1146 PMID:2252233

Schampp, D. (1978). *A cross-cultural study of multinational companies*. New York: Praeger.

Scheick, D. M. (2011). Developing self-aware mindfulness to manage countertransference in the nurse-client relationship: An evaluation and developmental study. *Journal of Professional Nursing*, *27*(2), 114–223. doi:10.1016/j.profnurs.2010.10.005 PMID:21420044

Schein, E. H. (1985). Defining organizational culture. *Classics of Organization Theory*, *3*, 490-502.

Schein, E. (1992). *Organizational culture and leadership: A dynamic view*. San Francisco: Jossey-Bass.

Schein, E. (2003). *Organisationskultur*. Bergisch Gladbach: EHP.

Schein, E. H. (1978). *Career dynamics: Matching individual and organizational needs* (Vol. 6834). Addison Wesley Publishing Company.

Schein, E. H. (1982). *What to observe in a group: Reading book for human relations training*. Bethel, ME: NTL Institute.

Schein, E. H. (1996). Culture: The missing concept in organization studies. *Administrative Science Quarterly*, *41*(2), 229–240. doi:10.2307/2393715

Schein, V. E. (1992). *Organizational Culture and Leadership* (2nd ed.). San Francisco: Jossey-Bass.

Scherer, F. M. (2012). Inter-industry technology flows and productivity growth. *The Review of Economics and Statistics*, *64*(1), 627–634.

Scherer, F. M. (2012). Schumpeter and plausible capitalism. *Journal of Economic Literature*, *30*(3), 1416–1433.

Schermerhorn, J. R. (2008). *Management*. John Wiley & Sons.

Schief, S. (2010). Does location master? An empirical investigation of flexibility patterns in foreign and domestic companies in five European countries. *International Journal of Human Resource Management*, *21*(1-3).

Schiepek, G., Wegener, Ch., Wittig, D., & Harnischmacher, G. (1998). *Synergie und Qualität in Organisationen. Ein Fensterbilderbuch*. Tübingen: dgvt-Verlag.

Schultz, P. W. (2001). The structure of environmental concern: Concern for self, other people, and the biosphere. *Journal of Environmental Psychology*, *21*(4), 327–339. doi:10.1006/jevp.2001.0227

Schultz, P. W., Gouveia, V. V., Cameron, L. D., Tankha, G., Schmuck, P., & Franek, M. (2005). Values and their relationship to environmental concern and conservation behavior. *Journal of Cross-Cultural Psychology*, *36*(4), 457–475. doi:10.1177/0022022105275962

Schultz, P. W., & Zelezny, L. (1999). Values as predictors of environmental attitudes: Evidence for consistency across 14 countries. *Journal of Environmental Psychology, 19*(3), 255–265. doi:10.1006/jevp.1999.0129

Schulz, M., Damkroger, A., Heins, C., Wehlitz, L., Löhr, M., Driessen, M., & Wingenfeld, K. et al. (2009). Effort-reward imbalance and burnout among German nurses in medical compared with psychiatric hospital settings. *Journal of Psychiatric and Mental Health Nursing, 16*(3), 225–233. doi:10.1111/j.1365-2850.2008.01355.x PMID:19291150

Schumpeter, J. (1942). *Capitalism, socialism and democracy*. London: Allen&Unwin.

Schwaninger, M. (2000). Managing Complexity – The Path Toward Intelligent Organization. *Systemic Practice and Action Research, 13*(2), 207–241. doi:10.1023/A:1009546721353

Schwaninger, M. (2006). *Intelligent Organizations – Powerful Models for Systemic Management*. Berlin, Germany: Springer.

Schwartz, B. (2009). *Our Loss of Wisdom*. Retrieved from https://www.ted.com/talks/barry_schwartz_on_our_loss_of_wisdom

Schwartz, S. H. (1999). A Theory of Cultural Values and Some Implications for Work. Applied Psychology: An International Review, 48(1), 23-47. doi:10.1111/j.1464-0597.1999.tb00047.x

Schwartz, S. (1994). Beyond individualism/collectivism: New cultural dimensions of values. In U. Kim, H. C. Triandis, Ç. Kagitçibasi, S.-C. Choi, & G. Yoon (Eds.), *Individualism and collectivism: Theory, method, and applications* (pp. 85–119). Thousand Oaks, CA: Sage Publications.

Schwartz, S. (2008). Personal values and socially significant behavior. *International Journal of Psychology, 43*(3-4), 168–168.

Schwartz, S. H. (1992). Universals in the content and structure of values - theoretical advances and empirical tests in 20 countries. *Advances in Experimental Social Psychology, 25*, 1–65. doi:10.1016/S0065-2601(08)60281-6

Schwartz, S. H. (1994). Are there universal aspects in the structure and contents of human values? *The Journal of Social Issues, 50*(4), 19–45. doi:10.1111/j.1540-4560.1994.tb01196.x

Schwartz, S. H. (2011). Studying values: Personal adventure, future directions. *Journal of Cross-Cultural Psychology, 42*(2), 307–319. doi:10.1177/0022022110396925

Schwartz, S. H., & Bilsky, W. (1987). Toward a universal psychological structure of human-values. *Journal of Personality and Social Psychology, 53*(3), 550–562. doi:10.1037/0022-3514.53.3.550

Schwartz, S. H., Schmidt, P., & Davidov, E. (2004). Values in Europe: A Multiple Group Comparison with 20 Countries Using the European Social Survey 2003. *Sixth International Conference on Social Science Methodology*.

Schwarz, N. (2005). When Thinking Feels Difficult: Meta-Cognitive Experiences in Judgment and Decision Making. *Medical Decision Making, 25*(1), 105–112. doi:10.1177/0272989X04273144 PMID:15673588

Schwenk, C. R. (1995). Strategic decision making. *Journal of Management, 21*(3), 471–493. doi:10.1177/014920639502100304

Seers, A., Petty, M. M., & Cashman, J. F. (1995). Team-member exchange under team and traditional management a naturally occurring quasi-experiment. *Group & Organization Management, 20*(1), 18–38. doi:10.1177/1059601195201003

Segal, J., & Smith, M. (2014). *Emotional intelligence: Key skills for raising emotional intelligence*. Retreived May 12, 2015 from: http://www.helpguide.org/mental/eq5_raising_emotional_intelligence.htm

Seider, S. C., Rabinowicz, S. A., & Gillmor, S. C. (2011). The impact of philosophy and theology service-learning experiences upon the public service motivation of participating college students. *The Journal of Higher Education*, *82*(5), 597–628. doi:10.1353/jhe.2011.0031

Seligman, M. E. P., Steen, T. A., Park, N., & Peterson, C. (2005). Positive Psychology Progress: Empirical Validation of Interventions. *The American Psychologist*, *60*(5), 410–421. doi:10.1037/0003-066X.60.5.410 PMID:16045394

Sellgren, S. F., Ekvall, G., & Tomson, G. (2008). Leadership behaviour of nurse managers in relation to job satisfaction and work climate. *Journal of Nursing Management*, *16*(5), 578–587. doi:10.1111/j.1365-2934.2007.00837.x PMID:18558928

Selmer, J. (2000). A quantitative needs assessment technique for cross-cultural work adjustment training. *Human Resource Development Quarterly*, *11*(3), 269–281. doi:10.1002/1532-1096(200023)11:3<269::AID-HRDQ5>3.0.CO;2-6

Selznick, P. (1957). *Leadership in administration: A sociological interpretation*. New York: Row Peterson.

Semler, S. W. (1997). Systematic agreement: A theory of organizational alignment. *Human Resource Development Quarterly*, *8*(1), 23–40. doi:10.1002/hrdq.3920080105

Shalley, C. E., & Perry-Smith, J. E. (2001). Effects of social-psychological factors on creative performance: The role of informational and controlling expected evaluation and modeling experience. *Organizational Behavior and Human Decision Processes*, *84*(1), 1–22. doi:10.1006/obhd.2000.2918 PMID:11162295

Shamay-Tsoory, S. G., Aharon-Peretz, J., & Perry, D. (2009). Two Systems for Empathy: A Double Dissociation between Emotional and Cognitive Empathy in Inferior Frontal Gyrus versus Ventromedial Prefrontal Lesions. *Brain*, *132*(3), 617–627. doi:10.1093/brain/awn279 PMID:18971202

Shamim, S., & Abbasi, A. S. (2012). Interethnic Culture Orientation of Business Managers in Pakistan. *Middle-East Journal of Scientific Research*, *12*(5), 632–642.

Shane, S. (1992). Why do some societies invent more than others? *Journal of Business Venturing*, *7*(1), 29–46. doi:10.1016/0883-9026(92)90033-N

Shane, S. (1993). Cultural influences on national rates of innovation. *Journal of Business Venturing*, *8*(1), 59–73. doi:10.1016/0883-9026(93)90011-S

Shane, S. (1995). Uncertainty avoidance and the preference for innovation championing roles. *Journal of International Business Studies*, *26*(1), 47–68. doi:10.1057/palgrave.jibs.8490165

Sharma, N., & Singh, V. K. (2015). Differential association and imitation as moderators of workplace deviance. In *Twelfth AIMS International Conference on Management* (pp. 2515–2520). Retrieved from http://papers.ssrn.com/sol3/papers.cfm?abstract_id=2548091

Sharma, C., & Mitra, A. (2015). Corruption, governance and firm performance: Evidence from Indian enterprises. *Journal of Policy Modeling*, *37*(5), 835–851. doi:10.1016/j.jpolmod.2015.05.001

Shatzer, R., Caldarella, P., Hallam, P., & Brown, B. (2014). Comparing the effects of instructional and transformational leadership on student achievement: Implications for practice. *Educational Management Administration & Leadership*, *42*(4), 445–459. doi:10.1177/1741143213502192

Shea, C. M., & Howell, J. M. (1999). Charismatic leadership and task feedback: A laboratory study of their effects on self-efficacy and task performance. *The Leadership Quarterly*, *10*(3), 375–396. doi:10.1016/S1048-9843(99)00020-X

Shein, E. H. (1990). Organizational culture. *The American Psychologist*, *45*(2), 109–119. doi:10.1037/0003-066X.45.2.109

Shenhar, A. J., & Dvir, D. (1996). Toward a typological theory of project management. *Research Policy*, 25.

Shenhav, Y., Shrum, W., & Alon, S. (1994). Goodness concepts in the study of organizations: A longitudinal survey of four leading journals. *Organization Studies, 15*(5), 753–776. doi:10.1177/017084069401500506

Shepherd, D. A., Zacharakis, A., & Baron, R. A. (2003). VCs decision processes: Evidence suggesting more experience may not always be better. *Journal of Business Venturing, 18*(3), 381–401. doi:10.1016/S0883-9026(02)00099-X

Shi, X., & Wang, J. (2011). Interpreting Hofstede Model and GLOBE Model: Which Way to Go for Cross-Cultural Research? *International Journal of Business and Management, 6*(5), 99. doi:10.5539/ijbm.v6n5p93

Short, D. C., & Shindell, T. J. (2009). Defining HRD scholar-practitioners. *Advances in Developing Human Resources, 11*(4), 472–485. doi:10.1177/1523422309342225

Shriberg, M. (2002). Institutional assessment tools for sustainability in higher education. *International Journal of Sustainability in Higher Education, 3*(3), 254–270. doi:10.1108/14676370210434714

Siegrist, J. (2002). Reducing social inequalities in health: Work-related strategies. *Scandinavian Journal of Public Health, 30*(59 suppl), 49–53. doi:10.1177/14034948020300030801 PMID:12227965

Sikavica, P., Hunjak, T., Begičević Reƌep, N., & Hernaus, T. (2014). *Poslovno odlučivanje*. Zagreb: Školska knjiga

Simon, F. (2004). *Gemeinsam sind wir blöd? Die Inteligenz von Unternehmen, Managern, Märkten*. Heidelberg: Carl-Auer Verlag.

Simon, F. (2013). *Einführung in die systemische Organisationstheorie*. Heidelberg: Carl-Auer Verlag.

Simon, H. A. (1959). Theories of decision-making in economics and behavioral science. *The American Economic Review, 49*, 253–283.

Sims, R. L., Gong, B., & Ruppel, C. P. (2012). A contingency theory of corruption: The effect of human development and national culture. *The Social Science Journal, 49*(1), 90–97. doi:10.1016/j.soscij.2011.07.005

Sitte, W., & Wohlschlägl, H. (2006). *Beiträge zur Didaktik des Geographie und Wirtschaftskunde*. Wien: Institut für Geographie und Regionalforschung der Universität Wien.

Skakon, J., Nielsen, K., Borg, V., & Guzman, J. (2010). Are leaders' well-being, behaviours and style associated with the affective well-being of their employees? A systematic review of three decades of research. *Work & Stress: An International Journal of Work, Health & Organisations, 24*(2), 17–139.

Skarzynski, P., & Gibson, R. (2008). *Innovation to the core*. Boston: Harvard Business Press.

SKFU. (2014). *Russia and Hungary are at the crossroads of European history: the almanac* (1st ed.). Stavropol-Kaposvar-Moskva.

Skogstad, A., Einarsen, S., Torsheim, T., Schanke Aasland, M. S., & Hetland, H. (2007). The Destructiveness of Laissez-Faire Leadership Behavior. *Journal of Occupational Health Psychology, 12*(1), 80–92. doi:10.1037/1076-8998.12.1.80 PMID:17257068

Slappendel, C. (1996). Perspectives on innovation in organizations. *Organization Studies, 17*(1), 107–129. doi:10.1177/017084069601700105

Smircich, L. (2013). Concepts of culture and organizational analysis. *Administrative Science Quarterly, 28*(1), 339–359.

Smith, J. A. (1995). Semi-structured interviewing and qualitative analysis. In Rethinking Methods of Psychology. Sage. doi:10.4135/9781446221792.n2

Smith, K. (2016). *Marketing: 96 amazing social media statistics and facts for 2016*. Retrieved July 19, 2016, from https://www.brandwatch.com/2016/03/96-amazing-social-media-statistics-and-facts-for-2016/

Smith, P. B., & Schwartz, S. H. (1997). Values. Handbook of Cross-Cultural Psychology, 3(2), 77-118.

Smith, J. O., & Pate, R. N. (2016). Cultures Around the World: A Unique Approach to Youth Cultural Diversity Education. *Journal of Youth Development*, 2(2), 174–179. doi:10.5195/JYD.2007.354

Smith, P. B. (2004). Acquiescent response bias as an aspect of cultural communication style. *Journal of Cross-Cultural Psychology*, 35(1), 50–61. doi:10.1177/0022022103260380

Smith, P. B., Huang, H. J., Harb, C., & Torres, C. (2011). How Distinctive Are Indigenous Ways of Achieving Influence? A Comparative Study of Guanxi, Wasta, Jeitinho, and Pulling Strings. *Journal of Cross-Cultural Psychology*, 43(1), 135–150. doi:10.1177/0022022110381430

Smith, P. B., Peterson, M. F., & Schwartz, S. H. (2002). Cultural values, sources of guidance, and their relevance to managerial behavior: A 47-nation study. *Journal of Cross-Cultural Psychology*, 33(2), 188–208. doi:10.1177/0022022102033002005

Smith, P. B., Torres, C., Leong, C.-H., Budhwar, P., Achoui, M., & Lebedeva, N. (2012). Are indigenous approaches to achieving influence in business organizations distinctive? A comparative study of guanxi, wasta, jeitinho, svyazi and pulling strings. *International Journal of Human Resource Management*, 23(2), 333–348. doi:10.1080/09585192.2011.561232

Song, M. X., & Parry, M. E. (2013). The determinants of Japanese new product success. *JMR, Journal of Marketing Research*, 34(1), 64–76. doi:10.2307/3152065

Song, M. X., Souder, W. E., & Dyer, B. (2015). A causal model of the impact of skills, synergy, and design sensitivity on new product performance. *Journal of Product Innovation Management*, 14(2), 88–101. doi:10.1016/S0737-6782(96)00076-8

Sørensen, J. B. (2012). The strength of corporate culture and the reliability of firm performance. *Administrative Science Quarterly*, 47(1), 70–91. doi:10.2307/3094891

Sorrentino, R. M., Otsubo, Y., Yasunaga, S., Kouhara, S., Szeto, A., & Nezlek, J. (n.d.). *Uncertainty Orientation and Emotional Responses to Everyday Life Within and Across Cultures*. Retrieved from http://iaccp.org/ebook/xian/PDFs/5_4Sorrentino.pdf

Sorrentino, R. M., Hudson, G., & Huber, G. L. (2005). Umysl spoleczny a style reagowania na niepewnosc – roznice indywidualne w kontekscie interpersonalnym. In J. P. Forges, K. D. Williams, & L. Wheeler (Eds.), *Umysl spoleczny. Poznawcze i motywacyjne aspekty zachowan interpersonalnych*. Gdansk: Gdanskie Wydawnictwo Psychologiczne.

Sosik, J. J. (2005). The role of personal values in the charismatic leadership of corporate managers: A model and preliminary field study. *The Leadership Quarterly*, 16(2), 221–244. doi:10.1016/j.leaqua.2005.01.002

Sowa, J. E., Selden, S. C., & Sandfort, J. R. (2004). No longer unmeasurable? A multidimensional integrated model of nonprofit organizational effectiveness. *Nonprofit and Voluntary Sector Quarterly*, 33(4), 711–728. doi:10.1177/0899764004269146

Spałek, S. (2004). *Omowienie podstawowych czynnikow wpływających na niepowodzenie przedsięwzięcia*. Paper presented at the Project Management Conference, Profesjonalizm, Stowarzyszenie Project Management Polska, Jelenia Góra.

Spear, R., & Bidet, E. (2005). Social enterprise for work integration in 12 European countries: A descriptive analysis. *Annals of Public and Cooperative Economics*, 76(2), 195–231. doi:10.1111/j.1370-4788.2005.00276.x

Spector, P. E. (2006). *Industrial and Organisational Psychology: Research and Practice* (4th ed.). John Wiley & Sons.

Speier, C., & Frese, M. (1997). Generalized self-efficacy as a mediator and moderator between control and complexity at work and personal initiative: A longitudinal field study in East Germany. *Human Performance*, *10*(2), 171–192. doi:10.1207/s15327043hup1002_7

Spiegel, T. (2011), *O processo cognitivo e a tomada de decisão: articulações necessárias* (Unpublished doctoral dissertation). Rio de Janeiro Federal University, Rio de Janeiro, Brazil.

Spiegel, T. (2014). An Overview of Cognition Roles in Decision-Making. In J. Wang (Ed.), *Encyclopedia of Business Analytics and Optimization* (pp. 74–84). Hershey, PA: IGI Global. doi:10.4018/978-1-4666-5202-6.ch008

Spielberger, C. D. (1972). *Anxiety: current trends in theory and research* (Vol. 1). New York: Academic Press.

Stachowicz-Stanusch, A. (2004). *Zarządzanie poprzez wartości. Perspektywa rozwoju wspolczesnego przedsiebiorstwa.* Gliwice: Wydawnictwo Politechniki Slaskiej.

Stake, R. E. (2006). *Multiple case studies analysis*. New York: The Guildford press.

Stark, D. (1996). Recombinant property in Eastern European Capitalism. *American Journal of Sociology*, *101*(4), 993–1027. doi:10.1086/230786

Stead, V., & Elliott, C. (2009). *Women's leadership*. New York: Palgrave Macmillan. doi:10.1057/9780230246737

Steel, G. D., Rinne, T., & Fairweather, J. (2012). Personality, nations, and innovation: Relationships between personality traits and national innovation scores. *Cross-Cultural Research*, *46*(1), 3–30. doi:10.1177/1069397111409124

Steers, R. M., & Porter, L. W. (1991). *Motivation and work Behavior*. New York: McGraw Hill.

Stern, P. C. (2000). Toward a coherent theory of environmentally significant behavior. *The Journal of Social Issues*, *56*(3), 407–424. doi:10.1111/0022-4537.00175

Stern, P. C., & Dietz, T. (1994). The value basis of environmental concern. *The Journal of Social Issues*, *50*(3), 65–84. doi:10.1111/j.1540-4560.1994.tb02420.x

Stets, J. E., & Turner, J. H. (2007). *Handbook of the Sociology of Emotions*. New York: Springer.

Steurer, R., & Konrad, A. (2009). Business-society relations in Central-Eastern and Western Europe: How those who lead in sustainability reporting bridge the gap in corporate (social) responsibility. *Scandinavian Journal of Management*, *25*(1), 23–36. doi:10.1016/j.scaman.2008.11.001

Steyn, E., & Steyn, T. F. J. (2009). The challenge to incorporate teamwork as a managerial competency: The case of mainstream South African newsrooms. *Journal of Media Business Studies*, *6*(2), 47–65. doi:10.1080/16522354.2009.11073484

Stoner, J. A. F., Freeman, R. E., & Gilbert, D. R. (2000). *Vadyba*. Kaunas: poligrafija ir informatika.

Stoner, J. A. F., Freeman, R. E., & Gilbert, D. R. (1997). *Kierowanie*. Warszawa: PWE.

Storti, C. (1994). *Cross-cultural dialogues: 74 brief encounters with cultural difference.* Yarmouth, ME: Intercultural Press.

Subotzky, G. (1999). Alternatives to the entrepreneurial university: New modes of knowledge production in community service programs. *Higher Education*, *38*(4), 401–440. doi:10.1023/A:1003714528033

Sullivan, C., & Smithson, J. (2007). Perspectives of homeworkers and their partners on working flexibility and gender equity. *Journal of Human Resources Management*, *3*(3), 448–461. doi:10.1080/09585190601167797

Sullivan, E. J., & Garland, G. (2010). *Practical leadership and management in nursing.* Harlow: Pearson Education Limited.

Supovitz, J. A., & Taylor, B. S. (2005). Systemic education evaluation. *The American Journal of Evaluation, 26*(2), 204–230. doi:10.1177/1098214005276286

Sutherland, A. M., & Dodd, F. (2008). NHS Lanarkshires leadership development programs impact on clinical practice. *International Journal of Health Care Quality Assurance, 21*(6), 569–584. doi:10.1108/09526860810900727 PMID:19055267

Suzuki, K., Ohida, T., Kaneita, Y., Yokoyama, E., Miyake, T., Harano, S., & Uchiyama, M. et al. (2004). Mental Health Status, Shift Work, and Occupational Accidents among Hospital Nurses in Japan. *Journal of Occupational Health, 46*(6), 448–454. doi:10.1539/joh.46.448 PMID:15613767

Svanström, M., Lozano-García, F. J., & Rowe, D. (2008). Learning outcomes for sustainable development in higher education. *International Journal of Sustainability in Higher Education, 9*(3), 339–351. doi:10.1108/14676370810885925

Swanson, D. M. (2009). Where have all the fishes gone?: Living uBuntu as an ethics of research and pedagogical engagement. In D. M. Caracciolo & A. M. N. Mungai (Eds.), *In the spirit of Ubuntu: stories of teaching and research* (pp. 3–21). Rotterdam: Sense.

Swanson, D. M. (2010). Value in shadows: A critical contribution to values education in our times. In T. Lovat, R. Toomey, & N. Clement (Eds.), *International research handbook on values education and student wellbeing* (pp. 137–152). Dordrecht: Springer. doi:10.1007/978-90-481-8675-4_8

Swiatek-Barylska, I. (2016 June). *Socio-demographic characteristics as determinants of person-organization relations. Results from empirical research.* Paper presented at the International Conference of Leadership and Innovations, Berlin, Germany.

Swiatek-Barylska, I. (2013). Zrodla zaufania grupowego we wspolczesnych organizacjach, *Acta Universitatis Lodziensis. Folia Oeconomica, 282,* 261–270.

Syrek, M. (1997). *Menedzer we wspolczesnym przedsiebiorstwie – sylwetka, kwalifikacje, style zarzadzania.* Katowice: Wydawnictwo WSZM i Jo.

Sy, T., & Côté, S. (2004). Emotional intelligence: A key ability to succeed in the matrix organization. *Journal of Management Development, 23*(5), 437–455. doi:10.1108/02621710410537056

Sy, T., Côté, S., & Saavedra, R. (2005). The contagious leader: Impact of the leaders mood on the mood of group members, group affective tone, and group processes. *The Journal of Applied Psychology, 90*(2), 295–305. doi:10.1037/0021-9010.90.2.295 PMID:15769239

Szabo, E., Reber, G., Weibler, J., Brodbeck, F. C., & Wunderer, R. (2001). Values and behavior orientation in leadership studies: Reflections based on findings in three German-speaking countries. *The Leadership Quarterly, 12*(2), 219–244. doi:10.1016/S1048-9843(01)00070-4

Sztompka, P. (2007). *Zaufanie Fundament Spoleczenstwa.* Krakow: Wydawnictwo Znak.

Taghinejad, H., Suhrabi, Z., Kikhavani, S., Jaafarpour, M., & Azadi, A. (2014). Occupational Mental Health: A Study of Work-Related Mental Health among Clinical Nurses. *Journal of Clinical & Diagnostic Research, 8*(9), WC01–WC03. PMID:25386506

Tani, N. S., & Parnell, S. G. (2013). Use the appropriate decision process. In S. G. Parnell, A. T. Bresnick, N. S. Tani, & E. R. Jonson (Eds.), *Handbook of Decision Analysis* (pp. 92–109). John Wiley & Sons. doi:10.1002/9781118515853.ch5

Tannenbaum, R., & Schmidt, W. (1973). How to choose a leadership style. *Harvard Business Review, 51*(3), 58–67.

Tannenbaum, R., & Schmidt, W. H. (2007). Jak wybrac styl przywodztwa. *Harvard Business Review Polska, 4,* 131.

Tannenbaum, S. I., Mathieu, J. E., Salas, E., & Cohen, D. (2012). Teams are changing: Are research and practice evolving fast enough? *Industrial and Organizational Psychology: Perspectives on Science and Practice*, *5*(1), 2–24. doi:10.1111/j.1754-9434.2011.01396.x

Tanzi, V., & Davoodi, H. (1998). Roads to nowhere: How corruption in public investment hurts growth. *Economic Issues*, *12*, 1–12.

Taras, V., Kirkman, B. L., & Steel, P. (2010). Examining the impact of Cultures consequences: A three-decade, multi-level, meta-analytic review of Hofstedes cultural value dimensions. *The Journal of Applied Psychology*, *95*(3), 405–439. doi:10.1037/a0018938 PMID:20476824

Taras, V., & Steel, P. (2009). Beyond Hofstede: Challenging the ten testaments of cross-cultural research. In C. Nakata (Ed.), *Beyond Hofstede: Culture frameworks for global marketing and management* (pp. 40–61). Chicago, IL: Macmillan/Palgrave. doi:10.1057/9780230240834_3

Taras, V., Steel, P., & Kirkman, B. L. (2012). Improving national cultural indices using a longitudinal meta-analysis of Hofstedes dimensions. *Journal of World Business*, *47*(3), 329–341. doi:10.1016/j.jwb.2011.05.001

Taris, T. W., & Kompier, M. A. J. (2005). Job demands, job control, strain and learning behavior: Review and research agenda. In A. S. Antoniou & C. L. Cooper (Eds.), *Research companion to organizational health psychology* (pp. 132–150). Cheltenham, UK: Elgar. doi:10.4337/9781845423308.00015

Taylor, M. Z., & Wilson, S. (2012). Does culture still matter?: The effects of individualism on national innovation rates. *Journal of Business Venturing*, *27*(2), 234–247. doi:10.1016/j.jbusvent.2010.10.001

Teasley, S. D. (1997). Talking about reasoning: How important is the peer in peer collaboration? In L. B. Resnick, R. Saljo, C. Pontecorvo, & B. Burge (Eds.), *Discourse, tools, and reasoning: Essays on situated cognition* (pp. 361–384). Berlin: Springer-Verlag. doi:10.1007/978-3-662-03362-3_16

Teece, D. J. (2015). Firm organization, industrial structure and technological innovation. *Journal of Economic Behavior & Organization*, *31*(1), 193–224.

Terelak, J. F. (2005). *Psychologia organizacji i zarządzania*. Warszawa: Difin.

Terman, L. M. (1904). A Preliminary Study of the Psychology of Leadership. In *Handbook of leadership Research: A Survey of Theory and Research*. Riverside, N.Y.: Free Press.

Thagard, P., & Toombs, E. (2005). Atoms, categorizations and conceptual change. In H. Cohen & C. Lefebvre (Eds.), *Handbook of categorization in cognitive science* (pp. 243–254). New York, NY: Elsevier. doi:10.1016/B978-008044612-7/50065-2

The American Institute of Stress. (2011). Retrieved from http://www.stress.org/about/

The Statistics Portal. (2016). *Leading social networks worldwide as of April 2016, ranked by number of active users (in millions)*. Retrieved July 19, 2016, from http://www.statista.com/statistics/272014/global-social-networks-ranked-by-number-of-users/

The World Databank. (2014). *World Databank*. Retrieved April 20, 2014, from http://databank.worldbank.org/data/home.aspx

The World of Civilizations: The Post-1990. (n.d.). Wayback Machine.

Thielen, K. (2001). Varieties of labour politics in the developed countries. In P. A. Hall & D. Soskice (Eds.), *Varieties of Capitalism: The institutional foundations of comparative advantage* (pp. 71–103). New York: Oxford University Press. doi:10.1093/0199247757.003.0002

Thiry, M. (2002). Combining value and project management into an effective programme management model. *International Journal of Project Management*, *20*(3), 221–227. doi:10.1016/S0263-7863(01)00072-2

Thomas, M. P. (2009). *Regulating Felxibility. The Political Economy of Employment Standards*. Montreal: McGill-Queen's University Press.

Thorpe, J. R. (2015). Do women suffer mental illness more than men? 8 factors behind the gender imbalance in treatment. *Bustle*. Rerieved 28 July, 2016 from: http://www.bustle.com/articles/83245-do-women-suffer-mental-illness-more-than-men-8-factors-behind-the-gender-imbalance-in-treatment

Thorsteinsson, R. B., Brown, R. F., & Richards, C. (2014). The Relationship between Work-Stress, Psychological Stress and Staff Health and Work Outcomes in Office Workers. *Psychology (Savannah, Ga.)*, *5*, 1301–1311.

Tlaiss, H., & Kauser, S. (2011). The importance of wasta in the career success of Middle Eastern managers. *Journal of European Industrial Training*, *35*(5), 467–486. doi:10.1108/03090591111138026

Tompos, A. (2014). Hungarian societal values through business negotiators' practices.*Proceedings of the 14th International Academic Conference*.

Transparency International Website. (2014). *Corruption perception index*. Retrieved April 11, 2014, from http://www.transparency.org/cpi2012/results

Triandis, H. C. (1995). *Individualism & collectivism* (Vol. 5). Boulder, CO: Westview Press.

Triandis, H. C. (1995). *Individualism and Collectivism*. Boulder, CO: Westview Press.

Trocki, M., Grucza, M., & Ogonek, M. (2009). *Zarzadzanie projektami*. Warszawa: PWE.

Trompenaars, F., & Hampden-Turner, C. (2011). *Riding the waves of culture: Understanding diversity in global business*. Nicholas Brealey Publishing.

Tschopp, C., Grote, G., & Gerber, M. (2014). How career orientation shapes the job satisfaction–turnover intention link. *Journal of Organizational Behavior*, *35*(2), 151–171. doi:10.1002/job.1857

Tsutsumi, A., Kayaba, K., Tsutsumi, K., & Igarashi, M. (2001). Association between job strain and prevalence of hypertension: a cross sectional analysis in a Japanese working population with a wide range of occupations: the Jichi Medical School cohort study. *Occupational and Environmental Medicine*, *58*(6), 367–373. doi:10.1136/oem.58.6.367 PMID:11351051

Turner, M. E. (2014). *Groups at work: Theory and research*. Psychology Press.

Turró, A., Urbano, D., & Peris-Ortiz, M. (2013). Culture and innovation: The moderating effect of cultural values on corporate entrepreneurship. *Technological Forecasting and Social Change*, *88*, 360–369. doi:10.1016/j.techfore.2013.10.004

Tushman, M. L., & O'Reilly, C. A. (1997). *Winning through innovation: A practical guide to leading organizational change and renewal*. Boston: Harvard Business School Press.

Tushman, M. L., & OReilly, C. A. III. (1996). The ambidextrous organizations: Managing evolutionary and revolutionary change. *California Management Review*, *38*(4), 8–30. doi:10.2307/41165852

Tuulik, K., & Alas, R. (2005). The impact of the values of top managers upon their subordinates. In R. Lang (Ed.), The End of Transformation (pp. 439-454). München: Hampp.

Tversky, A., & Kahneman, D. (1973). Availability: A heuristic for judging frequency and probability. *Cognitive Psychology, 5*(2), 207–232. doi:10.1016/0010-0285(73)90033-9

Tversky, A., & Kahneman, D. (1981). The framing of decisions and the psychology of choice. *Science, 211*(4481), 453–458. doi:10.1126/science.7455683 PMID:7455683

U.S. Department of Health and Human Services. (n.d.). *Public Health Service Centers for Disease Control and Prevention National Institute for Occupational Safety and Health*. Retrieved from https://www.cdc.gov/niosh/docs/99-101/

Udo, V. E., & Jansson, P. M. (2009). Bridging the gaps for global sustainable development: A quantitative analysis. *Journal of Environmental Management, 90*(12), 3700–3707. doi:10.1016/j.jenvman.2008.12.020 PMID:19500899

Ulman, S.-R. (2013). Corruption and national competitiveness in different stages of country development. *Procedia Economics and Finance, 6*(13), 150–160. doi:10.1016/S2212-5671(13)00127-5

Ulrich, D., & Black, S. (1999). Worldly Wise. *People Management,* 42-46.

Ulrich, W. (1994). *Critical Heuristics of Social Planning – A New Approach to Practcal Philosophy*. Chichester, UK: John Wiley and Sons.

Upenieks, V. V. (2003a). The Interrelationship of Organizational Characteristics of Magnet Hospitals, Nursing Leadership, and Nursing Job Satisfaction. *Health Care Management (Philadelphia, Pa.), 22*(2), 83–98. PMID:12785545

Upenieks, V. V. (2003b). Nurse Leaders Perceptions of What Compromises Successful Leadership in Todays Acute Inpatient Environment. *Nursing Administration Quarterly, 27*(2), 140–152. doi:10.1097/00006216-200304000-00008 PMID:12765106

Usunier, J., & Lee, J. (2005). *Marketing across cultures*. Harlow, UK: Financial Times/Prentice Hall.

Vadi, M. (2005). The relationships between subtypes of collectivism and organizational culture in Estonia. In R. Lang (Ed.), The End of transformation (pp. 267-280). München: Hampp.

Vahey, D., Aiken, L., Sloane, D., Clarke, S., & Vargas, D. (2004). Nurse burnout and patient satisfaction. *Medical Care, 42*(2), 1157–1166. PMID:14734943

Van De Valk, L. J. (2008). Leadership development and social capital: Is There a Relationship. *Journal of Leadership Education, 7*(1), 47-64.

Van den Bossche, P., Gijselaers, W. H., Segers, M., & Kirschner, P. A. (2006). Social and cognitive factors driving teamwork in collaborative learning environments team learning beliefs and behaviors. *Small Group Research, 37*(5), 490–521. doi:10.1177/1046496406292938

Van Der Vegt, G. S., & Bunderson, J. S. (2005). Learning and performance in multidisciplinary teams: The importance of collective team identification. *Academy of Management Journal, 48*(3), 532–547. doi:10.5465/AMJ.2005.17407918

Van Looy, B., Landoni, P., Callaert, J., van Pottelsberghe, B., Sapsalis, E., & Debackere, K. (2011). Entrepreneurial effectiveness of european universities: An empirical assessment of antecedents and trade-offs. *Research Policy, 40*(4), 553–564. doi:10.1016/j.respol.2011.02.001

Vecchio, R. P. (1987). Situational Leadership Theory: An examination of a prescriptive theory. *The Journal of Applied Psychology, 72*(3), 444–451. doi:10.1037/0021-9010.72.3.444

Vestal, K. W., Fraliex, R. D., & Spreier, S. W. (1997). Organizational culture: The critical link between strategy and results. *Hospital & Health Services Administration*, *42*(13), 339–365. PMID:10169292

Vester, F. (2008). *Die Kunst vernetzt zu denken. Ideen und Werkzeuge für einen neuen Umgang mit Komplexität. Der neue Bericht an der Club of Rome*. München: Deutscher Taschenbuch Verlag.

Viegas, C. V., Bond, A. J., Vaz, C. R., Borchardt, M., Pereira, G. M., Selig, P. M., & Varvakis, G. (2016). Critical attributes of sustainability in higher education: A categorisation from literature review. *Journal of Cleaner Production*, *126*, 260–276. doi:10.1016/j.jclepro.2016.02.106

Vigoda-Gadot, E., & Meiri, S. (2008). New public management values and person-organization fit: A socio-psychological approach and empirical examination among public sector personnel. *Public Administration*, *86*(1), 111–131. doi:10.1111/j.1467-9299.2007.00703.x

Virkus, S. (2009). *Dimesnions of Culture: Geert Hofstede*. Tallinn University. Retrieved from: http://www.tlu.ee/~sirvir/IKM/Leadership%20Dimensions/globe_project.html

Vitak, J., Crouse, J., & LaRose, R. (2011). Personal Internet use at work: Understanding cyberslacking. *Computers in Human Behavior*, *27*(5), 1751–1759. doi:10.1016/j.chb.2011.03.002

Vitell, S. J., & Hidalgo, E. R. (2006). The impact of corporate ethical values and enforcement of ethical codes on the perceived importance of ethics in business: A comparison of us and spanish managers. *Journal of Business Ethics*, *64*(1), 31–43. doi:10.1007/s10551-005-4664-5

Vogl, F. (1998). The Supply side of global bribery. *Finance & Development*, *35*(2), 30–33.

Volberda, H. W. (1998). *Building the Flexibility Firm. How to Remain Competitive*. New York: Oxford University Press.

Volonté, C. (2015). Culture and corporate governance: The influence of language and religion in Switzerland. *Management International Review*, *55*(1), 77–118. doi:10.1007/s11575-014-0216-5

von Bertalanffy, L. (1969). *General System Theory. Foundations, Development, Applications*. New York: George Braziller Inc.

Von Winterfeldt, D., & Fasolo, B. (2009). Structuring decision problems: A case study and reflections for practitioners. *European Journal of Operational Research*, *199*(3), 857–866. doi:10.1016/j.ejor.2009.01.063

Vrba, M. (2007). Emotional intelligence skills and leadership behavior in a sample of South Africa. *Management Dynamics*. Retrieved 22 July, 2016 from https://www.questia.com/library/journal/1P3-1357960571/emotional-intelligence-skills-and-leadership-behaviour

Vroom, V. H., & Yetton, P. W. (1973). *Leadership & decision-making*. Pittsburgh, PA: University of Pittsburgh Press.

Waddington, K., & Fletcher, C. (2005). Gossip and emotion in nursing and health-care organizations. *Journal of Health Organization and Management*, *19*(4/5), 378–394. doi:10.1108/14777260510615404 PMID:16206920

Waddock, S., & Bodwell, C. (2007). *Total responsibility management*. Sheffield, UK: Greenleaf Publishing.

Waldman, D. A., de Luque, M. S., Washburn, N., & House, J. R. (2006). Cultural and leadership predictors of Corporate Social Responsibility Values of Top Management: A GLOBE Study of 15 Countries. *Journal of International Business Studies*, *37*(6), 823–837. doi:10.1057/palgrave.jibs.8400230

Wang, J., Tian, J., & Shen, Z. (2013). The effects and moderators of cyber-loafing controls: An empirical study of Chinese public servants. *Information Technology Management*, *14*(4), 269–282. doi:10.1007/s10799-013-0164-y

Wang, X. (2001). Dimensions and current status of project management culture. *Project Management Journal, 32*(4), 4–17.

Wardle, I. (2013). The Drug Treatment Workforce: Lifeline Project. Academic Press.

Ward, S., & Chapman, C. (2003). Transforming project risk management into project uncertainty management. *International Journal of Project Management, 21*(2), 234–236. doi:10.1016/S0263-7863(01)00080-1

Warner, M. (1997). Chinas HRM in Transition: Towards Relative Convergence? *Asia Pacific Business Review, 3*(4), 19–33. doi:10.1080/13602389700000041

Warren, C., White-Means, S., Wicks, M., Chang, C., Gourley, D., & Rice, M. (2011). Cost burden of the presnteeism health outcome: Diverse workforce of nurses and pharmacists. *Journal of Occupational and Environmental Medicine, 53*(1), 90–99. doi:10.1097/JOM.0b013e3182028d38 PMID:21187792

Warr, P. B., Cook, J., & Wall, T. (1979). Scales for the measurement of some work attitudes and aspects of psychological wellbeing. *Journal of Occupational Psychology, 52*(2), 129–148. doi:10.1111/j.2044-8325.1979.tb00448.x

Warwick, P. (2016). An integrated leadership model for leading education for sustainability in higher education and the vital role of students as change agents. *Management in Education, 30*(3), 105–111. doi:10.1177/0892020616653463

Waterman, R. H. Jr, Peters, T. J., & Phillips, J. R. (1980). Structure is not organization. *Business Horizons, 23*(3), 14–26. doi:10.1016/0007-6813(80)90027-0

Watts, D., & Strogatz, S. H. (2008). Collective dynamics of small world networks. *Nature, 393*(1), 440–442. PMID:9623998

Waxman, S. R. (2012). Social categories are shaped by social experience. *Trends in Cognitive Sciences, 16*(11), 531–532. doi:10.1016/j.tics.2012.09.007 PMID:23026021

Way, M., & MacNeil, M. (2006). Organizational characteristics and their effect on health. *Nursing Economics, 24*(2), 67–77. PMID:16676749

Weatherbee, T. G. (2010). Counterproductive use of technology at work: Information & communications technologies and cyberdeviancy. *Human Resource Management Review, 20*(1), 35–44. doi:10.1016/j.hrmr.2009.03.012

Webb, N. (1992). Testing a theoretical model of student interaction and learning in small groups. In R. Hertz-Lazarowitz & N. Miller (Eds.), *Interaction in cooperative groups: The theoretical anatomy of group learning* (pp. 102–119). New York: Cambridge University Press.

Weber, E. U., Shafir, S., & Blais, A. R. (2004). Predicting risk sensitivity in humans and lower animals: Risk as variance or coefficient of variation. *Psychological Review, 111*(2), 430–445. doi:10.1037/0033-295X.111.2.430 PMID:15065916

Weick, K. (1979). *The Social Psychology of Organizing*. McGraw-Hill.

Weick, K. (1985). *Der Prozeß des Organiesierens*. Frankfurt am Main: Suhrkamp Verlag.

Weir, D. (2003). Human resource development in the Middle East: A fourth paradigm. In M. Lee (Ed.), *HRD in a Complex World* (pp. 69–82). London: Routledge. doi:10.4324/9780203410158_chapter_5

Weir, D., Sultan, N., & van de Blunt, S. (2016). Wasta: a scourge or a usement management and business practice. In M. A. Ramady (Ed.), *The Political Economy of Wasta: Use and Abuse of Social Capital Networking* (pp. 23–32). New York: Springer International. doi:10.1007/978-3-319-22201-1_2

Weiten, W. (2008). *Psychology: Themes and Variations*. Cengage Learning.

Welch, C., Piekkari, R., Plakoyiannaki, E., & Paavilainen-Mäntymäki, E. (2010). Theorising from case studies: Towards a pluralist future for international business research. *Journal of International Business Studies, 42*(5), 740–762. doi:10.1057/jibs.2010.55

Wellins, R., & Weaver, P. (2003). From c-level to see-level leadership. *Training & Development, 57*(9), 58–65.

West, A. (2014). Ubuntu and business ethics: Problems, perspectives and prospects. *Journal of Business Ethics, 121*(1), 47–61. doi:10.1007/s10551-013-1669-3

West-Burnham, J. (2002). *Leading and Managing for High Performance*. Australia Principals Center Ltd.

West, C. P., Tan, A. D., Habermann, T. M., Sloan, J. A., & Shanafelt, T. D. (2009). Association of resident fatigue and distress with perceived medical errors. *Journal of the American Medical Association, 302*(12), 1294–1300. doi:10.1001/jama.2009.1389 PMID:19773564

Westerman, J. W., & Cyr, L. A. (2004). An integrative analysis of person-organization fit theories. *International Journal of Selection and Assessment, 12*(3), 252–261. doi:10.1111/j.0965-075X.2004.279_1.x

Weyland, A. (2011). Engagement and talent management of Gen Y. *Industrial and Commercial Training, 43*(7), 439–445. doi:10.1108/00197851111171863

Whitley, R. (1992). The social structuring of Business Systems. In R. Whitley (Ed.), *European Business Systems: Firms and Markets in their National Contexts* (pp. 5–45). New York: Sage.

Whittlesea, B. W. A., Brooks, L. R., & Westcott, C. (1994). After the Learning is over: Factors controlling the selective application of general and particular knowledge. *Journal of Experimental Psychology. Learning, Memory, and Cognition, 20*(2), 259–274. doi:10.1037/0278-7393.20.2.259

WHO. (2001). *World health report. Mental disorders affect one in four people*. Retrieved 21 July, 2016 from at: http://www.who.int/whr/2001/media_centre/press_release/en/

WHO. (2013). *WHO Nursing and midwifery progress report 2008-2012*. Retrieved 20 July, 2016 from: http://www.who.int/hrh/nursing_midwifery/progress_report/en/

WHO. (2016a). *Hospitals*. Health Topics. Retrieved 20 July, 2016 from: http://www.who.int/topics/hospitals/en/

WHO. (2016b).*Mental health: strengthening our response*. Media centre. Retrieved 20 July, 2016 from: http://www.who.int/mediacentre/factsheets/fs220/en/

WHO. (2016c). *Gender and women's mental health*. Gender disparities and mental health: The Facts. Retreived 28 July, 2016 from: http://www.who.int/mental_health/prevention/genderwomen/en/

Wickens, C. D. (1984). Processing resources in attention. In R. Parasuraman & D. R. Davies (Eds.), *Varieties of attention* (pp. 63–101). London, UK: Academic Press.

Wilhite, A. (2006). Protection and social order. *Journal of Economic Behavior & Organization, 61*(1), 691–709. doi:10.1016/j.jebo.2004.07.010

William Todorovic, Z., McNaughton, R. B., & Guild, P. (2011). Entre-u: An entrepreneurial orientation scale for universities. *Technovation, 31*(2–3), 128–137. doi:10.1016/j.technovation.2010.10.009

Williamson, I. O., Burnett, M. F., & Bartol, K. M. (2009). The interactive effect of collectivism and organizational rewards on affective organizational commitment. *Cross Cultural Management: An International Journal, 16*(1), 28–43. doi:10.1108/13527600910930022

Williams, R. (1977). *Marxism and literature* (Vol. 1). Oxford University Press.

Wilms, F. (Ed.). (2012). *Wirkungsgefüge. Einsatzmöglichkeiten und Grenzen in der Unternehmungsführung.* Bern: Haupt Verlag.

Winter, M., Smith, C., Cooke-Davies, T., & Cicmil, S. (2006). *Rethinking project management—Final report. EPSRC Network 2004–2006.* Retrieved February 10, 2008, from http://www.mace.manchester.ac.uk/project/research/management/rethinkpm/final.htm

Wold, H. (1975). Path models with latent variables: The NIPALS approach. In H. M. Blalock, A. Aganbegian, F. M. Borodkin, R. Boudon, & V. Capecchi (Eds.), *Quantitative sociology: International perspectives on mathematical and statistical modeling* (pp. 307–357). New York: Academic Press. doi:10.1016/B978-0-12-103950-9.50017-4

Wong, C., & Law, K. (2002). The effects of leader and follower emotional intelligence on performance and attitude. *The Leadership Quarterly, 13*(3), 243–274. doi:10.1016/S1048-9843(02)00099-1

Wood, D. J. (1991). Corporate Social Performance revisited. *Academy of Management Review, 16*(4), 691–718.

World Values Survey. (2017). Retrieved from: http://www.worldvaluessurvey.org/

WorldatWork. (2015). *Trends in Workplace Flexibility. A report by WorldatWork, underwritten by FlexJobs.* Retrieved from https://www.worldatwork.org/waw/adimLink?id=79123

WorldBank. (2013). *Learning outcomes.* Retrieved 15. September 2013, Retrieved from http://go.worldbank.org/GOB-J17VV90

Wright, P., Szeto, W., & Cheng, L. T. (2002). Guanxi and professional conduct in China: A management development perspective. *International Journal of Human Resource Management, 13*(1), 156–182. doi:10.1080/09585190110083839

Wright, T. S. A., & Wilton, H. (2012). Facilities management directors conceptualizations of sustainability in higher education. *Journal of Cleaner Production, 31*, 118–125. doi:10.1016/j.jclepro.2012.02.030

Xin, K. K., & Pearce, J. L. (1996). Guanxi: Connections as substitutes for formal institutional support. *Academy of Management Journal, 39*(6), 1641–1658. doi:10.2307/257072

Xu, K., & Li, Y. (2015). Exploring guanxi from a gender perspective: Urban Chinese womens practices of guanxi. *Gender, Place and Culture, 22*(6), 833–850. doi:10.1080/0966369X.2014.917279

Yahchouchi, G. (2009). Employees' perceptions of Lebanese managers' leadership styles and organizational commitment. *International. The Journal of Leadership Studies, 4*(2), 127–140.

Yalom, D. Y. (2002). *The Gift of Therapy.* Kinneret, Israel: Hebrew.

Yammarino, F. J., Dionne, S. D., Chun, J. U., & Dansereau, F. (2005). Leadership and levels of analysis: A state-of-the-science review. *The Leadership Quarterly, 16*(6), 879–919. doi:10.1016/j.leaqua.2005.09.002

Yang, M. M. (2002). The resilience of guanxi and its new deployments: A critique of some new guanxi scholarship. *The China Quarterly, 170*, 459–476. doi:10.1017/S000944390200027X

Yaniv, I. (2004). Receiving other peoples advice: Influence and benefit. *Organizational Behavior and Human Decision Processes, 93*(1), 1–13. doi:10.1016/j.obhdp.2003.08.002

Yeganeh, H. (2014). Culture and corruption. *International Journal of Development Issues, 13*(1), 2–24. doi:10.1108/IJDI-04-2013-0038

Yerkes, R. M., & Dodson, J. D. (1908). The Relation of Strength of Stimulus to Rapidity of Habit-Formation. *The Journal of Comparative Neurology and Psychology, 18*(5), 459–482. doi:10.1002/cne.920180503

Yeung, I. Y., & Tung, R. L. (1996). Achieving business success in Confucian societies: The importance of guanxi (connections). *Organizational Dynamics, 25*(2), 54–65. doi:10.1016/S0090-2616(96)90025-X

Yılmaz, F. G. K., Yilmaz, R., Öztürk, H. T., Sezer, B., & Karademir, T. (2015). Cyberloafing as a barrier to the successful integration of information and communication technologies into teaching and learning environments. *Computers in Human Behavior, 45*, 290–298. doi:10.1016/j.chb.2014.12.023

Yin, R. K. (2009). Case Study Research Design and Methods (4th ed.). Sage.

Yogun, A. E. (2015). Cyberloafing and innovative work behavior among banking sector employees. *International Journal of Business and Management Review, 3*(10), 61–71.

You, J., & Khagram, S. (2005). A comparative study of inequality and corruption. *American Sociological Review, 70*(February), 36–57.

Young, A. (2010). *Empathy, Cruelty, the Origins of the Social Brain*. Paper presented at Interacting Mind Workshop, Aarhus, Denmark.

Young, H. P. (2013). The evolution of conventions. *Econometrica, 61*(1), 57–84. doi:10.2307/2951778

Young, H. P., & Burke, M. A. (2011). Competition and custom in economic contracts: A case study of Illinois agriculture. *The American Economic Review, 91*(1), 559–573.

Yukl, G. (1989). *Leadership in Organizations*. Prentice-Hall.

Yukl, G. (2006). *Leadership in organizations*. Upper Saddle River, NJ: Prentice Hall.

Yukl, G. (2008). How leaders influence organizational effectiveness. *The Leadership Quarterly, 19*(6), 708–722. doi:10.1016/j.leaqua.2008.09.008

Yukl, G., & Mahsud, R. (2010). Why flexible and adaptive leadership is essential? *Consulting Psychology Journal: Practice and Research, 62*(2), 81–93. doi:10.1037/a0019835

Yum, J. O. (2007). Confucianism and Communication: Jen, Li, and Ubuntu. *China Media Research, 3*(4), 15–22.

Yusof, A. A. (2014). *The human side of human resource management*. Kedah, Malaysia: UUM Press.

Zak, P. J., & Knack, S. (2001). Trust and growth. *The Economic Journal, 111*(470), 295–321. doi:10.1111/1468-0297.00609

Zandi, A., Sayari, R., Ebadi, A., & Sanainasab, H. (2011). Abundance of depression, anxiety and stress in militant Nurses. *Iranian Journal of Military Medicine, 13*(2), 103–138.

Zeytinoglu, I. U. (Ed.). (2005). Flexibility in Workplaces: Effects on Workers, Work Environment and the Unions. Geneva: IIRA/ILO.

Zeytinoglu, I. U., Cooke, G. B., & Mann, S. L. (2009). Flexibility: Whose Choice Is It Anyway? *Relations Industrielles. Industrial Relations, 64*(3), 555–574. doi:10.7202/038873ar

Zgusta, L. (2006). *Lexicography Then and Now: Selected Essays* (F. Dolezal & T. Creamer, Eds.). Tübingen: Walter De Gruyter. doi:10.1515/9783110924459

Zhang, H., Zhao, H., Liu, J., Xu, Y., & Hui, L. (2015). The dampening effect of employees' future orientation on cyberloafing behaviors: The mediating role of self-control. *Frontiers in Psychology*, 1–18. doi:10.3389/fp??g.2015.01482 PMID:26483735

Zhang, L. (2008). Thinking Styles and Emotions. *The Journal of Psychology*, *142*(5), 497–515. doi:10.3200/JRLP.142.5.497-516 PMID:18959222

Zhang, Y., & Wu, Y. (2012). Huawei and Zhengfei Ren: leadership in a technology-innovative firm. In C. Petti (Ed.), *Technological Entrepreneurship in China: How Does it Work?* (pp. 103–122). Northampton, MA: Edward Elgar. doi:10.4337/9780857938992.00013

Zhou, K. Z., Tse, D. K., & Li, J. J. (2006). Organizational changes in emerging economies: Drivers and consequences. *Journal of International Business Studies*, *37*(1), 248–263. doi:10.1057/palgrave.jibs.8400186

Zimbardo, P. (2008). *The Lucifer Effect: How Good People Turn Evil*. New York: Random House Publishing Group.

Zlatanović, D. (2015). A Holistic Approach to Corporate Social Responsibility as a Prerequisite for Sustainable Development: Empirical Evidence. *Economic Annals*, *60*(207), 69–94. doi:10.2298/EKA1507069Z

Zlatanović, D., & Mulej, M. (2015). Soft-systems approaches to knowledge-cum-values management as innovation drivers. *Baltic Journal of Management*, *10*(4), 497–518. doi:10.1108/BJM-01-2015-0015

Zopiatis, A., & Constanti, P. (2010). Leadership styles and burnout: Is there an association? *International Journal of Contemporary Hospitality Management*, *22*(3), 300–320. doi:10.1108/09596111011035927

СаатиТ. Л. (1993). *Принятие решений. Метод анализа иерархий* (пер. с англ.). Москва: Радио и связъ.

About the Contributors

Zlatko Nedelko, Ph.D. (in Business), is an assistant professor at the Faculty of Economics and Business, Department of Management and organization, University of Maribor, Slovenia. His main research interests are management, leadership, personal values, business ethics, transitional issues in CEE and innovativeness. He has been involved in international projects tackling with business optimization, enhancing innovativeness and creativeness of management in catching up economies. Recently he was a guest researcher for nine months at Vienna University of Economics and Business, Austria. Dr. Nedelko has published his articles in peer reviewed scholarly journals including, but not limited to International Journal of Physical Distribution & Logistics Management, Journal of enterprising communities, Research in social change, Logistics & sustainable transport, Engineering Economics, and Actual problems of Economics.

Maciej Brzozowski has received his PhD in management science in 2006 from Poznan University of Economics and is currently hired as Assistant Professor at the Department of Strategic Management of Poznan University of Economics and Business. He writes and presents widely on issues of strategic management, project management, managers' personal values and design management.

* * *

Raghida Abdallah Yassine, with an undergraduate degree in Computer Science from the American University of Beirut and a Master's degree in Human Resource Management from the LER program at the University of Illinois Urbana Champaign, is currently a PhD student at the University of Illinois with an emphasis in Human Resource Development. She has accumulated five years of working experience in human resource development (HRD) and human resource management (HRM) in the healthcare industry as well as two years of teaching HR related courses in Lebanon. Possessing strong work ethic and an integrated and strategic knowledge of HRM, business/technical issues, and organizational change, Raghida has demonstrated the ability to develop and implement, in a demanding environment, coherent HR strategies encompassing improved internal processes consistent with project deadlines. Her research interest lie in national workforce development, structured on-the-job training, employee development in healthcare industry as well as organizational performance.

Niksa Alfirevic is a professor of management and an assistant professor of sociology at University of Split, Croatia. He also serves as a researcher with the national center of scientific excellence in school effectiveness and educational management.

Kseniia Baimakova is a PhD student in the Doctoral School of Safety and Security Sciences at Óbuda University in Budapest, Hungary. However she is also senior lecturer and deputy of the director of Entrepreneurship technologies institute on international affairs in State University of Aerospace Instrumentation, Saint-Petersburg, Russia. Her research interests are security and safety conscious behaviour, trust and organisational behavior, countries' cooperation in the sphere of innovation, the EU economy, innovative models of countries' economic development.

Richard Glavee-Geo holds a PhD from Molde University College, Specialized University in Logistics, Norway. He is an Associate Professor at the Norwegian University of Science and Technology (NTNU), Aalesund campus and teaches export management, marketing research and logistics & supply chain management to undergraduate business students and international marketing to postgraduate Master students. Though his research interests are specifically in the areas of B2B marketing/interorgarnizational relationships, buyer-supplier relationships, consumer and organisational buying behaviour, he has a broad interest in the use of second generation structural equation modeling techniques in organizational/management research.

Peter Holicza is a PhD student in the Doctoral School of Safety and Security Sciences at Obuda University in Budapest, Hungary, where he also serves as President of the PhD Student Union. He holds a Masters' degree in economics, specializing in business development. During his studies, he was granted funding by the Erasmus Programme multiple times to study and work in the following countries: Portugal, Malta, The Netherlands and the United Kingdom. His research interests include: international affairs, security politics, education and culture, international mobility.

Tomasz Kopczyński has received his MS in Economics from the Poznan University of Economics (Poland) in 1997. The same year he was hired as Assistant Lecturer at the Department of Management Systems and Technics of Poznan University of Economics. In 2003 Tomasz Kopczyński has received his PhD in management science from Poznan University of Economics and is currently hired as Assistant Professor at the Department of Strategic Management of Poznan University of Economics and Business. He writes and presents widely on issues of strategic management, project management, managers' personal values.

Manoj Kumar received his PhD in Mechanical Engineering from the Indian Institute of Technology, Delhi, India. He is presently working as Director, Mother Parwati Education Services, New Delhi, India. He has authored or co-authored over 80 research papers in journals and conferences. He has authored or co-authored 20 chapters of book. He is reviewer in 11 international research journal. His biographical note is published in Asia/pacific who's who (vol. XII)- 2013, Biography India-2014, Famous India: nation's who's who-2015.

Kornélia Lazányi is an associate professor at Óbuda University's Keleti Faculty of Business and Management. She, as the Vice-Dean for Research, is responsible for coordinating researches conducted at faculty level and organising funding for them. She strongly believes in talent management, hence has 6 PhD students from all over Europe and many more scientific research assistants from bachelor and master studies to work on topics connected to Organisational Behaviour, Organisational Safety Issues and the Development of SMEs. She is an editorial board member of 4 international journals, and has been part of the organising committee of over 20 international conferences.

Ping Li, Doctoral student in Human Resource Development, MSc Candidate in Business Administration at the University of Illinois at Urbana-Champaign, USA, and BSc in Economics from China. Her professional work experience includes Dept. of Management of the United Nations Headquarters in New York, and multinational companies in China and Germany.

Mateja Lorber is an assistant professor at the University of Maribor, Faculty Health Sciences from 2005. Before she worked 11 years at the University of Clinical Center Maribor as a registered nurse at the Clinic for Internal Disease. She obtained her BSc degree at the Faculty of Organizational Sciences University of Maribor, her MSc at the Faculty of Management, University of Primorska, and her PhD at the Faculty of Economics and Business, University of Maribor. Her main areas of interest and lecturing are gerontology, managing chronic disease, leadership and research in nursing. She has presented her work at international scientific conferences and published original scientific papers in domestic and foreign scientific journals.

Anne Namatsi Lutomia is a doctoral candidate in Human Resource Development at the University of Illinois at Urbana-Champaign. She holds a Bachelor of Education degree in Administration and French from Kenyatta University, Kenya and a Masters degree in Nonprofit Management from Hamline University in Minnesota, US. Her research interests span international network collaborations, leadership, adult learning, labor mobility and nonprofits organizations. She has published an article and two book chapters on women organizations and leadership. She has worked in the corporate and nonprofit sectors in Kenya and the United States.

Chi Maher lectures in Business Management at St Mary's University Twickenham, London. Dr Maher has published a book and several research papers in national and international scientific journals such as, Business Leadership Review, International Business and Entrepreneurship Development and the International Journal of Globalisation and Small Business. Her research interest lie in national and international Social enterprise management, Career management, Third sector development and partnerships, Social entrepreneurship and Human resources management. Dr. Maher is a reviewer for several scientific journals. Besides those academic activities, she has many years' experience of developing and managing projects in the public sector. and the third sector.

António C. Moreira obtained a Bachelor's degree in Electrical Engineering and a Master's degree in Management, both from the University of Porto, Portugal. He received his PhD in Management from UMIST-University of Manchester Institute of Science and Technology, England. He has a solid international background in industry leveraged working for a multinational company in Germany as well as in Portugal. He has also been involved in consultancy projects and in research activities. He is Assistant Professor at the Department of Economics, Management, Industrial Engineering, and Tourism, University of Aveiro, Portugal, where he headed the Bachelor and Master Degrees in Management for five years. He is member of GOVCOPP research unit.

Damijan Mumel obtained his PhD in psychology. He works as a Professor of marketing and a Head of Marketing institute at the University of Maribor, Faculty of Economics and Business. His main areas of interest and also lecturing are consumer behaviour, research methodology, qualitative research and communication. His scientific bibliography consists of 50+ published scientific articles. He is a member of the Slovenian Marketing Association, and the Slovenian Psychologists' Association as well as European Marketing Academy (EMAC).

Ghulam Mustafa is an Associate Professor of Organization and Management at the Department of International Business, at the Norwegian University of Science and Technology (NTNU), Norway. He holds a PhD from Norwegian School of Economics (NHH) and an MPhil from the University of Bergen. His research interests include leadership, work attitudes, work team effectiveness and cross-cultural management. Mustafa has published several articles in journals of international repute including the Journal of Cross-Cultural Management, Journal of Leadership studies and Eurasian Business Review.

Jelena Nikolić is an Assistant Professor on the following subjects: Introduction to Management, Decision Making Theory, Corporate Governance at the Faculty of Economics, University of Kragujevac, Republic of Serbia. She received her PhD from the University of Kragujevac, Faculty of Economics and her research interests focus is on strategic decision making, corporate governance and corporate entrepreneurship.

Rasa Pališkienė is a PhD student at Vilnius Gediminas Technical University. He is the author or co-author of over ten articles.

Anna Piekarczyk has received his MS in Economics from the Poznan University of Economics (Poland) in 1997. She completed also MBA course in Berlin (Germany). In 2000 she was hired as Assistant Lecturer at the Department of Management Systems and Technics of Poznan University of Economics. In 2007 Anna Piekarczyk has received her PhD in management science from Poznan University of Economics and is currently hired as Assistant Professor at the Department of Organization and Management Theory of Poznan University of Economics and Business. He writes and presents widely on issues of quality of management, personal management and network analysis.

Irma Rybnikova, after graduation in Psychology at Vilnius University (Lithuania), received her PhD in business and administration at Dresden University of Technology (Germany). Currently, Irma is preparing her habilitation on solidarity, resistance and participation in organizations at the Chemnitz University of Technology (Germany). Her main research interests include organization and leadership theories, voice and silence in organizations and industrial relations in Central and East European countries. Irma's research has been published as textbooks, books, books chapters and journal articles in German, English and Lithuanian.

Nira Shalev is the lecturer at the Open University in Israel.

J-Ho Siew Ching is currently a PhD student in School of Management, Universiti Sains Malaysia, Malaysia.

Pedro Miguel Silva has a Bachelor's degree and a Master's degree in Business Management at the University of Aveiro, Portugal. He is currently a PhD candidate in Marketing and Strategy in the Universities of Minho, University of Aveiro and University of Beira Interior. He has previous experiences in a multinational company and participated in research projects on the internationalization field.

Ilona Skačkauskienė, Doctor of Social Sciences, Associate Professor, Head of Department of Social Economics and Management, Vilnius Gediminas Technical University. She has published over 40 publications in her scientific research period and read reports in Lithuania and international conferences, and actively participated in national projects as the head, expert and executor. Her research interests: social and economic development, management theory, tax system evaluation.

Beata Skowron-Mielnik received PhD and Dr hab. degrees from Poznan University of Economics and is currently hired as Associate Professor at Department of Management and Corporate Resources Analysis at Poznan University of Economics and Business. She is engaged in research issues of human resources management, enterprise management, job design, flexible work arrangements, working time management and work performance management.

Thais Spiegel is an Associate Professor in the Industrial Engineering Department of Rio de Janeiro State University. Her research interests include operations management and design, process modeling, decision making, logistic and supply chain management. The author is pioneer in the convergence of cognitive sciences and industrial engineering in Brazil. She works on the premise that, in order for decision-making to be understood "completely" and improved, the underlying cognitive processes must be examined. It thus sets out to identify how decision-making is shaped by the cognitive processes of the agents involved.

Ilona Swiatek-Barylska is an Associate Professor in Department of Management at the University of Lodz, Poland. She teaches courses in Management Methods, Organizational Behavior and Human Resource Management on postgraduate and doctoral studies, as well as in a variety of executive programs for the managers. She is a visiting lecturer at the Universities in different European countries (Cyprus, Holland, Italy, Portugal, Spain, Turkey). She is a principal investigator of the research project "Multidimensional Analysis of Organizational Behaviour (MABO).The methodology and measurement tool." Grant for the years 2014 – 2016 awarded by the National Science Centre in Poland. Author and co-author of 4 books and 43 scientific papers. Experienced management consultant. For several years president of international human resource management consulting company.

Ramayah Thurasamy is currently a Professor of Technology Management at the School of Management, Universiti Sains Malaysia, Visiting Professor King Saud University, Kingdom of Saudi Arabia and Adjunct Professor at Multimedia University and Universiti Tenaga Nasional, Malaysia. He has taught courses in Statistics, Operations Management, Research Methods and at undergraduate level. He has supervised numerous PhD/MA/MBA students in the fields of Information Systems, Operations Management, Marketing Management and Organizational Behavior. He has conducted Structural Equation Modeling (SEM) workshops in Malaysia, Australia, Indonesia, Thailand and India. He has conducted workshops in Monash University, Sunway University, UUM, UKM, UTM, UiTM, UMK, UMS, UNIMAS, USIM, UMT, UMP, UTHM, UNISZA, INTAN and Polytechnic Colleges in Malaysia. He has also presented numerous papers at local and international conferences having won 5 "Best Papers" award. His publications have appeared in Information & Management, Journal of Environmental Management, Technovation, Journal of Business Ethics, Internet Research, Journal of Travel Research, International Journal of Operations & Production Management, Journal of Business Economics and Management, Computers in Human Behavior, Resources, Conservation and Recycling, International Journal of Information Management, Cross Cultural & Strategic Management, Evaluation Review, Information Research, Asian Journal of Technology Innovation, Social Indicators Research, Quantity & Quality, Service Business, Knowledge Management Research & Practice, Journal of Medical System, International Journal of Production Economics, Personnel Review and Telematics and Informatics among others. He also serves on the editorial boards and program committee of several international journals and conferences of repute. His full profile can be accessed from http://www.ramayah.com.

Xiaoping Tong is a Ph.D. candidate in Human Resource Development at the University of Illinois at Urbana-Champaign. She currently works as a Graduate Research Assistant at the Office of E-Learning in the College of Business within the same university. She holds a Bachelor of Science degree in Educational Technology from Beijing Normal University and a Master of Education degree in Educational Technology from Peking University, Beijing, China. Her research interests include leadership, Confucianism, female education, human resource development professional accountability, and corporate university. A native of China, Xiaoping has extensive experience in Chinese culture. She has published several journal articles and presented conference papers on topics about Chinese educational technology and human resource development. She has worked in multiple roles such as instructor, teaching assistant, graduate assistant, and so on in China and the United States.

Sonja Treven, PhD, Professor, is employed at the School of Business and Economics at the University of Maribor in Slovenia for the field of human resource management. She is the Head of the Department for management and organisation. She is the author of 3 books (Management stress, International organisational behaviour, Human resource management) and co-author of 13 books as well as more than eighty scientific articles. She participated in more than 100 domestic and international conferences with her papers as an author or co-author. She also participated in various domestic and international projects.

Grzegorz Wojtkowiak has received his PhD in management science from Poznan University of Economics and is currently hired as Assistant Professor at the Department of Management and Corporate Resources Analysis of Poznan University of Economics and Business. He writes and presents widely on issues of decision making process and human resources.

Dejana Zlatanović is an Assistant Professor on the following subjects: Economic Cybernetics and Management Science, at the Faculty of Economics, University of Kragujevac, Republic of Serbia, where she received her PhD degree. Her research interest focus is on systems thinking and its application in business economics, i.e. holistic conceptualizing and solving the management problems in enterprises as well as systems methodologies for problem situations structuring.

Index

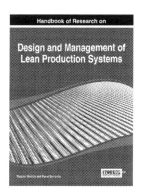

Stay Current on the Latest Emerging Research Developments

Become an IGI Global Reviewer for Authored Book Projects

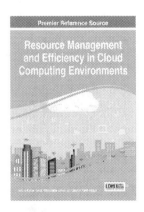

The overall success of an authored book project is dependent on quality and timely reviews.

In this competitive age of scholarly publishing, constructive and timely feedback significantly decreases the turnaround time of manuscripts from submission to acceptance, allowing the publication and discovery of progressive research at a much more expeditious rate. Several IGI Global authored book projects are currently seeking highly qualified experts in the field to fill vacancies on their respective editorial review boards:

Applications may be sent to:
development@igi-global.com

Applicants must have a doctorate (or an equivalent degree) as well as publishing and reviewing experience. Reviewers are asked to write reviews in a timely, collegial, and constructive manner. All reviewers will begin their role on an ad-hoc basis for a period of one year, and upon successful completion of this term can be considered for full editorial review board status, with the potential for a subsequent promotion to Associate Editor.

If you have a colleague that may be interested in this opportunity,
we encourage you to share this information with them.

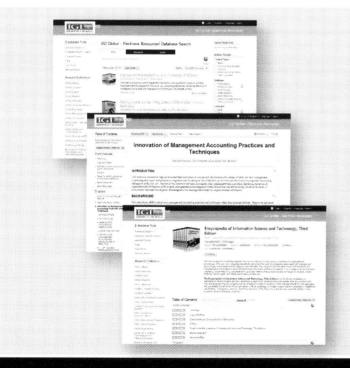

Information Resources Management Association

Become an IRMA Member

Members of the **Information Resources Management Association (IRMA)** understand the importance of community within their field of study. The Information Resources Management Association is an ideal venue through which professionals, students, and academicians can convene and share the latest industry innovations and scholarly research that is changing the field of information science and technology. Become a member today and enjoy the benefits of membership as well as the opportunity to collaborate and network with fellow experts in the field.

IRMA Membership Benefits:

- **One FREE Journal Subscription**
- **30% Off Additional Journal Subscriptions**
- **20% Off Book Purchases**
- Updates on the latest events and research on Information Resources Management through the IRMA-L listserv.
- Updates on new open access and downloadable content added to Research IRM.
- A copy of the Information Technology Management Newsletter twice a year.
- A certificate of membership.

IRMA Membership $195

Scan code or visit **irma-international.org** and begin by selecting your free journal subscription.

Membership is good for one full year.

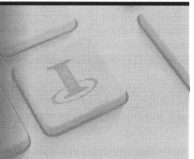